A SHORT

HISTORY

OF THE

MOVIES

.

A SHORT HISTORY OF THE MOVIES

GERALD MAST

Second Edition

The Bobbs-Merrill Company, Inc.
Indianapolis

Copyright © 1976 by the Bobbs-Merrill Company, Inc.
Printed in the United States of America
All rights reserved. No part of this book shall be
reproduced or transmitted in any form or by any means,
electronic or mechanical, including photocopying, recording,
or by any information or retrieval system, without written
permission from the Publisher:

The Bobbs-Merrill Company, Inc.
4300 West 62nd Street
Indianapolis, Indiana 46268

First Edition
First Printing 1976
Designed by Trezzo/Braren Studio

Library of Congress Cataloging in Publication Data

Mast, Gerald   1940–
    A short history of the movies.

    Includes bibliographical references and index.
    1. Moving-pictures—History.   I. Title.
PN1993.5.A1M39 1976   791.43'09   75–14302
ISBN 0–672–63719–7

Contents

Preface to the Second Edition   vii

Acknowledgments   x

1   Introductory Assumptions   1

2   Birth   9

3   Film Narrative, Commercial Expansion   33

4   Griffith   53

5   The Comics: Mack Sennett and the Chaplin Shorts   91

6   Movie Czars and Movie Stars   115

7   The German Golden Age   159

8   Soviet Montage   181

9   Sound   219

10   France Between the Wars   239

11   The American Studio Years: 1930–1945   263

12   Years of Transition   315

13   Neorealisms and New Waves   341

14   Emerging National Traditions   403

15   The Fourth American Era   475

Appendix: For Further Reading and Viewing   505

Index   545

Preface

to the Second Edition

find it extremely gratifying that the response to the first edition of *A Short History of the Movies* has allowed me to do a second. I am pleased to have had the opportunity to do the book over again—reassessing old judgments, adding new material that brings the book both to where I am and where the movies are today. If the appearance of a new edition less than five years after the original seems odd, it is simply a sign of the rapid changes in both film and film thinking over the past five years. In adding new material, I have tried to follow two general principles: first, to weave the additions invisibly into the original matter, so that the result remains one book rather than a book with parenthetic items stitched and patched on; and second, to preserve the spirit, approach, and attitudes of the original edition, which seem to have had so much to do with the book's acceptance.

This new material is of three basic kinds. First, I have altered or expanded information and judgments about some of the "Old Masters," trying to eliminate those pesky (and inevitable) errors of detail and to add the relevant results of my own recent research. Second, I have brought my discussions of the "New Masters" up to date, treating many of their more recent films, styles, and directions. Finally, I have added sections that never existed in the original edition—in particular, a discussion of the Japanese,

Indian, and Czech cinemas, as well as of the American Underground. The result is that the second edition devotes a far greater proportion of its attention to the sound film in general and to the postwar cinema in particular than did the original. Although this never-very-short "short" history is now even less short than it was, I hope it will also be more useful, more relevant, and more interesting.

I wish to thank all those people who helped both the first and second editions to exist—and to exist so felicitously. First, let me thank once again all who added their judgment and knowledge to the creation or re-creation of the manuscript: Joe Adamson, Richard Meran Barsam, Jeanne Eichenseer, Antonin J. Liehm, Richard Dyer MacCann, Ned McLeroy, John Mong, Leonard Quart, William Reiter, and Burnell Y. Sitterly. Let me also thank all of you who considerately sent me your constructive suggestions, especially those anonymous readers who so conscientiously detailed their suggestions, corrections, and opinions at the request of the publisher. The revisions in this edition are the surest sign of my respect for the validity of those ideas.

Next, I would like to thank all those commercial film exchanges who lent their aid and their prints to my research: to Walter J. Dauler of Audio-Brandon Films (and where would film teaching and viewing be without this magnificent collection?); to Murray Glass of Em Gee Films (surely the best rental resource of pre-1920 films in America); to Bill Franz and Peter Meyer of Janus Films (one of the great pioneers of the "art film" movement of the 1950s); and to Darrell Flugg and Adam Reilly, who both served so ably and helpfully with Contemporary Films/McGraw-Hill.

The book's collection of stills merits a whole battery of thanks by itself. In response to several inquiries, let me explain that the stills from the silent films exist nowhere else because they were made specifically for this book. Using a Hasselblad camera with close-up and slide-mount attachments, these stills were shot directly from 35mm prints of the films in the storage vaults of the Museum of Modern Art. The poor quality of some of the stills in the first edition was due partly to the inescapable fact that many of the films are themselves old and worn and partly to the decision to integrate text and pictures in the first edition, necessitating a standard text, nonglossy paper for the illustrations. This latter decision has been changed for the second edition, and I hope the stills are sharper (if more distant from the relevant discussion) now. Steven Jack took the pictures; Margareta Akermark, Jean Lenauer, and Donald Richie of the Museum of Modern Art were kind enough to give their permission and make the arrangements to do so.

Speaking of the Museum of Modern Art, it is simply not possible to speak of it often enough. I am indebted to Mary Corliss, Charles Silver, and Steven Harvey of the Museum's Film Department for their aid, encouragement, efficiency, courtesy, and patience. Without people like this and a research resource of this kind there simply would be no scholarly film writing at all in America. It seems time for the various foundations and granting organizations to recognize the indispensable contribution of the Museum to American film study, a resource that has done its very best with inadequate funding and facilities.

ACKNOWLEDGMENTS

The author and publisher wish to thank the following for permission to reprint photographic stills:

from *Wavelength;* used by permission of Anthology Film Archives.

A Kinetoscope Parlor and *Fred Ott's Sneeze;* reprinted by Arno Press, Inc., 1970.

from the films *Potemkin, Mother, October, Arsenal,* and *The End of St. Petersburg;* used by permission of R. & S. Madell, Russian Film Library.

from the films *Diary of a Country Priest, Accatone, 8½, Closely Watched Trains, Intimate Lighting, Viridiana, Pather Panchali, Throne of Blood,* and *The Bicycle Thief;* used by permission of Audio-Brandon Films.

from the film *La Strada;* used by permission of Avco-Embassy Films.

from *On the Waterfront;* courtesy of Columbia Pictures Television, a Division of Columbia Pictures Industries, Inc.

from the films *Breathless, Vivre sa vie, The Children of Paradise,* and *À Nous la liberté;* used by permission of Contemporary Films/McGraw-Hill.

from *A Trip to the Moon, The General, The Pawnshop, One A.M., The Last Laugh,* and *Easy Street;* used by permission of Em Gee Film Library.

from *My Uncle;* used by permission of Jacques Tati.

from the films *The 39 Steps, The Rules of the Game, Jules and Jim, The 400 Blows, L'Avventura, Citizen Kane, Ugetsu, Wild Strawberries, The Seventh Seal, The Blue Angel,* and *Grand Illusion;* courtesy of Janus Films.

from *Scorpio Rising;* used by permission of Kenneth Anger.

from *The Passion of Joan of Arc;* used by permission of La Societé Nouvelle des Establishment Gaumont.

from *Lola Montès;* used by permission of Les Films de la Pléade.

from the MGM releases: *2001: A Space Odyssey,* copyright © 1968; *Singin' in the Rain,* copyright © 1952 Loew's Inc.; *An American in Paris,* copyright © 1951 Loew's Inc.; *North by Northwest,* copyright © 1959 Loew's Inc.; and *Greed,* copyright © 1925 Metro-Goldwyn Pictures Corporation, copyright renewed 1952 by Loew's Inc.

from the films *Seven Years Bad Luck, Rescued by Rover, Queen Elizabeth, The Lonely Villa, The New York Hat, The Birth of a Nation, Intolerance, Broken Blossoms, The Surf Girl, High and Dizzy, The Cabinet of Doctor Caligari, The Joyous Microbes, Motion Painting #1, Le Zoetrope,* and Muybridge's leaping horse; used by permission of The Museum of Modern Art.

from *Paper Moon,* copyright © 1973 by Paramount Pictures Corp. All rights reserved.

from *The Informer* and *Swing Time;* courtesy of RKO Radio Pictures, a Division of RKO General, Inc.

from *The Red Desert;* used by permission of Rizzoli Editore Corporation.

from *The Gold Rush;* copyright © Roy Export Company Establishment.

from *Breathdeath;* used by permission of Stanley VanDerBeek.

from *Metropolis;* used by permission of Standard Film Service.

from *Nosferatu* and *Destiny;* used by permission of Transit Films.

from *Stagecoach;* used by permission of TV Cinema Sales Corporation.

from the films *The Jazz Singer, Golddiggers of 1935, Red River, Persona,* and *Sleeper;* used by permission of United Artists Corporation.

from the films *Trouble in Paradise, The Scarlet Empress, The Blonde Venus,* and *Blind Husbands;* courtesy of Universal Pictures.

from *Steamboat Willie;* used by permission, copyright © Walt Disney Productions.

from the motion pictures *Rebel Without a Cause,* copyright © 1955; *Day for Night,* copyright © 1974; and *A Clockwork Orange,* copyright © 1971; courtesy of Warner Bros. Inc.

Chapter

1

INTRODUCTORY ASSUMPTIONS

The first audience watched a motion picture flicker on a screen in 1895, only some eighty years ago. In those eighty years the movies have developed from a simple recording device—the first films merely captured a scenic or not-so-scenic view—to a complex art and business. The first movie audiences were delighted to see that it was possible to record a moving scene on film; today we debate the desirability rather than the possibility of capturing an image. The important question for the first film audiences was, "Is the image discernible?" rather than, "Is the image meaningful?" From the simple beginning of turning a camera on to record a scene, the filmmaker has learned that his art depends on the way his camera shapes the scene he is recording. Analogous to the novel, the finished movie is not just a story, but a story told in a certain way, and it is impossible to separate what is told from how it is told. Just as novelists discovered that narrative technique can either be subtly invisible—as in Dickens or Hemingway—or intrusively self-conscious—as in Joyce or Faulkner—so too the filmmaker can construct a lucid, apparently artless story or a complex, almost chaotic maze for traveling to the story. The wonder is that while the evolution of narrative fiction can be tracked back to Homer, the movies have evolved such complex techniques in only eighty years.

No one takes the movies more for granted than the present generation of moviegoers. For these "third-generation" audiences, who grew up with the polished, technically perfect sound films of the last thirty years, there is no consciousness of the way an entertainment novelty evolved into an art. Although the current "film generation" prefers seeing movies to reading novels, prefers making movies to writing poetry, and has pushed the movies into university curricula, it is surprisingly ignorant of the cumulative progress of the movie art—especially surprising since each student filmmaker lives through the identical historical evolution of film in learning his craft. He begins by trying to record technically correct pictures on film, perfecting his ability to obtain clearly focused, properly exposed images. He then realizes the power of different pictorial compositions, the strategies of long shots and close-ups, the effects of different lenses and filters. Then he discovers the power of editing in creating a film's meaning and tone. The student's first film is usually a black-and-white silent film with musical accompaniment: precisely the kind of film that evolved during the first thirty-five years of film history. Only after he gains some confidence with this kind of film does the new filmmaker experiment with color and synchronized sound.

The history of the movies is, first of all, the history of a new art. Though it has affinities with the novel, the drama, the dance, painting, photography, and music, like each of these sister arts it has a "poetics" of its own. When the early films turned from scenic views to fictional stories, directors suspected that the "poetics" of the film was the same as for the stage. Stage acting, stage movement, stage stories, stage players, and stage perspectives dominated the first story films. The camera was assumed to be a spectator in a theatre audience, and just as the spectator has only one seat, the camera had only one position from which to shoot a scene.

Time and experimentation revealed that the camera was anchored by analogy alone—and that the analogy was false. The scene—the locale—is the basic unit of the stage because space in the theatre is so concrete. The audience sits here, the characters play there, the scenery is fixed in space behind the action. But space in the film is completely elastic; only the screen is fixed, not the action on it. Directors discovered that the unit of a film is the shot, not the scene, that shots can be joined together in any number of combinations to produce whole scenes and that scenes can be varied and juxtaposed and paralleled in any number of ways. Unity of place, a rather basic and practical principle of the stage, does not apply to the movie. More applicable is a principle of an appropriate succession of images which produces the desired narrative continuity, the intended meaning, and the appropriate emotional tension of the film as a whole. By the end of the silent era this principle had not only been discovered but demonstrated.

The discovery of sound raised doubts about the discoveries of the preceding thirty years. Once again the analogy with the stage was suspected; once again stage actors, stage writers, stage directors, and stage techniques flooded the movies. And once again, the analogy was refuted. Just as the stage is anchored visually in space, so too it is anchored by sound. Sounds come from the speaker's mouth; you see both the speaker and his mouth. But movies were free to show any kind of picture while the words came from the speaker's mouth. Synchronization of picture and sound also allowed for the disjunction of picture and sound. Further, the freedom of the movies from spatial confinement allowed a greater freedom in the kinds of sounds they could use: natural sound effects, musical underscoring, distortion effects, subjective thoughts, and so forth. Whereas the history of the silent film could be summarized as the discovery of the different means of producing an evocative *succession* of visual images, the history of the sound film is the discovery of the different means of producing an evocative *integration* of visual images and sound.

Just as the history of the novel is, to some extent, a catalogue of important novels and the history of drama a catalogue of important plays, the history of film as an art centers around important films. In film history, a discussion of the significant films is especially relevant, for not only are the individual films milestones on an historical path, but also significant artistic discoveries that immediately influenced other directors. Although Shakespeare drew from Seneca, and Brecht from Shakespeare, even more immediate was the influence of Griffith on Ford or Ford on Bergman. Without years of stage tradition to use as a well, film artists have drawn insights from the excitement generated by contemporary discoveries. The internationalism of film distribution has always guaranteed the rapid influence of any significant discovery.

A study of eighty years of film history has led this author to make one basic assumption: no great film has ever been made without the vision and unifying intelligence of a single mind to create and control the whole film. Just as there is only one poet per pen, one painter per canvas, there can be only one creator of a movie. The *"auteur* theory" is as valid for films as for any other art. Whether the *auteur* improvises the whole film as he goes along—as Griffith did—or whether he works according to a preconceived and scripted plan, a single mind must shape and control the work of art. The difficulty with movies, however, is that their very massiveness and complexity work against their having such an *auteur*. The director is often no more than a mechanic, bolting together a machine (often infernal) that someone else has designed.

Those who view the film as an inferior artistic medium most frequently argue that the conditions of making a commercial film nullify its chances for artistic success. The great work of film art is the exception, the mediocre factory product the rule. To see the history of films as just a few dozen great movies is to simplify the history. All movies, great or small, have been made in the context of the entire film industry. Any film history that intends to reveal the genesis of today's film world must, in addition to discussing the film as art, discuss three related problems that have always influenced the artistic product—and continue to influence it today: the film as business, the film as entertainment, and the film as machinery.

Movies today are a billion-dollar business. The choice of directors, stars, and scripts is often in the hands of businessmen, not in the heads of artists. The company that invests $5,000,000 in a picture ought to be able to insure the safety of its investment. Commercial values outweigh artistic ones. The name Hollywood is for some synonymous with glamor, for others synonymous with selling out. For decades Hollywood's commercial crassness has served American novelists—from F. Scott Fitzgerald and Nathaniel West to Gore Vidal—as a metaphor for the vulgar emptiness of the "American Dream." If the gifted young director today seems to face a distasteful dilemma—sell out or get out—it has been equally true that directors have faced the same dilemma for fifty years.

The awesome financial pressures of Hollywood are partly responsible for the growing number of independent and underground films—just as Broadway production demands are responsible for the Off-Broadway and Off-Off-Broadway theatres. Young filmmakers often prefer to work alone with the life and life-styles around them; their sole expense is equipment and film. These filmmakers are, in a sense, regressing to the earliest period of film history. But every artistic innovation since then has ironically necessitated spending more money. If lighting was a step forward in film toning, it also required spending money on lighting equipment and on men who knew how to control it. If acting was to be improved, the proven actors would have to be retained. And as actors supplied greater and greater proofs, they demanded higher and higher salaries. Longer films required more film, more actors, more story material, and more publicity to insure a financial return on the greater investment. It took only twenty-five years for the movies to progress from cheap entertainment novelty to big business.

Making a film is such a massive and complex task it is a wonder that an artistically whole movie can be made at all. The huge sums of money required to make a movie merely reflect the hugeness of the task of taking a movie from story idea to final print. Shooting is painfully slow. It takes time to perfect each setup: lights must be carefully focused and toned, the shot's composition must be attractive and appropriate, the set must be dressed, background action (extras) must be coordinated with the action of the principals, actors must have mastered their interpretations of lines so that a single shot fits into the dramatic fabric of the whole film, make-up must be correct, costumes coordinated, the positions of the players must match those in the preceding shot. And so forth. Because it takes so much time to set up a shot, producers economize by shooting all scenes together that require the same location or setup, regardless of their position in the film's continuity. But even with such economies, to get five minutes of screen time "in the can" is a healthy day's work. Sometimes, on location with mammoth spectacle pictures, a whole day can be devoted to a fifteen-second piece of the finished film—until the sun, the caravans, the camels, the soldiers, and the gypsy maidens reach their proper places. The devastating effect of accomplishing so little each shooting day is that a film's budget is calculated on the number of days it will take to shoot, the average expense for a color film being in excess of $75,000 per day. Whereas the novelist or poet or painter can sit alone and perfect his art with a minimum of expense (and waste), the film artist is the servant of an uneconomical master. Even the ten-minute student film can cost over $1,000 for film stock and laboratory costs alone—exclusive of the original cost of the equipment.

Because movies cost so much to make, the men who spend that money are understandably concerned about getting it back again. The only way to retrieve expenses is with ticket receipts. Not only is the film artist at the mercy of expensive machines and services, but he is also dependent on the consent of the entertained. The history of the movies as a business is inextricably linked with the history of the movies as a mass entertainment medium. To get the public to spend its dollars at the box office, the producer must give the public what it wants, or make the public want what it gets. History indicates that the public has gotten some of both. The crassest movie maxim is the famous, "The box office is never wrong." The validity of the maxim is dependent on the kinds of questions you ask the box office to answer.

Just as film art has changed radically in the course of its eighty-year history, so too film audiences have changed. The first movie patrons in America were also patrons of vaudeville houses and variety shows. When those audiences tired of the same kinds of film programs, the movies found a home with lower- and working-class patrons. Small theatres sprang up in poor sections of cities; admission was a nickel or a dime. The rich and educated saw movies only on an evening of slumming. As film art and craft improved, larger and more expensive movie theatres opened in respectable and central areas of the cities. Films tried to appeal to a wide range of tastes and interests, much like television today. In this period there was little consciousness of movies as an art; they were mass entertainment. And as with today's television, the educated, the literati, and the serious shunned the movies. H. L. Mencken sardonically lauded the movies as the appropriate artistic attainment of the American "booboisie." Similes linking movies with tastelessness and movie patrons with morons continually pop up in fiction and articles of the 1920s and 1930s. Only recent American audiences, the third generation of movie-goers, expect the film to be art and not formulaic entertainment. Current audience surveys indicate that the overwhelming majority of steady movie patrons are between seventeen and twenty-nine, with Bachelor degrees either in sight or in hand. The present movie audience takes its movies as seriously as it does the products of the novelist and poet. The new influence of the intellectual movie critics, who now exert more power and attract more attention than the critics of any other art, is merely a symptom of these new audience expectations. As usual, producers are giving the public what it wants. Although the existence of Radio City Music Hall, drive-in theatres, and neighborhood movie houses (steadily dwindling in number) proves that the mass entertainment film is not dead, it is really the "art" cinema that is alive and well in American cities.

A final influence on any discussion of the history of the movies is the fact that film art is dependent on machines. Appropriately enough, our technological century has produced an art that depends on technology. The first filmmakers were not artists but tinkerers. The same spirit that produced a light bulb and a telephone produced a movie camera and projector. Their goal in making a movie was not to create beauty but to display a scientific curiosity. The invention of the first cameras and projectors set a trend that was to repeat itself with the introduction of every new movie invention: the invention was first exploited as a novelty in itself and only later integrated as one tool in making the whole film. The first camera merely exploited the fact that it could capture images of moving things. The first synchronized-sound films exploited the fact that the audience could hear the words that the actors' lips were mouthing. Most of the first color films were merely colorful, many of the first wide-screen films merely wide.

Perhaps no invention so clearly demonstrated the ephemerality of pure gimmickry than the short-lived 3-D movie. There were obvious limits to the number of knives, spears, arrows, hatchets, and swords that could be thrown at an audience before it would begin to take itself elsewhere. The technical gimmickry of 3-D was so pervasive that the innovation could never be assimilated into a greater artistic whole. The same extinction seemed to threaten Cinerama, with its inevitable rides on roller coasters, hydrofoils, stagecoaches, dogsleds, and anything else that moved, until Stanley Kubrick made a lady of her with *2001*. Novelty became an artistic tool; rather than exploiting movement for its own sake, Kubrick used movement to echo the subjective impressions of his characters. However, *2001* may have indeed been the ultimate Cinerama film, for there has not been another artistically significant film made in the process since.

No other art is so tied to machines. Some of the most striking artistic effects are the products of expanding film technology. For example, the awesome compositions in depth and shadow of Welles's *Citizen Kane* are partially the result of the conversion from carbon-arc lamps to incandescent lighting in the studios and the development of high-speed panchromatic film, which allowed much greater depth-of-field. Research has converted the camera from an erratic, hand-cranked film grinder to a smooth, precise clockworks. Research has silenced the camera's noise without using clumsy, bulky devices to baffle the clatter. Research has developed faster and faster black-and-white stocks, enabling greater flexibility in lighting, composition, and shooting conditions. Research has developed color film stocks that are not only accurate in recording color but can also provide different effects for different artistic purposes. Research has improved sound recording and sound reproduction, has developed huge cranes and dollies, has perfected a wide assortment of laboratory processes and effects, has invented special lenses and special projectors and special filters. Film equipment is so sophisticated that no film artist can master all of it; he is dependent on mechanics as well as machines.

Because they are mechanical, because they are big business, because they pander to audience tastes, movies have never before been ushered into the temple of high art by those who guard the doors. Throughout their eighty-year history the movies have carried on a parasitic flirtation with the stage. Feeling the cultural superiority of the older art, movie producers and artists borrowed properties and people from Broadway. The typical route to Hollywood for a story idea was from fiction to Broadway to sound stage. But in the 1970s a significant detour on this route is a sign of the changing times; Broadway now regularly adapts screenplays into stageplays. Despite the difficulties of money and machine, the movies have become the dominant and the liveliest living art.

This short history will follow the road the movies have traveled to get here. To keep a short history short has required several decisions. First, this history aims at revealing significant trends and turns along the road rather than exhaustive lists of titles, directors, and dates. For further reading in any particular period, the reader should consult the bibliography. Second, because the history of the American film is most relevant to American readers—as well as being the dominant film force in the world—this short history allots more space to a discussion of American movie practices. But to write a history of the art that neglects the influences of non-American films is impossible. Third, the particular films that have been singled out for detailed discussion are not only significant contributions to film art, but are readily available in 16mm. prints for rental and viewing. A list of these films and their distributors appears in the Appendix. Finally, this history concentrates on the fictional film almost exclusively. The aesthetic principles of the nonfiction (documentary) film are different enough from those of the fictional (or story) film, so that the documentary or factual film deserves a separate study of its own.

Chapter

2

BIRTH

Although some film historians trace the origin of movies back to cave paintings or Plato's Cave of the Shadows, the history of the movies proper begins with the steps leading to the invention of the movie camera and projector. This era in movie prehistory is the province of inventors, not artists. The nineteenth-century mechanical mind created machines for travel, machines for work, machines for the home, and, in the process, machines for entertainment. In the second third of the nineteenth century, three kinds of mechanical experimentation began which, by the end of the century, had combined to create the motion picture: research in the phenomenon of persistence of vision, research in still photography, and research in mechanized audience entertainments.

Persistence of Vision

Movies are an optical illusion. We believe we are watching completely continuous, fluid motion on the screen. In fact, we watch short, jerky, discontinuous bits of the motion, which the eye sees as continuous because of the way the eye sees and the way the brain interprets that information.

The brain retains the images of the eye for a fraction of a second longer than the eye actually records them. If it did not, we would be conscious of the hundreds of times a day that the eyelids blink. The mind has no consciousness of blinking because although the lids cover the eyeball for a fraction of a second, the mind retains the preblink image. The same principle accounts for the fact that a flashlight rotated in a circle in the darkness appears to produce a circle of light. The brain blurs the individual points of light into a circular figure. If the eye saw sixteen individual but related figures of a moving object in rapid succession, the brain would connect the pieces to make a single, fluid sequence out of them. This optical phenomenon is known as persistence of vision.

Persistence of vision makes movie action seem as fluid and continuous as live action. It cancels out the differences between the event and the recording of the event. The genuine difference between the two can easily be grasped by an understanding of the way motion pictures record movement. The movie camera exposes a single frame at a time; each frame is a single, fixed, still photograph. The succession of frames produces the appearance of movement. To record an image on film, the camera's shutter remains open about one-thirtieth of a second. The shutter exposes, say, sixteen (the approximate, although not standard, silent speed) of these images each second. Simple mathematics indicates that one second of film thus exposed contains only 16/30ths of a second of exposed action and 14/30ths of a second of darkness (of blinking) between the frames. Whereas, in viewing, a second of film appears to be a continuous line, _____, it is really a discontinuous one, ---. The eye's persistence of vision fills in the blank spaces.

Persistence of vision, known by the ancients, was investigated and demonstrated by European thinkers and tinkerers between 1820 and 1835. One of the early discussions of the phenomenon was written by Peter Mark Rôget, author of the famous thesaurus. Another English scientist, Sir John Herschel, bet a friend that he could show him the head and tail of a shilling at the same time. And then Sir John spun the coin. The eye blurred the spinning sides of the coin into a single image. In 1825, Dr. John Ayrton Paris had developed a little toy based on this same spinning-coin principle. On one side of a circular board was a parrot, on the other an empty cage. By holding the board by two attached straps and then spinning it, the viewer saw the parrot inside the cage. Again, two images had melted into one. Paris called his little toy the Thaumatrope.

Four years later, in 1829, Joseph Antoine Ferdinand Plateau published his investigations on persistence of vision, and three years after that (1832) he patented his own toy to demonstrate his theoretical research. Painted on a flat, circular piece of board were individual designs in slightly varying positions. When the board was grasped by a handle, held up in front of a mirror, and then spun, the individual designs became a continuous, animated sequence. In order to see the designs moving (rather than as a blur), the viewer looked into the mirror through little slits cut into the circular board of the toy. Plateau called his toy the Phenakistiscope. Plateau's researches were important, for in the course of them he discovered that sixteen images per second were an optimal number for producing continuous movement. The early filmmakers would also discover the utility of sixteen frames per second. In addition, Plateau's machine required moments of darkness, of nonimage, in order to make the images appear to move. The eye needed momentary resting time to soak in the images. A successful projector would not be invented until Plateau's principle of slits was reapplied.

A German inventor, Simon Ritter von Stampfer, developed the same machine as Plateau's Phenakistiscope in the same year; he called it the Stroboscope. Based on the same principle as the Phenakistiscope and Stroboscope, many refined versions of this toy appeared throughout the nineteenth century. In 1834, William George Horner created a stroboscopic machine that used a circular drum rather than a flat, circular board. Horner's machine could be fitted with exchangeable paper strips to wrap inside the circular drum. When the viewer looked at the spinning paper strip inside the drum—again through slits in the drum, allowing moments of darkness—the same sequential movement delighted him. Horner called his toy the Zootrope (or Zoetrope).

Also in 1834, Baron Franz von Uchatius began combining stroboscopic toys with the magic lantern—what today we would call a "slide projector," using candle power rather than electricity. Uchatius lined up a series of projectors side by side and focused them on the same screen. In each lantern was a slide with a slightly different phase of movement. By running with a torch from lantern to lantern, Uchatius threw an apparent sequence of movement on the screen. The result was the progenitor of the animated cartoon. Uchatius's experiments with lanterns continued, and by 1853 he had developed a Projecting Phenakistiscope, combining a phenakistiscopic disc with a single magic lantern. When the operator spun the disc, the lantern threw the sequential animated movement on the screen.

By the end of the nineteenth century, hundreds of variations on these toys abounded, each with its own name, either simple or ornate: Praxinoscope, Choreutoscope, Wheel of Life. All of these stroboscopic toys shared, in addition to the common use of persistence of vision, several traits that were to continue as trends in later movie history. Most striking was the inventors' passion for fancy Greek and Latin names to dignify their dabblings: Thaumatrope, Phenakistiscope, Viviscope, Zootrope. This passion for nominal embroidery would later dominate the first era of motion pictures—Kinetoscope, Bioscope, Vitascope, Cinématographe—and beyond it—Vitaphone, Technicolor, CinemaScope, television, stereophonic. Also striking is the simultaneity of discoveries by different men in different countries. Many different heads and hands applied themselves to the same problems, primarily in France, England, Germany, and the United States. Such simultaneous experimenting produced a confusion that would continue throughout the century, so that even today these four countries all claim to have invented the motion picture. Each chauvinistic historian supports his claim with solid evidence. The validity of each claim is contingent upon whether one defines the motion picture as invented when it was conceived, when it was patented, when it was photographed on film, or when it was projected in public.

All the stroboscopic experiments and toys used drawn figures. Before the movies could progress from stroboscopic toy to motion pictures of the natural world, the means to record the natural world had to be discovered. Simultaneous with the scientific dabblings in persistence of vision were scientific dabblings with photography.

Photography

Before there could be motion pictures, there had to be pictures. A moving picture was born from the union of the stroboscopic toys and the still photograph. The principle of photography dates back to the Renaissance and Leonardo da Vinci's plan for a *camera obscura*. This device—literally translated as dark room or chamber—was a completely dark enclosure that admitted light only through a small, lensed hole. The *camera's* lens projected an inverted reproduction of the scene facing it on the wall opposite the lens. The only thing needed to turn the *camera obscura* into a camera was a photographic plate to replace the wall. Nineteenth-century scientists set out in pursuit of this plate that could fix the inverted image permanently.

As early as 1816, Nicéphore Niepce, a Frenchman, captured rather fuzzy and temporary images on metal plates, which he called Heliographs. But it was another Frenchman, Louis Jacques Mandé Daguerre, who in 1839 determined the future of photography by making clear, sharp, permanent images on silvered copperplate. The exposure time required for an image was fifteen minutes, and the first sitters for Daguerreotypes (the first photos were named after their father) had to sit motionless for fifteen minutes, their heads propped up to keep from wiggling. Before photography could become more practical, exposure time would have to be cut. There obviously could be no motion pictures, which require multiple exposures per second, until the photographic material was sensitive enough to permit such shutter speeds. (Indeed, the first still cameras did not even use a shutter.) After Daguerre's original perfecting of the basic principle, photographic stocks became faster and faster, allowing for a three-minute exposure by 1841. Before thirty years had passed, the shutter had been invented and faster photographic plate allowed for exposures of a fraction of a second.

The first attempts at motion photography were posed stills that simulated continuous action. The stills were then projected with a Projecting Phenakistiscope to give the appearance of movement. But a real motion picture required a continuous action to be first analyzed into its component units and then resynthesized, rather than a simple synthesis of static, posed bits of action. The first man to break a single process into discrete photographic units was an Englishman transplanted to California, Eadweard Muybridge. Muybridge, whose career was as bizarre as the spelling of his first name, was a vagabond photographer and inventor, who had been involved in a divorce and murder scandal over his wife. In 1872, he was hired by the governor of California, Leland Stanford, to help him win a $25,000 bet. Stanford, an avid horse breeder and racer, bet a friend that at some point in the race-horse's stride all four hooves left the ground. In 1877, after five years of unsuccessful research, Muybridge set up twelve cameras in a row along the racing track. He attached a string to each camera shutter and stretched the string across the track. He chalked numerals and lines on a board behind the track to measure the horse's progress. Stanford's horse then galloped down the track, tripping the wires, and Mr. Stanford won $25,000 that had cost him only $100,000 to win.

For the next twenty years, Muybridge perfected his multiple-camera technique. He increased his battery of cameras from twelve to forty. He used faster, more sensitive film. He added white horizontal and vertical lines on a black background to increase the impression of motion. He shot motion sequences of horses and elephants and tigers, of nude ladies and jumping men and dancing couples. He mounted his photographs on a Phenakistiscope wheel and combined the wheel with the magic lantern for public projections of his work. He called his invention—really just a variation on Uchatius's Projecting Phenakistiscope—the Zoopraxiscope, another very fancy name for a not-so-fancy machine. Muybridge traveled to Europe where he gave special showings of his Zoopraxiscope to admiring scientists and photographers. Despite Muybridge's imitators, and despite his international honors, his discovery was obviously a dead end. There were limits on the number of animals in motion that one could find interesting. Muybridge's later refinements never surpassed the importance of his first set of motion photographs. Continuous motion had been divided into distinct frames, but it had not yet been photographed by a single camera.

One of Muybridge's hosts in Paris was another scientist, Étienne-Jules Marey, who was experimenting with motion photography. In 1882, Marey was to shoot the first motion pictures with a single camera. "Shoot" quite literally applies to Marey's experiment, for his camera looked like a shotgun. Marey's photographic gun is probably the etymological source of our present "shooting," which we use synonymously with photographing. The photographic gun used a long barrel for its lens and a circular chamber containing a single glass photographic plate. The circular plate rotated twelve times in the chamber during a single second of shooting, leaving all twelve exposures arranged in a ring around the glass plate. Like Muybridge, Marey photographed men and animals: runners, jumpers, fencers, trotting horses, falling cats, flying gulls. But Marey's Chronophotographs produced a much more fluid analysis of motion, the finished print resembling a surreal multiple exposure. In 1888, Marey replaced the glass plate with paper roll film, allowing more and faster exposures. Photography had reached the threshold of motion pictures.

To produce a motion picture that was more than a one- or two-second snippet of activity, a material had to be developed that could accommodate not twelve or forty or one hundred images, as Marey's eventually did, but thousands of images. In 1884, George Eastman began his experiments with celluloid roll film, which he intended to use in his Kodak still camera. By 1888 the camera and film were ready; photography, which had been the sole property of professionals, was now any man's hobby. Eastman's celluloid film, intended originally for still photography, became the natural material for further experiments in motion photography. This American discovery of celluloid film shifts the history of the movies back across the Atlantic from France.

Thomas Edison

Appropriately enough, the American father of the movies is the ultimate representative of the ingenious, pragmatic American inventor-businessman—Thomas Edison. The supreme tinkerer threw his support behind the new tinker's craze of motion photography. But Edison gave the motion picture little more than support. Although he assigned employees and laboratory space to the photographic project, he himself gave motion pictures little thought, an oversight that was later to cost him both prestige and money. Edison's real interest in motion pictures was to provide visual accompaniment for the phonograph he had invented earlier. Pictures were not important in themselves, but merely to make the phonographic experience fuller. His original idea was to etch tiny photographs on a wax cylinder in much the same way as sound was recorded on his phonograph cylinders. The same cylinder would contain both sound and picture and could be reproduced by a single machine. The idea was theoretically good enough, but the practical problem of reducing photographic images to pin points was unsolvable. Reproduction of the images was poor and the cylinder was too small to hold a long enough segment of pictorial action. After Eastman's perfection of celluloid film, Edison's director of the motion picture project, William Kennedy Laurie Dickson, convinced the "Wizard" to give up cylinders for celluloid. Dickson sent his first order to Eastman in 1889.

Dickson had been shooting motion pictures in the Edison laboratory for cylinders as early as 1888. According to legend, one of his chief actors was Fred Ott, one of Edison's mechanics, who was a very comical fellow. One of Fred's specialties was sneezing on command. Dickson later selected Fred as the subject for one of his first film strips on celluloid. Of course, Fred froze in front of the camera for the first few takes, but eventually he sneezed his comical sneeze and the first celluloid close-up was in the can— *Fred Ott's Sneeze*. The problem now confronting Dickson was how to share that sneeze with the public. The problem of recording images had now been conquered in 1889; the problem of reproducing them had not. Edison traveled to Europe in the summer of 1889, leaving Dickson in charge of making filmstrips and perfecting a reproducing apparatus. On Edison's return in October of 1889, Dickson greeted his boss with a projected film on a screen, roughly synchronized with sound, which Dickson called the Kinetophonograph.

Despite the amazingly early projection and sound synchronization, Edison backed away from both inventions, apparently worried about the poor quality of the reproductions. Edison decided against projection. Rather than projecting films for large groups, the individual customer would put his eye to the hole of a machine and view a single filmstrip inside it. Edison's decision was based partly on his integrity as an inventor and partly on his greed as a businessman. He saw the greater clarity of reproduction in the little peephole machine; and he was sure he would make more money from the novelty if it were displayed to one man at a time, rather than filling up a hall with many people who would quickly tire of a silly novelty. Edison so underestimated the potential of moving pictures that he refused to spend $150 to extend his American patent rights to England and Europe. His shortsightedness would prove expensive.

In 1891, Edison applied for patents on his camera, the Kinetograph, and his peephole viewer, the Kinetoscope. Slowness of manufacture and distribution retarded the popularity of the invention, but within three or four years Kinetoscope Parlors, showing Fred's sneeze and other items, had sprung up all over the United States. Rows of Kinetoscope machines beckoned the customer to peek at the new marvel of mechanically recorded life.

The requirements and design of this Kinetoscope machine strongly influenced the films that Dickson shot for them. The film was necessarily a fifty-foot continuous band. Wound around spools inside the Kinetoscope, the film's ending led continuously into its beginning, exactly as the Phenakistiscope wheels or Zootrope strips had done. The space inside the Kinetoscope box limited the length of a filmstrip to fifty feet, and since Edison's cameras and viewers ran at forty-eight frames per second, the Kinetoscope contained less than a half-minute of action. The films for these machines were not edited; whatever Dickson shot became the finished film. The films had no stories, just a simple bit of action or movement. The most popular filmstrips were of bits of dancing, juggling, or clowning, of natural wonders from all over the world, and even of staged historical events.

Despite the crudeness of the first Edison films—and despite his blunder about projection—Edison left his mark on the future of film. His most important contribution was the decision to use perforations on the side of the film to help it roll smoothly past the shutter. The Edison-Dickson perforations quickly became the standard throughout the world and were known as the American Perforation. Edison was also the father of the movie studio. In order to produce filmstrips for the Kinetoscope Parlors, Dickson built a small room especially for motion pictures, adjacent to the Edison laboratories. Because the outside of the studio was protected with black metal plates, the room quickly became known as the Black Maria, at that time slang for paddy wagon. Dickson mounted his camera on a trolley inside the Black Maria so that it could move closer or further away, depending on the subject of the film. The camera, however, never changed position during the shooting. To light the action, the Black Maria's roof opened to catch the sunlight. The whole studio could be rotated with the sun, so that the scene would always be sufficiently lit.

The disadvantages of the Black Maria are obvious. The room was really a small, sunlit theatre, with the camera as single spectator. There was even a specified stage area where the juggler, dancer, comic, or animal performed. Mobility was further curtailed by the bulky heaviness of Dickson's camera and by Edison's insistence on using electricity rather than a hand crank to run it, which kept the machine perpetually indoors and inert.

Freeing the camera from its cage and freeing the filmstrip from its peephole box were the final steps in the evolution of the movie machine. For these steps the history of film travels back across the Atlantic.

The problem of projecting motion pictures was a surprisingly difficult one to solve. After the principles of motion photography had been discovered and a camera developed to demonstrate the principles, one would have thought that projecting the images would come easily. In fact, early projection attempts produced blurry images, ripped film, and a great deal of noise. Edison's decision to shelve projection was as much a realization of difficulties as a business blunder. On the other hand, it should have been clear to Edison, as it was to other inventors, that a projected motion picture was the next evolutionary step. For hundreds of years audiences had delighted in mechanically projected shows. Even before photography, audiences had sat in darkened rooms and watched projected images on a screen.

The invention of the magic lantern is attributed to Father Athanasius Kircher, who, in 1646, made drawings of a box that could reproduce images by means of a light passing through a lens. That box is the ancestor of today's slide projector. In the eighteenth century, showmen trooped across Europe giving magic-lantern shows, projecting drawings and, much later, photographs for paying customers. From the beginning, the magic lantern-ists sought to make their static images move. They developed lantern slides with moving parts and moving patterns. They used multiple lanterns to give the impression of depth and sequence. The most famous of these multiple-lantern shows was the Phantasmagoria, in which ghosts and spirits were made to move, appear, and disappear with the aid of moving lanterns and mirrors. The stroboscopic toys of the nineteenth century further enlarged the lanternist's bag of motion tricks.

The last in this string of premovie projection entertainments was the movie's closest ancestor—the photo play. In the late nineteenth century, Alexander Black combined the magic-lantern slide, photography, and narrative to produce a complete play with live narrator, live actors, and pictorial slides. Unlike the stroboscopic lantern shows, the goal of these entertainments was not the visual novelty of reproduced motion, but the same delight in stories and drama that drew audiences to the live theatre. Some of these photo plays lasted a full two hours and contained as many as four slides a minute. A striking connection between the photo play and the early movies is that both used the same melodramatic plots and stereotyped characters.

Such predecessors clearly indicated the potential popularity of projected movie shows. The problem was to develop a machine that could project the filmstrips. There were two specific difficulties, which Edison himself had faced and forgotten: the projector needed a powerful enough light source to make the projected image clear and distinct, and the film needed to run smoothly and regularly past the light source to duplicate the photographed movement without ripping, rattling, or burning. One of the first successful projections was made by a Virginia family of adventurer-inventors, the Lathams. Major Woodville Latham, former officer in the Confederate Army and former chemistry instructor, together with his two dashing sons, Gray and Otway, invented a camera and projecting machine in 1895 (called either the Panoptikon or the Eidoloscope) that produced better results than Edison's. The Lathams doubled the size of Edison's film to approximately 70mm. The bigger film produced a clearer, brighter, sharper picture. Although the Lathams gave a few showings in southern cities and in New York, their stay in the big city converted the two Latham boys from scientists to playboys. The Lathams and their invention ended in the obscurity of financial disaster.

A successful projector required more than just an enlargement of the film. It required a totally new principle of moving the film past the gate. The new principle, discovered and developed in Europe rather than America, was the intermittent movement of the film rather than a continuous one. Each frame stopped momentarily in front of the lamp and was then succeeded by the next frame, which stopped, and then the next, which stopped, and so forth. The intermittent movement allowed a clear, sharp image, for the stationary frame used the available light more economically. The intermittent motion was, in principle, precisely the same as the slits in the Phenakistiscope; rather than a continuous succession of whirring images, each image was separated from the others into an individual piece of the whole. The intermittent movement solved the problem of ripping film as well as of insufficient illumination. The moments of pause allowed the tension on the take-up reel to ease; the film did not rip as it did with continuous-motion projectors. The single problem that intermittent motion caused was the possibility of burning the film that remained momentarily stationary in the gate. To solve this problem, the intermittent-motion projector required some kind of cooling system to protect the film. Today, despite all the changes and improvements in movie equipment, our projectors are the same in principle as those invented in the final years of the nineteenth century.

As early as 1888, a Frenchman working in England, Louis Augustin Le Prince, patented machines that both shot and projected motion pictures, using intermittent motion in both processes. He also shot several filmstrips with a machine that used perforated film and a much slower film speed than Edison's (twenty frames per second). Le Prince's influence on the history of film is minor, however, for in 1890 he mysteriously disappeared from a train between Dijon and Paris; he was never found. In 1893, an Englishman, William Friese-Greene, patented a combination camera-projector, guaranteeing intermittent motion in both, but there is no evidence that the machine ever successfully photographed or projected any films. The two most significant projectors were developed by men who began, ironically, by buying Edison Kinetographs and analyzing them. Edison's oversight in neglecting European rights allowed an Englishman, R. W. Paul, and, more important, two Frenchmen, appropriately named Lumière, to invent a functional projector and build a more functional camera.

Auguste Marie Louis Nicolas Lumière, the elder, and Louis Jean Lumière, the younger and more important of the two inventor brothers, started dabbling with Edison's Kinetoscope and Kinetograph in 1894. Their father, an avid photographer, had founded a factory in Lyon for manufacturing photographic plates and, later, celluloid film. Interested by the new motion photography, these scientist-industrialist-mechanic brothers developed their own machine within a year. Unlike Edison's bulky indoor camera, the Lumière camera was portable; it could be carried anywhere. The operator turned a hand crank rather than pushed an electric button. In addition, the same machine that shot the pictures also printed and projected them. Intermittent motion was guaranteed for projection.

Early in 1895 the Lumière brothers shot their first film, *Workers Leaving the Lumière Factory*. Beginning in March of the same year, the Lumières showed this film and several others to private, specially invited audiences of scientists and friends throughout Europe. The first movie theatre was opened to the paying public on December 28, 1895, in the basement room of a Paris café. The Lumières showed several films, among them *Workers Leaving the Lumière Factory,* a Lumière baby's meal (*Le Repas de bébé*), a comical incident of a gardener who gets his faced doused by a boy's prank (*L'Arroseur arrosée*), and a train rushing into a railway station (*L'Arrivé d'un train en gare*). The last film provoked the most reaction, as the audience shrieked and ducked when it saw the train hurtling toward them. In Jean-Luc Godard's *Les Carabiniers*—Godard's films are filled with historical tidbits—a farm boy watches his first movie, which is also a train arriving at a station, using the same camera angle as Lumière's, of course. The boy shrieks and ducks, just as the first movie audiences did in the café theatre. Audiences would have to learn how to watch movies.

The Lumière discovery of 1895 established the brothers as the most influential and important men in motion pictures in the world, eclipsing the power and prestige of Edison's Kinetograph and Kinetoscope. Within five years, the power of the Lumières would also fade. The brothers were more interested in the scientific curiosity of their discovery than the art or business of it, although eventually their film catalogue included over one thousand filmstrips for purchase. Despite their brief importance, the Lumière discoveries established several patterns and practices that have remained standard throughout the history of film. The Lumières standard-ized the film width at 35mm., still the standard width of film today. The Lumières established the film speed of sixteen frames per second, the ap-proximate standard speed until the invention of sound required a faster one for better sound reproduction. The slower film speed allowed their projector to run more quietly and dependably. Edison, still maintaining the visual superiority of forty-eight frames per second, scoffed at the Lumière speed as destroying the sensation of continuous movement; only a few years later Edison himself adopted the Lumière speed. And a final Lumière contribution was the fancy name they coined for their inven-tion—the Cinématographe; it is one of the few Greco-Latin names to sur-vive the first era of invention. In many countries today, as well as in the columns of many sophisticated film reviewers, the movies are the cinema.

Almost simultaneously with the Lumières, experimenters in England, Germany, and America were making progress on their own machines. In England, R. W. Paul and Birt Acres also borrowed Edison's unpatented machines for their own discoveries. In Berlin, Max and Emil Skladanow-sky entertained audiences with their Bioscope, a camera and projector they had developed independently of any other invention. In America, a young inventor named Thomas Armat independently discovered the Lumière principle that the film movement must be intermittent. In addition, Armat discovered that the film ran more smoothly with a small loop to relax the film tension just before and behind the film gate. This loop was quickly adopted around the world and called the American or "Latham" loop, which all projectors still use today. The loop also proved the legal loophole that dragged Edison into the courts for the next ten years in an attempt to get back the money he had lost from his initial mistake. But the story of the lawsuits comes later. Early in 1896, Thomas Armat and Thomas Edison came to a business agreement. Edison would sell Armat's projector as his own invention, enhancing the prestige and sales potential of the machine. Armat would silently receive a handsome percentage of the sales. The Edi-son company announced its latest invention, the Vitascope, a projecting version of the "Wizard's" Kinetoscope.

The first public showing of a projected motion picture in the United States is difficult to fix. The Lathams projected films in a store in 1895. Thomas Armat demonstrated his projector in Richmond, Virginia, before selling it to Edison. Several other American inventors—Jean-Aimé le Roy, Eugene Lauste, Herman Casler—also demonstrated projection machines to limited audiences. But the first official public showing for a paying audience was on April 23, 1896, at Koster and Bial's Music Hall, on 34th Street and Broadway in New York City—the present site of Macy's. The "amazing Vitascope" was only one act in a vaudeville bill; movies were

The Zoetrope.

Muybridge's leaping horse.

A Kinetoscope Parlor: Phonographs at left (complete with handkerchiefs for wiping the ear pieces), Kinetoscopes on the right.

The first movie studio: Edison's Black Maria.

Lumières' first film: **Workers Leaving the Lumière Factory.**

A "home movie": Lumières' **Feeding Baby.**

The freedom of the outdoors and the excitement of motion: Lumières' **Boat Leaving the Port.**

The Mutoscope.

Méliès' **A Trip to the Moon:** a chorus line of ladies bids farewell to the space ship.

Cohl's **The Joyous Microbes:**
the disease of drunkeness.

Rover jumps out the window . . .
swims the stream (and shakes
himself off) . . . finds the shanty
where Baby has been hidden . . .
comforts Baby . . . leaves the shanty . . .
swims back across the stream . . .
trots down the street . . .
leaps back into the house . . .
tells the news to his grieving master . . .
leads master back down the street . . .
back across the river and . . .
back to the shanty door. Rover's reward.

The precise establishment of locations
and the repetition of setups produces
both awareness of the process and
emotional participation in the event.

QUEEN
ELIZABETH

Sarah Bernhardt: stage composition and
stage acting, with no help from the camera.

SEVEN
YEARS
BAD LUCK

Max (Max Linder) fooled into thinking that his butler
is his reflection in a mirror that doesn't exist.

typically part of vaudeville shows in the United States until they started filling their own theatres shortly after the turn of the century.

For the first Vitascope program, Edison converted several of his Kinetoscope strips for the projector; he also "borrowed" a few of the R. W. Paul films that Edison had pirated from England. One good piracy deserved another. As with Lumière's first showings, the most exciting films were those with action that came straight out at the audience. During the showing of a filmstrip of *The Beach at Dover* patrons in the front rows ran screaming from their seats, afraid they were about to be drenched. Those cynics who were unimpressed were sure that the film had been shot in New Jersey.

The First Films

The first film audiences were amazed to see that living, moving action could be projected on an inert screen by an inanimate machine. The first films merely exploited their amazement. The films that Louis Lumière shot for his Cinématographe and that Dickson and others shot for the Vitascope were similar. A film lasted between fifteen and ninety seconds. The camera was stationed in a single spot, turned on to record the action, and then turned off when the action had finished. These films were really "home movies"—unedited scenery, family activity, or posed action—that depended for their effect on the same source as today's "home movies"— the wonder of seeing something familiar and transitory reproduced in an unfamiliar and permanent way. Nowhere is the home-movie-like quality of the first films more obvious than in Lumière's *Le Repas de bébé,* which has been duplicated uncounted times in contemporary 8mm. versions. A major difference between the first Edison films and the first Lumière films is that Lumière's have more of this home-movie quality of merely turning the camera on to record the events that happened to occur around it. The Edison films, despite their lack of editing and plot, were gropings toward a fictional, theatrical film; they were indoor films. The Lumière films took advantage of the outdoors—they were freer, less stilted, better composed, more active.

The categories of the Lumières' catalogue indicate their conception of what the filmstrip would provide its audience. The catalogue breaks its filmstrips into different kinds of "views"—mere visual actualities—General Views, Comic Views, Military Views, Views of Diverse Countries. The most interesting views are those containing the most interesting patterns of movement: a boat struggling out to sea against the waves, a cavalryman mounting and dismounting from his horse in the accepted military style, the charge of a line of cavalry horses, the crumbling of a demolished wall.

The most celebrated of the Lumière films is the comic jest, *L'Arroseur arrosée*. This comic incident, staged, but shot outdoors, contains the seeds of what was to blossom into one of the most important contributions of the silent film—physical comedy. While a gardener waters a lawn, a boy sneaks behind him and steps on the hose. Seeing the hose is dry, the gardener picks up the nozzle and stares at it. The boy steps off the hose, water gushes out of the nozzle into the gardener's unsuspecting face. The boy laughs. The gardener catches the boy and spanks him (although the camera's refusal to pan with the action makes the final action more difficult to catch than the boy).

This little film contains so many elements of a comic art that would one day mature: the gag is completely physical; despite the improbability of the result, the causes are clear and credible; the butt of the joke is unjustly and unwittingly the victim of circumstances of which he is un-aware; despite the victim's ignorance, the audience participates in the joke with the boy; the comic punishment is more a blow to the ego than to the body; the comic participants have obvious one-dimensional traits and roles so that complexity of character cannot interfere with the force of the jest.

The early Edison films lack the freshness and freedom of Lumière's. Typical is the staged heaviness of *The Execution of Mary, Queen of Scots* (1895). In less than a half-minute of film, besheeted guards lead Mary to the block, push her on it, and whack off her head. The audience then gets the thrill of seeing Mary's head bound off like a basketball. Despite the clumsiness of the film, two elements of it are worth some attention. First, the camera clearly thinks of itself as a spectator in the theatre. The characters move left and right in a single plane, rather than using the full depth that films were later to discover. Further, the film has a strong sense of entrance and exit, two more stage devices the mature film would dis-card. This stage mentality would continue to dominate the movies for over fifteen years. Second, the film shows one clear realization of the potential of the film medium. After Mary sets her head on the block, the camera stops to allow a dummy head to substitute for Mary's real one. The ability to stop the action and start it again is one of the advantages that the camera enjoys over the stage. Within a very few years, the Frenchman, Georges Méliès, would make much out of this camera advantage.

A second interesting Edison film, and certainly the most famous, is the *John Rice-May Irwin Kiss*. Shot originally for the Kinetoscope in 1896, this kiss, when projected on the large screen, excited the first wave of moralistic reaction to movie romance, which has remained a constant in film history. John Rice and May Irwin were the romantic leads in a current

Broadway stage success; Edison convinced them to enact their climactic kiss in his Black Maria. When moralists and reformers saw their large, projected mouths meet in lascivious embrace, they showered the local newspapers with letters and the local politicians with petitions. Upon seeing *The Kiss* today, the viewer would probably find more obscenity in the dumpy unattractiveness of the two bussers than in their "torrid" kiss, which seems a quarter-second peck. The players spend more time coyly and clumsily puckering up than they do in physical contact.

Although Lumière specialized in actualities and Edison in theatrical and staged scenes, the success of each in their particular genre led to imitations in the same genre by the other. Edison's *Washday Troubles* (1898) is a clear descendant of Lumière's gardener film, as a tub of washing douses those who are tending it because of a boy's prank. After seeing Edison's success with them, Lumière began staging historical scenes such as *Marat* and *Robespierre* in 1897. In addition to borrowing successful formulas—a practice that would continue throughout movie history and even into today's television programming—the two companies literally stole each other's films, made up duplicate prints (dupes) and sold them as their own. In addition to competing with and stealing from each other, Edison and Lumière faced both competition and thievery from rivals who were springing up in England, America, and France. The next ten years of film history would be ones of commercial lawlessness as well as aesthetic discovery.

Chapter 3

FILM NARRATIVE, COMMERICAL EXPANSION

The two film rulers of 1895, Lumière and Edison, would encounter crafty and powerful competitors within a year. In France, the Lumière superiority was attacked by an artist on one side and by industrialists on the other. Georges Méliès, owner-prestidigitator of the Théâtre Robert-Houdin, saw the movies as a means of inflating his bag of magical tricks. He immediately recognized the cinematic possibilities for fantasy and illusion. In 1896 he asked the Frères Lumières to sell him a camera and projector. When the Lumières refused to sell a Cinématographe, he bought one of R. W. Paul's Theatrographs in London. Méliès shot his first film of illusory tricks, *A Game of Cards*, in the spring of 1896. By 1900, Méliès was supplying the world with films and the Frères Lumières had almost ceased production.

Two other Frenchmen, Charles Pathé and Léon Gaumont, also began building their huge film empires in 1896, several colonies of which still exist today. Charles Pathé and his three brothers formed Pathé Frères, which began by copying the successful Lumière formulas of "views" and "actualities." But the Pathé goal was not entertainment but conquest: to control all branches of the French film industry. Within a very few years the Pathé factory embraced everything to do with motion pictures. Their company manufactured cameras and projectors, it manufactured the raw film stock (after acquiring George Eastman's European patent rights), it produced the filmstrips, and it owned a chain of theatres for showing them. The American film industry would grope hesitatingly toward this monolithic control that the Pathés quickly perceived. Léon Gaumont's perceptions were similar; he founded a second French film empire that ranged from manufacturing machine parts to collecting receipts at the theatre door.

The English film between 1896 and 1906 was perhaps the most innovative in the world. R. W. Paul, who had been displaying the products of his Theatrograph for almost a year, began attracting other inventor-photographers to experiment with moving pictures. This group, which has become known as the "school of Brighton," produced the first original ideas to take cinematic form. G. A. Smith, James Williamson, and Cecil Hepworth made significant and rapid progress with the principles of editing, realizing that the effect of a filmed story was a function of the way the individual pieces of celluloid were stitched together. Until the emergence of D. W. Griffith some ten years later, the films of these British directors were the slickest on the screen, precisely because they had discovered the importance of editing for both building a story and driving the story's rhythm.

An American, Charles Urban, joined the native Englishmen to enrich the British film further in this period. Urban, who had unsuccessfully tried to peddle his Edison-imitation camera (called the Bioscope) in America, journeyed to London to try his luck there. Fearing the stigma of Americanism, Urban christened his London concern the Warwick Trading Company. Despite the name, the Urban company pioneered in its production of scientific films using micro-cinematography and in its development of the first successful color process, which Urban called Kinemacolor. These British pioneers discovered the elements of film construction that Griffith would later fuse into more powerful movie chemistry: the close-up, the cross-cut, superimposition, the traveling shot, and the pan shot.

In the United States, artistic and industrial progress was much slower than in England or France. The era of tinkering, piracy, and imitation lasted until after the turn of the twentieth century. By 1897, however, the two companies that would share the power with Edison had begun making and showing films. The American Mutoscope and Biograph Company manufactured both a peepshow machine and a projecting machine that outperformed Edison's. The inventive intelligence behind "Biograph," as the company was to be called, was Edison's own film pioneer, W. K. L. Dickson. Dickson, who had left Edison, because of tensions and dissatisfaction, to go to work for the Lathams, then left the "fast" Lathams (Dickson's own testimony) to become the "D" of the K.M.C.D. syndicate. The early film companies often took their names from the initials of their owners; Dickson's initial joined Eugene Koopman's, Henry Marvin's, and Herman Casler's.

The K.M.C.D.'s first project was the Mutoscope, their peephole machine, whose effectiveness put the Kinetoscope out of business. Like the Kinetoscope, the Mutoscope offered a series of moving photographs to the eyes of a single viewer. Unlike the Kinetoscope, however, the Mutoscope pictures were large photographs mounted on individual cards. The viewer flipped the series of cards with a hand crank, his persistence of vision blurring each card into the other to produce the same appearance of movement as a motion picture. The large picture cards made the Mutoscope pictures clearer, more detailed, and more lifelike than the Kinetoscope's. The hand crank added to the viewer's pleasure by allowing the motion to go either forward or back, to go slower, faster, or stop altogether. The ultimate testimony to the Mutoscope is that of all the archaic and outdated machines of the invention era, it alone survives today—in penny arcades and amusement parks—delighting children with some of the identical photographs that their great-grandparents flicked through eighty years ago.

The K.M.C.D. motion picture machine also bested its Edison opponent. Like the Latham projector, the Biograph used much larger film than Edison's or Lumière's. The similarity of the oversized film implies that Dickson may have developed the Latham machine as well as the Biograph. The Biograph camera's huge pictures could either be mounted on Mutoscope cards or, when combined with its intermittent-motion projector, throw the sharpest, clearest images that had yet been seen on a screen. Dickson's films were also more interesting, more active than Edison's: the Empire State Express (yet another thrilling train shot), President McKinley receiving a letter at home, the parade honoring the Japanese ambassador, the actor Joseph Jefferson performing scenes from his famous *Rip van Winkle*.

As he had done at Edison's West Orange laboratories, Dickson built a special studio for shooting staged scenes. Unlike the Black Maria, the first Biograph studio was outdoors, on the roof of the Biograph offices near Broadway and 14th Street. As in the Black Maria, the stage of Dickson's roof theatre rotated to keep the sun at the best lighting angle. From this nuts-and-bolts beginning the company evolved that was to give its name to moving pictures in some parts of the world (in South Africa today the movies are still called the biograph; both Chicago and London still have theatres called the Biograph) and that was to launch the careers of D. W. Griffith, Mack Sennett, Mary Pickford, the Gish sisters, and many others.

Edison's second major competitor was the Vitagraph Company, which had a less spectacular career than Biograph, but a longer one. Vitagraph's founder and director of production was J. Stuart Blackton, another Americanized Englishman, who began as a reporter and cartoonist for the *New York World*. Blackton first became interested in moving pictures when he visited Edison at the Black Maria; he even performed his sketching act for Edison's Kinetograph. Edison soon leased Blackton a Vitascope franchise. Blackton repaid Edison's kindnesses by copying Edison's machine and making pictures on his own. Realizing the power of the Edison company, Blackton and his partners, William "Pop" Rock and Albert E. Smith, chose a name for their company that was as close to Edison's as the law would allow—Vitagraph. Vitagraph's first film, *Burglar on the Roof* (1897), was appropriately filmed on the rooftop of their office building in Chelsea. For several years Manhattan rooftops doubled as film studios. Another interesting early Vitagraph film was *Tearing Down the Spanish Flag* (1898), an attempt to capitalize on the Spanish-American War. Although the film claimed to have been shot in the heat of battle, Blackton actually staged it in the heat of Manhattan on his friendly rooftop. Blackton had not been a journalist for nothing.

Other men all over the country were catching the movie craze, assembling machines, and capturing images. In Chicago, three men began tinkering independently: George Kleine, George K. Spoor, and "Colonel" Selig. Kleine would one day become the "K" of the Kalem (K.L.M.) Company that produced the first *Ben Hur* in 1907. Spoor would one day become the "S" of Essanay (S&A) who, with his partner, "Broncho Billy" Anderson, would shoot the first series of westerns. In Philadelphia, Sigmund Lubin began several tricky activities, including "duping" (illegally duplicating) the films of others to eliminate the problem of paying for them and re-enacting events like a heavyweight title bout or the Oberammergau Passion Play on his Philadelphia rooftop. Movie projectionists trooped across the country with their filmstrips much as the magic lanternists trooped across Europe with their slides a century earlier. One of these projectionists toured the Caribbean, drawing audiences and applause with the adopted name of Thomas Edison, Jr.; his real name was Edwin S. Porter.

Narrative

Despite the frenzy of movie activity in the United States, the films did not change much. The new films imitated the successes of earlier ones; like television and film producers today, the earliest film producers copied successful formulas. The new films were longer, of course, freed from the fifty-foot limit of the Kinetoscope box. But the same rushing trains, ocean and mountain views, one-joke pranks, and historical vignettes dominated the screen. Audiences began to yawn at these same predictable film subjects. The motion picture, formerly the highlight of a vaudeville bill, became the "chaser," the part of the program that was so dull that it chased the old audience out so the new one could file in. By 1900 the movies were suffering the first of a series of business crises.

The rope that pulled the movies from the abyss was the development of a new kind of screen entertainment. The rope-abyss metaphor is an apt one, for the new kind of movie, the story film, was to use this and other similar heart-stopping devices to weave its spell. The movies were born into the age of Belasco; they have never quite outgrown that heritage. The Belasco theatre era traded on violent emotional effects—violent tears, violent suspense, violent laughter. The two dominant theatre genres were melodrama and farce; they were to become the two dominant film genres as well. The most respected playwrights were Scribe and Sardou, Jones and Pinero, Dion Boucicault, Bronson Howard, and Augustin Daly. In these plays, good and evil were as clearly distinct as black type on a white page. Though evil triumphed over good for the first two hours of the play, good miraculously won out in the last fifteen minutes. Melodrama was a world of pathos, not of tragedy, of fears and tears, not of ideas. There was no action that was irreversible; no matter what mistake the good-hearted character made, the mistake would eventually be erased by his or her essential goodness. The era's face was just as extroverted; a series of comic mistakes would arise, entangle, and explode until the denouement put all the pieces of the puzzle together. There was no reason why the film could not tell the same kinds of stories.

The problem was to translate these dramatic stories into film terms. There had been early attempts at screen narrative (Blackton's *Burglar on the Roof,* for example). But the method of making these early narrative films was merely to piece together the same kinds of static, unedited scenes that were shot for the first Kinetoscope, to expand a fifty-foot strip to a whole reel. A good example of one of these films is *Pullman Honeymoon* (1898). This Edison product records a series of events that might take place in one of George Pullman's sleeping cars involving porters and passengers, lovers, comics, bandits, and the police. The film is strikingly inert. The movie set is a stage set: the berths line the frame at left and right; the center aisle of the Pullman car serves as the stage-center playing area. Although the film lasts almost ten minutes, the camera never shifts its viewing angle nor its distance from any of the action. As in the earliest Edison strips, the camera is the single spectator at a staged play. The only noticeable participation of the camera in the action is that it stops after each incident and then starts again. But the slight jumps between the scenes indicate that the filmmaker tried (and failed) to make these gaps invisible, to keep the camera from participating in the event, refusing to exploit the cinema's ability to manipulate chronological time. Further, because the film uses only one setup, the effect is ploddingly static; the passive camera never picks out the details or facial reactions that give a film emphasis, empathy, and movement. No action, character, or object is more important than anything else. Despite its length, *Pullman Honeymoon* represents no real improvement over *The Execution of Mary, Queen of Scots*.

The Frenchman, Georges Méliès, was a much better film storyteller, precisely because he exploits the very difference between time in nature and in the cinema that *Pullman Honeymoon* tried to cover up. The Méliès films owe their superiority to the wild imagination and subtle debunking humor of their master. Méliès was by trade a magician; just as earlier magicians had adopted the magic lantern, Méliès adopted moving pictures. He saw that the camera's ability to stop and start again brought the magician's two greatest arts to perfection—disappearance and conversion. Anything could be converted into anything else; anything could vanish. One of Méliès's films, *The Conjuror* (1899), is nothing but a series of vanishings and conversions. The magician (played by Méliès himself) vanishes, his lady assistant vanishes, she turns into snow, he turns into her, and she turns into him. It may not be entirely accidental that one of Ingmar Bergman's striking films uses the same metaphor of the magician's art as a parallel to the filmmaker's.

Méliès's most famous film is *A Trip to the Moon* (1902), which successfully combines his fantasy and his humor into a naively charming film. The film's humorous touches almost outweigh the trick effects. Méliès parodies the intellectual doings of academics in the opening scene as a crazy professor (Méliès again) earnestly demonstrates his points and makes his ideological opponents disappear. Méliès's parody of the intelligentsia continues in his later films: *The Doctor's Secret* (1908) and *The Conquest of the Pole* (1912). Delightfully whimsical in *A Trip to the Moon* are the rocket ship's landing with a splat in the eye of the man in the moon, the lines of chorus girls in their short panties who wave goodbye to the moonship and lend their faces to the seven stars of the Pleiades, and the jerky, jumpy gymnastics of the little moon creatures who go up in puffs of smoke when the scientists whack them with their umbrellas. Méliès was an experienced showman; he made sure that his plots inevitably required the services of one or more scantily attired ladies. He also made sure that the films used plenty of tricks. In *A Trip to the Moon*, telescopes turn into stools, moon creatures disappear into smoke, stars and planets twirl about the heads of the sleeping scientists, and the explorers gesticulate with delight when they see the earth rise.

For all of his camera trickery, Méliès was still very much a stage creator shaping effects for a passive camera. Méliès's art was one of plaster, pulleys, and paint. The camera remained in its single position—just as in *Pullman Honeymoon*—while the magician pulled wires. The earth's rising was contrived by pulling up the earth and pulling down the rear part of the moon's crust; the ship's landing on the moon was contrived by moving the moon closer to the camera, not by moving the camera closer to the moon. Méliès clearly saw the film as a stageplay, and he referred to his technique as making "artificially arranged scenes." The structure of *A Trip to the Moon* reveals his thinking in terms of scenes. Though the film shifts locations (*Pullman Honeymoon* did not), each scene is presented in a single, unedited, unchanging shot.

Méliès also composes the scenes as on a stage; he is conscious of right and left, of entrances and exits. This staging is clear in those scenes in which the performers line up in a row across the screen: the row of scientists in the first scene, the row of chorines in the departure scene, the row of moon creatures in the moon court. The staginess of Méliès's technique is especially clear in his Oriental fantasy film, *Palace of the Arabian Nights* (1908), in which we can see the trap doors opening, the wires pulling, and the cardboard scenery sliding. Méliès took great pride in his scenic decor and effects, which he painted and plastered and conceived himself. But his insistence on making active scenery perform for a passive camera was not quite the essence of movie art.

Despite Méliès's uncinematic imagination, he is an important film figure because he was the first to have an imagination of any kind. Film theorists of a later generation—particularly Siegfried Kracauer and André Bazin—observed that Méliès and his contemporary, Lumière, established the two potential directions of the cinema in the very infancy of the art: Lumière's realism (the rendering of the world as it is) and Méliès's fantasy (the recreation of the world by the filmmaker's imagination). Interestingly, these theorists find Lumière's realism the more legitimate path. But such a judgment overlooks the fact that in contrast to the impersonal, accidental, soulless filmstrips of Lumière, the Méliès films reveal a wit and mentality behind the camera's lens still capable of producing laughter and delight in an audience that has seen the seventy-five years of films that followed in Méliès's wake. The Méliès films, abounding in surreal surprises and audacious sight-gags-in-time (unlike the later custard pie, which is a sight-gag-in-space), were the first to prove that a motion picture could be the result of the human act of creation.

Méliès's peak year as a creative artist and as a businessman was probably 1902. His trademark, the star, was seen all over the world. That star steadily declined in the first decade of the century, and by 1914 he had made his last film and disappeared, like one of the moon creatures in his film. Fourteen years later a journalist discovered him selling toys and candy at a kiosk in the Gare Montparnasse. His fame and films (many of which Méliès himself had destroyed out of bitterness) were revived. After receiving a small pension from his cinephile admirers, he died in a sanitarium in 1938.

Méliès had an immense influence on other directors in France and all over the world. The second most imaginative French filmmaker of the decade, Emile Cohl, also delighted in the irrational surprises of a world of tricks. Cohl applied the tricks that Méliès played with the natural world to animated drawings. The surreal illogic of the Cohl cartoons is much closer in spirit to the wildly surreal transpositions of objects in the early Disney cartoons or in *Yellow Submarine* than to the more realistic later Disney cartoon. Cohl delighted in converting one kind of drawn figure into another: a stick that becomes a man that becomes a window, an angry woman whose head rolls off and turns into a parrot, a pool cue that becomes a straw. One of Cohl's most delightful films is *The Joyous Microbes* (1909) in which tiny microbic dots flow together to depict the diseases they supposedly cause. In another Cohl film, *The Neo-Impressionist Painter* (1910), a painter tries to sell his very artsy abstract canvases to a buyer (the film is still topical today). As he describes each painting, the events and qualities he discusses come alive in line drawings on the canvas.

Méliès's success also influenced the films of Ferdinand Zecca. Zecca who was director of production at Pathé, made films in all the popular genres: social commentaries, farces, and melodramas. But Zecca also made trick films like *Whence Does He Come?* in which a man leaps out of the sea and begins putting on clothes that also leap out at him. Méliès's influence is also clear in many of Zecca's chase films. The chase was almost obligatory in the first decade of the century; the excitement of people running after other people compensated for the stasis of the camera and the slowness of unedited films. Zecca was one of the masters of the chase, but he added new excitement when he combined the chase with trick shots. In *Slippery Jim* (1905), the police chase a criminal who successfully eludes them because he has the ability to disappear, to appear in two or three places at once, to fly in the air on a bicycle, to unscrew his feet and remove the fetters, to wriggle out of any container or bind. Emile Cohl also made chase-trick films. In *The Pumpkin Race* (1907), the pursuers try to corral some nature-defying pumpkins that persist in rolling all over town, in windows, up steps, chimneys, Méliès's success accounts for the trick films of G. A. Smith and Charles Urban in England, for trick films in Denmark and Germany, and for Edwin S. Porter's *The Dream of a Rarebit Fiend* (1906).

One of the most influential French filmmakers in the first decade of the twentieth century was more famous for his performing than for his directing of the films in which he starred. Max Linder was the first internationally famous star of motion pictures and the first film clown. *A Skater's Debut* in 1905, in which a clumsy man meets a pair of iceskates for the first time, was also the debut of a comic character, Max, who was to become the leading figure of hundreds of comic one-reel films over the next decade. By 1910 Linder's yearly salary had jumped to over one million francs, and his face had become one of the most familiar in Europe (few of his films were ever shown in America). Linder, like Chaplin, Keaton, Lloyd, and Langdon who followed him, was a tiny man, and he used his smallness deliberately to contrast with the bigger opponents and obstacles he frequently faced. Linder's dancing moustache and dandyish manner-isms with hat and cane also set a pattern that Chaplin would follow (and expand). Linder specialized in drunken routines (also a Chaplin specialty) as in *Max and the Quinquina* (1911), in which a woozy Max makes a series of comic mistakes with both people and houses. He also specialized in debunking the intellectual, pretentious, and arty (like Méliès before him and Sennett after) as in *Max Plays at Drama* (c. 1912), which par-odies classical tragedy and romantic melodrama, primarily by means of delightful anachronisms.

Because of his European popularity and American anonymity, the Essanay company brought Max over to America in 1917 after Chaplin had left them. Both Max and Essanay soon failed. Although the films he made in America were slick and funny (especially the features, *Seven Years Bad Luck,* 1921, and *The Three Must-Get-Theres,* 1922), they never recaptured the popularity of his earlier, cruder but livelier films in Europe. Max Linder remains an interesting historical footnote who merely pointed the way for the comic masters like Chaplin, partially because of his lesser comic gifts (particularly his lack of personal vision about both his own character and the world that character faced), and partially be-cause the cinematic medium in the first decade of the century had not yet become quite malleable enough to convey a personal comic style, as it would for Chaplin only a few years later.

Indeed, the films of Linder, Zecca, and Cohl—like the films of Méliès —had not yet grasped the construction principle of movies. For them, one shot equalled one scene; the finished film was a series of scenes, not of shots. Each scene progressed chronologically, following the central char-acter about. There were no leaps in time or space, no ellipses in the sequence of events. The camera was inevitably distant enough from the playing to include the full bodies of all the persons in the shot. The next step in the evolution of film construction was taken by an American. After Edwin S. Porter had returned from the Carribbean, he paid a visit on his "father," Mr. Edison, Sr., and asked for a job. Edison hired him as one of his cameramen; within a few years Porter became director of production for Edison's film company.

Edwin S. Porter shot his two most important films in 1903. *The Life of an American Fireman* begins with the fireman-hero falling asleep, the subject of his reveries appearing, comic-strip style, in a superimposed white space near his head. This convention, known as the "dream balloon," was the only accepted way of presenting a film character's thoughts until Griffith revealed the logic of simply cutting to the character's visions. As the fireman dreams of his wife and child, the film dissolves to a close-up of a fire-alarm box and a hand setting off the alarm. The film dissolves again to the fire station as the men tumble out of their beds and down the pole, and the horses and fire engines charge out of the station house. The scenes of the fire brigade charging out of the firehouse and down the street were bits of stock footage that Porter cut into the narrative. Like the early views of rushing trains, charging engines and horses were favorites with the first film audiences. Here Porter incorporates the delight with movement into a story, just as he would do with the train in *The Great Train Robbery*.

Up to this point in the film, Porter's cutting shows far more fluidity than Méliès's or Zecca's; he cuts freely from place to place, allowing the logic of the story rather than the scene-by-scene progress of the focal characters to determine his cutting. In the film's final scene—the fireman rescuing his own wife and baby from the burning house—Porter may have taken an even more imaginative step. There are two conflicting versions of this rescue scene: one of them using the one-shot, cutless method of Méliès, the other using a more complicated editing plan. The rescue scene tells its story from two setups: from inside the house (point of view of the wife and child awaiting rescue), and from outside it (point of view of the fireman making the rescue). In one of the extant versions of the film, the audience sees the whole rescue first from inside the house and then repeated again from outside the house. This method, in the stock tradition of sticking with the focal character throughout, makes little narrative sense. The fireman could not possibly go through the entire rescue operation twice; such games with time would await Alain Resnais's *Last Year at Marienbad*.

The second editing plan of the scene is much more daring but also more credible in the film's narrative. In this version, Porter cuts freely from interior of house to exterior, making the two setups melt into a single sequence. The fireman climbs up the ladder (outside), steps into the room and saves his wife (inside), climbs down the ladder with his wife and then up again (outside), climbs into the house again to save the baby (inside), and then down the ladder again with the child (outside). Porter seems to have realized that the basis of film construction was not the scene but the sequence of shots that could be built into a scene. Further, the final rescue sequence reveals Porter's perception of what the Soviets later called "creative geography." The outdoor shots were clearly shot outside a real house and the indoor shots just as obviously inside a studio. Porter seems to have intuited that the cinema's logic creates a unity of place where none exists in nature.

Because of the doubts about the editing of *Fireman's* last scene, Porter's later film of 1903, *The Great Train Robbery*, receives more critical attention. The first series of shots in the film shows the same kind of step-by-step, one-shot–one-scene editing of the Méliès films. The outlaws enter the telegraph office and tie up the operator, board the train as it stops for water, rob the mail car and shoot the railroad man, seize the locomotive, unhook it from the rest of the train, rob all the passengers and shoot one who tries to escape, run to the locomotive and chug off, get off the locomotive and run to their horses in the woods. Up to this point in the film any director might have made it, except for the flow and careful detail of the narrative sequences and the beauty and vitality of the outdoor shots. The very last scene of the sequence reveals a new editing idea. It is clearly an elliptical jump in time, and it contains a pan shot that follows the outlaws through the woods.

But the next shot identifies the director's cinematic imagination more clearly. He cuts back to the opening shot, the telegraph office, and shows the discovery of the assaulted operator. Although the scene is a backward leap in time and deserts the spatial focus of the film (the outlaws), it makes perfect sense in the story's continuity. It answers the question which the audience naturally asks: how will the outlaws be caught? Porter's next shot reveals yet another ellipsis. Rather than sticking with the new focal characters (the operator and, presumably, his daughter) it jumps to a barn dance, into which the operator and girl eventually enter to tell their tale. And then another ellipsis. The posse is tailing the outlaws in the woods. Again, the audience makes the connecting links that the director has purposely omitted. Porter was demonstrating a familiar artistic maxim in film form: the most effective way to shape a work is to omit the inessential. Although Porter may have discovered the power of ellipsis accidentally and unconsciously (according to legend, he was running out of film and needed to economize), the finished film demonstrates that power nonetheless.

In the film's final shoot-out, three of the four bandits meet operatic, hands-in-the-air, pirouette-and-fall deaths. The fourth had already fallen off his horse in the chase scene. Ironically, this one gunman who did not know how to ride (he even had trouble mounting up in an earlier scene) later became the world's first cowboy star: "Broncho Billy" Anderson (né Max Aronson). Another irony of the film is that the final close-up of a bandit firing at the audience was intentionally unrelated to the whole film. Like 3-D of later years, the shot merely thrilled customers with a direct assault. The exhibitor could put the shot either at the beginning or end of the film, depending on his personal taste.

Porter's other films do not show the same freshness in cutting as *The Great Train Robbery*. His version of *Uncle Tom's Cabin*, also 1903, is completely bound by the stage and staging. Later films, like *The Dream of a Rarebit Fiend*, despite its comedy and imaginativeness, copied the Méliès formula. Perhaps the freedom of being outdoors influenced Porter's editing plan in *Train Robbery,* the vast spaces being so clearly different from the boundaries of four theatre walls. Indeed, one of the striking characteristics of all American films before 1912 (including Griffith's) is that their outdoor shots look vital and fresh while the indoor shots look static, flat, and dead. Once outdoors, the accidental attractions of nature compensated for the filmmakers' lack of craft and consciousness. Porter's studio films, like those of his contemporaries, revert to the principles of the first films in Edison's Black Maria.

While Porter was developing the tools of continuity and ellipsis in America, the "school of Brighton" was making similar and even more rapid progress in England. Cecil Hepworth's *Rescued by Rover* (1905) is one of the most slickly edited pre-Griffith films, a decided advance over Porter in narrative construction and rhythm. In the first expositional shot, a nurse wheeling a baby carriage insults a lady gypsy, who vows revenge. In the second shot the gypsy steals the baby as the nurse chats with a beau. Then Hepworth makes a huge elliptical jump. Rather than sticking with nurse, watching her discover the loss and running home to tell baby's parents, the film's third shot begins with nurse bursting into the family living room to tell her news. As she recites her tale, Rover, the family collie, listens intently; he jumps out the window in search of lost baby.

Then begins the most remarkable sequence in the film: a series of individual shots showing Rover finding baby, returning to tell his master, and leading master back to baby. The sequence unfolds in the following shots: 1) Rover jumps out of window; 2) runs down the street toward camera; 3) turns corner; 4) swims across stream toward camera (with a delightful moment as Rover shakes himself off after emerging from the water, probably the first naturalistic detail in a fictional film); 5) Rover searches a row of shanty doors; 6) cut to inside shanty where gypsy wench sits guzzling booze; gypsy exits, Rover enters, nuzzles baby; 7) Rover runs out door of shanty, same setup as 5; 8) Rover swims across stream away from camera, same setup as 4; 9) Rover runs around corner, away from camera, same setup as 3; 10) Rover runs down street away from camera, same setup as 2; 11) Rover jumps into house window, same setup as 1; 12) cut to inside house, Rover "tells" master; 13) Rover and master run down street, same setup as 2 and 10; 14) Rover and master cross stream, same setup as 4 and 8; 15) Rover leads master to door of shanty, same setup as 5 and 7; 16) master finds baby, takes her out of shanty; gypsy returns to find baby gone; she is comforted by baby's clothes and her bottle of booze. In the film's final scene baby, master, mistress, and Rover are happily united in their living room; Hepworth has elliptically omitted the process of returning home, knowing that the sequence was not necessary to the emotional tension of the film.

Hepworth's careful editing of *Rescued by Rover* produced two effects that had not been achieved before, which communicated themselves to the audience in completely cinematic terms. His careful use of the same setups to mark Rover's progress both toward and away from baby firmly implanted in the audience's mind exactly where Rover was in relation to the object of the rescue (the gypsy hovel) and the agent of the rescue (the master's house). Without any titles or explanations the audience had a complete understanding of the rescue process. Second, this technique produced not only awareness but suspense. Because the audience knew where Rover's path was leading, it could participate in the excitement of Rover's finally reaching the end of it. Hepworth increased this excitement with the smooth fluidity of cuts from one setup to the next. Although the locations were undoubtedly far apart, the impression of Hepworth's cutting was that Rover ran continuously from one location to the next. Hepworth cut consistently as Rover was in motion across the frame (Eisenstein and Pabst would later develop the power of cutting on movement), impelling the viewer's eye into the next shot and producing both fluidity and visual energy. The lengths of the shots were perfectly timed to increase the rhythm of excitement. Hepworth did not repeat the shot-by-shot sequence after baby had been rescued because he realized that the effectiveness of the process was dependent on our not knowing how and if baby would be saved.

Perhaps the ultimate testimony to the quality of the primitive British films can be seen in the satirical comedy, *A Suffragette in Spite of Himself*. Produced by the new British branch of the Edison Company in 1912, this little film is the story of an anti-feminist male chauvinist who inadvertently carries a profeminist sign on his back all around London, the sign having been stuck there by some pranksterish boys. (The film is a clear extension of the Lumière prank film, effectively complicated by detailed characterization and social satire.) The film's acting is so subtle, its satire so relevant, its plot construction and editing so fluid, its composition so interesting (one shot even uses extreme depth-of-field with both foreground action inside a room and rearground action outside a window that might be said to foreshadow Renoir), its visual texture so consistent between indoor and outdoor shots, that it was far superior to any of the contemporary offerings of the parent Edison Company.

Between 1895 and 1905, the movies had progressed from static, one-shot "views" to increasingly fluid sequences of shots that produced a continuous if not necessarily complex narrative. The next evolution of narrative would require a master with a firmer and bolder sense of the cinematic elements. D. W. Griffith would display it some three or four years later.

Business Wars

While movie directors gradually discovered the elements of film construction, American movie exhibitors gradually converted commercial chaos into order. In the last five years of the nineteenth century, the American picture business enjoyed the protection of neither law nor professional ethics. Cameramen and exhibitors blatantly ignored machine patents, pirating and duplicating any instrument that could make them money. Even more vulnerable were the filmstrips themselves, which were not yet protected by copyright laws. The French and English films, especially those of Méliès and Lumière, were the most vulnerable; although many Méliès films were shown in the United States, his Star Film Company made no money from the prints that had been smuggled out of France and duped in America. A cold war, which on occasion became a very hot one, entangled all producers and exhibitors of motion pictures.

In 1899, for example, Biograph set up a huge battery of hot lights on Coney Island to record the Jeffries-Sharkey fight. The film would be the first to use electricity instead of sunlight. While the Biograph camera was grinding away in the front row, the Vitagraph camera was grinding away twenty rows back. When the Biograph boys discovered the Vitagraph camera, they sent a crew of Pinkerton detectives to seize the machine and film. The fight fans surrounding the Vitagraph camera, unaware of the causes of the attack, manfully protected their neighbor, producing more action outside the ring than in it. Eventually Vitagraph's Albert E. Smith recorded the whole fight, smuggled the film out of the arena, and developed it that night in the Vitagraph lab. The next morning Smith discovered that the pirated film had itself been pirated out of the lab by some late-night delegates from the Edison company. Ironically, although Biograph went to the trouble and expense of lighting the fight, Vitagraph and Edison (both eventually released prints of it) were the only ones to make any money on it.

In December of 1897, Thomas Edison served his first legal writ, announcing his intention to eliminate all competitors in motion pictures. Edison, in the next ten years, would bring suit against any company that used a loop of film in either a projection machine or camera, claiming he owned the rights to all loops because of the Armat patent on the "Latham

Loop." Ironically, although the Lathams used a loop of film in their patented camera, only Armat used a loop in his projector. But film loops had been identified with the Lathams, and so the "Latham Loop" became the generic name for all loops in all film machines. Edison's private detectives roamed the country searching for shooting companies, serving any they discovered with legal writs or extralegal wreckage. Edison steadily coerced the smaller companies into accepting his terms, eventually bringing suit against the big ones like Vitagraph.

Then Thomas Armat took to the courts, dissatisfied with Edison's taking full credit for the Vitascope. Edison had double-crossed Armat commercially by manufacturing his own projecting machine, the Projecting Kinetoscope, just two years after marketing Armat's. Armat, like Edison, brought suit against everyone who used his loop projector; he also sued Edison. Biograph, meanwhile, was preparing its own legal dossiers. With some careful bargaining it bought both the Armat patents and the Latham patents, thereby arming itself with plenty of ammunition to use against Edison. For ten years the motion picture companies busied themselves with suits and countersuits, in addition to grinding out an ever-increasing number of films. Some 500 legal actions were taken, over 200 of them making their way into court. The reams of court testimony from this era proved to be valuable for the film historian, if for no one else.

While the company lawyers were busy at each other's legal throats, the movie companies continued making and selling films. Originally, when movies were part of vaudeville bills or amusement arcades, the film company sold the finished picture directly to the exhibitor at between ten and twenty-five cents per foot, depending on the expenses of the film, its potential popularity, whether it was hand-tinted (a common practice of the time), et cetera. The exhibitor then owned the film and could show it as often as he liked—until the print wore out. Then he would buy a new one.

But a new exhibiting development, just after the turn of the century, produced a new distributing practice. In 1902, an enterprising Los Angeles showman opened a small theatre in a store specifically for the purpose of showing motion pictures. Thomas L. Tally's Electric Theatre was the first permanent movie theatre in the United States. More and more of these store theatres sprang up, until, in 1905, a Pittsburgh store theatre opened that was a bit plusher, accompanied its showings with a piano, and charged its customers a nickel. It was the first nickelodeon. Within three or four years there were over 5,000 of these nickelodeons in the United States.

The permanent movie theatre forced a fundamental change in the relationship of the movie exhibitor and movie producer. The nickelodeon required a large number of films each week; about six films of one reel each (sixty minutes of film) made up a single program, and to keep the customers coming, programs had to change several times a week, if not daily or several times a day. The theatre owner had no use for buying a film outright; after several showings his regular patrons would not want to see it again. Between the film producer and the film exhibitor stepped a middleman who either bought the film or leased it from the producer and then rented it to the many exhibitors. The exhibitor paid less money for a larger supply of films; the producer was certain of selling his films. The three-part structure of the American film industry, producer-distributor-exhibitor, worked out well for all parties. The structure, with some wrinkles, survives today.

Edison would try to use this three-level structure to bring peace and regularity to the chaotic American film world. Pressure, threats, bankruptcy, and collusion led to a combining of the nine leading film companies of 1908: Edison, Biograph, Vitagraph, Essanay, Lubin, Selig, Kalem, Méliès, and Pathé (the latter two had both begun producing in America). The combine, called the Motion Picture Patents Company, agreed to share the legal rights to the various machine patents, agreed to buttress each other's business procedures, and agreed to keep all other men and machines out of the film business permanently. The Motion Picture Patents Company could make its rules stick because they also agreed not to sell or lease to any distributor that bought a film from any other company. The exchange (distributor) who wanted to handle Patent Company films—the best pictures then on the market—could not handle any other company's films. Further, the Patent Company made an exclusive contract with George Eastman's factory; Eastman would sell raw film stock to the Patent Company and only to the Patent Company. The Patent Company was such a big account that Eastman could not afford to sell to interlopers. After ten years of piracy and bickering the "War of the Patents" was over. American film production was the exclusive property of nine companies: they leased their films only to those distributors who would accept their terms and pay their fees; and these "licensed" film exchanges, soon to become amalgamated as the General Film Company, rented only to exhibitors who paid a weekly licensing fee ($2.00) and agreed to show Patent Company pictures exclusively. From first shot to final showing, law and order had theoretically come to motion pictures.

Theoretically. Unfortunately for the Motion Picture Patents Company and the General Film Company, some distributors and exhibitors were unhappy about this monopolistic control. It eliminated bargaining, it eliminated profits from duping and, it raised prices. Within months after the peace had been signed, two distributors, William Swanson of Chicago and Carl Laemmle of New York, decided to "go independent." The two pacesetters urged other film exchanges to follow their example. The Patent War had ended; the Trust War had begun.

The independent distributor faced one problem: he needed films to distribute that were not made by a Patent Company studio. One of the obvious solutions was for a distributor to turn producer. Carl Laemmle, film exchangeman, became Carl Laemmle, film producer, and gave birth to the organization that would eventually become Universal Pictures. William Fox, distributor and theatre owner, became William Fox, producer, and the organization that would eventually become Twentieth Century-Fox was born. Fox also retaliated against the Patent Company by suing them and their General Film Company as an illegal trust. The lawyers were back in the movie business.

For almost ten more years movie companies fought in the courts and fought in the streets. Jeremiah J. Kennedy, a major executive of the Patent Company, sent gangs of gentlemen to visit unlicensed studios, leaving bits of wreckage about for calling cards. Despite the strong-arm tactics of the Trust, the Independents prospered. Adam Kessel and Charles Bauman, two former bookies, formed the Bison Life Motion Picture Company, which eventually founded the film careers of Thomas Ince, Mack Sennett, and Charles Chaplin. Edwin S. Porter left Edison to go independent, making films for his own Rex Company; it would one day be swallowed by Paramount. Most successful of all the Independents was Laemmle's Independent Motion Picture Company (known as Imp).

The Trust's solid barriers sprung other leaks. Unable to buy film stock from Eastman, the Independents bought stock from English and French factories. In addition, legitimate, licensed film companies and film exchanges ran unlicensed, independent companies and exchanges on the side. When the smoke of this second film war had cleared some ten years after the first armistice, not only had the Motion Picture Patents Company been busted in court as an illegal trust, but also the individual companies who formed the Trust were either dying or dead. The independent companies, for reasons that we will see, propelled the movies into their next era. Many of the original independent companies survive today. The last of the original Trust companies, Vitagraph, died in 1925.

The Film D'Art

An important film influence was to make itself felt toward the end of the new century's first decade. In 1907, a French film company announced the intention of creating a serious, artistic cinema, of bringing together on film the most important playwrights, directors, actors, composers, and painters of the period. The company, which rather pretentiously called itself the Film d'Art, produced its first film in 1908—*The Assassination of the Duke of Guise.* Featuring actors from the Comédie Française and incidental music by Saint-Saëns, the film was hailed as introducing the nobility and seriousness of the stage to the film. Ironically, the movie was a huge cinematic step backward from the level attained by Porter and Hepworth. The Film d'Art ran the movies headlong back into the theatre: theatrical staging, unedited scenes, theatrical acting, theatrical set painting. The Film d'Art showed no more cinematic thinking than Méliès films had, and a lot less imagination. The French Film d'Art was the first in a series of attempts to produce "canned theatre," the most recent of which was the American Film Theater with its filmed productions of plays like *The Homecoming, The Iceman Cometh,* and *A Delicate Balance.* Described by its producers as a "bold, new experiment" in 1973, the idea for the American Film Theater was sixty-six years old.

The first of these Films d'Art to be seen in the United States was *Queen Elizabeth* (1912), featuring Sarah Bernhardt and members of the Comédie Française, directed by Louis Mercanton. This bombastic film version of Elizabeth's love for Essex, whom she must eventually send to the block, reveals all the plodding staginess of the Film d'Art technique. Characters enter and exit from right and left; groups of soldiers, ladies in waiting, or courtiers stand immobile in the background, just as they are supposed to do on the stage; the actors, Miss Bernhardt included, indulge in a grotesque series of facial grimaces, finger gesticulations, arm swingings, fist clenchings, breast thumpings (once even raising dust from the costume), and quadruple takes. And yet these were among the most skillful stage actors in the world!

One of the clear lessons of the Film d'Art was that stage acting and film acting were incompatible. The stage, which puts small performers in a large hall, requires larger, more demonstrative movements. The artificiality of this demonstrativeness does not show in a theatre for two reasons: first, the live performance sustains the gestures with the "vibrations," the vitality of the living performer's presence, which assimilates gesture as only one part of a whole performance; second, the performer's voice adds another living note that makes facial expression and gesticulation also merely parts of a whole. In the Film d'Art of *Queen Elizabeth,* gesture and grimace were not parts, but the wholes themselves.

However, the only way to improve film acting was not just to make the actors underplay, but to let the cinematic technique help the actors act. A camera can move in so close to an actor's face that the blinking of an eye or the flicker of a smile can become a significant and sufficient gesture. Or the camera can cut from the actor to the subject of the actor's thoughts or attention, thereby revealing the emotion without requiring a grotesque, overstated thump on the chest. Film acting prior to Griffith, not only in the Film d'Art but in Méliès and Porter and Hepworth as well, had been so bad precisely because the camera had not yet learned to help the actors.

In *Queen Elizabeth*, for example, there is a scene in which Elizabeth bids adieu to Essex (he's off for Ireland) and then, after all the court has left, she sinks down on her throne in abject sorrow; she can be a queen, but not a woman. The entire scene—adieu, exit, sorrow—is filmed in one setup. The single take is ridiculous, unrelated to both the content and the composition of the scene. The first part of the scene is a big one: Essex kneels screen left, Elizabeth sits screen right, the courtiers watch, standing around and behind the principals. But after Essex and the court leave, Elizabeth still stands far screen right—alone. What a natural spot for the camera to pan so that she fills the frame; what a natural spot for a close-up so that we can see her sorrow. No wonder Sarah acts her unhappiness in such a big way; we can hardly see her way off on the right edge of the screen.

Although the Film d'Art had nothing to do with film art, it had a lot to do with the direction that film art would take. *Queen Elizabeth*, despite its leaden technique, was a huge success. Its success launched the career of its American distributor, Adolph Zukor, who decided to form an American Film d'Art called Famous Players in Famous Plays, which would one day become Paramount Pictures. Its success also proved that quality pictures and, more important, long pictures could make money. The Motion Picture Patents Company maintained that the public would not sit through a single picture of over fifteen minutes. It was to their advantage to maintain the theory, for the whole film business they had solidified was dependent on one- and two-reel pictures exclusively. Longer pictures would scramble the whole industry; the General Film Company purposely would not distribute any films longer than two reels. *Queen Elizabeth*, a six-reeler, squashed the Trust myth; meanwhile, D. W. Griffith's epics were only two years away.

Chapter

4

GRIFFITH

David Wark Griffith never intended to make movies. The accidental path that eventually led him to films stretched from his rural Kentucky home to selling books, picking hops in California, reporting for a Louisville newspaper, and finally writing and acting for the legitimate stage. The young Griffith had decided he was a playwright. One of his plays, *A Fool and a Girl,* even played two tepid weeks in Washington and Baltimore. Like the movies themselves, Griffith's dramatic apprenticeship was rooted in the world of Belasco. It would be Griffith who would most successfully translate the Belascian effects for the screen—melodrama, suspense, pathos, purity. Although today there is a certain pejorativeness in the term that press agents concocted to describe Griffith—"the Belasco of the screen"—there is an ironic aptness in the label that was not then apparent. Griffith began with the same dramatic structures, the same sentimental characters, and the same moral assumptions of the Belasco stage, and he never deserted them, even when his audiences did.

Griffith's playwriting ultimately brought him to the movies. Like all stage actors, Griffith regarded the moving pictures as an artistic slum. But he had written an adaptation of *Tosca,* which he failed to peddle as a stageplay. He then decided to try to sell it to the films. In 1907, out of work, he took his manuscript up to the new Edison studios in the Bronx.

The film companies had deserted city rooftops for more spacious and secretive quarters in the Bronx and Brooklyn. Edwin S. Porter, by then head of production of Edison, thought Griffith's *Tosca*, with its many scenes and lengthy plot, too heady for the movies; this was five years before the Film d'Art's *Queen Elizabeth*. Instead of buying Griffith's script, Porter offered him an acting job at five dollars a day. Griffith, recently married to Linda Arvidson, needed the money and took the job. But he insisted on playing under the assumed name of Lawrence Griffith, thinking he would save his real name for the day when one of his plays opened on Broadway. Things would work out differently.

Apprenticeship

In Griffith's first role for Porter he played a lumberjack (a very thin lumberjack!) and father in *Rescued from an Eagle's Nest*. When his wife informed him that baby had been swooped away by a huge black bird, Griffith scaled the bird's mountain lair (shot partly inside a studio and partly outdoors on the Palisades, producing a very obvious mismatching of shots), fought the puppet "eagle" to the death, and brought baby back home. This melodramatic film was not without significance for Griffith's later career. First, Edwin S. Porter provided Griffith's introduction to film technique—Porter being the only American director before Griffith who understood the power and logic of editing in building a story. Second, the thin melodramatic plot was to find its reincarnations in later Griffith movies throughout his career, both in the early short films and in the long epics. Whether Griffith acquired the taste for the melodramatic suspense of the last-minute rescue from the Belasco stage or the Porter screen, by the time he started to direct his own films that taste had become his own.

After a short career with Edison, Griffith took a job with the Biograph studio, performing the same kinds of acting chores for the head of production there, Wallace C. ("Old Man") McCutcheon. By 1908, the devouring nickelodeon's demand for films was so great that Biograph needed to step up production from one to two reels per week. The studio needed a second director for that second reel of film. Griffith, whose imagination had been spotted by Biograph cameraman Arthur Marvin (brother of co-owner Henry Marvin), was offered the job. Griffith wasn't sure he wanted it. He was content with the daily five-dollar wage; failure as a director might cost him the steady income from acting. Biograph promised him that he could go back to acting if he failed as director. The sincerity of the promise was never tested. Griffith directed his first film, *The Adventures of Dolly*, in June of 1908.

The Adventures of Dolly is a clear sign of Griffith's thorough knowledge of the successful formulas of the past. Dolly's one-reel adventures are terribly familiar. An insulted gypsy takes vengeance on a family by kidnapping its baby, Dolly, and hiding her in a water cask. As the gypsies ride away, the cask falls off their wagon and into a stream, where it starts moving steadily toward the vicious rapids. Dolly eventually escapes a watery death when her cries attract the attention of some nearby boys who are fishing; the picture ends with the inevitable happy family reunion. Griffith uses two motifs that had become standard in filmed melodrama: the spurned gypsy's revenge and the perilous danger to an innocent child. Its clear ancestors are films like *Rescued by Rover, Rescued from an Eagle's Nest,* and *The Lost Child* (1904), an American imitation of a Zecca chase film in which a mother thinks her baby has been spirited off by a gypsy and runs off in pursuit. Despite its debt to the past, the dangerous rapids would recur in later Griffith films, most notably in *Way Down East,* made twelve years later, in which Lillian Gish floats toward the falls on an ice-cake. In this first film, Griffith's handling of conventional motifs was itself completely conventional. His only innovative gesture in the film was a slightly more careful attention to the casting of the roles.

The innovations would come later. Griffith, shouldering the production demand of directing a one-reel picture every week, had been given an ideal laboratory for experimentation and development. In the five years between 1908 and 1913, clearly Griffith's apprenticeship period, he directed over 400 films, giving him the opportunity to test a new idea immediately, seeing how and if it worked, and then returning to the technique the next week and developing it further. Griffith did not innovate abstractly; he could test each method weekly in front of the camera, rejecting the tools that failed, sophisticating the ones that worked. Griffith's discoveries were empirical, not theoretical. Those discoveries embraced every component of visual, black-and-white cinematic technique.

Griffith realized that the content of the shot had to determine the camera's relationship to it, whereas the accepted shot in the film world of 1908 was what would be called the full shot or far shot today. This shot necessarily included the full figures of all the characters in the scene, plus enough of the scenery so that the audience could see exactly where the characters were and how carefully the set had been painted. This standard shot enjoyed the official blessing of the Motion Picture Patents Company, whose reasoning seemed sensible: why should the public pay the full price to see half an actor when it can see the whole actor for the same money? Griffith revealed the effectiveness of showing half an actor, or an even smaller percentage of him.

In his apprentice years, Griffith developed a full series of different shooting perspectives. Beginning with the standard full shot, he moved the camera closer to the players to produce the medium shot, including, say, two actors from the knees up (a shot later christened, the "American shot"). And then the camera was positioned still closer to produce the close-up, including only the face and shoulders of a single actor, or the extreme close-up, revealing only the eyes, nose, and mouth. Griffith also saw that he could move the camera in the other direction, further away from the actors. He produced the long shot—a much more distant view of one or more players—which emphasized more of the scenic environment than the far shot. And then he moved the camera still further from the players, producing the extreme long shot that would emphasize huge vistas and panoramas rather than the human figures.

Griffith, of course, was not the first to use these shots. Many of the Lumière "views" were of vast panoramas. *Fred Ott's Sneeze* and the closing shot of *The Great Train Robbery* both used medium to close shots. G. A. Smith's *A Big Swallow* (1900) uses an extreme close-up of a man's mouth (he was supposedly swallowing the camera), and Porter's *Life of an American Fireman* used a close-up insert of a fire-alarm box. But these earlier films used the nonstandard shot for some special photographic or narrative effect (as even the term insert implies). Griffith made all of these shots standard and combined them into sequential wholes; he thereby proved that the very idea of standardness was a cinematic lie. One could cut freely between long and medium, close and medium, close and long to produce a whole scene. Griffith broke the theatrical scene into the cinematic unit of shots.

In a sense, his method really was another kind of analogy with the stage, but a much more subtle one than film directors had earlier perceived. Although a scene on the stage is anchored in immovable space, it really is a series of shifting "beats," of emotional pivots and pirouettes, of thrusts and parries, of comings together and splittings apart. Despite the stasis of the setting and the audience's viewing angle, the theatrical scene is not static; it is constantly shifting, changing, and evolving. Griffith translated these stage "beats" into film terms. When the mood shifted, when the emotions changed, the camera shifted. It caught that intimate moment when a single member of a group made up his mind to take a significant emotional leap; it caught the smallness of a solitary soldier in the midst of a huge army on a vast battlefield. Griffith discovered that the emotional content of the scene, not the location of the scene, determined the correct placement of his camera and the correct moment to cut from one perspective to another. This discovery is frequently called the grammar and rhetoric of film because Griffith discovered that—as with words—there was a way of combining film shots to produce both clarity and power.

Griffith discovered, at the same time, the power of two moving-camera shots: the pan shot and the traveling shot. Again, both of these shots had been used before. There were pans in the "school of Brighton" films and in *The Great Train Robbery*. There were traveling shots in early Lumière views (a trip through Venice by gondola in 1897) and in an American film show called Hale's Tours, in which the audience sat in a theatre designed as a railroad car and watched films of moving scenery actually shot from a moving railroad car. But Griffith realized that these special shots were just two more potential units in creating the whole. The pan shot, with its horizontal sweeps from left to right or right to left, is not only functional for following the moving action but also transfers its feeling of sweeping movement to the viewer. The eye is sensitive to such shifts in the field of vision and it telegraphs this sensitivity to the brain, which translates it into a physical sensation. The traveling shot (sometimes called a tracking shot because the camera's dolly is often mounted on a track) produces an even more magnified sensation of physical movement: the perfect tool for communicating the internal excitement of people riding rushing trains and galloping horses and racing wagons. Griffith integrated these two moving shots into his cinematic language, using their special emotional qualities when his shot needed that effect. Griffith's restraint in using the traveling shot—reserved for brief and occasional moments in the midst of a climactic chase or "race for life"—shows how thoroughly he understood its kinetic power.

Griffith also realized that just as the camera was not the servant of space, neither was the final editing of a film the servant of space or time. The early films—Méliès's, for example—had been the slavish followers of a focal character from place to place, unable to leap to other places and other people regardless of the needs of the narrative. Griffith discovered that two places vastly separate in space or time could be brought together in the audience's mind. This editing technique, called the cross-cut (or parallel cut, switch-back, or several other synonyms), which produced closeness out of distance, became a standard Griffith tool, fulfilling two primary functions. The cut could be either a leap in space (from the victims of an attack to the potential rescuers of the victims) to increase the audience's suspense or awareness, or a leap controlled by the character's mind (from the face of a sad girl to a shot of her husband lying dead on the battlefield) to reveal the character's motivations or perceptions. Both kinds of cross-cuts were attempts to mirror internal human sensation in a concrete, externalized, visual form—either the fear and frenzy of a rescue from a violent attack or a reflective reverie in a quiet moment of joy or melancholy. But Griffith's first cross-cuts seemed illogical to the Biograph management; no one will be able to follow the story, they said. Griffith's answer revealed both his insight and his influences: "Doesn't Dickens write that way?"

Griffith's innovations went beyond the camera and the editing table. Almost simultaneous with Griffith's debut in films came the debut of the electric light in the studios. Artificial lighting gradually replaced the sun's harsh and inconstant performances. When film companies left Manhattan rooftops for the Bronx and Brooklyn, they also left the sun and the muslin (used for diffusing its harshness) behind. But the first film directors merely used the new arc lights as though they were the sun—to produce bright, even, untuned light with no regard to the tonal and narrative requirements of the scene. Does the scene take place indoors or out? During night or day? Should it feel harsh or gentle, cool or warm? Griffith realized the importance of such questions and the potential effectiveness of lighting in answering them. Indeed, one of the primary reasons that indoor scenes in early American films looked so unnatural and artificial (in addition to their obviously painted, flat settings) was that the flat, even sunlight could not possibly duplicate the texture and atmosphere of indoor life. And so Griffith lit one early film (*The Drunkard's Reformation*, 1909) with a dim, flickering, low-angle light that convincingly imitated a firelight's glow. The scene was not only one of the first indoor scenes in an American film to look like life; it was also tonally and metaphorically related to the film's plot—the drunkard returning to the warmth and comfort of his home and family. In *Pippa Passes* (1911) Griffith indicated the passage of time, from morning to night, with lighting alone. Again the Biograph management, and Bitzer, Griffith's own cameraman, said the effects were impossible, that films required bright light. After they saw his mellow results, Griffith suggested that they cash in on the dimness by advertising it as "Rembrandt lighting." Griffith's complete mastery of tonal lighting would culminate in 1919 with *Broken Blossoms*, which is dependent on lighting effects not only for its atmosphere and tone but also for the metaphoric contrast that underlies the film's moral system.

Griffith was as innovative with people as with machines. Early film acting was laughably bad; Griffith set out to improve it. First, he demanded underacting: no more huge gestures and demonstrative poses. Of course, because he had developed the expressive power of his camera and editing he had the tools to allow a player to underact and still be understood. Second, he showed a much greater attention to selecting actors to play the roles, realizing that the actor's physical type was a crucial element in conveying his emotional and intellectual states. Despite the obvious limitations of type-casting, a purely visual medium like the films communicates as much or more with physical presences than with flexible, dynamic acting talents—a principle the films still respect today. The very casualness of Griffith's getting a job with Porter reveals how shoddy the early directors were in selecting either actors or types. Third, Griffith shocked his employers with what they considered an obvious waste of time—rehearsals.

The actors rehearsed the scenes before Griffith shot them. In an era when directors could scream their instructions during the shooting, Griffith's method seemed extravagant and unnecessary. Griffith, however, had doubts about creating moods with his actors while he was screaming at them. Finally, Griffith realized the applicability of one of the key artistic principles of the stage: a whole production requires an ensemble, not a collection of individual players. Griffith began building the Biograph stock company as a cohesive group of talented, attuned performers. His success is reflected in the number of important screen actors that Griffith's stock company produced, either for his own films or for the films of others. Mary Pickford, Lionel Barrymore, Lillian and Dorothy Gish, Mae Marsh, Blanche Sweet, Henry B. Walthall, Robert Harron, and Donald Crisp all had worked for Griffith by 1913.

A close look at three specific Griffith one-reelers reveals his growing mastery of the film form. In *The Lonely Villa* (1909), Griffith's skill in cutting adds excitement to a melodramatic trifle about a wife and children who are attacked by two intruders in her home. Early in the film, Griffith's fluid and rhythmic cutting adds pace to a rather clumsy and unclear exposition that establishes the fact of the husband's leaving home while the two assailants hide outside in the bushes. The opening sequence is full of fluid match-cuts—shots from different angles and distances that have been assembled to give the impression of fluid, continuous movement—as the husband walks through the house and out the front door. These match-cuts also establish the various domains of the house: the hallways and rooms that will play a significant role in the film's climactic sequence as the wife retreats further and further from the intruders.

That climactic sequence reveals the power of Griffith's cross-cut. As the intruders begin their assault, Griffith cuts to the husband, many miles distant and ignorant of the danger to his family. The wife retreats to the telephone to inform her husband; Griffith cuts to the husband receiving the call, firmly linking the two distant locations in the narrative flow, despite the separation in time and space. Griffith then cuts back and forth between the besieged wife trying to hold out against the attackers and the husband furiously driving home to the rescue. Griffith tightens the screws by cutting each shot shorter and shorter, increasing the tension, excitement, and suspense. When the husband arrives home—just in time—the audience feels as much relief as the besieged wife; we, like her, relax after the driving finish.

The Lonedale Operator (1911) drives to its climax even more excitingly. The whole film shows a surer and more fluid technique than *Lonely Villa*. The exposition, establishing the relationship of the girl and her beau, establishing that he is a railroad engineer and she a telegraph operator, is much clearer and more detailed than the exposition in the earlier film. The acting is much quieter, much more natural than in *Villa;* the scene in which he proposes to her is humanly credible and warmly touching. Griffith captures the girl's spirit and her joy as she unexpectedly leaps on one of the railroad tracks and walks, tightrope-style, on the track while she talks to her beau. As soon as she and the beau separate, he to his engine and she to her telegraph office, Griffith builds toward the climax with a series of fluid match-cuts showing her entering the office and setting to work. Once the attack begins on her and her office, Griffith begins his relentless and rhythmic cross-cutting, which alternates between three clearly established locales: the attackers on the outside trying to get into the office, the operator inside the office trying to protect herself from the assault, the speeding train (traveling shot) on its way to answer the distress signal that the operator intelligently wired to the next station. Griffith cuts quicker and quicker from outside to inside to train, outside, inside, train, until the beau arrives just in time to find his sweetheart holding the culprits at bay with a wrench she has disguised as a pistol. The girl has brains as well as energy.

Both of these films are pure stories of suspense with very similar devices, although the later one has more human detail, greater realistic texture, and stronger narrative construction. Much more human still is *The New York Hat* (1912), which dispenses with the melodramatic, suspenseful rescue altogether. With a screenplay by Anita Loos (her first, for which she received $15 and an offer to write more), featuring Mary Pickford and Lionel Barrymore, *The New York Hat* is the story of the birth of love. Young Mary longs to escape her drab life and clothing, to attract a gentleman's eye. The young reverend of the parish buys her a stylish hat from New York that she fancies. The town biddies start gossiping, linking Mary and the reverend in sin. He finally silences their talk with a letter from Mary's dying mother asking him to look after the girl. He takes advantage of this opportunity to declare his romantic intentions; she accepts his proposal of marriage.

Griffith puts human flesh on the story's potentially bare bones. To establish Mary's longing for a hat, Griffith breaks down an expositional scene between Mary and her father into two different setups, alternating between a medium two-shot (a shot with two equally important figures) that includes both Mary and her father and a close-up of Mary alone making wistful faces in a mirror. The two alternating setups in the scene establish the crucial emotional premise of the exposition: the gulf between Mary's little-girl relationship with her moralistic father and Mary's womanly longing to be pretty. And Griffith makes the mirror a key leitmotif of the film, for when Mary finally gets her hat, she returns to the mirror (and the camera to precisely the same setup) to see how charming she looks. Griffith similarly breaks the hat-buying scene into several setups: from Mary's point of view (desiring the hat), from the reverend's point of view

Griffith's cross-cutting. Wife and family under attack . . .
while the husband gallops home to the rescue.

THE
NEW YORK
HAT

The gentlemen thumb their noses at the gossipy matrons.

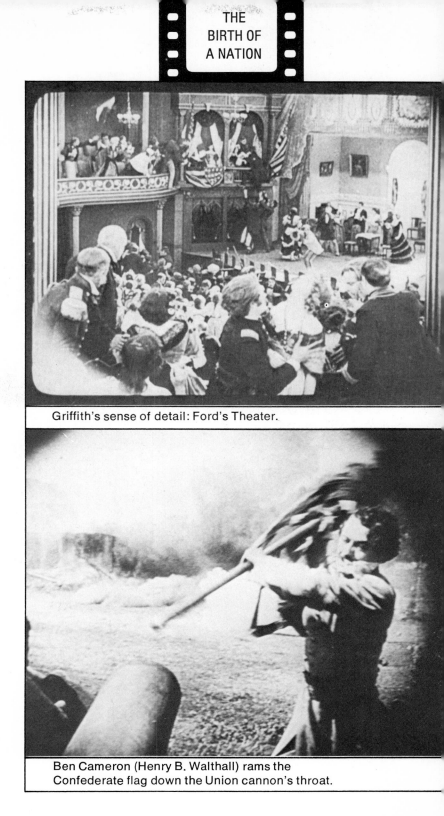

Griffith's sense of detail: Ford's Theater.

Ben Cameron (Henry B. Walthall) rams the
Confederate flag down the Union cannon's throat.

From War's fury to "War's Peace."

The street as emotional barometer: the total emptiness
and loneliness of the "Little Colonel's" return from the War.

Elsie (Lillian Gish) and Ben (Walthall)
see the City of God replacing the strife of the world.

Both bigness and intimacy.
Belshazzar's Feast and the faces of women:
The Mountain Girl (Constance Talmadge) and
The Little Dear One (Mae Marsh).

INTOLERANCE

The immensity
of the walls
of Babylon and
Belshazzar's Feast.

The poignant detail: The Little Dear One grasps her stolen baby's booty.

Flowers bloom in the rocking cradle (Lillian Gish).

BROKEN
BLOSSOMS

Chen Huan (Richard Barthelmes) and
Lucy (Lillian Gish) in their idealized Kingdom of Peace.

(seeing she wants the hat), and then a close two-shot when he makes the purchase, bringing their two heads together, instantly suggesting the direction of their affections.

The film is full of other sensitive human touches. Mary's faces in the mirror are coy and charming; the ugly, snide town gossips are perfect comic caricatures. Griffith would draw fuller portraits of these comic, nasty ladies in *Intolerance* and *Way Down East*. Most personal of all in the film is the disdainful masculine flick of the head that the all-male church elders give, in unison, to the gossipy ladies after their reverend has washed the taint of sin from his relationship with Mary. Griffith is also thumbing his own nose at these morally near-sighted ladies of reform and "uplift."

With a film like *The New York Hat*, Griffith had gone as far and as deeply as he could with the ten-minute picture. Those five years of one-reel films show Griffith laying the foundation not only for his technical achievements but also for the themes and motifs that would dominate his later films. He had made films about periods of American history (i.e., *1776, or The Hessian Renegades*), films about the contemporary social problems of poverty and vice (i.e., *The Musketeers of Pig Alley*), films that were stylistically careful adaptations of literary classics (Shakespeare, Browning, Longfellow) and contemporary novels (Frank Norris, Helen Hunt Jackson). Griffith particularly excelled at the close and affectionate study of American rural life—either the gently comic, tender study of rural customs and courtship, as in *A Country Cupid* (1911), or the compassionate view of the difficulty of rural living and survival, as in the hauntingly slow, lyrical, almost mystical shots of the farmer and his horse sowing and planting in *A Corner in Wheat* (1909), establishing the beautiful and natural unity of man, beast, and fields.

Although no member of the audience yet knew Griffith's name (no Patent Company director or actor received screen credit until after 1912), they all knew that Biograph pictures were the best on the market. But by 1913, Griffith wanted to break loose from the one-reel limit on his thoughts. He had earlier made two-reel films, but the General Film Company insisted on releasing them in two parts, one reel at a time. Now that Griffith had discovered how to say things in the cinematic form, he found he had things he wanted to say.

Griffith made no technical innovations in his longer films that he had not already begun or perfected in the short ones. The longer films used the earlier innovations to assimilate and communicate more complex and more solid material. And that material was simply the Truth, the humanistic gospel according to Saint D. W. He no longer wanted to tell melodramatic stories that culminated with the last-minute rescue, although he never dispensed with either melodrama or the rescue. He wanted the images on the screen to illuminate his personal vision of good and evil. Griffith was not just the cinema's first technician; he was also its first moralist, poet, *auteur*. A cliché in the criticism of Griffith is that his moral system is essentially that of the Victorian sentimentalist. The positive values are social order, peace, the home and family, womanhood, motherhood, and marital fidelity. The negative values are, correspondingly, social change, war, high life, sexual license, and the broken home. But these specific values are really consequences of Griffith's central vision rather than the vision itself.

The two poles of Griffith's moral world are gentleness and violence. From gentleness come all the virtues of Woman, Peace, and the Home. The figures of gentleness are almost always female; Griffith's women are really girls—luminous, soft, sweet, blonde, frail, child-like, symbols of a delicate ideal rather than living, breathing creatures. Gentleness for Griffith, however, is the ideal, whereas violence is the reality. From violence issue the evils of social upheaval (hence Griffith's hatred of social reformers), war (hence Griffith's pacifism), and sexual libertinism. The figures of violence are almost always men, for it is man's way to fight and seduce and conquer and reform. Ironically, Griffith's adoration of love and gentleness and simplicity is precisely the same, in its own terms, as that in the later *Easy Rider, Midnight Cowboy,* and *Last Picture Show.*

Griffith's difficulty was integrating his vision into his melodramatic, plotty films. All too often Griffith fell back on two artificial devices that seemed superimposed on the films rather than an integral part of them. One of them was literally superimposed. He often thrust allegorical meanings on the films by superimposing angels and visions up in the heavens to comment on the earthly action. His allegory also extended to giving characters allegorical names—the Dear One, the Friendless One, the Evil Eye. In one of his short films, *Man's Genesis* (1912), he told his own story of Darwinian evolution. The characters' names—Lilywhite (the girl, of course), Bruteforce (the violent man), and Weakhands (but strong head, the other man)—reveal their allegorical functions. A second Griffith device was to soup up the film's meaning with purple, rhetorical titles that literally told the audience what moral conclusions it should draw from the actions it was about to witness. The titles constantly tell us that war's slaughter is *bitter* and *useless* (italics Griffith's), that women turn to social reform when they can no longer turn a man's fancy, that "looms of fate" weave death that opens up its "opal gates." One of the discoveries about film that Griffith did not make was that the silent film should include as little of its information in titles as possible. One reason that his last-minute rescues were so exciting was that they needed (and used) no titles at all.

Several four-reel films that Griffith shot between the one-reelers of 1912 and the epic films of 1914–15 show both his artistry in transition and his difficulties in wedding moral significance with film action. *Judith of Bethulia* (filmed 1913, released 1914) was the last film Griffith made for

Biograph. It is a curious mixture of cinematic strengths and weaknesses. Because Griffith felt self-conscious about his biblical style and subject, his actors were much more stilted and much less carefully observed than in *New York Hat*. Griffith's rendering of the evil of the invader, Holofernes, is also formulaic and hollow. The "orgies" in his tent, metaphoric for the man's evil mind, are represented as a series of clumsy and unevocative semihula dances by the "Maids of the Fishes." Those Fish Maidens revealed a flaw in Griffith's vision that was to persist throughout his film career. Although Griffith knew what purity and goodness were, he never really knew what sin and degeneracy were all about. The abstractness of the lives of sin that people lead in his films inevitably keeps those lives from having any real or credible impact.

Balancing the film's artificiality and the fable-like thinness of the characters is Griffith's skill at cutting and construction. His opening expositional sequence effectively establishes the peacefulness and fertility of life in Bethulia, the importance of the well to its survival, and the thickness of the town walls for its defense. Here is Griffith's civilized ideal of peace and gentleness. Then Griffith introduces the conqueror Holofernes and his attacking army, the forces of violent destruction. The branches in the foreground part, revealing the awesome hordes ready to descend on peaceful Bethulia. Griffith magnifies the horrifying intensity of the battle scenes with his skillful cutting from side to side, from inside the walls to outside, and back again. These battle scenes clearly show Griffith warming up for the huge sequences in *The Birth of a Nation*, although in *Judith* the battles feel slightly pinched and confined by their being anchored to the walls of the city, a problem he would solve in *Intolerance*. Much freer is Griffith's cutting at the end of the film when the attacking hordes, without their leader, retreat in chaos. Griffith cuts from one shot in which the horses and men run furiously from screen right to screen left to the next in which men and horses stream down a hill at the top of screen left into a valley that is at the bottom of screen right. This collision of contrary movements would not only dominate the battles in *Birth of a Nation* but would also contribute to Eisenstein's theory of the shock value of colliding images.

Also noteworthy in the film are the cross-cuts between the Bethulians starving inside the walls and Judith inside Holofernes' tent preparing to ease their starvation (clearly a variation of the last-minute rescue); or the cross-cuts between Judith's hesitation before killing Holofernes, with whom she has fallen in love, and her vision of her own starving people (the vision that ultimately moves her to commit the murder). Despite Griffith's continuing technical skill and despite the film's vastness, it remains a rather tepid and artificial production.

By 1914, Griffith's innovativeness, the growing lengths and costs of his films, had irked Biograph into kicking him upstairs, making him director of studio production and relieving him of the opportunity to direct films personally. Griffith, however, wanted to make feature films; both his own vision and the new feature-length imports from Italy (*Cabiria, Quo Vadis?*) pointed the way toward longer films. Griffith left Biograph for the independent company, Mutual, signing a contract that gave him the freedom to make one picture of his own each year, in addition to making several program pictures of the company's choosing. It was a new beginning for Griffith; it was the end for Biograph. Not only did Griffith leave, but so did his cameraman, G. W. "Billy" Bitzer, and the whole Griffith stock company of actors.

One of Griffith's program pictures for Mutual, *Home Sweet Home* (1914), is another transitional mixture of good and bad; it showed where Griffith had been and indicated where he was to go. Like the later *Intolerance, Home Sweet Home* uses four strands of action. Unlike the later film, Griffith does not weave the strands together but keeps them separate, using only the leitmotif of the song, "Home Sweet Home," to unite the four stories (the song parallels the rocking cradle that unifies *Intolerance*). In the framing story of *Home Sweet Home,* the composer of the famous song, John Howard Payne, deserts home, mother, and sweetheart for the big city. There he falls to wenching, drinking, degeneracy, and poverty, summoning up just enough of his old home spirit to write his famous song. Payne later dies of unspecified causes in a foreign land, and his home-town sweetheart dies at the same time, presumably from E.S.P.

The second story in the film is the most human and delightful. An Eastern slicker falls in love with the earthy, out-west hash-slinger, Apple Pie Mary, played energetically by Mae Marsh. Griffith adds a human, comic touch when Mary first sees the slicker; she immediately starts pulling the curlers out of her hair, revealing her attraction to him. When he later returns to her, she goes through the same curler business again. In this section, the Easterner is about to reject Applie Pie Mary (two different worlds) when he hears a fiddler playing "Home Sweet Home." He rushes back to her—a delightful reunion scene with her crawling under the bed to hide from him—and they marry and live happily ever after. Interestingly, this section, the comic, earthy, rural sequence of the film, is the most entertaining part of it, just as the earthy, comic, down-east sequences of *Way Down East* are the best sections of that film. Griffith repeatedly demonstrates that his best film subjects are those he intimately knew and loved.

The third section of *Home Sweet Home* is a melodramatic Cain-and-Abel story in which brother murders brother. Their mother, about to commit suicide after the dual slaughter, hears another fiddler playing "Home Sweet Home." She gives up her thoughts of suicide and continues living, now resigned to life. The fourth section of the film is a domestic tale of potential marital infidelity. A young wife flirts with a lascivious admirer; as she is about to run off with him to a sinful amour, she hears a fiddler playing "Home Sweet Home." (Those fiddlers are everywhere.) She rejects the lover, returns to her husband, and in the next shot we see the happy married couple, aged and gray, surrounded by a bushel of kids.

The implication of all three stories is clearly that Mr. Payne's song, despite his faulty life, did great good. The film's epilogue picks up this moral nail and drives it home. We return to Payne in some unclear locale; he is either slaving away in Hell or fighting in a foreign war in which he met his death. Payne's home-town sweetheart (played by Lillian Gish) appears to him as a white diaphanous angel, superimposed in the heavens. Her image multiplies until there are many images of her fluttering and floating and beckoning from up there; Payne's image flutters up to join hers. The point Griffith makes is obviously that the results of the man's work cancel out the depravity of the man's life; furthermore, that Payne had the potential for good in him (he could write such a song), but the potential was corrupted by decadent, big-city life.

There is obviously much that is soft-headed in the film. Griffith announces with his opening title that the film is allegorical and not biographical; but the slender, melodramatic stories and the artificial unifying device (that fiddle) cannot support the film's ponderously heavy theme. You can't ask a bon-bon to be a steak. The film's titles are no help either. In the epilogue Griffith tells us:

Master Lust Thoughts
Master Carnality
Master Brutality
Master Worldly
They Pull Hard.

The Bunyanesque personifications seem disproportionate to the slim tales. An earlier title sums up Griffith's sentimentality as Lillian Gish tells her fiancé, " 'Til the end of the world and afterward, I shall wait for you." Despite the absurdity of the idea, she makes good on her promise.

The Birth of a Nation and Intolerance

For his own independent project for 1914, Griffith chose a novel by Thomas Dixon, *The Clansman,* for his property. The book appealed to Griffith for several reasons. It was a vast story, covering the final years in the graceful life of the old South before the Civil War, the turbulent, violent years of war, and the painful, political years of Reconstruction. Griffith, a southerner whose father served in the Confederate Army, was also attracted by Dixon's slant. Dixon, also a southerner, saw the Reconstruction era as a period of chaos in which the white South struggled, but survived. It was this film, with dangerous social and political implications, that Griffith set out to make.

No one on the set knew exactly what Griffith's film was all about. Griffith used no shooting script, creating all details of the vast cinema pageant out of his head as he went along. The players only knew that the project was vast: it took six weeks to rehearse and nine weeks to shoot, an incredible amount of time in an era when a director cranked out a film (*Home Sweet Home,* for example) in only a week. It required thousands of men and animals and countless huge and detailed indoor sets. Its cost, $125,000, was the most ever invested in a motion picture. At the film's premiere in Clune's Auditorium in Los Angeles on February 8, 1915, audiences finally saw how huge Griffith's plan and project were. The film was still called *The Clansman* at that opening. When the author of the novel, Thomas Dixon, finally saw the film, however, he told Griffith, in his enthusiasm, that the original title was too tame. Griffith should call his film *The Birth of a Nation*.

The Birth of a Nation is as much a document of American social history as of film history. Though President Wilson described the film as "history written in lightning," its action, which openly praises the Ku Klux Klan, is a very difficult morsel for today's liberal or social activist to swallow. It was just as difficult for the liberals of 1915. The N.A.A.C.P., the president of Harvard University, Jane Addams, and liberal politicians all damned the work for its bigoted, racist portrayal of the Negro. The film was suppressed in some cities for fear of race riots; politicians spoke for or against it according to their dependence on the black vote. At a revival of the film some ten years after its original opening, mobs poured into Chicago to see it as well as to attend a Ku Klux Klan convention. With all of the controversy over the film, it might be wise to look at Griffith's handling of the black man a bit more closely, and then to move on to the cinematic qualities of the film.

First, a close examination of the film reveals that two of the film's three villains—Lynch (the false reformer) and Sarah (Stoneman's mistress)—are not pure Negroes but mulattoes. Both possess qualities that Griffith had already damned in white men—hypocrisy, selfishness, social reforming, and sexual license. That they were mulattoes indicates that Griffith's main target was not the blacks but miscegenation; the miscegenation theme flows through the movie—in the black legislature, in signs at the black-dominated polling place, in Lynch's attraction to Elsie. The mixing of bloods is the source of evil. Griffith's stance against miscegenation stems from an assumption about blacks and whites that is perhaps more central to the film's offensiveness. For Griffith, whites are whites and blacks blacks; the white race is naturally superior; each race has "its own place." If Griffith's view seems outrageous today, it is certainly a part of his general moral system in which he viewed all social establishments as good because they are established and all attempts to change the Establishment as bad because they are disruptive, violent, and disorderly.

There are good blacks and bad blacks in Griffith's film. The good ones are the "faithful souls" who work in the fields, "know their place," and stay with their white family after the war. If Griffith's separation of good and bad seems an old-fashioned partiality to Uncle Tom, it should be pointed out that *Gone with the Wind,* twenty-five years newer fashioned than *Birth of a Nation* and released every five years to a still adoring public, makes the same distinction between good and bad "darkies." Perhaps Griffith's most offensive scene is the one in which the empty state legislature suddenly (with the aid of superimposition and dissolve) springs to life, full of black lawmakers with bare feet on desks, swilling booze, and eating—what else?—fried chicken. But Griffith's treatment of these blacks is not an isolated expression of racial prejudice, but a part of his whole system of the evil of social change and disruption. And cinematically this legislature scene is a visual marvel!

The brilliance of *The Birth of a Nation* is that it is both strikingly complex and tightly whole. It is a film of brilliant parts carefully tied together by the driving line of the film's narrative. Its hugeness of conception, its acting, its sets, its cinematic devices had not been equalled by any film before it and would not be surpassed by many that followed it. Yet surprisingly, for such an obviously big picture, it is also a highly personal and intimate one. Its small moments are as impressive as its big ones. Though Griffith summarizes an entire historical era in the evolution of the nation in general and the South in particular, his summary adopts a human focus: two families, one Northern (the Stonemans), one Southern (the Camerons), who, despite the years of death and suffering, survive the war and the reconstruction. The eventual marriage between the two families becomes metaphoric for Griffith's view of the whole nation. Human values —love, sincerity, natural affection—triumph over social movements and social reformers. The close observation of people and their most intimate feelings, the techniques of which Griffith had been developing for five years, propels the film, not its huge battle scenes, its huge dances and political meetings, its detailed "historical facsimiles" of Ford's Theatre and the Appomattox courthouse. The big scenes serve as the violent social realities with which the gentle, loving people must contend.

Even in the mammoth battle sequences Griffith never deserts his human focus. His rhythmic and energetic editing constantly alternates between distant, extreme long shots of the battles and close concentration on the individual men who are fighting. Griffith takes the time for such touches as his cut from the living, fighting soldiers to a shot of the dead ones who have found "war's peace," his cuts from the valiant human effort on the Union side to shots of a similar effort on the Confederate, including Ben Cameron's heroic charge of the Union lines, ramming the Southern flag down the Union cannon's throat. Griffith increases the power, the violence, the energy of these battle sequences with his sensitivity to cutting on contrary movement across the frame, to cutting in rhythm with the action, and to cutting to different distances and angles that mirror the points of view of the different participants. But in the midst of such violence, Griffith takes the time for quiet, tender moments: the moment when the two boys, one Cameron and one Stoneman, die in each other's arms; the moment in which a weeping mother on a hilltop views the destructiveness of the invading army in the valley.

This shot, one of the most celebrated in the film, shows Griffith's control of the masking- or irising-effect, another of the innovations he developed in his apprentice years. The iris-shot masks a certain percentage of the frame, concentrating the viewer's attention completely on a circle or rectangle or some other shape of light within the blackened screen rectangle. The iris, analogous to the theatre spotlight or today's zoom lens, either shrinks the audience's focus from the whole field to a single point or expands our focus from the single point to the whole field. In *Birth of a Nation*'s famous iris-shot, Griffith begins tightly on the weeping mother's face and then irises out to reveal the awesome army below her, the cause of her sorrow. This use of the mask-shot to reveal cause and effect is only one of many in the picture.

Griffith's attention to human dramatic detail dominates the film. He uses animals to define his characters and their emotional states. In the film's opening sequence depicting the gentle, peaceful life of the old South (analogous to the opening sequence of *Judith of Bethulia*), Griffith shows Mister Cameron gently stroking two puppies. Significantly, one of the puppies is black and the other white; also significant is the fact that a kitten soon begins to play with the pups. The animals become visual metaphors for Griffith's idealized prewar South, a happy mixture of different races and different social classes. Later in the film Griffith cross-cuts between the two lovers, Elsie and Ben, gently playing with a dove while the savage Lynch mistreats a dog. The attitudes of the characters toward animals ultimately reveal their attitudes toward people.

Another of Griffith's artistic devices is his use of the main street in the Piedmont town as a barometer of the film's emotional and social tensions. At the film's opening the street is full of people and carriages: active, sociable, friendly. As the Confederate soldiers first march off to war, the street becomes a carnival: fireworks, cheering townspeople, rhythmic columns of men on horses. Then, when "the little Colonel" (Ben) returns home after the war, the street is desolate, empty, ruined, dusty, dead. And finally, when the town is overrun with carpetbaggers and reconstructionists, drunken gangs of black men rove the street; the street has become a very unfriendly, ungentle place. By capturing human emotion in concrete visual terms Griffith successfully renders human feeling rather than a parody of feeling, as in *Queen Elizabeth*.

Birth of a Nation is part mammoth spectacle and part touching human drama. It is also part melodrama and part allegorical vision. Griffith never deserts the constructional principles of his early melodramatic one-reelers as the means to keep his story moving. The suspense and excitement of Griffith's cross-cutting create the dramatic tension of many of the sequences: the attack of a band of black renegades (significantly their captain is white) on the defenseless town and the Cameron home (and women); the assassination of Lincoln in Ford's Theatre; the rapacious Gus chasing the littlest Cameron girl through the woods until she falls to her death. The most thrilling sequence of all is, appropriately, the final one in which Griffith gives us not one but two last-minute rescues. Not only does Griffith cross-cut from the victims to the potential agents of their rescue; he cuts between two sets of victims and their common saviors—the Ku Klux Klan—furiously galloping forth to eradicate the forces of rapine and death. Not only is this rescue sequence Griffith's most complex up to this point; it is also his most sensitive to the kinetic excitement of editing rhythms and the moving camera. Some of Griffith's cuts are fewer than eight frames long.

But after the dust from the galloping climax has settled, Griffith celebrates the peaceful union of Elsie Stoneman and Ben Cameron with a superimposed allegorical pageant in the heavens. Elsie and Ben see Christ replacing the military general (Alexander the Great?); Christ cuts the Gordian knot and all humanity rejoices as the City of God replaces the Kingdoms of the Earth. There are several remarkable things about this closing vision: its audacity, its irrelevance, and the passionateness and sincerity of Griffith's commitment to it. But, as in *Home Sweet Home,* there is a striking disparity between the film's generalizations and the specific evidence on which they are based, between realistic melodrama and mystical allegory. Exactly how is this City of God to become a reality? Certainly not by the efforts of the Ku Klux Klan alone. It is the evil in the human soul that must be exorcised. And once again Griffith reveals his near-sighted probing of what he considers evil.

All the evil in the film is instigated by three people. They are evil: 1) because they are evil, or 2) because they have mixed blood. They succeed in doing evil because they entice the naturally good but easily tempted Congressman Stoneman. And his temptation stems from his physical vanity (Griffith's brilliant use of a wig to define this trait of

Stoneman's), which demands physical proofs of his prowess. According to the film's action, the chaos of the Civil War was the direct result of the nation's Stonemans who became entangled in an evil of which they were totally ignorant or about which they were helpless. Even granting Griffith this preposterous premise (suitable for melodrama but not for history or philosophy), how is one to be sure that the future contains no Stonemans? *Birth of a Nation's* final vision is an innocent wish rather than the intellectual consequence of what has preceded it. The film remains incredibly solid as human drama and cinematic excitement, incredibly flimsy as abstract intellectualization.

Precisely the same is true of *Intolerance*. This next major film grew directly out of the controversy over *Birth of a Nation*. Griffith's treatment of the blacks provoked public condemnation of the man who put such ideas on film. The criticism stung Griffith deeply, especially since he had watered down many of Thomas Dixon's most inflammatory, anti-Negro passages. Griffith began defending himself against the charges of bigotry and hatred; he angrily protested the film's suppression in several cities, writing a pamphlet championing the "Freedom of the Screen." *Intolerance* was to be his cinematic defense, his pamphlet against intellectual censorship in film form. Fortunately for Griffith, *Birth of a Nation* not only stirred a lot of talk; it also made a lot of money. Griffith would need all that money for *Intolerance*, its cost reputed as high as $2,000,000, its conception so huge that it was to *Birth of a Nation* in scope and complexity as *Birth of a Nation* was to *Judith of Bethulia*.

Intolerance was not one story, but four. In Belshazzar's Babylon, the evil high priest conspires against the wise and just king, selling the city to the Persian conqueror, who destroys the nation's happiness and murders its ruler. In Judea, the jealous Pharisees intrigue against Christ and contrive to send the wise and just savior to the cross. In Renaissance France, evil courtiers convince the Catholic king to slaughter all the Protestant Huguenots. In twentieth-century America, a Boy is falsely convicted of a murder and his wife unjustly robbed of her baby by a group of social reformers; the facts eventually surface to save the Boy from the gallows.

Tying the four stories together are its consistent themes: the machinations of the selfish, the frustrated, and the inferior; the divisiveness of religious and political beliefs; the constant triumph of injustice over justice (except in the modern story); the pervasiveness of violence and viciousness through the centuries. Also tying the stories together is Griffith's brilliant control of editing, which keeps all the parallels in the stories quite clear, and which creates an even more spectacular climax than in *Birth of a Nation*.

In *Intolerance*, there are four frenzied climaxes; the excitement in each of the narrative lines reinforces the others, all of them driving furiously to their breath-taking conclusions. Griffith's last-minute rescues cross-cut through the centuries. And finally, tying the four stories together, is a symbolic mother-woman, rocking a cradle, bathed in a shaft of light, representing the eternal evolution of humanity, fulfilling the purpose of the creator. This woman, inspired by Whitman's lines, "Endlessly rocks the cradle, Uniter of Here and Hereafter," is a figure of peace, of light (a shaft of light grows steadily brighter on her as the film progresses), of fertility (flowers bloom out of her cradle at the end of the film), of the ultimate goodness of man that will eventually triumph.

The film's bigness is obvious: the high walls of Babylon, the hugeness of the palace (and the immense tracking shot that Griffith uses to span it), the battle sequences, the care with each of the film's periods and styles. The costumes, the lighting, the acting styles, the decor are so distinct in each of the four epochs that the viewer knows exactly whether he is in the squalid, drab poverty of a contemporary slum, the elegant tastefulness of the French court, or the garishness of ancient Babylon. But as with *The Birth of a Nation*, *Intolerance* is a big film that works because of its little, intimate moments. The film revolves around the faces of women—from the bubbling, jaunty, comically vital face of the Mountain Girl in the Babylon story to the luminous, tear-stained, soulful faces of Brown Eyes in the Huguenot story and the Dear One in the modern story. *Intolerance* makes it perfectly clear that social chaos takes its toll on the women, who are the helpless sufferers of its violence. Significantly, Griffith's mother-symbol of historical continuity is also necessarily a woman. Along with the close-ups of faces, the film is equally attentive to close-ups of hands, particularly in the modern story: the Dear One's wrenched hands as the callous court pronounces judgment on her husband; her hand grasping her imprisoned husband's cap, a tender memory of his warm presence; her hand clutching one of her baby's booties after the social uplifters have carried the infant away.

The film is also rich in the same kind of metaphoric detail as *Birth of a Nation*. The Dear One shows her humanity and tenderness as she lovingly throws grain to her chickens; when she moves to the oppressive city she keeps a single flower in her flat, a metaphor for all that is beautiful and natural and alive. Significantly, flowers bloom in the symbolic cradle at the end of the film. And flowers become the same kind of symbol of love and beauty in Griffith's later *Broken Blossoms*. Yet another touching metaphoric detail is the little toy cart, pulled by two white doves, in the Babylon sequence—a metaphor for the tender, fragile love between Belshazzar and his queen. After the two have been slain, Griffith hauntingly cuts to a shot of the tiny cart and doves, a touching evocation of a passion that was, but is no longer.

Although the film is very deeply felt, Griffith's ideas are once again very shallowly developed. *Intolerance* makes quite clear what kinds of humans and human activities Griffith thoroughly detests: rich meddlers in false charities, unsympathetic judges and courts of law, callous entrepreneurs and businessmen, religious hypocrites, political schemers, white slavers who take advantage of the poverty of the poor, anyone who kills or destroys. Griffith's technique is as effective at conveying hatred as it is at evoking tenderness. His social-reforming ladies are vicious, ugly caricatures of gossiping old ladies; his intriguing priests and politicians and Pharisees are equally grotesque. One of Griffith's most effective devices of caricature is the cross-cut—particularly the sequence in which he captures the cold, unfeeling inhumanity of the factory owner. Griffith cuts from the shots of the workers being mowed down by police rifles (violent, quick cutting, frenetic) to a shot of the owner of the factory sitting alone in his vast office (a long take, perfectly still, shot from above to emphasize the size of the office and the smallness of the man). The contrast of action and inaction, passion and deadness, in the two shots clearly defines the man's unsympathetic inhumanity to his slaughtered workers. Ten years later Eisenstein would build a whole film, *Strike,* out of such cross-cuts.

Although Griffith's dislikes are clear, the intellectual cement uniting the four stories (and the rocking cradle) is not. The film could as easily have been called "Injustice" or "Intrigue" as *Intolerance*. Griffith was interested in the word intolerance simply because he felt himself the victim of it. But in none of the four stories does intolerance seem so much the cause of evil as pure human nastiness (exactly as in *Birth of a Nation*). And when the film ends with its almost obligatory optimistic vision—more superimposed angels in the heavens; the fields of the prison dissolve into fields of flowers; flowers bloom in the cradle—we once again witness a thematic *non sequitur,* an interpolated wish rather than a consequence of the film's action. Though there may be hope in the Boy's last-minute reprieve, it hardly seems enough to balance a whole film of poverty, destruction, suffering, and injustice.

The audience of 1916 was not so much aware of intellectual inconsistencies in the film as it was of its confusing complexity and its general unpleasantness. The fact that Griffith films can be probed for intellectual and artistic wholeness at all, despite the results of the probe, shows how far Griffith had taken the feature film in only three years (since *Queen Elizabeth*). But unlike *The Birth of a Nation, Intolerance* aroused no social protest; worse, it aroused little audience interest of any kind. Perhaps the film was unpopular because its structural complexity asked too much from its audience. Or perhaps the film was a victim of an historical accident, its obviously pacifistic statement being totally antipathetic to a nation preparing itself emotionally to send its soldiers "Over There." Thomas Ince's pacifist-intellectualistic film, *Civilization,* had made money only six months earlier. Whatever the reason, *Intolerance* was a financial disaster costing Griffith (its ballooning budget forced him to invest in it personally) all his profits from *Birth of a Nation*. The failure of *Intolerance* began Griffith's financial dependence on other producers and businessmen, from which he would never recover.

The cliché of criticism of Griffith is that with *Intolerance* the director reached a peak from which the only direction was down. The final years of Griffith's career are often dismissed as years of repetition, a retreat into sentimentality, and a lack of attention to audience tastes. There is some truth in the cliché. In the final period of his career, Griffith was no innovator; the cinematic advances of his youth had solidified into a stable, controlled mastery of the film form beyond which he would or could go no further. Some of his major pictures were unsuccessful at the box office and do not seem striking artistic wholes today: *Hearts of the World* (1917), *Orphans of the Storm* (1921), *America* (1924). After the financial fiasco of *Intolerance*, Griffith also had to look to his wallet, a concern that led to many uninspired program pictures to fulfill contracts: *True Heart Susie* (1919), *The Idol Dancer* (1920), *One Exciting Night* (1922), *Sally of the Sawdust* (1925), *That Royle Girl* (1926), and perhaps a dozen more.

Despite Griffith's financial problems and lagging artistic imagination, he made two films during his final period that rank just behind his two epics in power and interest. In fact both of the films, *Broken Blossoms* (1919) and *Way Down East* (1920), are more entertaining and easier to sit through for today's audiences than either of the huge epics. *Broken Blossoms* is Griffith's most polished, most finished gem. This film, smaller in conception than the two epics, is a tight triangle story of one woman between two men. Out of this triangle come the film's values, rather than from Griffith's subtitles and allegorical visions. If the film is less weighty than the two epics, it is also less pretentious, less intent on intellectualization, and less insistent on its high seriousness. Like so many Griffith films, *Broken Blossoms* is an adaptation of a work of fiction—Thomas Burke's "The Chink and the Child," from his collection *Limehouse Nights*. As with *Birth of a Nation*, Griffith took another man's work and made it his own, as the film's metaphoric title so clearly shows.

The film is Griffith's gentlest, his most explicit and poetic hymn to gentleness. The typical Griffith film shows violence destroying gentleness; the focus of the films is usually on the violent disrupters: war, social upheaval, union protests, political chicanery, sexual debauches. In *Broken*

Blossoms, the aura of ideal gentleness dominates the action, only to be punctuated by the violent jabs of the real world. The gentle man in the film comes from the Orient to bring the message of the gentle Buddha to the vicious, violent men of the West. Once he arrives in London's Chinese slum, Limehouse, Cheng Huan runs into the "sordid realities of life"—gambling, whoring, opium smoking—that constitute life in the West.

Then in the film's second section, Griffith switches to the female figure of gentleness, Lucy. Raised by the prize fighter, Battling Burrows, Lucy is an unloved child who spends her time wandering around the Limehouse district, trying to scrape up enough tin foil to buy herself a flower. Flowers, of course, are the visual metaphor for gentleness in the film, as the title clearly indicates. Lucy's gentleness, however, like Cheng Huan's, runs into sordid realities. Her reality is her foster father, Burrows, a brute who uses Lucy as both slavish servant and defenseless punching bag. One of the most poignant touches in the film is Burrows's insistence that Lucy smile for him, regardless of her real feelings. Since she is unable to summon a genuine smile, she uses two fingers to force one.

The next section of the film necessarily brings the two gentle figures together. Cheng Huan is attracted by Lucy's gentle purity, which he instantly perceives. They first meet, appropriately, over the purchase of a flower. She later collapses in his shop after a terrific beating by her foster father. Cheng Huan enthrones her in his room as a Princess of Flowers, and the two celebrate a brief but beautiful union of gentle love. Lucy even smiles without the aid of her fingers for the first time, and Cheng Huan's one weak moment of animal lust (brilliantly communicated by a painfully tight close-up) is soon conquered by his realization of the ideal perfection of his guest and their relationship.

But the realities break in upon the ideal. Burows finds her at Cheng Huan's, drags her back to their slum room, and begins his inevitable attack. She retreats to a closet; he smashes it open with an axe, and Griffith creates one of the most accurate renditions of human frenzy in screen history as Lucy frantically starts rushing in a circle inside the closet—trapped, flustered, terrified. The death of all three characters is imminent. Lucy dies from this final beating, Cheng Huan shoots Burrows and then commits *hara-kiri.* Blossoms, despite their loveliness, cannot survive for long in the soil of mortality.

This simple story could descend into either boredom on the one side or sentimental claptrap on the other. Griffith walks a tight-rope between the two abysses. He suffuses the film with the atmosphere of dreams and haze. The two actors who play the gentle figures—Richard Barthelmess and Lillian Gish—have perfectly harmonious faces of inner calm and peace. Their acting is so restrained and so perfectly matched that the two even begin to look alike. The two feel like a single being. Griffith also succeeds in giving the violent villain—played by Donald Crisp—both energy and credibility. Because he is a prize fighter, Burrows comes alive by sustaining the metaphor of boxing; Griffith makes Crisp walk, stand, sway, stagger like an animal in the ring. After Cheng Huan shoots Burrows, Griffith adds one of those observant touches that brilliantly makes the moment come to life. Burrows, reeling under the shot, instinctively puts up his dukes and begins dizzily jabbing at his opponent; after a few weak and faltering feints, Burrows collapses. This realistic detail at the moment of death—for once Griffith gives his villain as much naturalistic attention as his heroes—parallels Lucy's final living gesture in which she uses two fingers to poke her face into a last smile.

Griffith's lighting also sustains the film's mood; *Broken Blossoms* remains one of the most beautifully lit films in screen history. The lighting of scenes in Cheng Huan's shop and room is an atmospheric blend of beams of light and pools of shadow. Lillian Gish, as the Princess, becomes luminous, surrounded by the gray and black regions of her flowery kingdom. Griffith uses low-key lighting exclusively for these scenes. The lighting is not only atmospheric; it is also a precise visual translation of the film's metaphoric contrast between gentleness and violence. While Lucy is enthroned in Cheng Huan's room, Battling Burrows fights his title match. Griffith cross-cuts between the place of love—the room—and the place of hate—the ring. The boxing ring is harshly lit with bright, even white light; the room is suffused with shafts and shadows. Although *Broken Blossoms'* single mood asks a lot less of its audience than the earlier epics, it keeps its promises.

Way Down East, although more uneven than *Broken Blossoms,* contains sections that are as fine as anything Griffith ever did. The most famous sequence in the film is the climax, the last-minute rescue of Anna Moore (Lillian Gish again), floating steadily toward the deadly falls. Anna Moore's unfortunate sexual error has been discovered by her adopted down-east family; she rushes out of their house into a blinding blizzard, the savagery of the wind and snow becoming visual metaphors for the rage and misery in her own heart. Then Griffith's cross-cutting, his most useful and enduring tool, drives the film's climax by alternating between three separate but related locations: Anna Moore alone in the storm, prostrate on a moving ice-cake; her down-east boyfriend (Richard Barthelmess again) searching for her—the agent of her rescue; the ominous falls, toward which the ice-cake is moving—the danger from which she must be saved. The falls that Griffith used for these cuts were none other than Niagara Falls; Griffith merely spliced in bits of stock footage. Here was the ultimate proof of the logic of cross-cutting: although the actress was really nowhere near any falls (especially not Niagara), the audience felt her nearness because of the narrative links that bound the three locations. Soviet filmmakers would soon seize on this Griffith editing principle, giving it the name of "creative geography."

The uneven, weaker parts of *Way Down East* are the plotty remnants of the original stage melodrama, whose rights Griffith purchased for $175,000 ($50,000 more than the entire budget of *Birth of a Nation* and a sure indication of the industry's rising costs). Everything in *Way Down East* related to the evil doings of the rich folks reveals the artificial, heavy, and abstract hand of Griffith trying to depict a life-style for which he had neither sympathy nor understanding. After all, rich people have more things to do with their money than hold fancy-dress balls, act snobbish toward the pure of heart but poor of purse, and seduce innocent virgins with fake marriage vows. Griffith's handling of the rich in the film is a throwback to the Fish Maidens of *Judith of Bethulia*. But the film has two compensating virtues. First, there is the face of Lillian Gish, radiant, luminous, charming, alive. If the problems that the plot gives her seem foolish and artificial, the touching reactions of her eyes and mouth make sense of them. Griffith knew the power of the Gish face; he rivets our gaze on it with close-up after close-up, most of them key-lit to give her hair that shiny, diaphanous glow. The real action of the film takes place not in the film's society but on the Gish face.

The second virtue of the film is Griffith's tender, careful, comic observation of down-east life. He loves the warmth of these rural people, their pettiness, laziness, and short-sightedness as well as their sincerity, simplicity, and compassion. For Griffith, the down-east life, despite its lack of wealth and sophistication, is a model of gentleness, of peacefulness, of poor eyes balanced by rich hearts. In down-east life Griffith saw a mirror for the gentle and fertile life of the South (which he had depicted in the opening section of *Birth of a Nation*) before the violence of military and political wars ripped that life asunder. In his final important film, Griffith again demonstrates that no director could more convincingly and lovingly render the things he knew and loved, and could more laughably and artificially render the things he gathered from books and literary clichés.

There are several theories that attempt to explain Griffith's creative decay in the final fifteen years of his career. Perhaps he ran out of innovative ideas, both technically and intellectually. The solidifying of his cinematic technique may have contributed to the congealing of his ability to make exciting, moving, powerful films. Because his vision was so consistent and yet so thin he may have gone sour on saying the same things without being able to say them in a new way. There might never have been an *Intolerance* to equal or surpass *Birth of a Nation* if the controversy over the first epic hadn't fired Griffith's anger and imagination. A second popular theory is that Griffith's ideas had become outmoded in the twenties. The flapper morality of the jazz age rejected the sentimentality of Griffith's Victorianism. Belasco's melodrama had been supplanted by urbane, domestic comedy-dramas of sexual innuendo and verbal wit. The high life, which Griffith depicted so blackly and so clumsily, was what audiences vicariously wanted to experience. Griffith did not give the public what it wanted. A third theory is that Griffith's own artistic integrity had been corrupted by wealth and success. Renowned as the director-laureate of the world, Griffith substituted dreams of power—ten-hour-long films, chains of movie theatres and studios all bearing his name, The Griffith—for his artistic seriousness and skill.

The truth probably lies somewhere among the various theories. On the one hand, Griffith certainly seemed to be running out of creative gas. On the other, since his pictures became more and more formulaic he was more and more dependent on public acceptance of his formulas. His formulas were, however, as formulas, ten to twenty years out of date. Without the Griffith mastery to make Victorian formulas exciting, the audiences saw the bare bones of sentimentality and took itself to other directors' pictures. *Broken Blossoms* and *Way Down East,* both heavily Victorian and sentimental, both released in the early years of the jazz age, were also huge box-office successes, as big financial successes as Griffith ever had. If Griffith's later films in the 1920s had been as powerful as those two, they also might have pulled the customers in.

Griffith's *America* (1924) is a sure symptom of his hardening of the creative arteries. Despite its lovely photography, its careful re-creation of American life in 1776, and its brilliantly edited sequence of Paul Revere's ride, the film is an obvious remake of *The Birth of a Nation,* substituting the Revolution for the Civil War. Again there are two families, one Southern, one Northern. Again one of the families is misguided in its political loyalties but not in its moral instincts. Again the villain is an idealization of evil who uses political theory to mask his own selfish drives of sexual, material, and political conquest. And again the film's last-minute rescue resolves its melodramatic problems as well as its political ones, uniting hero and heroine, North and South, Yankee and Tory, common man and aristocrat. The film might just as well have been called *The Birth of a Nation,* that title being at least as appropriate to it as to the film of almost a decade earlier. Griffith was obviously repeating himself.

The final years of Griffith's career were scarred by his disastrous fling with the sound picture. In *Abraham Lincoln* (1930), he returned to American history. *The Struggle* (1931) was a sentimental and overstated sociological study of alcoholism. In the true Griffith manner, he depicts alcoholism as a product of the social-reforming ladies who thrust prohibition on a beer and wine-drinking nation, converting it to whiskey as a result. The fact that people might drink because they are unhappy, because they want to or need to, does not seem to occur to him. The film was so unsalable that its producers changed Griffith's title to *Ten Nights in a Barroom,* presumably hoping to lure a few alcoholics off the street to see the film. The Hollywood brass was convinced that Griffith was old-fashioned, that his day was done. He spent his final seventeen years living in Los Angeles, barred from an art that he had practically fashioned by himself, his only contribution being several sequences for Hal Roach's *One Million B.C.* in 1941. The years of mouthed praise for his achievements did not ease the bitterness of his rejection by the business. He died in Hollywood in 1948.

THE COMICS:
MACK SENNETT AND
THE CHAPLIN SHORTS

Chapter

5

n the same year that Griffith took his ride on the "El" up to the Edison studios in the Bronx (1907), Mack Sennett took the same ride for the same purpose. Like Griffith, Sennett then wandered from Edison to Biograph to take up a longer residence there. Like Griffith, Sennett later moved from his apprenticeship at Biograph to maturity as an independent producer and director. Sennett even worked for Griffith at Biograph, as director, actor, and writer (he wrote the screenplay for Griffith's *Lonely Villa*). In his years with Griffith, Sennett absorbed many lessons on cutting and shooting and construction. Sennett would later repay his teacher by both adopting his fluid cutting methods and by parodying Griffith's plots and last-minute rescues. Unlike Griffith, however, Sennett always wanted to make comic films. For years he tried to get Biograph to let him make a comic film about cops. He finally got his chance with the independent company, Keystone, in 1912.

The marriage that Sennett effected between visual, physical, burlesque comedy and the silent film was one of those happy, inevitable unions. The purely visual film medium was perfectly suited to the purely visual comic gags that Sennett concocted. The popularity of Lumière's first comedy, *L'Arroseur arrosée*, foreshadowed the future of the physical gag. Although there were comic films before Sennett—particularly the comic surprises of the trick films—no one before him so forcefully revealed the comic effects of motion, of human bodies and machines and inanimate objects hurtling across the screen and colliding into each other. It may not be coincidence that one of the most famous essays on comedy—Henri Bergson's *Le Rire* (1900)—was contemporary with the early films. Sennett— and later Chaplin, Keaton, Lloyd, Laurel and Hardy, et cetera—would unknowingly apply the Bergson theories. No theoretical aesthetic ever had the advantage of such concrete and convincing data. The Bergsonian principle that Sennett best demonstrated was that the source of the comic was the conversion of a human being into a machine. We laugh at the mechanical, inelastic motions of a man who fails to alter his responses to suit some change in the environment: the man who slips on a banana peel but continues walking as if no peel were under him until he inevitably falls. Further, we cannot laugh if we have any real fears for the man's safety; we must view him externally as a kind of imperishable machine, rather than as a man who can suffer pain and broken bones and bruises.

This conversion of men into machines is at the center of Sennett's comic technique. The characters zip across the screen like mechanical toys, crashing and colliding into pies, walls, furniture, and each other. Sennett furthers the impression of human machines with his undercranked camera. He discovered that by recording the action at only eight to twelve frames per second and then projecting it at sixteen or twenty the action became so speeded up that the effect became even more mechanical, more frantic, and hence, more comical. There is never a sense of the Sennett characters as people; reflection and feeling are human activities they never experience. The characters have no real human personalities; their individuation is strictly in terms of physical type—fat, thin, short, tall, dark, fair, and so forth. They are purely externalized creatures, not differing at all, really, from the inanimate objects and moving machines with which they collide. In one of the Sennett films, *The Clever Dummy* (1917), Ben Turpin actually plays a robot—the perfect metaphor for all Sennett's people. The use of people as objects, rather than as feeling, thinking beings, makes them perfectly suited to run into trouble with the other objects and machines in their universe. Whatever terrific collisions they suffer, we know that the injury will be no more serious than a dent in an automobile fender. Although many Sennett characters brandish guns that shoot bullets, the audience knows that a bullet is no more lethal than a kick in the pants or a pie in the face. Their automobiles smash into each other at fifty miles an hour, their boats sink, their roller-coaster cars fly off the tracks, they fall down wells, they fall off roofs. Disasters resulting in death in the real world produce only a few dazed moments in the Sennett world. Machines do not feel pain; machines do not die. We can laugh at the Sennett characters because we know they are machines and not people.

Like Griffith, Sennett depended heavily on improvisation. A rough plot outline was the basis for staff meetings each week when Sennett, his cast, and crew would get together to see what wild and zany bits they could inject into the story line. Sennett liked to have an imaginative outside observer, whom he called his "wild card" or "joker," sit in on the staff meetings, his function being to toss out the wildest, most far-fetched and irrelevant gags he could think up. After a series of gags had been hammered together in the meeting, there was further improvisation and gagging in the course of the shooting. Sennett adhered to only one principle of construction: a gag had to begin, develop, and finish itself off within a hundred seconds. Because Sennett cared so little about whole plots—the individual gag was the beginning and end of his cinematic technique—the films are loosely structured, holding together only by the pace of the movement within them. The stories seldom go anywhere; they end when the series of gags has been played out and the reel of film has been shot. One of the most common Sennett endings is for the clashing characters to end up dazed and exhausted or doused in a pool of water, the ocean, or a well —for example, *Tillie's Punctured Romance, The Surf Girl,* and *The Masquerader.* When the characters are all wet, the action stops.

Sennett films usually conform to one of three structural patterns. One of the most common is that Sennett takes some conventional, almost melodramatic plot—the kind that Griffith used—and then peppers it with gags wherever he can. The plot merely serves as a kind of string to hold the gags together. This kind of structure is a clear sign of the loose script outline that gets gagged up at staff meetings. The plot becomes totally formulaic and passes by unnoticed; only the frenzied movement of the mechanical men attracts the eye. The second kind of Sennett structure is even less plotty. This structure could best be described as "riffing"—taking some place or situation and then running through all the gags they can think of that might occur there. The third Sennett structure is more whole than the first two. Sennett had a great taste for parodying both the styles and the themes of other famous directors and pictures. In the parody pictures, Sennett not only used individual gags but shaped the whole film in accordance with the model he was burlesquing.

Sennett's first feature film, *Tillie's Punctured Romance* (1914), is a good example of the formula plot that merely serves as a string to tie the gags together. The plot is a completely conventional story of a farm girl who falls prey to the false advances of a city slicker; he only wants her for her money. She leaves the farm for the evil city, inherits money from an uncle who is presumed dead, gets mixed up with rich city folk, has troubles with her fiancé who has another girlfriend, and finally discovers his duplicity. (The film sounds as if it could have been made by Griffith.) But Sennett discards the plot entirely and spends his time sticking in whatever gags he can, gags that are fundamentally irrelevant to the plot.

Tillie, the farm girl, is played by the enormous Marie Dressler; her city-slicker boyfriend is the small and skinny Chaplin (before he adopted the tramp character exclusively). Sennett plays with the disproportion in their sizes, showing Tillie besting her beau in all sorts of contests in which Charlie winds up with a brick or a stone or a boot hitting him in the head or seat of the pants. The "other woman" in the film is played by Mabel Normand, a coy and subtle comedienne who indulges in her own comic shenanigans as a fake waitress at Tillie's grand ball. Sennett includes a hilariously comic dance number with the tiny Charlie and the immense Tillie, he adds a hilarious drunken "elephant" sequence when Tillie over-indulges in a café, he draws on the incompetent Keystone cops for the final chase, and he throws all the main characters off the Santa Monica pier and into the Pacific Ocean to end the film. Tillie's enormous bulk is eventually hoisted from the waves by a mechanical winch that predictably slips and throws her back in again several times before fishing her out. The plot of the film is almost nonexistent; the best things in the film are the gratuitous gags, the surprises that Sennett throws in. That which is gratuitous ultimately becomes that which is essential.

Mabel's Dramatic Career (1913) has the same kind of structure. Mabel (Normand), a country gal, and Mack (Sennett), her country swain, are deeply in love. Sennett acted in his films, too, usually portraying the oafish, sluggish country boy. Mack's mother objects to the match. The story is further complicated by another woman who arrives from the city and steals Mack's heart away from Mabel. Mack gets his ring back from Mabel, and Mabel slinks sadly off toward the big city. Some unspecified time later, Mack journeys to the city and sees a nickelodeon displaying Mabel's picture. (Many of the early film comedies were about the film business itself.) Mack goes into the theatre to see the show; he sees Mabel attacked by the villain (Ford Sterling) in a typical film melodrama. Mack, who does not realize he is watching a fiction, fails to keep his aesthetic distance. He pulls out his six-shooter and starts firing at the screen, scaring the shocked customers out of the theatre. Mack also runs out and catches a glimpse of the screen villain at home; naturally, off-screen Ford is a kindly father and husband. But Mack starts shooting again. Someone douses him with a pail of water and the film just stops, now that the menace has been soaked. The plot of the film is merely a convenience to get Mack to the movie theatre; the film is built around the single gag that Mack cannot separate screen life and real life. The early rural romance is merely expository; it pads the film out so that it fills up a reel; it gives Sennett the chance for a few boy-girl gags.

The Sennett "riffing" films are even more fun; the director does not even pay lip service to any kind of narrative line. These films are structured as a pure series of gags, held together only by pace and by the general locale or situation. Several of the films Chaplin made for Sennett use the "riffing" structure. In *The Masquerader* (1914), Sennett and Chaplin pull as many gags as they can on the premise that a disruptive actor on a movie set can wreak havoc in a studio. Chaplin is the actor; Charlie Murray is the director who boots him out; Charlie sneaks back in as a seductive woman; chaos follows until Charlie winds up in a well, soaked, and the "riffing" stops. *The Rounders* (1914) "riffs" on the troubles that two drunks (Charlie and Fatty Arbuckle, two obviously contrasting physical types) can get into, and on the reactions of their two shrewish wives. *Getting Acquainted* (1914) "riffs" on the theme of flirtation and mashing in the park.

The Surf Girl (1916) is one of the zaniest of the "riffing" pictures. Wild gag relentlessly follows wild gag for two reels. The film takes the beach as its starting point and then runs off every gag it can imagine in a beach setting. Sennett uses the ocean, a swimming pool, a roller coaster, a ferris wheel, a beach-front saloon, dressing rooms for changing into bathing suits, showers, beach cabañas, an amusement park, an aviary, motor boats, et cetera. The strong man with the hammer not only rings the gong but sends a fellow surfer flying up the gauge and off into the sea. The swimming pool is a crowded casserole of frantic aquatics—Sennett's undercranked camera makes the pool activities a kind of water ballet turned St. Vitus' dance. An immensely fat man rolls down a slide and into the pool. Everyone in the pool (Sennett uses reverse motion of the camera brilliantly) is vomited out of the water by the impact of the fat man's splash. The two life-guards, courting a young lady, discover that an ostrich has swallowed her locket. They chase and ride the awkward bird until he finally disgorges the chain. Another lifeguard, swinging on the rings over the pool, loses his pants; the lady who has been pushing him unintentionally flies off with the pants into the pool. An old man suspected of lechery takes shelter in the ball-throwing booth, pretending to be one of the moving mannikins the customers try to hit. Sure enough the customers try to hit him.

This wild mêlée of gags and movement ends with a great anti-climactic joke. The cops hustle all the soaked, brawling surfers into the paddy wagon. As the wagon pulls into the station, the top part strikes the roof of the entrance and separates from the frame. (Those incompetent cops can't even build the right-sized garage.) The surfer-felons slowly walk away from the cops, using the top part of the paddy wagon as a shell and cover for their retreat. As the dozen or so legs walk off, looking like a huge beetle, the film comes to a halt. A sure sign of the film's "riffing" premise is that despite its title not a single surf girl plays a role in the picture.

The Sennett parody films are less zany but more whole. Parodying the latest movie hit was a staple of the comic shorts. Chaplin parodied *Carmen* in 1915, the same year that two serious versions of the story were released; there were parodies of stage and filmed melodrama: for example, Vitagraph's delightful *Goodness Gracious;* both Sennett and Hal Roach parodied hits like *The Iron Horse* (*The Iron Nag*) and *The Covered Wagon* (*The Uncovered Wagon, Two Wagons Both Covered*). Some of Sennett's best parodies were of Griffith, not only of his melodramatic stories but also of his famous last-minute rescues. An early Griffith parody, *Barney Oldfield's Race for a Life* (1913), features a villain (played by Ford Sterling) who ties the young damsel (Mabel Normand) to the railroad tracks and then steals a train (perhaps a parodic glimpse at films like *The Great Train Robbery*) for the express purpose of running over her. Her boyfriend, played by Sennett, is flying to the rescue in an automobile. The cops, also alerted to the danger, furiously pump to the rescue on a handcar. Sennett, in the best Griffith tradition, cuts between four locales: Mabel on the tracks, anxious; Ford in the train, looking forward gleefully to squashing Mabel; Mack and Barney in the auto; the cops on the handcar. Sennett pokes fun at Griffith by drawing out this rescue to an impossible length; the train, which we know is not very far from Mabel's bound body, takes forever to get to it, just long enough for Mack and the cops to get there in time. The film's ending is also intentionally silly. Ford shoots all the cops—who obviously do not die—and then, for some reason, decides to shoot himself. Having no bullets left, he chokes himself, does a pirouette, twirls, and falls, apparently dead of dizziness.

Teddy at the Throttle (1916) is a later, longer, and funnier parody of the same kind. The film not only parodies the Griffith cross-cut but also the Griffith plotting. The story is a triangle. The young man (Bobby Vernon) drops his true girlfriend for the rich society gal; the young man is being manipulated by the villain (Wallace Beery), who thinks he will make money from the society match. The society gal (large) drags the young man (small) out into an unbelievably intense storm—with winds that blow the clothes off the guests at a fancy ball when the door opens, with oceans of rain driving down, with pools of mud several feet deep. She is insistent on getting married pronto. The true girl (Gloria Swanson), who has discovered the deception, pursues them into the storm. The next morning, after a hilarious sequence of rolling around in the water and mud, the villain ties the true girl to the railroad tracks. Her dog, Teddy, carries a message explaining her terrible plight, which she has miraculously managed to write, to her boyfriend. Then comes the Griffith cutting. From Gloria tied to the tracks, to the train chugging toward her, to the agent of her rescue (the dog), who finds the boyfriend and leads him back to Gloria. Gloria is, of course, saved just in time, and Teddy continues his canine heroism by treeing the nasty villain.

The Sennett films set a comic standard for zaniness, *non sequitur,* and physical activity that has served as a model ever since—for René Clair, for

Richard Lester, for Louis Malle. Not as technical a cinematic innovator as Griffith, Sennett still realized that the tricks the camera could play with motion were highly suited to physical comedy. In a sense, Sennett's method took Méliès's stop-action principle one step further by combining rapid physical activity with the camera's tricks. Sennett also realized that in a world as physically active as his, the camera and editor should do a lot less work than in Griffith's films, so as not to detract from the purely physical fun. Sennett had no need for the close-up, which personalizes and indi- vidualizes, which conveys human emotions. The standard Sennett setups are the far shot and long shot, revealing the figures only as types, not as individual people. Whereas Griffith developed his screen grammar and rhetoric to transmit human emotion and personality, Sennett purposely needed no such method since his comedy negated both.

In 1916 Sennett scrapped his independent Keystone Company to begin producing comedies for the giants like First National, Paramount, and Pathé. By the mid-1920s Sennett had become a producer, ceasing to direct films personally, and his films had become more expensive and pol- ished, losing much of the improvisatory, slap-dash, slap-happy quality of the Keystones that starred Chaplin, Normand, Sterling, Arbuckle, Chester Conklin, and Mack Swain. But Sennett's parody still created his hilarious 1920s films that starred the cross-eyed, antiheroic Ben Turpin; Sennett's devotion to frantic movement, irrational surprises, and impossible non- sense created his 1920s films that starred Billy Bevan, supported by in- credibly agile machines like tin lizzies and airplanes, or by menacingly awesome beasts like wild lions and even a viciously snapping oyster. The Sennett style lasted as long as the silent film, which was its natural me- dium. The particular qualities of the Sennett style become most obvious when compared with the completely different method and emphasis of his most distinguished disciple.

Charlie

In 1913 Charles Chaplin was touring the American vaudeville stages with an English music-hall act, Fred Karno's English Pantomime Troupe. Either Adam Kessel, the bookmaker-turned-owner of the independent Bison Company, or Sennett himself saw Chaplin's performance as a comic drunk in *A Night in a London Club,* one of the Karno features. They offered Chaplin a job with Sennett's comic branch of Bison, Keystone, thinking Chaplin's comic gymnastic talents perfectly suited to Sennett's style. Chaplin wasn't sure he wanted the job; like many stage performers he shared the prejudice against working for the films. He also distrusted the impermanence and novelty of the movie business. After Chaplin drove Kessel's offer up from $75 to $150 a week, including a one-year guarantee, he decided the risk was worth it. Chaplin joined Keystone late in 1913.

Sennett immediately tried to use Chaplin as one more mechanical cog in his factory of human puppets. Sennett capitalized on Chaplin's gymnastic abilities: his ability to fall and stagger and roll and bounce off both people and the floor. Chaplin's smallness was the perfect foil for the fatness of Arbuckle or the hugeness of Dressler. Sennett used Chaplin as mechanical toy. In *The Knockout* (1914), Chaplin makes a brief appearance as referee in a boxing match, ducking, sliding, squirming, and falling between the punching pugilists and the ropes. This was Chaplin as pure physical comic. Sennett used the same gymnastic potential in *The Rounders,* in which Chaplin recreates his drunk act from Karno's troupe.

But tension soon developed between Chaplin and Sennett. Sennett's rapid, pure-motion principle bothered Chaplin, who wanted to add character and individuality to his gymnastics. Chaplin began to evolve the tramp character at Keystone, borrowing the idea of using a cane and hat from the earlier French film comic, Max Linder, borrowing an old pair of Ford Sterling's shoes (much too big for Charlie's feet) and an old pair of Fatty Arbuckle's pants (obviously too big for Charlie). Such individuation was both unwanted and unneeded in Sennett's mechanical world. Sennett neither took the time nor placed the camera close enough to make such characterization count. After one year with Sennett, the gymnastic comic with the hat, cane, and shoes had become so familiar in the nickelodeons that he could negotiate a contract to make his own pictures. In 1915 he left Sennett's Keystone Company for Essanay, which agreed to pay him $1,250 a week and give him the freedom to write and direct his own pictures.

Temperamentally, Chaplin never could see comedy the way Sennett saw it. For Sennett, the comic world was a world of silly surfaces; for Chaplin the comic world was a way of getting at the serious world of men and society. For Sennett, comedy was an end; for Chaplin, it was a means. Chaplin's own experience played a tremendous role in shaping his outlook. With his father and mother separated, and his mother battling ill health and insanity, Chaplin spent almost two years of his young life in a workhouse for the poor. Chaplin admits that as a boy in the workhouse the power of wealth and social status became apparent. The young Chaplin was an outsider, beyond the embrace of social and material comforts. The screen character he created, Charlie (the French call him Charlot), is also an outsider. He is either a tramp, a criminal, an immigrant, a worker—someone excluded from the beautiful life. And yet Charlie yearns desperately for that life: he longs for money, for the pretty society girl, for legitimacy, for social station, for etiquette, for superiority, for recognition.

Ironically, Charlie as outsider serves to show both the gleaming attractiveness of the beautiful life for those who don't have it and the false emptiness of the beautiful life for those who do. Chaplin was mature enough an artist to show the ambivalence of power and wealth, its attractiveness and its emptiness, an ambivalence that Chaplin the man felt when he became rich and powerful.

The Chaplin comic aesthetic was radically different from Sennett's. The cliché is that Chaplin slowed Sennett's dizzy pace down. He did slow it down; but he did so to put something else in. The *structures* of the films reveal a key shift. If Sennett's films are merely strings of gags, Chaplin's films are structured as three or four beads on a string. Like Sennett's, Chaplin's film structures break into clear and distinct pieces. But whereas Sennett's pieces are thirty to ninety seconds long, Chaplin's are five to ten minutes long. He exhausts a situation completely rather than flipping from gag to gag. His Essanay film, *The Tramp* (1915), breaks into four sections: Charlie the tramp protecting the pretty girl from other, meaner tramps; Charlie as farmhand on the girl's farm; Charlie foiling the other tramps' plot to rob the farm; Charlie losing the girl when her wealthy boyfriend arrives. A later film he made for Mutual, *The Adventurer* (1917), also breaks into four sections: Charlie's escape from the police; Charlie rescuing the drowning rich man; Charlie attempting to join the *haut monde* at the rich man's swank party; Charlie's second escape from the police when the rich man betrays him, coupled with his expulsion from the house by the pretty rich girl. This shift in film structure from the gag to the scene demands that each of the sequences be more detailed, fuller; each requires attention to either the situation or the character—rather than the gags alone—to sustain it.

The Chaplin structure not only allows for the examination of character but demands it. The long sequences deny the possibility of a mere string of gags; the gags revolve around the location, the objects, and especially the people in the sequence. The gags actually define the characters. When Charlie twirls his cane at a fancy party (in *The Count*, 1916), and then accidentally stabs the turkey, which he inadvertently swings above his head, he makes us laugh at a hilarious gag; he also defines his sociable attempts to be suave and his frustrating lack of success at it. Charlie's sly and jaunty crap shooting and card shuffling when surrounded by big, mean opponents (*The Immigrant*, 1917) show he has guts as well as style. Despite the size of his opponents and the social obstacles, Charlie always insists on enjoying the last laugh or the last kick in the pants. His attempts to enjoy the last boot are not only ingenious and funny; they also define Charlie's pluck. Though Charlie is comically incompetent at mastering the social graces of the *haut monde,* he consistently makes up for his lack of etiquette with his wiry toughness and his pragmatic cleverness. Though he eats *pêches melba* very badly (*The Adventurer*), he is very adept at dodging the police. Chaplin's gags alone define Charlie's ironic synthesis of naïveté and pragmatism.

Another dimension of the Chaplin tramp is that despite the toughness and dishonesty that help him survive, he has a kind and generous heart. He never mistreats those who genuinely deserve his sympathy. He demonstrates this trait repeatedly by using a Griffith-like woman who evokes Charlie's milder qualities. The Chaplin woman is invariably pure, blonde, and kind, instantly perceiving the redeeming characteristics in the unworldly tramp. For years Chaplin used the same actress, Edna Purviance, to portray her. For Chaplin, the woman was not just a sentimental character—although she certainly was that; she was also a metaphor for natural human beauty uncorrupted by social definitions and unburied by material possessions. In film after film Charlie shows his affinity with the naturally good and beautiful spirit by allying with her against those who can do him more material good. In *The Tramp* and *Police* (1915), he refuses to ally with fellow robbers and protects Edna instead. In *The Tramp* and *The Immigrant,* he retrieves Edna's stolen money and, without letting her know it, slips it back into her pocket. And yet Chaplin's sense of character and reality is such that after stuffing a whole wad of bills in Edna's pocket, he thinks better of it and takes a few back for himself.

Chaplin's handling of character also comments on the values of the society that produces such people. The villain in the short Chaplin films is invariably Eric Campbell, a huge brute of a man whose superblack, upturned eyebrows look as though they alone contained enough poison to kill a man Charlie's size. Like Sennett, Chaplin uses physical types for comic effect. Unlike Sennett, the physical type also implies moral, social, and psychological values. Eric Campbell, the heavy, is invariably a member of the film's social in-group; he naturally hates Charlie because Charlie is not a member of that group. Eric is the physical giant in *Easy Street* (1917), a very uneasy street that values physical toughness alone; Charlie is the contrasting runt. Eric is the waiter in *The Immigrant* who enjoys pommeling those patrons who are only ten cents short of paying the bill; Charlie is the diner without any money. Eric is the lecherous rich man in *The Rink* (1916); Charlie is the poor waiter (but good skater!). Eric is the believable count in *The Count;* Charlie is merely the clumsy pretender. If the social "ins" are as brutal, as coarse, as empty, as vicious as Eric, then there is some human value in being "out," like Charlie. And how pathetic are Charlie's attempts to get "in" considering he is physically and emotionally incapable of besting Eric for more than a second or two.

Some of the differences between Sennett and Chaplin become most clear when comparing similar devices and motifs they both used. Both Sennett and Chaplin used cops. For Sennett, the cops were purely comic characters, whose good will was balanced by their energetic but cross-eyed incompetence. Despite their efforts and frenzy, Sennett's cops can do nothing right. Their cars crash; their boats sink; they fall all over each other as they swarm to answer a call. They are as earnest and as functional as toy soldiers. Chaplin's cops, though not precisely what contemporary radicals would call Pigs, were not very far from it. In *Police*, the cops spend their time leisurely journeying by motor car to answer an emergency call for help; they drink tea and fluff their uniforms and show no concern at all for Edna's distress. The cops in *The Adventurer* are not as satirical, but they do shoot rifles at the escaping Charlie, and their bullets, unlike the bullets in Sennett comedies, look as though they could kill. In one of the films Chaplin himself directed for Sennett, *Getting Acquainted* (1914), the differences between the two comic perspectives are clear; in this film, the cop patrolling the park indiscriminately clubs anyone on the head who seems to be a masher.

Both Sennett and Chaplin use the ocean; for Sennett the ocean is a location for watery gags, but for Chaplin the ocean is a place where people can drown. Both Sennett and Chaplin use the chase, but Sennett emphasizes more of the pure motion and frenzy of it whereas Chaplin emphasizes the cleverness and skill of Charlie at avoiding capture. The chase scene at the beginning of *The Adventurer*, the chase up and down the escalator in *The Floorwalker* (1916), the chase on roller skates in *The Rink*—all show Charlie's adeptness at escaping his Establishment pursuers. Chaplin's chases seem more like choreographed ballets whereas Sennett's seem more like flying, colliding bowling pins after the ball has thrown them askew. Both Chaplin and Sennett use the motif of the bum who substitutes for the man of wealth and position. But in Sennett (*Comrades*, 1912), the tension is between two bums: one is enjoying the fruits of the masquerade (food, flirtations, a snooze in a real bed) and the other, lacking a costume, is not. In Chaplin's *The Count*, the tension is entirely between the bum and the problems of the situation itself, his unsuccessful attempts to manipulate the social tools that make a count a count (eating, drinking, dancing).

Most of the short Chaplin films contain obvious and pointed social commentary in the action as well as the characters. The comedies treat several controversial themes that we might think the rather exclusive property of our own generation: drug addiction, poverty, hunger, crime on the streets, homosexuality, religious hypocrisy. In *Police*, Charlie learns that those who want him to go straight only intend to eliminate him as a competitor. He discovers that the preacher who urges him to reform has stolen a man's watch that Charlie considered stealing but didn't because of the preacher's sermon. Charlie's instincts are far more human and unselfish than the platitudes of preachers and reformers. In *The Immigrant*, Charlie juxtaposes the Statue of Liberty with a cattle-boat full of immigrants. As soon as a title announces, "The land of liberty," government officials rope all the immigrants together and start checking their identification tags. Men in uniform are inevitably damned in the Chaplin shorts, whether the uniform is a policeman's, a fireman's, a government official's, or a banker's.

Easy Street is perhaps the most social of the early short films. In the opening sequence, Charlie gets uplifted in the Hope Mission, singing hymns and feasting on Edna's pure face. He is so uplifted that he gives back the collection box he has stolen. Charlie goes off into the world uplifted only to discover that the world is a vicious place, full of hunger, poverty, thieves, drug addicts, bullies and rapists; Easy Street is not so easy, a jungle world of animals striving to survive. Charlie as cop (still an outcast despite the uniform) subdues all the foes of goodness. In the final sequence, the den of thieves has been miraculously transformed into the New Hope Mission; all the thugs, including the ominous Eric Campbell, have dressed in their Sunday suits and Sunday smiles, all of them marching meekly and politely into the mission for their own uplifting.

This deliberately contrived, Pollyannaish ending is Chaplin's deliberate way of reducing social optimism to the absurd. The social evils admit of no easy solutions; in fact, they seem to admit of no solutions at all. As Brecht's *Threepenny Opera* put it ten years later with its similarly contrived happy ending, "Victoria's messenger does not come riding often." Chaplin's endings frequently imply this social dimension of false happiness and solution as in *The Vagabond* and *The Immigrant*. In *The Bank* (1915), Charlie wakes up only to discover that the happy ending literally was a dream. The other typical Chaplin ending (*The Tramp, The Adventurer*), less socially oriented but more poignant than the faked happy one, shows Charlie losing in the end, shuffling off down the road again after failing to satisfy his longings.

Though the social and moral implications of the Chaplin shorts are very striking, Chaplin never deserts the objective tool of comedy for making his points. If the endings of the films contain the social and psychological implications, the beginnings of the films are brilliant lessons in the comic way of making an entrance. In film after film Charlie shocks the audience with a daring comic surprise at the beginning from which it never recovers. One of the most brilliant is the beginning of *The Bank*. Charlie strides into the bank, goes directly to the safe, twirls the dials of the huge safe, checking his cuff to make sure that he remembers the combination, finally opens the door of the safe, steps in, and brings out his mop and pail. Not only does Charlie demonstrate the difference between capital and labor; he does it in a stunning surprise of our expectations. At the beginning of *The Immigrant*, people are lying about the boat, obviously seasick. The camera cuts to a heaving Charlie leaning over the side of the pitching ship. We expect he is sick like all his fellow passengers.

Charlie turns around holding a fish that he has just caught. In *The Tramp,* he enters walking down a dusty road; a car rushes by, spraying him with dust—another contrast of rich and poor. Charlie takes out a brush, whisks himself off, buffs his fingernails, and continues on his way. (There is Charlie's spunk as well as Chaplin's comic technique.) In *A Woman* (1915), Charlie enters by walking through a sprinkler. In *The Floor-walker,* he enters by inquiring about the price of a leg of one of the mannikins in the department store. In *The Adventurer,* he enters by digging himself out of his hiding place, a hole in the sand.

Another of Chaplin's great comic gifts was his ingenuity in using objects. As in Sennett, objects were a crucial part of Chaplin's technique. Unlike Sennett, however, Chaplin did not use objects solely as comic weapons (Sennett's famed pies); the object could be either weapon or tool, could define the character using it, could be used in a surprising and unfamiliar way, could either foul Charlie up or help him out. One of the consequences of Chaplin's structure—to exhaust a situation of some length before moving on to the next—was that one of the ways of exhausting a situation was to exhaust all the objects in it. And in exhausting an object, Chaplin frequently transformed it into a completely different thing before our very eyes, not by stopping the camera, as Méliès had, but by simply manipulating it in a surprising and unexpected way. Chaplin, like Méliès was a kind of magician, but his was a magic without trick.

Chaplin's most famous short film with objects is *One A.M.* (1916). With the exception of a cab driver in the first sequence, Charlie is the only character in the film—except for a roomful of objects. In the film Charlie returns to one of his favorite incarnations, the drunk; the play with objects begins in the first section when the drunken Charlie, returning from a night on the town, gets tangled with the taxi door and then with the taxi meter. Charlie can't find the key to his front door so he climbs in the window, stepping in his goldfish bowl as he does so. Inside the house he finds the key in his vest pocket. Back out the window he goes (foot in goldfish bowl again) so that he can enter properly through the door.

In the film's second section, Charlie is in the living room using every piece of inanimate matter with which he has decorated the set. He feels he is being attacked by the tiger rug on the floor. He tries to walk on a circular table toward a bottle of booze and seltzer; the table spins giddily and Charlie walks a treadmill, unable to reach the booze as he spins faster and faster. He tries to walk up the stairs only to discover himself at the bottom again. Second and third tries to ascend end with him rolled up in the rug covering the stairs. He finally succeeds in getting upstairs by climbing a coatrack. Upstairs he unsuccessfully tries to dodge the huge pendulum of the clock that swings back and forth in front of his bedroom door.

Then, in the film's third section—Charlie and the bed—the game with objects culminates in a five-minute duel between the drunken tramp and a Murphy bed, which seems to operate according to its own laws. The bed flips down, flips up, reverses itself, loses its frame, bounces, rises, falls as it pleases. Charlie finally beds down in the bathtub. With the bed, Chaplin has literally succeeded in bringing an inanimate object to life. Though he excludes living people to play against in *One A.M.*, Chaplin has not excluded living opponents. Yet another sign of his shrewdness is his refusal to cut or edit in the final bed sequence. The whole episode is practically a single long take. If we are to believe in the bed's vitality, we must not feel that the director has tricked the bed effects with camera and editing scissors. The lack of cutting rivets our attention on the two combatants. All consciousness of the cinematic medium disappears.

Chaplin's other objects lack the bed's personality and vitality, but are equally functional. His cane is not just a suggestion of the dandy; Charlie uses it both as tool and weapon—to keep an opponent at bay, to lift a lady's skirt, to trip a pursuer by the heels. In *The Adventurer*, Charlie temporarily escapes his pursuers by putting a lamp shade on his head and posing as a lamp. In *The Immigrant*, Charlie has difficulties eating a dish of soup because the ship is pitching from side to side. In *Behind the Screen* (1916), Charlie runs into trouble with chairs, pillars, and the lunch of one of his fellow workers. He tries to blow the stench of onions away with a bellows; he sneaks in a few bites from an enormous drumstick that the co-worker inadvertently sticks in Charlie's face. When he is caught, he puts up his paws and begs like a dog for another bite.

In *The Pawnshop* (1916), Charlie dismembers a clock that a needy customer has brought in to pawn; his deft part-by-part dissection combines the methods of a surgeon, plumber, dentist, jeweler, and butcher. When Charlie sees the guts of the clock dancing before him on the counter (a unique Chaplin use of Méliès's stop-action), he matter-of-factly turns to the customer and tells him that his clock is unpawnable. There are other objects in *The Pawnshop*; Charlie and a rival worker (he cannot even get along with members of his own class) sling baking dough at each other in the kitchen. When the boss walks in, Charlie nonchalantly starts kneading the dough and then suavely runs it through the wringer of the washing machine. He later tries to dry the dishes by running cups and saucers through the same wringer. When he tries to eat one of Edna's doughnuts it seems a bit heavy to him. He instantly transforms the doughnut into a dumbbell by doing weight lifting exercises with it and then blithely caps his routine by tossing it in the air to catch on his plate. The dumbbell-doughnut smashes the plate to bits and crashes through to the floor.

The most striking and most popular element of the early Chaplin shorts is their pure comic inventiveness. The creation of the tramp character and the objective, concrete depiction of social realities are themselves

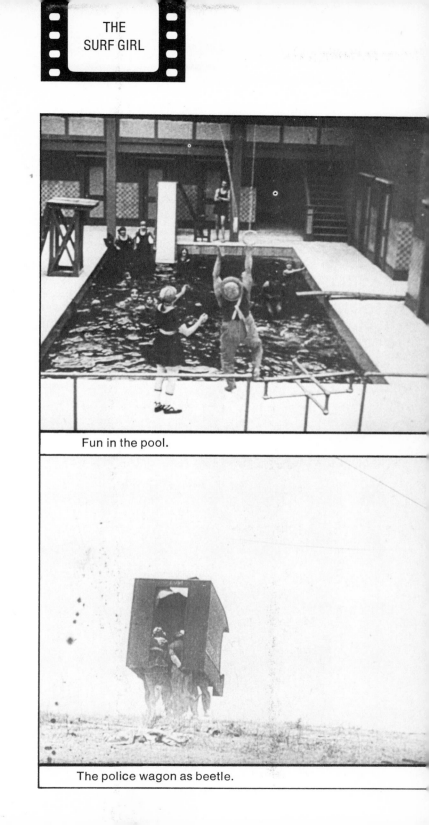

Fun in the pool.

The police wagon as beetle.

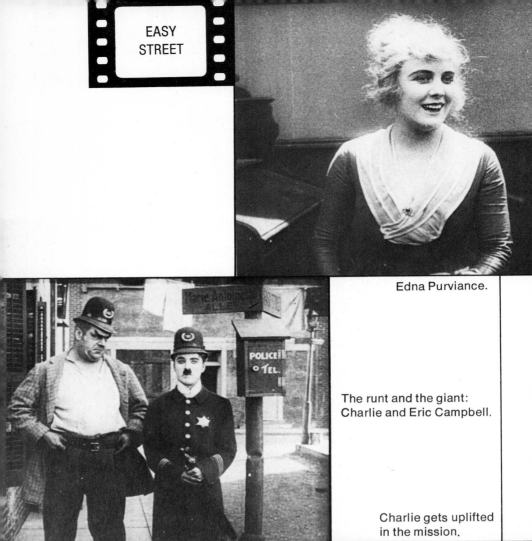

EASY
STREET

Edna Purviance.

The runt and the giant:
Charlie and Eric Campbell.

Charlie gets uplifted
in the mission.

Charlie and the tiger rug.

THE
PAWNSHOP

The clock as patient and
as jewel (Charlie and Albert Austin).

Von Steuben (Erich von Stroheim) prepares
himself for the evening's amour.

Margaret (Francelia Billington) reads von Steuben's note
in her bedroom—with a cross in the background.

GREED

The two tones of von Stroheim. An accurate, detailed, sarcastically humorous view of bourgeois customs in the wedding ceremony (ZaSu Pitts and Chester Conklin, as her father) and the violent brutality of human beings who act like cannibalistic animals (ZaSu Pitts devoured by McTeague—Gibson Gowland).

Harold Lloyd with
a sleepwalking lady
(Mildred Davis)
on a scary ledge.

Charlie's forks dance
the "Oceana Roll,"
a moment of comedy
and pathos.

THE
GENERAL

Johnny Gray (Buster Keaton) chops wood not realizing his train is carrying him behind the advancing enemy's lines.

Johnny Gray, the pragmatist, turns obstacles into tools.

functions of the comedy. Like Griffith, Chaplin would make longer and more famous films after his apprenticeship period. Also like Griffith, Chaplin's later work reveals the increasing self-consciousness and seriousness of the artist. Unlike Griffith, however, Chaplin's expanding self-consciousness demonstrated the richness and complexity of the artist's vision—his thorough understanding of both the character he had created and the world in which that character (and all men) function—rather than exposing its pretentiousness and banality. Whereas Griffith's simplistic system pitted idealized goodness against idealized evil, Chaplin's system showed the inherent contradictions within the definitions of good and evil themselves. The comic tramp was himself a walking contradiction, a figure who loathed (and feared) the falsity of the established order and who yearned toward the purity of the ideal but also envied the comforts and rewards of the established society and realized that he had better administer a kick unto others before they kicked unto him. This tension between naïveté and instinctive, tough pragmatism in the Charlie tramp produces the moral ambivalence of the mature Chaplin films: the contrast between societal definitions of paternity and more human ones in *The Kid* (1921), the contrast between societal definitions of morality and more human ones in *The Pilgrim* (1922), the ambivalent contrasts between rich and poor in *City Lights* (1931) and between civilization and nature in *Modern Times* (1936).

But most unlike Griffith, Chaplin's contribution to the cinema has much more to do with what he does on film than with what he does with film. Whereas Griffith is most important for his building the devices of cinema into a coherent cinematic language, Chaplin is most important for making all consciousness of the cinematic language disappear so completely that we concentrate solely on the photographic subject rather than the process. This does not mean (as many have claimed) that Chaplin was "uncinematic," that he was ignorant of the means of manipulating the cinematic language. Quite the opposite. One indeed manipulates a language skilfully when all consciousness of manipulation disappears and the language serves solely to communicate the subject matter with complete lucidity. This lucidity allows us to view the hypnotic magic of the Chaplin performance far more intimately and closely than we could if he were on the stage. And Chaplin's insistence on unobtrusive, middle-distance composition and "invisible," restrained editing sustains the spell by producing this hypnotic magic without sleight-of-hand.

Chaplin's early films not only demonstrated the magic of a human performance on film but the magical appeal of the performer on the minds of the public. His millions of new fans rushed to the novelty shops that sold mechanical tramp dolls and plaster tramp statues in his image, much as more recent generations of kiddies have bought Mouseketeer and Beatle paraphernalia. In his first five years in the business, 1913–18, Chaplin worked for four different companies; each new job brought him more money and more artistic freedom. From $150 a week as a Sennett pawn, he progressed to $75,000 for a year with Essanay in 1915–16, to $670,000 for a year with Mutual in 1916–17, to $1,000,000 beginning in 1918 with First National Pictures, a firm which then only distributed and exhibited films. This last move left Chaplin as a totally independent producer and owner of his own film studio. With First National the later phases of his career began—with the silent and sound feature film. But these are later stories.

MOVIE CZARS
AND
MOVIE STARS

G riffith, Sennett, and Chaplin were the three major artists of the moving picture's second decade, 1905–15. Significantly, all three made their films in America. All three were both the causes and the effects of the rise of the American film in this second decade. After trailing the industries of England and France in the first decade of commercial film-making, the American film asserted its dominance in the years just pre-ceding World War I and, with the help of that war, established a commercial supremacy that has never yet been challenged. The secret of the American rise was both art and industry. The increasing demand of American audiences to see moving pictures, the increasing admissions at the nickelodeon theatres, led, in turn, to greater demands on production and more opportunities to experiment and invent methods that were better than the competition's. The art of a Griffith was partially the result of the audience's demand that the Biograph studio turn out two reels a week. The necessity of just making films allowed Griffith's imagination to discover ways of making them better. His discoveries, in turn, produced greater popularity and esteem for the movies, and hence further demands for more films and for better films. The successes of Chaplin and Sennett worked in the same circular way.

World War I came at an opportune time for the American film business. In 1914, just at the time when the European film imagination was beginning to atrophy and the American to swell, the war came along to kill off the European industry. The same chemicals that produced raw film stock were also the essential ingredients of gunpowder. The European governments, given the choice of guns or movies, made the obvious decision. American films, suddenly without any competitors, ruled the screens of America and Europe during the war and just after it. When the film industries of France, Germany, Russia, and Scandinavia finally recovered, their roles in world film production were as fertile, imaginative innovators rather than as equal competitors with the dollar doings of Hollywood.

Wealth began flowing into the American film world just as the industry was pulling itself out of the legal and commercial chaos of its infancy. In 1910, the war against the Trust was raging as the impish Independents valiantly kept fighting and producing pictures. Ten years later all but one of the original Trust companies had folded, and the leaders of the opposition had themselves become more tyrannical and more powerful than their earlier Establishment adversaries. Carl Laemmle, William Fox, Adolph Zukor, Jesse Lasky, Marcus Loew, Samuel Goldfish, Lewis J. Selznick, Louis B. Mayer were all lucky enough to be in the right place at the right time. They were fortunate to be running a studio or buying up theatres at the moment when everyone in America started going to the movies and when everyone abroad went to American movies because there were few others. These men, who became the first movie moguls, had outlasted their Trust competitors simply because they rode the crest of the new wave of film merchandising rather than trying to dam it.

The Trust studios and distributors were unalterably opposed to the feature film. Their business was to market one-hour programs of short films; the new feature film, usually lasting two hours, demanded more personnel and more money than they were ready to invest. For a studio to produce fifty-two feature films a year (the equivalent of one film program per week) would require a huge permanent staff of actors, writers, directors, and technicians, a major investment in equipment, a complex administrative office for scheduling the shooting and selling the films, and so on. Zukor, Goldfish, Laemmle, Fox, and a few others made the investment; the Trust companies did not, certain that the new feature craze was just a passing fancy. The fancy never passed; the Trust companies did. Although the Trust officially lost the battle in the courts in 1915, it had already lost the war to such opponents as *Queen Elizabeth, Quo Vadis?, Cabiria, The Last Days of Pompeii,* and *The Birth of a Nation.* The public wanted to see feature films.

The years between 1910 and 1920 determined the direction the American film industry would take. By 1915 the film program consisted of a single feature film supplemented by a short or two, the same practice that survives today. A second current practice was born at the same time—the star system. In the healthy days of the Trust no actor ever received screen credit. Performers were either known by the names of the characters they played—"Little Mary"—or by the studio—the Biograph Girl. There even seems to have been some doubt in the minds of the earliest patrons about whether they were watching a dramatization or real life. The confusion in the mind of the country boy about fiction or reality in *Mabel's Dramatic Career* may have been quite common a few years earlier.

The Trust opposed giving screen credit for the same short-sighted commercial reasons that it opposed the feature film. The Trust reasoned that star actors would cost more than anonymous faces on a screen. Their reasoning was quite correct. But the Independents reasoned that although a star would cost more, a film with a star would earn more. As with the feature film, the Independents had the stronger argument: to make more it was necessary to spend more. The Independents launched their career by stealing the Biograph Girl in 1910 and featuring her in Imp pictures under her real name—Florence Lawrence. They did the same with "Little Mary" Pickford, King Baggott, Arthur Johnson, and many other formerly anonymous players. The power of the star system was such that in 1917—only a few years after its inception—two stars, Chaplin and Mary Pickford, were vying with producers and with each other to become the highest paid performers in the business, both of them signing contracts for over $1,000,-000. And every major producer in the industry was trying to sign them and pay them that million.

The movie star, no longer an anonymous character in a film but a human being in his or her own right, instantly seized the imagination of the American public. In 1912, just after audiences started learning their favorites' names, America's first motion picture magazines appeared. The fan magazines featured pictures, stories, and interviews that made the figure on the screen an even more intimate and personal being for each member of the audience. Producing companies needed publicity departments to sell the stars as well as the pictures to the public. In the middle of the second decade of the century, the exotic and erotic activities of the stars first became items of household gossip. One of the earliest and most impressive of the grand publicity jobs was the packaging of the "lusty, seductive siren," Theda Bara, who made her debut in *A Fool There Was* (1915). Born in Chicago as Theodosia Goodman, the publicists transformed her into Theda Bara, the Arabian beauty clad in black who survived less on oxygen and victuals than by wrecking homes and devouring men. She was a mystic semisorceress; her name, they pointed out, bore an anagrammatical relationship to Death (Theda) and Arab (Bara); the blood of the Ptolemies flowed in her veins; and her astrological signs matched Cleopatra's. The character she played—a sexual vampire—was abbreviated to vamp, adding a new noun and verb to the English language. More significant than all the drivel of the Bara legend was the fact that the public loved the drivel and swallowed it, obviously because it wanted to. Movie publicists had discovered the ease of selling something the public wanted to buy.

The greatest stars of the silent films created their own images and types; the lesser stars merely filled the patterns that the great stars had already sketched. There were imitations of Mary Pickford's spunky, goodhearted, pranksterish little girl with the golden curls. There were sultry sirens in the Theda Bara image, many of them imported from Europe. There were gentle, soulful juveniles—Richard Barthelmess, Charles Ray. There were exotic Latin leading men—Rudolph Valentino, Ramon Novarro. Perhaps even Douglas Fairbanks's conversion from zippy American go-getter to swarthy swashbuckler in the twenties was the result of the influence of this new sexual type. There were lecherous, jaded roués, often from decadent foreign shores—Erich von Stroheim, Owen Moore, Adolphe Menjou. There were stars from the opera, the stage, and even the swimming pool—Geraldine Farrar, Mary Garden, Alla Nazimova, Annette Kellerman. There was the basically pure woman who was inevitably tainted by experience (Lillian Gish); there was the stubborn, sophisticated, and often tragic lady (Gloria Swanson); there was the strong, competent, virile male (Thomas Meighan); there was the serious, tough cowboy with the sad eyes (William S. Hart); there was the fat (John Bunny, Fatty Arbuckle), and the little (Chaplin, Harold Lloyd, Buster Keaton), and so forth. The star and not the play became the thing that caught the consciousness of the public. Hollywood also used the star to catch the public's wallet.

The third major development of the American film's second decade was the move west. As early as 1907, production companies—usually evading the law or the Patent Company wrecking crews—discovered the felicities of southern California. During the Trust War, the independent companies also took advantage of California's distance from the Trust headquarters in New York and its closeness to the Mexican border, where the company could quickly flee with its negatives and machines. But gradually the more legitimate virtues of California struck the filmmakers. The vast, open plains, the predictability of the sun, the nearby mountains and deserts and ocean, all attracted the eyes of men whose art depended on the power of the visual. D. W. Griffith brought his company west in the winters of 1910 and 1911 and 1912. *The Birth of a Nation* and *Intolerance* were both filmed in California. By 1915 most of the film companies had permanently settled down to business in the Los Angeles suburbs— the most famous of them known as Hollywood. Real estate speculators, who suddenly discovered that miles of apparently useless land were of great use to the movie men, sold it to them by the tens of thousands of acres, and at absurdly reasonable prices. Vast studios, like Thomas Ince's Inceville (which became MGM) and Carl Laemmle's Universal City, with rows of shooting studios, office buildings, storage buildings, back lots (for the outdoor sets), and even vast ranches completely stocked with cattle and horses and other four-legged beasts, sprang up near Los Angeles. The founding of the movie capital was the result of three coincidental accidents: weather, topography, and real estate values. Enjoying the harvests of chance, the accidental emperors of the new film world now ruled vast, tangible empires.

The Emperors and Their Rule

The most significant accident in the history of the American film is that this first generation of influential movie producers, those gentlemen who made the concrete decisions about the artistic and moral values worthy to be included in films, were themselves deficient in formal education and aesthetic judgment. The first Hollywood producers were not just businessmen; they were a very specific breed of businessmen. Most of them were either Jewish immigrants from Germany or Russia or Poland, or the sons of Jewish immigrants. Most of them came to the movies by accident. They sold herring or furs or gloves or second-hand clothes. They jumped from these businesses into running amusement parks and penny arcades, just at the time when Edison's Kinetoscope and the Mutoscope were bringing new life to the novelty business. When movies left the peep-show box for the screen, these arcade owners converted their stores into nickelodeons. They built more and more of these theatres, which became more and more plush. Soon they began producing films for their theatres, what with the pressures of the Trust and its licensing fees. Such was the series of small steps that a Goldwyn (né Goldfish) or Zukor or Mayer took from the Jewish ghetto to multimillion-dollar arbiter of national artistic tastes. It is doubtful that a first generation of producer-aesthetes would have made better movies (look at the likes of *Queen Elizabeth*); but this first generation of film men and film values has left its legacy of sacrificing taste for dollars that Hollywood films have never completely outgrown.

The most powerful film company of the silent era was Paramount Pictures. Paramount was the child of Adolph Zukor, the final stage in the evolution of his Famous Players in Famous Plays. Zukor, who began by distributing *Queen Elizabeth*, jumped aboard the feature-film wagon at the very beginning—and therein lies one of the chief reasons for his success. Zukor's Famous Players company initiated three kinds of pictures:

Class A (with stage stars and stage properties, the artsy films); Class B (with established screen players); and Class C (cheap, quick features). Zukor discovered that the Class B films, the ones with Mary Pickford, were far more popular than the high-toned Class A. Zukor dropped the stagey films and made Class B's exclusively. He soon absorbed Jesse Lasky's Feature Play Company, Lewis J. Selznick's Picture Company, Edwin S. Porter's Rex Pictures, Pallas Pictures, and Morosco Pictures; he also absorbed a distributing exchange called Paramount Pictures, which eventually gave its name to the final amalgamation. Zukor bested his competition by buying it out. The huge company then had the power and the money to hire the most popular stars and demand the highest fees from exhibitors who wanted the films of his stars.

A second powerful combine emerged in the mid-twenties: Metro-Goldwyn-Mayer. The monolith was assembled by theatre owner Marcus Loew, who wanted to control the profit from the pictures that he showed in his vast national chain of theatres. In 1924, Loew bought the struggling Metro Picture Company and the struggling Goldwyn Picture Company. Goldwyn had himself left his own company shortly before the merger, bitter about losing one of those power-financial struggles that dominated the early years of the film business. Loew then put Louis B. Mayer, another theatre owner recently turned producer, in charge of production at Metro-Goldwyn. Mayer brought a young assistant, Irving Thalberg, with him to supervise the shooting of the pictures. With these individual parts, Loew assembled the most solid film factory in America. MGM took over the Goldwyn lot to shoot its films (Goldwyn had earlier taken it over from Ince); the studio then distributed its films to all of the Loew theatres. Loew had finally succeeded in creating the kind of empire that Gaumont and Pathé had established twenty years earlier; he controlled all three processes of commercial film: production, distribution, and exhibition.

Zukor was not slow to follow suit. His company had been working in a similar, octopal manner, snatching up theatres as well as studios and exchanges. One of Zukor's commercial innovations was the system of block booking. The theatre owner had to agree to buy all of Zukor's products to get any of them. If he wanted Mary Pickford or William S. Hart, he had to buy all fifty-two weekly programs from Paramount. But even block booking, tyrannical as it was, was less efficient than owning the theatres. The studio owner not only had to produce films but had to guarantee that each of them would be shown. What better guarantee than to own the theatres to show them?

Understandably, the theatre owner did not enjoy the strong-arm pressures of block booking nor the unavailability of those popular films that had been made by the studios for their own theatres. In 1917, a group of theatre owners joined together specifically as an antidote to Zukor's commercial poison, calling themselves the First National Exhibitors Circuit. First National, managed by W. W. Hodkinson (himself elbowed out of Paramount by Zukor) and J. D. Williams, intended to eliminate the film production company from filmmaking, just as the film production companies were trying to eliminate the independent exhibitor. First National contracted with individual stars (Chaplin, for example, and Harry Langdon) to make pictures for their theatres. The star gained independence and financial backing; the theatre owner gained the lucrative products of popular, established stars. The idea was so felicitous that First National became the third power of the 1920s film world.

Yet another new producing wrinkle was the emergence of the artist himself as producer. If film producers could turn theatre owners and if theatre owners could turn producers, then an artist could also turn producer and work for himself. In 1919, D. W. Griffith, Charles Chaplin, Mary Pickford, and Douglas Fairbanks joined together to form the United Artists Corporation. Each would produce his own films, which would then be distributed by the common company, United Artists. United Artists owned neither studio nor theatre; it merely released the finished products for distribution. However flimsy such an organization seemed compared with the Goliaths like Paramount, MGM, and First National, the company survived and still does today. In fact, the idea for the company was years ahead of its time, foreshadowing the commercial practices of the 1960s and '70s. Today, the major "studios" themselves are primarily distributors for pictures that have been filmed by independent producers.

The Hollywood film studios of the twenties had traveled a long way from Edison's Black Maria. Vast expanses of land and a complex maze of buildings had replaced the single, little armored room that pirouetted with the sun. The Hollywood studio had become an entertainment factory; like any factory it broke the manufacture of its product into a series of parts, and each cell of the whole organism fulfilled its particular function. There was a specific section for writers in the studio—those who conceived the original story ideas, those who wrote the final scenarios, and even those who created the film's subtitles, a separate and highly developed art of its own. There was a specific section for costuming, one for the construction of sets, and another for the care and maintenance of the increasingly complicated equipment, still another for the shooting of the films, and one for publicizing, marketing, and financing the finished product. The arts of the costumer, the cinematographer, the electrician, and the writer had become as significant as the contributions of the director and actor.

The growth and evolution of the film studio were paralleled by the growth and evolution of the theatre that showed its films. Almost simultaneous with the birth of the feature film came the huge, plush, comfortable movie theatre to show feature films. The two births are interrelated: the same feature phenomenon that turned the studios into rich dinosaurs turned the theatres into rich dinosaurs. The earlier nickelodeons were small and often dirty; the movies migrated from these little stores in the low-rent districts to huge theatres on Broadway. The first of the new palaces was the Strand, constructed on Broadway in 1914, followed immediately by the Vitagraph (now the Criterion). The new theatres could accommodate over two thousand patrons, who trod on carpeted floors and relaxed in plush, padded chairs. The manager of the Strand Theatre, Samuel L. Rothafel (né Rothapfel), soon went on to buy, build, and conceive huge movie palaces of his own. Roxy (his nickname) opened or salvaged a string of mammoth New York houses: the Rialto, Rivoli, Capitol, Roxy, and the Radio City Music Hall, his finale and *chef d'oeuvre*. Roxy brought the same tone of quasi-gentility to the movie theatre that his colleagues, like Zukor and Mayer, brought to the films themselves. Roxy supplemented the film showing with symphony orchestras, corps de ballets, and live variety acts. Whereas vaudeville had supported the movies in their first years in America, the movies had now begun to support vaudeville. The last survivor of the Roxy era in this country is, of course, Radio City Music Hall, whose live stage show is a major tourist attraction simply because it is a unique anachronism.

Roxy decorated the insides of his theatres with the same kinds of flouncing that he used for the film showings. The ushers wore colorful silken uniforms that matched the carpets and walls and were consistent with the theatre's architectural motif. The theatre walls offered ornate carvings in stone, brass, and wood; gargoyles stared from the balconies; plaster copies of Greek statues (attired in fig leaves covering the appropriate areas) gazed down from trellised cupolas, bathed in a red or green floodlight. The Roxy of the West Coast, Sid Grauman, paid as much attention to the outsides of his theatres as Roxy paid to the inside. His Chinese Theatre welcomes the patron with a complex system of pagoda roofs and Oriental carvings; his Egyptian Theatre offers the patron a waterfall and a wishing well as he walks in the door. The pretentiousness, the tacky splendor of these huge movie houses today seems metaphoric of most of the films they showed on their screens.

Morality

The movies have waged a perpetual cold war with the forces of religion and righteousness. In 1897, the moralists denounced the improprieties of the *Rice-Irwin Kiss*. Another 1897 film, *Fatima*, which depicted the bumps and grinds of a noted hooch dancer of the day, so offended some members of certain communities that exhibitors superimposed broad white stripes across the screen to cover the areas where Fatima displayed her most lascivious wares. Without question, the censored version of the film is far more offensive and obscene than the original since the two heavily streaked regions of the frame inform the viewer quite precisely about what areas of the body he should consider nasty.

Throughout the nickelodeon era the movies had been criticized as cultivators of iniquity; the theatres had been attacked as unsavory or unsafe. The protests of the moralistic few did not deter the entertainment-minded many from going to the nickelodeons. The parallels between the twentieth-century moralistic controversy over the movies (still continuing today) and the sixteenth-century moralistic controversy over the Elizabethan theatre (also criticized as a breeder of licentiousness and laziness) are striking. The vocal moralists preached; the public continued to go to their favorite public entertainment. The movie cold war suddenly became a very hot one in the early 1920s.

First, the content of films, reflecting the new materialism and moral relativism of the decade, became spicier and more suggestive. The sentimental films of the Griffith era had not disappeared; Griffith's own films, Mary Pickford's, and pictures like Henry King's *Tol'able David* perpetuated the tradition of innocence and purity. But alongside these Victorian films were others suggesting that lust was indeed a human emotion, that married couples indeed indulged in extramarital flirtations (at the least), and that the urbane and wealthy and lustful were not inevitably evil and unhappy. The new materialistic audience (who spent as much as two dollars to get into the plush movie palace) enjoyed films that idolized the material as well as the spiritual. The spiritual sermonizers intensified their letter-writing and speech-making campaigns with concerted public action. Clergymen and laymen united to form panels and committees that would not exactly censor films, but would advise parishioners and the public about which films to see and which to avoid. The National Board of Review, the Federal Motion Picture Council in America, and even the W.C.T.U. launched their "advisory" campaigns. Behind the censorship drives of some of these organizations lay a thinly veiled antisemitism (an interesting parallel with the similarly antisemitic campaigns against the Hollywood "Reds" of some thirty years later). The moral deficiencies of the movies were yet another strategem of the Jewish infidels, once again poisoning the wells of a Christian nation.

The moral ambiguities of the offerings on the motion picture screens were soon accompanied by the scandalous doings of the motion picture people off the screen. In the early twenties, several national scandals rocked the film industry far more severely than had the letters and speeches of the zealots. Hollywood did not just sell pictures to the public; it sold the stars who sold the pictures. Scandal in the life of a star was more serious than any extra-marital wink on the screen. In 1920, Mary Pickford, "America's Sweetheart," quietly went to Nevada with her husband, Owen Moore, to get a divorce. Three weeks later "Little Mary" married her male counterpart in innocence and purity, Douglas Fairbanks. The public was not shocked by the divorce alone, since divorces in Hollywood had become old news. But this divorce, followed by the abrupt marriage of these two supposedly healthy, happy, all-American people, was something special. The Pickford-Fairbanks marriage was further complicated by the possibility of the divorce proceeding's being improperly executed ("Little Mary" eventually avoided the stain of bigamy). Though Doug and Mary had done nothing illegal, their illicit premarital romance seemed contradictory to their screen purity. The tremendous public interest in the petty domestic affair clearly revealed the new social importance of the film industry and its vulnerability to attack by newspaper headlines.

In 1921, two consecutive Fatty Arbuckle scandals fed the headlines. In July of that year newspapers reported a mysterious Arbuckle party in Massachusetts that had taken place in 1917. The mysterious detail was that the District Attorney of a Massachusetts county received a $100,000 gift just after the party. The public wondered what the District Attorney had discovered that was worth such a sum to keep quiet. Then in September of 1921, Arbuckle threw a second party, this one in San Francisco's St. Francis Hotel. The next morning one of Arbuckle's guests, Virginia Rappe, was found dead in her hotel room. A week later Arbuckle gave himself up to the police, was eventually tried for involuntary manslaughter, and found not guilty. His innocence in the eyes of the law did not affect his standing in the eyes of the moralists. The Hollywood producers, acceding to the cries of the preachers, barred the evil Fatty from pictures. The great comedian worked in only one more film, James Cruze's bitter satire of Hollywood (*Hollywood*, 1923), although he continued to direct films under an assumed name (Will B. Good!). The Hollywood producers threw Arbuckle to the moralists, hoping to still the hissing tongues; the money men preferred a safe surrender to a possibly unsettling and unprofitable confrontation. Some thirty years later the industry made the same choice when it sacrificed "the Ten" directors and writers to the Red-baiters.

In 1922, "handsome" Wallace Reid died suddenly and mysteriously, generating posthumous scandal when the newspapers discovered he had used drugs. Early in the same year, a minor director, William Desmond Taylor, was found dead in his apartment, another scandal with a vague mixture of sex, murder, and drugs. The Taylor murder hurt the careers of Mabel Normand, the pretty comedienne, and Mary Miles Minter, a little-girl imitation of Mary Pickford, who were both friends of the director. The press, satisfying the hunger of its readers, turned these friendships into something salacious. There was no defense against vague rumor and veiled implication. Two more careers were thrown to the yapping dogs to keep them quiet.

Such notoriety brought the film business to the attention of the United States Congress and the edge of federal censorship—the last thing any producer wanted. The industry decided to clean its own house, to serve as its own censorship body. Recalling the success of the baseball owners at finding a moralistic commissioner to cleanse the black-sox scandals, the esteemed Judge Landis, the film producers sought their own respected commissioner. In 1922, they found Will H. Hays, President Harding's campaign manager, Postmaster General of the United States, Presbyterian elder, and Republican. Hays became president of the Motion Picture Producers and Distributors of America, known colloquially as the Hays Office, which he headed for over twenty years. Rather than taking concrete censorship actions, the Hays Office sought to counter bad publicity with good, to keep the press from magnifying its tales of Hollywood debauches, to regularize business procedures, and to encourage producers to submit their films voluntarily for prerelease examination. The loose, informal advising of the Hays Office in the twenties was the first in a series of successful Hollywood attempts to keep films out of the hands of government censors.

Films and Filmmakers, 1910–1928

The ever-increasing problem of the American film director was how to make an individualized, special film in a factory system geared toward standardization and mass production. The Griffith era of anarchy and improvisation was rapidly passing, even as Griffith himself went to work for Zukor. For a director to assemble his own company and begin production without a shooting script and production schedule became unthinkable. Rather than being the artistic creator of his own films, the director was more and more expected to be the mechanic who hammered together the machine that other men, the producer and writer, had earlier designed. Griffith himself noted with dismay the widening gap between producer and director, between the business of making a film and the art of making a film. Each film, rather than being an important work in itself, became only one unit of the studio's yearly output. Though the films had gotten longer and the film business more complex, studio owners considered only the total yearly product, exactly as they did in the Patent Company days of the one-reeler. This industrialization of the film business is most relevant to the career of Thomas Ince, Griffith's contemporary and, after Griffith, the most interesting American director of non-comic films before 1919.

Ince's films are almost the paradigmatic opposites of Griffith's. Whereas Griffith's technique aimed at developing the characters, their emotions, and the metaphoric implications of the action, Ince concentrated ruthlessly on the narrative flow. Ince was as avid a film cutter as Griffith, but whereas Griffith cut to develop rhythm and emotion, Ince cut to keep the story moving. Whereas Griffith consistently used the close-up for intimacy and detail, Ince consistently used the long, far, and extreme far shots, rarely picking the characters' feelings out of the flow of the action. Griffith's interest was primarily on why the characters did something and what that implied symbolically; Ince's focused almost exclusively on what they did. If, on the surface, Ince's method seems thinner and less interesting than Griffith's, he compensated for it by eliminating Griffith's sticky sentimentality and symbolism. Ince's pretentiously symbolic *Civilization* (1916) is an obvious exception (and an obvious attempt to copy the Griffith formula). However, more typical of Ince is a film like *The Coward* (1915), another Civil War story made the same year as Griffith's, which avoids all the symbolic freight of *Birth of a Nation* to concentrate exclusively on one young man's earning his "red badge of courage." The two titles of the films (the specificity of Ince's, the abstractness of Griffith's) are indicative.

Ince was also one of the first directors to discover the power of shooting outdoors. Ince movies could have been made nowhere else but in California and the West. The openness and movement that Griffith used for battle scenes and chases were the bases of Ince's films: the stagecoach sweeping down a mountain trail flanked by mountains and plains and sagebrush, the Indians pursuing the rushing stage, the posse galloping across the prairies, the Indians' circle of death as they revolve about the isolated victims, the dust and smoke and powder of the gun battle (a brilliant visual translation of sound into visual terms), the dust of the horses' hooves, the silhouettes of the tribe of Apaches on the mesa awaiting the moment to join the attack. One of the most common (and beautiful) Ince images is smoke—the swirling, enveloping movement of gunpowder or dust, the refractions of light through this haze. This smoky haze is an effective contrast with Ince's usual clean, crisp, deep-focus photographic style (yet another marked contrast with Griffith, who depended on soft-focus photography).

Ince movies moved. And they moved because they had the space to move in. The outdoor freedom that Porter accidentally discovered for *The Great Train Robbery* became a conscious artistic tool for Ince. It was a tool he would pass on to his successors—John Ford, Howard Hawks, Sam

Peckinpah, and many others—who also used the visual contrast of small, moving men in vast western vistas.

Ince, unlike Griffith, quickly tired of directing films. Instead, he became a supervisor of production (a position Griffith rejected), in effect a producer, keeping his finger on several different film projects at the same time. Unlike Griffith, Ince insisted on a detailed shooting script, which he eventually approved and stamped, "Shoot as is." The Ince director then went about the business of constructing from the producer's blueprint. Ince supplemented the shooting script with a detailed production breakdown and schedule, making sure that all the people and animals and equipment went to the right place at the right time for the fewest number of hours. If Griffith was the film's first real director, Ince was its first important producer, instituting the system that uncomfortably divides the artistic responsibility for the film between two men. Ince showed the future studio heads how to run a studio.

Ironically, Ince's career waned in the studio era itself. He was the hardest hit by the failure of the Triangle Film Corporation, which depended on his films and his Culver City studio. In 1915, the president of the Mutual Film Corporation, Harry Aitken, was ousted by his partner, John R. Freuler, in another one of those power struggles for control. Aitken, who personally owned the Mutual contracts of Griffith, Sennett, and Ince, took the three with him to build the Triangle Film Corporation, with the three important directors as the tips of the triangle. But Griffith produced several unimportant program pictures, and Sennett's and Ince's drawing powers were feebler than they had been. The triangle collapsed in 1919. Ince, the movie man of system and efficiency, died mysteriously (another of those strange Hollywood deaths) in 1924, just when the era of system and efficiency had officially arrived with the Mayer-Thalberg rule at MGM, Ince's old lot.

The films of Douglas Fairbanks also reveal the changing values of Hollywood. Fairbanks broke into films with Griffith at Triangle; the young actor was so athletic, so bouncy, so perpetually in motion, that Griffith gave up on him and suggested he go see Mr. Sennett. Triangle eventually let Fairbanks go his own way, pairing him with the scenario writer, Anita Loos, her director-husband, John Emerson, and cameraman, Victor Fleming. Between 1915 and 1920, the group produced a series of breezy, parodic, energetic comedies that combined the star's athleticism, energy, and sincerity with the writer's and director's wit and style. For today's "film generation," which only thinks of Fairbanks as the cavalier who duelled while swinging from a chandelier (Gene Kelly parodied this Doug in *Singin' in the Rain*), his early films are refreshing surprises. They are parodies which make fun of a personality trait (American snobbishness, the fascination with royalty, the hunger for publicity, the ambition to achieve the impossible) or a genre of films (the western, the mystery, the melodrama). Doug is the center of the parody, the magnified version of whatever the film is satirizing. But Doug, because of his naïveté, because of his enthusiasm, because of his obvious love of life and people, always succeeds in engaging our sympathies at the same time that we laugh at him. Loos and Emerson took advantage of the fact that Doug overdid everything; they made a virtue of overdoing. And Doug's athleticism, his physical exhilaration, his constant movement, become a delight to watch. Doug can jump around madly, can swing from the beams of the ceiling, can jump from balconies, can ride horses and twirl a rope, can tumble down (or up) a ravine. Doug's acting technique seemed to center around such questions as: why enter a room through a door when you can jump in through the window? why walk up a flight of stairs when you can leap up them, or swing upstairs on a lighting fixture, or vault through a hole in the downstairs ceiling?

The glorification of the physical in the Fairbanks film led to several key moral principles which the films implicitly, and sometimes explicitly, extolled. One of the key contrasts in the films is between the dull, routine, banal life that Doug must live in conventional society and the imaginative, free, vigorous life he wants to live. Fairbanks was the foe of the dull and regimented; the row upon row of similar desks in the button factory of *Reaching for the Moon* (1917) was an image of everything Fairbanks hated. A consistent metaphor for the routine and businesslike in Fairbanks's films was the opaque accountant's sunshade; whenever Doug feels the need to drive free and imaginative thoughts out of his head, he clamps on the sunshade and gets to work. The physical emphasis of Doug's talent also led the star to value the source of the physical, the body. The character Doug played, though guilty of an overly fertile imagination and far-fetched ambitions, was rarely guilty of abusing his body. Doug supplemented his on-screen cleanliness with magazine articles lauding the healthy life and disparaging the unhealthy lures of drink, tobacco, and gluttony.

Yet another Fairbanks moral principle was—despite the joys of the imagination and the tortures of routine—one's imagination should not be too imaginative, and should really bend its efforts to make the conventional, routine life less routine. In *Reaching for the Moon*, Doug tells us that the moon is not worth having because we can't get it. The plot is a sputteringly delightful parody of skullduggery and spying in a small, mythical middle-European kingdom (Vulgaria). But affixed to the plot is the explicit message that one should indeed concentrate and aspire, but only toward that which is worth attaining. Whereas Doug aspires to be a king, his girl only aspires to a husband, house, and children (in New

Jersey). In the end she gets her wishes and Doug renounces his "moon shot," returning to the hateful button company, supposedly to use his imagination there; there is a rather uncomfortable vagueness about just how he is going to go about doing so.

The later Fairbanks films of the twenties make quite a contrast with these earlier, breezy ones. Doug is still a great athlete; he still has his smile and energy. But, most significantly, he is no longer a contemporary American trying to strike a blend between his own imaginative impulses and the conventions of society. Doug has been transported to faraway, romantic lands of centuries ago. He is free to perform bizarre and exotic deeds, and although he is usually some kind of thief, he is not, paradoxically, dishonest. In addition to his daring exploits, the faroff themes and places allow Doug to become an explicit sex symbol, gliding through most of the films without his shirt, with limbs clearly defined by a pair of tights or slightly exposed by the scanty cloth that teasingly covers his middle. The transformation of Doug from pure American to gallant, sexy swashbuckler may be due to several causes. Perhaps the naiveté and innocence of the American Doug was out of touch with the earthier tastes of the jazz age. Perhaps the new popularity of ornate costume spectacles prompted Doug's decision. Perhaps the Pickford romance necessitated a less virgin-like image. Perhaps the new popularity of exotic Latin types (Doug even grew a moustache and let his hair grow) contributed to the transformation.

The Thief of Bagdad (1923) is one of the best of Doug's costume films. He and his director (Raoul Walsh) borrow both the plot devices and the cinematic gimmicks of Fritz Lang's *Destiny* without borrowing any of the German's mysticism. The result is a rather long, empty, and yet entertaining film of adventures and cinematic tricks. Doug's energy still holds the stringy plot together; only his dash, his zest, his immense good will (despite the fact that he plays a thief) keeps us interested in his success at winning both wealth and the girl. Though Doug has been whisked off to some mythical Oriental land, his goals are the standard ones of domestic comedy and the materialistic American society of his early films. The film is impressive visually: a rope hangs suspended in midair (Doug climbs it of course); Doug rides a flying horse and flying carpet (both borrowed from Lang, but used more slickly); the city of Bagdad itself is a glimmering, shiny synthesis of a marble temple and a birthday cake. The film adds up to a slick, pleasant show, but that sum seems less significant than the incisive wit, the cleverness, the insight of the early Doug films.

No two directors more clearly show the problems of the filmmaker in the 1920s than Erich von Stroheim and Cecil B. DeMille. Like Griffith and Ince of a few years earlier, the two are almost paradigms for the whole industry. Von Stroheim gave the public what he wanted, DeMille gave it what he thought it wanted. Von Stroheim was a ruthless realist committed to his art and his vision, DeMille was willing to throw any hokum into a film that was faddish or striking. Von Stroheim's greatest tools were close observation and detail, DeMille's were size and splash. Significantly, DeMille's greatest popularity was in the twenties and fifties, the two decades most devoted to size and splash. Von Stroheim's films, despite their symbolic excesses and occasionally overstated moralizing, were controlled by the director's taste and intelligence; DeMille's films had everything but taste and intelligence.

Both DeMille and von Stroheim served several apprentice years before emerging as major directors. DeMille shot his first film in 1913, *The Straw Man*, for Jesse Lasky's Feature Play Company. Later he and his brother, William, joined the new production company of Samuel Goldfish and Edgar Selwyn (hence, Gold+wyn, which eventually became Goldwyn). DeMille began keeping track of national trends and tastes. Von Stroheim began as a studio adviser on European military details, then began playing vicious "Huns" (dubbed "the man you love to hate") for Griffith, and finally, in 1919, convinced Carl Laemmle to let him direct and perform in his own films.

No two films more clearly reveal the differences in the two men than DeMille's *Male and Female* and von Stroheim's *Blind Husbands*. Both films were released in the same year, 1919; both capitalized on the new audience interest in sexual amours and the doings of the rich. Both suggested the importance of sex in human relationships. But there the similarities stop. *Male and Female* is a lavish, pretentious, and inconsistent examination of the class question; DeMille's point of view is so vague that he seems to suggest two things at the same time: that masters may marry their servants and that masters may not marry their servants. Although some of the film's confusion stems from J. M. Barrie's play, *The Admirable Crichton*, that DeMille was adapting, the most dazzling stupidities are DeMille's "additions": for example, the film begins with a sequence that does not exist in the original play, a series of shots of oceans and the Grand Canyon, followed by a biblical quote, "God created man in his own image." Both the quotation and this whole "Creation" sequence is irrelevant to anything that follows in the film, an obvious plea for high seriousness, and a theft of Griffithisms. The stentorian seriousness of the DeMille film's beginning—the implication that the film one was about to see was Very Significant Art and may even come directly from God—was a consistent DeMille trait that continued into the sound era. Even a modest, war-time biography, *The Story of Dr. Wassel* (1944), begins with a "Voice of God" narrator.

DeMille then plunges into the affairs of a contemporary British household, spending most of his time showing the elegance of Gloria Swanson taking a bath (scented with rose water), the water temperature being checked carefully by her maid, Gloria striding carefully and sliding gently into the sunken tub. One of DeMille's titles asks why shouldn't the bathroom express as much elegance as anything else in life, and the fact that he is interested in asking such a question is at the heart of what is empty about the film. Meanwhile, DeMille contrasts the high-falutin' ways of Lady Mary (Gloria), who rejects a piece of toast because it is too soft, with the simple ways of Tweeny, her maid. Simple Tweeny is in love with the butler, Crichton (Thomas Meighan). But, alas, he is not simple; he loves Lady Mary; he reads aloud poetry that Tweeny cannot understand but Lady Mary can.

Then the whole family takes a yachting trip and runs aground. A title tells us that they have sailed into "uncharted seas," but we recognize Catalina. Now that the group must survive on a desert isle, DeMille can add yet another locale and style of decor to the film. Having already filmed the Creation and a chic English drawing-room comedy, he can go about filming a kind of Swiss Family Robinson. On the island, it turns out that he who is lower-class in one society is upper-class in another. Crichton, the butler, becomes the king of the group and they become his servants, simply because he is competent and able to survive, while they are all numbskulls trying to play at being posh in the middle of the wilderness. The only unaltered element is that Crichton still loves Mary (now no longer a Lady); and she discovers that she loves him. One night, fearing for her safety, Crichton follows her to the haunt of the lions where he slays a beast that is about to attack her. The male and female vow their love. And now comes the kitchen sink.

There is an instantaneous and unmotivated cross-cut to some Oriental dream kingdom, presumably Babylon (the scene does not exist, of course, in Barrie's play). The only motivation for the shift is the line of poetry that Crichton and Mary have read in the film (whereas Barrie uses the line just once, DeMille repeats it several times so you don't miss it), "If I were a king of Babylon. . . ." DeMille is not one to leave his ifs iffy. In this Babylon sequence, Crichton is indeed king, and Mary, a title informs us, is a Christian slave. The fact that Babylon had evaporated hundreds of years before Christ does not offend DeMille's sense of history. Despite the irrelevance of the shift, DeMille can trade in the cave man, leopard skin costumes of the island sequence for the lavish, gaudy silks and satins of Hollywood's version of Babylon. Gloria Swanson, slave though she is, appears in flowing gowns and peacock headdress. Because she refuses to share her man with other concubines, the king of Babylon tosses his reluctant mistress to the sacred lions of Ishtar. She is not reluctant at all about these lions as she strides majestically into their lair. All DeMille then shows us is a sacred lion licking his chops and Gloria's empty gown (unbloodied) lying on the floor.

Meanwhile, back on the desert island, Lady Mary and Crichton are in the middle of their marriage ceremony (they luckily happened to have a clergyman in their yachting party) when they spot a ship. Lady Mary says forget the ship; Crichton, however, for some incomprehensible reason, decides that they must go back to society and must not wed. They go back; they don't wed; the picture ends. The tastelessness of the individual episodes is overwhelmed by the tastelessly irrelevant method of stitching them together. The film is clearly one of the bastard progeny of *Intolerance* in its combination of different epochs and locations in a single film. But in *Male and Female,* the diversity is for diversity's sake, merely using the splashiness of set and costume changes. The moral spinelessness of the film, which flirts with unconventionality and then upholds convention for no dramatic or human reason, became a staple of DeMille's fifty-year career. His racy films flirt with naughtiness and sell conventionality; his religious films flirt with righteousness and sell lewdness. In both versions of *The Ten Commandments,* DeMille was more interested in the splashy, sinful doings around the golden calf than in the righteous thunder and lightning on the mountain.

Von Stroheim's *Blind Husbands* is a far less complicated story than *Male and Female.* A doctor and his wife travel to the Alps; he pays her insufficient sexual attention. A German military officer sees the young wife and desires her; she cannot stop herself from desiring him, for she has no other outlet for her desires. The husband's blindness finally clears up; on a climactic hiking trip, the two males confront each other on the pinnacle, and the lecherous rival perishes, more a victim of the mountains and of fate than of the husband. The power of the film lies in von Stroheim's reduction of the quantity of incidents (quantity was DeMille's credo) in order to develop the quality, the feeling, the texture of the incidents he includes. Details develop the film's emotional dynamics: the calm husband's pipe; the wife's provocative ankles and shoes; the German's handling of his monocle and his careful primping with brush, comb, and vaporizer of cologne to make himself sexually attractive; the soulful tune that Margaret (the wife) plays on the piano, joined by von Steuben (the German) on the violin, which shows both her loneliness and her desire (we need no sound to hear the kind of tune the two are playing together).

Von Stroheim's attention to detail inevitably allows him the luxury and subtlety of understatement. Several of the seduction scenes between von Steuben and Margaret take place in rooms, or hallways, or fields where a cross can distantly but clearly be seen in the background; von Stroheim never cuts to a close-up of the cross. Just before von Steuben's plunge from the pinnacle we see, for no more than a few seconds, a dark, shadowy, unexplained figure looking at him from the distant background. Von Stroheim never explains the figure nor cuts to a close-up of him; he remains a vague and mystifying presentiment of death. The one way to turn that presentiment into twaddle would have been to let us see more of him. Von Stroheim, mature artist that he is, knows the power of allusion.

The director's technique owes its greatest debt to his first master, Griffith. Like Griffith, his two principal tools are the creation of atmosphere and cutting. Von Stroheim's care with sets, lighting, costumes, and decor is so meticulous in creating his seamy world that you can almost smell it. In *Blind Husbands,* the details of the inn courtyard, of the dining room with its posters and crockery, of the individual bedrooms (so important to the film's plot), of the fog and mist on the pinnacle, all contribute to the tone of the film and the power of each scene.

Von Stroheim's care extended to his editing of the films, using the two Griffith devices of the cross-cut (to show parallel events in different places at the same time) and the subjective cut (to show the mental projection of a character at a particular moment). In *Blind Husbands,* von Stroheim's cross-cutting develops both tension and irony. For example, he shows the doctor delivering a baby at the same time that von Steuben courts his wife, obviously trying to perform the act that produces babies. The most striking subjective cut in *Blind Husbands* comes just after the husband has discovered the Prussian's designs on his wife. Von Stroheim suddenly cuts to a menacing, spot-lit head of the German looming out of the darkness until it eventually fills the frame; it leers grotesquely and points an accusing finger at the doctor.

The grotesque, the ugly, and the repellent are dominant motifs in von Stroheim. André Bazin described von Stroheim's "one simple rule for direction": "Take a close look at the world, keep on doing so, and in the end it will lay bare for you all its cruelty and ugliness." Beneath the elegant surfaces of von Stroheim's characters—their polished manners, white gloves, and spray perfume—there is animal rapaciousness, viciousness, and lust. His films are populated by physical cripples and mental defectives; their physiological ugliness is clearly metaphoric of the moral ugliness of this world. In *Foolish Wives* (1921) the fake Russian Count (von Stroheim again) attempts to rape a helpless, mentally retarded child. At the end of the film, the girl's father kills the "Count" and dumps his body into the sewer so it can be swept out to sea with the other garbage.

Despite the overwhelming viciousness of the von Stroheim films, these close and careful examinations of bedroom tensions between husbands and wives were very popular with the public. Their less-than-American nastiness and the haughty independence of their non-American director were less popular with the heads of studios and their flunkies. Irving Thalberg, then Carl Laemmle's assistant at Universal, removed von

Stroheim from *Merry-Go-Round* (1922) in the middle of shooting, firing him for his "inefficient" (i.e. perfectionist and uncompromising) production methods, his wasteful expenditures on "invisible" details (which were actually quite visible in the convincing realism and texture of the overall film), and for his insubordination. Metro Pictures, then in financial trouble, engaged von Stroheim to keep them alive, as he had Universal. (Thalberg would get the chance to fire von Stroheim twice.)

Von Stroheim's first project at Metro was an adaptation of Frank Norris's brutal novel, *McTeague*. The novel attracted von Stroheim for several reasons. Norris's view of the human dog exactly matched von Stroheim's, whose consistent metaphor was to depict human behavior in animal terms. Like von Stroheim, Norris was a ruthless realist with a taste for the ugly and grotesque. Further, the German family in the novel paralleled von Stroheim's own heritage, and the familiar San Francisco and Oakland settings of the novel appealed to a man who had lived there before he went to Hollywood. The director decided to shoot a precise, literal translation of the novel, scene by scene, page by page. He went on location to San Francisco (in an era of almost exclusive studio shooting) and Death Valley (during the summer!) to obtain absolutely authentic details. As his teacher had done with Lillian Gish in the snow, von Stroheim's passion for authenticity put one of his players, Jean Hersholt, in the hospital after the gruelling takes in the sand of Death Valley.

The original version of the film ran forty-two reels (*Birth of a Nation*, Griffith's longest film, ran thirteen). Von Stroheim cut it to twenty-four and said he could cut no further. His friend and director-colleague at Metro, Rex Ingram, cut the film to eighteen reels and felt he could cut no more without mutilating it. Irving Thalberg (who had come to Metro with Louis B. Mayer while von Stroheim was at work on *Greed*) turned the film over to the Metro cutting department, where a hack film cutter (Joe W. Farnham) finished the hatchet job. *Greed* was released in ten reels, and the remainder of the negative was purposely destroyed. Whether a nine-hour, literal translation of a novel is one of the authentic aesthetic possibilities of the cinema will perhaps never be known.

The *Greed* that exists must therefore be judged on the strength of its parts rather than its whole. For one who hasn't read Norris's novel, the film's narrative (certainly its details) are almost incomprehensible. The concrete process of the dissolution of McTeague and Trina's relationship makes no sense in the film at all, for in the novel Norris carefully charts it by moving the couple to shabbier and shabbier living quarters. Each degradation in physical surroundings implies emotional and moral degradation. But in *Greed*, although we might notice that the walls of the McTeague household change as the film progresses, we never know exactly when, why, and where the couple has moved. Although in one shot we might notice that Trina's bandaged hand is lacking several fingers, we never learn from the film that she lost them because they became infected as a result of her husband's biting them. The dissolution from happy, human marriage to vicious, selfish animal combat—which is the subject of at least half of the Norris novel (and which also must have been of central interest to von Stroheim)—does not exist in the film.

Another reason this sense of dissolution does not exist is that the ten-reel version had to do without two other "love" relationships in the novel that undoubtedly seemed quite superfluous to a hack film cutter but which are really essential. The relationship between Trina and Mac is bounded, on the one hand, by Old Grannis and Miss Baker, an idealized couple of old folks who carry on a pure, genteel, spiritual, "Victorian" love affair, and, on the other, by Zerkow and Maria Macapa, two slovenly human beasts whose "love" is based solely on Zerkow's almost sexual pleasure of listening to the equally insane Maria's story of her hoard of gold. The only element remaining of this story in *Greed* are the two extremely bizarre, expressionistic shots of long, skinny arms playing with a pile of metallic objects (taken out of the Maria-Zerkow context, these shots in *Greed* seem irrelevantly and pretentiously symbolic). In the novel, we understand the original love of Mac and Trina as a median between the pure spirituality of the old folks and the crazed passion of the gold lovers. Trina begins as Miss Baker's close friend, somewhat repulsed by Maria's crudeness, and gradually drifts into becoming Maria's confidante. Mac and Trina even move into the squalid hovel where Zerkow and Maria lived (and which became vacant when Zerkow cut Maria's throat). Without the two poles of these other couples, *Greed* has no barometer to measure the direction and degree of decay in the central couple.

Despite the incompetence and incoherence of *Greed* as a whole, several of the sequences are visual and dramatic marvels. The wedding ceremony is a mixture of the comic and the somber: a delightful parody of bourgeois wedding customs that is overshadowed by the sight of a funeral cortege through an open window (and a clear premonition of the direction the marriage will take). The scene in which Trina realizes that she is alone—with no one to protect her except the stranger who is her animal-sensual husband—is a touching, sensitive examination of internal feelings and sensations. Von Stroheim ends the sequence brilliantly as Trina rushes into the room where Mac sits patiently alone, throws herself helplessly into his huge arms, kisses him desperately, and rises instinctively and involuntarily onto her toes. Von Stroheim's use of animal symbolism, particularly his likening the evil Marcus Schouler to the sneaky cat that constantly prowls about the cage of McTeague's bird, is quite effective. And most awesome visually are the endless wastes of Death Valley—a seeming infinity of caked sand and dust under a pitiless, dead sky—the ultimate stopping place on a journey in which a dead metal seems the only goal worth pursuing.

But von Stroheim's point is not so much a moralistic warning against the evils of Mammon as it is a minute examination of what gold does to the human animal. Gold is the stimulus that turns men into vultures, viciously preying on the flesh of their fellows to peck out a profit. Von Stroheim depicts his society of animals with a series of the most realistically detailed scenes in any American film prior to the new naturalism that followed World War II: the tawdriness of the middle-class American home; the brutal lust for wealth that turns husband and wife into murderous enemies; the human irony that the thirst for gold, an inanimate object, can overpower the natural human need for life-sustaining water, chaining a man to a corpse and a cask of gold in the midst of a vast desert where his body can only become food for vultures. It is von Stroheim's view of man, not gold, that dominates the surviving scenes of *Greed*.

That same view of man dominates even the fluffy trifle of a film that Thalberg assigned von Stroheim after *Greed*. *The Merry Widow* (1925) was a safe property, a Viennese operetta that Thalberg was sure von Stroheim could not destroy. Von Stroheim apparently did not destroy it; the film was one of his greatest commercial successes. But von Stroheim, in adapting this operetta fairy tale, devotes a disproportionate amount of attention to the widow's first husband (before she became a widow) rather than her resulting merry widowhood. The husband is a deformed cripple (von Stroheim accentuates the deformity). Worse, he is a cripple with a very obvious sexual fetish; he is attracted to healthy feet—a theme that von Stroheim develops with pointed cutting. Worse still, he is so excited on his wedding night that he collapses and dies on top of his bride, worn out from dragging his gnarled body up to the bed of love. Von Stroheim's handling of this unsavory relationship is not exactly operetta fare. Another brilliant von Stroheim stroke is his depiction of the mental attitudes of the girl's three suitors. All three come to watch her perform at the theatre; all three stare at her through opera glasses. Then von Stroheim cuts to the object of their stares: the cripple watches her feet; the lecherous suitor watches her groin; the young hero watches her face. Such naturalistic touches turn von Stroheim's operetta into a very subtle and salacious parody of an operetta.

Because his production methods seemed extravagant, because he seemed mean and tyrannical, unwholesome and unpleasant, Erich von Stroheim was very easy to fire, even if his films made money. *The Merry Widow* was his last film for MGM. He went to work for Zukor and had as little success with him as with Thalberg. After two projects in 1928, *The Wedding March* and *Queen Kelly*—the latter ending with the cataclysmic introduction of sound that shelved the film—Erich von Stroheim directed only one other film, *Walking Down Broadway* (1932). For over twenty years von Stroheim continued acting in films, most memorably as the German count in *Grand Illusion* and the chauffeur in *Sunset Boulevard*. The irony of this last film was that not only did von Stroheim play a character whose career in films echoed his own, but that he also played the devoted, adoring servant of Gloria Swanson, who was with him at the stormy end of his Hollywood road.

Another interesting and important descendant of Griffith's methods was Henry King's *Tol'able David*. The Soviet director, V. I. Pudovkin, found King's use of cutting to build a scene as instructive and effective as Griffith's. Although *Tol'able David* (1921) is often shrugged off as a piece of American regionalism or a retreat to a bygone era, it is a very powerful film in its own right. King, the student of Griffith and the employee of Ince, combines the very best of both Griffith and Ince in the film. King's world in *Tol'able David* is similar to the Griffith world of *Way Down East:* rural, homey, gently comic, touching, peaceful. Into the peaceful world come the violent figures from outside, three fugitives from justice, who are as vicious, as nasty, as psychotically mean as Battling Burrows. Like Griffith, King uses the characters' responses to animals to define them (Pudovkin called it the use of the "plastic material"): David lovingly plays with his dog Rocket; the invaders consider stoning a sleeping cat and eventually kill the playful Rocket out of pure meanness. Like Griffith, King uses cutting both to reveal the characters' feelings and to develop narrative suspense, especially in the climactic showdown between David and the crooks. But like Ince, King avoids the sentimentality of Griffith; the film is sentimental without sentimentality. King shuns Griffith's symbolism and overstated subtitles. And like Ince, King makes the film's narrative flow, never adding any detail of characterization that does not keep the story moving.

Tol'able David is a David and Goliath story. The three villainous Hatburns, who have cast their shadow (literally) on the sunny rural town, kill David's dog, cause his father's death from a heart attack, and cripple David's older brother, Alan. The villains have destroyed David's home (the source of his comfort and happiness), which the family must leave now that the breadwinners have either died or become disabled. David, who had happy dreams of an adult life in his town, is reduced to a poor clerk. He finally gets the chance to prove his mettle, however, by disposing of all three Goliath Hatburns in brutal and exciting combat; David shows he is a lot more than tol'able.

King shows how to bring a story alive with significant and memorable detail, by manipulating the visual, "plastic material." Richard Barthelmess, Griffith's own figure of gentleness and sincerity, plays David; his face and presence contribute greatly to the charm, warmth, and sympathy of the story. King's cutting consistently drives the emotions of the tale; the horror of Alan's injury, its impact on Rose, his wife, comes alive as King repeatedly cuts from the crippled, helpless Alan in bed to a shot of Rose, sitting in a rocking chair, holding their new infant, rocking relentlessly back and forth, back and forth. King's cutting transforms the emotionally neutral act of rocking into a moment of pain, of determination, of savagery, of misery, as the shots of the invalid in bed create the emotional climate for the wife's silent rocking. The rocking is far more successful than the cradle in *Intolerance* because the human focus and the specific causes and effects of the act of rocking are so much more concrete.

Also effective in the film are its details of brutality, which clash, intentionally, with the sweeter strains of the picture. Unlike Griffith and more like Ince, King actually depicted malicious violence on the screen: the death of David's dog, Hatburn's digging his finger into the gunshot wound in David's shoulder, the excruciating, exhausting pain of David's final fight with the last Hatburn. Even in Griffith's *Broken Blossoms,* the beatings of Lucy were more implied than graphically depicted. Also Ince-like is the irreparability of the disaster that has befallen the characters. Unlike the damage done in *Way Down East,* the pieces of David's life can never be patched together again. His dog and father are dead and his brother is an incurable invalid; there can be no miraculous resuscitations. His home is gone; his innocence will never return.

Several other directors made interesting films in the twenties. Some of those filmmakers would never make the transition to sound; some of them had only begun a career that would take a clearer shape in the era of sound. James Cruze, whose specialty was satire, made the most celebrated western epic of the decade—*The Covered Wagon* (1923). Rex Ingram, whose most famous film was *The Four Horsemen of the Apocalypse* (1921), was a pictorial master of composition and atmosphere. Josef von Sternberg began his control of physical detail and cinematic atmosphere in *Salvation Hunters, Underworld,* and *Docks of New York.* John Ford made his first important western film, *The Iron Horse,* in 1924. King Vidor effectively mixed wartime humor, antiwar propaganda, and a saccharine love story in *The Big Parade* (1925).

Most significant of all the newcomers was the German director, Ernst Lubitsch. Hollywood had begun importing many of the leading directors of Europe: Mauritz Stiller, Victor Sjøstrøm, Fritz Lang, F. W. Murnau, E. A. Dupont. But none found Hollywood so comfortable and so amicable a home as Lubitsch. Mary Pickford imported him specifically to direct a costume spectacle, *Rosita,* for her. Miss Pickford, like her husband, sought to change her adolescent image: to grow up, cut her curls, and show she was a woman. Lubitsch, who had directed a string of costume pageants in Germany (*Gypsy Blood, Passion, Deception*) which had become popular in America for their comic "humanizing" of history, was Miss Pickford's choice. *Rosita* proved the beginning of the end of Mary Pickford's career, the beginning of Lubitsch's. He immediately turned to polite, witty, understated drawing-room comedies: *The Marriage Circle* (1924), *Lady Windermere's Fan* (1925), *So This is Paris* (1926). His cleverness, his ability to imply so much with a trivial detail, his pictorial sense all would later help him make some of the best early American sound films.

A striking statistic of the American film in the twenties is that, despite the fact that thousands of films were made and hundreds of directors made them, very few individual men and works of the period are memorable (or even remembered). Very few films were asked to be memorable and very few directors were asked to use their own inventiveness and insight to make them so. The director was responsible for finishing the film that had already been designed; and the designers, not knowing what new ideas would work and what new ideas the public would accept, ultimately fell back on the old ideas which had the virtue of being tested. The formula picture, deadening to creativity and the imagination, was a means of making the studio product as standardized and, consequently, as stable as the product of any other factory. From the film's earliest days, competing directors copied each other's successes, but not until the 1920s had high finance made the necessity of copying so binding. If the film conformed to a familiar pattern—western, melodrama, spy story, war story, domestic comedy, spine-tingling serial, biblical epic, historical romance—it could be made. The most creative directors either invented new formulas or, much more likely, injected their own personal vision into old ones. The films of von Stroheim and Lubitsch were part formula (the general situation and plot outline) and part individual (development of the story, illumination of characters, implications of the action). DeMille's great gift was to whip up any formula so furiously that the audience could not tell that the immense edifice was built of whipped cream.

There were a few directors of the 1920s who worked outside the fences of the Hollywood formulas. One of them was Robert Flaherty, the father of the documentary film, who had been taking his camera and film to Hudson Bay since 1913; the eventual result was *Nanook of the North* (1922). Flaherty discovered that only the documentary filmmaker enjoyed the freedom of the solitary, individual artist, shaping his material with his own methods according to his own perceptions. He enjoyed the freedom of a Griffith or Sennett in the early years when man, camera, and idea were still one, without studio middlemen.

Flaherty's *Nanook* is significant for the beauty of its photography of the white, frozen plains of ice and for its care in revealing the life and life-style of the man who lived there. Flaherty's greatest asset was Nanook's total lack of inhibition about the filming process. Although he was clearly conscious of being filmed, he did not quite know what a film and camera were (just as he tried to eat a phonograph record in an early sequence of the film). He did not pose for the machine; he did not act. He merely lived his life while Flaherty's camera recorded and, inevitably, commented. The comment was not only that Nanook's life was hard, a perpetual battle to survive, a continual struggle for two absolute necessities, food and shelter; Flaherty also found a virtue in the hardness, in the struggle itself, for Nanook had no consciousness that a life could be lived in any other way. So for Nanook life was not hard, it merely was. In Nanook's simplicity, in his strength, his competence, his ability to survive, in his inability to formulate existential questions, Flaherty depicted a life of fulfillment. Nanook's life was ultimately full and filled. Life, in fact, could be no fuller.

Flaherty's later sound film, *Man of Aran* (1934), also develops the fulfillment of the hard, vital life that leaves no space for self-conscious questioning. But by then Flaherty had fled to England. Hollywood, rewarding the dollar success of *Nanook* with more dollars, asked Flaherty to make pictures for commercial release. For Paramount he made *Moana* (1926)—an idyllic study of the life on a South Seas island, a life whose warmth and total easiness were as fulfilling for the natives as Nanook's coldness and hardness were for him. Hollywood, which expected native dancing girls dancing the hula, was disappointed and teamed Flaherty with other directors, W. S. Van Dyke and F. W. Murnau, for his later films. The fiction directors were expected to add formulaic stories to snatches of Flaherty's documentary photography. The idea was contrary to Flaherty's intentions and inimical to all three directors. Flaherty left for England to preserve his independence; a whole group of filmmakers applying his principles had begun to produce films there.

The Comics

One other group of 1920s films maintained an inventiveness and individuality that remain as fresh today as they were fifty years ago. The silent film, which had already proved itself the ideal medium for physical comedy, continued to nurture its most legitimate children. Several new comic imaginations joined the established Sennett, who still supervised films, and Chaplin, who had begun to make feature films: most significantly, Harold Lloyd, Buster Keaton, Harry Langdon, and Laurel and Hardy. Laurel and Hardy were minor figures in the silents, just beginning their teamwork at the same time that sound began seeping into Hollywood. They became popular comics of the sound era, and although sound did nothing to detract from the comic principle they had discovered in the silents, it did little to add to it either. The Laurel and Hardy team had been patched together by Hal Roach, a major producer of comedies, who reasoned that one of his fat players and one of his thin ones might go well together. The premise was an entirely Sennett-like one, and indeed Laurel and Hardy's method was a return to the completely comic, externalized, surface world of Sennett gags.

But Laurel and Hardy films were far more controlled and far more tightly structured than the loose Sennett romps. Their films inevitably demonstrate the "snowball" principle that Bergson had developed in *Le Rire*. Like the snowball rolling down the mountain, the Laurel and Hardy film gathers greater and greater momentum, greater and greater bulk, as it hurtles toward the valley. Their films demonstrate the classic structure of farce—of Plautus and Feydeau: to begin with a single problem and then multiply that problem to infinity. Compared with the random movement in Sennett or the leisurely tangents of Chaplin, the Laurel and Hardy films are very tightly structured indeed. If an auto gets dented in a traffic jam at the start of the film, every car on the highway gets stripped by the end of it; if a Christmas tree branch gets caught in a door at the start of the film, the tree, the house, the salesmen's car must be totally annihilated by the end of it; if the two partners have trouble with a few nails and tacks when starting to build a house, the film must inevitably end with the house collapsing into a pile of rubble. There is an insane yet perfect logic about the whole process.

As in every great silent-film comedy, the Laurel and Hardy films depend on physical objects; the purely visual, physical medium demands the use of concrete, visible things. But for Laurel and Hardy an object is merely something to be destroyed; their films are built around breaking things. The childishness of this willful destruction demands that the primary emotion of the films be a childish one—spite. They are all children squashing each other's mud pies. Both Stan Laurel and Oliver Hardy themselves play men who are merely overgrown kiddies. Stan is the weepy, puling, sneaky, and covertly nasty kid, while Oliver is the pompous, bullying, show-off, know-it-all, and inherently incompetent kid. His dignity is as false as Stan's tearfulness; they are both ploys to cover their spiteful pettiness. If the premise of the films is much thinner than Chaplin's, or even Sennett's, it is also true that the spiteful emotion they capture is a genuine one. They mirror our feelings when another car zips in to steal the parking place that we have patiently waited for. Their single-keyed emotion and their taut, unidirectional structure did limit their success, however, to the short film. Though they made many features in the sound era, the longer films are more interesting in their parts rather than their wholes.

Harold Lloyd, another Hal Roach product, was almost a combination of Chaplin and Fairbanks. Like Charlie, he was a little guy, slightly inept, trying to succeed. Like Fairbanks, he was energetic, athletic, and engagingly charming. Like Doug, his smiles were calculated to snare us as well as the girl. Like Charlie, he had trouble both with objects and the world while trying to achieve his desires; but unlike Charlie—and like Doug—he invariably does achieve those desires, and they are the same material and romantic treasures that Doug always wins. Also like Doug—and unlike Charlie—Lloyd films never imply that the prize he has won was not worth the winning.

Rather than developing character or social commentary, Lloyd generates pure comedy from the situation, from topical satire, from his own limber body, and from the daring stunts he would dream up for it. In *High and Dizzy* (1921), one of the few Lloyd films that is still in circulation, he demonstrates the variety of his comedy. The film is constructed like the Chaplin shorts, with three rather isolated episodes loosely tied together by the thinnest of narrative threads (but without Chaplin's thematic unity). In the opening sequence, Lloyd plays a young doctor, recently out of medical school, whose practice is so dismal that his phone is gathering cobwebs. When a potential patient appears in his office, the young doctor goes through a series of clever improvisations and disguises to make the patient think the doctor is very busy. In the midst of these frenzied activities, he falls madly in love with the lady patient who, it turns out, walks in her sleep.

In the film's second section, he strolls down the hall and gets stinking drunk with another young doctor who has distilled some hooch in his medicinal laboratory. Lloyd's topical satire of doctors, admittedly rather gentle, is the same kind that he would use to sketch his comic portrait of the twenties' college generation in *The Freshman* (1924). The two drunken doctors also allow Lloyd to demonstrate his ability and agility as pure physical comic, as the two friends, one fat, one thin, dizzily weave down the street and into their hotel. The purely surface, physical comedy instantly suggests Chaplin and Fatty in *The Rounders*. But Lloyd's drunken business is more choreographed, more precisely timed. He and his friend get their feet interlocked; they try to put on the same overcoat; they get hung up (literally) on a lamp post. In the hotel, Lloyd's virtuoso gymnastics (tumbling over the bell desk to get his key; trying to stagger into the elevator) show the kind of physical control and clever responses to a situation that make the clothes-ripping sequence of *The Freshman* so funny.

Lloyd introduces his "comedy of thrills" in the film's third section. It just happens that the lady sleepwalking patient, with whom he is in love, lives in the same hotel. She starts sleepwalking out on the hotel ledge, many frightening stories above the hard pavement below. Harold goes out on the ledge to save her and, predictably, gets locked out there when she decides to stroll inside. Lloyd tightropes, trips, stumbles out on the ledge, playing on many different emotions in us at the same time. We feel suspense because he might fall; yet we laugh because we know he won't. We wonder if he was really on the ledge when he shot the sequence (the camera angle and lack of editing trickiness make us suspect he really performed the stunt). We laugh at the man's fright and perplexity; we admire his underlying competence and control. It was this same synthesis of cliff-hanging serial and burlesque comedy that created the excitement and success of his feature, *Safety Last* (1923). Ultimately, Lloyd's comedy is one of sensations alone and not of thought. He merely asks us to like the earnest, affable, bespectacled guy he plays, to enjoy his ticklish and dangerous scrapes, and to feel both comfort and delight when he pulls himself out of them successfully.

Harry Langdon was Lloyd's opposite: a comic style constructed almost exclusively of internal sensations and emotional reactions with almost no dependence on external business and physical gags. His career was also the shortest of any of the comic stars of the silents. He broke into films at Mack Sennett's studio in 1924, reached stardom with a series of features directed by Frank Capra in 1926 and 1927, and fell from popularity just as suddenly in 1928 when Langdon went off to direct his own films and when sound invaded Hollywood.

The union of Capra and Langdon was significant for both men, for like Capra's later heroes, Langdon was a figure of innocence trapped in a mean, brutal world where foolish angels should indeed fear to tread. Langdon was a Mr. Deeds or Mr. Smith distilled into their essential and purest naïveté, innocence, and childishness. He was an overgrown baby with a puffy baby body, pudgy baby face, and tiny, slow baby brain. The Langdon-Capra films put this overgrown infant into difficult and dangerous situations from which the child-man could only escape by means of a miracle (for only a miracle could save an infant in a lion's den).

In *Tramp, Tramp, Tramp* (1926) Harry enters a cross-country walking race to try to win enough money to save his father's business from ruin (a clear Capra motif). Harry's opponents in this athletic contest of strength eventually include not only men who are bigger, tougher, and stronger, but even the natural universe itself. Harry miraculously triumphs over an awesome cyclone that levels an entire town but that turns around and goes away after Baby Harry hurls a few pebbles at it. In *The Strong Man* (1926) Harry is a weight lifter's assistant who is unexpectedly forced to substitute for his boss. He miraculously manages to subdue a whole gang of bootleggers in the course of his act, ridding a small town of the nasty mobsters who have usurped it (more Capra). Harry's small-town girlfriend in this film, Mary Brown, is blind, a figure as physically helpless and spiritually pure as little Harry himself (and a possible influence on Chaplin's use of a blind girl in *City Lights*). At the end of *The Strong Man* the couple of meeklings inherit the earth. But in *Long Pants* (1927) Harry is unhappy with the purity and innocence of small-town life. He deserts the small-town gal and runs off to the "Big City," in pursuit of an exotic "Bad Woman" who drove through his small town and fueled his romantic dreams. After a series of scrapes with criminals, thieves, and the police, Harry discovers that the apparent Lady of his Dreams is no lady, and he hurries back to his small-town family and sweetheart, a sadder and wiser child.

Although Harry Langdon lacked the comic range and physical gifts of the other silent clowns, his comic style revealed how restrained, how subtle, how slow, how non-physical a silent, physical comedian could be. His films were constructed so that a tiny smile, a blink of the eyes, the wave of a hand, or even, as James Agee observed, a twitch of the muscles at the back of the neck were as significant as a whole sequence of Lloyd's spectacular slips and falls on top of a skyscraper.

Of the new comics, only Buster Keaton could rival Chaplin in his insight into human relationships, into the conflict between the individual man and the immense social machinery that surrounds him; only Keaton could rival Chaplin in making his insight both funny and serious at the same time. On the one hand, the Keaton canon as a whole is thinner, less consistent than the Chaplin canon. The character Keaton fashioned—with his deadpan, blank reaction to the chaos that inevitably and inadvertently blooms around him—lacks the range, the compassionate yearnings, the pitiable disappointments of Chaplin's tramp. On the other hand, Keaton made a single film, *The General* (1926), that is possibly more even, more unified, and more complex in both conception and execution than any individual Chaplin film.

The key difference between Keaton and Chaplin is that Charlie longs to better himself, to accomplish grand things, whereas Keaton merely desires to go about his business. If he fails to reach his modest goal it is not because of his own incompetence or ineptitude but because of the staggeringly huge obstacles the environment throws in his path to keep him from getting there. Objects inevitably play a role in Keaton films, but unlike the objects in a Chaplin film—which are small and manageable and which Charlie can hold in his hand, or lie in, or sit on—the objects in a Keaton film are immense machines that dwarf the little man. Keaton plays against huge things: an ocean liner he must navigate by himself, a locomotive, a steamboat, a hurricane, a herd of cattle. When he runs into trouble with men, it is never with a single figure (an Eric Campbell); he runs into rivers of antagonists, into armies of opponents: a whole tribe of jungle savages, the entire Union and Confederate armies. Like Charlie, Buster

THE CABINET OF DOCTOR CALIGARI

Faces of paint:
Caligari (Werner Krauss) . . .
and Cesare (Conrad Veidt).

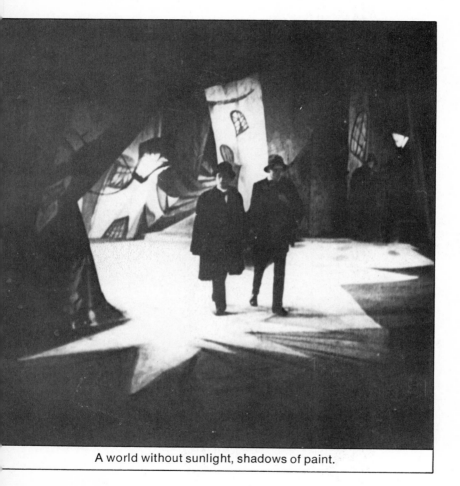

A world without sunlight, shadows of paint.

DESTINY

Lang's geometry: revelers in Venice.

The Cave of the Candles: thin, fragile white shafts as metaphors for human life (Lil Dagover and Bernhard Götzke).

METROPOLIS

Human beings reduced to a disspirited
mass of geometrical architecture.

The vampire (Max Schreck) brings the demons of Hell into the regions of nature.

NOSFERATU

THE LAST
LAUGH

The subjective camera in **The Last Laugh.**
The hungover porter sees his neighbor
(Emilie Kurz) bring him the morning coffee.

The Porter (Emil Jannings) with his uniform and without it.

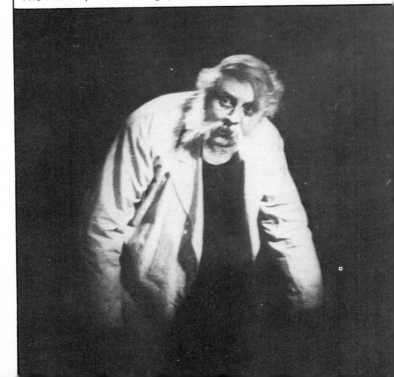

has his troubles with cops, but never with one or just a few cops; in *Cops* (1922), in *Daydreams* (1922), Buster runs into the entire police force. Given the size and complexity of his problems, Buster can take no sensible or meaningful action, despite his most sensible efforts. The perfect metaphor for the Keaton man is in the short film, *Daydreams,* in which Buster, to avoid the police force, takes refuge in the paddle wheel of a ferryboat. The wheel begins turning; Buster begins walking. And walking. And walking. He behaves as sensibly as a man can on a treadmill that he cannot control, but how sensible can life on a treadmill ever be?

Chaplin and Keaton are the two poles of silent comics. Chaplin's great strength is his development of character and the exhausting of a particular comic and social situation; Keaton's strength is the tightness of his narrative structures and his contrast between the numbers one and infinity. Chaplin is sentimental; his gentle, smiling women become idols to be revered. Keaton is not sentimental; he stuffs his females into bags and hauls them around like sacks of potatoes; he satirizes their finicky incompetence and even raises his fist to the silly lady in *The General* who feeds their racing locomotive only the teensiest shavings of wood. It was especially appropriate and touching to see the two opposites, Chaplin and Keaton, united in *Limelight* (1952), both playing great clowns who were losing their audiences and their touch. It may be no accident that one of the most significant literary works of our era, *Waiting for Godot,* was produced in the same year as *Limelight* and used the same metaphor of two old vaudeville tramps whose act (in *Godot* their act is their life) had become a bomb. If the Godot of Beckett's title suggests Charlot, it should also be remembered that Beckett wrote a film script especially for Buster Keaton, *Film.* The influence of the pair of comics continues to be felt.

No two films more clearly reveal the contrasting strengths and interests of the two clowns than *The Gold Rush* and *The General,* both of which were made at about the same time (1925–26). Like the short comedies, *The Gold Rush* is an episodic series of highly developed, individual situations. The mortar that keeps these bricks together is a mixture of the film's locale (the white, frozen wastes), the strivings and disappointments of Charlie, and the particular thematic view the film takes of those strivings (the quest for gold and for love, those two familiar goals, in an icy, cannibalistic jungle). All the Chaplin features, including those he made with synchronized sound, would share this common episodic structure. *The Gold Rush* also benefits from the circular pattern of the sequence of episodes: Prologue (the journey to Alaska), the Cabin, the Dance Hall, New Year's Eve, the Dance Hall, the Cabin, Epilogue (the journey home).

The individual sequences of *The Gold Rush* are rich both in Chaplin's comic ingenuity and his ability to render the pathos of the tramp's disappointment, his cruel rejection by the woman he loves. Several of the comic sequences have become justifiably famous. In the first cabin scene, a hungry Charlie cooks his shoe, carves it like a prime rib of beef, salts it to taste, and then eats it like a gourmet, twirling the shoelaces around his fork like spaghetti, sucking the nails in the soles like chicken bones, offering his friend one of the nails as a wishbone. This is the Chaplin who treats one kind of object (a shoe) as if it were another kind of object (a feast), the same minute observation he used in dissecting the clock in *The Pawnshop*. In the dance hall, Charlie hastily ties a rope around his middle to keep his sagging trousers up. He does not know that the other end of the rope is attached to a dog, who then trots around the dance floor following his dancing master. Charlie, however, must follow the leader when the dog takes off after a cat.

But the comic business is matched by the pathos that Charlie can generate, often itself growing out of the comic business. Charlie's saddest moment is when Georgia, the woman he loves, whose picture and flower he preserves beneath his pillow, callously stands him up on New Year's Eve. When Charlie realizes that it is midnight and that she is not coming, he opens his door and listens to the happy townspeople singing "Auld Lang Syne." The film cuts back and forth between Charlie, the outsider, standing silently and alone in a doorway, and the throng of revelers in the dance hall, clasping hands in a large circle and singing exuberantly together (excellent use of Griffith cross-cutting here). But this pathetic moment would have been impossible without the previous comic one in which Charlie falls asleep and dreams he is entertaining Georgia with his "Oceana Roll." Charlie's joy, his naive sincerity, his charm, his gentleness, all show on his face as he coyly makes the two rolls kick, step, and twirl over the table on the ends of two forks. The happiness of the comic dream sequence creates the pathos of the subsequently painful reality.

If the reality proves painful for Charlie, it is because the lust for gold makes it so. The film's theme is its consistent indictment of what the pursuit of the material does to the human animal; as in *Greed*, it makes him an inhuman animal. Charlie, the least materialistic of men, has come to the most materialistic of places—a place where life is hard, dangerous, brutal, uncomfortable and unkind. Unlike the life of Nanook (might Chaplin have been influenced by Flaherty?), in which hardness becomes a virtue in itself, the men who have rushed for gold want to endure hardship only temporarily, just long enough to snatch up enough nuggets to go home and live easy. The quest for gold perverts all human relationships in the film. It creates a Black Larsen who casually murders and purposely fails to help his starving fellows. It creates a Jack, Georgia's handsome boyfriend, who treats his fellow men and women like furniture. Just as Charlie's genuine compassion reveals the emptiness of Jack's protestations of love, Chaplin's film technique makes an unsympathetic villain out of the conventional Hollywood leading man.

The rush toward gold perverts both love and friendship. Georgia herself, though Charlie perceives her inner beauty, has become hardened and callous from her strictly cash relationships with people in the isolated dance hall. And Charlie's friend, Big Jim McKay, is one of those fair-weather friends whose feelings are the functions of expediency. When Big Jim gets hungry, he literally tries to eat Charlie; although Jim's seeing his buddy as a big chicken is comic, the implied cannibalism of the sequence is not. Later, Big Jim needs Charlie to direct him to his claim; once again Charlie becomes a friend because he is needed. But when Jim and Charlie get stuck in the cabin that teeters precariously on the edge of a cliff, the two men turn into dogs again, each trying to scramble out of the cabin by himself, stepping on each other to do so.

Whereas *The Gold Rush* combines a thematic unity with the episodic structure of exhausting the individual situations, the thematic coherency of *The General* is itself the product of the film's tight narrative unity. *The General* is the first, probably the greatest comic epic in film form. Like every comic epic, *The General* is the story of a journey, of the road (albeit a railroad). As in every comic epic, the protagonist suffers a series of hardships and dangerous adventures before achieving the rewards and comforts of returning home. As in every comic epic, the protagonist's opponents are both men and nature (particularly those two natural enemies, fire and water). As in every comic epic, there is a comic insufficiency in the protagonist and a disparity between his powers and the task he is asked to accomplish; but like every protagonist in the comic epic, Buster triumphs despite his insufficiencies. Everything in the Chaplin film, every gag, every piece of business, every thematic contrast, is subordinate to the delineation of the lonely tramp's character and the qualities that make him both lonely and superior to the men who have betrayed their humanity to keep from being lonely. Everything in *The General*—every gag, every piece of business—is subordinate to the film's driving narrative, its story of Johnny Gray trying to save his three loves: his girl, his country, and, most important of all, his locomotive. *The Gold Rush* is a comedy of character, *The General* a comedy of narrative.

The great question *The General* poses in the course of its narrative is how to perform heroic action in a universe that is not heroic. Buster, with his typical dead-pan expression, merely tries to go about his business while the world around him goes mad. A metaphor for the feeling of the whole film is the shot in which Buster is so busy chopping wood to feed his engine that he fails to notice that the train is racing past row after row of blue uniforms marching in the opposite direction. Johnny Gray has inadvertently propelled himself behind the enemy's lines. Johnny Gray simply wants to run his train; unfortunately, the Union Army wants to steal the train and use it to destroy his fellow Confederates. In the course of merely trying to save the train, Johnny rescues his lady love and accidentally wins a terrific victory for the South.

That heroism occurs as an accident in *The General* is at the center of its moral thrust. It is an accident that the cannon, aimed squarely at Johnny, does not go off until the train rounds a curve, discharging its huge ball at the enemy instead of at the protagonist. It is an accident that Buster's train comes to a rail switch just in time to detour the pursuing Union train. Whereas wealth, material success, is accidental in *The Gold Rush* (and an accident not worth waiting for), heroism and successful military strategy are accidental in *The General*. And just as Charlie's character exposes the folly of the accidents of wealth, Buster's character exposes the folly of the accidents of heroism. For how less heroic, how less aspiring, less grand can a man be than little Buster? Buster merely uses his shrewd common sense against impossible odds, and he is lucky to get away with it.

The denigration of the heroic is as constant an element of *The General*'s narrative as the denigration of gold is in the sequences of *The Gold Rush*. The plot is triggered by Johnny Gray's rejection by the Confederate Army. He fears he has been found wanting, but the Confederacy needs him vitally at home, running his locomotive. Nevertheless, his girl and her family ostracize Johnny as an unheroic coward, a shirker, and the rest of the film demonstrates what heroism really is and what it is really worth. Johnny uses the most pragmatic, least heroic of tools for defeating the northern army: boxes of freight, pieces of wood from a fence, the locomotive's kerosene lantern. Hard-headedness, not gallantry, wins the day.

The gallant and romantic are explicitly burlesqued in the film's final sequence, the battle in which victory comes as a combination of stupidity and chance. The northern general, certain that the bridge Johnny earlier set afire is still strong enough to support his supply train, orders it across. The general is wrong; the train and bridge topple magnificently into the river below. In the pitch of battle, Johnny sees the Confederate standard about to fall to the ground. He hastily climbs to what he thinks is a hilltop in a gallant gesture to support the falling flag (a parody of Griffith?), only to discover the embarrassment of feeling the hilltop move. The hilltop is really a disgruntled soldier's back. When the northern officer surrenders to the South according to all the articles and procedures of war— the sequence uses all the formal rigamarole of military honor—Johnny Gray accidentally fires his pistol, disrupting the dignified formality of the ceremony.

Even the film's ending burlesques the conventions of heroism, war, and romance: Johnny wraps his arms around his girl for the final clinch;

since he is now an officer, all soldiers must salute him and he must salute in return. In the midst of his embrace, the entire battalion troops past him. After interrupting his embrace for a while, he, in his pragmatic manner, devises a better method. He continues saluting perfunctorily and mechanically, never taking his lips or his eyes away from hers.

Such antiheroism is common to all the Keaton films; he is always the sensible little guy who inadvertently runs up against senseless objects that dwarf him. The thing that distinguishes *The General* is that the senseless object, the huge infernal machine of this film, is war. Men themselves have been transformed into a machine (an army), and the business of this machine is murder and destruction. This antiheroic comic epic must necessarily become an antiwar story, too, for the military heroism *The General* consistently debunks is the Circe that turns men into murdering and destructive swine. Buster is never hypnotized, and his film makes sure we keep our eyes open, too. There is absolutely nothing sentimental in the world of *The General*. As soon as Johnny Gray gets a bit sad, Keaton immediately slams him with a joke to rip the pathos off him.

The film is as shrewd, as caustic, as hard-edged as Johnny Gray himself. His girl, a typical figure of sentiment and romance (her name is Annabelle Lee!), is degraded into an incompetent and feeble representative of romantic notions; Johnny Gray ultimately must fight her as well as the pursuing army. There is no place in the world of *The General* for sentiment, for the same reason that there is no place for heroism. Romance and heroism are twins, and *The General* wages war on both. Unlike the Chaplin films, there are no flowers, no roses, in *The General*. As soon as you admit a rose, you must also admit a gun to fight for it.

True, the character Buster plays, Johnny Gray, is a southerner, a seemingly romantic choice. But Buster chose to play a rebel because the South lost the war, because the South was romantically blind about fighting the war, and because the South—like Buster—was the little-guy underdog. Though Johnny plays a southerner, the film is impartial; ultimately Johnny must sneak his train (even its name is a military one) past both the Union and the Confederate lines. Despite the film's comic conclusion and inventive gags, *The General*, with its mixture of burlesque and grimness (many men die in this film), is the spiritual ancestor of that more recent mixture of laughs and war horrors, *Doctor Strangelove*.

The ultimate proof of the power of *The Gold Rush* and *The General* is that they need not be referred to as great silent films; they are merely great films. They require no qualification of any kind, unlike even Griffith's greatest work. For both of them, silence was not a limitation but a virtue. It is inconceivable that the two films could have been any better with sound; in fact, by removing our complete concentration on the visual they could only have been worse.

The power of the Chaplin film comes from the expressiveness of his pantomime. Mime is mute. To reveal the significant gestures and facial flickers, Chaplin, as is his wont, uses the range of shots from full to close. Only expository shots—the opening shots of the men treking north, the establishing shots of the dance hall, et cetera—pull away from the characters. Chaplin's unobtrusive editing consistently allows the pantomime to play itself out without a cut—for example, the roll dance.

The power of the Keaton film comes from the contrast between his simple efforts and the immense problems surrounding him. Keaton, the character, is as tight-lipped as he is expressionless. His character is essentially mute. His blank stare says everything that can be said about the chaos he sees. To reveal the contrast of man and chaos, Keaton, as is his wont, uses the range of shots between full and extreme long. His camera works further away from the characters than Chaplin's, consistently comparing them with their surroundings. His cutting is slightly quicker than Chaplin's—to increase the pace and to reveal the different perspectives of man and environment—but never so quick or obtrusive as to make the stunts seem faked.

With such control of physical business, of thematic consistency, of appropriate structure, of placement of the camera, and of functional editing, neither *The Gold Rush* nor *The General* requires speech to speak.

Chapter

7

THE GERMAN GOLDEN AGE

In the final year of World War I, the German government wondered if its preference for bullets to pictures had not been a tactical error. Whatever the results of the battles at the front, the German nation and German character were losing terribly on the screens of the world. In the early years of the war, the American film, mirroring the nation's neutrality, did not take a consistent side in its view of the conflict in Europe. Some American films expressly advocated neutrality; others, like *Civilization* and *Intolerance*, preached pacifism. But as America herself prepared to enter the war, her films began to prepare her to prepare. In 1916, Vitagraph's J. Stuart Blackton made *The Battle Cry of Peace*, the first of a series of films urging "defenseless America" to defend herself. Blackton was continuing his tradition of making patriotic war films some twenty years after *Tearing Down the Spanish Flag*. The American war films predictably painted the enemy as a villainous, vicious Hun; the evil, sinister, outwardly polished and inwardly corrupt Erich von Stroheim was the perfect stereotype of this newest movie bad guy.

There was no screen antidote for this single stereotypic portrait. The German government decided to produce one. In November of 1917, the government collected the tiny, chaotic fragments of the German film industry together into a single, large filmmaking unit, Universum Film A.G., known subsequently to the world as U.F.A. Ufa's job was to make movies that would boost the German spirit at home and sell the German character and position abroad; the war ended before Ufa could accomplish either goal. But the huge movie company, with its studios at Neubabelsberg near Berlin, was still standing after the armistice had been signed. The great era of German films was born in those studios.

The German Golden Age of film was a very short one, from the making of *The Cabinet of Doctor Caligari* (1919) to Hitler's absorption of the German film industry in 1933. The great burst of artistic activity that followed the fall of the Kaiser and the founding of the Weimar Republic, the new spirit of intellectual and creative freedom in Germany, made itself felt in all the arts (in the pictorial and plastic arts, the founding of the Bauhaus group by Kandinsky and Klee; in the theatre, the plays of Brecht and the staging of Erwin Piscator), but especially in the cinema. The great German contribution in these years of intellectual freedom and artistic innovation was, as almost all post-Griffith cinematic innovations have been, merely a refinement of one of the potentialities of the medium that Griffith had himself discovered. If Griffith's two great accomplishments were his realization of the power of atmosphere and texture within a shot and the power of editing to join shots, it was the genius of the German film to refine and develop the former (the Soviet film developed the latter). The German film, in an era of silence, made the aura, the mood, the tone of the shot's visual qualities speak. It made them speak so well that the best German films of the era contain the barest minimum of subtitles, or none at all.

Further, the German filmmakers realized that the emotional tensions and sensations in a film need not be performed solely for a passive, objective camera. The camera—rather than taking the stance of a distant, impartial observer—could itself mirror the subjective feelings of a single character experiencing an event. To use an analogy with the novel, the German filmmaker realized that the camera, like the pen, could narrate a story in the first person as well as the third. Griffith used an occasional flight into subjectivity—his flashbacks to reveal a character's thoughts, the tracking camera galloping with the horses to the rescue—but Griffith's subjective moments were always in brackets. He used specific conventions to inform the audience that it was entering the personal experience of a single character. The subjectivity in the German film is never set off in brackets; the boundary between subjective and objective perceptions becomes as blurry in the films as it is in our own post-Pirandellian lives.

The dependence of the German film on the evocations of its visual elements led to its becoming completely a studio product. The only way to make sure that the lighting, the decor, the architectural shapes, the relationships of blacks, whites, and grays were perfect was to film in a completely controlled environment. Even outdoor scenes were shot inside the four walls and ceiling of a studio. The vastness, the freedom of the outdoors that had become one of the sources of power of both the American and Swedish film was rejected by the Germans. The result was not only a perfect control of style and decor but also a feeling of claustrophobia that enhanced the mood of many of the best films, which were also claustrophobic in their content. The totally studio-produced films emphasized the importance of the designer, whose job was to conceive and decorate enormous indoor cities. These designers came to films from painting and, especially, from architecture, having absorbed the styles of many of the new artistic movements of postwar Europe: expressionism, cubism, constructivism, other forms of abstraction. The German film could never have exerted its influence without its talented painter-architect designers, the most notable of whom were Hermann Warm, Walther Röhrig, Walther Reimann, Robert Herlth, Albin Grau, and Ërno Metzner.

The emphasis on the studio production and the consolidation of talent in a single studio produced a very different kind of studio system from Hollywood's. Unlike the competing factories of Hollywood, the German studio was far more a combination of artists working with each other because they were devoted to their product rather than to receipts. Although there were competitors with Ufa in the twenties, many of them worked so closely with the major producer that merger was inevitable (Decla-Bioscop, for example). Ufa's great producer, Erich Pommer, was a man of artistic judgment and taste who stimulated mediocre directors to do their very best work (E. A. Dupont's *Variety,* for example) rather than the reverse. Rather than building a star system, the German studio developed a repertory company, emphasizing the play and not the player, the character and not the personality. The German film actor needed variety and range, not a single trait that he milked over and over again. The greatest of the German repertory actors were Emil Jannings, Werner Krauss, Conrad Veidt, Fritz Körtner, Lil Dagover, Asta Nielsen, Lya de Putti, Pola Negri, and Greta Garbo. Hollywood imported most of them and tried to turn them into stars; the attempt was inconsistently successful.

The German studio also gave a great deal of freedom to its cameramen; they were encouraged to develop new and revealing ways of looking at things. The Hollywood cameraman had become more and more tied to the most functional, most familiar way of recording a scene. Two German cameramen in particular, Fritz Arno Wagner and Karl Freund, used their freedom to show how much a camera could really do.

The German films of this great era were of two types: either fantastic and mystical or realistic and psychological. One was steeped in the traditional German romanticism of love and death, the other revealed the new German intellectual currents of Freud and Weber. In the film of fantasy, the action revolves around the occult, the mysterious, the metaphysical. These are films of fantastic monsters in human dress, of the kingdom beyond the grave, of dream kingdoms of the past and of the future. The German architect-painters could use their imaginations to turn these eerie, abstract, intangible regions into concrete, visual domains. In the realistic film, the action revolves around the inner thoughts and feelings of the characters, their needs, their lusts, their frustrations. Of the Americans, only von Stroheim, perhaps showing his Teutonic origins, made such internalized, sensation-centered films. Unlike the fantasy films, which are inevitably set in some romantic time and place, the psychological films are set in a squalid and seamy middle-class present. The architect-painters could use their imaginations to turn the tawdry, dirty, depressing rooms, streets, and suburbs into complex and detailed studio slums.

Fantasy

The film that signaled the start of the new German era, *The Cabinet of Doctor Caligari,* appropriately combined both the mystical and the psychological. Although Ernst Lubitsch had been making his historical costume films since 1918, those witty, lavish entertainments were more relevant to his own personal career than to the eventual development of the great German films. Perhaps the one significant influence of the Lubitsch films was the respect and attention they commanded for the art of the designer. It was *Caligari* that set the German film mind in motion for the next decade.

Its central plot was a story of horror, of murder, of superhuman powers. An enigmatic and menacing hypnotist (Werner Krauss) opens a stall at a fair in the town of Holstenwall; his act demonstrates his mastery over another human being whom he has hypnotized, Cesare (Conrad Veidt). Mysteriously a rash of murders breaks out in the town. The police have no clues. The film's protagonist, Francis, suspects the hypnotist, shadows him, and eventually discovers that he forces his slave, Cesare, to murder the innocent victims while the hypnotist substitutes a wax image of Cesare in the coffin-like box to fool the police. Francis continues to follow the murderous master who, it turns out, is also the director of the state insane asylum. The keeper of the insane is himself an insane murderer, a monster who has discovered the medieval formula of Caligari for subduing men's minds. Francis exposes the monster; the monster goes mad. The orderlies stuff Caligari into a strait jacket and lock the door of his cell. This is as far as the central plot of *Caligari* goes. It is also as far as its writers, Carl Mayer (who would become the most influential of the German scenarists) and Hans Janowitz, wanted it to go.

But *Caligari* goes further. The entire central plot has a frame. The film begins with Francis informing a listener (and us) that he has a most horrifying tale to tell. To set a horrific, supernatural tale within a frame is, of course, a traditional literary device (for example, Henry James's *The Turn of the Screw*), the means to anchor a fantastic story in reality and thereby increase our credulity. The setting of this opening, framing sequence seems like a park—there are trees, vines, a wall, benches. But there is something vaguely disturbing about it: it is too bare, too cold; the girl who walks past seems somnambulistic, ethereal. Only at the end of the film do we discover that the setting for the entire tale is not a park but an insane asylum, that Francis himself is a patient, that many of the characters in his tale are also patients, and that the so-called Caligari is the director of the asylum. And it is not Caligari who winds up in a cell with a strait jacket but Francis, whose feverish accusations of the director have necessitated his confinement. The surprise at the end of the film is our discovery that the tale we assumed to be one of horror and of superhuman powers is really the product of the imagination of a subhuman brain, a paranoid's fantasy, a madman's hatred of his doctor.

Our discovery of the disease in the narrator's brain suddenly illuminates the principle of the film's decor. Throughout the film the expressionist-cubist world of the horror tale has been striking: the grotesque painted shadows on streets and stairs; the irregular, nonperpendicular chimneys, doors, and windows; the exaggerated heights of the furniture; the two-dimensional, painted rooms; the painted skin and wrinkles of the characters' faces. The grotesque world is not simply a decorative stunt; it is a precise translation of the way Francis, the madman, sees the world. The world of the film is the product of Francis's subjective vision, not of the director's objective one. Robert Wiene, *Caligari*'s director, has intentionally used the decor of the film in a perpetual war against nature.

The striking effect of the film's design (by Warm, Röhrig, and Reimann) is not just the look but the unnatural feel of it. Walls, floors, and ceilings bear a structurally impossible relationship to one another; buildings so constructed could never stand. Skin, that soft and most malleable material of nature, becomes caked and frozen with paint. Windows are painted in gnarled and impossible shapes. And most unnatural of all, the world of *Caligari* is a world without sunlight. Shadows of light and dark, shafts where the sun would normally cast its shadow, have been painted on the sets. To use paint to make a shadow where the sun would normally make one, emphasizes the fact that no sun exists. The outdoor scenes feel as if they were shot indoors. And they were. Here was the perfect use of the total studio film. The deliberate unnaturalness of the film is so striking that it is difficult to tell if the acting is intentionally or unintentionally stilted. In any case, it is appropriate.

The interest in *The Cabinet of Doctor Caligari* is not only in the way the film looks but in the ambiguities that the film-within-a-film generates. Wiene's structure clearly reveals that *Caligari* is no simple horror story. The film is no simple tale told by an idiot either. True, Francis is mad; he has clearly leaped the gulf between control and lack of it. But what pushed him over it? How did he manufacture this particular story and in such detail? Is there no truth at all in his story of the Holstenwall murders? And if the kindly doctor is really not the demented Caligari, why does he look like Caligari when he puts on his glasses? And why does the asylum look no more natural in the frame of the film (supposedly an objective point of view) than it did in Francis's narration? And what is the relevance of the film's clear antagonism to bureaucracy? Wiene ridicules the police and the authorities with their ridiculously high, skinny desks and their red-tape insistence that the hypnotist obtain a permit to perform at the fair—a permit, essentially, to murder. The insane asylum that the doctor heads is yet another bureaucratic enterprise with its procedures, methods, and assistants. Is one bureaucratic institution better than another? Are the assumptions and definitions of one superior to those of the other?

Unfortunately for the critic, *The Cabinet of Doctor Caligari* raises these questions without answering them. Perhaps there are no answers. Perhaps the film's ambiguities stem from the unintentional carelessness of the director with a few details or the conflict between the writers, who conceived one kind of story, and the director, who filmed another. Whatever the underlying reason, the ambiguities of *Caligari* seem to enrich it. How can a world as askew and ajumble as this one give us clear and unambiguous answers?

Perhaps no major work in film history has attracted as many theoretical sticks and stones as *The Cabinet of Caligari*. The major film theorists—André Bazin, Erwin Panofsky, Siegfried Kracauer—are unanimous in their opinion that the film is a cinematic mistake, that it "prestylizes reality," that it violates the inherent photographic realism of the medium, that it substitutes a world of painted artifice for the rich resources of nature. Despite these later arguments of the theorists, the film was immensely influential on other filmmakers, not only in Germany but in France, where "Caligarism," though detested by some, inspired many of the early avant-garde experiments in abstract cinema, in film as "painting-in-motion" rather than as realistic narrative of natural events in natural settings. And despite the arguments of the theorists, *The Cabinet of Doctor Caligari* has been capable of intriguing and fascinating audiences, of weaving its mysterious, hypnotic spell, for over fifty years.

Of the mystical children of *Caligari*, Fritz Lang's *Destiny* (1922) is the most interesting. Lang, in collaboration with his author-wife, Thea von Harbou, is more famous for a series of psychological studies of the activities of gamblers, murderers, and spies (*Doctor Mabuse, Spies, M*). But he also made several metaphysical-fantasy films. In *Destiny,* a young girl and her lover enter a new town; on the road they encounter a dark, shadowy, spectral stranger. The stranger has bought a piece of land near the town's cemetery and has enclosed it with an immense stone wall that lacks a door or any other physical means of entering the region beyond the wall. The girl's lover disappears; when she discovers that he is a prisoner beyond the wall she frenziedly starts to drink a poisonous drug. Lang immediately cuts to the huge wall where she sees the transparent, spectral images of souls entering the region beyond the wall. The means to enter the wall is metaphysical, not physical.

The wall surrounds the kingdom of death; the mysterious stranger is Death himself, and a tired, sad Death he is, superintending the candles of human life that inevitably flicker out. The girl pleads for the life of her lover; Death tiredly offers her a chance to save him, pointing out three candles whose lights have begun to flicker. The girl claims that love can conquer death, and she sets off to save at least one of the three lights. Each of these "lights" is a story in a far-off land: a middle-eastern Moslem city, Renaissance Venice, and a magical China. In all three, the girl and her loves are reincarnated as two young lovers whose monarchs have declared war on their love. In all three reincarnations, the young man dies; the girl's love does not conquer death. After her failure, Death gives the girl one more chance; she can return to life and redeem her lover's being if she can offer another life in trade. She soon runs into a burning hospital to save an infant trapped there. Death meets her inside and asks her for the child as the pawn. She considers and then refuses; she will not kill the infant to save her lover. Instead, the girl herself dies in the fire; her soul and her lover's are thereby reunited as their transparent images climb a hill and stand against the sky. Love, in dying, has, ironically, conquered death.

The power of the film lies in its combination of the pictorial sense of the director and the magnificent visual creations of the designers (Warm, Röhrig, Herlth). The huge, gray wall of Death dwarfs the little, black-clad human figures who stand in front of it; its horizontal and vertical lines run off the frame at top, right, and left—the perfect visual metaphor for the infiniteness and inaccessibility of fate. Death's cave of the candles— a dark, hazy (a special distortion-lens effect), smoky den, punctuated by a numberless collection of thin, white candles with bouncing, waving flames—is an equally perfect visual metaphor for the fragility of human life, the irreversible direction of its progress, and the inexorable control of fate over that progress. Equally memorable is the care taken in creating each of the fantastic kingdoms for the stories of the three lights: the minarets and mosaics of the Arabian city; the canals, the flights of steps, the arched bridges streaming with revelers of the Venice sequence; the flying horse, the flying carpet, the tiny army that emerges from beneath the magician's legs of the China sequence. Lang uses the trick effects of the camera as well as the atmospheric architecture of the designers: superimposition (to depict the souls of the dead), dissolve (to show a dead infant suddenly materializing in Death's arms), vertical masking (to emphasize the height and narrowness of arches and steps), Méliès-style stop-action (to metamorphose a man into a cactus or a pig).

The gimmickiness of the film may make it seem as superficial and banal an exercise as *Male and Female* or *The Thief of Bagdad*, with which it has obvious affinities. Like the DeMille film, *Destiny* uses multiple locales and hence is enhanced by the splash of multiple sets, costumes, and customs. Like the Fairbanks film, it presents the spectator with an entertaining series of surprising cinematic tricks. The Lang film, however, keeps its artistic seriousness because of the unity and consistency of its theme (the war of love and death), because of the clear purpose of its structure (a film descendant of the medieval romance in which the protagonist must face the challenge of a series of tests), and because of the fatalism and melancholy of its tone. If the film resembles DeMille or Fairbanks, it also has unmistakable affinities with the work of the later film metaphysician, Ingmar Bergman. The opening scene in the forest in which the coach stops for the stranger feels like the opening sections of both *The Magician* and *The Seventh Seal*. Bergman's coach and forest at the beginning of *The Magician* reveal the same eerie tone as Lang's; the awesome, black-cloaked figures of Death in *Destiny* and *The Seventh Seal* are cousins. And the two directors photograph them the same way: in shadow, as silhouettes against the sky, back-lit so that the faces are only discernible in close-ups. In its mysticism, in its romantic struggle of love and death, which ends in a romantic truce (both triumph), *Destiny* is more than a surface picture of visual splash.

The same cannot be said of a later Lang film of a similar type, *Metropolis* (1926). Although *Metropolis* is a fantasy of the future and technology rather than a fantasy of the past and romance, like *Destiny* it uses a never-never-land setting to demonstrate an abstract theme. Unfortunately, *Metropolis* is all eyes and no brain, all visual with no convincing vision. The film depicts a world of the future where the rich and intelligent live on the earth's surface with their airplanes and trams and skyscrapers, and the workers—who make the society go—live beneath the surface in dark, imprisoning caverns. Here was Lang's visual translation of the class structure. The banker's son, a young rebel, rejects his father's upper world and goes to live and struggle with the workers of the underworld. There he meets the spirit of the workers—Maria, a proletarian version of the Virgin Mary and Christ all in one—who urges peaceful change and passive progress.

Maria is a Christian-Democrat-Humanist (literally Christian since she delivers her political sermons in a white, candle-lit cave full of crosses) who formulates the film's political argument: the heart must mediate between head and hands.

The young hero's banker father will have none of this. He hires the evil scientist, Rotwang, to manufacture a violent, vicious robot who looks exactly like Maria and who will incite the workers to riot; the father's troops can then use the riot to enslave the workers. The workers riot, flood the city, and almost destroy the whole society, until the real Maria appears to tranquilize them with her abstract words of political love. The banker learns his lesson, and his son, appropriately, is designated as the society's official "heart" to mediate between head (his daddy) and hands (he shakes hands with the foreman of the workers).

The film demonstrates the dangers of the purely architectural-pictorial premise of the German studio film. *Metropolis* is a series of stunning pictures with the silliest, wateriest intellectual and dramatic paste to hold the pictures together. Lang's primary compositional device was to create geometrical patterns of men and machines: configurations of row upon row of black-clad workers against the white walls at Maria's political prayer meeting; the geometrical machines and the geometrical patterns of workers who serve them; the circle of workers around the warning gong as the water seeps into the lower city; the fleeing workers in the flooded streets, a river of rushing human bodies that parallels the river of rushing water engulfing their homes. The film resembles nothing so much as a kaleidoscope, a shifting series of interesting visual patterns, from its opening montage of whirring machines to its final triangular configuration of head, heart, and hands.

The emptiness of the film, however, lies in this kaleidoscopic premise. To reduce people to patterns—to units of geometrical architecture—is to convert them from the living into the dead. The whole film is lifeless, inanimate; even the principal players are dead abstractions. The acting in the film is abominable—overstated, inhuman, unconvincing. A further failing of the film is not only the reduction of men into cyphers, but the reduction of complex political concepts into romantic drivel. The political opposition—head versus hands—with its facile solution is as theoretically silly as it is blantantly overstated. The political conflict in the film has been drained of as much vitality as the human conflict.

The implications of *Metropolis,* however, did not pass unnoticed in its time. It was one of Hitler's favorite films, and after he had seized control of the Reichstag he invited Lang, a leftist and half Jew, to make films for the Nazis. That Lang diminished men into wooden puppets and political problems into romantic abstractions exactly suited Hitler's hypnotic purposes. Perhaps the film's romanticized stupidities and unconscious (or is it conscious?) fascism was more the responsibility of Thea von Harbou, who remained in Germany to join the Nazis after her husband fled. Lang, trained as an architect, may have decided to tend to the film's pictorial architecture, leaving his scenarist wife to tend to the ideas. What is most vicious about *Metropolis* politically is its portrayal of the general lot of men as a mass of undistinguished and undistinguishable ciphers, incapable of thought, growth, or development, incapable of the mental energy to look after themselves, totally dependent on the beneficence of the ruler above. The film sees the benign despot as the only means of shepherding a human race of plodding sheep.

Despite the fascistic implications of the action and *mise-en-scène,* *Metropolis* is a clear forerunner of many later developments in the American film. Its progeny include, of course, all the science fiction films about the world of the future; several sequences seem to have leaped directly into *Flash Gordon,* particularly the conflict between the blond, Buster-Crabbelike hero (Gustav Fröhlich) and the evil, Emperor Minglike magician (Rudolf Klein-Rogge). The whirring machines, sparking Jacob's ladders, and bubbling retorts that are necessary to bring the Robot alive in Rotwang's laboratory are the progenitors of all that similar apparatus which transfers the juices of life into the monster in the laboratory of Doctor Frankenstein. Rotwang himself leads directly to yet another evil colleague, Doctor Strangelove, who—forty years later—wears Rotwang's black glove to cover permanently the remains of one hand, undoubtedly sizzled or gnarled in the course of one of their hellish experiments. If Lang had stuck to such imaginative details rather than decorating them with intellectual bombast (Lang's decorative version of the *Niebelungen,* 1924, suffers from the same pretentiousness), he might have duplicated the success of his madman, crook, and spy films, which are understandably more popular today.

Of the other films of fantasy and the supernatural, Paul Leni's *Waxworks* (1924) combined the setting of *Caligari* (a fairground "cabinet") with the structure of *Destiny* (three separate stories—of Haroun Al-Raschid, Ivan the Terrible, and Jack the Ripper—in three bizarre and decorative locales). Paul Wegener's and Henrik Galeen's *The Golem* (1920, but previously made by the pair in 1914)—the story of a magician Rabbi who brings a clay statue to life to protect the Jews in the Ghetto—is significant for the twisted architecture of its settings (designed by Hans Poelzig) and the fiery, demonic special effects in the scene when Rabbi Loew brings the man of clay to life (more clear evocations of the later Frankenstein *genre,* including the monster's attraction to an innocent, playing child). Their second version of *The Student of Prague* (1926, previously made by Stellan Rye in 1913) is the mythical story of the *Doppelgänger,* the man who sells his shadow only to effect a divorce between his internal and external selves. Arthur Robison's *Warning Shadows* (1922) is interesting for its complex and consistent use of the visual effects of shadows: as an element of the film's action, as the profession of one of the main characters, as a means of creating a mysterious mood and mystical atmosphere, and as one of the film's key metaphoric motifs.

Perhaps the most noteworthy of the purely horrific descendants of *Caligari* was F. W. Murnau's *Nosferatu* (1922), the first in a long series of movie versions of Bram Stoker's Dracula story. This film, Murnau's first major success, was distinguished in the aura of horror and gloom with which it surrounded the vampire's neck-piercing activities. Unlike the later incarnations of Dracula, Bela Lugosi and Christopher Lee, Murnau's vampire (Max Schreck) was no sexy, suave, debonair figure who stole the lady's heart before he stole her blood. Murnau's vampire was hideously ugly—a shriveled, ashen little man with pointed nose, pointed ears, and pointed head.

Unlike later Dracula films, in *Nosferatu* the vampire's victim did not die with the first kiss of the count's teeth. The victim remained alive, growing steadily weaker with each successive loss of life-juice that the vampire sucked out of him. The longer relationship of the vampire with each victim gives *Nosferatu* a feeling of mystical parasitism, of the way that death perpetually feeds off the living. Also memorable are the shots that evoke the deadly emanations of the vampire: the rats scurrying in the streets; the phantom ship sailing by itself with no humans to sail it; the tricky use of negative film and single-frame exposure to depict the gulf between the natural world and the supernatural world of the vampire's castle; the bare, stony walls of the castle itself. Significantly, the underlying theme of *Nosferatu* is the same as *Destiny*'s: the conflict of love and death. The film's heroine consciously seduces the deadly menace, who is attracted to her beauty; she keeps him out of his coffin until after the sun rises, and he dissolves into the morning air. Just as Cesare could not kill the beautiful Jane in *Caligari*, the vampire cannot kill beauty in *Nosferatu*. Love is the strongest power in the mystical German film.

Realism

F. W. Murnau's *The Last Laugh* (1924) is the most influential of the realistic sons of *Caligari*, and is probably the most even and most satisfying film of the whole German era. *The Last Laugh* teamed the greatest talents of the German film: director, Murnau; producer, Erich Pommer; writer, Carl Mayer; photographer, Karl Freund; designers, Röhrig and

Herlth; and central figure, Emil Jannings. The plot is as simple as the plots of the mystical-fantasy films were complex; its emotions are as personal, as human, and as carefully motivated as the concepts of the metaphysical films were abstract.

A porter at a posh hotel (Emil Jannings) bases his self-respect and centers his being on his belief in the importance of his job, which is symbolized by his passionate devotion to his ornate porter's uniform. The uniform both defines his existence and is the only feature that impresses his less fortunate neighbors. Because he is old and feeble the porter is stripped of this uniform and given a new one; he now wears the white linen jacket of the lavatory attendant. The film then details the impact of this loss of dignity on his emotions and on his family and acquaintances. Rather than leaving the porter stooped in abject despair, the film "takes pity on him" and gives him a happy ending: a sudden inheritance of money that turns him into a kindly but gluttonous gobbler of caviar. The effect of this deliberately contrived ending will be discussed in a moment. Worthy of the fullest and most immediate attention in the film is the rendering of the steady degeneration of the porter's soul once he has lost the uniform that covers his body.

One of the film's great virtues is the performance of Jannings, his clear yet subtle portrayal of the two states of the porter's mind. Wearing his uniform Jannings walks quickly and erect; his gestures are smart and precise; his smile and buoyancy make him seem a very young man. His whole body exudes pride and self-esteem, as well as smugness and vanity. Without the coat he ages fifty years—his body stoops, his gestures are vague and languid, he barely moves at all—he becomes a hunched, old, broken man.

But Jannings does not need to do it alone. The director and cameraman have given him a new and useful ally—the camera itself. Freund's camera tracks and swings and tilts and twirls at key moments in the film. The key principle is not so much that the camera moves, but that it has been freed of its tripod. The camera actually serves as the emotional mirror of the old man's soul; its lens is his own pair of eyes. When the world becomes blurry or confusing or insufferable for him, the camera photographs the way the world feels to him, the way he responds to it. The real action in the film is not between Jannings and other characters (there are no other important characters in the film), but between the warring thoughts and feelings inside the porter's own head. The camera makes this internal warfare clear and becomes, in effect, the other major character with whom Jannings plays his scenes.

The power of the sweeping camera strikes the viewer in the film's first scene: the camera tracks down the elevator and through the bustling lobby of the Atlantic Hotel as if it were one of the guests there, continues through the revolving doors, and stands with the porter in the rain as he hails a cab. The sequence not only imparts excitement with its movement, but also establishes every crucial expository detail the film's action requires: the size and importance of the hotel, the conscientious devotion of the porter to his job, the indifference of the revolving door, which later becomes a metaphor for the circular, inhuman, insensitive relationship of a man to his vocation. The vocation remains; the individual man disappears. Further, the bustling excitement of the moving camera precisely mirrors the porter's own excitement about the significance of the hotel and his high position in it.

When the porter receives his dismissal notice from the manager, the camera shows us the letter and then blurs; the porter can no longer read the piece of paper. When the porter gets frenziedly drunk at his daughter's wedding party, the room starts whirling around madly; the spinning camera mirrors the porter's spinning head. In his drunken reverie, the whole world becomes blurred and distorted; the faces of the musicians look like faces in the distorting mirrors of a fun house; the revolving door of the hotel becomes distorted into an immensely high, narrow space that could crush and dwarf a man. And Murnau even translates sound into subjective visual effects by blurring the shots of the musicians' trumpets, implying that the porter can only hear them as a blur. Whereas the distortion and superimposition in a film like *Destiny* reveal the supernatural and the immaterial, those same techniques in *The Last Laugh* reveal natural sensations and responses; the effect of a technique is defined by the context of the whole film.

Compared with the externalized, narrative emphasis of Hollywood films, the emphasis on the internalized, emotional state of the character in *The Last Laugh* is striking. With the exception of Chaplin or von Stroheim, the Hollywood filmmakers consistently subordinated character development to telling a story. Even Griffith developed only those feeling states that were functional to the narrative sweep of the entire film. Another radical departure of *The Last Laugh* from the Hollywood films of the twenties was its avoidance of preaching, its depiction of a world of moral grays rather than blacks and whites. On the one hand, the film condemns the inhuman and insensitive social process that values the man's function rather than the man himself. The society (the callous hotel manager serves as its symbol) welcomes the rich in its posh hotels and posh dining rooms, it caters to the rich with a huge staff of personnel, and it sends the functionless members of that staff packing through the revolving door (as one man revolves out, another revolves in). The circle is truly vicious. On the other hand, our particular hotel porter is foppish and vain, egotistical and falsely self-satisfied. For a man to define his essence in terms of a uniform is false and foolish.

On yet another side, the other members of the porter's own lower-middle-class world are themselves callous and petty, unsympathetic and inhumane. They are as vicious as the hotel manager is indifferent. They snigger behind the porter's back when the bent, broken man walks down the street and into his house. Even his own family turn their backs on him. These vicious, gossiping beings are totally unresponsive to the misery of their fellows; they have lost any sense of camaraderie, of compassion for the plight they all share. On still another side, the very social pressures to survive are partially responsible for their petty viciousness. And the porter, to some extent, deserves their unpitying torture, for his earlier attitude toward them, as he smugly paraded down the street in his uniform like a peacock, was as callous as their present one. The complexity of the film's moral system contributes to the feeling that it mirrors life rather than forms some simplistic paradigm for it. In its rendering of character and its relativity of values, *The Last Laugh* was not only a mature contrast with the escapist Hollywood product; it also set a kind of pattern that has, with exceptions of course, continued through the years: the Hollywood film has traditionally been the film of action and clear-cut values, the European film of character and moral ambiguities.

The one questionable note in the whole film is its ending: the porter's unexpected discovery of a pot of gold at the end of the rainbow. The contrivance of the legacy is emphasized by the fact that the film's only subtitle wrenches us out of the story and tells us that the rest of the film is chimera. Whereas the film had not previously required a single title to clarify the thoughts or feelings of its characters, it suddenly uses one to show that the filmmaker is sticking something on with narrative paste. The key question about the ending is, is it a deliberate contrivance (a parody of Hollywood's happy ending) or a deliberate attempt to emulate Hollywood and give us a happy ending? Perhaps it is a little of both.

Like the endings of both *Easy Street* and Brecht's *Threepenny Opera*, the artificiality of the film's conclusion is so obvious, the solution so facile, so inconsistent with the social realities that the film itself has defined, that our mind immediately sniffs parody and social comment. However, our hearts are also gladdened by the man's good fortune, particularly because he shares that fortune with the only human being in the film who showed compassion for his suffering—the night watchman. The porter's goodness showers on all those who really need it; he discovers the humanity, the compassion for his fellows that he lacked at the beginning of the film. He has no compassion, however, for those who turned their backs on him. He makes the hotel manager eat crow, and his own family is noticeably absent in his moment of good fortune. The ending satisfies our sense of poetic justice at the same time that it reveals the insufficiency of natural justice. Alas for the real porters of the world—and all of us—poetic justice and natural justice are incompatible.

After the success of *The Last Laugh,* the same producer, photographer, and leading actor combined to make another film—*Variety* (1925). The only shift in personnel was the substitution of E. A. Dupont for Murnau as director. Despite the shift in directors, the two films are clearly similar. The film begins in a prison as its warden tells a prisoner (Jannings) that he can be released if he will finally tell his story, confess his motivation for committing murder. The expressionism of this prison sequence—the prisoners shuffling in a circle in their murky, light-streaked den; the bare white walls of the warden's office; the prisoner's hunching back with the number twenty-eight seemingly burnt into the cloth of his uniform—is a descendant of both *Destiny* and *Caligari.* The rest of the film is the realistic story of the prisoner's motivation.

He is Boss Huller, a trapeze artist in a sleazy circus; his pretty young lover (Lya de Putti), who is also his trapeze partner, is his great joy. He, oafish and clumsy bear that he is, waits on her like a servant: cooking, cleaning, trying to satisfy her lusts in bed. One day the two aerialists are needed as assistants for the great circus artist, Artinelli. Even as an aerialist Huller is the oafish servant, the strong-man who supports the tricks of the graceful and lithe Artinelli. The suave Artinelli and the woman drift into an affair. Huller eventually discovers it. He murders Artinelli; the woman, in fear and frenzy, trips on the stairs and tumbles to her death. The prison director, touched by the tale, grants Huller his freedom. The heavy, iron gates of the prison swing open as Huller once again sees the trees and the sky.

Though even more successful commercially than *The Last Laugh, Variety* is not as even a film. The film's addition of a melodramatic love-triangle shifts the attention away from a pure examination of the prisoner's soul to an understanding of his motivations for performing a melodramatic act. The acting in the film—Jannings's included—is not as subtle, as internally suggestive as that in *The Last Laugh;* the actors' overstatement may also have been the result of the film's melodramatic foundation. But the picture's real similarity to *Last Laugh,* and its greatest asset, lies in Karl Freund's subjective camera work. When Huller discovers that he is a cuckold, he picks up a café table and starts twirling around madly to show his strength and his frenzy. The camera spins rapidly around the room. When Huller considers murdering Artinelli by dropping him in the middle of their trapeze act, the camera swings back and forth on the trapeze bars themselves, twisting, turning, flying through space, mirroring Huller's indecision and increasing our suspense. As Artinelli, a sexual spider, waits for his lady fly to walk down the hall into his web, he stands at the door of his room, ear pressed to the wood. The camera tracks in toward his ear as a small pair of legs dissolves into his eardrum and then grows steadily bigger, moving toward the camera. Artinelli hears his prey walking down the hall. Freund again translates sound into visual image.

If one kind of German realist film was the close examination of a single man's psyche, the other was a sociological examination of a whole political or social milieu. These films, which have since acquired the label, "street films," consistently use the word street in their titles: Karl Grune's *The Street* (1923), Bruno Rahn's *Tragedy of the Street* (1927). They consistently use the unifying locale of the street as a means of tying together diverse kinds and classes of people and diverse kinds of human activities. In a sense, the street films can be seen as related to the street sections of *The Last Laugh* in which the porter walks between his home and the hotel—the many people he meets on the street, their attitudes, their aspirations, their successes and failures. The street becomes a microcosm for society as a whole.

Perhaps the most interesting of the street films is *The Joyless Street* (1925), the first important film of G. W. Pabst. Pabst's street runs through postwar Vienna, a city of striking contrasts, of rich and poor, of feast and starvation, of family traditions and whoring. The street of Pabst's film is the synthesis of Vienna's two faces: the ugly, starving reality and the courtesan's painted mask. On Pabst's street the poor wait doggedly and frustratingly in line in front of a butcher's shop, hoping that the brutal man will give them a shred of meat. In the same building as the butcher's shop is Mrs. Greifer's night club, a frivolous, gay, orgiastic late-night gathering spot for the rich, which also serves as a brothel. The film examines several lives on that street of contrasts where the women must inevitably choose between the poverty of standing in the slow line for the butcher's meat or the fast line to riches at Mrs. Greifer's (where the butcher is a steady customer). Two women take opposite paths. One (Asta Nielsen) sells her body and eventually commits murder; the other (Greta Garbo) holds out as long as she can and is rescued from selling herself at the last minute. Pabst's street is joyless because it is a dead end of prostitution and early death.

Pabst's realism typically combines a social theme with melodramatic action. Despite the artificiality and contrivance of the film's tubercular whore who murders one of her rivals, the real unity of the film lies in Pabst's consistent condemnation of the society that allows such poverty and such opulence to exist at the same time, that gives no choice to the poor except starvation or capitulation to the perverted values of the opulent. Pabst's innovative technique, befitting the objectivity and moral consciousness of the film, rejects the subjective use of the moving camera. Pabst's camera does move: it tracks down passageways, pans a line of starving faces, walks along a street with its dwellers. But the movement is less intended to mirror the inner feelings than it is to keep the film moving, exciting, vital.

Pabst's cutting, far more important in his films than it is in *Last*

Laugh or *Variety,* also aims at cinematic fluidity rather than developing a character's sensations. Pabst's great refinement in cutting was to realize that the director can charge a scene with invisible energy if he cuts in the middle of a character's motion. The moving hand or arm or leg, the rising body, the opening door all hide the fact that the camera has shifted its distance and angle while propelling the eye into the next frame. The consistent cuts on movement in *The Joyless Street* keep the story, for all its overstatement, flowing. In an occasional sequence—for example, Pabst's rendering of the frenetic emptiness of the night club with its tapping toes, clapping hands, bouncing knees, bobbing heads—his cutting alone produces energy and rhythm. The later Pabst film, *The Love of Jeanne Ney* (1927), another melodramatic love story played against a political backdrop, develops his principle of cutting on movement still further.

Pabst's cinematic sense and his political vision contributed to his making some of the best early sound films. Pabst brought the traditions of the German studio film into the sound era. His *Westfront 1918* (1930) is an antiwar piece that uses World War I to condemn all militarism. The primary difference between Pabst's film and the similar contemporary American one, *All Quiet on the Western Front,* is that Pabst's war story is less overt, less active than Milestone's. Almost nothing happens in *Westfront 1918:* the soldiers live in the trenches, a young man runs a "heroic" errand to inform the commander that his trench is under attack, a soldier visits a soldier's club to sing and see a show, another soldier returns home on leave to find his wife in bed with a delivery boy, the principal soldiers all die. The power of the study in *Westfront 1918* is that the war is so claustrophobic. The men seem buried in the trenches, and some of them literally are. Life and events merely plod on; the war is a boring treadmill.

Pabst's camera work, feeling the restrictions of the bulky sound equipment, is not as active and fluid as it had been in the silents, but he still manages interesting tracking shots through the trenches, emphasizing that the men are dogs caught in a ditch. A revealing comparison between *Westfront* and *All Quiet* is that whereas Pabst's favorite tracking shot was the claustrophobic one running parallel to the trench, Milestone's favorite track was the sweeping movement of the camera from right to left as lines of soldiers charge over the trenches and toward the camera, a machine gun grinding away in the foreground. Milestone's track is sweeping and active, Pabst's is slow and confined.

Pabst's later sound film, *The Threepenny Opera* (1931), shows a mastery of the new sound medium. His camera tracks through the studio-built streets of a sleazy beggar's London, descends stairways, marches along with the army of the poor. Bertolt Brecht unsuccessfully sued Pabst for corrupting his play, for changing his antiromantic, anticonventional, deliberately contrived theatre-piece into a romantic, conventionally plotted, realistic movie. Despite Pabst's social views, which paralleled Brecht's, Brecht's condemnation of Pabst's more conventional, melodramatic treatment—always a Pabst weakness—was quite valid. Pabst converts the story into a conventional boy-girl tale; Mackie meets Polly in the first scene and their lustful amour blooms. Brecht's play avoids how or why Mackie and Polly first meet; he has no interest in this kind of exposition and motivation. Pabst makes a twenty-minute scene of the business. Pabst's film milks the antics of the thieves, particularly their comic-clumsy attempts to steal a grandfather clock. It milks the pathos of the march of the poor (pathos is one of those emotions that is absent from the Brecht canon). It blurs the deliberate contrivance of Brecht's ending by supplying Mackie's release with a motivation: his wife, Polly, and his gang have themselves founded a bank, so Mackie is respectable. Pabst's emendation is pointedly social. The founding of the bank is a clear jab at the extralegal power of capital and a rather explicit reference to Hitler, the crook who was becoming legitimate. But the Pabst ending blunts the satiric force of the original; Brecht's play is funnier, more bitter, more biting, sharper-edged than Pabst's adaptation. Pabst has weighed Brecht down with unneeded freight: a linear plot and a minutely detailed, atmospheric world of film decor. On the other hand, the cinematic qualities of that world are marvelous. The seamy streets, the smoke-filled, mirrored and paneled café where Mackie first seduces Polly, the cavernous, expressionistic interiors of Peachum's house, the sumptuous, sparkling splendor of the wedding banquet, the tacky gentility of the whorehouse are all exquisite visual creations. Pabst's visuals unfortunately work contrary to Brecht's vision.

The End of an Era

The key question about the death of the German film is whether it came with a bang or a whimper—with Hitler's tyranny over the imagination of the individual artist or in the gradual decay that had been afflicting the German film mind for a half-dozen years before Hitler came to power. There is evidence that the claustrophobia of the studio production, the dependence on architecture and paint, which had so liberated the visual imagination in 1920, began to inhibit it by 1926. Lang's *Metropolis* was the triumph of the dead, decoration for the sake of pure decorativeness. One year after *Metropolis*, 1927, the great writer of studio films, Carl Mayer, and the great photographer of studio films, Karl Freund, broke out of the studio completely to shoot a candid documentary of Berlin life. Edited and constructed by the abstract artist and architect, Walther Ruttmann, *Berlin: Symphony of a Great City* was the antithesis of the traditional German film. It used no story; it was merely a chronological progression of some twenty hours in the city's life, from the arrival of an early morning train to the late-night activities of the Berliners. The film lacked a human protagonist; its protagonist was the city itself. And, as any great city is, the protagonist of this film is both good and bad, kind and cruel, cold and warm. It is a place of great activity—which is of questionable meaning or value. It is a place where people sit in cafés in the warm sun and where litter clogs a storm drain. It is a place where people see Charlie Chaplin on a screen and where a girl commits suicide by jumping off a bridge. The film's ultimate comment is that life in Berlin certainly exists in staggering quantity, but whether that life is good or bad, beneficial or brutal is impossible to say. It has all and none of these moral qualities. It is as neutral as life itself.

The power of *Berlin* lies in its candid photography and its rhythmic cutting. To guarantee the authenticity of filming the city at work and play, Karl Freund, the careful craftsman of both *The Last Laugh* and *Variety*, hid his camera in a truck and drove about the city, hastily and fleetingly shooting the movement that accidentally caught his eye. Though the shooting of the film was mostly accident, Walther Ruttmann's editing of it was not. His two controlled editing principles were form and rhythm (this was, after all, two years after *Potemkin*). As he cut from shot to shot, Ruttmann capitalized on either parallels in form (circles, verticals, heavy masses) or contrasts in form. To combine whole sections of shots he used the principles of musical composition, endowing the sequence with a rhythm and tone appropriate to its content. The opening movement of the film, the train approaching the sleeping city, is *allegro moderato*—rhythmic, pulsating, alive with expectation, but a bit cautious, sleepy, hesitant. The next sequence, of the sleeping city waking, is a *largo*—slow, quiet, peaceful. As the city wakes and goes to work, the tempo changes to *allegro vivace*—vibrant, alive, active. There is an *andante* at the lunch hour when work stops, another *allegro* when it begins again, and another *andante* in the quiet, gear-changing hours of the evening between work and play. The film ends with a *presto finale,* a fast, frenzied sequence of neon lights, night life, dancing, music, movies. With its use of pure visual form, musical rhythms, and real life, *Berlin* is clearly an attempt to break the bounds of studio production.

Another iconoclastic film is *Kuhle Wampe* (1932), Brecht's attempt to redress his movie injury by writing a script of his own. The work rejects the lighting, the atmosphere, the control of the German studio film completely. The film, like the *Berlin Symphony,* feels more Russian than German; its creators (Brecht and Slatan Dudow, the director) are clearly influenced by both Marx and Eisenstein: the montage of bicycle wheels rolling endlessly through the streets, unsuccessful at taking their riders to a job; the montage of rising prices, of evictions for not paying the rent, of the fact that every human necessity bears a price tag. The film's total rejection of a plot, its use of actual locations, its subordination of people to political discussion are also signs of its rupture with the German film tradition.

Unfortunately, though the film clearly condemns the capitalistic system that puts prices on everything and then causes depressions so that no one can pay the prices, it is not exactly clear what political system will take capitalism's place. The camp where the evicted workers have all collected, Kuhle Wampe, is itself a petty, unhappy, unworkable society. The young leftists, with their festival of outdoor athletic contests, confuse the issue still further. The accent on physical prowess smells suspiciously like the Hitler youth groups with their subordination of the mind to the body. And though at the end of the film the young leftists march off singing the equivalent of "We Shall Overcome," we know that at that very moment the Black Shirts were marching and singing similar ditties. *Kuhle Wampe* is more interesting in its total rejection of the German filmmaking conventions than as a convincing film in its own right.

Perhaps the limitations of the studio film had begun to cramp the German imagination. Another possibility is that the exodus of the best film talent to Hollywood had not left enough imaginations in Germany to get cramped. Murnau had gone to Hollywood where, after making the sensitive, internalized, and highly praised study of a married couple's antagonism and reunion (*Sunrise*, 1927), he died in an automobile crash in 1931. Lubitsch had gone to Hollywood, never to return. Pommer had gone to Hollywood and returned, but he may have caught the dollar influenza after being exposed to it. But even for those filmmakers who never went to Hollywood, the influence of Hollywood was unavoidable. As the German film industry had more and more financial difficulties, it was more and more underwritten by Hollywood production dollars. With dollars came influence. Perhaps the Germanness of the German film was bought out.

On the other hand, it is possible that there was no real decline, that Hitler's victory killed a reviving and thriving film imagination with a swift and terrible suddenness. The early German sound films were as good as anyone's. Or better. *The Blue Angel*, despite its American director (von Sternberg), was a completely German film. Its heritage is evident in its careful studio-controlled atmospheres (the contrast between the smoky chiaroscuro of the night club and the bright, clean, ordered whiteness of the professor's classroom), in its close examination of a Jannings character's soul (Professor Unrat's steady degeneration into a beast), and in its cynical portrayal of the nasty, callous insensitivity of the German populace to human suffering. The film was as careful with sound as with pictures: the contrast of Lola's singing and the traditional tune chimed by the town clock, the contrast between the noisy chaos in Unrat's classroom before he enters and the deadly silence when he does. Von Sternberg never made a better film (or as good a one?). Pabst's use of sound was also developing: the wheeze and crash of exploding shells in *Westfront 1918,* the effective contrast of singing soldiers and dying ones, the use of musical leitmotifs in *Threepenny Opera.* So was Lang's: the asynchronous handling of sound and picture in *M:* the haunting echoes as a mother calls in vain for the daughter who has been murdered, the repeated whistling of a Grieg theme, the importance of a blind man (who is totally dependent on sound) in identifying the murderer, the clever use of objects that contrast with the sound track (shadows, a glass window, a "Wanted" poster, the little girl's balloon, the dishes on the table for the meal that will never be eaten). Rather than dying slowly, the German age may well have been translated abruptly from one of gold into one of iron.

Ironically, the great era of German films can be seen as merely developing the means that a Hitler would use to manipulate the minds of the public. The German sense of architecture and composition, the rhythms of cutting and movement, would be reincarnated in the masterful propaganda films of Leni Riefenstahl, who lent her great art to bending the German mind. The heroic architectural configurations of her *Triumph of the Will* (1935) are descendants of *Metropolis* and *Niebelungen;* the stirring integration of musical motifs, the control of camera angle, the incorporation of mythic elements all aim at presenting the Führer as a combination of Pagan god of strength and Christian savior of mildness. In *Olympia* (1936–38), the techniques for consecrating and glorifying the body, the athlete, the purely physical are the descendants of the rhythmic editing of Ruttmann and Pabst. With the exception of providing the world with a series of lessons on the use of the film to bend the public's mind, the German film has been remarkably invisible since 1933.

Chapter

8

SOVIET MONTAGE

The Russian film was born with the Russian Revolution. Before 1917 the Russian film industry was a colony of Europe—of Pathé or Lumière or Scandinavia's Nordisk. No film was shot in Russia by a Russian company until some ten years after the invention of the moving picture. The films of the next ten years (1907–17) were strictly for local consumption (very few of them were exported). Costume films, horror films, and melodramas—the typical formulas of Europe and America—were the staples of the pre-1917 Russian film diet. The revolution changed all that.

Marxist political and economic philosophy, which had evolved in the age of machines, adopted the machine art as its own. Lenin considered the cinema the most influential of all the arts. Movies not only entertained but, in the process, molded and reinforced values. The film was a great teacher; with portable power supplies it could be shown to huge groups of people at the same time in every remote corner of the new Soviet Union. While the flickering images held their audiences captive, the events on the screen emphasized the virtues of the new government and encouraged the Russian people to develop those traits that would best further it. Whereas the American film came into the world as an amusing novelty, the Soviet film was created explicitly as teacher, not as clown. In 1919, after a chaotic year in which the Soviets let the film industry go its own commercial way, the Russian industry passed under government control. The first harvest, however, would not come for six years.

"The foundation of film art is editing," wrote Pudovkin in the preface to the German edition of his book on film technique. Whereas the German innovators concentrated on the look, the feel, the pictorial values of the individual shot, the Soviet innovators concentrated on the effects of joining the shots together. Like so many of the earlier innovations in film technique, the Soviet discoveries were the products of experience and experiment rather than abstract theorizing. Two significant accidents determined the paths the experimentation would take. The first was the shortage of raw film stock. As in the rest of Europe, film stock was scarce in Russia during and just after the war years. The Russian film famine was even more severe, for the still fighting Red and White armies erected blockades against each other to keep supplies from getting through. Lacking quantities of stock, the Soviet filmmakers had to make the most of what they had.

One of the first to make something was Dziga Vertov, who traveled about the country shooting newsreel footage with his camera, which he called his "Kino-Eye." Vertov then assembled this absolutely unstaged footage (Vertov insisted on unstaged reality throughout his career) into a newsreel called *Kino-Pravda*, creating powerful emotional effects and educational results from the way he joined this real footage together. Vertov brings the ordinary, laborious tasks of building or rebuilding a nation to life (laying an airstrip, planting crops, finishing a tram line) by examining the progress of the task from many stirring and awesome angles that succeeded in endowing the ordinary with wonder. Vertov succeeds in giving inanimate machines both stature and vitality, revealing, as many of the later Soviet films would do, the powerful potential, the almost sexual fertility of the union of men and machines. Of course, one of the reasons for Vertov's dynamic editing was that he had to shoot with mere scraps of film stock, and many of those scraps were very short.

The scarcity of film stock also created the film workshop of Lev Kuleshov. Kuleshov, who taught a workshop class at the newly established Moscow Film School, led his students in a series of editing experiments. Pudovkin was to become the most famous of those students, but even those filmmakers who did not study with Kuleshov (for example, Eisenstein) could not escape his influence. Lacking the film stock to make whole films of their own, the Kuleshov workshop experimented in drafting scenarios, in editing and re-editing the pieces of film they already had on hand, and in re-editing sequences of feature films imported from the West. The second of the influential accidents directly affected the Kuleshov group. In 1919, a print of Griffith's *Intolerance* successfully wriggled through the anti-Soviet blockade. *Intolerance* became a Kuleshov primer. His students examined its boldness in cutting—cuts to drive the narrative, to integrate tremendously diverse and disjointed material, to intensify emotion with its rhythms, to mirror internal thought and sensations. The Kuleshov workshop screened *Intolerance* until the print disintegrated; they re-edited its sequences to examine the resulting effects on the film's power and the reasons for Griffith's particular choices. With such a thorough mastery of the principles of Griffith's cutting, the Soviet directors would extend those principles to their limits—when they got the money and the film.

Until then they experimented. Each of the experiments furthered their control of the effects of editing and their conviction that editing was the basis of film art. Several of the Kuleshov experiments have become classics. In one, Kuleshov used some stock footage of the prerevolutionary actor, Ivan Mozhukin. Mozhukin had fled to Paris (with the majority of the Czarist film industry), where he became a matinee idol of French films. But, unknowingly, he left his face behind on a piece of film to aid the dreaded Bolsheviks. Kuleshov cut the strip of Mozhukin's face into three pieces. He juxtaposed one of the strips with a shot of a plate of hot soup; he juxtaposed the second with a shot of a dead woman in a coffin; he juxtaposed the third with a shot of a little girl playing with a toy bear. When viewers, who had not been let in on the joke, saw the finished cutting they praised Mozhukin's acting: his hunger when confronted with a bowl of soup, his sorrow for his dead "mother" (their interpretation), his joy when watching his "daughter" (another interpretation) playing. Mozhukin's expression was identical in all three cuts; the actor's emotion never changed. The context of the juxtaposed material evoked the emotion in the audience, which then projected it into the actor. Editing alone had created the emotion—as well as a brilliant acting performance!

In another Kuleshov experiment the audience sees a series of five shots: 1) a man walks from right to left; 2) a woman walks from left to right; 3) they meet and shake hands, the man points; 4) we see a white building; 5) the two walk up a flight of steps. The audience connects the five pieces into a single sequence. A man and woman meet; they go off toward a building that he sees. In reality, the two individual shots of the man and woman walking were made in two distant and different parts of the city; the building he points to is the White House, snipped out of an American film; the steps they ascend belong to a church in yet a third section of the city. Kuleshov's experiment revealed that the impression of geographical unity in a film was unrelated to geographical unity in space. Kuleshov called the result "creative geography." It was the same method Griffith used when he spliced Niagara Falls into the climax of *Way Down East*. A third Kuleshov experiment might, by analogy, be called "creative anatomy." Kuleshov created the impression of a single actress by splicing together the face of one woman, the torso of another, the hands of another, the legs of yet another.

The Kuleshov student learned that editing served three primary purposes in building a film. First, a cut could serve a *narrative* function. For example, a man walks toward the camera; suddenly, something to his right catches his attention and he turns his head. The audience's natural question is: what does he see? The director then cuts to an old tramp who pulls a pistol on the man. The audience's next question is: how will the man react to this attack? The director cuts back to the man to show his fear. And so forth. The narrative cut allows the director to analyze an action into its most interesting elements and then to resynthesize these elements of the event into a powerful sequential action. Another kind of narrative cut is the flash back or forward—a cut that furthers the action by revealing a character's thoughts at a particular moment. A woman stares dreamily into space; the director cuts to her husband in a faraway prison; the director then cuts back to the woman's face. Yet a third kind of narrative cut is the cross-cut. While the tramp attacks the man with a pistol, the police, aware of the attack, charge to the rescue. These lessons of cutting had all been learned from Griffith.

But the Soviet film students realized that a cut could do more than narrate. They also found that a cut could generate an *intellectual* response. One kind of intellectual cut was the metaphorical-cut or associational-cut. From a group of workers being mowed down by the rifles of soldiers, the director could cut to the slaughter of an ox in a stockyards (as Eisenstein did in *Strike*). The image of the slaughtered ox comments on the action of the slaughtered workers. The director can cut from a streaming procession of striking workers to a shot of a river thawing in the spring, a mass of ice flowing steadily toward the sea (as Pudovkin did in *Mother*). The naturalness, the inevitability of the progress of the streaming ice comments on the force of the streaming workers. A second intellectual effect could be produced by the contrast-cut. The director cuts from the dinner table of a poor man, who eats only a few pieces of bread, to the table of a rich man laden with meats, candles, and wine. The contrast of the two tables comments on the injustice of the fact that two such tables can exist at the same time. The parallel-cut produces a third kind of intellectual response. From the condemned man sentenced to die at five o'clock, the director cuts to a thief who murders a victim at precisely five o'clock. The parallel acts of violence at the same time reinforce each other. Significantly, the intellectual cut—metaphoric, contrast, or parallel—also has an emotional dimension. The director not only uses the slaughter of the ox but also the sickening, horrifying violence and bloodiness of the murder to make his point. He not only comments on the injustice of the rich man's dinner but

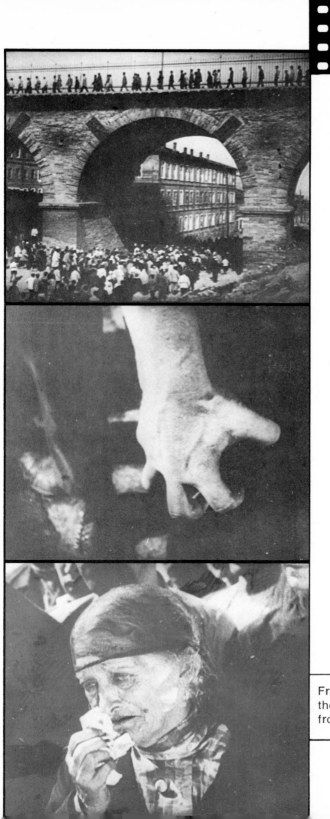

From the mass to
the individual detail,
from geometry to people.

POTEMKIN

The plate-smashing sequence.
A brief action broken
into a dramatic process:
Close-up of the man's face
deciding to smash the plate . . .
medium shot as
he pulls his arm back . . .
medium shot of
the withdrawing arm . . .
close shot of his right arm
and shoulder pulling back . . .
medium shot of the arm
starting forward . . .

medium shot of his determined
motion . . . close shot
showing his determination . . .
medium-close shot of his face
and arm in action . . .
medium shot of the table
about to receive the blow . . .
close shot of relaxed shoulder . . .
medium shot of the table where
the dish has been smashed.

A world of objects.
Eisenstein
deflates material
things into the ugly
and the dead.

MOTHER

Pudovkin builds the scene of mourning with four shots:
sorrowing Mother (Vera Baranovskaia) and
dead husband together . . .
the Mother alone . . .
the dead man alone . . .
while the water drips slowly into the bucket.

MOTHER

The beginning of the slaughter.
Gloved hand of commanding
officer raised, close-up . . .
Soldiers raise their rifles,
full shot . . . Workers see rifles and scurry,
far shot . . . The Mother and Pavel
embrace, medium shot . . .
Commanding officer's gloved hand drops,
close-up. Rifles fire, full shot . . .
Fallen worker's body crashes in pool
of muddy water, close shot . . .

Another worker plunges face first into water,
close shot . . . Body falling, close-up
on midsection . . . Red flag starts
to fall, silhouetted against the sky,
close shot . . . Falling flag and bearer
reflected in water as they fall in mud . . .
Mother and Pavel continue to embrace
medium close . . . Pavel falls, still
locked in embrace.

Pudovkin's use of the "plastic material." Defining a bureaucratic policeman by his gloved hands.

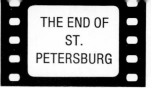

THE END OF
ST.
PETERSBURG

The deflation of war.
Soldiers without heads:
medals, sabres, sashes,
and uniforms, but no heads.

From the glories of war
to the realities.
Flags fly and
the people cheer . . .

an orator makes fancy
speeches (note the
extreme upward angle
to burlesque him) . . .

as men die
in the smoke
and carnage on
the battlefield.

ARSENAL

The horrors of war.
Frozen statues of
death in silhouette...

a mad laugh...

a frozen smile . . .

a hand.

ARSENAL

Dovzhenko's eye. A composition in light and space.

makes us hate the rich man for his gluttony and pity the poor man for his need.

The third kind of cut that the Kuleshov students discovered is a purely *emotional* one: the very method of joining the strips of celluloid together, rather than their content, produces an almost subliminal kinetic response in an audience that the director can unobtrusively control. First, the director can cut a sequence rhythmically. He can use shorter and shorter pieces of film, increasing the tempo and tension of the action. Or he can cut a sequence with long pieces of film, producing a feeling of slowness and languidness. By stitching together a series of strips of equal length the director can produce the feeling of a regular, measured beat. The tonal-cut is the director's second method of manipulating an audience's emotions without its conscious awareness of manipulation. He can cut a sequence with steadily darker pictures, producing the impression of oncoming night and growing despair, or with steadily lighter pictures, producing the impression of dawn and rising hope. A third kind of emotional editing is the form-cut, cutting on a similarity or difference in the form of the object in the frame. The director can cut from a spinning roulette wheel to a turning wagon wheel, from a plodding ox to an efficient tractor, from a jabbing pencil to a thrusting sword. A fourth kind of kinetic editing is the directional-cut, in which the director uses the direction of movement across the frame either to keep the action flowing or to produce a dynamic collision. The director can cut from a group of workers streaming from right to left, to a group of foot soldiers streaming from right to left, to a group of Cossacks on horseback streaming from right to left. Or he can cut from a group of workers streaming from right to left to a group of Cossacks streaming from left to right. Whereas the first series of directional cuts would produce the feeling of speed, continuousness, and flow, the second would produce the sensation of two huge masses smashing into one another. Significantly, a cut that is intended to have an intellectual effect—from pencil to sword—may also serve as a form-cut, as part of a tonal sequence, as part of the film's increasing rhythm, and as a shift in the film's narrative structure all at the same time. A single cut can function on all three levels —narrative, intellectual, emotional—at once. In fact, the Soviet directors discovered that most cuts *must* function on all three levels at once.

To this discovery they gave the name "montage." In French, the word simply means editing; for the Soviet director, the word signified the particular way he used editing to control the film's structure, meaning, and effect. By 1924, the Kuleshov students had acquired the film, the equipment, and the budgets to turn their lessons into films. Each went out to use his notion of montage. The surprise was that despite the similarities in theory, the individual filmmakers produced strikingly individual and personal films.

Sergei M. Eisenstein

Eisenstein was the greatest filmmaker to apply the principles of Kuleshov, the greatest master of montage. It was Eisenstein's sense of cutting that transformed his didactic lessons on the virtues of brotherhood and Marx into dynamic, moving works of art—even for the non-Marxist. The Eisenstein films break all the rules of narrative construction. They lack a protagonist and focal characters; they lack a linear plot of the rising or falling fortunes of a single man. Although the Eisenstein films lack a conventional plot, they lack neither compelling action nor a unified structure. Although they lack individualized and rounded studies of human personality, they lack neither character nor human compassion.

The Eisenstein film holds together by means of its theme rather than its story: the experience of the workers who learn what it means to strike and to take collective action against a wicked state, the ability of a single revolutionary action on a battleship to unite a whole people, the replacement of a false revolutionary government by a true one, the superiority of the new agricultural and social methods to the old ones. The theme gets its flesh from Eisenstein's depiction of the people who embody it. Although the central character of the Eisenstein film is the mass, the people as a whole, he never forgets that the mass is a combination of individuals. Although the Eisenstein film is full of magnificent shots of streaming rivers of men, he invariably shows the viewer the impassioned faces of the men and women in that river. Like Lang, Eisenstein has the visual ability to convert huge groups of people into complex and striking geometric shapes. Unlike Lang, Eisenstein constantly reminds you that his subject is man and not a visual pattern. Also unlike Lang, Eisenstein's geometric compositions, as careful and as visually attractive as they are, are never static. The individual shots are full of dynamic movement; they are not static, metaphoric, or quasi-ballet as in *Metropolis*. That was one of Eisenstein's advantages in shooting outdoors; he had the freedom to move. And Eisenstein's montage increases the sense of movement and tension as the individual shots collide, crash, explode into each other.

Eisenstein defined his principle of montage as one of collision, of conflict, of contrast. He does not simply edit the shots together but sees each frame as a unit with a dynamic charge of a particular kind. His goal is to bring the dynamic charge of one frame into conflict with the charge of the next. For example, the shots can conflict directionally—a group of men running from right to left, followed by a shot of soldiers marching from left to right. The shots can conflict in rhythm—a group of people running quickly and chaotically, followed by a group of soldiers marching steadily, slowly, and inexorably. The shots can conflict in bulk—from a mass of workers to a shot of a single worker's face. The shots can conflict in emphasis—from a shot of four silent workers' faces to a shot of a single worker's fist clenched at his side. The shots can conflict in camera angle—from an extreme downward angle on a large crowd to a noble upward angle shot of a member of the crowd. The shots can conflict in the intensity of light—from a dark, dim shot to a blazing, bright one. The shots can conflict in the intensity of emotion—from a shot of fighting, struggling workers to a shot of a single worker's lifeless body, dangling quietly outside the struggle. The shots can conflict in their vitality—from a shot of a living man to a shot of a stone statue. And so forth. Eisenstein's great films are the products of the combinations of his many and diverse gifts—his visual sense of composition, his feeling for rhythm and tempo, his ability to understand and manipulate human emotion, and his perceptive intellect, which could create meaning by joining two seemingly unrelated images.

Eisenstein formally studied engineering and architecture. During the Civil War of 1917, he organized an impromptu theatre troupe in the Red Army. Attracted to the theatre, he started directing plays in Moscow after the war, where he was heavily influenced by the innovative, anti-naturalist director, Vsevlod Meyerhold. In one of Eisenstein's productions, *The Wise Man* (1922), he used a short film sequence within the context of the play. He staged his last play, *Gas Works* (1923), in the Moscow Gas Works. Eisenstein could go no further with stage reality; the leap into films was inevitable. His first film, *Strike* (1924), revealed the bold, broad strokes of a new film master. From the film's opening montage sequence—of whirring machines, spinning gears, factory whistles, of traveling shots along the length of the factory complex, of dynamic, dizzying movement—the film proclaimed that a brilliant cinematic imagination was at work.

The film contains many of the traits that make an Eisenstein film pure Eisenstein. The director's control and alternation of moods: from the peaceful, idyllic sequences of the striking workers at rest and play to the violent, vicious slaughter of the workers in their tenements. The satirical treatment of the rich and the informers for the rich: the company finks are depicted as sneaky animals (a Griffith touch here); the rich factory owners sip cocktails while the workers starve and die (Griffith cross-cutting, of course). The director's visual sense of composition: the geometrical patterns and shapes of the factory and of the workers' tenements where the Cossacks attack. Eisenstein's use of metaphor to comment on the action: the sickening slaughter of the dumb and defenseless ox, which comments on the slaughter of the workers. And uniting the film is the Eisenstein vision—the capitalistic, Czarist system is fundamentally inhuman and inhumane, an obstacle not only to physical survival but also to human fellowship and brotherhood.

Potemkin (1925) was Eisenstein's next film. The work was originally intended to depict the entire workers' revolt of 1905. Instead, Eisenstein pared down his conception to a single event in the revolt—the rebellion on the battleship Potemkin and the resulting reprisals from the Czarist army —to serve as a microcosm for the whole year's events. (Ultimately, of course, it foreshadowed the workers' eruption of 1917.) The film's five parts form a taut structural whole: from the unity the sailors build on the ship, to the unity between ship and shore, to the unity of the entire fleet. In the first part, subtitled "Men and Maggots," Eisenstein builds the dramatic reasons for the sailors' discontent. The food is infested with maggots; the Czarist doctor looks at the meat closely through his spectacles and declares the meat wholesome, despite the fact that his glasses magnify the presence of the worms. The officers beat the men and treat them like cattle. Eisenstein brilliantly shows a worker's pain by merely photographing the twitching muscles of his back as he sobs.

In the film's second section, "Drama on the Quarterdeck," the men have had enough. They refuse to admit that their food is edible; when the captain orders all dissenters to be shot, the sailors rebel. By the end of this violent sequence, the ship belongs to the workers. The film's third section, "An Appeal from the Dead," is a quiet, elegiac requiem, a pause between the violent capture of the ship and the violence to follow on the Odessa Steps. One of the sailors has been killed in the battle; his body lies in state on the shore. The workers of Odessa file past it, united in spirit by the sailor's sacrifice. The dead man's action touches and unites the people of Odessa.

The fourth section of the film, "The Odessa Steps," begins gaily enough. The workers of Odessa race out to the Potemkin in their boats, carrying food and joy to their fellow-workers on the ship. There is a union of ship and shore, of sailors and citizens. Other Odessans watch and wave from the shore. Suddenly, Czarist troops march down the steps, butchering every person in their path. The citizens scurry for protection. The soldiers' guns mercilessly fire, slaughtering young and old, men and women, children and mothers. The fifth section of the film, "Meeting the Squadron," is another emotional contrast. From the violence and chaos of the previous section, the mood becomes subdued, tense, expectant. The single battleship races toward the fleet; the ship prepares for battle. Eisenstein builds the suspense with shots of whirring gears, pumping pistons, rising guns. Will the fleet fire? The fleet does not. The comrades of all the fleet cheer one another. The Potemkin has united them all.

The techniques that are uniquely Eisenstein's bring the film to life. The power of his cutting is unmistakable. At the end of section one, Eisenstein wants to emphasize the fact that the men have had it, that the last straw has been laid on the camel's back. A sailor washing the dishes sees a plate inscribed, "Give us this day our daily bread." The biblical platitude infuriates him since they have no decent daily bread. He smashes the plate. To emphasize this act of smashing, Eisenstein divides this physical action, which takes only two or three seconds, into ten different shots [see photographs on pages 186–87]: 1) a close-up of the man's face reflecting his decision to smash the plate; 2) a medium shot as he pulls his arm back with the plate in his right hand; 3) a medium shot of the withdrawing arm; 4) a close shot of his right arm and shoulder pulling back; 5) a medium shot of his right arm starting forward; 6) a medium shot of his determined motion; 7) a close shot of his face showing his determination; 8) a medium-close shot of his face and arm in action; 9) a medium shot of the table about to receive the blow; 10) a close shot of his relaxed shoulder; 11) a medium shot of the table where the dish has been smashed. Dividing an action into such a process makes the event more violent, more purposeful, and more memorable as a pivotal point in the film. The edited version of the action takes longer than the physical act itself.

Other sequences use a different but equally effective editing plan. No better example of tonal montage exists than in the opening passage of the film's third section, "An Appeal from the Dead." The entire sequence is saturated in the lyric calm of the sailor's death. Eisenstein cuts slowly from shot to shot, each of them growing lighter, revealing the rising of the sun through the fog. In the languid cuts, the sea is calm as glass, ships glide through the mist, their masts silhouetted in the fog, gulls quietly hover in the air. The quiet editing creates a lyrical moment of slow-moving, dark shapes sliding through a gray mist. The editing of the mourning Odessans in the final section of this "Appeal from the Dead" adds a note of strength and human determination to the moody silence. Eisenstein cuts from far shots of the immense mass of people to medium shots of three or four faces, to close-ups of single faces, clenched fists, and outstretched arms. When an antisemite screams, "Down with the Jews," Eisenstein shows the fierceness of the people's unity in a rhythmic editing sequence that shows heads turning, wheeling, in angry response to this voice of narrow inhumanity.

And the most dazzling editorial sequence of all in the film is the slaughter of the innocent Odessans on the steps. Eisenstein weaves this magic with a series of different kinds of shots: far shots from the bottom of the steps showing the workers running chaotically; traveling shots along the side of the steps that reinforce the movement of the running workers; shots from the top of the steps showing the relentless, metric pace of the marching soldiers, only their boots, their bayonets, and their awesome shadows in the frame; close-ups of the individual workers, their faces expressing horror, fear, sorrow, anger. Eisenstein weaves this tapestry by intercutting the different shots, alternating them according to different principles of his montage of collisions, each of them sustained on the screen for the rhythmically correct number of seconds (or fractions of seconds). And as in the plate-smashing scene, the film time for the sequence on the Odessa Steps is longer than the actual time it would take a group of people to run down a flight of steps. Subjective time, the way it felt to be there, replaces natural time.

But *Potemkin* is more than montage, more than a series of dazzling editing techniques. For a film with a mass protagonist, the faces of individual people are strikingly memorable. Out of the brilliant geometric organization of sailors' hammocks emerge the individual faces of the young sailor who gets beaten and Vakulinchuk, the sailor who leads his comrades in revolt. The sharp-featured, beady-eyed faces of the sneaky ship's doctor, the cunning ship's mate, and the egomaniacal captain capture Eisenstein's condemnation of the vicious ruling class. The most maniacal and vicious face of all is that of the priest, his hair streaming in close-ups framed with light and smoke, his huge iron cross more a dangerous weapon (it sticks in the ship's deck like a dagger) than a symbol of love and mildness. To enhance the lyrical quietness of the "Appeal from the Dead," Eisenstein evokes our sympathies with loving shots of the sorrowing faces of old and young, of men and women. And the most memorable faces of all are those in the most active and violent sequence of all—the Odessa Steps. Eisenstein creates the horror of the slaughter not just with mass murder and chaotic movement but with the individual reactions and sensations of the people who experience the slaughter: the elderly lady with the pince-nez, the mother with her young son, the student with the glasses, the legless man scurrying at the feet of the crowd. As the soldiers attack, Eisenstein follows the fortunes and reactions of each of these individual faces, using their emotional responses to evoke ours.

If *Potemkin* seems to be Eisenstein's most unified, most satisfying, and most *emotionally* effective film, it is perhaps because so many of its devices are felt rather than noticed. For example, the famous montage of the stone lions (three sequential shots of three statues—a lion sleeping, waking, and rising—so edited as to produce the impression of a single, natural, connected action) has drawn extensive critical and theoretical attention. Clearly the sequence is a rather explicit metaphor (condemned by André Bazin for its explicitness) for the rising of the people's power and anger, enraged at the slaughter on the Odessa Steps. But a much more subtle and less explicit metaphor in the film (drawing no commentary at all, despite the fact that the metaphor runs throughout the film) is Eisenstein's handling of the battleship's guns. At the beginning of the film the guns are lifeless, inert. In the middle of the film the guns come alive to send the ship's defiance to the shore in answer to the slaughter on the Odessa Steps. By the end of the film, the guns are alive with power: rising, turning, and twisting toward the enemy. The guns have come to life because they have now acquired a soul, working as the tools and servants of the true spirit of the people.

But Eisenstein's use of the guns may be even more subtle, for he may be giving the general metaphor of the new soul within the machine a specifically sexual connotation. Early in the film the guns play a passive, androgynous, a sexual role. When a sailor inserts a swab into one of the huge guns, the potential instrument of power serves as a mere receptacle, secreting a gooey oil. Later—in response to the slaughter on the Steps— the guns rise for the first time in the film (and the low angle increases the sexual implications of this rising), and then shoot their answer into a Czarist edifice, knocking it flat. (Only then do the stone lions arise, being born, in a sense, from the semen of the guns.) In the film's final sequence, the guns continue to stand erect and alert, becoming a mechanical extension of the new potency of the men who control them.

Another element of the film that is felt rather than noticed is the sheer musicality of Eisenstein's montage. Although Eisenstein (and most historians and critics) have devoted their time exclusively to discussing the intellectual and argumentative effects of montage, the editing of the strips of film in *Potemkin* also functions on a purely sensual level. Because Eisenstein's major period of theoretical writing followed the making of *Potemkin* by almost a decade, one can argue that he might well have lost touch with a quality of his work that he had manipulated instinctively and spontaneously in his youth. (Such a view would explain the drier, more academic, less exciting sound films that he made after his years of theorizing.)

So much of the viewer's experience of *Potemkin* proceeds not from the eyes to the brain (the film's ideological statements) but from the eyes to the nerves. Like music, one *feels* the film as rhythm, mood, tone, and texture in addition to perceiving its concrete images. Eisenstein's "music" might be generally described as tensely violent, as a nervous, surging, discordant dissonance—a feeling that would parallel it with the modern music then being written by his countrymen and contemporaries, Dimitri Shostakovich and Sergei Prokofiev. Interestingly, both composers later wrote music for the Soviet sound film, and the effective collaboration of Eisenstein and Prokofiev on *Alexander Nevsky* and *Ivan the Terrible* revealed how kindred were the spirits of these two "musicians."

Eisenstein's next film, called either *October* or *Ten Days That Shook the World* (1927), is not nearly as careful, consistent, or effective in its manipulation of the sensual effects of visual "music" as *Potemkin*. The film, a loose historical survey of the months between the February Revolution of 1917 and the Bolshevik Revolution of October, is more intellectual, more satirical, and more specifically political than *Potemkin*. Its historical structure also makes it less unified dramatically, less consistent thematically, and less effective emotionally. Unlike *Potemkin,* its parts are far more striking than its whole.

The film's montage still drives its rhythms. During the scenes of rebellion, Eisenstein uses tremendously quick cuts (two frames long!) that smash the viewer with an impression of violence, shock, and frenzy. To emphasize the fact that St. Petersburg has been cut in half, Eisenstein extends, slows down the scene of the raising of the bridges, just as he draws out the plate-smashing scene and the Odessa Steps sequence in *Potemkin*. Two halves of a drawbridge pull apart and rise with infinite slowness. On one of the halves lies the body of a woman whose hair streams into the gap between the halves. On the other half lies the body of a horse, still attached to a wagon. The horse falls into the gap; the wagon remains on the bridge; the horse remains suspended in midair, like the girl's hair, as the bridge continues to rise. After an agonizing wait, the two bodies fall into the river. Significantly, immediately after they fall in the river, Eisenstein cuts to a shot of Bolshevik leaflets and banners falling in the river. The real revolution is as dead as the girl and horse. The new provisional government, the result of this February Revolution, is a failure for the real revolutionists.

The striking device of *October* is less in the emotional power of its montage than in the intellectual commentary of Eisenstein's cutting. His consistent method in this film is to use inanimate objects to comment on the activities of men. The film's dead things ironically give it its life. Whereas Eisenstein used the method only once in *Potemkin, October* is full of "stone lions" that come to life.

A series of objects comments on the values of Kerensky, leader of the provisional government. As Kerensky poses, Eisenstein cuts to a statuette of Napoleon. Eisenstein further debunks Kerensky by showing all the possessions in his palace: gleaming china plates, goblets of cut glass, chalices of silver, an army of toy soldiers. The burlesque of Kerensky dominates the film. During the Bolshevik Revolution, Kerensky furtively calls the Cossack barracks for help, but the Cossacks have joined the Bolsheviks. The only response to his furtive call is a series of shots of the buttocks of horses, implying both that he is a horse's ass and that even the animals are breaking wind in the false leader's face. Most damning of Kerensky is the series of shots that shows him fleeing in his Rolls Royce, a little American flag firmly planted on the radiator. Eisenstein repeatedly cuts to the flag to show both Kerensky's flight and his loyalties.

Eisenstein uses other objects satirically. To burlesque the glories of war, he shows a collection of gaudy medals; to burlesque the emptiness of religion (a consistent Eisenstein theme) he shows a series of church icons: crosses, statues of Buddha, wooden figures of primitive gods. All of the statues are inanimate and ugly; all of them emphasize the artificiality of turning the abstraction of a deity into a tangible (and expensive) object. To burlesque the futility of the government officials, Eisenstein plays geometric games with the empty coffee glasses on their conference table.

The glasses jump into a circle, a line, a curve, a square; though the patterns of the glasses change, the results of the conference do not. To burlesque the idealism of the Mensheviks, a group that advocated peaceful change rather than revolution, Eisenstein cuts from one of their speakers to a group of harps plucked languidly by graceful, feminine hands.

The dominant mood of *October* is parody and burlesque. Symptomatic of the tone of the film is Kerensky's action when he hears that the Bolsheviks are attacking: he buries his head under the cushions of a sofa and flails his arms and legs frantically and childishly in space. The constant use of inanimate objects is a perfect burlesque tool, a way of turning human activity into wood or glass or stone. The parodic tone of the film's spirit holds together its sprawling, semihistorical structure.

Eisenstein's next film, his last silent, returns to the human world of *Potemkin*. In *Old and New* (1929), Eisenstein demonstrates the difficulties and the virtues for the peasant of discarding the old ways of farming and thinking, of adopting the new collective ways and the new machines. The film represents some departures for Eisenstein. In the manner of Pudovkin, he uses natural (rather than inanimate) imagery—fields, soil, animals, and crops—and he also uses a central figure rather than a mass to embody the film's social progress (although unlike Pudovkin, Eisenstein merely observes the peasant woman's behavior rather than probes or develops her thoughts and feelings).

But Eisenstein was beginning to run into trouble with the Soviet line and leaders. Stalin was dissatisfied with the ending of *Old and New,* finding it untrue to the spirit of the new nation and the people. Eisenstein, an iconoclast, a devoted artist, an avid reader of everything from T. S. Eliot to Joyce and Kafka, from Dickens to Haiku poetry, began to feel the pinch of tightening state control. He did not complete another film for ten years.

Several factors contributed to his silence. Sound had suddenly overtaken the world's film industries and Eisenstein needed time to study the new medium. He spent several years in America studying, trying to get Paramount to accept one of the scripts that they had contracted him to direct (*Arms and the Man, The War of the Worlds, An American Tragedy*). Paramount rejected them all. In 1932, Eisenstein and his cameraman, Edouard Tisse, went to Mexico to film an epic of the Mexican people, *Que Viva Mexico!*, financed by Upton Sinclair. Eisenstein fought with Sinclair and the film was cancelled. Eisenstein never got the chance to edit the finished footage, much of which he never saw. A bowdlerized version of the film, assembled by Sol Lesser, was released in 1933 as *Thunder Over Mexico*. Returning to the Soviet Union, Eisenstein submitted several film projects that were rejected by the state film committee. Eisenstein was accused of formalism—the great sin of Soviet art. He paid too much attention to the beauty of the work and not enough to the utility of it. His methods were wasteful and time-consuming. His perfectionism was demanding and unconcerned about budgets and schedules. Then in 1938 he completed *Alexander Nevsky*.

Eisenstein's theory of the sound film was that the "talkie" was a fundamental error in the use of the medium. There was no artistic purpose in showing a man's lips move while the audience hears the words pour out. For Eisenstein, sound was to be used asynchronously, to do something that the picture did not do. And the picture should continue to do what sound could not do. Sound was to become one more element of a film's montage. The visuals and sound should play against one another, not sing in unison. Although Eisenstein's theory of the sound film was contrary to the practice of his contemporaries, years of experience with the sound film have since proved the solidity of his theory.

Eisenstein, whose use of images had always been musical, was especially interested in the precise synchronization of visual images with musical passages and motifs. One of Eisenstein's best demonstrations of his musical theory is in "The Battle on the Ice" sequence in *Alexander Nevsky* as the invading Teutonic hordes encounter the valiant Russian people who have collected to defend themselves. Aided by the power and complexity of Prokofiev's score, Eisenstein turns "The Battle on the Ice" into a cinematic symphony. The successive tones and rhythms of the Prokofiev music—slowly expectant, playfully fast, steadily victorious—play both with and against the content of Eisenstein's images of battle and the rhythms and shapes that control the cutting of the images.

Eisenstein's only other completed works before his death in 1948 were two of the three intended parts of *Ivan the Terrible*. In Part II, he experimented with color in two sequences. As with sound, Eisenstein believed that color should not be exploited for its novelty, its colorfulness, but that color should play a functional role in controlling the film's tone and effects. Again, the years would prove his sensitivity to the real potential of a cinematic device. But the most striking fact of Eisenstein's twenty-five-year career in films is that he made four pictures in his first five years and three in his next twenty. Eisenstein became a teacher and theoretician; he taught at the State Film School; and he wrote lengthily and convincingly on the powers and effects of montage. But his greatest achievements in filmmaking had been accomplished before the end of the silent era. Indeed, his sound films display a self-consciousness in his handling of montage that was deadening to the vitality and the exuberance of the method he applied instinctively in his youth.

To some extent his career mirrors the artistic vitality of the Soviet film as a whole. The Russian film made the transition into the sound era with the greatest difficulties, partially because the Soviet cinematic method was so visual, partially because the great Soviet directors became politically suspect, partially because the Soviet industry had great difficulty acquiring reliable machines to shoot and project sound pictures.

Vsevlod I. Pudovkin

Pudovkin and Eisenstein were friendly opponents. Whereas Eisenstein's theory of montage was one of collision, Pudovkin's was one of linkage. For Pudovkin, the shots of the film combine to build the whole work rather than conflict with one another in dynamic suspension. Although the linkage-collision argument may seem a war of words, of similar but different-sounding abstractions, nothing so clearly reveals the differences between the two directors than a comparison of their films. Whereas the tone and pace of the Eisenstein film is generally nervous and tense, the tone and pace of the Pudovkin film is more languid and relaxed. He reserves the shocking, violent montage effects for occasional sequences of fighting and rebellion. Whereas Eisenstein's usual human focus is the mass, Pudovkin's is the individual, a single human's revolutionary decision rather than the revolutionary action of a whole group. Whereas Eisenstein's montage is rich in intellectual commentary, Pudovkin's usually develops the emotional tone and human feelings within the scene.

Pudovkin, unlike Eisenstein, depended heavily on the performances of individual players; like Griffith, Pudovkin realized that the context of the scene, the immobile face of an actor in close-up, a flickering in the eyes, could communicate more than overt gestures. Pudovkin took Kuleshov's experiment with Mozhukin's face seriously—far more seriously than Kuleshov himself took it (as the overacting in Kuleshov's own film, *By the Law*, shows). Pudovkin believed that the "plastic material"—concrete physical objects—could communicate emotions and ideas more effectively than an actor's grimaces.

Whereas the imagery in Eisenstein's films is primarily inanimate, the imagery in Pudovkin's films is primarily natural: trees, rivers, the sky, the wind. When Eisenstein does use a natural image, for example the sea in *Potemkin*, his choice is a huge, violent natural image rather than a calm, peaceful one. The Eisenstein film is a more exciting, jostling emotional experience; the Pudovkin film is a warmer one.

Like Eisenstein, Pudovkin came to the arts not as artist but as scientist. After studying physics and chemistry, Pudovkin decided to work in films (originally intending to act rather than direct). His admiration for Griffith's *Intolerance* strongly influenced his decision. In 1920, Pudovkin began his studies at the State Film School, entering Kuleshov's workshop two years later. His scientific training ably suited him for his first major film project, *Mechanics of the Brain* (1926), a cinematic investigation of Pavlovian research in conditioned reflexes in animals and children. He took time off from the Pavlov picture to shoot his first fiction film, *Chess Fever* (1925), an ingenious and charming short comedy that paid homage to his teacher, Kuleshov.

Unlike the American comedies, *Chess Fever* is a comedy of editing. Pudovkin surprises us with gags that are solely the results of montage. In the opening sequence, we watch a chess game from underneath the table, seeing only the feet and arms of each of the players making his move. Only later does Pudovkin pull back to show us a single chess player playing the game by himself—he is that infected with the chess fever. Pudovkin's editing fooled us into believing that there were two players, the usual and expected number. The whole film is built out of such Kuleshovian tricks. During the filming of *Chess Fever,* an international chess tournament actually took place in Moscow. Pudovkin sent his camera crew—masquerading as newsreel photographers—to film the tournament and the champion players. Pudovkin then spliced the "newsreel" footage into the plot of the comedy, making the film's action seem to revolve around the tournament. For example, a girl is so upset by her boyfriend's fanatic devotion to chess that she throws one of his chess pieces away. Pudovkin then cuts to a shot of the chess champion, Capablanca, standing and holding a chess piece. It looks as though he caught the piece that the girl just threw. Purely an editing trick! Pudovkin took Kuleshov's notion of "creative geography" and produced "creative continuity."

Pudovkin's unique style emerged in his later fiction films. In *Mother* (1926), he reveals his ability to combine sensitive treatment of a human story, fluid narrative editing that uses the shock effects of montage for isolated, showcase effects, and natural images that comment on the action and reinforce the film's values. *Mother* is an adaptation of a Gorky story (later adapted by Brecht into a play): a tale of a woman who learns that radical action is ultimately the only protection against a wicked state. Her husband is lured into helping a group of strikebreakers; he is shot and killed in a scuffle. The mother then betrays her own son, Pavel, revealing that the boy was in collusion with the workers. At her son's trial, she sees the corruption of justice. The judges are more interested in dozing or breeding race horses than in administering justice; the unsympathetic gallery has come to the trial for a good sadistic show. The unjust social process turns the old lady into a radical herself. She helps her son escape from prison and together they march in the forefront of a workers' demonstration. Although both she and Pavel die, cut down by the bullets and bayonets of the Cossacks, the story of her education serves as a model for all the workers of Russia and a metaphor for the results of their education that would suddenly surface in 1917.

Pudovkin's handling of his actors and shaping of the scenes is exceptional. His principle of acting—that actors do not really act in films, that the film's context, its decor, its business, its use of objects, create an acting performance—is demonstrated throughout the film. A most effective example is the scene of mourning in which the mother sits by the corpse of her dead husband. Pudovkin alternates between several shots: a far shot of the mother sitting beside the bier, the walls gray and bare behind her; a close shot of water dripping in a bucket (the scene's "plastic material"); a close shot of the mother's face, motionless. The mother's face needs no motion. The bareness of the room, the steadily dripping water, our knowledge of the husband's death create all the emotion the scene needs. Her still, quiet face mirrors all the sorrow that has been built around her.

A similar principle creates the viciousness of the strikebreakers, the Black Hundreds. As they make plans in a saloon, Pudovkin uses three kinds of shots: shots of the musicians playing a jolly tune, shots of a man's hands dismembering a fish (the "plastic material"), and shots of the strikebreakers' faces. These men need not grimace and glower to reveal their nastiness; by juxtaposing their discussion with happy, frenetic music and the brutal gutting of a fish, Pudovkin creates all the viciousness he needs.

Significant also is the camera angle Pudovkin uses to shoot a scene. The far shot of the mourning mother beside the corpse is a down-shot from a high camera position. Pudovkin discovered that the downward angle emphasizes the character's smallness, his feeling of being alone, his insignificance. Conversely, the extreme upward angle can magnify the self-importance of a character, his smugness and petty self-esteem. Pudovkin uses extreme upward angles for his satiric shots of the factory owners, of the corrupt judges, of the egotistical, self-important policeman (played by Pudovkin himself) who comes to search the mother's house for the strikers' guns. A slight upward angle produces not satire but ennoblement of the figure, making the character grand without delusions of grandeur. Pudovkin's final shots of the mother marching nobly at the head of the demonstration are slight upward shots. In fact, Pudovkin mirrors the state of the mother's mind and the progress of her education with his choice of camera positions. He shoots her from above before her conversion, he shoots her from below to ennoble her after it. With such control of scene and camera angle, Pudovkin allows his actress, Vera Baranovskaia, to give a brilliant performance. Her performance, of course, is partially the result of his cutting and camera placement.

Pudovkin relies primarily on the narrative cut, on the lessons he had learned from Griffith. Like Griffith, he works for fluidity in building a scene, a fluidity that hides the cut from the viewer so that we synthesize the complete emotional experience. Most reminiscent of Griffith is the flashback in which the mother remembers her son hiding the guns; Pudovkin even uses a Griffith-like iris-in and -out to mark the flashback. Such fluid, narrative cutting was infrequent in Eisenstein. But like Eisenstein, Pudovkin could also use tricky montage effects when he needed the power of a physical assault. To reveal the joy in Pavel's heart when he discovers that his comrades will soon free him from prison, Pudovkin splices together a series of images to evoke the sensation of joy. The director's sensitivity to the actor's needs told him that merely to show a smile on Pavel's face would be fakey and punchless. Instead, Pudovkin cuts from Pavel's face to a series of beautiful natural images: a flowing river, tree-lined fields, a happy child playing. Pudovkin uses the identical method to reveal the other prisoners' thoughts of home when they hear of the intended escape: he uses cuts of fields, of horses, of plowing, of hands feeling the soil. Like Eisenstein's cuts, the shots are related thematically, not narratively; unlike Eisenstein, the images are natural rather than artificial, warm and human rather than satirical. Pudovkin's famous ice shots, with which the film ends, also echo Eisenstein's metaphorical cuts. Pudovkin cuts repeatedly from the shots of marching workers, steadily growing in mass, rhythm, and purpose, to shots of ice flowing on the river, steadily growing in mass, rhythm, and direction. Although the image of the ice-cake echoes Griffith's *Way Down East,* the intellectual function of it does not.

Yet another use of montage for a nonnarrative effect is Pudovkin's cutting of violent sequences; like Eisenstein, Pudovkin knew how to ana-lyze a quick action into its component movements to add emphasis, shock, and drama to the event. For example, in the final demonstration sequence, Pudovkin emphasizes the brutality of the slaughter by breaking the mo-ment of the soldiers' initial attack into thirteen shots [see photographs on pages 190–91]: 1) a gloved hand of the commanding officer is raised, close-up; 2) the soldiers raise their rifles, full shot; 3) the workers see the rifles and start to scurry, far shot; 4) the mother and Pavel embrace, me-dium; 5) the commanding officer's gloved hand drops, close-up; 6) the rifles fire, full shot; 7) a fallen worker's body crashes in a pool of muddy water, close shot, very quick; 8) another worker plunges face first into the water, close, very quick; 9) another body falling, close-up on midsection, quick; 10) the red flag starts to fall, silhouetted against the sky, close; 11) the falling flag and its bearer reflected in the water as they both fall into the mud; 12) the mother and Pavel continue to embrace, medium close; 13) Pavel falls, still locked in the embrace. Out of the violence and chaos of this moment the mother gains courage, picks up the fallen flag and starts walking slowly toward the advancing troops (excellent series of cuts with contrasting directions and rhythms). Though the mother dies, she dies a new woman and a new metaphorical mother of the nation that is born with her death.

Like *Mother, The End of St. Petersburg* (1927) is a story of political education, of a character who betrays the revolutionists early in the film only to join them before the end of it. A young peasant boy from the country must leave for the city to survive; there is neither enough land nor enough food on the farm to support him. Pudovkin draws a visual contrast between city and country with the opening shots of animals, fields, rivers, and trees (precisely the same images as in *Mother*) contrasted with later shots of factories and city buildings and statues. The boy feels dwarfed in the city of St. Petersburg. Pudovkin shoots from high angles down at the boy, making him seem small and worthless in comparison with the huge statues, high buildings, and vast public squares.

The boy, ignorant of political realities, becomes a strikebreaker and betrays the leaders of the strike, one of whom is his own cousin. The boy feels guilty for his betrayal. He returns to the man's home to give the man's wife the piece of silver he received for his information. Pudovkin's skill in narrative cutting and manipulating detail creates a memorable scene. The boy enters the room. He and the wife look at each other, faces motionless, saying nothing. He slowly walks toward her. In a close-up of his right hand we see him slowly and fumblingly pull the piece of silver from his pocket and put it on the table, the same table where the whole family had eaten together earlier in the film. The wife says nothing; she just looks at his face and his coin. The boy says nothing. He slowly turns and walks out the door. The woman's grim silence, a small, seemingly trivial action, teaches him the meaning of his betrayal of another human being.

The second half of the film is a sharp structural shift. Pudovkin abandons the narrative focus on the boy to treat the political events of 1915–17 that converted St. Petersburg into Leningrad: World War I, the February Revolution, Kerensky's Provisional Government, and the October Revolution. Like Eisenstein's *October, The End of St. Petersburg* was intended to commemorate the tenth anniversary of the revolution. Although the film's second half lacks narrative unity (the thin unifying thread is the boy's development into a Bolshevik soldier), it contains some powerful thematic contrasts that Pudovkin draws with his control of montage.

The film makes a brilliant visual contrast between the idealistic glories and the horrifying realities of war. When war is declared Pudovkin shows a procession of marching soldiers, smartly filing into formation. Pudovkin's shot reveals only their bodies from the neck down—their sabres, their uniforms, their medals, their gold braid, their boots. Not their heads. They obviously have no heads. As the parade of soldiers marches off to war, Pudovkin cuts the sequence rhythmically to look and feel like a gaudy carnival: trumpets blare, flags wave, drums rattle, arms wave, girls throw flower petals, an orator speaks (extreme upward angle to burlesque his grandiloquence). From the rhythmic shots of celebration, Pudovkin cuts to a quiet shot of the sky; suddenly a shell explodes, splattering the earth in the foreground. The glory of war has been replaced by the reality. Pudovkin continues with horrifying shots of trenches, fire throwers, smoke, bodies. Not content to let the contrast rest there, Pudovkin cuts back and forth between the violent war at the front and violent men haggling at the stock exchange. While men die in the military war, other men get rich in the financial war. While men die on the battlefield, other men barter at the stock exchange. While men sleep in the trenches, the rich Lebedev sups in his posh dining room.

Pudovkin's next film, *Storm Over Asia* (1928), is yet another story of revolutionary education, of potential betrayal converted into political camaraderie. A young Mongol hunter learns that the value of his pelts is fixed by the greed of the capitalists, who buy them as cheaply as they can. When the Mongol is captured by his people's enemies (he has since joined the Partisan guerrilla army in their struggle against the imperialists), the young man produces papers that seem to prove him the heir of the great Genghis Khan, papers that he has acquired accidentally and that make him the hero's heir only in the sense that all Mongols rightfully share that heritage. The imperialist rulers (the British Army in the original version, the White Army in the American one), however, try to use the lad to keep his own people in bondage. The young Mongol perceives their viciousness, rejects the rich and soft life they offer him, breaks free from his captors, and leads his people in an uprising that sweeps the usurpers off the land.

The film is remarkable in the restraint of the acting (particularly the performance of V. Inkishinov as the Mongol) and in the flowing, exciting sweep of its narrative. *Storm Over Asia* is perhaps the most engaging, most thrilling story of the whole Russian silent era. In addition to Pudovkin's fluid, well-paced, dynamic tale, the film contains three specific devices that are remarkable indications of the director's control of the form. The first is a montage sequence that both deflates the sanctity of religion (probably influenced by *October*) and deflates the pretentions to gentility of the imperialists. Pudovkin cuts back and forth between the religious icons, which are being scrubbed and brushed and polished for a religious festival, to shots of the rich imperialists, who are also being scrubbed and powdered and dressed to attend the festival. These parallel and intercut activities turn the religious objects into pampered dolls and turn the pampered imperialists into dead wood.

Pudovkin's second brilliant device is his use of a puddle of muddy water, an exemplary use of his notion of "plastic material." A puddle blocks the town's main road. When a soldier leads the young Mongol to be shot, the Mongol walks directly through the puddle; the soldier carefully walks around it, taking care not to soil his boots. The puddle instantly delineates the class conflict (reminiscent of Chaplin), the difference between the rulers and the people. Interestingly, when the soldier is later commanded to save the Mongol, he runs directly through the puddle in his frenzy and haste.

The film's third remarkable device is the metaphor with which it ends, a howling, furious wind that strips the branches off the trees and the imperialist soldiers off the land. The wind, like the flowing ice in *Mother,* is a natural image; it symbolizes the spirit of the people, rising irresistibly to blow the foreign element from their soil.

Like Eisenstein, Pudovkin believed that the value of the sound film would be its asynchronous, tonal use of sound rather than a synchronized dialogue and picture. In discussing how he would have used sound in the silent *Mother,* Pudovkin said he would have evoked the sorrow of the mourning scene not with the synchronized sound of the mother's weeping but with the steady, hollow sound of the water dripping into the bucket. Like Eisenstein, Pudovkin had difficulty putting his theories into practice. *The Story of a Simple Case* (1932) was originally intended as a sound picture; it was finally released silent. It is uncertain whether the film's difficulties with sound stemmed from the clumsiness of the director with sound or the clumsiness of the Soviet sound machines and technicians. His next sound film, *Deserter* (1933), is his most respected; it is the story of a young German worker who, like the protagonists of Pudovkin's silent films, receives an education in political radicalism. It was originally intended as a German-Soviet coproduction, but the emergence of Hitler forced Pudovkin to finish shooting in Russia. Pudovkin continued directing and acting in films for the next twenty years, until his death in 1953; during those twenty years he directed only about a half-dozen major films. Like Eisenstein, he was castigated for his formalism and his fictional manipulating of official Soviet history; like Eisenstein, he spent much of his later life teaching and writing. But Pudovkin's few sound films lack the stature of his silent films; he ran out of creative gas when his purely visual method was forced to add sound to his control of the "plastic material."

Dovzhenko and Others

Alexander Dovzhenko was the third of the great Soviet directors. Though he shared both the political philosophy of Marx and the montage methods of Kuleshov with Eisenstein and Pudovkin, Dovzhenko's style was completely original. Unlike Eisenstein and Pudovkin, Dovzhenko came from the provinces, not the capital, from the Ukraine, not Moscow or St. Petersburg. As a result, Dovzhenko's films are saturated in local Ukrainian life and customs as well as in the folk-legend spirit and poetry of the province. Dovzhenko's films desert realism and linear construction even more completely than Eisenstein's or Pudovkin's. His is a world where horses talk, where paintings of heroes in picture frames roll their eyes at the bastardization of their principles, where animals sniff the revolutionary spirit in the air. The Dovzhenko film is structured not as story or even as mass political action, but purely as visual metaphor that develops a theme and allows the filmmaker immense elliptical jumps in time, space, and continuity.

Typical of Dovzhenko's films is *Arsenal* (1929), the first of his mature film poems. Made after three years of apprentice directing in which he converted himself from painter of static scenes on canvas to director of moving ones on a screen, *Arsenal*'s subject is, roughly, the birth and growth of the revolutionary spirit in the Ukraine. Whereas Eisenstein would develop such a theme by showing the action of a human mass in relation to a single historical event, and Pudovkin would develop it by showing a single Ukrainian's revolutionary decision, Dovzhenko's treatment of the theme is unique. The film's structure feels as though the filmmaker spread all the events of the revolutionary years before him on a table and then selected those images and those vignettes that appealed to him. The film darts from place to place, from social class to social class, from political meeting to war to church procession to factory to a train chugging through the snow.

Somewhat like the second half of Pudovkin's *St. Petersburg*, Dovzhenko uses a central figure, a soldier who deserts the czar to serve the revolution, as a loose peg on which to hang the film's action. Scenes with the soldier flow through the film's many vignettes. In the final sequence, the White Army captures the soldier, leads him in front of a firing squad, and shoots him. The Ukrainian soldier does not die; the bullets do not strike him. He stands there defiantly. Although the forces of tyranny can capture a single arsenal, although they can shoot a single rebel, they cannot murder the spirit of rebellion and freedom in the hearts of the people. The Ukrainian becomes a metaphor for that spirit. His presence throughout the film has been as metaphor, not as traditional protagonist. Dovzhenko's films are not narrations of events but metaphors for the feeling and the significance of the events.

Individual images and vignettes of a film like *Arsenal* stand out from the whole. Whereas Eisenstein's geometric compositions show him building with the eye of an architect, Dovzhenko's striking compositions in light and space reveal the eye of a painter. Vast shots of sky and clouds, framed at the left by a tall tree and with the thinnest strip of land at the bottom with a group of tiny men trooping across it, are among Dovzhenko's favorite views. A similar principle of composition controls his snow sequences—vast expanses of white, a peasant wife huddled in black beside a grave in the lower-right corner of the frame, a team of horses bearing the husband's body to the grave in the center reground. Dovzhenko's painter's eye sees the power and tension of shooting with the tilted camera, on an angle to rather than parallel with the world he is filming.

But Dovzhenko's compositions are as impressive for their content as their look. His shots of war, which dwarf men as tiny dots on the horizon or turn them into motionless statues in silhouette against the sky, also evoke the horrors of useless human slaughter. If Pudovkin deflates war by comparing it with theoretical glories on the one hand and financial realities on the other, Dovzhenko deflates it with haunting images of sheer horror. Dovzhenko cuts repeatedly to the frenzied laughter of a German officer who has been gassed, to a frozen smile on the face of a corpse (a smile of death), to a frozen hand sticking out of a pile of dirt (a single reminder that a whole man once breathed the air).

Dovzhenko's style is also dependent on extended metaphors; whole sequences, not just an occasional montage (Eisenstein's slaughtered ox, Pudovkin's ice), are pure metaphor. In *Arsenal*, Dovzhenko shows the journey of a train, loaded with soldiers of the czar. The train has no brakes; it hurtles faster and faster down the track until its inevitable and disastrous crash, murdering the men who are still aboard. The train becomes a metaphor for the unquestioning servants of political tyranny, blindly accepting the murderous orders of their government. Dovzhenko brings the metaphor alive with his control of montage: tracking shots of the speeding train, of some soldiers frenziedly leaping from it just before the collision, of other soldiers contentedly listening to accordion music in ignorance of their impending doom, and swirling cuts when the train crashes into the station. Dovzhenko dramatizes the death of the soldiers by following the career of the accordion, the former instrument of pleasure. Tossed from the train in the collision, the accordion lies on the ground full of air; suddenly it collapses as all the air goes out of it. The "death" of the accordion is a metaphor for the death of all the soldiers on the train.

Dovzhenko's films are of metaphors within metaphors within metaphors, of isolated vignettes, of scenes and characters manifesting themselves without preparation or introduction, playing themselves out on the screen and then disappearing, often never returning to the film at all. The film's general theme and the unity of the director-poet's imagination keep the apparently random scenes together. Dovzhenko's second great silent film-poem, *Earth* (1930), is another series of images and vignettes, this one revolving around the earth, the harvests, the relationships of men, machines, and the cycles of life. His sound films, *Ivan* (1932), *Aerograd* (1935), and *Schors* (1939), were equally daring, equally episodic, equally imagistic. Not surprisingly, Dovzhenko ran into stiff Soviet criticism; he was the most elliptical director of them all. How could his films be socially useful if the audiences could not follow them? Dovzhenko made only two films in his last fifteen years; he died in 1956. The Pudovkin-Eisenstein pattern had asserted itself again—the great innovative mind stifled by the state's ever-narrowing definitions of artistic utility.

Lesser film minds enjoyed healthier and longer careers. Abram Room, whose great silent film, *Bed and Sofa* (1926), combined a sensitive, human study of a love triangle with the social problems of abortion and inadequate housing, continued to make competent films in the sound era. Room's realistic human focus and more conventional narrative plotting were more consistent with the new official aesthetic of "socialist realism" than were the methods of the more adventurous silent masters. Dziga Vertov, innovator of the Kino-Eye, made a trick-montage documentary (*The Man with the Movie Camera*, 1929) that combined his devotion to unstaged reality with his delight in the gymnastic abilities of his recording machine. Vertov's later *Three Songs of Lenin* (1934) combined documentary footage with lyrical passages in homage to the founding father. Esther Shub used montage effects to bring old newsreel footage to life, providing a striking, imaginative, and officially sanctioned view of what it was like to live in *The Russia of Nikolai II and Lev Tolstoy* (1928) and other eras.

In the early years of sound, the more realistic and less elliptical directors triumphed. Perhaps their methods were more congenial with the theoretical demands of the new sound filming. But behind the struggle between realism and abstraction in the films lay a more general battle that was being waged between two conflicting forces in all the Soviet arts: the struggle between socialist realism and constructivism for control of the "true path" of the People's Revolutionary Art. The central arena for the struggle was the theatre, where the principles of Stanislavski's Moscow Art Theatre (detailed, realistic characters; lucid stories of human interaction in a clear social setting) triumphed over those of Vsevlod Meyerhold's "constructivism" (more abstract and symbolic settings; epic stories of vast social forces and movements). The official canonization of the Stanislavski method (despite the Moscow Art Theatre's Czarist and elitist origins) led to the vilification and ostracizing of Meyerhold. (Bertolt Brecht, who first fled Hitler's Germany for the Soviet Union, found a very cool reception there in 1933, for Brecht and Meyerhold held similar theories of the stage.) This conflict of values in the theatre necessarily spilled over into the cinema, where several film directors (Eisenstein, for example) had been extremely influenced by Meyerhold.

Nikolai Ekk, whose *The Road to Life* (1931) was the first great success of the Soviet sound film, found the new socialist-realist assumptions very congenial. His film is both a close, warm study of human feelings and exertion as well as a social lesson on how the "wild boys" of Russia—the homeless juvenile delinquents roaming the streets—found a purpose in life through collective labor. The Vasiliev Brothers' *Chapayev* (1934) became the model for the study of Revolutionary heroes, the human portrayal of a military leader whose great strengths are his energy, his passion, his humor, and his love for the people, and who overcomes his great weaknesses—excessive individuality, a stubborn refusal to study the new ways—to unite his heroic band of guerrillas with the spirit of the entire Red Army. The difference between the Vasilievs's Chapayev and Eisenstein's Nevsky is the difference between the leader as a man of the people and the leader as totem pole or as opera singer in buskins.

The most successful realist directors of the first decade of sound also included Yakov Protazanov, one of the few film directors of the Czarist era to return to Soviet Russia; Kozintsev and Trauberg, who founded the actor-oriented "FEX" group (Society for Eccentric Actors) in the silent period in answer to the montage-oriented Kuleshov group and who continued to make films into the 1960s, including the respected color version of Pasternak's translation of *Hamlet* (1964); and Mark Donskoi, who made the careful, literate biographical trilogy of Maxim Gorky's growth from youth to maturity (*Childhood of Maxim Gorky*, 1938; *Out in the World*, 1939; *My Universities*, 1940).

But for almost twenty-five years the imagination and creativity of the Soviet film was tightly reined by a government policy and aesthetic that found it exceedingly difficult to force innovative minds into the prescribed channels of film expression. During the most critical years of film history, from 1929 to 1937—the transitional years between silence and sound—the Russian film industry was controlled by Boris Shumyatsky, a business-minded bureaucrat who viewed his job as bringing the eccentric, "formalistic" artists in line. Shumyatsky's "bringing the artists in line" was as responsible for the silence of Eisenstein in those ten key years as the triumph of socialist realism. Stalin dismissed Shumyatsky in 1937 for failing to produce enough films and enough significant films; the Soviet filmmakers then enjoyed three years of freedom. But the war against Germany in 1940 imposed restrictions on Soviet directors again; certain kinds of films were needed to boost morale at the front and at home. After the war, Stalin clamped down on the directors again. Only since his death in 1953 have Soviet films regained prestige on international screens with such powerful and personal films as Mikhail Kalatozov's *The Cranes are Flying* (1957) and Grigori Chukhrai's *Ballad of a Soldier* (1959).

The five greatest years of Soviet filmmaking, 1924–29, demonstrated how powerful and important are the effects of simply joining the pieces of celluloid together. In Hollywood, the Eisenstein methods were so admired in the late 1920s that producers began installing metronomes on sets and in cutting rooms to control the rhythms of the movement and cutting. (The metronomic parade and battle sequences in King Vidor's *The Big Parade* would never have been made without Eisenstein and, especially, Pudovkin.)

In the early years of sound, Hollywood did an about-face and began discrediting the jangling, discordant effects of montage. In the 1960s and 70s, however, the quick cutting of television commercials, the tense, violent cutting of action films like *Bullitt, The French Connection,* and the James Bond series, the subjective flashes into the past of *Joanna* and Z, the satiric cross-cutting in *Medium Cool,* and the clichés of cutting in so many student and experimental films, all show that montage is once again very much "in."

Chapter 9

SOUND

According to legend, sound unexpectedly descended on the film industry from the skies, like an ancient god out of a machine, when *The Jazz Singer* opened on Broadway on October 5, 1927. Although the success of *The Jazz Singer* ripped apart the film industry of 1927 with incredible speed, the preparation for sound's entrance had been building for over thirty years. The idea for the sound film was born with the film itself. W. K. L. Dickson even produced a rough synchronization of word and picture as early as 1889.

For the first twenty years of film history inventors worked to wed sight and sound. Many of the same inventors who had developed the first cinema cameras and projectors turned to sound synchronization after the film artists had taken their toys and put them to use. In France, between 1896 and 1900, Auguste Baron, Henri Joly, and Georges Demeny patented various processes of synchronizing moving pictures with sounds recorded on a disc. Between 1900 and 1910, Léon Gaumont demonstrated various synchronized-sound pictures, both at the World Exposition of 1900 and in his own Paris theatres. In 1910, the German film pioneer, Oscar Messter, produced a film with synchronized sound, *The Green Forest*. And in America, the Edison Company had produced a fifteen-minute, synchronized (vaguely), musical version of *Mother Goose Tales* (shot in one continuous take!) as early as 1912. Like the pioneers of an earlier film era, the first sound pioneers decorated their inventions with fancy-sounding Greco-Latin names that practically required a special apparatus to pronounce: Phonorama, Graphonocone, Chronophone.

The first practical, dependable synthesis of picture and sound came just after World War I. There were two primary problems that confronted the inventor of a sound-film process. The first, obviously, was synchronization. How were the film and the sound to be kept permanently and constantly "in synch." The method of coupling a projected film with a recorded disc was dangerous; with two separate machines it was terribly easy for the two to slip "out of synch." The film could break; the stylus could skip. The film musical, *Singin' in the Rain* (1952), a marvelous parody of the transitional era from silent to sound films, revealed the unintentionally comic results when the cavalier's voice issued from the damsel's moving lips. Although the first successful American sound-film process, the Vitaphone, synchronized a recorded disc with the film projector, a more stable method had been developed as early as 1919. Three German inventors had discovered the means of recording the sound track directly on the film itself. Using the principle of the oscilloscope, which converts sound into light beams, the three Germans converted the sound into light beams, recorded the beams on the side of the strip of film next to the image, and then built a reader on the projector that could retranslate the light beams into sound. This German discovery, known as the "Tri-Ergon Process," became the ruling sound-film patent of Europe ten years later. In America, a similar sound-on-film process had been developed by Dr. Lee de Forest in the early 1920s.

An earlier de Forest invention solved the second problem of the sound film—amplification. The sound not only had to be synchronized. It had to be audible. A film had to make enough noise to reach the ears of the thousands of patrons who filled the huge movie palaces. The earliest phonographs and radios, lacking the means of amplification, could entertain only one listener, who stuck the listening tube in his ears (similar to the stereo systems on today's jet airplanes). In 1906, de Forest patented the audion tube, the little vacuum tube that magnified the sounds it received and drove them into a speaker. De Forest's tube gave birth to many children—radio, the public address system—and grandchildren—television, the high-fidelity music system. It also gave birth to the sound film. Whatever the system of synchronization, the audion tube magnified the sound so that an entire audience could hear it.

By 1923 de Forest was making and showing little synchronized-sound films of variety acts, singers, and famous comedians, analogous to the first film strips that Edison made in his Black Maria. De Forest also gave a filmed lecture-demonstration of his sound-on-film process, which he called the Phonofilm. *Singin' in the Rain,* historically relevant as well as brilliantly funny, satirizes the good professor de Forest with its film clip of a horse-faced, nasal-voiced scientist, his nose and forehead grotesquely distorted by a wide-angle lens, stupidly and tautologically telling the audience that it is watching a talking picture. Despite de Forest's success with his sound-on-film process, the Bell Telephone Company's research laboratory, Western Electric, developed and marketed its sound-on-disc process, called the Vitaphone, in 1925.

Western Electric offered the Vitaphone to the biggest producer in Hollywood, Adolph Zukor. Paramount did not want it. Neither did any other major company. Their reasons for rejecting sound were obvious; it was an untried and expensive innovation that could only disrupt a business that had become increasingly stable and increasingly profitable. Sound recording was ticklish and expensive; it would only slow down production schedules. Sound equipment was expensive to buy, and especially expensive for the theatre owners whose houses would have to be converted before any sound film could be shown.

Rejected by all the powerful producers, Western Electric offered Vitaphone in 1926 to Warner Brothers, a family of struggling film producers whose company was near bankruptcy. The Warners had nothing to lose. They were being forced out of the business by the bigger companies, not necessarily because the Warners made poorer pictures (Lubitsch was one of their directors), but because the Warners owned fewer theatres for showing them. Loew, Zukor, and First National controlled enough theatres to choke the market for Warner films. The Warners bought Vitaphone. Three years later Warner Brothers swallowed First National and absorbed many of the theatres in their chain.

The Warner sound films started cautiously enough. On August 5, 1926, Warners presented a program of short sound films; the first was an address by Will Hays praising the possibilities of the sound film, followed by short performances by leading artists of the opera and the concert hall. The Vitaphone shorts were no different from de Forest's earlier Phonofilm novelties. In addition, Warners presented a feature film on the same program, *Don Juan,* with a synchronized musical score. A canned orchestra had merely replaced the live one in the pit. For over a year the Warners presented a series of similar film programs: short, musical sound-films and a feature with synchronized score.

Like the Warners, another lesser producer, William Fox, was a film businessman who enviously gazed up at the Zukors and Loews on the heights; he decided to use sound the same way as the Warners did. Early in 1927 Fox began presenting mechanically scored films to match the Warners'. Like the Warners, Fox also presented a series of short novelty films—performances with famous variety artists and conversations with famous people. In addition, Fox inaugurated the first newsreel film with synchronized narration, the Fox-Movietone News. Unlike Vitaphone, the Fox system, called Movietone, was a sound-on-film process, exactly like de Forest's Phonofilm. One of de Forest's assistants, Theodore Case, had apparently pirated the inventor's system, made some slight modifications, and then sold it to Fox.

Fox exploited the novelty of coupling the sound of the human voice with the picture of his moving lips. In the Movietone short, *Shaw Talks for Movietone* (1927), the audience is amused solely by seeing the image of the crusty playwright, by hearing his voice, by enjoying his garrulous, improvised pleasantries, and by recognizing the mechanical reproduction of other natural sounds like birds chirping and gravel crackling on the garden path. Visually the film is static and uninteresting. It uses only two setups: a brief far shot as Shaw walks down the path; a medium shot of Shaw's head and torso that lasts for the duration of the film (at least five minutes without a cut). Perhaps the only reason the film "splurged" with the second setup is because the honk of an automobile horn (clearly audible on the sound track) "spoiled" the first take a few minutes after the camera started rolling. The moving pictures had become a simple recording device once again. The camera had stopped speaking, speech had replaced pictures.

The tendency of the Movietone shorts to use picture as merely an accompaniment for human speech also became the tendency of the first sound films that tried to integrate human speech and fictional action. *The Jazz Singer* was neither the first sound film nor the first film to synchronize picture with human speech and song. It was, however, the first film to use synchronized sound as a means of telling a story. Most of the film was shot silent and the musical score later synchronized with the finished picture. In this respect Warners' *Jazz Singer* went no further than their earlier *Don Juan*. But four sequences used synchronized speech. In one, the jazz singer returns to his orthodox Jewish home to visit his parents. His mother both enjoys seeing him and listening to his "jazzy" singing. His father, a cantor, does not and orders an end to all profane jazz in his sacred house. The father's command to stop the music is the cue for the film to revert to silence again. In another of the synchronized sequences, Jolson sings his "Mammy" number to an audience in a theatre. The number is exactly like the vaudeville shorts recorded earlier on the Phonofilm, the Vitaphone, and the Movietone—with two differences. In addition to singing his song, Jolson both spoke to the audience and performed for two specific people who were watching him: his girl (backstage) and his mother (in the audience). Jolson not only sang and spoke, but his song played a functional role in the action of the film: the jazz singer had become a successful entertainer.

The schizophrenia of this first sound feature—part silent, part sound—revealed both the disadvantages and the advantages of the new medium. Whereas the silent sections of the film used rather flowing camera work and terse narrative cutting, the synchronized sections were, like the 1912 *Mother Goose Tales,* cinematically static and inert. For Jolson's first song, "Blue Skies," the camera was restricted to two shots: a medium shot of him sitting at the piano; a close shot of his mother responding (used sparingly). Most inert of all is the dialogue sequence: a rambling, improvised series of Jewish jokes that follows the song—a full shot of Jolson and mama, one long take. The two actors obviously squeeze and huddle together so that their voices can be picked up by the microphone that had been hidden somewhere between them. Although the later "Mammy" sequence uses four shots—a full shot of the singer, a medium shot of his girl responding, a close shot of mama responding, a reverse shot from behind Jolson of the audience—the director (Alan Crosland) depended on the first of these for almost ninety percent of the sequence. When the film starts making synchronized noises, the camera stops doing everything but exposing film.

On the other hand, the vitality, the acting, the spirit of the film is infinitely superior in the sound sections than in the silent. Jolson was a poor mime, with hammy, overstated gestures and expressions. But when the actor acquires a voice, the warmth, the excitement, the vibrations of it suddenly convert the overgesturing hands and overactive eyes into a performance that really sparkles. The addition of a Vitaphone voice revealed the particular qualities of Al Jolson that made him a star.

Problems

The Jazz Singer was a huge hit; it put new zip in a film business that had begun to sag in 1927. The movie czars who resisted sound because it would disrupt their stable business now had to convert to sound to stay in business. Although studio executives predicted that the sound and silent films would continue to coexist, the admission dollars of the public punctured the theory. Americans no longer wanted to see silent films; they quickly deserted the old mistress for a more attractive new one. Silent films had taught them to see; the new invention of radio had taught them to hear. They would not leave their homes and spend their money if they could not both see and hear at the same time. By 1929 the silent film was dead in America; Hollywood produced a few silent versions of sound films for foreign theatres and for rural American houses that were not yet equipped for sound. In 1926 a few silent films used synchronized music and sound effects as a commercial novelty; in 1929 a few synchronized-sound pictures were released silent as a commercial necessity.

Although Hollywood leaped quickly into sound production, it did not leap without stumbling. The new sound film caused filmmakers and film critics three primary problems: artistic, technical, and commercial. The camera, which had spent the last thirty years learning to become an active participant in filmed fiction, suddenly became motionless and mute. The camera stood still while the players mouthed their lines. Cuts were rare; visual images became functional rather than expressive. Although the post-Griffith silent film had declared its independence from the stage, the early sound film became the vassal of the theatre once again. Films became canned theatre again; now they could even duplicate the dialogue of the stage hit in an identical film version. The moving picture stopped moving and stopped using pictures. Critics and directors sang a requiem for the film art and said amen.

Typical of the aesthetic blunders of the early sound films was a Warner Brothers "all-talking" film, *The Lights of New York* (1928). The camera stood still to record scenes of seemingly endless dialogue. The director cut sparingly if at all. The characters huddled together so they could all be heard by the single microphone. In a scene in a barbershop, a character began a speech at one end of the room, walked across the room, and started talking only when he had come to a complete rest at the other end. He could not speak until he had parked himself under the mike. In a later scene, two thugs talk to their mobster boss in his office; the crooks sit on the edge of the sofa leaning toward the boss; the boss sits in his desk chair leaning toward his boys. All three actors strain to make sure that their voices can be heard by the single microphone, obviously buried in a canister on a ludicrous table that has no other function in the scene except to hide the microphone.

Worse, the film not only strains to record the dialogue, but the dialogue, once recorded, is not worth hearing. The film's speech is crammed with mixed metaphors ("You think you can take any chicken you want and throw me back in the deck?"), with clichés ("You needed me to stick by you through all the tough times")—with the blatantly obvious and unnecessary. Especially ludicrous are the actors' attempts to render their versions of gangster slang with the most precise, articulate diction. Although the films had learned to talk, they had not learned to talk well. Compared with the fluidity of a gangster film like von Sternberg's *Underworld* (1927), with its completely effective moments of tough violence and subtle humor, *The Lights of New York* was an abominable regression. The outcry of theorists and critics was understandable.

Many of the aesthetic shortcomings of the early sound films were less the result of theoretical problems than of the practical and technical problems of mastering the new machines. Just as the first generation of film directors had to learn to paint with lens and film, the new generation of directors had to learn to both paint and score at the same time. The stasis, the inertia of the early sound films was partially attributable to the difficulty of silencing the whirring camera and partially to the difficulty of recording with a single, fixed microphone. To baffle the camera's clatter, the machine and its operator were imprisoned in a soundproof glass booth. The camera could neither tilt nor travel. The most it could manage was a slight pan. In the era before sound mixing and the microphone boom, a single microphone had to be buried in a pivotal, stationary spot on the set. Of necessity, the microphone nailed the action to a tiny circle. The comic attempts to hide the mike in *Singin' in the Rain*—in a bush, in the star's bosom—are exaggerated but accurate. Movies could not move if they wanted to be heard.

Yet another problem of the new sound equipment was its tremendous expense. Studios invested huge sums for the new machines to record the voice and new soundproof stages to record it in. The theatre owner also faced big expenses, being forced to buy new sound projectors, new speakers, and new wiring to link the two. Both studios and theatres borrowed from the banks to convert to sound. The movies, big business though they were, became subsidiaries of the banks. The two major sound processes in 1930, Western Electric's and R.C.A.'s, were themselves subdivisions of the Morgan and Rockefeller holdings. Studios borrowed from these very banks to buy the equipment that bank money had developed. This interrelationship of movies and high finance has continued for the past forty-five years.

The new invention caused commercial problems with people as well as with paper. Studios suddenly discovered that the popular stars and directors of the silent films were now liabilities in the era of speech. The incoming tide of foreign talent—the Negris and Jannings and Stillers and de Puttis—suddenly reversed and started flowing back to native shores. The actor or director with faulty English had no place in the Hollywood world of dialogue film. Lubitsch, Murnau, Garbo stayed, but most returned home. Native American stars also had troubles with dialogue; their voices had to harmonize with the visual images they had projected in the silent era. The beautiful actress with a nasal rasp, the handsome Latin with a squeaky twang might as well have been unable to speak English at all. Diction coaches suddenly opened offices in the studios to polish the pronunciation of those voices that did not irreparably offend the microphone. Along with the diction coaches came dialogue writers, many of them novelists or playwrights, whom the studios also needed. Old stars and old jobs died; new ones were born.

Eisenstein predicted that the sound film would try to solve its problems by taking the path of least resistance: by drifting into dialogue films, by synchronizing picture and sound, by merely exploiting the audience's interest in seeing a picture and hearing a sound at the same time. Hollywood did just that, grandly advertising its films as "all-talking" and even as "100% all-talking, all-singing, and all-dancing." Gunshots, twittering birds, ringing telephones, banging doors became mandatory sound-film effects. Musical numbers became obligatory. Hollywood imported Broadway directors, Broadway players, and Broadway plays. At least the talk in a play had already been proven and its actors had demonstrated their ability to speak it. As in their earliest years, moving pictures became the hand-servants of the theatre, seemingly forgetting the twenty-five years of development that had created a unique narrative art.

Solutions

While film aesthetes sang the blues, a few creative film artists worked to turn talkies into moving pictures with sound. Two of the greatest directors, René Clair and Eisenstein, refused to throw their handfuls of dirt on the film's grave, certain that the movies could absorb sound rather than the other way round. Hollywood quickly began to solve some of the technical problems. Although the noisy camera had to be encased, it could be released from its glass prison for a few sequences that did not require synchronized dialogue. In *Hallelujah* (1929), King Vidor let his camera roam silently over the fields and then dubbed in the singing of the Negro spirituals. Music in *Hallelujah,* its rhythms precisely synchronized with the visual action and emotional "beats," became one of the powerful sources of the film's meaning and effect—either the exuberant joy of jazz or the soul-heavy sorrow of the spiritual. In *The Love Parade* (1929), Ernst Lubitsch shot ladies sitting in Parisian windows or soldiers marching gallantly in formation with a silent, tracking camera and then dubbed in the song that Maurice Chevalier or Jeanette MacDonald sang. In *All Quiet on the Western Front* (1930), Lewis Milestone shot battle scenes with silent sweeping tracking shots of the lines of attacking armies and then dubbed in the sounds of machine guns and grenades later.

Soon even the dialogue scenes gained mobility with the invention of the camera blimp, a device that slipped over the camera to baffle its clatter without banishing it to a glass island. By 1929 Victor Fleming (in *The Virginian*) could shoot dialogue sequences outdoors, including tracking shots in which men on horseback spoke to passengers on a moving train. And by 1930 Ernst Lubitsch (in *Monte Carlo*) could shoot a long tracking shot on a gravel path in which camera movement, dialogue, and editing worked together with complete fluidity (and cleverness).

Hollywood solved the microphone problem, too. Rouben Mamoulian, one of the directors imported from New York, showed filmic imagination when he suggested using two microphones to shoot a single scene, balancing and regulating the relative volumes of the two with a sound mixer. In Mamoulian's *Applause* (1929), two characters could speak to each other from opposite ends of the room without trotting together to speak into the same microphone. Mamoulian added zip to his film by recording indoor scenes with a moving camera, ceaselessly (sometimes too incessantly) tracking toward and away from the speakers. He shot other scenes on location, taking advantage of actual and interesting New York scenes like the Brooklyn Bridge, the Empire State Building, and the subway, then dubbing in the dialogue later.

An even more flexible method of capturing the voice was the invention of the "boom," a machine that kept the microphone hovering directly above the speaker's head, just out of the camera's frame. Whenever the actor moved, the microphone could move silently and faithfully with him. Although the invention of the principle has been credited to either sound technician Eddie Mannix (at MGM) or actor-director Lionel Barrymore, the idea for the machine was probably born when some director (perhaps Barrymore) improvised by tying the mike to a long stick rather than burying it in a bush or canister or telephone receiver.

Just as technicians began to conquer the mechanical problems of sound filming, film directors began to discover the means of using sound artistically in a primarily visual medium. Even a deadly talkie like *The Lights of New York* contained a few imaginative combinations of sound and picture: the opening sequence of the film evokes the excitement of the city with a montage of city sights and city sounds; the sequence in which the gangsters shoot a cop is staged in enlarged shadows on a wall coupled with the sounds of a shout, a policeman's whistle, a shot, and the racing motor of the getaway car. René Clair was particularly impressed with some of the effects of a mediocre all-talking, all-singing picture, *Broadway Melody* (1929). While Bessie Love watches the departure of her lover, the director (Harry Beaumont) keeps the camera riveted on her tearful face, dramatizing the departure with sound alone—the door slams, the lover's car drives off. In a later sequence, just as Bessie is about to break into tears, Beaumont fades the picture out, a single Love sob punctuating the blank, black screen.

Ernst Lubitsch's first two sound films, *The Love Parade* (1929) and *Monte Carlo* (1930), show a creative film mind wrestling with the problems of integrating sound and picture. Although *The Love Parade* has dull, static passages (the long, posed takes of Miss MacDonald's songs), this first Lubitsch sound film shows him beginning to weave his tapestry of witty dialogue, of clever and surprising uses of sound, and of deft images that imply much more than they show. The film contains many subtle effects that would have been impossible without synchronized sound: the coordination of the valet's physical business with the precise rhythms of his opening song, an adieu to Paris sung by a dog, Chevalier's flippant and charming asides to the camera, the parody of American tourists who do not look up from their newspapers until they hear how much the castle cost to build, the sexual implications of Chevalier's saying "Yes" in answer to the queen's question at the same time that his head is shaking "No," the parody of the wedding ceremony in which the minister emphasizes the reversal of the sexual roles by pronouncing the couple wife and man, the booming sound of cannon (a typical Lubitsch use of a comic Freudian symbol, combining both picture and sound), which both implies and interrupts the couple's wedding night amours.

Several of Lubitsch's juxtapositions of sound and film are dazzling indications of the comic ingenuity that would later develop into a sound-film masterpiece like *Trouble in Paradise.* As Chevalier starts to tell the queen's chamberlain a sexual anecdote (how Madame Curie cured him of a cold but gave him a French accent), Lubitsch cuts to a camera position outside the window. The remainder of the scene is silent; we cannot hear the joke at all. We don't need to. The slyness of silence is funnier than the joke itself. Similarly, as Chevalier and the queen dine tête-à-tête in her boudoir, Lubitsch, rather than showing us the scene inside the room, shows us the queen's ladies-in-waiting, ministers, and servants narrating the scene they can see from outside her window. Sound allowed Lubitsch to develop one of his favorite comic devices: a scene inside a room can be much more interesting and much more fun if the camera stays outside the room.

In *Monte Carlo,* another Jeanette MacDonald musical, Lubitsch's most famous device was his use of the song, "Beyond the Blue Horizon," which was actually a duet between the singer and a speeding train. As Miss MacDonald sings the song, the sounds of the train (chugging wheels, tooting whistle, puffing smoke) become her percussion accompaniment, underscored by the equally percussive rhythms of Lubitsch's cutting. Unfortunately, the Lubitsch innovation soon became a Hollywood cliché: those outrageous combinations of speeding trains, a rhythmic song on the sound track, a superimposed calendar with the dates flying off it to mark the passage of time, or a superimposed series of newspapers whose names reveal the train's progress across the country. Lubitsch's original idea had been an innovative and ingenious combination of picture, sound, and cutting.

The most innovative early sound films, however, were the animated cartoons of Walt Disney. Disney began as a commercial artist and cartoonist in Kansas City; he made his debut in films with animated ads and satiric, short cartoon films—Fred Newman's Laugh-O-Grams. He migrated to Hollywood in 1923, produced a series of short films that integrated cartoons

Jakey (Al Jolson) sings "Blue Skies" for his mother
(Eugenie Besserer) and a frozen, static camera.

The clever wedding of sound
and visual. A cow's teeth as a xylophone.

A film of faces. Joan's (Falconetti), smooth and passionate . . .

and her one compassionate accuser, Massieu (Antonin Artaud), on the right.

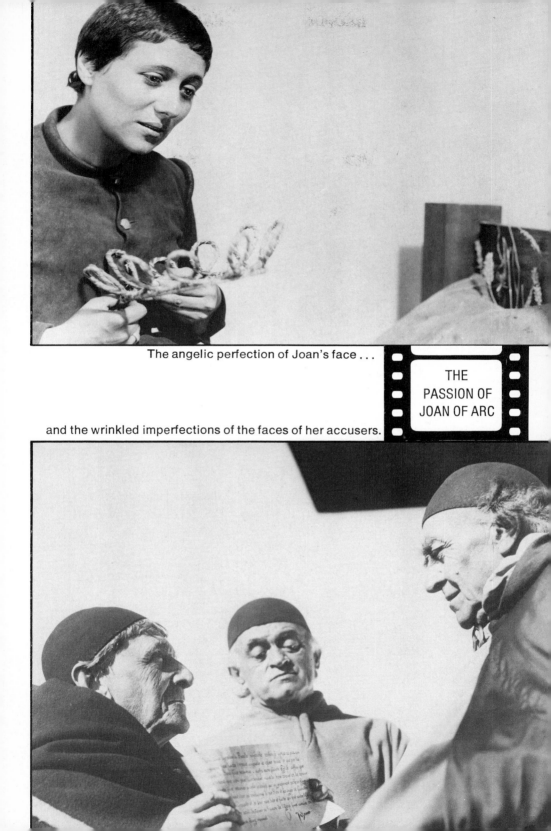

The angelic perfection of Joan's face ...

THE
PASSION OF
JOAN OF ARC

and the wrinkled imperfections of the faces of her accusers.

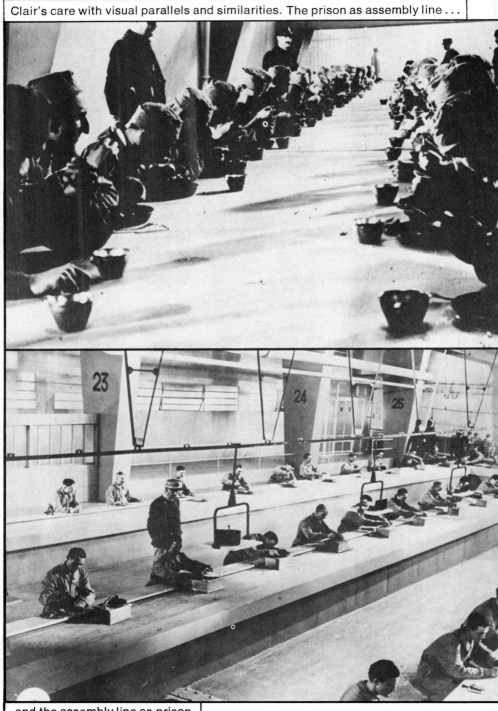

Clair's care with visual parallels and similarities. The prison as assembly line . . .

and the assembly line as prison.

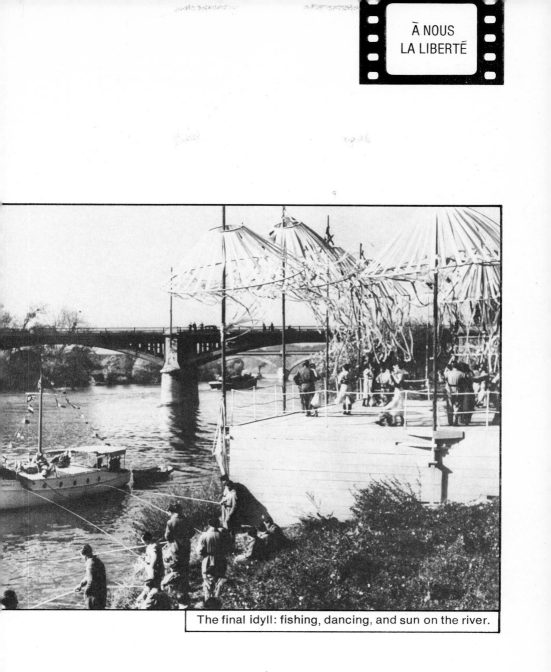

The final idyll: fishing, dancing, and sun on the river.

The coldness of stone and metal. Von Rauffenstein (von Stroheim), Boeldieu (Pierre Fresnay), and Maréchal (Jean Gabin) in the German prison.

Maréchal finds warmth on the little farm. A farm rather than a prison, straw rather than stone, loose clothing rather than rifles and uniforms.

GRAND ILLUSION

GT-13

THE RULES OF THE GAME

The perfect orderliness of conventionalized murder. The aristocrats at the hunt.

The Marquis (Marcel Dalio) with one of his mechanical pets, and Octave, the sponger (played by Renoir himself).

The seething activity in "the gods."

The theatre as life and life as the theatre. Frederick (Pierre Brasseur) as Harlequin, Garance (Arletty) as the Moon Lady, and Baptiste (Jean-Louis Barrault) as Pierrot.

with a living little girl (called Alice in Cartoonland), and, by the end of the silent era, he and his animator, Ub Iwerks, had mastered the methods and art of animation. The "Alice" films, except for the irrelevant, living Alice herself (Disney would again mix people and cartoons two decades later in *Song of the South*), were rich in the mature Disney imagination, particularly in his transposition of physical reality into almost surreal impossibility. For example, as a mouse (Mickey's progenitor) serenades his mousette (Minnie's) in *Alice Plays Cupid* (1925), a barrage of notes flies out of his guitar and streams into her face as she stands on her balcony. The mouse then uses these notes as a ladder, climbing them up to her chamber; that accomplished, he gathers them together with his tail, transposing the ladder of notes into a bouquet of flowers for his Juliet.

But it was sound that turned Disney into one of the most influential producers and respected artists in the film industry. Disney's animated cartoons, which were not compelled to photograph the real world, escaped the tyrannies of sound recording that enslaved the directors of theatrical features. The cartoon—which is pure fantasy, is free from all natural laws, from all human and spatial realities—also granted its creator the same freedom in playing with sound. Just as the pictures could depict impossibilities—animals that act like people, physical stresses that a living organism could never endure—the sound track could be equally free and fanciful. Fantastic, unreal pictures could combine in fantastic and imaginative ways with unreal and clever sounds. The imaginative Disney sound cartoon united three of the great traditions of silent filmmaking and carried them into the sound era: the wacky, speedy physical comedy of Mack Sennett; the fantasy and unreality of the world of Méliès and Emile Cohl in which that which cannot happen happens; and the Chaplin genius for transforming one kind of object into a totally different one.

Disney's first sound film, *Steamboat Willie* (1928), shows complete mastery of the possible counterpoint of picture and sound. The most imaginative sequence is the "Turkey in the Straw" number. A billy goat has eaten a guitar and a copy of the tune, "Turkey in the Straw." Mickey Mouse starts twisting the goat's tail; the notes again become visible, pouring out of the animal's mouth; the music on the sound track accompanies the visual notes. Then Mickey runs all over the boat using whatever he can find as an accompanying percussive instrument. He rattles on a garbage pail and on a series of different-sized pots; he scratches a washboard; he twists a cat's tail to produce syncopated shrieks; he squeezes a duck's throat to produce rhythmic quacks; he pulls the tails of nursing piglets to produce percussive squeaks; he bangs on a cow's teeth to produce the tones of a xylophone. Whereas the method of the silent film was to create meaning by juxtaposing two dissimilar images, Disney perceived the similarity of apparently dissimilar sounds and images. An Eisenstein simile that the workers (visual) are like oxen (visual) contrasts with Disney's that a cow's teeth (visual) are like a xylophone (sound).

The Skeleton Dance (1929), the first of the Silly Symphonies, is an even more skillful weaving of visual action, music, and rhythm. The film's opening sequence—an atmospheric painting of the mood of midnight and goblins—combines the eerie, tense whine of violins with percussive effects produced by an owl hooting, bats' wings flapping, wind whistling, and cats screeching. Then the skeletons creep out of their graves. The surprising activities of the bones are carefully coordinated with the percussive beats of the score's rhythm. Disney is not only sensitive to the possibilities of the kinds of sound that a visual image might generate, but also to the punch of coordinating animated movement with the rhythmic effects of the score. This sensitivity to musical rhythms became the outstanding feature of all the Silly Symphonies, eventually culminating in the cinematic tone-poem, *Fantasia* (1941), and in the wildly surreal evaporations of one object into another of the "Pink Elephants" dance in *Dumbo* (1941). Disney's synthesis of image, music and rhythm had begun with his first sound films. The means of turning sound into a virtue of the film rather than a liability were being found.

Chapter 10

FRANCE
BETWEEN
THE WARS

The French film in the first decade of sound may have been the most imaginative, the most stimulating of its generation: a subtle blend of effective, often poetic, dialogue, evocative visual imagery, perceptive social analysis, complex fictional structures, rich philosophical implication, wit and charm. The maturity of the French film mind in the decade between 1930 and 1940 was partially the result of the growth of the French film mind in the previous decade between 1920 and 1930. The final ten years of the silent film laid the foundations for the great sound structures that would follow in the next ten. René Clair, Jean Renoir, Jacques Feyder, Julien Duvivier, and Jean Epstein all conquered purely visual expression before they began combining picture and word. The sharp chasm that divided the two Hollywood film worlds before and after 1928 was less apparent in the Paris film world. The innovative, experimental minds of the French twenties energetically accepted the artistic challenge of the new talking machine. Although many French plays and playwrights found a welcome on the new French sound stages, just as American plays and playwrights had in America, the French sound film never turned its back on visual expression. The French filmmakers of the silent twenties had learned some very powerful and convincing visual lessons.

Paris of the 1920s was the avant-garde capital of the world in art, music and the drama. It was the city of Picasso and Dali, of Stravinsky, Milhaud, Poulenc, and Satie, of Cocteau and Stein. The urge to experiment, to invent new forms, to challenge artistic norms that had grown so strong in music, painting, poetry, and drama also dominated the new machine art of the motion picture. Paris was the city of many isms— surrealism, cubism, dadaism. Painters exulted in manipulating the pure shapes and textures and colors of paint on a canvas. The painting did not need to mirror life's external reality; it could mirror its moods, its feelings, its tones, its dreams. The world was irrational; art could mirror that irrationality. Plays did not tell logical stories of rational men; playwrights exulted in the irrational, the *non sequitur*. Jean Cocteau wrote a drama about an absurd wedding party at the top of the Eiffel Tower; Gertrude Stein and Tristan Tzara wrote plays whose value was inherent in the sounds of the words rather than their meaning. Colonies of artists would gather at parties to show each other little works they had sculpted, or painted, or written—works devoted to form and sensation rather than to logic and meaning. At these parties some of the artists would show little movies, created on the same formal principles, to their gathered friends. They discovered that of all the arts, the moving picture was capable of the most bizarre tricks with form: a series of purely visual images, of shapes, of lights, of double exposures, of dissolves, a series of worlds out of focus, moving too fast or too slow, upside down or inside out. The lens and crank could be even more devoted to pure irrational form than chisel or brush.

Ironically, the great experimental leap forward of the French film in the 1920s was also a step backward into the past. In 1919, at the dawn of this avant-garde decade, Louis Delluc and Ricciotto Canudo, two zealous film buffs, founded the first of many subsequent French societies for the presentation and preservation of great films of the past. Delluc and Canudo canonized the movies as the Seventh Art and urged attention to the directors of an earlier era: to Méliès, Zecca, Cohl, Max Linder, Jean Durand, Louis Feuillade. The "Seventh-Art adventists" leaped back into the film past about ten years, ignoring the theatrical, stagey, Comédie-Françaiseish, Film d'Arty pictures of the decade of the war. This first generation of *cinéastes* urged a return to the irrational fantasy of Méliès, to the action-filled chases of Zecca and Sennett, to the tricks with camera speed and motion of Jean Durand's *Onésime Horloger* (1910), in which a magical clock makes the world dizzily speed up or lethargically slow down. Like the French *cinéastes* of the sixties—Godard, Truffaut, Malle—the Paris filmmaker of the twenties not only used film history to pack his movies with historical echoes but also to embellish earlier film ideas with his own distinct and personal extensions of them. The Parisian avant-garde filmmaker of the 1920s used one hand to rip up accepted film conventions and assumptions and the other to pull the traditions of the film past into the movies of the present.

The experimental French films of the twenties were of three approximate types: 1) films of pure visual form; 2) surrealistic film fantasies in which tricks with visual form create the surrealistic-symbolic-irrational film universe; 3) naturalistic studies of human passion and sensation in which symbols and surreal touches aid the rendering of elusive human feelings. The three types were far from distinct. A film could begin as an essay in pure form and then change into a surreal dream-fantasy (René Clair's *Entr'acte*, 1924). Sometimes the film would begin as a surreal journey and change into a study of form (Man Ray's *Mysteries of the Chateau Dé*, 1929). Or the film could begin as an impressionistic study of human emotions and relationships only to end as a dream (Jean Renoir's *Little Match Girl*, 1928). Dadaism, surrealism and poetic naturalism flowed into one another to create new and surprising compounds in the movies.

The films of Man Ray are the purest examples of movie dada—of a collage of visual shapes and patterns without any meaning other than the interesting forms themselves. Ray's films began quite literally as collages: he randomly scattered paint, nails, glue, scraps of paper over strips of film, and then processed the results. Ray gradually abandoned such accidental methods for more controlled essays in form: *Return to Reason* (1923), a highly ironic title since the film consciously rejects reason, and *Emak Bakia* (1927). In these films a pair of spinning dice become a pair of spinning lights which become a pair of spinning sticks which become a pair of dancing legs. And so forth. Visual similarities and differences of form control Ray's choice of images. *The Mysteries of the Chateau Dé* moves away slightly from pure visual form; Ray examines the architectural shapes and views of a friend's mammoth villa. In the process he turns his friends in the villa into architectural shapes, too—statues, balls. *Étoile de Mer* (1928) sets a love poem to film, with Ray using two devices to convert words into visual images. He uses the starfish as consistent visual symbol; he consistently shoots the two lovers through softening and distorting panes and prisms of glass. Fernand Léger's rhythmic *Ballet Mécanique* (1924) and Marcel Duchamp's comic jest of spinning spirals and nonsense words (closely resembling Ionesco's puns and plays with sound), *Anaemic Cinema* (1926), also begin with the premise of using a succession of visual images related in form, shape, and rhythm rather than in meaning.

The most famous of the surreal films is the Salvador Dali-Luis Buñuel fantasy, *Un Chien andalou* (1929). Like the title, the film is a series of *non sequiturs*, scenes that seem to be related logically and yet are not related. The film teasingly suggests thematic unities and some kind of structural logic. Its action consistently pairs the same man and woman; sexual desires and tensions clearly dominate their confrontations. Dali-

Buñuel seem to contrast sexual desire and social convention: the stigmata and ants in the man's hand suggesting Christian sin and human mortality, the man fondling the woman's breasts, the two puritans laboriously being dragged along with the equally heavy burdens of pianos and burros, the doorbell in the shape of a cocktail shaker, the asocial bawdiness of the man in his jester's costume. Despite the whiffs of consistent meaning, *Un Chien andalou* is pure dream, irrational, a series of daring and imaginative vignettes with no rational paste between them. From the opening sequence in which Buñuel slits a lady's eyeball with a razor (in intentionally gruesome closeup) to the final one in which the man and woman wander inexplicably on a rocky beach "in the springtime," the film's goal is to excite, to shock, to tickle, to surprise rather than to preach or explain.

On the other hand, Jean Epstein's *The Fall of the House of Usher* (1928) uses surreal dream effects to create the atmosphere for his lucid Poe plot. Epstein uses the tools of cinematic surrealism—slow-motion effects, out-of-focus lenses, contrasts of light and shadow, distortion, cavernous, dream-world sets—as a means of rendering Poe's eerie tale. Dada and surrealism become a means for Epstein, not an end—the means of turning the House of Usher into a house of mirrors.

Even the naturalistic psychological studies of human interaction try to probe beneath familiar surfaces to reveal man's irrational, chaotic passions, often using the devices of the surrealists to illuminate this subjective world. Alberto Cavalcanti's *Rien que les heures* (1926), on the surface a documentary study of twenty-four hours of Paris life, relies on cinematic tricks to paint the city's moody picture: on freeze frames, double exposures, split-screen effects, obtrusive wipes. Louis Delluc's *Fièvre* (1921), a tense story of desire and death in a seamy waterfront saloon, weaves images of gliding ships and a symbolic rose into its tapestry of naturalistic human conflict in the café. Dimitri Kirsanov's *Menilmontant* (1926) uses quick cutting and the sordid atmosphere of Paris slums to tell its story of two girls from the country who drift into prostitution in the city. The films of Germaine Dulac (*The Smiling Madame Beudet,* 1923) and Marcel L'Herbier (*The Late Matthia Pascal,* 1924) use the tricks of slow motion, distortion, and soft focus subjectively to illuminate thought and emotion.

The most grandiose films of the decade—Abel Gance's *J'Accuse* (1919), *La Roue* (1923), and *Napoléon* (1927)—play tricks with the camera's speed, with exaggerated attention to visual shapes and forms, and even with the width of the screen itself. Gance, perhaps the most important commercial French director of the decade, applied the surrealists' concern with cinema form, tricks, and devices to the narrative feature film. Like the surrealists, his tricks functioned to increase a film's subjectivity, its close rendering of a character's personal experience, thereby heightening both the emotional impact and psychological insight for the audience. In his biggest film, *Napoléon,* Gance even adopted a three-screen process (called Polyvision) for his huge crowd scenes, a predecessor of the later Cinerama and other multi-screen processes. The film also included sequences shot in color and in what would later be christened 3-D.

The French director of the 1920s delighted in the games he could play with his camera, in its visual surprises, in its ability to make the familiar world look bizarre. The isms of twentieth-century French painting had also captured its cinema.

The culmination of this decade of film painting was a feature falling somewhere between impressionism and abstract painting, Carl-Theodore Dreyer's *The Passion of Joan of Arc* (1928). Despite its Danish director and German designer (Hermann Warm, the designer of *Caligari*), the film's aesthetics and effects are pure French. Narratively, the film chronicles Joan's long trial and eventual execution at the stake; but the film's narrative structure is merely a skeleton. The picture has no real plot; it is pure passion. The details of Joan's trial are very blurry; the enormity of her suffering, her sorrow, her spiritual fire, her warmth are very clear. The film examines Joan the immense emotional being rather than Joan the historical figure, Joan the militant, or even Joan the religious iconoclast. The sainthood of Dreyer's Joan (played by Falconetti) is not inherent in her words or deeds; it exists within her; it is inherent in her intense ability to feel and suffer and glow. Dreyer's Joan contrasts strikingly with Shaw's, although the film uses some of the identical dialogue as Shaw's play. But in Shaw's play Joan's comments are witty and intelligent and shrewd; in Dreyer's film her words seem totally inconsistent with her passion and suffering. Dreyer's Joan, with her glowing face and shiny, tear-filled eyes seems incapable of verbal expression. Words are irrelevant to her passion. Shaw's Joan is pure mind, Dreyer's pure passion.

Dreyer's film is more a musical Mass in film form than a dramatic story; it is a St. Joan's Passion in the same way that Bach composed a St. Matthew's Passion. Like Eisenstein, Dreyer's sense of cinematic form is more musical than logical. Unlike Eisenstein, whose "music" was the rhythmic, violent dissonance of the twentieth-century symphony, Dreyer's music is the spiritual, passionate calm of the organ fugue or church chorale.

To create a feature film of almost musical sensations rather than story, Dreyer fills the frame with faces rather than events. His camera travels ceaselessly over the faces of the judges and the face of the girl. Huge asymmetrical compositions of human faces fill the screen. The bare white walls of the sets make the richly textured human features and human skin leap out at the viewer. The bareness and whiteness of Warm's decor give the film the flavor of medieval starkness and the texture of abstract painting's clean, sharp lines.

To contrast the passionate saint with her fallible accusers, Dreyer uses two different photographic methods. He shoots the accusers in motion. The judges and priests twist, pivot, and lunge with their bodies and faces; Dreyer keeps his camera moving when photographing them to sustain an even greater impression of movement. The accusers are constantly in motion; Joan is always still. Dreyer shoots her motionless with a motionless camera. The maid's passionate calm contrasts with her accusers' nervous activity, her passivity with their action. Dreyer's camera also contrasts the potential ugliness, the deformities, the faults in the faces of the accusers with the smooth, glowing perfection in the face of the maid. The camera prowls over the faces of the judges, settling on a wart, a wrinkle, a misshapen nose or chin, a roll of facial fat. The shots of Joan, glowingly lit from behind rather than ruthlessly from the front, turn her skin into a milky silk to contrast with the crust and crevices of the skin of her accusers.

For many critics, *The Passion of Joan of Arc* was the ultimate silent film, the ultimate example of the power of purely visual expression. Comparisons of its pictorial beauty and expressiveness, of its artistic wholeness, of its intellectual and emotional maturity with the silly, static talking pictures that were already playing at competing theatres were ludicrous. Critics and aesthetes justifiably watched with horror as the *kitsch* of a Crosland swallowed the art of a Dreyer.

But even the *Joan of Arc,* as moving as its pictures were, contained its own kind of limitations. Although sound and talking were obviously bothersome gimmicks, printed titles—the necessary evil of the silent film—became uncomfortably intrusive in Dreyer's *Joan.* Just as there is something anomalous in his Joan's uttering any words at all, there is something anomalous in interrupting the passionate conflict of human faces to flash printed words on the screen. The titles disrupt the pictorial unity of *Joan of Arc* just as obviously as sound disrupted the pictorial imagination of early talkies. To sustain an unbroken flow of visual images, the film needed sound rather than printed words to perform its vital narrative functions. *Joan of Arc* needed the means of showing us what those compelling faces were thinking, what those mouths were saying. A purely visual cinema, perfectly suited to short, abstract, surreal films, had its own kinds of limitations in the full-length narrative film.

René Clair

Like so many French filmmakers of the era, René Clair mastered the purely visual cinema, the painting-in-motion of the twenties, before he began his assaults on both eye and ear in the thirties. Clair began as cinematic trickster, a choreographer of irrational film ballets; later he used his cinema tricks to turn the realistic and rational world into a place of fantasy and song. Clair looked back with admiration at the zany, frenetic worlds of Sennett, Zecca, and Durand, and that looking backward allowed his own kind of zany frenzy to move forward. Despite Clair's historical influences, despite his maturing as an artist, despite the new adjustments that the talking machines forced him to make, a René Clair movie—silent or sound—is unmistakably Clair. The clearest Clair traits are his delight in physical movement and his comic fancy (falling somewhere between wit and whimsey), which converts two things that are obviously different into things that are surprisingly the same: a funeral becomes a wedding party, a prison is a factory and a factory is a prison, a tussle for a jacket becomes a football game, a provincial French café becomes an Arabian harem. Clair's constant dissolving of differences into similarities is fanciful as well as satirical, designed as much for wildly fantastic, imaginative fun as for social commentary. However, Clair's best silent film, *The Italian Straw Hat* (1927), and his best sound film, *À Nous la liberté* (1931), are those in which his flights of visual fancy drop the most explosive intellectual bombs on the director's two favorite targets—social convention and money.

Clair's first two films, both silent, contained the seeds of everything that would grow afterward. *Paris qui dort* (*The Crazy Ray*, 1923) is the story of a crazed scientist, appropriately named Dr. Craze, whose mechanical ray has put the populace of the world to sleep, paralyzed in the midst of their activities. Only a handful of Parisians avoid the professor's paralyzing power, those who were above the beams of his machine on the top of the Eiffel Tower or in an airplane. Most Clairish in the film is not its story —although the director would always feel comfortable with fantasy—but the clever translation of its premise into visual and physical terms.

Clair has great fun with the frozen human statues that dot the streets of Paris, interrupted unsuspectedly in their daily pursuits: the pickpocket paralyzed as he flees with the wallet he has just lifted from a frozen victim, the unfaithful wife frozen in the arms of her lover, frozen diners in a café, the paralyzed waiter holding the anticipated bottle of champagne. The witty plights of Clair's frozen people are matched by his comments on social values. One of the first plans of the nonparalyzed survivors is to rob the sleeping banks of all their cash; unfortunately they discover that their hordes of wealth have no value in a sleeping society in which there is nothing to buy. Equally pointed is the way the characters resume their old social roles as soon as Doctor Craze reverses his ray and gets society going again. While the city sleeps, crook and cop, socialite and socialist live and play together; when the city reawakens, the familiar social distinctions also reawaken.

Clair's second film, *Entr'acte,* is less satirical and less logical than his first, but it is more fun. The film is pure movement, pure romp, the whimsical, choreographic Clair rather than the social satirist. The film begins with a series of dadaist *non sequiturs:* two men playing checkers on a high building, two others hunting birds on skyscrapers, a ball dancing on jets of water, a ballerina (shot from underneath) whose billowing skirt spreads and shuts like the petals of a flower. Clair masquerades as pure irrationalist, pure film dadaist. But he quickly reveals the sly comical logic in his cinema madness. The two checker players surprisingly see the Place de la Concorde materialize on their checker board; the dancing ball dangles inexplicably in midair, defying gravity, after the spurting water jets have been turned off; the ballerina turns out to be a bearded man. Clair's irrational images are anomalous, nonsensical surprises rather than a "serious" collage of pure form.

The delightful silliness continues in the second half of the film, which develops a more coherent structure. One of the bird hunters has been accidentally killed; society gathers for his funeral. But the mourners surprisingly dress in white; they gleefully throw rice at the departing hearse; a Sennettesque jet of air blows the ladies' skirts up. The hearse itself is incomprehensibly drawn by a camel; the mourners break pieces of the funeral wreaths off the hearse and eat them like pretzels. Suddenly, the hearse starts running away by itself; the mourners rush off after it. A Zecca-Sennett chase begins. Clair uses fast motion, slow motion, traveling shots, interpolated cuts of a roller coaster to add energy and interest to the chase. Eventually the coffin falls off the hearse, the corpse miraculously rises from the box and blithely makes everyone disappear (Méliès stop-action). The film apparently ends as the word *"Fin"* flashes on the screen. But Clair has one more joke up his sleeve: the characters suddenly come bounding through the word on the screen, like dogs bounding through a paper hoop in the circus. The characters cavort in slow motion and then bound back (reverse motion) through the hoop. Clair's bizarre, nonsensical romp finally comes to its final *"Fin."*

Clair's silent feature, *The Italian Straw Hat,* combines the director's romping spirit with his sarcastic sniggers at the pettiness of middle-class conventions. A young bridegroom's horse eats a young lady's straw hat as the groom drives to meet his bride. Since the young lady lost her hat while enjoying an extramarital afternoon with a beau, she must replace the rare hat to allay her husband's suspicions. The young groom must juggle his wedding party with his frantic attempts to replace the mangled hat. He leads the wedding party out of the church and through the city in an energetic chase that eventually culminates in the town jail. Throughout the chase Clair supplements the physical fun with satiric jabs at the tawdry wedding festivities, the pettiness of the silly, middle-class guests, and the inane social conventions that have created both the tacky wedding and the chase for an Italian straw hat.

The addition of sound gave Clair even more opportunities for comic inventiveness. In his first sound film, *Sous les toits de Paris* (1930), Clair—always the choreographer—discovered the effectiveness of using music as one of the film's leitmotifs and as a means of creating the film's fantasy-like breezy spirit. Clair's films became musical films; music became the perfect unrealistic accompaniment for the ballet-like Clair fantasy world.

Clair's next film, *Le Million* (1931), is an even wilder mixture of movement, sound, and music. The film revolves about two favorite Clair motifs—money and the chase. A poor French artist discovers that he has won a million francs in the state lottery; unfortunately, the lottery ticket is in the pocket of a coat that has been stolen by a fleeing thief. The film becomes a furious chase for the elusive jacket, carrying the artist through the streets of Paris, into a den of brainy thieves, and finally onto the stage of the Paris Opera. The ballet-like film appropriately ends in a joyous dance as all members of the eventually successful chase join hands in a singing, dancing circle of celebration.

On their way to this final rejoicing, Clair engages his characters in a series of wild adventures that reveal a startlingly imaginative combination of sound and visual images. When the young man finds his coat at the Opera, he grabs it, only to find that the vain, fat tenor insists on using the old coat as part of his atmospheric pauper's costume. The young man, the tenor, and the police engage in a mock-heroic struggle for the jacket. Clair comments on these mock-heroics by adding crowd noises, officials' whistles, and cheering to the sound track while the men play keep-away in the Opera's corridor. The coat has become a football, the struggle has become a game.

Clair later uses the sounds of the operatic performance on stage to comment on the difference between real love and the operatic clichés of love. As two genuine lovers sit behind the set on stage pledging their love, the fat tenor and the fat soprano, who hate each other, pledge their troth in grandiose song. Clair juxtaposes the saccharine lyrics of the fakey aria with the sincere protestations of the real lovers. Clair then caps his contrast of fake and real love with a dazzling visual joke—by dropping fluttering leaves on both pairs of lovers. The stage hands in the flies let loose a horde of artificial autumnal leaves designed to flutter down on the two operatic lovers on stage. The wonder is that whereas the fakey theatricality of the device underscores the artificiality of operatic love, it, at the same time, converts the more genuine love of the two real, backstage lovers into a tender, lyrical, even magical moment.

But Clair's next film, *À Nous la liberté,* remains his best. Clair combines his comic inventiveness with the thematic wholeness and seriousness that make a great film. Two convicts escape from prison. One of them, using stolen money, builds a huge factory to manufacture phonograph records and machines; the other, his friend in prison, eventually becomes a worker in that factory. The business tycoon eventually discovers that the life of a "respectable" factory owner, with its rules, its social obligations, its emotional infidelities, its devotion to money and machines, is no different from the life of a prisoner. Neither businessman nor prisoner is truly free. The film ends as the businessman and the worker turn their backs on the factory and on money to stroll off down the road, two tramps, finally free of restraint and convention.

Uniting the film is its consistent examination of the term liberty in its title. For Clair, society and freedom are incompatible. Everyone attached to the factory—Clair's microcosm for society as a whole—is a prisoner of his role in the system: owner, member of the board, worker, foreman, secretary, all are prisoners of their particular functions. The film's brilliance lies in the director's translation of this Marxist-humanist cliché into imaginative film terms. The two central characters, one tall and fat, the other short and skinny, are two spirits from the world of silent comedy, reminiscent of Fatty and Charlie, of Laurel and Hardy. Their ultimate choice of vocation —tramp—also echoes the asocial yet human choice that Charlie makes over and over again. If Clair's tramps seem indebted to Charlot, Chaplin later collected the debt by borrowing one of *Liberté's* assembly-line scenes for *Modern Times.* Clair's little prisoner, the Chaplinesque dreamer, sits in his place on the monotonous assembly line. As the unfinished machines roll past him on the conveyor belt, he, dreaming of his blonde lady love (another Chaplin echo), fails to put his particular screw into the destined hole. He scampers down the line following the machine, trying to remedy his error. The assembly line quickly becomes chaos, a heap of unfinished machines and brawling workers. Clair's assembly-line chaos is not only Chaplinesque but a perfect way of showing man's inhuman enslavement to the machines that he himself has built.

Clair's consistent technique for illuminating the lack of liberty is visual parallel. The film opens with shots of men in prison, manufacturing little toy horses as they sit in rows on the prison's assembly line; they eat their meals as they sit in rows in the prison's dining room. Later, Clair shows the factory workers sitting in the same rows as the men in prison, eating in the same formations as the men in the prison mess hall. Factory and prison are visually identical. Prison uniforms have become factory uniforms; prison guards have become factory foremen; prison numbers have become workers' numbers.

Clair emphasizes these visual parallels with his decor. The vertical bars of the prison are echoed by other verticals throughout the film: vertical rows of flowers (they look like flowered bars) in front of the young girl's window, vertical wood paneling in the factory owner's office, vertical bars on the windows of the factory. The factory's bare courtyard looks exactly like the prison yard. The film's music also emphasizes parallels. Its title song, a bouncy march about "liberty," recurs throughout the film; it often has little to do with liberty. As in *Le Million,* Clair juxtaposes the words of a song with contrasting events. The prisoners sing the "Liberty Song" as the film opens; they sing it lifelessly and dully as they work dispiritedly on the prison assembly line. The chorus line of convicts singing about liberty is not only ironic, but also introduces the typical Clair spirit of unreality and fantasy at the beginning of the film. Later, a pretty young miss sings the "Liberty Song" at her bowered window (the one with the flowery bars). Suddenly her song slows down and stops. She was only mouthing the words to a record: another Clair device that is surprising, funny, ironic, and a clever comment on the lack of liberty. Of course, Clair's choice of making the factory a phonographic one is just as much a part of the film's metaphorical wholeness as his use of the prison and the ironic "Liberty Song." The factory turns music into an artifact; that which should be spontaneous and free becomes a machine. Even music lacks liberty in this society.

The film hits its visual and thematic climax in the wild scene in which the social elite gather to honor the great factory owner (former crook) who has created this phonographic empire. The ceremony begins with perfect formality: the guests wearing top hats and tails (symbols of social convention), the orators sitting stiffly on the rostrum, the men standing in formation listening to the boring, droning speeches. Suddenly a wind sweeps (both visual and sound effect) through the factory courtyard. It drowns out the silly speech of the old rhetorician; it blows the top hats all over the courtyard; it scatters the factory's profits—bills of money—all over the ground. The liberating wind turns the factory into a swarming mass of chaotic, free activity. In the most Sennettesque manner, the dignitaries abandon their dignity to chase their blowing top hats and the blowing bills all over the courtyard in frenzied, choreographed patterns.

After this climax, the film's final section—a quiet, peaceful coda— shows the effect of this whistling wind of freedom. The two prisoners become tramps; all the factory's workers sit by the river dreamily fishing; the now totally automated factory continues producing phonographs without any workers at all. In Clair's idyll, the men are free to be men, leaving the machines to tend the machines. It is work itself, and the society that requires its men to work to survive, that ultimately deprives a man of his liberty. Work and freedom are antithetical. If Clair's idealistic solution of this dilemma seems too idyllic, too fanciful in the film's final scene, perhaps the director had the same kind of solution in mind as Chaplin had in

Easy Street or *The Gold Rush*. The obviously facile solution magnifies the problem.

With *À Nous la liberté* René Clair hit an obvious peak of both style and vision. After two less important films in France, Clair made his first English-language film, *The Ghost Goes West* (1936), a fantasy about a social-climbing American who buys a Scottish castle and transports it, block by block, back to Florida. He also transports the ghost that haunts the castle. The film has some very Clairish satire of the American *nouveau riche* (played by Eugene Pallette), but otherwise it is a rather sticky creampuff. During the war years, Clair understandably stayed in Hollywood where he made more fantasies (*I Married a Witch*, 1944), and the most ingenious comedy-mystery by a director other than Hitchcock, *And Then There Were None* (1945). When Clair returned to France after the war, his wit was gentler, the whimsey thicker, the decor more lush. Later Clair films never matched the combination of exuberance, style, cinematic control, structural parallel, and thematic consistency of *À Nous la liberté*.

Jean Renoir

Like René Clair, Jean Renoir started making films in the twenties and reached the peak of his powers in the thirties. Like Clair, Renoir was a social satirist. But there the similarities between the two directors very clearly stop. Renoir's satire was bitter and melancholy whereas Clair's was ebullient and whimsical. Clair's satire condemned institutions and praised the spirit of man; Renoir's satire declared hollow institutions as the inevitable products of erroneous men. Like Clair, Renoir saw that the claims of nature and civilization were antithetical; unlike Clair, however, Renoir never resolves the dilemma by simplistically espousing one of the two alternatives. For Renoir realized both the naïve attractiveness of nature and the incontrovertible fact that human beings require civilization and that for human beings civilization is nature.

Clair's roots were firmly planted in ballet and in song, Renoir's in painting, in the sensitivity to light and shadow, form and texture that he inherited from his father. Clair's physical comedy instantly found itself a home in exciting silent films; Renoir's method matured slowly, requiring dialogue and the structural complexities of the dialogue film before his pictures could paint his personal view of the human condition. If Clair's visual cleverness quickly hit its peak, it just as quickly fell from it. Renoir's canon was fuller, richer, with significant films stretching into the color and wide-screen eras of the 1950s. Clair was the more ingenious, Renoir the deeper, more perceptive artist.

The Renoir silent films are darker, slower, more brooding than Clair's. In *The Little Match Girl* (1928), Renoir adapts Andersen's fairy tale of the little match-seller who dreams of happiness in toyland and perishes in the snow of reality. The film is suffused with the heavy atmosphere of death. The opening sections, Renoir's depiction of reality in the cold, snowy city, reveal the director's impressionistic eye. He paints the world with exaggerated harshness, with extreme blacks and whites: glaring lamps (obvious spot lighting), black silhouettes, grotesque shadows. Renoir's impressionism makes the real world surreal; the visual contrasts of dark and light are that intense.

In the second sequence, the little girl's dream, Renoir is free to play with all the devices of the French cinematic tricksters: double exposures, irrational sequences of images, blurred focus, superimposition. But again the results are strikingly different from Clair's effusive use of the same tricks. Even in the toy shop window the atmosphere is heavy and dark. The shapes of this toy world are jagged and sharp; the lighting emphasizes harsh tones of over-darkness and extra-whiteness. Whereas Clair's lighting is appropriately even and bright, Renoir's is consistently tonal and moody. Even the toys threaten the little girl—soldiers in formation, an aggressive ball, the ominous jack-in-the-box who becomes the pursuing figure of death.

In the final section of the film, the girl and her soldier-protector futilely flee from this black pursuer. Their flight through the clouds becomes a horrifying, nightmare chase, not a joyfully Clairish one; it ends in the girl's dream-death in an impressionistic cemetery. The petals of flowers descend onto her dying body; the petals of the dream dissolve into the snowflakes of reality. The little match girl lies frozen, buried under a mountain of snow. Only a few scattered boxes of matches reveal that she once existed.

Although later Renoir films became less fantastic, the effects of tonal lighting, the overhanging mood of death, the underlying bitterness beneath the superficial gaiety were all constants. Even the utopianly comic *Crime of Monsieur Lange* (1936) ends with a murder and the probable disintegration of a happy human society. A publishing house becomes a joyous communistic utopia for the production of western movies, chronicling the adventures of the cowboy hero, Arizona Jim. Renoir shows his particular debt to the film past with his satiric handling of a movie cowboy, clearly based on William S. Hart, known in France as Rio Jim. Arizona Jim's creator, M. Lange, who has never been to Arizona, becomes founder and father of the happy commune; all workers benefit equally from the films that they jointly produce and in which they all joyfully perform. In this particular film's conflict of art and nature, it is artifice that is truly benign.

But the old capitalistic owner returns to seize possession of his now successful publishing house. To preserve the house's freedom, Lange shoots the boss and becomes a fugitive from justice. The continued success of the

Arizona Jim commune is highly doubtful. Despite the brief era of social perfection and happiness, reality returns to awaken men from the dream world. The disintegration of the social idyll in *Monsieur Lange* seems to speak directly to Clair's creation of such an idyll in *À Nous la liberté*.

Throughout the 1930s Renoir's films threw a cold, hard-edged light on the crumbling social and political structures of Europe. Renoir juxtaposed the tinkle of ironic laughter with the overwhelming sense of dissolution and decay of an effete aristocracy gradually sinking beneath the weight of its own artificial and lifeless conventions, and the new rising classes barrenly following in the empty steps of their former masters. The thirties, in France as well as in America, had become the age of the scenarist, and Renoir's scenarios (which he wrote himself in collaboration with one or two other writers) novelistically emphasized parallel events, parallel structures, parallel characters, parallel reactions, parallel details. The attention to visual and intellectual parallels gave the Renoir film the richness and complexity of the novel. But the literary structures of the films were supported by Renoir's sensitivity to the visual: shots of nature, of faces, of social groupings that visually generate the film's meaning and control its tone. *Boudu Saved From Drowning* (1932), an exuberantly comic clash between a tramp, a pure man of nature, and the stifling conventions of polite, bourgeois society, *Toni* (1934), a sensitively tragic clash between the passions of love and the societal conventions—law, marriage—that unsuccessfully attempt to harness those passions, and an adaptation of Gorky's *The Lower Depths* (1936), which attracted Renoir with its bitter microcosmic study of man in society, all show the director warming up for his greatest films at the end of the decade.

Grand Illusion (1937) is also a microcosmic study. Its superficial action is the story of two French soldiers who eventually escape from a German prisoner-of-war camp during World War I. Its real action is metaphor: the death of the old ruling class of the European aristocracy and the growth of the new ruling classes of the workers and bourgeoisie. The prisoner-of-war camp is Renoir's microcosm for European society. The prison contains French and Russian and English, professors and actors and mechanics and bankers, nobility and capital and labor.

At the top of the social hierarchy is the German commander, Rauffenstein (played by Erich von Stroheim), and the French captain, Boeldieu (played by Pierre Fresnay). Though the two men fight on opposite sides, they are identical: they both use a monocle; they both wear white gloves; they both share the same prejudices and snobberies, the same tastes in wines, foods, and horses. The supreme irony of the film is that the German commander must kill this man to whom he feels most closely allied because the rules of the war game demand that the commanding officer of the prison shoot men trying to escape, and the same rules dictate that the prisoner-gentleman's duty is to escape. The two men are unalterably frozen in their codes, their rules, and their duties. Though the French prisoners live better than their German guards, though they sip fine wine and sup on *pâté de foie gras,* their duty is to escape.

The two tougher, hardier prisoners do escape, while Boeldieu, attired in his white gloves, smartly covers for them and gives up his life in gentlemanly sacrifice. Maréchal (played by Jean Gabin), a mechanic, and Rosenthal (played by Marcel Dalio), a Rothschildean Jew whose family owns banks, land, and several chateaux, escape together from the German prison. The animosities, the tensions, the prejudices of the two men surface when the going gets rough, but the two finally make it to Switzerland—and they make it together. They are the new Europe.

Renoir sustains the film's metaphor with his sense of style, construction, and imagery. The film opens on a gramophone horn; the machine plays "Frou, Frou, Frou," a popular French song; we are in the French camp. A few minutes later, the camera captures a second gramophone horn; the machine plays a Strauss waltz; we are in the German camp. The songs have changed; the camps are the same. Most indicative of the film's tone and statement is the drag-show sequence in which the French prisoners entertain each other dressed as cancan girls in the latest imported Paris frocks. Just before the show, the French prisoners receive word that the German army has captured the French town of Douaumont. Despite their sadness, the show must go on—to show their *esprit.* In the middle of the drag show, the French receive word that the Allies have recaptured Douaumont. Maréchal makes the announcement; the cancan boys stop dancing and rip off their wigs to cheer; they all sing the "Marseillaise." Renoir's shots of these rouged, lipsticked men singing the patriotic hymn—moments before they had been singing a frivolous tune—equates the two songs and exposes the falseness of the emotion, the patriotism, and the seriousness of these prisoners. The patriotic display becomes merely tawdry. Renoir caps the tawdriness by revealing that the Germans recapture Douaumont right after the song. The war is a silly ping-pong game; the men who play it merely puppet transvestites.

Music is one of the film's leitmotifs. The musical trifle, "Frou, Frou, Frou," recurs several times. Another unifying tune is "Il était un petit navire," which we hear for the first time as Boeldieu's ruse to help Maréchal and Rosenthal escape. Boeldieu plays the song on his little toy flute; the tune diverts Rauffenstein's attention, but leads to the French captain's death. Later, on the icy road, when the crippled Rosenthal and the impatient Maréchal quarrel and threaten to separate, Rosenthal starts singing, "Il était un petit navire," in defiance and anger. As Maréchal stalks away from his lame comrade he unconsciously starts to sing the same song. The song ultimately brings Maréchal back to his wounded comrade; he will not desert him again.

Consistent visual imagery is another source of the film's unity. Renoir's camera contrasts things that are hard, cold, and dead with things that are soft, warm, and vital. The story is set in winter; the consistent pictures of snow and frozen ground throw their cold, damp shadow over the entire film. The two escaped prisoners must struggle across an immense meadow of snow to reach safety in Switzerland. Yet ironically, the Swiss border, the place of refuge, is invisible. It is impossible to distinguish different nations beneath a common blanket of snow. Only the German officer's announcement that the two have made it informs us where the snow of Germany ends and the snow of Switzerland begins. That one can make such nationalistic distinctions between things that are really the same is one of the film's grand illusions, an illusion that freezes the human heart and condition to death.

Equally cold is the bare, stony castle that keeps the prisoners captive. And unforgettable is the piece of iron replacing Rauffenstein's chin; it supports his face since his real chin has been shot away. Rauffenstein himself is literally held together by metal—in the chin, the back, the knee—the living embodiment of the film's contrast of the vital and the dead. The one warm thing in the prison-castle is Rauffenstein's little geranium, which he carefully guards and nurtures. When Boeldieu dies, Rauffenstein lops off the one blossom himself; he knows that his world is dead. Emphatically warm and vital are the woman and child, Elsa and Lotte, that Maréchal and Rosenthal encounter on their flight. Elsa's warmth touches the soldier Maréchal, as does her little daughter, Lotte, with her sparkling blue eyes. Maréchal vows to return to this warmth after the war is over. But will he?

In a film so full of disastrous political illusions, it is difficult to determine which is the "grand" one. That war can resolve political issues? That national boundaries exist? That national boundaries do not exist? That class distinctions do not exist? That national distinctions are stronger than class distinctions? That class distinctions are stronger than national distinctions? Whichever of these intentionally paradoxical illusions is the grander, *Grand Illusion* pointedly condemns the decadent, wasteful artificiality of the ruling class that has caused the very war that will kill it. With World War I, the aristocracy of Europe committed elegant suicide. To turn life into a cold murderous game with a series of artificial rules is ultimately to turn life into death.

This implication in *Grand Illusion* becomes the specific theme of one of Renoir's next films, perhaps his greatest, *The Rules of the Game* (1939). The film depicts the dead values of a dead society—two dead societies, in fact—the society of wealthy masters, and the society of genteel, parasitic servants who ape their masters. Both masters and servants value good form over sincerity and the open expression of human emotion. The inevitable result is death.

Renoir's complex structural parallels play two love stories off against each other. In the main plot, a young, romantic aviator, André Jurieux, openly confesses his love to a stylish, upper-class, married lady, Christine de la Chesnaye. Although the rules of the game do not prohibit adultery, they do condemn such frank, open, sincere expressions of it. In the subplot, the adulterous lady's maid begins her own adulterous dabbling with a new servant, Marceau, a poacher, an outsider (like André), not a genteel servant like her own husband, Schumacher. The servants, who ostracize Marceau, are just as snobbish and conventional as their masters who ostracize André because he is romantic and Christine because she is foreign. The two love plots cross paths. The maid's jealous husband, who also has problems observing the rules of the game, mistakenly shoots the aviator, thinking that André is his wife's new suitor. The romantic aviator dies but the game goes on. Marquis de la Chesnaye, Christine's husband, formally announces to his guests that André has met with a "regrettable accident"; the group willingly and unemotionally agrees to accept the baron's obvious lie as a gentlemanly display of good form.

Renoir's sense of style and imagery again sustain the film. Its most memorable visual sequence is the rabbit hunt, a metaphor for the society's murderous conventionality and insensitivity. The wealthy masters go off to shoot rabbits; this hunt, like the lives of the rich, has its etiquette, its rules, its gentility. It is a totally destructive, yet conventionalized form of killing. The servants also serve as accomplices in the murder, for their job is to beat the trees and bushes, driving the pheasants and rabbits out of their cover and into the open where they can be gunned down. Servants and masters are partners in this murderous game. Renoir fills the screen for five minutes with an agonized ballet of helpless, dying animals: they run across the screen accompanied by the bushy scamper of their little feet on the sound track, we hear the crack of a rifle, the furry animal stops, flips, spins, and stretches out (in slight slow motion) to die. The sickening, horrifying beauty of this dance of death is at the heart of the film's meaning and tone. The whole film is a dance of death. While the skeletons dance on stage at the marquis's evening party, men shoot real bullets at one another in the audience.

Visually significant, also, are the faces of the marquis and his guests: they are overly powdered, with tweezed eyebrows and pencilled lips— effete. One of the marquis's friends is overtly homosexual; his effeminacy is merely an extension of that of all the other game players. Yet another of the film's visual metaphors is the marquis's collection of mechanical toys —ornate, clockwork birds and music boxes. The marquis converts the living into the dead, the body into a machine. He collects people—his wife and mistress—the way he collects toys, and he prefers stuffed but predictable machines to breathing, unpredictable people. The marquis's delight in the mechanical mirrors his society's worship of mechanical social rules rather than respect for people, for whom the rules have theoretically been written. The aviator uses his machine to reach his beloved; the marquis uses his as a substitute for loving. The rules of the game and love are incompatible. The sincere, loving, naïve aviator is gunned down—like a rabbit.

And yet Renoir's method is not so naïve as to condemn artifice and praise the simplicities of spontaneity. For one thing, the Marquis de la Chesnaye—Renoir's representative of civilization—is a compassionate, considerate man who is trying not to hurt anyone, whereas the aviator—Renoir's representative of spontaneity—is a selfish, blundering fool. La Chesnaye's human problem is that he would like to achieve an impossible ideal—a world in which the demands of love and order are harmonious rather than mutually exclusive. As he tells his gamekeeper, he wants no fences around his property and he also wants no rabbits. It is not La Chesnaye's fault that the perfect grace of the eighteenth century (the century that produced his chateau, his lifestyle, and the Mozart on the sound track), a world in which the demands of spontaneity and convention might have been properly balanced, no longer exists in the twentieth century with its airplanes, motor cars, bourgeoisie, and the Nazis massing on the borders of France. As in *Grand Illusion,* the source of evil in *The Rules of the Game* is extremely complex: it exists partly in the human personality, partly in the demands of social convention, partly in nature itself, and partly in history, which has posed dilemmas greater than the powers of men can solve.

Renoir's comedies of manners were dark, bitter, and very uncomical. The death, the decay, the antisemitism, the organized murder that Renoir depicted in his films prophetically surfaced with World War II. Renoir, like Clair, made films in the United States during the war: *Swamp Water* (1941), *The Southerner* (1945), *Diary of a Chambermaid* (1946). After the war, he, as did Clair, returned to France. But Renoir's talents had been less dulled by the war and the years in Hollywood. His eye, his sense of style, his perception of social structures and human relationships were still keen. Renoir would serve as an historical bridge, uniting the tradition of French literary filmmaking with the emerging cinematic breeziness of the *nouvelle vague.*

Vigo, Carné, and Others

Not all the French films were successful at combining literariness with the visual powers of moving pictures. As in America, the early sound years in France produced a curious and inert hybrid, the filmed play. "Canned theatre" became one obvious but clumsy way of solving the dialogue problem in French as well as American films. The success of the French playwright, Marcel Pagnol, as a producer and director of dialogue films was symptomatic. But in translating plays for the camera, Pagnol showed more cinematic sense than many theatre-inspired Hollywood directors. He often preferred shooting outdoors to shooting on the sound stage, a very untheatrical choice. He also had the vision to ask cinematically-minded directors to work for him, like Jean Renoir (*Toni*).

The young iconoclast, Jean Vigo, however, was totally unfettered by the theatrical and literary biases of the early thirties. Vigo made only four films—two shorts, one of medium length, one feature—before his death in 1934 at the age of twenty-nine. That Vigo should be free of the deadening conventions of canned theatre was entirely appropriate, for freedom was Vigo's primary theme. Unlike Clair, whose ballet-like romps created a naïve dream-world for the free human spirit, and unlike Renoir, whose films evoke a bitter, sardonic laugh at the human attempts to wriggle free from suffocating social conventions and their own fallibility, Vigo's films show the determined and successful efforts of his characters in creating temporary pockets of freedom in the midst of the society that confines them.

Zéro de Conduite (1933) contrasts the energetic, joyous freedom of childhood with the constrictiveness and restraint of the prison-like school which the children must attend. The boys eventually rebel against their captors, staging a demonstration on alumni day in front of all the wooden guests. They lower the flag of France and raise the skull-and-crossbones. They stand erect against the sky as the film ends. The differences between Vigo's film and the later restatement of it, *If. . . .* (1968), are striking, and clearly reveal the sources of Vigo's imagination. *If* combines its social rebellion with a series of obligatory contemporary clichés: various sexual permutations, a Pirandellian insecurity about illusion and reality, and physical violence; *Zéro de Conduite* tells its story with wild imaginativeness, visual surprises, and comic grotesqueries. The freedom of Vigo's surprising images reveals the spirit of this film about freedom. The one humane teacher consciously imitates Charlot; a line drawing on his desk unexpectedly comes to animated life in the manner of Émile Cohl. Vigo, like Clair and Renoir, had studied his film history.

Surprisingly beautiful in the film is the slow-motion pillow fight in the bare, sterile dormitory. The scene is a metaphor for the whole film: in the midst of the confining, regularized room the children leap and bound, swing pillows, spill feathers in ballet-like slow motion, the feathers falling about their laughing faces and bodies like snow. Indicative of the film's tone is Vigo's handling of the teacher-jailers as comic grotesques (perhaps the Eisenstein influence here). The teachers have sharp, ugly faces or fat, round bodies. They sneak around corners; they steal the kids' candy. Most grotesque of all is the school's principal—a three-foot dwarf with a pointed beard. The highest authority of the system is the smallest man; his mind is as small as his body. Not surprisingly, this snide, iconoclastic film was banned by the French government in 1933 because it ridiculed authority. The film was not shown in France until after the war in 1945 when all forms of repression and restraint became understandably unpopular.

If *Zéro de Conduite* was the young director's youthful, rebellious, sarcastic swipe at authority and the system, his next film, *L'Atalante* (1934) is a mature investigation of two people discovering what is important within the system. Two young people, recently married, discover each other's love, then drift apart and separate, and then find each other again, now knowing how empty their lives are without one another. Tying the film together is the river barge, L'Atalante, where the newlyweds must live. The young man owns the barge, and running the boat is his life. Juliette (the young bride) longs for life on the shore. The barge becomes the source of the plot's complication, the rival that drives the young man and woman apart. What Juliette does not know is that L'Atalante is Atlantis, that life on the shore is brutal, false, a place of hunger, thieves, police, corrupt commerce, unemployment. Vigo develops a Huck-Finnish contrast of ship and shore. The barge, adrift on the river, gliding on the water, in the sunlight, through the fog, becomes an ideal community—man, wife, old crew member, young apprentice—because it is not contaminated by contact with society at all.

The film's opening sequence begins the contrast of ship and shore. The man and woman are married on shore; the wedding party is stiff, formal, wooden; the marriage ceremony feels more like a funeral; the guests seem dead; their faces are unfeeling; they wear black. Only on the barge do the two young people loosen up and begin to feel what getting married really means: not a deadening social ceremony but a fertile union of two minds and bodies. Vigo's gorgeous traveling shots of the barge on the water, either from extremely high or low angles, consistently evoke the beauty of river life. His sincerity in rendering human emotions, which he accomplishes by means of understatement and implication, is evident in the images that imply so much more than they say: Juliette's desire to listen to the radio, her one contact with the shore; the lonely Juliette sitting huddled up alone in the fog; the separated man and woman, each sleeping alone in separate beds (before, they had always slept together). Vigo's sense of the grotesque—a carry-over from *Zéro de Conduite*—adds a unique and symbolic air to the old sailor (Michel Simon), who has made the sea his home, and the clownish peddler (reminiscent of the jester in *Chien andalou*), who evokes Juliette's longings for the life on shore. Because the two young people really love each other, and because Vigo has rendered that love so intimately and so sincerely, we feel complete relief and delight when they return to each other and the idyllic life on L'Atalante. The barge casts off and continues its journey up river.

Like the films of Renoir, the films of Jacques Feyder and Marcel Carné took their literariness from the novel rather than the stage. In this age of the scenarist, both directors were served by talented minds to write their scripts. Charles Spaak (who also wrote *Grand Illusion* for Renoir) wrote the scripts for Feyder: *Le Grand Jeu* (1934), *Carnival in Flanders* (1935), *Pension Mimosas* (1935). Even more fruitful was the collaboration of the novelist-poet, Jacques Prévert, and Carné. Prévert, whose poetic obsessions with fatalism and death dominated even his light comedies (*Bizarre, Bizarre* [1937]), wrote Carné a series of scripts in which admirable men die (for no reason other than that men die), in which men are dragged against their wills into complicated webs of human interactions from which there is no escape, in which men lose what they want and achieve what they do not want, in which symbolic figures of death weave pointedly through the realistic action, in which images of fog and gloom and chaos dampen the film's tone and symbolize the world's emptiness.

Like Renoir, the Carné-Prévert theme, clearly the key theme of the 1930s, is freedom. But whereas freedom is restricted by social convention in Renoir, for Carné-Prévert the limit to man's freedom is the nature of man himself: his fallibility, his mortality, his existence in a completely irrational, indifferent universe. Prévert's existential void is the precursor of Camus's or Beckett's; his characters not only wait for Godot (love is clearly their Godot), but wait for it very incompetently, never attaining the desired love because of some failing within themselves, within the desired lover, or merely within the cosmos. Although the Carné-Prévert films echo the decay, the waste, the death of Renoir's, they lack the surface level of ironic comedy, of polished manners, of genteel laughter. The serio-comic irony of Renoir contrasts with the hollowness, the sadness, the profound despair of Carné.

In *Port of Shadows* (1938), a young soldier, past unknown (all we know is that he is running away from something), is steadily dragged into a complicated human net of murderers, thieves, and outcasts, all because of the woman he loves, who loves him in return. One of the film's leitmotifs is a small dog who follows the soldier (Jean Gabin) everywhere, instinctively, irrationally attached to this man who helped save his life at the beginning of the film. In the same way, the soldier is instinctively, irrationally attached to Nelly. He abandons his own attempts to escape, protects Nelly instead, and is suddenly and unexpectedly gunned down at the end of the film, the victim of his love, his self-sacrifice, his commitment to a human being outside of himself.

The film is dominated by the empty, seamy people who surround the soldier and Nelly: the fat owner of the toy shop, Zabel (Michel Simon), who is Nelly's foster father and also her lecherous captor; the slimy, petty mobster who takes the loss of Nelly as a blow to his self-importance; the nihilistic painter (a Prévert surrogate) who paints death in all his pictures and eventually commits suicide so that the fleeing soldier can use his passport and clothes. The film is dominated also by images of shadows and fog—of rain, of dimly lit streets, wet pavements, shadowy figures in silhouette. The gray muteness of the film is the perfect visual accompaniment to the inexorable closing of the jaws of the trap around the soldier and his love. The trap is life itself; his two ways of facing the trap—fight or flight—are equally unsuccessful.

The richest, the most complex of the Carné-Prévert films, probably the greatest literary-novelistic film of all time, is *The Children of Paradise* (1943–45). As with Dostoyevsky, or Tolstoy, or Dickens, the viewer of *Les Enfants du Paradis* feels he has lived through a very complicated series of interlocking events with a great many complex and interesting figures over a long period of time. The feeling of complexity, of immensity, and of depth in the film is overwhelming. There are four central characters: two actors, a woman, and a murderous thief. Each has difficulty deciding what he really wants; each achieves tremendous material success only to discover that the success is meaningless.

Central to the film is the contrast between the two actors: one, Frederick Lemaître (Pierre Brasseur) is the man of words who acts with his mouth; the other, Baptiste Deburau (Jean-Louis Barrault), is the mime who acts with his body. Although both Frederick and Baptiste are historical figures—two famous French actors of the nineteenth century—the film treats them as metaphorical opposites rather than as biographical subjects. Frederick is the man of surfaces, of words, of fine talk and phrases; he becomes a huge success in cheap, hack dramas which he saves with his own imaginative theatrics; he runs up debts, trifles with the ladies, treats his colleagues with contempt. His life is richly barren. Baptiste is the man of real feeling and the real artist; he is moon-struck; his ability to feel and love makes him the artist that he is. Although Frederick is the matinee idol of Paris, Baptiste's ethereal mime is the delight of artists, thinkers, and the common people.

Between the two actors stands a woman named Garance (Arletty), after the flower, who casually becomes Frederick's mistress although Baptiste is the man who really loves her. The young Garance thought that love was very simple, that bodies were to be tasted and then tossed away when they were empty. Her view of love's simplicity conflicted with the complexity of Baptiste's passion; when she casually offers him her body, he, seeing her as a pure spirit of beauty, declines the offer. Only years later, after she has found wealth and glamor as the mistress of a rich count, does she realize the power of Baptiste's passion, the same power that makes him a great mime. And only then does Baptiste realize that he should never have declined Garance's offer. But when she returns, Garance sees that Baptiste is saddled with a wife, whom he does not love, and a child. The two are just as far apart as ever.

The fourth character, Lacenaire (Marcel Herrand), is not a man of the theatre, but a thief with a taste for murder, a man who lives his life as though it were the theatre. Lacenaire, like Frederick, is another man of words; he writes plays in private and makes embroidered, fatalistic, lengthy speeches about the futility of life in public. He is a glossy, empty servant of death who treats both life and the living as banal jokes; his one passion is indulging his contempt for others and his vain love for himself. He is a man of costumes: of overstarched, overwhite shirts, fancy canes, curled hair, finely spun words.

Carné and Prévert use the theatre as the film's central metaphor. The first and second parts of the film both open on a theatre curtain; the curtain rises to reveal the world of *Les Enfants* behind it. Both the first and second parts of the film end with the curtain coming down. Although the theatre is Carné's metaphor, the film never degenerates into the static talkiness of the canned-theatre films. (Ten years later, both Max Ophuls and Jean Renoir would use the theatre or circus tent as a metaphor without inhibiting the film's cinematic freedom.) Carné sustains his theatre metaphor by paralleling the dramatic, fictional roles of the actors on stage with their actual longings and choices as human beings off stage. In the playlets on stage there are bandits, lovers, police, and deaths; in their off-stage lives there are bandits, lovers, police, and deaths. The on-stage character that Frederick plays—Harlequin—is, like Frederick, bouncy, playful, spirited, charming, superficially happy. Baptiste's dramatic role as Pierrot is like Baptiste himself: sad, mellow, moon-struck, tender, unfortunate. Just as Pierrot loses the beautiful moon lady (played by Garance) to Harlequin, Baptiste loses Garance to Frederick. The theatre is life and life is the theatre.

The title of the film itself is part of its theatre metaphor. The "Paradise" of the title is not a heavenly, metaphysical one, but an earthly one: it is the slang name for the second balcony, the highest, cheapest seats in the theatre, the seats where the masses sit, those who love the theatre and mix intimately in all its passions. The chaotic, seething, energetic masses (the "gods") in "Paradise" parallel the masses just outside the theatre on the teeming, vital, packed Boulevard du Temple, also known as the "Street of Crime." There is no particular order or reason or meaning for all the human activity in "Paradise" or the "Street of Crime." The life merely is; it exists in all its energy, its contradictions, its desires, its disappointments, its feelings. It, ironically, is the only kind of paradise there is. Out of this huge human "audience," Carné and Prévert have merely selected four specific performers to demonstrate their roles. The ending of a drama in life, however, is not always happy, as it is on the stage (except in Baptiste's mimes, which always have unhappy endings). In fact, given Prévert's nihilism, the ending in life is never happy; at the most it is ambiguous.

Weaving through the film is an old-clothes man called Jericho, who is Prévert's symbolic reminder of the sordid, mortal realities beneath all our dreams of the ideal. Jericho, with his prophetic biblical name of death and dissolution, is also a thief, an informer, and an eavesdropper. He spies on people's lives, spreading gloom and doubt wherever he goes. Baptiste hates Jericho, for the old tramp reminds him of the etherealness, the unreality of the moonbeams on which he bases both his life and his art. Baptiste hates Jericho so much that he creates a character just like him for one of his mime plays whom Pierrot kills. In an original version of the script, Baptiste was also going to kill Jericho.

Instead, Jericho merely stands at Baptiste's side at the end of the film. Baptiste has just lost Garance once more, perhaps never to see her again. He follows her through the "Street of Crime," vainly calling her name, trying to attract her attention. But Garance cannot hear him; the swirling masses of humanity slow Baptiste's pursuit, effectively choking him off, keeping him from reaching his love. At his side stands Jericho, a metaphor for broken dreams, unfulfilled hopes, irrational fate, human mortality—the true "crimes" of human existence. Surrounded by all this human activity, so alive and yet so senseless, Baptiste is swallowed by the crowd, by his "audience," and the curtain falls.

Les Enfants du Paradis was a kind of intermission in an era which had lasted for some twenty years before World War II and would last for another fifteen after it. *Children of Paradise* could not be finished and released until after the Liberation liberated both the creative energy and the necessary francs. For the first fifteen years after the war the best French films—those of Ophuls, Bresson, and Renoir—very clearly looked backward to the literary-scenario films of the prewar era. Not until 1959 would the French film imagination strike off in a new direction.

Chapter

11

THE AMERICAN STUDIO YEARS: 1930~1945

In the 1930s Americans went to the movies; in the 1970s they go to a movie. The difference is not merely semantic. In 1938 there were some 80,000,000 movie admissions every week, a figure representing sixty-five percent of the population of the United States. In 1973 there were fewer than twenty million movie admissions every week, less than ten percent of the population of the United States. Over 500 feature films were produced in the United States in 1937; fewer than 175 were produced in 1973. The film industry of the 1930s thrived on a felicitous circle of economic dependence on attendance, exhibition, and production. The huge number of movie admissions necessitated a huge number of theatres, which necessitated a huge number of films to be shown in the theatres, which necessitated large, busy studios that could produce enough films to keep the theatres filled. Only after World War II did the circle of dependence reverse itself and turn vicious.

The need for enormous quantities of films guaranteed the survival of the studio system, which was geared for production in quantity. The huge studios of the 1920s converted to sound by merely adding new departments to their already complex organizations; specialization and division of labor, two pillars of the silent-film factories, became even more essential to the sound-film factory. New departments of music, of sound mixing and dubbing, of sound technicians and machinery joined the older, established departments on the studio lot. The writing department became even more specialized; some writers roughed out general treatments, others broke the treatment into its shot-by-shot elements, and still others added the necessary dialogue.

The film property traveled through the studio, from department to department, from story idea to finished script, until it finally landed in the hands of its director, often on the day before shooting began. After fifteen to thirty shooting days, the director relinquished the negative to the cutting department, which edited and determined the form of the final film, as instructed by the film's producer. Only the most important directors enjoyed the opportunity of shaping the script before shooting and cutting the exposed footage after it. From the cutting department the film went to distribution offices, and from them to the waiting chains of theatres that the company itself owned. The film product rolled down the assembly line from original idea to final showing, all stages controlled by the studio factory. The film industry had evolved its structure for the next fifteen rich years, from 1930 to 1946.

The years of wealth were not without their moments of worry. The Wall Street crash of 1929 exerted curiously little effect on the film business at first. Although America was officially broke, Americans kept scraping up dimes, quarters, and dollars to see movies. The economic sag first hit the movie industry in 1933; admissions sagged, theatres closed, production dropped. But prudent studio economy measures, the aid of government dollars, and a new moralistic path of righteousness nursed the film business back to health.

In 1934, Joseph Breen went to work for the Motion Picture Producers and Distributors of America; Breen's special responsibility for the Hays Office was to serve as official arbiter of movie morality. Breen, a Catholic layman, was pushed into office by the newly formed Catholic Legion of Decency, which advised the faithful to avoid those films that were objectionable either as a whole or in part. Breen published and enforced a formal moral code to keep the films from being objectionable. Movies were to avoid brutality (by gangsters and especially by the police), they were to avoid depicting any kind of sexual promiscuity (unwedded, extramarital, or perverted), and they were to avoid making any illegal or immoral life seem either possible or pleasant (goodbye to the gangsters who lived well until the law gunned them down). The Breen Code made marriage more a sacred institution than a sexual one; the bedroom (with obligatory twin beds) of a married couple became more ornate and holy than a cathedral. Even more restrictive were the new code's specific prohibitions against certain words. Not only were "sex," "God," "hell," and "damn" forbidden, but so were such flavorful and healthy Americanisms as "guts," "nuts," "nerts," and "louse," which were considered deficient in gentility and "tone." Ironically, the code, which Hollywood adopted for business reasons in 1934, perished some thirty years later for the same reasons. The very words and deeds that cramped sales in the 1930s spurred them in the 1960s.

In addition to soothing its audiences' moral fears, Hollywood pulled itself out of the Depression by appealing to its audiences' greed. Double features—two pictures for the price of one—became standard in all but the poshest of first-run theatres. Hollywood added a third attraction to the two movies; audiences could play exciting games between the films—Keno, Bingo, Screeno—which promised to send them home with cash or a set of dishes as well as with many hours of uplifting entertainment. The studios survived the financial crisis of 1933 and profits shot up in 1935; they survived the crisis of 1938 and profits shot up in 1939. The boom years of the war eliminated all money crises for several more years. The film industry enjoyed its biggest business year in 1946.

The studio-system produced an obvious tension between film art and film business. Art cannot be mass produced; creativity does not work in departments and on schedules. Although Hollywood produced some 7,500 feature films between 1930 and 1945, only some two dozen directors and two hundred films maintain their original power and entertainment value (as opposed to their "camp" value) today. Despite the tension between commerce and creativity, there are surprising parallels between the Hollywood film of 1930 to 1945 and the rich era of English drama, 1576 to 1642. Like the Renaissance drama, the studio films were tremendously popular with vast audiences of diverse social, economic, and educational backgrounds. The Elizabethan plays and players were products of repertory theatre companies with a permanent staff of writers, actors, technicians, managers, costumers, and designers, just as the films were products of repertory film studios with similar permanent staffs. Like the Elizabethan theatre company, the film studio spread the acting parts among its regular stable of actors, each of whom played a specific kind of role over and over again—old man, comic, juvenile, leading man or lady, dancer, singer, child. Just as Shakespeare's Will Kemp or Richard Burbage bounced from comic or tragic part to comic or tragic part, Mickey Rooney and Clark Gable bounced similarly for MGM. And like the films of the studio era, the Elizabethan plays were drenched in the theatrical customs, clichés, and conventions of their age: the tragic scenes of Senecan gore, the bawdy use of the comic Vice, the pastoral convention of a magical, fanciful forest. And just as a Shakespeare, a Marlowe, or a Jonson could turn a convention into a trait of personal style, so too a Lubitsch, a von Sternberg, or a Ford could make a studio convention completely his own. The most striking differences between Elizabethan plays and the studio films are, first, that the studios produced no Shakespeare (but then neither has any other art at any other time) and, second, that thousands of the hack, completely conventional, and clichéd films of the 1930s still survive, but only a few hundred (presumably the best) of the thousands of plays written between 1576 and 1642 have not been lost.

There are two ways of looking at the artistic products of a repertory system for the manufacture of popular dramatic entertainment. The critic can look at the greatest products of the system—its Shakespeares and Jonsons—or at its most typical and conventional products. Any fair assessment of the studio system must do both.

Film Cycles and Cinematic Conventions

The studio system controlled both the subjects of film narrative and the cinematic style in which they were shot. Formulas for fictional construction, characterization, decor, and photography dominated Hollywood's films. A key principle in the selection of story material was simply that an idea which had worked before would probably work again. Films were not special, individual conceptions but tended to bunch together as types, in cycles. The new sound equipment introduced audiences to the hard-bitten, tough argot of mobsters; Hollywood produced a cycle of pictures that made the tough talk of gangsters as common as polite conversation around the family dinner table. The first gangster cycle glorified the amoral brutality of the underworld: *Little Caesar, Scarface, Public Enemy*. Later gangster cycles, purified by the anti-violence, anti-illegality sections of the Breen Code, merely put the tough-talking guys on the right side of the law—i.e., on the other side of the badge—*Public Hero Number 1, The Last Gangster*. A cycle of films about prisons, "the big house," spun off from the mobster films; the big house also had its euphonious argot, its underworld morality, its tough characters both behind bars and behind the warden's desk: *The Big House, San Quentin, The Criminal Code*. Yet another close relative of the mobster cycle was the journalism cycle. The newspaperman often seemed like a gangster who accidentally ended up behind a typewriter rather than a Tommy gun; he talked and acted as tough as the crooks his assignments forced him to cover: *The Front Page, Big News, The Power of the Press*. It is no accident that Ben Hecht, the greatest screen writer of rapid, bullet-like, flavorful tough-talk, wrote gangster pictures, prison pictures, and newspaper pictures. The pictures were all variations on the same brutal, tough-guy cycle. And Hecht, of course, had scores of imitators.

A succession of musical cycles accompanied the cops-and-robbers cycles. Just as synchronized sound brought the pungent, brittle crackle of thug talk to American audiences, synchronization also brought the possibility of complex rhythmic and musical effects. Singing and dancing could be synchronized to the exact beat; picture and sound could be wed in their own kind of sound-visual montage. The earliest talking pictures were inevitably singing pictures. De Forest's earliest Phonofilms and Warner's earliest Vitaphone shorts used singers and vaudeville entertainers. *The Jazz Singer* was more a singy than a talky; even *The Lights of New York*—the first of the gangster talkies—used several long musical numbers in Hawk Miller's night club. Musical sequences were almost obligatory in early talkies (even *The Blue Angel* and *Morocco*).

The first musical films were either filmed versions of Broadway shows with their original stars or suave, continental musical-comic pictures *à la* Lubitsch with Maurice Chevalier, Jeanette MacDonald, Jack Buchanan, or Miriam Hopkins. The second cycle of musicals was a series of "backstage" stories—the struggling young composer (who happens to be a slumming millionaire but wants to make it on his own talents), the young hopeful in the chorus (who is catapulted to stardom when the leading lady falls ill), et cetera—with the musical numbers directed by Busby Berkeley. The Berkeley musicals were highly schizophrenic mixtures of the blandest, thinnest dramatic sections and the most dazzling, kaleidoscopic visual style for the musical sections. The effect of the new Hollywood Code on these backstage musicals was especially obvious—particularly in the difference between the tough, vulgar, sexually frank dialogue of *42nd Street* and the saccharine, virginified dialogue of *Golddiggers of 1933*, only six months later.

Other musical cycles included the smoother, more intimate and integrated comedies-of-romance-with-music with Fred Astaire and Ginger Rogers or the ornately costumed operettas with Nelson Eddy, Jeanette MacDonald, Allan Jones, and Risë Stevens. America's greatest composers for the musical theatre, the Gershwins, Jerome Kern, Rodgers and Hart, Cole Porter, wrote original songs and scores for Hollywood musicals. There were musicals with children (Shirley Temple and Bobby Breen); musicals with the fresh, young ingenue, Deanna Durbin; musicals on ice (Sonja Henie); and later, even musicals under water (Esther Williams).

Any successful Hollywood film spawned a dozen imitations. Hollywood's studio years were like the 1960 television years when one successful spy show begot a dozen progeny on all three networks. Like television, the Hollywood of the thirties faced the weekly pressure of entertaining a huge percentage of the national population; like television, fear of a dollar disaster was a constant spur to producing safe mediocrities. The parallels with television programming are even more obvious with those successful films that spawned not only imitations but sequels. The film series was the ancestor of the television series: .the Andy Hardy pictures, the Maisie series, the Charlie Chan films, Mr. Moto, Philo Vance, Henry Aldrich, and—the closest parallel with television of all—the series of films springing from MGM's *Young Doctor Kildare*. Yet another studio formula was to patch together a film with all the available stars on the lot, using some flimsy narrative thread to unite the stars' fragments: Paramount's *Big Broadcasts* (of 1932, 1936, 1937, and 1938), MGM's *Broadway Melodies* (of 1936, 1938, and 1940). The studios made the same films over and over again, with similar titles or different ones.

Formulas for style were as binding as formulas for plotting. Despite the hundreds of different Hollywood directors in that decade, the Hollywood films, with surprisingly few exceptions, looked strikingly alike. The studio system was as pervasive in erasing stylistic differences as it was in blurring differences of theme and story. The director not only inherited a detailed scenario that he could not alter but a completed series of sets and costumes and a studio crew of cameramen, electricians, and soundmen. Any director's impulses toward personal style were suppressed before shooting began by the studio's general policies of lighting, design, cinematography, and cutting.

The key characteristic of film style in the studio era was that sound-films were talking films. The talk was better, now that writers of screen dialogue were men who knew how to write screen dialogue. The scenes of talk were smoother, now that the speakers could move from place to place and both camera and microphone could follow them. But talk, rather than images, still propelled the talkies. The reign of talk produced further stylistic consequences. The camera's position and angle illuminated the speaker and the other characters' reactions to his speech rather than obscuring them in the hope of illuminating something else. Extreme high and low angles, extreme close shots, extreme far shots, tilts, and whirls were uncommon in even the most visually imaginative films. Cutting was as functional as the shooting. Quick cutting distracted the audience from the speaker's words. Montage, one of the most expressive tools of silent films, was reserved for occasional and obvious showcase effects: passage of time, summary of a character's activities. Film lighting was also functional rather than tonal—clear, bright, even—so as not to detract from the speakers. Scenes were lit for the stars, not for the dramatic atmosphere. Designers and cameramen used light to make the pretty people even prettier, shaping their heads with light to make those box-office faces stand out from the backgrounds.

Despite the common assumptions and conventions which the studios all accepted, each of the studios displayed a unique personality in its application of them. Perhaps the two giants—MGM and Paramount—were the most distinctive and the most different from one another. MGM was the studio with almost dictatorial central control—exerted by Louis B. Mayer and Irving Thalberg. Paramount, under B. P. Schulberg, was a much

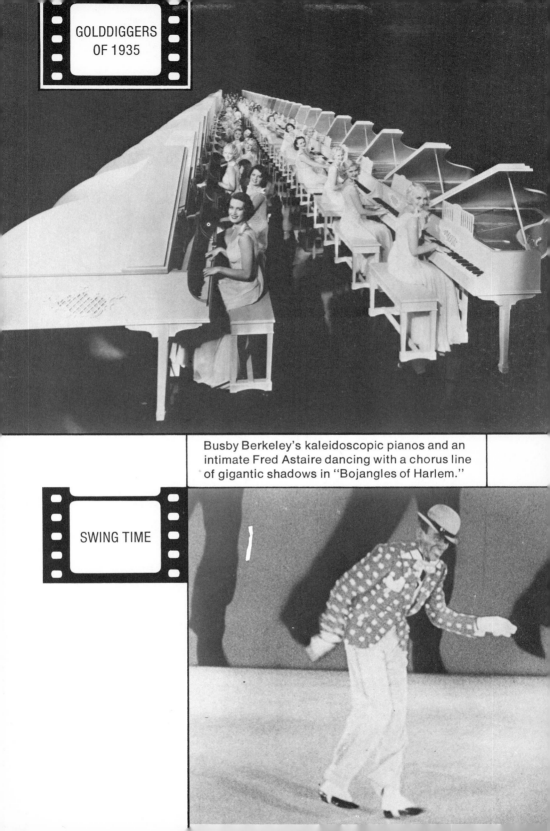

GOLDDIGGERS OF 1935

SWING TIME

Busby Berkeley's kaleidoscopic pianos and an intimate Fred Astaire dancing with a chorus line of gigantic shadows in "Bojangles of Harlem."

Elegant veneers. The two thieves (Miriam Hopkins and Herbert Marshall) use an elegant supper as an occasion for fleecing one another.

TROUBLE IN
PARADISE

The smoky, hazy, chaotic clutter of the night club . . . the antiseptic order and clarity of the classroom. Visual contrasts lead to the film's theme.

THE
BLUE ANGEL

THE BLONDE
VENUS

Von Sternberg putting his Venus through hoops.
Dietrich as sleazy whore and international star.

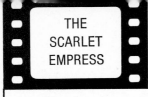

THE
SCARLET
EMPRESS

Von Sternberg's spectacular wedding sequence.

Ford's feeling for people
is reflected in the strength
and humanness of
his characters' faces.

THE
INFORMER

STAGECOACH

Bringing civilization to the wilderness.
Ford's stagecoach slices through the barren beauty
of Monument Valley; inside a rustic shack, Ford's
microcosm of society breaks bread together.

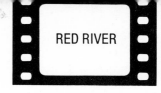

RED RIVER

The climactic clash of egos
(Montgomery Clift and John Wayne).

THE
39 STEPS

Hitchcock's sound-and-picture montage.
The landlady enters the room, turns to scream,
and the film cuts to the shriek of a speeding train.

CITIZEN
KANE

The styles of **Citizen Kane:** the flat
overexposure of the newsreel as the
"newsreel cameraman" tries to get a peep
through the fence at a secluded Mr. Kane . . .

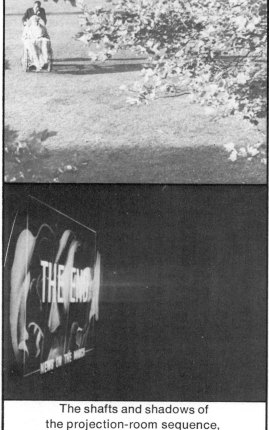

The shafts and shadows of
the projection-room sequence,
almost totally lit from behind . . .

The expressionism of Kane's death . . .

The baroque shadows of Kane's ultimate loneliness.

CITIZEN
KANE

The shot in depth. Jed Leland (Joseph Cotten) and Bernstein (Everett Sloane)
speak in the foreground while Charlie Kane (Orson Welles)
dances with chorus girls in the rearground.

The erosion of time. The youthful Leland, Kane, and Bernstein (Cotten, Welles, Sloane) and the aged Thatcher, Kane, and Bernstein (George Coulouris, Welles, Sloane). In his youth Kane signed his "Declaration of Principles"; as a man broken by both age and the Depression, he signs away his holdings.

Welles' "dissolve-montage." As Jed Leland tells his story
in the foreground, the events dissolve into the frame in the rearground—
a technique Welles borrowed from the stage.

CITIZEN
KANE

looser organization, granting more freedom to individual producers, directors, and writers. MGM was a studio of stars: Greta Garbo, Jean Harlow, Joan Crawford, Norma Shearer, Katharine Hepburn, Clark Gable, Lionel Barrymore, Spencer Tracy. Paramount was a studio of writers and directors: Ernst Lubitsch, Josef von Sternberg, Cecil B. DeMille, Leo McCarey, Preston Sturges, Billy Wilder. In the early 1930s Paramount was the iconoclast's haven: the home of Mae West, W. C. Fields, and the Marx Brothers. The studio permitted the sexual excesses of von Sternberg and the sexual sniggers of Lubitsch. MGM flattened all excesses into a shiny, respectable wholesomeness. When the Marx Brothers left Paramount for MGM they quickly lost their lunacy and their spark. Ironically, in the 1930s the MGM policy seemed the much wiser of the two, for Louis B. Mayer's devotion to family entertainment made MGM the most respected (and successful) film factory in Hollywood, while B. P. Schulberg's chaotic individuality ran Paramount into severe financial difficulties, resulting in the studio's loss of many of its stars (they lost Jeanette MacDonald and the Marx Brothers to MGM) and Schulberg's loss of his job.

None of the other studios were as distinctive as these two at the extremes. Warner Brothers, which invested less money in production values (sets, costumes, crowds), was more dependent on good talk, and the dialogue in the early Warner's pictures was as sharp, as fast, and as good as anyone's. The studio specialized in gangster films, biographies, and musicals, directed by Howard Hawks (until 1933), William Wellman, Mervyn LeRoy, William Dieterle, Michael Curtiz, and Busby Berkeley, and starring such sharp talkers as James Cagney, Edward G. Robinson, Paul Muni, Humphrey Bogart, Bette Davis, Ida Lupino, Dick Powell, Ruby Keeler, and Joan Blondell. Twentieth Century-Fox excelled in historical and adventure films directed by John Ford, Henry King, and Henry Hathaway with Tyrone Power and Henry Fonda, in show business musicals with Don Ameche and Alice Faye (and, later, with Betty Grable and Dan Dailey), and in the folksy comedies of Will Rogers and Shirley Temple. R.K.O. is most memorable for the smooth musicals of Fred Astaire and Ginger Rogers, the suave comedies with Cary Grant, and both the adventure and comic films directed by Howard Hawks. Universal excelled in the horror films—Frankenstein, Dracula, and the Wolf Man—directed by James Whale and Tod Browning, in the later comedies of W. C. Fields, and—at the opposite extreme—in the saccharine singing pictures of Deanna Durbin and Gloria Jean. The two "minor" studios, Republic and Monogram, specialized in cheap Westerns and cheap hoodlum pictures respectively. A later generation of French cinéastes has subsequently canonized the B-offerings of these cheapie-quickie studios as superior to most of the glossier offerings of the major studios.

The studio film of the thirties took the path of Ince rather than the path of Griffith: the American film became an externalized, narrative medium. What the characters did—and, as a corollary, what they said—became the movies' concern. Questions of why they did or said what they did or how it felt to do it or say it became almost irrelevant. Human psychology, the world of sensations and inner feelings, motivation, all became formulaic, the most functional kind of shorthand solely to serve the narrative incidents.

These studio conventions posed the greatest obstacle to the creativity of the individual filmmaker. Not only were the minor directors—the staff hacks, the directors of "B" pictures now needed as the thinner halves of the double features—dominated by studio producers and policies, but even some of Hollywood's most respected directors earned that respect by executing studio commands with the greatest economy, efficiency, and polish. Hollywood's directors were not expected to be poet-painter-thinkers like Renoir, Carné, or Vigo; American directors were more like sergeants than generals, draftsmen than architects. Even when Renoir, Clair, and Lang came to Hollywood to make films, their films—despite obvious touches of personal insight, theme, and composition—acquired Hollywood's slick, impersonal sheen.

The studios forced their best directors to be eclectic. A director jumped from jungle adventure to backstage musical to historical pageant to contemporary comedy to operetta to gangsters. The director's sole qualification for handling so many styles and settings was his ability to get any job done well. He was more director in the stage sense of the word, the man who puts together someone else's idea, rather than a film *auteur*. Discussions of studio directors so often dwell on one's fine sense of cutting, or another's clean use of light, or a third's close attention to costume and decor. To discuss a director as a competent mechanic is equivalent to discussing Shakespeare's control of metrics; it is substituting a means for an end.

Typical of the competent impersonality of the studio era are the careers of Warner Brothers' Mervyn LeRoy and MGM's W. S. Van Dyke. LeRoy, within a three-year period, directed *Little Caesar*, the tough story of a mobster's rise and fall; *I Am a Fugitive from a Chain Gang*, a tough tale of brutality in a southern prison; and the inane "dramatic" sections of the backstage musical, *Golddiggers of 1933*. In those same three years, 1930–33, LeRoy directed twenty other films, including journalism pictures, homespun comedies, and show-business musicals. LeRoy's later work was just as eclectic, from the patriotic adventure, *The F.B.I. Story*, to the heavy, sour musical pancake, *Gypsy*. Although a director like LeRoy obviously knows his craft, it seems impossible to say whether he knows or feels anything else. Woody Van Dyke's films are equally schizophrenic; there was adventure (*Trader Horn; Tarzan, The Ape Man*), light comedy (*The Thin Man* series), costume pageant (*Marie Antoinette*), historical romance with music (*San Francisco*), operetta (*Rose Marie, Sweethearts*), as well as contributions to MGM series pictures (*Andy Hardy Gets Spring Fever, Dr. Kildare's Victory*). To find any *auteur*ishness in the work of such directors is highly pedantic fishing.

The studio era produced several of these "smorgasbord" directors who could be depended upon to cook up a slick, palatable, occasionally powerful product regardless of its particular ingredients: Michael Curtiz (*Charge of the Light Brigade, Dodge City, The Private Lives of Elizabeth and Essex, Casablanca, Yankee Doodle Dandy, Mildred Pierce, Night and Day*), William Dieterle (*The Firebird, A Midsummer Night's Dream, The Story of Louis Pasteur, The Life of Emile Zola, Juarez*), Lewis Milestone (*All Quiet on the Western Front, The Front Page, Rain, Anything Goes, Of Mice and Men*), Victor Fleming (*Treasure Island, The Wizard of Oz, Gone with the Wind*, which was begun by Cukor and finished by Fleming).

In addition to asking their directors to select from the smorgasbord, the studios found that some directors did a better job with a single dish. Some directed comedies primarily: Gregory LaCava (*She Married Her Boss, My Man Godfrey*), Sam Wood (*A Day at the Races; A Night at the Opera; Goodbye, Mr. Chips*), Leo McCarey (*Duck Soup, Ruggles of Red Gap, Going My Way*), Edward Sutherland (*Mississippi, Poppy*). Other directors specialized in adventure films or mysteries: Tod Browning (*Dracula, Freaks*), William Wellman (*The Public Enemy, The Ox-Bow Incident, The Story of G.I. Joe, The High and the Mighty*), James Whale (*Frankenstein, The Kiss Before the Mirror, The Man in the Iron Mask*), Henry Hathaway (*Come On Marines, Lives of a Bengal Lancer*). George Cukor and Clarence Brown, because they worked well with actors and dialogue, specialized in adapting stageplays into films; Mark Sandrich and Roy Del Ruth directed musicals primarily. But even the specialists took their turn at the smorgasbord table—the comic director occasionally being served a costume pageant, the adventure director dishing up a musical.

If the conventional studio films displayed any consistent personality it was one that reflected the general moral assumptions and human values of the era as a whole rather than that of any individual director. Inherent in almost all the films was the view that the sincere, the sensitive, the human would inevitably triumph over the hypocritical, the callous, the chaos of social machinery. American movie audiences, escaping from the realities of the Depression outside the movie theatre, withdrew inside to see human grit triumph over suffering and human kindness triumph over financial, political, and moral chicanery. If the optimism of Hollywood films provided the audiences with the tranquilizer it needed, it also strengthened the audience's belief that eventually good people would make bad times better.

The American film offered not only escape but also subtle propaganda. Whereas the real American lacked the money to buy warm clothing, American movie characters wore fashionable gowns and well-tailored suits. Whereas the real American lacked the money to pay the rent, American movie characters lived in elegant flats filled with expensive furniture. The tasteful richness of the studio films, supported by the inevitable workings of poetic justice in their plots, answered a very deep need in a people working hard to achieve the kind of comfort, ease, and plenty that it saw in the films every week. Just as the cynical materialism of the 1920s succeeded the innocence and purity of the Griffith era, the optimism and wholesomeness of the 1930s succeeded the values of the jazz age. So many of the Hollywood studio films are more interesting as social documents than as personal, powerful works of art. As in the 1920s, the greatest individual directors were those who could avoid the clichéd convention or those who could inject their own personal insight and energy into the convention.

The Comics

Some of the most distinctive American films of the 1930s, as they had been for twenty years, were comedies. Chaplin survived the transition to sound by making no transition at all. His first two sound films, *City Lights* and *Modern Times,* used a synchronized score and sound effects but almost no synchronized speech (like *Don Juan* and other early Vitaphone features). Chaplin was certain that Charlie, the little tramp, was a man of mime, a character who could not survive in a world of words. In *City Lights* (1931), Charlie's pantomime takes him into the society of the rich, where he makes friends with a suicidal millionaire who is friendly and human when he is drunk, cold and callous when he is sober (a possible influence on Brecht's *Puntilla and his Knight Matti,* with the same kind of schizophrenic rich man). Charlie's closeness to the world of the rich allows him to help a poor blind girl who, significant in the Chaplin symbolism, sells flowers to keep herself alive. Charlie scrapes up enough money to pay for the girl's operation; she recovers her eyesight and eventually discovers her benefactor. But Charlie perceives that he and the girl are further apart than ever; she longs for a rich, respectable suitor—not the outsider, the tramp. An agonizingly poignant closeup of Charlie's face ends the film with an unanswered and perhaps unanswerable question. Does the girl accept Charlie for what he is and can the two possibly share a life together? Or are their worlds too far apart and must the tramp take leave of his lady of the flowers, the inevitable loser again?

In *Modern Times* (1936), the little tramp is at the mercy of the immense industrial machinery of our increasingly technological society. But

Modern Times would be Chaplin's last stand against the modern dialogue times and the last incarnation of the tramp. Certain that the pantomimic tramp had no place in a realistic dialogue world, Chaplin dropped Charlot for *The Great Dictator* (1940). Chaplin now played two roles: a little Jewish barber, closely akin to his underdog tramp, and the villainous top-dog Führer, whom Chaplin—with his short, toothbrush moustache—resembled. (Or did Hitler, who loathed Chaplin's spontaneous, compassionate, demystifying comedy, really resemble Chaplin?) The comic action of the film pleads eloquently and ironically for the rights of individual human expression against the stifling, murderous power of the tyrant. Unfortunately, Chaplin discovered that the dialogue film could plead with speeches as well as with comic action. The overt didacticism of the film's final speech, a sincere but clichéd appeal for peace and understanding, loses the power of Chaplin's comic objectivity, which scores its points with shrewd human observation and insight rather than with saccharine sentimentality.

The same overt moralizing and sentimentality cloud the brilliance of Chaplin's last two masterpieces, *Monsieur Verdoux* and *Limelight*. *Monsieur Verdoux* (1947), like *The Great Dictator,* begins with a brilliant serio-comic premise: a delightful, witty, urbane gentleman marries a series of rich women specifically to bump them off, using the dead ladies' legacies to support his crippled wife and child on an idyllic country estate. The film necessarily raises the question of the relationship of the means of an action to its end, whether murder is justifiable if its ultimate purpose is virtuous. The film develops its theme with a series of acidly hilarious vignettes in which Chaplin goes about his murderous business in the most fastidious, matter-of-fact way. Most hilarious of all are his frustrating attempts to dispose of the coarse, clumsy, big-mouth wife played in perfect counterpoint to Chaplin's diminutive suaveness by Martha Raye.

But as in *The Great Dictator* Chaplin deserts comic objectivity at the end of *Monsieur Verdoux* to turn the film's implications into rather bald and pedestrian prose: society commits the same crimes and accepts the same assumptions as Monsieur Verdoux, except on a much larger scale. The explicit accusation was unnecessary. The same blend of comic insight and uncomfortable sentimentality pulls *Limelight* (1952) in two directions. The flashback scenes that recreate the music-hall routines of the old vaudevillian are brilliantly funny and touching, the former music-hall clown's ultimate tribute to the genre that fathered his mime and art. The scenes in the present—of Calvero trying to control another human destiny now that he has lost control of his own—suffer from overstatement and melodrama.

Chaplin maintained his power and individuality in the studio era because he needed to make no concessions to Hollywood's commercial structure, to the new sound machines, nor to the new optimistic temper of the times. Chaplin ran his own studio; the success and popularity of his films guaranteed him theatres in which to exhibit them without having to own them and profits to make more of his own pictures as he wanted to make them without the interference of producer or president of the board. Chaplin's cinematic technique, even in the silent era, was never dependent on montage or intrusive camera work. The unobtrusive cinematic style of the talking films was perfectly suited to Chaplin, whose cinema style had always been unobtrusive, emphasizing what he was shooting rather than the way he was shooting it. Despite his hesitation in adopting dialogue, Chaplin's personal film style was completely consistent with the static conventions of the dialogue film. That consistency is especially obvious in Chaplin's most recent—and anachronistic—film, *A Countess from Hong Kong* (1967), which is striking in its static camera, its lack of attention to decor, its bland use of color, its sticky music (which Chaplin always composed himself), and its heavy, mannered acting by Sophia Loren and Marlon Brando, who were incapable of duplicating Chaplin's deft, perceptive way of adding salt to saccharine.

Walt Disney, like Chaplin, made the transition into the studio era by maintaining his commercial and, consequently, artistic independence. Disney, whose fantasies of sight and sound, drawing and music, movement and rhythm had evolved in the first years of sound, found one further ally in the 1930s—color. Whereas the realistic, live-action studio films were trying to tame the effects of color, to blur its garishness, to make its hues mirror nature rather than some color-mad dream world, Disney's animated fantasies could use such color madness as one more fantastic, unreal element. The counterpoint of picture and music in the Disney cartoon acquired a third contrapuntal line. Shifts in color could accompany the shifting tones of the music. When the action and music became ominous and eerie, the screen world could turn icy blue; when the action and music became heated and intense, the screen world could turn a torrid red-orange. Color, like rhythm and music, became kinetic, not naturalistic. The same advantage that Disney enjoyed over realistic films in the free use of sound also gave him the freedom to manipulate color. Disney brought color to his Silly Symphonies, to his animal characters (Mickey, Donald and Pluto), and eventually to his first feature film, *Snow White and the Seven Dwarfs* (1938).

The Disney fantasies of color and motion were perfectly suited to the audience's craving for happiness, wholesomeness, and optimism in films. His "Who's Afraid of the Big, Bad Wolf?" from *The Three Little Pigs* (1933), not only became a popular song but also a metaphor for the whole country's cheerful defiance of the big, bad social wolf, the Depression. But Disney's happy cleanliness began taking its toll on his visual imagination. *Snow White* was to be a foreshadowing of things to come. Disney gradually deserted the short for the feature, the fantasy-abstract film of color, music, and movement for the sentimental story film that attempted to blend fantasy and realism. Even in 1938 critics noticed a tension in *Snow White* between the fantastic rendering of the animals and dwarfs and the clumsy, sticky attempts at naturalism in rendering the people. The tension resolved itself as Disney moved steadily away from color-sound abstract painting (his *Fantasia* of 1941 was its culmination) toward turning human emotions into romantic, saccharine cartoons of emotions.

A third director of silent comedies found the new conventions of sound liberating rather than constricting. Ernst Lubitsch, whose camera had learned to comment on a character or situation by shooting an apparently insignificant detail that was loaded with implications, discovered that sound, as well as pictures, could make such touches. His first sound films, the continental musicals, taught him the means of mastering the new machines, of making the sound film as fluid and effortless as the silent one. But his greatest sound films were dialogue pictures, slick comedies of manners, translated by his cinematic imagination from the stage into his unique film terms: *Design for Living* (1933), *Angel* (1936), *Ninotchka* (1939), *To Be or Not To Be* (1942), and, especially, *Trouble in Paradise* (1932). *Trouble in Paradise* is such a subtle, deceptively artless film that its bold, imaginative mixture of picture and sound seems completely consistent with the shiny conventionalities of studio-era films.

Trouble in Paradise is the story of an urbane, elegant crook, whose charm and social graces allow him to work his way into the hotels and houses and hearts of the very rich where he performs his clever, high-stake thievery. Eventually the master crook, Gaston Monescu (Herbert Marshall), finds himself caught between his love for two women, Mariette Colet (Kay Francis), the rich perfume heiress he is swindling, and Lily (Miriam Hopkins), his clever accomplice in crime. Because he is a thief, because he is merely a pretender to propriety in the gleaming world of the rich and proper, because his past has determined his future, Monescu eventually leaves Mariette for Lily.

Lubitsch brings this droll carnival of thieves to life with his dry, witty control of picture, sound, and speech. The film opens on a shot of a garbage pail. A man picks up the pail and tosses its contents in his "truck." Except that "truck" turns out to be a gondola, for this is a garbage man in Venice, city of romance. As the garbage gondola journeys on its route, Lubitsch shoots the gleaming water of the canals and the picturesque *pallazos* surrounding them; the garbage gondolier sings plaintively, "O Sole Mio." The romantic song continues as the garbage gondola continues off-screen. Not only has Lubitsch deflated picture-postcard romance, one of the film's themes, but he also has underscored, metaphorically, the film's action, which reveals the "garbage" beneath the pretty surfaces in the lives of the film's "beautiful people."

A later blending of music and picture similarly deflates the world of the rich. When the characters go to the opera, that institution of snobbery and social status, Lubitsch summarizes the proceedings by concentrating on the conductor's score. With the camera riveted on that score, the soprano torridly sings (off-screen), "I love you, I love you." Then the pages begin to riffle, steadily turning by themselves to some point near the end of the opera. The soprano just as torridly sings (still off-screen) with the same notes, "I hate you, I hate you." The device is a brilliant means of handling the passing of time, of ridiculing opera plots and passions, and of burlesquing the values of high society that makes attending such drivel both fashionable and necessary.

Lubitsch handles Monescu's sexual relationships with his two ladies with the greatest wryness and subtlety. In the first sequence, Lily and Monescu fall in love by discovering each other's crooked cleverness. The two sit in Monescu's elegant hotel suite, eating supper and drinking wine. As the two trade polished banalities they subtly steal each other's watches, wallets, jewelry. After discovering and sorting out each other's goods, Monescu bends over to kiss Lily as she sits on a sofa. Lubitsch dissolves to an empty sofa. Then he cuts to a male arm, hanging a "Do Not Disturb" sign on the door of his hotel room. The implications of these cuts are obvious, clearly a sign of the screen's pre-Breen sexual maturity. Similarly pre-Breen are the sequences revealing Madame Colet's relationship with Monescu. Lubitsch enjoys keeping his camera in the corridor of Madame's house, coyly showing the two doors outside Madame's bedroom and outside Monescu's bedroom. One can never be sure whether Monescu will come out of his bedroom door or Madame's, or whether she will come out of hers or his.

Add to Lubitsch's subtle images and clever music his satiric handling of the minor characters, themselves rich fools or covert crooks (Edward Everett Horton, Charles Ruggles, C. Aubrey Smith), and Samson Raphaelson's sparkling, effortless dialogue, which consistently pins a new tail on an old cliché: "A bird in the hand is worth two in jail"; "If you behave like a gentleman, I'll break your neck"; "I love you as a crook, but don't become one of those useless, good-for-nothing heels"; "a member of the *nouveau poor*." The combined ingredients make *Trouble in Paradise* the most polished comedy of manners of the American film.

Frank Capra also directed comedies of manners. But instead of the suave manners of a shiny Europe in Lubitsch's films, Capra focused on the ingenuous, homespun manners of the most American America. Although Capra's career in films stems back to silent comedy when he was a gag man and staff director at both the Sennett and the Hal Roach studios, Capra became an important director in the era of the talkies after he had come to the then tiny Columbia studio. There he met Robert Riskin, the man who was to write all his important scripts. The Capra-Riskin film was generally a witty contemporary morality play that pitted a good man—inevitably a "little guy" who is naive, sincere, folksy, unaffected, unintellectual, apolitical—against evil social forces: money, politics, affectation, social status, human insensitivity. The "little guy" converts the social heretics to the human truth, usually by making the film's heroine, who embodies the false societal assumptions, fall in love with him. The "little guy" emerges from the struggle not only victorious but also wiser about the sorry ways of the world.

It Happened One Night (1934) examines the clash of a snooping newspaper reporter (Clark Gable) and a rich, society girl (Claudette Colbert) fleeing her wealthy father toward the worthless marriage she wants to make. The two travel cross-country by bus, discovering the hazards as well as the charms of rural, uncitified America—motels, bad roads, hitchhiking, and, most significantly, people. In Mr. Deeds Goes to Town (1936), a young man from the country (Gary Cooper) inherits a pile of money and comes to the city to discover how to spend it. The city folk belittle the country ways of the hero "hick," and leading the laughter is the snobbish lady reporter (Jean Arthur) with whom Deeds has fallen in love. Deeds eventually converts the lady and eventually discovers that he must use his money to help the poor and starving. A whole family of happy, poor, humane eccentrics struggles comically against the forces of money, sophistication, and industrialization in You Can't Take It With You (1938). In Mr. Smith Goes to Washington (1939), Mr. Deeds has merely changed his name to Smith and his problem has changed from money to politics. Although Capra was no cinematic innovator, and although his vision seems corny and populistic today, the consistency of Capra's material, his solid scripts, the perceptive comic characterizations, the informal, understated acting in his films all make them sincere and clever statements of the era's conventional optimism and folksy humanism.

As with the silent comedies, many of the sound comedies wore the personalities of their comics rather than their directors. Because Langdon and Keaton and other purely pantomimic clowns who were schooled in the silent tradition never successfully combined talk and movement, Hollywood imported clowns from Broadway who had already effected the combination. The Marx Brothers even shot their first films in New York. In 1929 they recreated their current stage hit, Cocoanuts, for the screen. The Marx Brothers combined the great traditions of American physical comedy with a verbal humor that perfectly suited their physical types. The Marx Brothers looked funny: Groucho's moustache and eyebrows and baggy pants, Chico's hats and bulbous eyes, Harpo's hair and silly smiles. The Marx Brothers talked funny: Groucho's nasal gravel, Chico's accent, Harpo's beeps. And the Marx Brothers walked funny. Like the Sennett silent comedies, the plots of the Marx Brothers' films were irrelevant: romantic clichés with obligatory musical numbers and sappy doings of the juvenile and ingenue. The zany comics inevitably dropped into this conventional world, and while it went about its predictable, Hollywoody business, they merely did their own unpredictable things.

Those unpredictable things were either visual insanities or verbal ones. The great silent comedies have no funnier sequences than many of those in the Marx films: the football sequence in *Horsefeathers* (1932), the mirror scene in *Duck Soup* (1933), the stateroom packed with human sardines in *A Night at the Opera* (1936) or the split-second timing of the bed-shifting sequence in the same film, the scene in which the brothers invade the midget's teeny room with the teeny furniture in *At the Circus* (1939), the "more wood" sequence in *Go West* (1940), in which the brothers strip a train to keep the locomotive racing. And for brilliant verbal double talk there is the "Why-a-duck?" sequence in *Cocoanuts* in which Groucho tries to sell Chico a piece of island property with a viaduct (why-a-duck), the "Party of the First Part" sequence in *A Night at the Opera* in which Groucho and Chico burlesque legalistic jargon by tearing apart a contract (literally) clause by clause, and there is the "Tootsie Frootsie Ice Cream" sequence of *A Day at the Races* (1937) in which Chico sells Groucho a coded manual for betting the ponies, and then another manual to decode the first manual, and then yet another manual to decode that manual, and so forth to infinity. The Marx Brothers films revealed the key elements of American sound comedy—comic physical types, suited to their comic personalities, suited to the physical-comic situations, suited to the verbal wit. Comic talkies had to move as well as talk.

Another Broadway import—Mae West—fulfilled the same comic formula. Miss West had her comic personality, a parody of the amoral, sensual female who frankly enjoyed nice clothes, nice food, and a nice tumble in the hay. She physically suited that personality. No petite, lithe, virginal ingenue was Mae, but a buxom, hefty broad who looked like a cross between a curvy stripper and a fullback for Notre Dame. Her rolling eyes, her gyrating hips, her falling, throaty voice consciously tried to unmask an opponent or undress a friend. And her comic lines fit the eyes, the voice, and the body: "Beulah, peel me a grape"; "Are you packin' a rod or are you just glad to see me?" Even her croaking "Oh" was more a sigh than an exclamation and said much more than oh. Like the Marx Brothers' plots, Mae West's film stories, which she wrote herself, were slender lines on which to hang her own personal business: her gyrations, her groans, her comments, her songs. The films' action inevitably ran Mae up against the wall of respectability and legality. And if she avoided prison and legal censure at the end of the film, it was primarily because her impulses were human and sympathetic even if her activities were against the law.

Ironically, only one Mae West film, *She Done Him Wrong* (1933), is, because of its pre-Breen date, a real Mae West film. Most suggestive (and most characteristic of Mae's style) in the film are her songs. One of them is her set of dirty lyrics to the familiar tune, "Frankie and Johnny"; after all, Frankie didn't shoot Johnny just because she saw him with another woman in a public bar. The second song was often referred to as "THAT song"; its noneuphemistic title was "I Like a Guy What Takes His Time" and its subject was exactly what the title implies it to be. A third song, "I Wonder Where My Easy Rider's Gone," was not about horse-back riding.

The effect of the Breen Code was obvious in Mae's film of only one year later, *Belle of the Nineties*. In this film she sings "My Old Flame," and, although the significance of the flame is clear in the innuendoes of her eyes and voice, it has no explicit life in the song's lyrics. Despite the financial success of *She Done Him Wrong*, Mae West's film career was cut up and cut short by the moralistic scissors of the Breen sanctions against sexuality and the glamorous portrayal of vice. In her later films—*Goin' to Town* (1935), *Klondike Annie* (1936), and even *My Little Chickadee* (1940) with W. C. Fields—Mae West becomes a sterilized, clean-scrubbed caricature of her own sexuality, which was, in its original frankness, a caricature of sexuality in the first place.

W. C. Fields was another great comedian of the sound stage. Like Mae West and the three Marx brothers, Fields's comedy stemmed from himself rather than from the stories in which he found himself. Like Mae West and the Marxes, Fields combined a comic personality, a comic physical type, and a style of verbal wit that fitted both his mind and body. Fields also came to films from the stage, but the former vaudevillian, so famous today for his gravelly, whiskey voice, began his film career in silent comedies directed by Edward Sutherland, Gregory LaCava, and—of all people—D. W. Griffith. Although it is impossible to imagine Fields without his voice, his roots in silent films emphasize the neglected fact that Fields's funniness, like that of all the great American screen comics, is fundamentally physical. An occasional sequence from one of the sound films reveals his powers as pure physical clown: his clumsy attempts to play croquet in *Poppy* (1936), the battle with bent pool cues in *Six of a Kind* (1934), and his deft juggling in *The Old-Fashioned Way* (1934). Physically funny, too, is the Fields body—the booze-bloated nose, the beer belly—which he tries to dignify with the spiffiest, most fastidiously selected period costumes.

Like his physical appearance, the Fields character is a mixture of external polish and inner nastiness. Fields is the great spinner of words—of melodious euphemisms, euphonious malapropisms, florid rhetoric. His affectation of polite speech is like all his other pretentions to politeness—pure sham. Beneath the fancy waistcoats and purple prose beats the heart of a dirty old man who drinks, smokes, swears, and gambles, who hates women (especially sweet old ones), children (especially cute little ones), animals, and all respectable social institutions (especially marriage, work, honest business dealings, and the law). In films like *Tillie and Gus* (1934), *It's a Gift* (1934), and especially *The Bank Dick* (1940), Fields—like the Marx Brothers and Mae West—was the foe of everything sentimental and nice. In an era of glamorized sentimentality and niceness, their essential vulgarity and comic crudeness were especially refreshing.

von Sternberg, Ford, Hawks, Hitchcock, Welles

Of the noncomic directors whose films were obvious exceptions to the studio rule, the films of Josef von Sternberg have perhaps worn the least well. Visually the von Sternberg films are gleaming gems, rich in atmospheric detail, shimmering pools of light and contrasting shadow, the excitement of a perpetually moving, prowling camera, the luminous face of Marlene Dietrich—in shadow, in blazing light, veiled, feathered, powdered, hazed. The von Sternberg film looks dazzling beside the stiff, static, neon-lit feeling of the typical studio film. But beneath the gleaming surfaces—the exotic locales, the symbolic details, the smoke, the shafts of light, the audacious sexual innuendoes that could only have gotten past the censors because they didn't understand them—von Sternberg's films suffer from some of the same ills of formulaic plotting and undeveloped characterization as their more stylistically conventional brothers.

The Blue Angel (1930), von Sternberg's second sound film, remains his best, for it suffers least from a hollowness in the guts. Ironically, von Sternberg shot the film in Germany for Ufa. In the early sound years, Hollywood suddenly discovered a new problem—breaking the language barrier. The silents simply substituted new titles in new languages as the film leaped from country to country. But with sound, before film distributors discovered dubbing and subtitling, Hollywood's plan was to shoot the same film in Europe with different languages and different casts. Von Sternberg went to Germany to take part in this cinematic internationalism.

The Blue Angel is a Circe story. A bewitching lady, the nightclub singer, Lola Lola (Marlene Dietrich), steadily turns an orderly, almost lifeless school teacher (Emil Jannings) into a beast; he even crows like a cock to show his transformation. Professor Unrat eventually dies from this dramatic change of air, his conversion from school teacher to night-club clown. The film is von Sternberg's best because the director renders every step in Professor Unrat's demise with the greatest intimacy and clarity, and he renders the sexual energy that destroys the man with an equal clarity. Atmosphere and visual images exist in the film not as independent entities but as a means of depicting the two conflicting characters and life-styles. Both picture and sound establish the two opposite worlds at the beginning of the film. Professor Unrat's classroom is white, clean, bright, desks arranged in geometric regularity; the Blue Angel club where Lola sings is smoky, hazy, chaotic, dim. Professor Unrat's classroom is silent except for the drone of his voice; the Blue Angel is noisy, bustling, full of shouts and song. The antiseptic silence of Unrat's classroom is emphasized by the song of a choir that drifts in through an open window; in the Blue Angel Lola sings songs of a far less spiritual kind.

Like the great silent films of Jannings's past, *The Blue Angel* refuses to draw either romantic or moralistic conclusions. Professor Unrat's ascetic life is sterile, schematic, so crammed with routine that it lacks the breath of life; he, like his caged bird, is dead. Lola's sensual life is totally selfish, amoral, blind to the existence of any other being but herself; she is committed to love, not to love someone—as her famous song, "Falling in Love Again," so clearly indicates. Neither of the two lives is superior to the other. The film's business is not moral comment but merely the human story of what happens to a man from one life who tastes a drop of another. The wine which at first makes him drunk eventually poisons him. Although Lola frees him from his cage at first and makes him sing, his song, like the man himself, becomes cracked and empty. His final metamorphosis is not into the singing bird, but into the same kind of pathetic clown that he saw in Lola's dressing room when he first met her. That clown both foreshadows Unrat's own fate and implies that Lola's collection of human husks is endless. The shattered professor creeps back to his old classroom to die. The only consistent moral comment in the film is on the professor's callous students who fail to see that as both strict disciplinarian and broken clown Unrat is a human being and deserves human sympathy. The film's young students are vicious, inhuman vultures, like the porter's neighbors in *The Last Laugh,* and rather obviously Nazis-to-be.

The von Sternberg–Dietrich American films are as dazzling visually as *The Blue Angel* (in fact, even more dazzling). They have individual moments of keen psychological insight. But they consistently pass off romantic formulas for human interaction, quickly turning a film's motivation (and hence plot) into cliché. For films that are supposedly psychological, von Sternberg's refuse to allow us beneath the sparkling surfaces. Take, for example, the final shot in *Morocco* (1930), the first of von Sternberg's Dietrich films made in this country. The hero (Gary Cooper), a member of the Foreign Legion, has marched off over the sands of the desert to fight. Marlene, in a wildly romantic moment, rejects her rich suitor and plunges off to follow Cooper over the sands, just as each peasant Arab woman follows her beloved Legionnaire, dragging her goods and her goats behind her. Now Marlene is not the kind of woman to travel with goats. The awkwardness of her crossing the desert is emphasized by her need to remove her high-heeled shoes before setting off over the sand dunes. To make such a wildly romantic gesture believable, the director's responsibility is to structure the whole film so that we believe Marlene really loves the soldier *that* much. But the Dietrich-Cooper relationship has no life in the film at all. He falls in love with her in public (she is a night-club singer again). They play only one scene together *in camera,* in which little is said and nothing is done. The ending remains an incredible romantic pose. On the other hand, if the final shot is dramatic drivel, it is visually gorgeous: a beautiful composition of waves of blowing white sand, a sliver of dark sky, black specks of human figures dotting the sand at the corners of the frame.

There are other beautiful things in *Morocco.* There is von Sternberg symbolism in the scene in which Marlene must decide between life with the rich suitor (Adolphe Menjou) and life with the man she loves. To emphasize the struggle and decision, Marlene hears the military trumpet call (fine use of sound as symbol) announcing the Legion's departure from the town; at the same time, she nervously fingers a string of pearls her suitor has given her (a metaphor for the rewards of the wealthy life). When Marlene makes up her mind she tugs so hard at the necklace that the string breaks and the pearls scatter all over the floor. The meaning of her decision is clear. The film's finest, most stunning psychological moment is Marlene's first appearance in the Moroccan night club. She is dressed as a man in tails; she sings, Evelike, about selling apples, which she offers as she sings. A lesbian is obviously attracted to the male-clad performer. Marlene, knowing the woman's intentions, toys with her while singing and then matter-of-factly walks up to her and kisses her on the mouth. Nothing that happens later in the film has the same psychological intensity or interest.

The von Sternberg films are consistently packed with beautiful pictures and flimsy human motivation. We are constantly told that each character has "a past," but we are never told what it was, making the whole concept of "a past" a Victorian cliché. The problem is especially clear in *Shanghai Express* (1932) in which the central emotional relationship hangs on this undeveloped and, hence, unconvincing hook. As in *Morocco,* von Sternberg captures the texture and look of an exotic locale with a brilliant opening sequence, relying on Lee Garmes's constantly tracking, moving, prowling camera to capture the bustling activity and scurrying people of the eastern railway station. As in *Morocco,* the pictures of Marlene Dietrich are luminous, her face radiant in a streak of light against a darkened backdrop; they even look striking in the stills. But perhaps there is too much of this posing-for-stills quality in von Sternberg's handling of his star.

The story of *Shanghai Express* is one of the reawakening of love between Marlene, now a shady lady in Shanghai, and her man, a proper officer in the British army (Clive Brook)—a story played against a background of robbers and revolutionaries in exotic China. The story of reawakened love is dependent on our belief that it had existed earlier and was put to sleep by some kind of misunderstanding between the two lovers. But the characters' discussions of their past are so cold, so abstract, and so sketchy that we cannot believe that anything really united them in the past and, hence, it is impossible to believe that anything really unites the exotic lady and the cold-fish man now, other than the obligatory script. Perhaps the von Sternberg films fall apart as stories of human emotion precisely because the consistently dull, flat performances from his male actors fail to convince us that the hypnotic Miss Dietrich could ever fall in love with such bland men.

The succeeding von Sternberg-Dietrich films became progressively more bizarre, as if the Austrian director were (like von Stroheim) daring the race of Puritans to stop him and, at the same time, were (like Lubitsch) laughing at the sexual childishness of the race of Puritans for accepting his mythic, Circean hogwash as the genuine sexual article. *The Blonde Venus* (1932)—which contains enough plot for four films—features Marlene as loving wife, tempted adulteress, devoted mother, cheap whore in a Southwestern border town, and international sensation of the music-hall. Despite the film's wandering and globe-circling plot, it is redeemed by its moments of sensual intensity and sexual audacity: the sensuous, tactile liquidity of the opening scene as Miss Dietrich swims in a shimmering, limpid stream (and as Herbert Marshall, impersonating a Boy Scout—at the age of 42!—voyeuristically watches this hypnotic Lorelei); the dusty, smoky chiaroscuro of the cheap dive in the Tex-Mex border town; the astonishing visual contrasts of the "Hot Voodoo" number, in which the Blonde Venus, complete with platinum fright wig, pokes her head out of the gruesome, black body of a gorilla's costume; Miss Dietrich in white top hat and tails (the lesbian motif again), the very masculine guise which attracts the applause and adoration of her masculine admirers. More than anything else, von Sternberg seems to wonder how many grotesque and outlandish hoops he can make his Blonde Venus jump through without his audience's catching on to the sardonic and satirically contemptuous game.

The coming of the Code to the Hays Office in no way inhibited the director's sexual fantasies but seemed to spur them to new heights. *The Scarlet Empress* (1934) begins with the dreams of the sweet, blonde, seven-year-old child who later becomes Catherine the Great of Russia. The child's nighttime visions are sado-masochistic fantasies, including the agonizing screams of tortured men on the rack and, in what may be the most deSade-like image ever filmed, the hanging of male bodies inside huge bells, so that their swinging legs and heels can bang against the bells and send their reverberating peels out over the town and countryside.

Later, the grown-up product of these dreams marries the madman who is the heir to the Russian throne, an idiot whose sexual activities are confined to drilling holes in people's walls so he can watch them and whose favorite playthings are inert, toy soldiers (clearly von Sternberg implies something about the Prince's own inert, toy soldier). The frustrated bride conceives a son by casually offering herself to one of the palace guards, and with the eventual support of the entire army (which obviously supports her because of the way she has been "supporting" it) she leads the Revolution and seizes the throne (riding a milk white stallion and wearing a white hussar's costume—the white/black and male/female tensions again). The bells of all Russia (and those bells have been a consistent visual and aural motif of the film since the film's opening dream sequence) peel out with something resembling joy.

What is equally striking about *The Scarlet Empress* is that it is essentially a silent film. Von Sternberg reveals his roots in the visual richness of the silents by shooting whole scenes with only musical accompaniment: the spectacular wedding ceremony that alternates long shots of the immense cathedral, its columns and candles, with agonizingly immense close-ups of Miss Dietrich's face shot through her lace veil; the Bacchanalian wedding feast with its sensational traveling shot spanning an immense table covered with steaming broths, littered plates, and the sugared carcasses of beasts. Most of all like the silent film, *The Scarlet Empress* does not attempt to tell its story with dialogue (or even with pictures). The film probably devotes more screen time to printed titles than any film made since 1930. But as in his other films, this is a sure sign that von Sternberg either could not or would not manage a narrative skilfully.

Von Sternberg broke away from Dietrich to direct films without her after 1935: specifically the unfinished *I, Claudius* (1937), with Charles Laughton, Emlyn Williams, and Merle Oberon; *The Shanghai Gesture* (1941) and *Macao* (1951), with their exotic, von Sternbergian Far-East locales; *The Saga of Anatahan* (1953), a film he directed for the Japanese film industry. But von Sternberg's most influential and prolific period as a director ended when he and Dietrich separated.

John Ford is the spiritual descendant of D. W. Griffith. Like Griffith, Ford's values are traditional and sentimental: the pure woman, the home, the family, law, decency, democracy. Like Griffith—and like the two other important Catholic directors of the studio era, Frank Capra and Leo McCarey—Ford was a populist who praised the little people and the institutions that protected the little people, while he damned those who selfishly twisted the system to grab money and power. Like Griffith, but unlike Capra or McCarey, Ford's method emphasized visual images rather than talk, and violent, dramatic action rather than wry comedy or tear-jerking. Ford also tended to use the myth of the settling of the West as his central metaphor for the spirit of Man and the spirit of America, bringing civilization and fruitfulness to the savage wilderness.

The Ford films are as striking visually as von Sternberg's. Like von Sternberg, Ford's technique paints with extremes of dark and light. But von Sternberg used darkness to emphasize the luminescence of his shafts of light; Ford used shafts of light to emphasize the darkness. The Ford world is one of night, fog, rain, and shadow. The dark form in silhouette replaces von Sternberg's light-saturated faces surrounded by darkness. The dominant photographic method of von Sternberg is his Germanically moving camera; Ford's camera, often managed by Joseph August or Gregg Toland, composes in space, width, and depth. Dominating Ford's films are the vast vistas of the plains, mountains, and sky, the shots-in-depth of a group of human faces or figures, tensely composed, shot slightly from below. But Ford never substituted picture taking for picture making. Although the films became almost allegories of good and evil—the misty lighting, the weather, the characterizations all support the allegory—Ford's best films never forgot the studio prescription that a film must tell a good story.

Ford's film career began early in the years of the silents, but he did not become a major influence until 1935 with *The Informer*. Ford, like Capra, never achieved real distinction until he found the proper scenarist-collaborator—Dudley Nichols. *The Informer* is a story of the Irish Revolution, with which Ford, an Irishman, was naturally in sympathy. Gypo, a former member of the I.R.A., betrays his closest friend and former comrades to the hated British. Gypo has been expelled from the party specifically because they fear his weakness. The film is the story of Gypo succumbing to that weakness and eventually paying, both physically and mentally, for his mistake. The film's power is its achievement in making Gypo's tortured mind manifest, in showing the man's hurts, hopes, fears, and conflicts.

Ford accomplishes his psychological translation by the consistently subjective use of Joseph August's camera, which mirrors Gypo's mind with dissolves, blurred focuses, and physical projections of the man's frightened mind. Ford bathes the film in fog. The fog is not only the perfect visual climate for the dim, damp story; it is also a metaphor for the era's moral fog and for the psychological fog inside Gypo's head. Like the storm scene in *King Lear* (and in Griffith's *Way Down East*), the physical universe in Ford films takes its tone from the insides of men's heads. Memorable in *The Informer* is not only the metaphorical fog but the metaphorical blind man—dressed in black, silhouetted in the mist, tapping steadily with his cane—who seems to follow Gypo everywhere. The blind man is both an internal and external symbol of Gypo's internal sense of guilt, which he cannot escape, and of the pursuit of the revolutionaries whose justice he also cannot escape. Ford's symbols consistently work (as von Sternberg's often do not) because they have a life on several literal and symbolic levels at the same time. Assigning them a specific, single meaning inevitably shrinks them into something smaller than Ford intended.

The Informer has other strengths. It has a series of fine performances in the smaller roles in which Ford depicts the way other Irishmen casually betray the cause and their fellows every day for money or booze. It has a series of brilliant scenes in which Ford depicts Gypo's growing irrationality and torment: his awkwardness in the house of mourning, his frenzy in spending the pieces of Judas money to buy drinks for the people he has betrayed, his final asking for forgiveness from his victim's mother as he lies dying in the church. As with Ford's visual symbols, his religious allusions in the film live on the dramatic level as well as on an intellectual one. Today the film's most glaring weaknesses seem to be an overstated performance from its star (Victor McLaglen) and a hackneyed musical score (by Max Steiner) in which the audience is instructed how to react by glaring exclamation points on the sound track. Ford, despite his talent, could not quite pull free from studio conventionality, and the score of *The Informer* is a reminder of his commercial bondage which lasted throughout his career. By his own admission, Ford claims that he made only about six films—out of over one hundred!—that he wanted to make and in the way he wanted to make them.

Ford's greatest weakness (other than studio policy, which he could not control) was, like Griffith's, to make his rather limited and traditional personal vision uncomfortably specific. Discussions of political and moral questions inevitably become simplistic and banal in Ford films. One of the most outstanding examples is James Stewart's classroom lecture on liberty and freedom in *The Man Who Shot Liberty Valance* (1962). The entire film, including the irony that the vicious villain bears the name of "Liberty," is an allegorical study of the bringing of democracy and civilization to the Old West, an allegory of liberty as opposed to license. When the film makes its point with story, characterization, or images (for example, the opening shot of the civilizing train slicing through the barren prairies) it is effective; when the film stops for a discussion of political or emotional issues, it is not. Action, character, and image fuse together in the best Ford films; among the best of them, because it is so active, so human, and so richly visual, is *Stagecoach* (1939).

For a film that masquerades as an action-packed western, *Stagecoach* is an intimate film of human interaction rather than exciting events. Although there is a thrilling Indians-versus-stagecoach chase in the final ten minutes of the film, followed by an obligatory (and very underplayed) gunfight just after the chase, *Stagecoach* is a film of faces and personalities for its first ninety minutes. The coach itself becomes Ford's metaphor for civilized society. Like the train in *The Iron Horse* and *Liberty Valance* and the truck in *The Grapes of Wrath*, the stagecoach is a machine built by civilized hands and heads for the taming of the vast, uncivilized western wastes. Although Ford's films examine what civilization does *to* men as well as *for* men, in *Stagecoach* the key dramatic conflict is between the humanness of the coach society and the savagery of the Apaches.

Inside Ford's stagecoach is a whole society of people, of different social classes and mental habits: banker, sheriff, outlaw, salesman, doctor, prim married lady, dance-hall "singer," gambler, stage driver. Ford and Dudley Nichols carefully distinguish between the human traits of each: the gambler's chivalry and polish, the outlaw's sense of fairness, the doctor's drunken kindness, the delicate lady's shedding of her former human prejudices, the sheriff's human concern for the outlaw's safety, the salesman's citified, dude-like cowardice. Beneath their superficial tensions and differences, all these people (with one exception) eventually reveal an underlying warmth, kindness, and camaraderie that makes them equally decent human beings. The doctor sobers up to deliver the lady's baby; the whiskey salesman overcomes some of his antiwestern squeamishness; the sheriff lets the good-hearted outlaw get away with his woman, the singer (a euphemism for prostitute), at the end of the film; the singer, despite her toughness, gently helps the doctor bring a baby into the world; the outlaw loves the girl despite the societally defined shadiness of her past.

The single unredeemed character in the film is the rich banker who has stolen $50,000 from his own bank and is now running away with it. Despite his selfish violation of the law, the banker is the most outspoken on the immorality of the doctor, singer, and outlaw, and the most dogmatic in pontificating on the government's duty to protect his own self-important person. The banker, whose view of the law is that it is written for his personal convenience, is pure Griffith. Ford's preference for the good-hearted, simple people—good-hearted despite their human fallibilities—to the evil-hearted rich is another Griffith dichotomy. And the prim, proper, moralistic, uplifting society of old hens, who viciously toss the doctor and singer out of town at the beginning of the film, seem to have leaped directly out of *Intolerance* or *Way Down East*. Despite the brilliantly exciting staging and cutting of the stagecoach's climactic battle with the Apaches, *Stagecoach* is a film about warm people and the important human values. So is *The Grapes of Wrath* (1940), *My Darling Clementine* (1946), and the other great Ford films.

If John Ford was the sound film's Griffith, Howard Hawks was its Ince. Compared with Ford, Hawks's films are more brutal and less sentimental, more active and less moralistic. Like Ince's, Hawks's movies are striking in their driving narratives rather than their examinations of psychology or emotional interaction. The psychological insight in a Hawks film functionally serves the narrative line. And if the Ince "soul fights" served that function in his films, the Hawks pictures contain similar fights between a man's outer actions and his inner urges. The typical Hawks study is the contrast between the tough, weak man and the weak, tough man: the man who is solid on the outside but has a heart underneath and the man who appears fragile on the outside but has a streak of tough competence underneath. During the course of the film the strong man cracks a bit, but doesn't break, the weak man toughens up, after several cracks, and the two stand and fight together. In *The Criminal Code* (1931), the tough warden and the weak prisoner unite at the end; twenty-eight years later, in *Rio Bravo* (1959), the solid John Wayne and the boozer Dean Martin fight side-by-side.

The Hawks world is almost exclusively a world of men. Women exist on the periphery of this world, but they never fill the same sentimental and almost allegorical civilizing roles that they do in Ford or Griffith. Hawks reserves his women for comedies, but even the delightfully wacky *Bringing Up Baby* (1938) has a tough, antisentimental core. Hawks runs Katharine Hepburn through swamps, mud, and thickets in a romantic chase after her man that has more to do with a tame leopard and a lost dinosaur bone than with love.

Whereas John Ford's stories of the West were of virtuous, self-sacrificing men bringing moral light to spiritual darkness, Howard Hawks's were of strong-willed men imposing their wills on weaker ones. Whereas Ford's essential human quality was a man's recognition of moral and social demands outside of himself, Hawks's essential human quality is ego. The Hawks character is completely wrapped up in himself: his job, his interests, his personal sense of integrity. The conflict in a Hawks film stems from the integrity of one character running up against the integrity of another. In *Red River* (1948) the older ego of John Wayne runs up against the younger ego of Montgomery Clift. The male ego of Humphrey Bogart runs up against the female ego of Lauren Bacall in *The Big Sleep* (1946). In *Bringing Up Baby* the scientist's ego (Cary Grant's) runs up against the feline ego of Katharine Hepburn. (She is far more predatory than her pet leopard, Baby.) *Twentieth Century* (1934) is perhaps the most complete and successful comedy of ego ever made, in which two people of the theater—John Barrymore and Carole Lombard, the Svengali and his ungrateful Trilby—fight to the egotistic death.

Ironically, in these egotistic battles there is also love, for if the characters didn't love one another they wouldn't bother to fight. Beneath all the egotism in Hawks's comedies, they, like most comedies, are stories of love triumphing over the obstacles. The obstacles in his comedies are the very egos themselves. There is also love in the noncomedies: in *Red River* (otherwise the two men would murder each other), in *Only Angels Have Wings* (1939), in *The Big Sleep,* and in many other Hawks films. Love in the Hawks film is a matter of mind, of one ego's perception that another is equally strong, worthwhile, "together." This is especially true because Hawks refuses to sentimentalize his women as well as his men. The strong woman for Hawks is exactly like the strong man: unswerving commitment to a purpose, a refusal to lie to others or to themselves. As a result, the underlying emotions in a Hawks film are almost never verbalized, for to put vague feelings into precise words is to tell a kind of lie. In *The Big Sleep* Humphrey Bogart hesitatingly tells Lauren Bacall, "Well, I guess I sort of love you." That is as articulately verbal as Hawks's emotions get.

Hawks's cinematic technique is far less striking, far less idiosyncratic than either von Sternberg's or Ford's. Like Frank Capra, Hawks was content with the studio styles of even lighting, eye-level, middle-distance composition, and functional narrative editing. But unlike so many of the room-bound studio films, many of Hawks's films—especially the westerns—enjoyed breathing the free air of the outdoors. Although his films seem to attempt less than Ford's, their tough, well-paced plots consistently fulfill themselves without wincingly banal or sentimentalized moments. Perhaps the ultimate testimony to Howard Hawks is that he created at least one film that could serve as the supreme example of the highest possible accomplishment in almost every significant American movie genre: the prison picture (*The Criminal Code*), the gangster movie (*Scarface*, 1932), the western (*Red River*), the whodunit (*The Big Sleep*), the newspaper picture (*His Girl Friday*, 1941), and the screwball comedy (*Bringing Up Baby*).

Although Alfred Hitchcock was a product of the British rather than American studio system, his work is very much a part of the American studio tradition. The British film industry has maintained a symbiotic relationship with Hollywood since the end of World War I, a relationship intensified by the sharing of a common language after the conversion to sound. Hitchcock's affinity with the American system is clear in the popularity of his British films in America and in his smooth, effortless emigration from the British studio to Hollywood in 1939. The assumptions of the British and American studio systems were essentially the same.

Although Alfred Hitchcock directed his first film as early as 1925 (*The Pleasure Garden*), he, like John Ford, did not become a major influence until 1935 with *The Man Who Knew Too Much* and *The 39 Steps*. *The 39 Steps* is a prototype Hitchcock film. The plot is a mad chase from London to Scotland and back again. The chase throws the crime-tracking runners into the most wildly diverse and incongruous settings: a Scottish farmhouse, a plush manor house, a vaudeville theatre. The action is a mad attempt to solve the film's great riddle, what Hitchcock called the "Mac-Guffin," the meaning of "the 39 steps." That riddle is buried inside the head of the vaudeville performer, Mr. Memory, who, when publicly confronted with the question in front of an audience, is torn by his commitment to his art (he prides himself in knowing all) and his commitment to his fellow conspirators.

As in so many of his films, Hitchcock delights in showing the most horrible crimes taking place in the most public places: amusement parks, concert halls, theatres, buses, trains. And like so many Hitchcock films, *The 39 Steps* is a completely apolitical story of political intrigue. Except for the war-time films (*Saboteur, Foreign Correspondent, Notorious,* and *Lifeboat*), which are explicitly anti-Nazi, and *North by Northwest,* which is fuzzily anti-Communist, the two political sides in Hitchcock films are us and them. He deliberately refuses to cloud a good story with ideology. For the same reason, Hitchcock films inevitably take place in the world of the rich; they are totally divorced from such social-realist problems as poverty, hunger, and injustice. The Hitchcock actors are smooth, slick males like Cary Grant, Ray Milland, and James Stewart and cold, sleek ladies (usually blonde with strong, almost sterile features) like Joan Fontaine, Ingrid Bergman, Grace Kelly, and Eva Marie Saint. *The 39 Steps* uses the slick Robert Donat and the cool Madeleine Carroll.

The Hitchcock films are a unique blend of story, style, and a deceptively complex technique. Hitchcock mixes the macabre and the funny, mystery and whimsey, suspense and sardonic laughter. While the film's gripping story drives relentlessly forward, Hitchcock takes time out to focus on a subtle physical detail or bit of human irony. The plots revolve about the wildest improbabilities in the most bizarre locales: vast, international conspiracies; little old ladies who are really spies; psychotic killers who impersonate their dead mothers; secret codes memorized by vaudeville entertainers; chases that culminate on carousels, in concert halls, in theatres, on the Statue of Liberty or Mount Rushmore. Beneath almost every Hitchcock film is the structure of the Sennett chase, the breathtaking, accelerating rush toward a climactic solution. But Hitchcock personalizes the wildly improbable chase by making each of the racers surprisingly human, comically vulnerable, fallibly credible. Murderers, psychotics, and spies become as human as the little old lady next door. The most insane, exotic tales hang on the tiniest, most trivial details—a rare brand of herb tea, a glass of milk, a bird cage, a glove, a native folk song, a cigarette lighter, an inquisitive cocker spaniel. Frenzied suspense and wry understatement are the ultimate Hitchcock ingredients, bizarre psychological states beneath the most banal surfaces the essential Hitchcock theme.

If there is a single Hitchcock theme that personalizes his vision and makes him more than the supreme technician and trickster, it is the fuzzy and indistinguishable line between normal and abnormal human behavior. The ordinary fears of normal human beings—of heights, of meeting a stranger on a train where no escape is possible, of being alone in a sleazy motel room—are subtly transformed into bizarrely abnormal occurrences. Perhaps the best Hitchcock example of this transformation is in *The Man Who Knew Too Much* (1934) in which everyone's fear of a trip to the dentist is transformed by the fact that this particularly menacing dentist is a member of an international conspiracy of murderers.

Hitchcock's two greatest technical tools are his command of cutting and his control of what Pudovkin called the "plastic material." Hitchcock's films are so rich in tiny yet revealing "plastic" details that if they had been made by Lubitsch the devices would have been called "Lubitsch touches." In *Suspicion* (1941), Hitchcock ingeniously reveals that Joan Fontaine is falling in love with Cary Grant. There is a close-up of a fashionable magazine; the pages flip until the book remains open on the picture of the handsome socialite (Grant). Then a lady's hand enters the frame and sets a pair of glasses down on the picture in the magazine. Because we know that Joan Fontaine wears glasses in the film, the scene instantly reveals that Miss Fontaine is looking at a picture of Grant and, further, that she has specifically removed the glasses in his photographic presence. The un-Hollywoodish, unglamorous use of glasses for ladies also functions in *Strangers on a Train* when the killer goes berserk upon staring into the face of a young girl with glittering glasses (the woman he murdered also wore glasses). Hitchcock's awareness of the power of concrete detail is such that when the detail is not exactly right in its natural state he fixes it up to emphasize it. In *Suspicion,* to hypnotize us with a glass of milk that Joan Fontaine thinks is poisoned, Hitchcock puts a tiny light inside the glass to make the milk truly glow in the darkness. In *Spellbound* (1945), he uses an immense, six-times-larger-than-life model of a revolver that truly dominates the foreground.

In an era of functional narrative cutting, Hitchcock's editing alone tightened the screws of suspense. As Sylvia Sidney slices roast beef at the dinner table in *Sabotage* (1936), Hitchcock's cutting shows her passion building until she drives the knife into her villainous husband. The same quick cutting creates the suspense of the final fight in *Saboteur* (1942) as the Nazi spy slips off the Statue of Liberty to his death, the frenzy of the spinning carousel at the end of *Strangers on a Train* (1951), the brutality of Janet Leigh's death in *Psycho* (1960) as Hitchcock cuts from shots of the victim's face, to shots of the slashing knife, to shots of the bloodstreaked water swirling down the drain of the shower.

Hitchcock films provide perfect "textbook" examples of the way to cut picture and sound together. In *The 39 Steps* (1935), the landlady walks into a room where she sees the shadow of a corpse; her eyes and mouth begin to erupt into a scream. Hitchcock immediately cuts to the shriek of a train whistle and a shot of the train racing toward Scotland. The screaming train replaces the human scream and startles us with its unnatural shrillness. Indeed, Hitchcock used the identical device—a mechanical scream replacing a human one when a landlady discovers a corpse—in his very first sound film, *Blackmail* (1929).

In *Strangers on a Train,* Hitchcock weds sound and cutting perfectly in the tennis sequence. The hero (Farley Granger) must play a tennis match knowing that the murderer (Robert Walker) is, at that very moment, trying to plant a clue that will erroneously prove him guilty. To avoid suspicion, Granger must finish off the tennis match before he finishes off the killer. Hitchcock makes the suspenseful delay unbearable with languid, rhythmic cutting from one player to the other to the crowd, player to player to crowd, underscoring the plodding sequence with no sound other than the steady plop, plop, plop of racquet hitting ball.

The 39 Steps is a mystery-with-psychology Hitchcock film (the other kind he makes being the psychology-with-mystery). In the course of running madly toward solving the film's cloak-and-dagger mystery, Hitchcock invests his film time in making the individual psychological moments of the picture come alive. In the opening scene between Robert Donat and the lady spy who is subsequently killed, Hitchcock enjoys the sexual matter-of-factness of the woman's inviting herself to a stranger's flat, where she calmly sits eating cheese and telling her outlandish story. In the scene in the Scottish farmer's house, Hitchcock deftly sketches with a few subtle strokes a whole lifetime's relationship between the moralistic farmer and his sympathetic wife. Most ironic of all the sequences is the one in which the fleeing Donat escapes his pursuers by rushing on the stage of a political gathering where he is mistakenly greeted as the anticipated orator. Donat then gives an impromptu political speech that brings the crowd to its feet cheering.

The flair of Hitchcock's breathless construction and subtly ironic sequences is matched by his complete control of his craft. To depict the death of the lady spy, a necessary but potentially dangerous starting point for the story, Hitchcock underplays the sequence by making the woman rush into Donat's room obviously upset and flustered, run toward the camera quickly, and then suddenly collapse on his bed, a knife sticking out of her back in the foreground of the frame. Then the phone rings (brilliant juxtaposition of visual and sound). To underscore Mr. Memory's confusion about telling the audience the truth about the 39 steps, Hitchcock shoots the man's face in tight close-up from below and on a tilt; the composition of the shot dramatizes the tension in his mind. Hitchcock's tilted camera constantly plays such dramatic functions in his films. Of course, Hitchcock subtly points the road back to Mr. Memory all along because Robert Donat unconsciously whistles the theme song of the man's act throughout the film. But Donat, no Mr. Memory, cannot remember where he heard the tune that keeps running through his head. Hitchcock repeatedly uses the sound medium by building entire films around musical leitmotifs.

The film's final scene is a brilliant synthesis of its action, irony, comedy, and psychology. Mr. Memory lies dying on the floor in the wings of the theatre. Though he is dying, he insists on telling the police the complicated formula he has memorized—his pride in his work is that great. Meanwhile, a line of chorines dances on stage (in the rearground of the frame). Meanwhile, Robert Donat puts his arm around Madeleine Carroll (in the foreground), and suddenly we discover the same dangling handcuff on his wrist that has been there for the last hour of the film. This final ironic detail undercuts completely the romance of the ending, a perfect indication of the Hitchcock style and tone.

Unlike Hitchcock, Lubitsch, Chaplin, Hawks, or Ford, whose reputations rest on a series of impressive films, critical respect for Orson Welles rests primarily on one film, *Citizen Kane*. The film's greatness can be discussed on several different levels: its technical innovation, its structural complexity, its controversy as a biography of a famous American, its philosophical search for meaningful human values, its sociological study of the "American Dream," its acting, its literacy, its individuality. Orson Welles, the young sensation of both the stage and radio, had been invited to bring his Mercury Theatre group to Hollywood in 1941 to make any film he chose. Welles was twenty-six. The film, *Citizen Kane,* was both his first and the last he would ever be so free to make. Like an earlier *enfant terrible* of Hollywood, Erich von Stroheim, Welles insisted on supervising everything himself: acting, directing, writing, editing, designing sets, even sewing costumes. And like von Stroheim, Welles soon saw the Hollywood lords giving his negative to other hands for slicing, and later found the gates of the lords' studios locked against him.

From its opening sequence, *Citizen Kane* is no ordinary film. It begins in quiet and darkness: a wire fence with a "No Trespassing" sign; a series of tracking shots and dissolves past a weird menagerie which bring us closer to the old, creepy house and eventually into the room of the dying man; his impressionistic death, with the echoing, rasping sound of the word "Rosebud" on the dying man's lips; the glass ball floating through space in slow motion before shattering; the nurse entering the room to attend to the dead man, seen in a distorted, extreme wide-angle shot. As if this beginning were not elliptical enough, Welles shatters the dark mood of death with the blaring music and glaring, overexposed images of the newsreel documentary. From moody expressionism, the film jumps to a brilliant parody of "The March of Time": the march-time music on the sound track, the booming "voice-of-God" narration, the overly descriptive printed titles, the purple prose, the little diagrams and maps, the clumsy newsreel photography, the flat interviews with reporters. The newsreel ends as abruptly as it began and is followed by a scene in the projection room in which the reporters discuss the newsreel's defects, a scene played entirely in shadow, drenched in smoke, backlit by shafts of light from the projection booth. The scene is as garishly shadowed as the preceding newsreel was flat and overexposed. Three sequences, three completely different film styles.

The film's technical brilliance continues throughout. Even today it seems striking in its extreme up-angle shots (how many Hollywood sets before *Citizen Kane* had ceilings?), its consistently extreme contrasts of dark and light (so much of the film was lit from behind), its vast shots in depth revealing interaction between foreground and rearground. Welles was lucky to have the cinematic eye of Gregg Toland behind his camera. He was also lucky to have the new fast film and the new bright lights.

But Welles also shows genuine cinematic imagination in editing several of the sequences. The most striking sequence reveals the widening emotional gulf between Kane and his first wife. As the two eat breakfast together at their dining table, Welles executes a montage series of vignettes, each of which shows the two moving further apart physically. At the end of the sequence, the two, who had begun sitting next to each other, talking cheerily, sit at opposite ends of the long table, not talking at all; she is reading a different newspaper—the supreme insult to a newspaper publisher, a wife who refuses to read his own paper.

Welles's control of sound is as careful as his manipulation of image. The years in radio made him aware of sound's dramatic power, an advantage he enjoyed over those directors who graduated to sound from the silents. The overloud narration of the newsreel sequence, the echoing emptiness of Mr. Thatcher's mausoleum-library, the contrast between the amplified and unamplified human voice at Kane's political rally, the shrieking tones of the opera singer trying to master her craft, the flat smallness of the voices in the immense rooms of Kane's huge chateau, all are examples of an ear trained in the power of the microphone and the loudspeaker.

Citizen Kane is also one of the most complexly structured pieces of film literature in cinema history. Resembling nothing so much as Faulkner's *Absalom, Absalom!, Citizen Kane* is, like the Faulkner novel, an immense jigsaw puzzle (like the puzzles Susan plays with in Kane's castle). The director and screenwriter (Herman J. Mankiewicz) lead the audience through a seemingly chaotic collection of events and human fragments until all the pieces of the puzzle are fitted together. Although both Welles and Faulkner seem to wander confusingly over an immense expanse of time and space, both artists carefully follow a well-charted if intricate map to the ultimate revelation. Although Welles and Mankiewicz may not have been directly influenced by Faulkner, they were also working at the time on a screen adaptation of Joseph Conrad's *Heart of Darkness,* whose complex story-within-a-story, imagery, theme, and central character (Kurtz—even the name is similar) bear obvious affinities to *Kane*.

The cinematic structure of *Citizen Kane*'s first sequence is a microcosm for the whole film. Just as Welles's camera begins outside the fence of Charles Foster Kane's house and then steadily moves closer until it comes to rest on the man himself, so too the whole film begins on the outside of Kane and steadily moves inward until it eventually exposes the emptiness at the man's core. The first section, the newsreel, is the most externalized report of all, a sweeping summary of the facts and dates of Kane's life with no attempt at understanding his motivation. The newsreel is useful for the film, not only because it gives us a completely surface report but also because it gives us a series of road signs, concrete incidents and dates, to which Welles will return later in the film, and which keep the film's sprawling structure moving in a clear, coherent direction.

The film's second section is narrated by Mr. Thatcher, the banker who first brought young Charles to the city. Or rather it is narrated by Mr. Thatcher's memoirs, since the man is now dead. Thatcher's section primarily covers Kane's boyhood and youth, from the time he left his parents in Colorado to the time he founded the newspaper in New York. Since Thatcher never cared for Kane, and since his written rather than spoken words tell his story, his report remains very much on the outside of Kane.

The film's third section, narrated by Mr. Bernstein, Kane's business associate, begins to turn inward. Bernstein begins where Thatcher left off—from the founding of the newspaper through the marriage with the first Mrs. Kane. But because Bernstein idolized Kane, and because Bernstein never deserted him, the section concentrates solely on the young, energetic, iconoclastic Charlie Kane, the man with spirit and vision. Bernstein never explores the hollow depths beneath the flashy shallows.

The fourth section, Jed Leland's, begins the depth sounding. Jed is Kane's former best friend, now his cynical enemy. Kane fired Jed when Jed refused to desert his principles to suit his boss; Jed's very presence reminded Kane of the principles he had left behind. Jed's section picks up where Bernstein's leaves off: from the marriage with the first Mrs. Kane to the Chicago opera debut of Susan Alexander, who has become the second Mrs. Kane. Whereas Bernstein's section takes Kane to the peak of his happiness and success, Jed's shows the beginning of Kane's bitter descent.

The film's fifth section, Susan Alexander's, continues the descent. The now booze-soaked singer in sleazy cafés begins her section with her operatic career under Kane and continues it through their horrifying life in the huge castle, Xanadu, that Kane supposedly had built for her; she ends with the time she finally walks out on him, despite his money, his screaming, and his threats. Kane, so attractively youthful and rebellious in the film's early sections, is now a broken, empty, ugly old tyrant.

The film's examination is complete, except for the epilogue, which mirrors the film's opening prologue. Like the prologue, the epilogue focuses on Xanadu, the house, as well as Kane, the man. In the epilogue, the reporter, whose presence has tied together all the film's sections, tries once more to find the meaning of the clue that has propelled his search, the meaning of Kane's last word, "Rosebud." The reporter, who has remained faceless throughout the film, gives up. (Welles consistently shot the reporter from behind, not wanting to blur the focus on Kane by adding the psychological complexity of his searcher). The reporter will never find Rosebud. After he resigns the search, Welles shows some workmen throwing piles of junk that Kane had collected during his lifetime into a furnace. One of the pieces of junk is Kane's childhood sleigh; its name is Rosebud. The wood goes up in flames. The camera pulls steadily away from inside the Kane house, dissolving steadily until it is once more outside the fence with the "No Trespassing" sign. The film's final sequence is a mirror image, an identical reversal of its opening one. The circle has been completed.

The film's key moral question is what happened to Charles Foster Kane. What did he do wrong? What destroyed his youthful hopes and excitement? The answer is a dark, sickly spot at the heart of Kane's values and, by implication, at the heart of the values of American life. The three abstract themes that constantly flow through *Citizen Kane* are wealth, power, and love. The questions that the film raises are whether the first two exclude the third, and whether a life that excludes the third is worth living at all. Kane obviously has wealth; his wealth bought him newspapers and his newspapers brought him power. But Kane thinks that money and power can buy him the affection of men. Kane is a man of quantities. He collects things in quantity: newspapers, *objets d'art*, junk. When he runs for governor, he attempts to collect the people's hearts in the same way that he collects statues and paintings. The word "love" echoes through his whole political campaign. But hearts cannot be bought and stored like statues.

Failing to earn the people's love, Kane decides to demonstrate his power by making them love his creation, the opera singer, Susan Alexander. But Kane is no Svengali; his Trilby is a dud. Despite Kane's mortal power he is not God; he cannot reshape nature; he cannot alter Susan's stringy tonsils. Kane fails to collect the people's hearts with his creation just as he failed with his political love-making. And so instead of collecting the hearts of the people *en masse*, Kane decides to collect a single human heart— Susan's. He becomes her absolute tyrant; he builds her a huge house, a private universe, where he is sole master of a single human destiny. The house becomes Susan's prison. It is full of dead statues and dead souls. Susan is merely one more piece of stuff that Kane has collected, the only living object in a house full of crates and crates of junk. Susan rebels; she leaves. Kane has not succeeded in collecting a single human heart. The most appropriate epitaph at his death is the silent cellar full of crated marble and stone, the dead objects he has ravished with his checkbook from the museums, cathedrals, and chateaux of Europe.

Rosebud, the sleigh, is also an object. But it is an object of Kane's youth, not his maturity, an object of wood rather than of stone. It is an object that he did not buy. He kept Rosebud around because, like his mother's old wood stove, the object had sentimental value. He was also sentimentally attached to snow and snowscapes: Kane's glass ball with the snow scene deliberately recalls the snowy images of Mr. Thatcher's visit to young Charles in Colorado. Young Kane was ripped away from his snowy childhood, his family, and life with Rosebud, by the discovery of the Colorado silver lode on the land that the Kane family fortuitously owned. And so Rosebud, in Kane's mind anyway, represented the opposite of everything his life had become, youth rather than corrupt maturity, life with living nature rather than dead objects, genuine human emotion (with his mother particularly) rather than cash substitutes. Rosebud was, in Frost's words, the road not taken. Even Kane himself told Thatcher that he could have been a really great man if he had not been rich. But what man, what American, would not have taken Kane's road? That question makes Kane's story both tragic and philosophically disturbing. Kane's barren, lifeless journey is so inevitable. One only misses the Rosebuds in life as a sentimental afterthought. For this reason, the Rosebud symbol is both poignant and silly, nostalgic and sentimentalized, important and totally unimportant to the reality of Charles Foster Kane's life.

Citizen Kane was shocking to its audiences in 1941. Instead of Hollywood's flat gloss, the film was sombre and grotesque. Instead of a tight, well-made story, the action sprawled over more than sixty years, requiring its performers to make tremendous transitions in acting and appearance. Orson Welles (as Kane) evolved from a dashing, Gablesque youth to a bald-headed ogre; Joseph Cotten (as Leland) evolved from a smooth Ivy Leaguer to a doddering, senile old man. Audiences found *Citizen Kane* distinctly unpleasant and brooding. There were no last-minute changes of heart, no romantic reconciliations. *Citizen Kane* followed its tragic premises to their logical, gloomy end. Even more disturbing for Hollywood was the enmity the film produced in the press, particularly in the Hearst chain. William Randolph Hearst saw obvious and infuriating parallels between himself and Charles Foster Kane, between Susan Alexander and his own artistic protégée, Marion Davies, between Kane's Florida castle, Xanadu, and his own California castle, San Simeon. The pressures of the press, and the film's unspectacular showing at the box office, led Welles's boss, R.K.O., to tie the reins around the director's head.

Welles's next film, *The Magnificent Ambersons* (1942), is certainly his next-best work. Like *Citizen Kane*, the film examines an egomaniacal, selfish mind that sees other human beings as his pawns. Like *Citizen Kane*, the film contains some striking compositions in depth and shadow, some brilliant montage sequences (particularly the opening section showing the passage of time—Joseph Cotten trying on each year's new fashions while facing a mirror), and some highly effective film acting. But Welles tacks a formulaic happy ending on the film as the vain, callous young Amberson (Tim Holt) undergoes a miraculous change of heart and sees the egotistical folly of his ways. Despite the Hollywood ending, the film did no better at the box office. R.K.O. relieved Welles of his duties on his next film, *Journey Into Fear*, before he had the chance to edit it. Later Welles films, *The Lady from Shanghai* (1947), *Macbeth* (1950), *Touch of Evil* (1958), *Mr. Arkadin* (1962), are, like *Citizen Kane*, obsessed with the themes of the corrupting influence of power and money, with the manipulation of human beings as mere pawns in a vicious game, with a human's choice between a selfish commitment to himself and a responsible commitment to others. But the later films, despite their striking moments, become, like Welles's acting itself, mannered caricatures of his greatest work. The Welles pose and the Welles cult have outlived the Welles genius.

Although Hollywood had won the battle with *Citizen Kane*, it would lose the war. The film, despite Hollywood's attempts to hide it and silence its creator, would become the most influential film in American film history after *Birth of a Nation*. Personal and individual rather than factory-made, iconoclastic rather than conventional, daring rather than safe, innovative rather than formulaic, bitter rather than sickly sweet, thoughtful rather than escapist, *Citizen Kane* would point the way toward the film things to come. In 1941 those things were not so very far away.

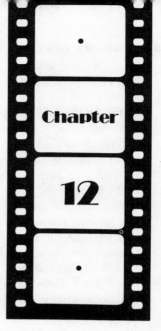

Chapter

12

YEARS OF TRANSITION

In 1946 the American film business grossed $1,700,000,000, the peak box-office year since the inception of the American film industry. Twelve years later, in 1958, box-office receipts fell below a billion dollars; by 1962 receipts had fallen to $900,000,000, slightly more than half the 1946 gross. While box-office income steadily fell, production costs—labor, equipment, materials—steadily rose along with the nation's soaring, inflated economy. The two vectors of rising costs and falling revenues seemed to point directly toward the cemetery for both Hollywood and the commercial American film. Yet in 1968, theatre box offices collected $1,300,000,000 (box office receipts having risen every year since 1963). In 1974 theatres grossed almost two billion dollars. The figures indicate that the American film industry has emerged from a difficult transitional period and has solidified itself commercially by redefining its product and its audience. Between 1948 and 1963 lay fifteen years of groping.

Even before World War II, the two forces that would crush the old Hollywood had begun their assault. First, United States courts had begun to rule that the corporate chains binding the picture studio to the theatres exhibiting their pictures violated the nation's antitrust laws. Block booking was unfair to the individual competitive exhibitor; the studio-owned chains of theatres gave the studio monopolistic control of the market for its own films. Hollywood knew that the day would come when the line that tied theatre to studio would have to be cut. The war postponed that day. Second, by the mid-1930s a new electronic toy that combined picture and sound—television—had been demonstrated by its scientist creators. At first Hollywood laughed at the silly toy; by the late 1940s, Hollywood had begun to fight; less than ten years later Hollywood had surrendered.

The war helped postpone the battle. A fighting America needed movies to take its mind off the war; both soldiers overseas and their families at home needed to escape to the movies. America also needed films for education: to train the soldiers to do their jobs, to teach them "why we fight," to give both information and encouragement to the folks at home who wondered how the fight was going and if the fight was worth it. Hollywood sent many of its best directors—Frank Capra, William Wyler, Fred Zinnemann, John Huston, John Ford, Garson Kanin—to make documentary films for the government and the armed forces. While Hollywood did its part, its profits conveniently rose. The government added special war taxes to theatre tickets; the American who went to the movies not only enjoyed himself but patriotically contributed to the war effort.

After the war, the Supreme Court's decision in the U.S. vs. Paramount case of 1948 was the ultimate court ruling that the studios must sell their theatres. The guaranteed outlet for the studio's product—good, bad, or mediocre—was dammed up. Each film would have to be good enough to sell itself. Meanwhile, more and more Americans bought television sets. Events like the 1948 Rose Bowl game and parade, the 1948 political conventions, and "Uncle Miltie," kept Americans looking at the box in their living rooms or, more than likely at first, in the living rooms of their neighbors. The movies declared war on the box. No Hollywood film could be shown on television; no film star could appear on a television program. So Americans stayed home to watch British movies on the box and the new stars that television itself developed.

The biggest, richest studios were hit the hardest. Two former assets suddenly became liabilities: property and people. In 1949, MGM declared wage cutbacks and immense layoffs. The giant studio's rows of sound stages and acres of outdoor sets became increasingly empty; the huge film factories now owned vast expanses of expensive and barren land. Even more costly than land were the contracts with people—technicians, featured players, and stars—that required the studio to pay their salaries despite the fact that it had no pictures for them to make. MGM allowed the contracts of its greatest stars, formerly the studio's richest commercial resource, to lapse. Every big studio extricated itself from the tangle of its obligations with financially disastrous slowness. A small studio, like Columbia, with very few stars under contract, a small lot, and no theatres, stayed healthier

ON THE
WATERFRONT

New York "method" naturalism in the famous car scene as Terry (Marlon Brando)
and his brother Charlie (Rod Steiger) discuss his taking another "dive."

Hitchcock's control of the "plastic material" as Cary Grant flees from a menacing plane in a flat, midwestern field.

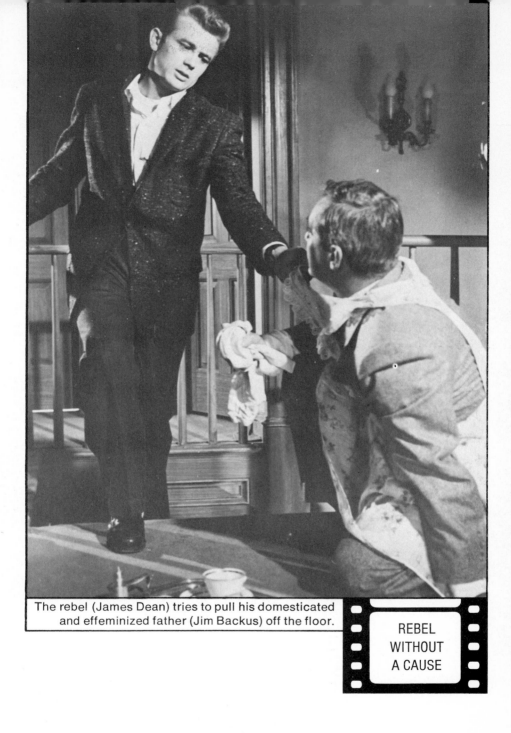

The rebel (James Dean) tries to pull his domesticated and effeminized father (Jim Backus) off the floor.

REBEL
WITHOUT
A CAUSE

Gene Kelly dances in the land of impressionism and in the rain.

in those years of thinner profits. The big movie houses suffered with the big studios. On a week night, only a few hundred patrons scattered themselves about a house built for three thousand. One by one the ornate palaces began to come down, replaced by supermarkets, shopping centers, and high-rise apartment buildings.

By 1952 Hollywood knew that television could not be choked. If films and television were to coexist, the movies would have to give the public what TV did not. The most obvious difference between movies and TV was the size of the screen. Television's visual thinking was necessarily in terms of inches whereas movies could compose in feet and yards. Films also enjoyed the advantage of over fifty years of technological research in color, properties of lenses, and special laboratory effects; the infant television art had not yet developed color or video tape. Hollywood's two primary weapons against television were to be size and technical gimmickry.

One of the industry's first sallies was 3-D, a three-dimensional, stereoscopic effect produced by shooting the action with two lenses simultaneously at a specified distance apart. Two interlocked projections then threw the two perspectives on a single screen simultaneously, the audience using plastic polaroid glasses to melt the two images into a single three-dimensional one. The idea was not new; even before the twentieth century, a viewer could see a three-dimensional version of a still photograph by looking at two related photos through a stereoscope. A popular American commercial toy, the Viewmaster, uses the same principle of fusing two pictures together to present a single, three-dimensional scenic view. Despite the familiarity of the stereoscopic principle, to see the principle become a full-length, active, feature film was a great novelty. Hollywood rushed into 3-D production in 1952 with *Bwana Devil, House of Wax, Creature from the Black Lagoon, The French Line, Kiss Me Kate, Murders in the Rue Morgue,* and *Fort Ti.* Audiences eagerly left their television sets to experience the gimmick that attacked them with knives, arrows, stampedes of animals, avalanches, and Jane Russell's bust; the thrill of 3-D was that the necessarily confined, flat, projected picture convincingly threatened to leap out of its frame at the audience.

Although there were long lines of eager patrons at the box office of *House of Wax,* the novelty, once experienced, did not bring many of them back again. Some blame the death of 3-D on the clumsy glasses that we had to wear; but the obvious cause of death was that any pure novelty, like the earliest filmstrips, becomes boring when it is no longer novel. Three-D was pure novelty; the thrill of being run over by a train is identical to that of being run over by a herd of cattle. Further, because 3-D required the theatre owner to make costly additions and renovations to his equipment, the exhibitors declared a war of neglect against the process and hastened its demise. Business at 3-D films fell off so quickly that Alfred

Hitchcock, who originally shot *Dial M for Murder* (1953) in the new process, released it in the conventional two dimensions. The only later attempts to revive 3-D have been in a few "sexploitation" films (for example, *Kiss My Analyst* or *The Stewardesses*) that promise especially titillating sequences for those who visit the "skin houses." Andy Warhol's decision to make his *Frankenstein* (1974) in 3-D undoubtedly reflected an awareness that the process could produce only two effects: the horrific and the pornographic.

A second movie novelty, released almost simultaneously with 3-D, also promised thrills. Cinerama, unlike 3-D, dazzled its patrons by bringing the audience into the picture, rather than the picture into the audience. Cinerama originally used three interlocked cameras and four interlocked projectors (one for sound). The final prints were not projected on top of one another (as in 3-D) but alongside each other. The result is a screen that is really three screens. The wide, deeply curved screen and the relative positions of the three cameras work on the eye's peripheral vision so that the mind believes that the body is actually in motion. The difference between a ride in an automobile and a conventionally filmed ride is that in an automobile the world also moves past us on the sides, not just straight ahead. Cinerama's huge triple screen duplicates this impression of peripheral movement.

Like 3-D the idea was not new. As early as the Paris World's Exposition of 1900, the energetic inventor-cinematographers had begun displaying wrap-around, multiscreen film processes. (Multi-screen experiments have long been popular at World Fairs, most recently at the New York fair of 1963–64 and Expo '67 in Montreal.) As early as the mid-twenties, Abel Gance incorporated triple-screen effects into his fictional feature film *Napoléon*. In 1938, Fred Waller, Cinerama's inventor, began research on the process. But when *This Is Cinerama* opened in 1952, audiences choked—quite literally—with a film novelty that sent them racing down a roller coaster track and soaring over the Rocky Mountains. A magnificent seven-track stereophonic sound system accompanied the galloping pictures; sounds could travel from left to right across the screen or jump from behind the screen to behind the audience's heads.

If Cinerama has survived much longer than its gimmicky brother, 3-D, it is not because Cinerama is less gimmicky. Lacking (at first) any fictional interest, Cinerama was even more dependent than 3-D on the surface grandeur of picture and sound. But Cinerama was more carefully marketed than 3-D. Because of the complex projection machinery, only a few theatres in major cities were equipped for the process. Seeing Cinerama became a special, exciting event; the film was sold as a "road-show" attraction with reserved seats, noncontinuous performances, high prices. Customers returned to Cinerama because they could see a Cinerama film so infrequently. And although Cinerama repeatedly offered its predictable postcard scenery and its obligatory rides and chases, the films were stunning travelogues and not embarrassing dramatic drivel like 3-D.

Cinerama faced new troubles when it too tried to combine its gimmick with narrative: *The Wonderful World of the Brothers Grimm* (1962), *It's a Mad, Mad, Mad, Mad World* (1963), *How the West Was Won* (1963). As with 3-D, what Aristotle called "Spectacle" (he found it the least important dramatic element) overwhelmed the more essential dramatic ingredients of plot, character, and ideas. In 1968, Stanley Kubrick's *2001* subordinated Cinerama's tricks to the film's sociological and metaphysical journey, letting the big screen and racing camera work for the story rather than letting the story work for the effects. The future of the Cinerama process is still uncertain today; the development in 1966 of special lenses that produce the Cinerama effect with one camera and one projector instead of three eliminates the bothersome joining lines and makes the process both easier to film and to exhibit. The ultimate health of the huge-screen process will depend on the artistic, creative, and imaginative uses to which it is put. In 1952, the gimmick successfully pulled Americans away from the small screen at home, but not enough of them at once to offer the film industry any real commercial hope. A sign that perhaps the Cinerama process is as doomed as 3-D was the 1973 rerelease of the original *This is Cinerama,* of twenty-one years earlier. The retreat into the past (*House of Wax* was rereleased in 1972) might indicate that the process has no future.

A third movie gimmick of the early 1950s also took advantage of the size of the movie screen. The novelty, christened CinemaScope, was the most durable and functional of them all, requiring neither special projectors, special film, nor special optical glasses (this lack of special equipment especially pleased the theatre owners). The action was recorded by a single, conventional movie camera on conventional 35 mm. film. A special anamorphic lens squeezed the images horizontally to fit the width of the standard film. When projected, with a corresponding anamorphic lens on the projector, the distortions disappear and a huge, wide image stretches across the theatre screen. Once again the "novelty" was not new. As early as 1928, a French scientist named Henri Chrétien had invented an anamorphic lens for the motion picture camera; in 1952, the executives of Twentieth Century-Fox visited Professor Chrétien, then retired to a Riviera villa, and bought the rights to his anamorphic process. The first Cinema-Scope feature, *The Robe* (1953), convinced both Fox and the industry that the process was a sound one. The screen had been made wide with a minimum of trouble and expense. A parade of screen-widening "scopes" and "visions" followed Fox's CinemaScope, some of them using an anamorphic lens, some of them achieving screen width by widening the film to 50 mm., 55 mm., 65 mm., or 70 mm.: Todd-AO, Metroscope, VistaVision, Panavision, Super Panavision, and Ultra Panavision.

Ultimately it was size, grandeur, that triumphed, not depth-perception or motion effects. As early as 1930, Eisenstein lectured on a flexible screen size, a principle he called the "dynamic square." Eisenstein reasoned that the conventional screen, with its four-to-three ratio of width to height, was an inflexible compromise. The screen, he reasoned, should be capable of becoming very wide for certain sequences, very narrow and long for others, a perfect square for balanced compositions. But Eisenstein's principles were much closer to Griffith's use of masking or irising than to the wide screen's equally inflexible commitment to width. George Stevens noted that CinemaScope made photographing a python more appropriate than a person. How could a horizontal picture frame, with a five-to-two ratio of width to height, enclose a vertical subject? As in the early years of sound, the new technological invention was a mixed blessing, adding some new film possibilities and destroying many of the old compositional virtues. But the wide screen, like sound, was an inescapable fact of film life and the artists would eventually come to terms with it. By the mid-1960s the wide-screen revolution was as complete as the sound revolution of the 1930s, and the wide screen, like sound, would become the basis of a new generation's film aesthetics.

The battle with television was partially responsible for another technical revolution in the 1950s—the almost total conversion to color. From the earliest days of moving pictures, inventors and filmmakers sought to combine color with recorded movement. The early Méliès films were hand-tinted frame by frame, but such meticulous painting was no substitute for color photography. Most silent films (Griffith's and Gance's most notably) were bathed in a color tint, adding a cast of pale blue for night sequences, a cast of red-orange for passionate, heated sequences, a yellow cast for certain effects, a green cast for others. Such coloring effects were obviously tonal, like the accompanying music, rather than an intrinsic part of the film's photographic conception. As early as 1908, Charles Urban patented a color photographic process, which he called Kinemacolor. But business opposition from the then-powerful Film Trust kept Kinemacolor off American screens.

In 1917, the Technicolor Corporation was founded in the United States. Supported by all the major studios, Technicolor enjoyed monopolistic control over all color experimentation and shooting in this country. Douglas Fairbanks's *The Black Pirate* (1926) and the musical *Rio Rita* (1929) used the Technicolor process, which added a garish grandeur to the costumes and scenery but sickly, unstable pinks or oranges to human flesh. In the 1920s Technicolor was, like Urban's Kinemacolor, a two-color process: two strips of film exposed by two separate lenses, one strip photographically sensitive to the blue-green colors of the spectrum, the other sensitive to the red-orange colors, then bonded together in the final processing. But by 1933 Technicolor had perfected a more accurate three-color process: three strips of film, one sensitive to blue, the second to red, the third to yellow, requiring a bulky three-lens camera for the three rolls of film. Hollywood could have converted to color at almost the same time it converted to sound. But expenses and priorities dictated that most talkies use black-and-white film, which was, itself, becoming faster, subtler, more responsive to minimal light, easier to use under any conditions. Color was reserved for special, novelty effects, for Disney cartoons, for lavish spectacles that needed the decorativeness of color and could afford the slowness and expense of color shooting (for example, Mamoulian's *Becky Sharp*, 1935; Fleming's *Gone with the Wind* and *The Wizard of Oz*, both 1939).

Before World War II, color was both a monopoly and a sacred mystery. Color negatives were processed and printed behind closed doors; special Technicolor consultants and cameramen were almost as important on the set of a color film as the director and producer. Natalie Kalmus, the wife of Herbert Kalmus who invented the process, became Technicolor's artistic director and constructed an official aesthetic code for the use of color (she preferred the quiet, muted effects of pastels), a code which was as binding on a film's color values as was the Hays Code on its moral values. Every film that used Technicolor was required to hire Mrs. Kalmus as "Technicolor Consultant."

The war, which demanded that the film industry keep up production while tightening its belt, generally excluded the luxury of color filming (with the notable English exception of Laurence Olivier's *Henry V*, 1944, in which the splendid color intensified the film's propagandistic appeal to the Englishman's traditional sense of courage). Most wartime American color films also had propaganda value—Minnelli's *Meet Me in St. Louis* (1944) which depicted the homespun life and traditions that the boys were fighting to save; DeMille's *The Story of Dr. Wassel* (1944), a hymn to an American war hero.

After the war, Hollywood needed color to fight television, which—at least until the 1960s—could offer audiences only black-and-white. Technicolor, formerly without competitors, had kept costs up and production down. Hollywood began encouraging a new, competing color process, Eastmancolor. The new process was one of the spoils of war, a pirated copy of the German Agfacolor monopack. The monopack color film bonded the three strips of color-sensitive film together in a single roll. A color film could be shot with an ordinary one-lens camera. Color emulsions became progressively faster, more sensitive, more flexible. A series of new color processes—DeLuxe, Metrocolor, Warnercolor—were all variations of Eastmancolor. During the 1950s black-and-white gradually became the exception, and color, even for serious dramas, little comedies, and low-budget westerns, became the rule. As the technology of color cinematography improved, film artists learned, as they did with sound, that a new technique was not only a gimmick but also could fulfill essential dramatic functions. Color movies ceased to be merely colorful and began using color to tell the film's story and control the film's tone.

While, on the one hand, the movies fought TV by offering audiences visual treats that television lacked, on the other, Hollywood finally capitulated to television by deciding to work with it rather than against it. If television was not to die, then it would use old movies and filmed installments of a series to sustain its diet. In 1951, Columbia Pictures established a subsidiary for making television films, Screen Gems, which produced such weekly shows as *Fireside Theatre* and *Ford Playhouse*. In the next few years, Walt Disney (*Disneyland*), Warner Brothers, Twentieth Century-Fox, MGM, and Universal began making 30- and 60-minute weekly shows —and commercials—for TV, while several new companies bought old film studios expressly to make television films: Revue bought the old Republic studio and Desilu the R.K.O. studio. Hollywood also lifted its ban against films and film stars appearing on television. In 1956, Hollywood first sold its films to television, the sole provision being that the film had to have been produced before 1948. Since 1956, however, Hollywood has sold more and more recent films to the networks; many of last year's movies appear on this year's television. In a sense, TV has replaced the old fourth- and fifth-run neighborhood movie houses, all of which have disappeared. By 1956, the war with television was over, and although the armistice had clearly defined the movies' future relationship with its living-room audiences, the future with its audiences in theatres was still uncertain.

Films in the Transitional Years

With the collapse of the studio structure, the dictatorial head of production, and the quantitative demands of a large yearly output, the producing of films became similar to the producing of stageplays. Like the theatre producer, the new film producer concentrated on shaping and selling a single project at a time, rather than a whole year's output of more than a dozen films. Like United Artists, David Selznick, and Samuel Goldwyn of earlier years, Hollywood feature-film production, even within the studios, had "gone independent." The more independent producer selected the property, the stars, and the director, raised the money, and supervised the selling of the finished film. He perhaps rented space on a studio lot; he perhaps used the studio's distribution offices to help sell the film.

But the producer, not the studio, made the picture. The producer usually owned no lot, no long-term contracts with stars, no staffs of writers and technicians. He assembled a company for a particular film, disbanded it when the film was finished, and assembled another company for his next film.

The individual producers, forced to make each film pay for itself, searched for stable, predictable production values. One of the axioms they discovered was that the most dependable films were either very expensive or very cheap. A very expensive film could make back its investment with huge publicity campaigns and high ticket prices at road-show engagements. The theory translated itself into practice with big films like *The Greatest Show on Earth, The Ten Commandments, The Robe, The Bridge on the River Kwai, Ben Hur,* and *Spartacus.* But the 1950s were also the years of *I Was a Teenage Werewolf, I Was a Teenage Frankenstein, Hercules, Hannibal, Joy Ride,* and *Riot in Juvenile Prison.* American-International Pictures, the only new producing company to be founded in a decade of studio collapse, built itself entirely on low-budget films with topical themes —horror, science fiction, rock and roll, juvenile delinquency, and beach parties—that could be shot in less than two weeks and budgeted at under $250,000. Joseph E. Levine built himself a commercial empire on films with Steve Reeves and a cast of Italians which were produced for under $150,000 in Italy and then dubbed into English. The very inexpensive film could make back its investment in two weeks of saturation booking at neighborhood theatres and drive-ins—yet another gimmick to pull Americans out of the living room. In an era of unstable business values the movies had become a lure for daring speculators, just as they had been before 1917.

For his major productions, the studio and independent producer became dependent on popular novels and popular plays, properties that had excited the public in other forms and would conceivably excite it again. American movies had been using the commercial power of a popular novel or play for forty years, ever since Kalem adapted *Ben Hur* in 1907 and later paid $25,000 in damages for failing to obtain legal rights to the book. In 1920, D. W. Griffith paid $175,000 for the rights to the old stage melodrama, *Way Down East,* and although no one had ever previously paid so much for a property, Griffith's financial investment was still a wise one. Throughout the studio years, both silent and talking, Hollywood adapted successful books, from *The Four Horsemen of the Apocalypse* to *Gone with the Wind.* But the percentage of adaptations that attempted to reproduce a book faithfully in return for trading on the book's popularity was rather low. Studios employed dozens of young writers either to invent totally original screenplays or to fashion almost original scripts loosely based on little-known stories and plays. If the studio years preceding World War II have been called the Age of the Scenarist, the years following the war must be called the Age of the Adaptation. Lacking large, permanent staffs of screen writers, both studio and independent producers bought established, already-written properties that merely needed translating into film form: *The Caine Mutiny, Marjorie Morningstar, Exodus, From Here to Eternity, Not as a Stranger, Tea and Sympathy, My Fair Lady, Sweet Bird of Youth,* and so forth, for several hundred titles. It was easier for a producer to raise money for a film that was considered "presold"; it was easier for him to sell one of these familiar properties back to the public after the film had been finished.

Because both fiction and the stage have traditionally remained freer of sexual and moral restrictions than films—there have never been any official codes for books or plays—it was inevitable that fresh breezes would blow from the original works into the screen adaptations of them. Because television applied even stricter moral regulations to its programs than the 1934 Breen Code did to films, film producers could lure audiences to the theatre with promises of franker, racier, "more adult" entertainment. The content of films adapted from novels like *Peyton Place, From Here to Eternity, Advise and Consent, Suddenly Last Summer,* and *Butterfield 8* could not possibly avoid references to adultery, fornication, or homosexuality, topics that were perfectly suited to Hollywood's audience war with television. In the search to find a tool that television lacked, film producers seized upon sexual relationships and social criticism.

But the sexual-social films of the transitional years were very different from 1970's "liberated" films. The sharp producer of the 1950s had merely found a clever way of injecting sexual tidbits and social questions into the old 1934 formulas for morality, motivation, and plotting. Otto Preminger and Stanley Kramer were particularly good at turning "explosive," "controversial" material into films that could offend no one. Preminger's *The Moon is Blue* (1953), the first major film to be released without the Code's seal of approval, merely added a few "naughty" words (for example, virgin and mistress!), a few leering eyebrows, and a few bedroom situations to a completely conventional, and stale, comedy of manners. The difference in the sexual maturity of this leering, juvenile treatment of sex and the treatment in a film like Lubitsch's *Trouble in Paradise* is the difference between mud pies and Sacher Torte. Equally puerile is Preminger's *Advise and Consent* (1962), which turns homosexuality into a melodramatic complication of the plot, and which, in the best Joe McCarthy style, turns the crusading leftist into an unscrupulous villain and the bigoted, filibustering southern crook into a nice old guy. Preminger's two most enjoyable postwar films, *The Man with the Golden Arm* (1955) and *Anatomy of a Murder* (1959), use very quiet, understated acting and very effective jazz scores (by Elmer Bernstein and Duke Ellington respectively) to make the stories more absorbing and the heavy-handed social commentary less obvious.

Stanley Kramer became the era's sentimental liberal. In *The Defiant Ones* (1958), he examined race relations by showing a black man and a white man escaping from a southern prison; since they are chained together, they are forced to come to terms with one another. The terms, the problems, and their solutions were completely predictable from the moment the men fled together. In *On the Beach* (1959), the entire human race is about to perish from atomic fallout. Kramer's film depicts this staggering human catastrophe as a nuisance that is about to interfere with several pretty love affairs. Kramer portrays the sentimental consequences of universal death, but none of its human or social causes. Perhaps the soul of Stanley Kramer is best presented by the judge in *Judgment at Nuremberg* (1961). Played by Spencer Tracy (who, along with Henry Fonda, was everyone's favorite movie liberal), the head judge at the Nuremberg trials defines himself as a Maine Republican who thought F.D.R. was a great man. Such a definition is specially designed to offend no one's principles. Amazingly, the film's *scène à faire,* in which the judge explains the legal principles on which he is going to find the German defendants guilty, never takes place. Kramer cuts from the judge asking for dissenting opinions, a clear forum for possible debate, to the judge pronouncing sentence on the guilty. The precise standard of guilt remains unclear. The film remains a vehicle for a predictable, melodramatic display of war horrors and the broken, psychotic, deformed humans who emerge from the war to parade to the witness stand and do their twitchy thing for Kramer's perpetually zooming lens.

The tension between social consciousness and Hollywood cliché is very strong in the films of the transitional era. The tension accounts for some of the pretentiousness and some of the staleness of those films today. William Wyler's *The Best Years of Our Lives* (1946) maintains its freshness because its social theme—the problem of the returning serviceman adjusting to civilian life—has been completely absorbed by a compelling story, a credible study of more general problems of human relationships, and Gregg Toland's subtly effective camera work. But Elia Kazan's *Gentleman's Agreement* (1947), a study of suburban antisemitism, and *Pinky* (1949), a study of a black girl who passes for white, seem both worn and thin because a rather obvious statement of a social problem has been substituted for both plot and people. Kazan, a cold-war liberal in the era of Hollywood blacklisting, had the problem of making social-problem films that would neither offend an audience nor cost him his job. He solved the problem in his best films by turning social statements into human statements—*A Streetcar Named Desire* (1951), *Viva Zapata!* (1952), *On the Waterfront* (1954), *East of Eden* (1955), *A Face in the Crowd* (1957)—all of which sustain their social issues with dynamic acting performances by Marlon Brando (the prototypic Kazan actor), Vivien Leigh, James Dean, Jo van Fleet, Rod Steiger, Andy Griffith, and others. In these films

Kazan brought the earthy, realist acting style of New York's Group Theater to Hollywood.

John Huston also faced the tension between cinema style and significant statement. His generally fine *Treasure of the Sierra Madre* (1948) is marred by heavy-handed symbolism (a money bag on a cactus) that is more in the spirit of MGM's *Greed* than von Stroheim's. If Kazan's films, with their credibly earthy acting, revealed his background in the theatre, Huston's revealed his background as a scriptwriter with their taut and subtle scripts in which individual human weaknesses usually destroy the best laid plans of mice and men: *The Maltese Falcon* (1941), *The Asphalt Jungle* (1950), *The African Queen* (1951), and *Beat the Devil* (1954). Huston, however, caught the pretentiousness bug, and his later films seemed to demand more than he could muster stylistically (*Moulin Rouge*, 1953; *Moby Dick*, 1956) or intellectually (*Freud*, 1963; *Night of the Iguana*, 1964).

The best films of the transition era were neither pretentious in size, spectacle, and grandeur, nor pretentious in their attempts at intellectual statement. The best American films of the fifteen years following the war were the same kinds of films that seemed best before the war: driving, engaging stories; credible, if not psychologically complex, characters; functional camera work and editing; appropriate and economical dialogue. The American film was still a narrative medium, not a thematic or psychological one.

Several of the directors who made the best films before the war also made the best films after it. Alfred Hitchcock, despite his opportunity to revel in the aberrant personality, never forgot to keep his stories driving toward a breathless climax. Hitchcock, always the technical innovator, accepted the challenge of the new technical devices (3-D, color, Cinema-Scope) of the transitional era with glee. His *Rope* (1948) was an audacious technical experiment in which Hitchcock decided to shoot his tale of murder and homosexuality in extremely long, ten-minute takes, using almost no editing devices at all (and this from a master of editing!). The decade from 1950 to 1960 was an extremely fertile one for Hitchcock, ranking with the English years of 1935 to 1940 as one of his two most significant periods. In *Strangers on a Train* (1951) Hitchcock juxtaposes murder and a bizarrely perverted sexuality with the conventional social assumptions about success and normalcy—exactly as he did with *Psycho* (1960), the film that closes the decade. In *Rear Window* (1954), *To Catch a Thief* (1955), and *Vertigo* (1958) Hitchcock examines the thin line between fantasy and reality, perversion and normalcy, vice and virtue. *The Man Who Knew Too Much* (1956) and *North by Northwest* (1959) return to the English films of the 1930s (quite literally with *The Man Who Knew Too Much*) in which slick, innocent, and endangered men run for their lives and run toward the vaguely political menace that has entangled them. As in his earliest films, Hitchcock remained the master of the "plastic material": the photographer's flashbulb in *Rear Window,* the sparkling jewels in *To Catch a Thief,* the crop-dusting plane in *North by Northwest.*

John Ford continued his mythification of the civilizing of the Old West: *My Darling Clementine* (1946), Ford's legend of Wyatt Earp; *Fort Apache* (1948), *She Wore a Yellow Ribbon* (1949), and *Wagonmaster* (1950), Ford's trilogy examining the role of the cavalry in the civilization process; and the allegorical *The Man Who Shot Liberty Valance* (1962). Ford also displayed his Irish background and commitment in the touchingly warm *The Quiet Man* (1952), as well as his commitment to America and Irish Americans in *The Long Gray Line* (1954) and *The Last Hurrah* (1959). Howard Hawks made his classics of toughness, *The Big Sleep* (1946) and *Red River* (1948), as well as the much later *Rio Bravo* (1959) and *El Dorado* (1967). Unlike Hitchcock, however, both Hawks and Ford seemed to belong exclusively to the styles of the earlier studio era. They both seemed stylistically uncomfortable with color and the wide screen. For Ford, color seemed irrelevant, and the wide screen tended to weigh his films down with a heavy, slow, and static nonrhythm. Hawks was so clumsy with the big screen (*Gentlemen Prefer Blondes,* 1953; *Land of the Pharaohs,* 1955) that his most lively later films deliberately used as small a screen as possible.

The western film remained one of the most exciting and entertaining of the transitional era: George Stevens's *Shane* (1953), Fred Zinnemann's *High Noon* (1952), Nicholas Ray's *Johnny Guitar* (1954), as well as several of the films of Budd Boetticher, Jacques Tourneur, Anthony Mann, and Samuel Fuller. But in the transitional era the conventions of this long-lived Hollywood genre began to stretch in several different directions. Some western films—most notably Anthony Mann's (*Winchester 73,* 1950; *Bend of the River,* 1951) and Budd Boetticher's (*Decision at Sundown,* 1957; *The Tall T,* 1957; *Buchanan Rides Alone,* 1958)—maintained the conventional attitudes of the genre toward violence and killing. Violence was a legitimate means to an end of establishing law and civilization or a legitimate assertion of a man's self and self-respect against elemental enemies.

But other westerns of the 1950s began taking the conventions of the genre toward their next evolutionary stage of the sixties and seventies. On the one hand, a director could use the mythic background of the Old West to discuss contemporary American values (disguise was an especially useful ploy in an era of blacklisting). *High Noon,* in its attack on the timidity of the respectable majority and its contempt for the think-alike, act-alike mentality, is clearly about the American social climate of 1952. The John Sturges westerns (*Bad Day at Black Rock,* 1954; *Gunfight at the OK*

Corral, 1957) similarly mix contemporary moralizing with the western's setting and action. On the other hand, a director could view the violence of westerns as symptomatic of deranged and psychotic human behavior; the "good" gunman who guns down the bad one becomes himself a brutal and brutalized semi-psychotic (most notably in *Shane* and in Samuel Fuller's orgies of violence, *I Shot Jesse James,* 1949; *Run of the Arrow,* 1957). *Johnny Guitar* may be one of the most bizarrely deranged westerns ever made, its tense hysteria magnified by the screeching gaudiness of its Trucolor, a two-color process as false as its name, favored by the quickie Republic studio because of its cheapness.

Another familiar Hollywood genre found its conventions stretching and pulling in the decade after the war. The gangster film began turning very dark, concentrating on the inevitability of crime in urban America, on crime as a symptom of the society's disease, on criminals who are not simply selfish and tough (like Rico or Scarface) but deranged, on policemen who are as diseased as the men they track down, on peripheral characters who are frequently physical or mental cripples, and on visual images that are consistently shadowy, dark, and dim. The French critics coined a name, the *film noir,* for this sub-genre of films about gangsters who are not tough but sick and about gangsterism which is incurably rooted in society itself. Edward Dmytryk's *Crossfire* (1947) is a black mixture of murder, antisemitism, and homosexuality. Robert Rossen's *Body and Soul* (1947) and Abraham Polonsky's *Force of Evil* (1949) both use John Garfield as a child of the slums facing the inevitable decision between an unprofitable honesty and lucrative crookedness. Garfield was perhaps the prototypic *film noir* hero and the "bad girl"—Gloria Grahame, Jean Hagen, Shelley Winters, the early Marilyn Monroe—its prototypically used and abused woman. The title of Huston's *The Asphalt Jungle* could serve as a metaphor for the whole genre. In Robert Siodmak's *Cry of the City* (1948), the cop becomes possessed with the task of tracking down the criminal, who happens to be his boyhood pal as well as a man that the cop secretly envies. Henry Hathaway's *Call Northside 777* (1948) uses real locations rather than studio interiors, giving it a sense of reality, immediacy, and urgency. James Cagney stars in Raoul Walsh's *White Heat* (1949), in which the old-style, breezy Cagney gangster has literally become psychotic. Jules Dassin depicts the brutality of prison life (*Brute Force,* 1947), the brutality of urban life (*Naked City,* 1948), and the commercial brutality of the San Francisco vegetable market (*Thieves' Highway,* 1949). In Fritz Lang's *The Big Heat* (1953) women become mere pawns (and the victims of gruesome crimes) in the war between cops and criminals.

An outgrowth of the *film noir* was a new genre that also showed marked affinities with the western. The "rebellious youth" films of the 1950s—particularly Laslo Benedek's *The Wild One* (1953) and Nicholas

Ray's *Rebel Without a Cause* (1955)—were also a violent reaction against a decaying and diseased society. But whereas the gangster chose violence as a defense against the brutal hardness of city life, the youths rebel against the sterility, monotony, and conformity of adult life. Despite Ray's ironic title, these rebels most certainly do have a cause. Just as the western hero has his horse, his means to freedom, and the gangster his automobile, his means of destruction, the youths have their motorcycles and automobiles, which are both instruments of freedom and destruction. The machines take the youths away from the confined mediocrity of adult life and give them the exhilaration of movement in open spaces (like the cowboy's horse); but the machines also destroy property, people, and even their masters themselves. The youth films developed new folk heroes, Marlon Brando and James Dean, who were to contemporary society what John Wayne, Gary Cooper, and Randolph Scott had been to the Old West.

American comic films after the war were particularly uninventive, especially considering the richness of the preceding thirty-five years. The newest comic performers were Bud Abbott and Lou Costello, who seemed to be built on the old physical premises of Laurel and Hardy or the Marx Brothers—one fat, one thin; one smart, one dumb; one clumsy, one suave. But despite their physical humor, Abbott and Costello were primarily verbal comics (Who's on first?); the only way to use them in a film was to plunge the bungling, cowardly, klutzy Lou into dangerous or horrifying situations. And so Abbott and Costello met murderers, the Invisible Man, Frankenstein, Dracula, and the Wolf Man in an attempt to squeeze laughs from spine-tingling contrasts of humor and horror.

Succeeding Abbott and Costello in 1950 were Martin and Lewis, another team combining a wacky, zany clown and a smooth "straight" man. Interestingly, none of the classic comedy-film teams—Laurel and Hardy, the Marx Brothers, the Sennett repertory clowns—had any use for a human being who was "straight." Martin and Lewis contrasted not so much physically as mentally: the one brash, noisy, nasal, the other cool, loose, controlled. But the weakness of their films is that their wacky personalities were drowned in predictable, overplotted situation comedies (so many of the American classic comedians were notoriously independent of plotting).

The same problem plagues the films that Jerry Lewis made alone after 1956. Although the French intellectual critics rate Jerry Lewis alongside Chaplin and Keaton, no American over fourteen can sit through a Jerry Lewis film. Lewis's problem seems to be a conflict between character and plot, a zany conception forced to march through a completely formulaic story. The first reel or two of a Lewis film is brilliantly funny as Lewis reveals the particular comic nuttiness of the main character. But then the exposition at an end, the nutty professor, shopkeeper, errand boy, or whatever, must trudge through more than an hour of, Will he get the girl? or,

Will he keep his job? Lewis runs out of comic ideas for a character or situation after about twenty minutes. Unlike any of the great American film clowns, Lewis's funniness stems entirely from technique rather than a unique personality and vision of experience.

The director-crafted comedy of manners also declined after the war. Frank Capra (*It's a Wonderful Life,* 1947; *State of the Union,* 1948; *Riding High,* 1950; *A Hole in the Head,* 1959) made films that were feeble shadows of his greatest work. Preston Sturges, who made several witty, satirical films during the war (*The Great McGinty,* 1940; *The Lady Eve,* 1941; *Sullivan's Travels,* 1942; *Hail the Conquering Hero,* 1944), made a few mellower, thinner comedies after the war (*Mad Wednesday,* 1947; *Unfaithfully Yours,* 1948; *The Beautiful Blonde from Bashful Bend,* 1949). The best postwar comedies of manners were Billy Wilder's, who, with his coauthor, I. A. L. Diamond, preserved the tradition of comic collaboration between director and scenarist.

Wilder's comedy juxtaposed verbal wit with a sinister, morally disturbing environment: comedy and the corruption of post-war Berlin (*A Foreign Affair,* 1948), comedy and a psychotic has-been of the silent screen (*Sunset Boulevard,* 1950); and a concentration camp (*Stalag 17,* 1953); and the gangster underworld (*Some Like It Hot,* 1959); and the corruption of Madison Avenue (*The Apartment,* 1961). The films vary in their balance of comedy and moral seriousness. *Sunset Boulevard* is most interested in the perversion of human values that turns Norma Desmond (Gloria Swanson) into a fanatic worshipper of her dead past and Joe (William Holden) into a male prostitute willing to sell head, heart, and body for the hope of an equally dead future. Wilder's film examines the human dreams and emotions a man must sell to purchase success. *Some Like It Hot,* the opposite extreme, tries to get as many gags as it can out of Jack Lemmon and Tony Curtis in drag with an all-girl orchestra. Outstanding among the postwar comedies of manners was George S. Kaufman's *The Senator Was Indiscreet* (1948), a brilliant political comedy in the Preston Sturges tradition, chronicling the hilarious attempts of a moronic senator to snatch the presidential nomination. But the film was an isolated stylish piece in an era when American comedy had lost its old style and had not yet found a new one.

Musicals in the postwar years were also undergoing a transition. This transition may have produced Hollywood's greatest musical films. Before the war, Hollywood musicals were slight concoctions inevitably centering around the doings of show folk. Musical numbers wove through a scanty plot about love among entertainers as Ruby Keeler, Dick Powell, Fred Astaire, Ginger Rogers, or Rita Hayworth sang and danced in the show-business world of theatres and night clubs. The films had no pretensions to psychological realism or serious human relationships; the plots were almost invisible trifles to hold the musical numbers together. In the 1960s, however, filmed musicals, following the pattern of Broadway shows (which, of course, they were adapting), became realistic and psychological. World War II and Nazis and street gangs and death had become subjects for Broadway musical comedy. The unserious fluff of Rodgers and Hart had been replaced by the romantic seriousness of Rodgers and Hammerstein.

In the "integrated" musical, as the Rodgers-Hammerstein type and its successors came to be known, one did not assume that singing and psychological interaction were mutually exclusive (which had been the assumption of earlier Broadway shows and Hollywood musical films). The "integrated" show tried to imagine under what conditions a human being might sing in reality. Although it was difficult to convince a Broadway audience that a group of juvenile delinquents would sing to each other before cutting each other's throats, the task was even more difficult for the films. The stage, at least, enjoys the unreality of cardboard and plaster and paint and spotlight. But how to make a film audience believe that a group of juvenile delinquents would pirouette down a real New York street with real graffiti on the walls and real garbage in the gutter? How to make an audience believe that a woman would sing a song standing on a real tugboat in the middle of New York harbor?

The director of early musical films did not have such problems. Musical films were obviously unreal, unserious spoofs that never pretended to credibility. A director like Busby Berkeley could twirl his camera, his dancers, their pianos, fiddles, and fountains, in such grandiose and grotesquely imaginative patterns precisely because his musical numbers owed no allegiance to either logic or reality. Although it is almost taken for granted that color is the musical's natural medium, it is worth mentioning that without black-and-white there would have been no Busby Berkeley or Fred Astaire—or not the same ones. Berkeley's kaleidoscopic visual conceptions depended on the contrast of white and black (say, white dresses gleaming off a polished black floor), and Fred Astaire, in top hat and tails, literally *was* black and white. Surely the decline in both careers after the 1930s must be partially the result of the death of the monochrome musical.

Musical films just after the war, while they did become lavish, ornate, Technicolor spectaculars (as so many films did), maintained their stylized unreality. The MGM musicals produced by Arthur Freed in particular combined surrealistically imaginative musical numbers, pleasant scores, an exciting use of color, and funny, spoofing plots that often still revolved around showfolk: Vincente Minnelli's *The Pirate* (1948), *An American in Paris* (1952), *The Bandwagon* (1953); Charles Walters's *Easter Parade* (1948), *Summer Stock* (1950); Stanley Donen and Gene Kelly's *On the*

Town (1949) and *Singin' in the Rain* (1952); Donen's *Seven Brides for Seven Brothers* (1954).

The best of the musicals were those with musical numbers conceived and choreographed by Gene Kelly, particularly *An American in Paris* and *Singin' in the Rain*. In *Paris,* Kelly's ballet, combining George Gershwin's tone poem with French impressionistic painting, received the most critical attention. Although the lengthy ballet borders on the pretentious and fits very clumsily into the film's plot (which is, itself, a concoction of clichéd hokum), the dream-ballet by itself is a brilliant demonstration of the powers of a purely abstract cinema. Its integration of music, color, dance, decor, costumes, and editing is as sensually and formally "pure" cinema as any abstract filmmaker has ever attempted. Equally exuberant and imaginative was the staging of "By Strauss" in a Paris bistro, the staging of "I'll Build a Stairway to Paradise" on a Paris music-hall stage, and Kelly's casual singing, hoofing, and whistling of "I've Got Rhythm" for a group of Paris kids.

Singin' in the Rain boasts perhaps the best screenplay for any musical film, by Betty Comden and Adolph Green, the best of Comden and Green's many Hollywood spoofs, both in films and on the stage. Every musical number in *Singin' in the Rain* combines both music and fun, pleasant movement and wry spoof: the opening musical montage in which Kelly rises from sleazy hoofer to movie star, the staging of the title song in which Kelly tap dances in rain puddles (!), the surrealistic ballet, "Gotta Dance," in which Kelly romanticizes a young entertainer's rise to the top.

Indicative of the shifting styles in film musicals is the difference between the love song, "You Were Meant for Me," of *Singin' in the Rain,* and the love song, "One Hand, One Heart," of *West Side Story* (1961). In the earlier film, Kelly leads his lady onto a sound stage, turns on atmospheric colored lights, turns on an artificial wind machine, and then sings, surrounded by stylized unreality. In *West Side Story,* girl and boy pledge their troth in her bedroom, shortly after climbing out of bed, the sheets of which are noticeably rumpled. Whichever style you prefer, the difference between the two is obvious. The shifting styles must partially account for the conversion of Gene Kelly's imaginativeness of *Singin' in the Rain* and *Les Girls* to the predictable dullness of *Hello Dolly!* (1969).

By the mid-1950s, MGM had already begun deserting original musical ideas, assigning Vincente Minnelli to adapting stage shows like *Brigadoon* and *Kismet*. The original screen musical died with the original screenplay. It also died with the studio system that produced a certain number of musical films each year and kept a stable of musical talent stocked expressly for that purpose. With the death of the studios that developed such musical talent America also witnessed the death of any future Gene Kellys, Judy Garlands, and Fred Astaires, who no longer had a school for study nor a showcase for displaying their wares. The repertory musical performer needs a repertory system.

Finding the Audience

Despite the gimmicks, despite the wide screen, despite the sexual innuendos, despite the industry's claim that "movies are better than ever," movie income and movie admissions continued to fall. In an effort to give the public what television could not, Hollywood discovered that it could not give much of it anything for very long. The public yawned respectfully through a big spectacle and returned to the television set; it bought a ticket for one supposedly racy film, discovered it was not very racy, and returned to the television set. In order to please its public, Hollywood had to discover who its public was. It could not assume, as Mayer and Zukor and Cohn did in the thirties, that its public was all of the people all of the time.

The signs that would eventually point the way had begun to appear just after the war. A series of foreign films—with DeSica's *The Bicycle Thief* (1948) being, perhaps, the first important import—proved that a particular kind of film, inexpensively produced, more obviously sociological and less escapist than the Hollywood film, could attract interested audiences to small theatres while slick Hollywood films played to empty houses in large ones. More and more little neighborhood theatres that could no longer do business as fourth-run houses for Hollywood films found a second life as "art houses" showing foreign pictures like *La Strada* (1954), *Les Diaboliques* (1955), and *Nights of Cabiria* (1957). The foreign film was certainly unlike anything that the networks could present on television: introspective, with dialogue requiring the audience to read printed words, sensitive to intellectual and social questions, sexually mature, with refreshing and un-Americanized insights into other cultures, other values, and other peoples. There had been a call for "art houses" and an "art movement" in the 1930s, which had been answered in a few major cities by a few theatres. But the small art house of under 500 seats, with its elitist fare, ran contrary to the old financial tides of 1940 (when the big movie palaces of several thousand seats filled up every night with customers eager to see Cary Grant or Greer Garson). With television, however, the commercial tides had turned.

Hollywood discovered that movies had indeed become an elitist, not a popular, art. Just as the legitimate theatre had been the art for *some* in the thirties when movies were the art for *everyone*, so movies had become the art for some when television became the art for all. Whereas movies had been the casual, everyday form of entertainment before the war, television supplied that kind of entertainment after it. Movies, then, had to be aimed at the minority audience that wanted the kind of show that television could not or would not provide. The elitism of the 1970 movie audience becomes clear when comparing the average cost of a ticket in 1946 and 1970. Although films grossed almost the same amount of money in both years, in 1946 the average movie seat cost a bit over forty cents; in 1970 the average seat cost a bit under two dollars. Parenthetically, the conversion of the movies into elitist entertainment has robbed the legitimate theatre of most of its audience. The theatre, with its enormous production costs, high ticket prices, and ever-decreasing number of large playhouses, has become such a superelitist art that it is a cultural relic, a living museum. In England, where the prices of theatre and film tickets are comparable, legitimate theatre still competes very healthily with films as the elite entertainment.

There is no clearer sign of the "generation gap" than in the difference between the television and movie audience in this country. The majority of filmgoers in the 1970s are under thirty, educated, and live in the cities. Hollywood aims its films at their values, their interests, their styles, using their themes, their music, their moral codes. If 1970s movies are directed at the young and urban, television, like films in the thirties, is aimed at rural and suburban families. The important rating systems that determine a show's popularity are very attentive to figures from the Midwest and South as well as from New York City. But for a new film to be successful, it needs favorable reviews from the big-city critics. Television programs are aimed at the kind of audience who went to the movies in the thirties and forties; in fact much of its audience is composed of those very people. Television formulas—family comedies, mysteries, westerns, hospital dramas, courtroom dramas—are the old movie formulas. They have not changed because the audience has not changed. Films and film audiences have changed.

The movies have learned to coexist with television. They have sent their old formulas to TV and deemphasized spectacle and bigness except for those few films each year consciously and sincerely intended as "General" (G) entertainment: *Funny Girl* (1968), *Oliver!* (1968), *Mame* (1973). They have scrapped their huge movie palaces and replaced them with 500-seat theatres that are easier to fill despite their three-dollar ticket prices. They have chopped big theatres into two or even three smaller theatres on the same property, a much more economical use of land and space in cities like New York and London where rent is very high: New York's Baronet/Coronet, Cinema I and II, Loew's State 1 and 2; London's Cinecenta 1, 2, 3, and 4, Paramount 1 and 2. Television, which threatened to swallow the film studios, has itself been swallowed. Over seventy-five percent of the film footage shot in Hollywood is for television production.

The old studios survived the years of drift and struggle solely on the steady income from TV filming. The same relationship that existed between "A" and "B" pictures in the studio era exists between feature and television production in the 1970s. Movies are Hollywood's proudest product; television shows and commercials are Hollywood's steady staples.

The fifteen years following World War II may have been the least exciting, least imaginative, least innovative years in the *art* of the American film since Griffith founded that art in 1908. The bustling production in quantity of the studio years had died; the imaginative production in quality of the last few years had not yet been born. Although some 4,000 films were made in those years—many of them good ones—the American film lacked the unifying spirit, direction, and purpose that distinguished it in its two previous major eras (1915–29, 1930–46). Hollywood slowly stumbled through the maze of conflicting production values, eventually emerging from what seems like a time warp.

Note that in the last sentence "Hollywood" has been personified. That personification is especially appropriate today when Hollywood, former world capital of film production, is now only a metaphor, a phrase that symbolizes the American film business, American film values, the movies. In 1968, there were almost as many films shot in New York City as in Hollywood (a fact that became an issue in the 1969 New York City mayoral campaign). "Hollywood" films included MGM's release of 2001 (made in Britain with an American director, an American technological process, and British crew), Paramount's release of *Romeo and Juliet* (an Italian film with an English cast) and *If . . .* (thoroughly English), and Twentieth Century-Fox's release of Richard Lester's totally English, *The Three Musketeers*.

In 1973 the MGM and Twentieth Century-Fox studios were both sold to make room for apartment houses, office buildings, and shopping malls. Although Leo the Lion still roars before several films each year, there is no more MGM studio where films are made, only a company that finances or distributes films. One of the only major Hollywood studios to remain intact, Universal, has done so by supporting itself almost completely with television production (both series filming and specially made-for-TV "movies"), with a large hotel on its grounds, and by advertising its tours as a major attraction for visitors to Southern California. In the Studio Golden Era no visitors were ever allowed on the lot when companies were filming, for they would disrupt the busy shooting schedules. Nineteen seventy-three was also the year that Central Casting closed. There were not enough jobs to justify the existence of a casting office that once sent thousands of extras each day to a dozen studios that were busily making films.

Although in the 1970s the American film business—yearly gross, weekly admissions, audience vitality and interest—is thriving, the theoretical capital of that business, Hollywood, is a movie ghost town, dead as a production center. With so many companies filming in New York, Europe, Mexico, and in the Great West, Hollywood itself is suffering the worst production crisis in its history. The new movie audiences have rejected not only the old Hollywood values but the Hollywood studios as well.

NEOREALISMS
AND
NEW WAVES

After World War II, European directors did exactly what they did after the first world war. They climbed out from under five years of wartime rubble and disrupted production, somehow scraped together enough money and film stock to assemble a motion picture, and began making films that showed extraordinary sincerity, perceptivity, and artistic control. While American films searched for a new identity, the best films came from Europe. The films were best not because they often revealed portions of naked bodies together in a bathtub or on a sofa, not because the actors spoke a chic but incomprehensible tongue, not because the films were bathed in obscure, symbolic, pretentious meanings, and not because American audiences had become cultural snobs—as so many chauvinistic American film critics and film executives claimed. The films were best because they raised the same questions in cinematic form that had been raised in the best novels, plays, poems, and philosophical essays of the twentieth century. And the Americans who had become the new movie audience, those who found it easy to leave their television sets, were precisely those who were reading the books.

To call the new European films more existential than the American would perhaps seem pretentious; it would also seem to give assent to those American critics who found the European films both dreary and depressing. But in the tradition of Mann, Proust, Pirandello, and Sartre (and, by the way, of Renoir, Carné, Murnau, and Pabst), the new European film searched for meaningful, life-giving human values in a world in which absolute values had obviously crumbled. This kind of film would almost inevitably produce what Hollywood would call (and has called) an unhappy ending. What are happy endings? Hollywood has traditionally, in thousands of films, used one of two—or both. In fact, there are only two happy endings: 1) Good triumphs over Evil; 2) John gets Jane. Historically these endings have always been appropriate to comedy—Plautus, Shakespeare, Molière—and melodrama. But they are inappropriate to tragedy, if we define tragedy as that kind of action pertaining to Man (whereas comedy pertains to men) which examines the human condition (whereas comedy examines the social condition). And the tragic human condition, as expressed by tragic dramatists from Aeschylus to Beckett, can be summarized by a single line from Albert Camus's play, *Caligula:* "Men die; and they are not happy."

The two Hollywood endings, and all comic endings, are incompatible with Caligula's cry. Previously, neither American producers nor American movie audiences had wanted such an idea to sneak into the local movie house. The only directors of American films who ever suggested such an idea were Erich von Stroheim, Charles Chaplin, and Orson Welles. All three of them were banned from Hollywood; all three of them have become extremely popular with the same audiences who enjoy foreign films. The American films prior to 1960 that do not end with either of the two familiar happy formulas make up a small and select group—among them, *Broken Blossoms, Greed, City Lights, The Grapes of Wrath, Citizen Kane, The Treasure of the Sierra Madre,* and *Sunset Boulevard.* (Not a bad group of American films!) Hollywood's victory of good over evil presented a severe problem in a world in which both terms were difficult to define. When Hollywood's John got Jane they lived happily ever after; when reality's John got Jane the problems of communication, compatibility, and day-to-day "unromance" began. Many European films began with a marriage rather than ended with one. A serious examination of tragic human problems could not be squeezed into the old Hollywood formulas—hence the tension between intellectual probing and melodramatic formula in the Kramer-Preminger films and other American films of the years that followed the war.

The great films of postwar Europe, despite the individuality of the particular directors, share several traits that contrast with the American films. First, very few of them were faithful adaptations of familiar books and plays. The films were often original conceptions, carefully shaped by the director and scenarist working in unison (in fact, the director was usually credited as coauthor). This collaboration of director and scenarist revealed a continuity in the European film tradition (before the war, its great films had been produced with collaborations like Murnau-Mayer and Carné-Prévert).

Second, the postwar European films continued the prewar tradition of structuring themselves around a theme or psychological problem rather than around a story. Like *Grand Illusion, The Children of Paradise, Potemkin,* or *The Last Laugh,* the films of Vittorio DeSica, Federico Fellini, Ingmar Bergman, and Michelangelo Antonioni were not so much narratives as they were comparisons of human conduct, human emotional states, and conflicts between the social whole and the human unit.

Third, the focus on psychology and theme brought these films into the mainstream of twentieth-century thought and literature. The thematic and psychological questions in these films could only be the same as those in Camus, Mann, Kafka, Beckett, and Ionesco.

Fourth, the European director knew that he was free to manipulate film style, that certain kinds of thematic inquiries or psychological states required a totally different handling of the camera and sound track. The directors of *Calgari, The Fall of the House of Usher,* and *À Nous la liberté* had earlier realized the same principle.

In effect, the postwar European cinema brought the movies into the mainstream of "modernism," the key twentieth-century movement that produced nonrepresentational painting, atonal music, absurd drama, and the stream-of-consciousness novel, and whose two tenets were the self-conscious questioning of all social and moral values and the self-conscious manipulation of the conventions of the art itself. Like the great European directors before 1940, the postwar European filmmaker was both thinker and poet. And the postwar film audience, especially in America, was receptive to his films, allowing him to make more and more of them. Although several American critics shuddered at the thought of "Antoniennui" or "come-dressed-as-the-sick-soul-of-Europe" pictures, the years after 1945 were remarkable in that so many European directors had something to say and knew how to say it.

Italian Neorealism

Not since 1913 had Italy been an important film power. The huge silent spectacles of 1912 and 1913 were swiftly replaced by the Griffith films which were not only big but active. Early Italian sound films traveled between the two poles of pro-Mussolini propaganda and escapist comedies and musical romances, so-called "White Telephone" pictures (because of the inevitable white telephone in the fancily decorated apartments that served as sets for these films). Italian films under Mussolini were remarkably similar to German films under Hitler. Despite the financial aid Mussolini extended to the film industry, despite his founding of a huge film studio (Cinecittá) and film school (Centro Sperimentale), the Italian film remained frozen by its commitment to either dogma or drivel. After the overthrow of Mussolini and the expulsion of the Nazis, the Italian filmmakers, well trained at their craft and highly experienced in film production, used the new freedom to combine their skill in making pictures with the subjects about which they wanted to make pictures. Just as the freedom following World War I unlocked the minds of the German and Soviet directors, the freedom following World War II released the Italian imagination.

Even as the Nazis were evacuating Rome, Roberto Rossellini began shooting *Open City* (*Roma, Città Aperta,* 1945). Rossellini made the film under the most difficult conditions, closely resembling the early production problems of the Soviet filmmakers: raw film stock was scarce, money for constructing sets was even scarcer, actors were difficult to find, slickness and polish were impossible without the controlled lighting of studio filming. Rossellini turned defects into virtues. He willingly sacrificed polish for reality, actors for people, settings for real locations, written scenes for improvisation, fiction for life. Rossellini often preferred laborers and peasants to actors (another striking parallel with Eisenstein and Pudovkin). He carried his camera all over the city and fleetingly shot the real city on the run.

Open City contrasted the humane, committed, unified struggle of the Italian people for freedom—the unity of priests, workers, intellectuals, adults, children—with the brutality of the Nazi invaders who used the most loathsome methods (torture, bribery, manipulation of the dependence on drugs or sexual gratification) to enslave the weaker Italians or to force them to betray their fellows. The two styles of the film—the natural, open, realistic, crisply lit texture of the scenes with the Resistance figures; the cramped, stilted, artificial, shadowy texture of the scenes with the Nazis—supported the film's thematic contrast. At the end of the film a single member of the Resistance, a committed priest, is executed by the Nazi oppressors for his service to the people. But as he dies, Rossellini's camera captures the activities of the children of Rome and a far shot of the city itself, for from the death of this one man will come the freedom of the future generation of this about-to-be opened city. *Open City* became the unofficial cornerstone of a new movement in Italian cinema—neorealism.

Cesare Zavattini, scenarist for so many of the neorealist Italian films, defined the principles of the genre: to show things as they are, not as they seem; to use facts rather than fictions; to depict the common man rather than silken heroes; to reveal the everyday rather than the exceptional; to show man's relationship to his real society rather than to his romantic dreams. The neorealist film developed the influence of the social environment on basic human needs: the need for food, shelter, vocation, love, familial comforts, sexual gratification. In the tradition of Marxist thought (yet another parallel with the classic Soviet films), the neorealist films repeatedly show that unjust and perverted social structures threaten to warp and pervert the essential and internal human values.

Vittorio DeSica's *The Bicycle Thief* (1948) is one of the best and most representative embodiments of the neorealist theories. DeSica, a popular stage and film actor in the 1930s and director of escapist fluff films in the early 1940s, directed the neorealist *Shoeshine* in 1946 (script by Zavattini), a poignant study of the perversion and destruction of a group of Roman children by both the gangsters and police who are using them. *The Bicycle Thief* (Zavattini script again) is another study of degradation and perversion. Its original title, *Bicycle Thieves,* is far more appropriate than the amended translation, simply because there are two bicycle thieves in the film: the man who steals the protagonist's bike and the protagonist himself, who eventually becomes a bicycle thief out of necessity.

From the film's opening shots DeSica begins his development of the kind of social environment that turns men into bicycle thieves: there are many men without work; there are very few jobs; the men have wives and children to support; the man with a bicycle is one of the lucky working few. To get his bicycle out of the pawn shop, Antonio's wife takes her wedding sheets to pawn in exchange for the bike. The poignancy of her sacrifice is underscored by DeSica's panning shot of row upon row upon row of pawned bridal sheets—other wives and families have been forced to make the same sacrifice of sentimental mementos for practical necessity. DeSica's camera constantly emphasizes the quantities of people and of things that are embraced by his story rather than implying that his tale is of the exceptional few. The film is filled with panning or tracking shots of rows and rows of men, of houses, of bicycles, of bicycle parts.

The film's narrative is Antonio's desperate search for his stolen bicycle. Without the bicycle he has no job; without a job his family starves. The man and his young son, Bruno, roam the streets, catching an occasional glimpse of the stolen bike or the shadow of the figure who stole it. Throughout the film the boy's relationship with his father serves as barometer of the effects of the agonizing search on the man's soul. Father and son drift further apart; the man even strikes the boy. When Antonio finally corners the thief, he discovers that the young man is as poor as he is. Even more pathetic, the thief is epileptic. The thief's mother and neighbors protect the young man against Antonio; the man who has been robbed discovers that he, in turn, has become the culprit in his attempts to get his bicycle back from a man who needs it as desperately as he does. The young bicycle thief is no thief but simply a starving, sick, desperate man like himself.

Realizing the impossibility of ever getting his own bicycle back, Antonio is tempted by the sight of the many unattended bicycles around him. The man cannot resist the temptation. He steals a bicycle himself, is swiftly caught, and then beaten and abused by the angry citizens who ignorantly denounce him as a villainous thief. The man's degradation is complete. Bruno both sees and hears his father's ultimate degradation. The father sits alone—empty, hurt, beaten. His son sits alongside him, silently. The boy slowly and gently slips his hand inside his father's. Despite the terrible social humiliation, the humanity and affection of father and son have been restored.

DeSica claims that an American producer offered him millions to make *Bicycle Thieves* with Cary Grant as Antonio. DeSica rejected both the money and the star. Instead, he cast a young metal worker, a nonactor, as the desperate father. DeSica's preference reveals many of the principles of neorealism. Reality rather than romance, earthiness rather than sparkle, the common man rather than the idol. Instead of Hollywood's bright sets and stylish clothes, the Italian directors showed primitive kitchens, squalid living rooms, peeling walls, baggy, torn clothing, streets that almost stank of urine and garbage (no telephones here, much less white ones!). Instead of the Hollywood love goddess, the neorealist lady-incarnate was Anna Magnani: coarse, fiery, indefatigable, too fat, too tough, too sweaty. Zavattini claimed that the neorealist film was as attached to the present as sweat was to skin. Both the idea and the imagery are significant.

The essential theme of the neorealist film was the conflict between the contemporary common man and the immense sociological forces that were completely external to himself and yet completely determined his existence: first the war, after it the means of making a living, and the struggle to keep a home and family together. In the three or four years following the war, many Italian directors developed their own variations on this essential theme: Rossellini's *Paisán* (1947); Allessandro Blasetti's *Un Giorno nella vita* (1946); Luigi Zampa's *Vivere in pace* (1946), *L'Onorevole Angelina* (1947), *Anni Difficili* (1947); Alberto Lattuada's *The Crime of Giovanni Episcopo* (1947) and *Senza Pieta* (1948); Giuseppi de Santis's *Caccia Tragica* (1947) and *Bitter Rice* (1949). In so many of these films, despite the social squalor and economic misery surrounding them, the central figures succeed at asserting the human and the humanity within themselves. The films are about misery without surrendering to misery.

But by 1950 neorealism had begun to change its course. Either the new stability of postwar Europe or the new prosperity of the Italian film industry shifted the Italian film's focus away from the sociological struggle with squalor. The films become increasingly psychological and less sociological. Although critics tried to elucidate the continuity of the movement by coining terms like poetic neorealism, romantic neorealism, or historical neorealism, such terms were incompatible with the original neorealist premise, if such a premise ever existed. The Italian film, while still valuing the realist actor and the realist milieu, had begun to use more polished scripts, more carefully constructed sets, more conventional fictional structures and themes. Even the original neorealist directors wandered away from earlier styles and themes. Rossellini became an international director, making carefully crafted and produced pictures all over the world, most of them starring his new wife, Ingrid Bergman. DeSica made a folk fantasy, *Miracle in Milan* (1951), and a highly personal study of old age, *Umberto D* (1952), that seemed far more interested in Umberto's mind and feelings than in old-age benefits. DeSica, however, probably strayed least from the original Zavattini principles, as his later *The Roof* (1956) and *Two Women* (1961) show. Sophia Loren won an Academy Award for her ability to play an unglamorous, Anna-Magnaniesque woman in *Two Women*, valiantly fighting the *Ur*-problems of neorealism: the war, hunger, and the assault on her family. In *The Garden of the Finzi-Contini's* (1971) DeSica again depicts the struggle of individual people and whole families against the viciousness of social systems and the brutalities of war. But this late film—with its nostalgic look backward at the world of the rich; its softer, more sentimentalized human beings; its dependence on lengthy discussions; and its lush color pictorialism—seemed antithetical to the style and spirit of the earlier DeSica.

The potential direction of Italian realism was predicted by the earliest of the films later hailed by critics as neorealist: Luchino Visconti's *Ossessione* (1942). Visconti's film, an unauthorized adaptation of James M. Cain's novel of sexual sordidness and passion, *The Postman Always Rings Twice*, uses squalid settings and realistic rather than romantic human types as background for its personal, psychological action. Social realism becomes the film's milieu, its soil, rather than its subject. Visconti's films consistently depart from the Zavattini definitions, using the social reality to define the personal problems of the characters rather than as the focus of the films themselves. For this reason, Visconti felt equally comfortable in the social reality of contemporary squalor: *Ossessione, La Terra Trema* (1948), *Rocco and His Brothers* (1960)—or historical sumptuousness: *Senso* (1954), *The Leopard* (1960), *The Damned* (1969), *Death in Venice* (1971).

That Visconti's interest was more in the interrelationship of human passion and stylistic decor than in societal forces can be clearly seen in the difference between his films in color and those in black and white. For Visconti (as, perhaps, for DeSica) black-and-white was the medium for depicting poverty, squalor, and the raw, baser human passions; color was the medium for depicting the rich, the elegant, and the more complex and contradictory thoughts and feelings. In *The Damned* the characters and their social system were both literally equated with the decor, for their corrupt and decadent passions were mirrored by the opulently decadent decor which was itself the mirror of the vicious political system these people had created and nurtured.

Visconti's late films put many of the commonly accepted views about film to their severest test: particularly that human beings are the focal interest of narrative films, and that film might be defined as a moving image. In his late color films, people seem to be reduced to mere puppets, mere elements of decor, and the image not only does not move but, in *Death in Venice* especially, seems subservient to the musical track. In his discussion of *La Terra Trema*, André Bazin referred to the extreme length—three to four minutes—of all of Visconti's shots as they tracked and panned endlessly, observing the characters' actions. In *Death in Venice* the shots are equally lengthy and the camera tracks and pans as much, assisted by a new ally—the zoom lens—which seems to slide through three of four maneuvers in every shot.

But unlike *La Terra Trema*, the dominant photographic subject of *Death in Venice* seems to be the characters' nonactions, as if they are posing for stills. They sit motionless—almost a Panavision postcard—allowing the eye to soak up the magnificent details of the decor: its elegance, its accuracy in re-creating an historical era, its visual taste and beauty. And as the eye absorbs this static scene, the only thing other than the camera that moves is the music of Mahler on the sound track, rising to heights of ecstasy. Whether the music successfully re-creates and transmits the passion in the main character's soul (clearly its intention) is a matter for debate, but the result (despite its pictorial and musical beauties) seems less complex and less compelling than the original novella by Thomas Mann.

Fellini, Antonioni, and Others

Although Federico Fellini's apprenticeship was in the most neorealistic of neorealisms—he assisted Rossellini and Sergio Amidei on the scenarios for both *Open City* and *Paisán*—the mature Fellini is a pure romantic. Fellini prefers the exotic places of romance—the circus, the variety theatre, the night club—to the squalid slums of reality. His characters search for happiness, for love, for meaning, not for social security. If Anna Magnani is the soul of neorealism, Giulietta Masina is the soul of Fellini; she is his wife off-screen and the central figure of many of his films, including *La Strada* and *Nights of Cabiria*, two of his greatest. Giulietta Masina, with the glowing eyes, the smirking mouth, the deep dimples, wildly joyful, wildly sad, is to Anna Magnani as a sun beam is to a pack horse. In both *La Strada* (1954) and *Nights of Cabiria* (1957) Miss Masina plays a pure spirit of love, a being of the heart not of the mind.

In the earlier film, she is Gelsomina, the clownish fool, apprenticed to the strong man, Zampano (Anthony Quinn), who uses her as servant, performer, cook, and concubine—a piece of human chattel. Despite her rough treatment from the boorish animal-man, Gelsomina comes to love this human with whom she shares her life. But he—afraid of human commitment, afraid of emotional strings—betrays her, leaves her alone to die in the snow. He kills her in the same careless and callous way that he killed the clownish acrobat (Richard Basehart) who had felt the rays of Gelsomina's hypnotic passion. Only after Gelsomina is dead, as the strong man hears the sad song that she once played on her trumpet, does the supposedly strong man learn how weak and alone he is as he sobs helplessly in a vast, cold, empty universe of sand, sea, and sky.

As Cabiria, Giulietta Masina plays once again the spirit of pure love that is trampled by the realities of human selfishness. Cabiria is the pure-hearted whore, forced to sell her love since no one will take it for nothing. The film opens with a boyfriend stealing her purse and throwing her in the river. Every sequence duplicates the disillusionment of this opening one. A film star casually picks her up and takes her to a fancy night club, using her as a weapon against his mistress whom he is trying to infuriate. The mistress ends up in the actor's bed; Cabiria spends the night in his bathroom, her only companion a tiny puppy. Cabiria goes to a music hall. A hypnotist entrances her into enacting all her romantic, childlike fantasies, symbolized by the appearance of her ideal lover, named "Oscar." Cabiria's tender dreams become merely sport for the hooting, crass members of the audience. Worse, a gentleman who has watched the performance, claiming that his name really is Oscar, introduces himself to Cabiria and begins her most serious romantic hope in the film. But after she sells her house and her furniture, gladly leaving her old life behind for the love of a man she knows almost nothing about, she discovers that he too only wants her purse.

Though he takes her money he cannot throw her into the sea. He cannot kill her as he had planned. Cabiria's final disillusionment is the ultimate magnification of the opening scene, the ultimate disappointment, the comedy of the opening scene turned tragic and horrifying by the compelling events between the two scenes. But Cabiria does not die. In one of the most truly ironic and metaphorical endings in film history, closely paralleling the ending of *The Children of Paradise,* the weeping, sobbing Cabiria encounters a group of festive, singing youngsters as she walks on the road back to town (and, metaphorically, to life). They sing as she sobs; they do not notice her tears; their singing does not stop her tears; but she continues walking with them, participating vicariously in their song. The laughter and tears of Cabiria's life, of Everyman's life, have been brilliantly juxtaposed.

Fellini's greatest works are inevitably works of laughter and tears. His sheer romanticism is underscored by his composer, Nino Rota, whose scores mix melodiousness and mysteriousness, exoticism and sweetness. Fellini gets into trouble when he deserts feeling for thought. *La Dolce Vita* (1959) is a sterile thematic exercise, an overstated contrast of Sensuality versus Spirituality. In the film's first sequence, a helicopter pilot, towing a wooden statue of Christ, looks down and waves at three girls in bikinis, sunning themselves on a Roman roof. The film, intellectually, is over. Christ has been petrified into wood; he is the tool of modern machinery (the helicopter); people are more interested in bosoms and bikinis than in Christ. Although the film has nothing more to say, Fellini continues for two hours, contrasting sensual things—night clubs, orgiastic parties, chic gatherings—with the corruption of spiritual things—a verbose intellectual commits suicide, a group of crazy children pretend to see a miraculous vision.

Weakest of all in the film is Fellini's symbolic summation of the dichotomy. A blonde adolescent child, dressed all in white, beckons to the central character (Marcello Mastroianni), but he, alas, cannot hear her. Her call is drowned by the sound of wind, waves, and human revellers. Although it is obvious that the girl symbolizes the abstractions of Purity, Innocence, Goodness, and Peace, it is not at all clear exactly what concrete, human life-choices she symbolizes. Is Fellini biblically asking us to become like unto pure little children? It seems difficult to believe that he could seriously advocate such brainless nudnickism. Is he saying that the yearning for serenity is understandable but impossible in the modern existential world? Whatever he is saying, the film has very fancy symbolic wrapping paper around a package that seems dramatically and emotionally empty.

Fellini's later film, *Juliet of the Spirits* (1966), suffers from the same hollowness. The film is another examination of the same duality—Sensuality vs. Spirituality—which must be considered Fellini's primary theme. Though the film also has Giulietta Masina, she fails to save the sterility of the thematic contrast, either because she has lost her sparkle or because the script does not allow her to sparkle as Giulietta Masina should. *Juliet's* one striking virtue is the dazzling use of color that Fellini manipulates to underscore the thematic opposition: pale green and lavender versus brilliant white, orange, and yellow. The director's later *Satyricon* (1969) is another dazzling technicolor show in praise of the free and sensual, but Fellini never interrupts the flow of his visual-sensual circus for symbolic dichotomies or abstract intellectualization. The result is a hypnotic journey through a surrealistic dreamworld that, like Fellini's other circuses, has no purpose other than to be savored and experienced for the way it looks and feels.

What substitutes for thought in Fellini is a romantic rebelliousness and an ambivalent reaction to the grotesque. A consistent Fellini target is the Catholic Church. For Fellini, the Church is a hypocritical and empty show that bilks its public by playing on its insecurities and fears. The Church is the arch sensualist masquerading as spiritualist. In *La Strada*, Fellini photographs a solemn Church procession, with a neon sign reading "Bar" prominently in the foreground; he further debases the religious spectacle by showing the tacky cardboard mounting on the backsides of the glowing pictures of the saints. In *La Dolce Vita*, the Church supports the lies of hysterical children because the lies will produce a profit in *lire* and souls. But one of Fellini's most devastating blows at the Church is in *Nights of Cabiria*. A society of human unfortunates takes a desperate outing to a religious festival, where they are greeted by canned prayers on loudspeakers (prominently in the foreground of Fellini's frame) and greedy vendors hawking sacred candles and secular candies. Fellini transforms a spiritual event into a commercial carnival. Even more grotesque, this delegation of prostitutes is led by a crippled pimp and dope pusher who has come to the festival specifically to be made to walk again. Perhaps he needs healthy legs to collect even more profits from the sales of body and needle. A much later Fellini swipe at the Church, that rivals *Cabiria* in its venom and cynicism, is in *Fellini—Roma* (1972) with its monstrously funny fashion show of clerical clothing and priestly paraphernalia. As in all his earlier films, Fellini's attack reduces the spiritual claims of the Church to the absurd by depicting its total preoccupation with the material and mundane.

Whereas Fellini treats organized religion with grotesque bitterness and comical contempt, he treats the glamorous world of the rich with a stylish grotesqueness that reveals both its emptiness and its fascination. Fellini films are jammed with the grotesque faces and costumes of the *haut monde*, ladies in long silken gowns and geometrically shaped lorgnettes, their teased hair climbing to the ceiling and their aquiline noses dragging toward the floor, effete gentlemen with fleeting eyes and fluttering hands. The lesbian ladies in the posh night club of *Nights of Cabiria*, the society party in *La Dolce Vita*, the patrons of the health spa in *8½*, the Roman revellers at feasts and orgies in *Fellini Satyricon*, are all examples of the grotesquely ugly—in costume, make-up, gestures, features, shapes, sizes—that Fellini finds hauntingly attractive. In *Juliet of the Spirits*, Fellini uses flashing, blinding color to make the wealthy sensualists even more beautiful-ugly. Fellini's social criticism of the fashionably idle pulls him one way; his hypnotized attraction to their visually stunning exteriors and their uncompromising sensuality pulls him another.

Fellini's greatest film, his most impressive synthesis of dramatic power, personal vision, and cinematic control, is probably *8½* (1963). Perhaps the quintessential modernist feature film, the subject of *8½* is simply itself.

It is not merely about filmmaking (like Truffaut's *Day For Night*); it is about the making of this very film, a film which the director finds impossible to make but which has been made nonetheless. The protagonist of the film (Marcello Mastroianni again) is a film director himself. Because of his nervousness and tension, he is relaxing, preparing for his next film, at a fashionable health spa. Preparing for the project, the director is flooded with images out of his film and memories out of his life, which get thoroughly and inextricably confused. He puts his living relationships into fictional structures; he draws his fictional ideas from his personal experiences of the past and present (just as Fellini does later in *Amarcord, 1974*). The director's emotional problem in the film—and undoubtedly Marcello represents Fellini here—is wondering whether he is successful at either life or art, wondering whether he hasn't prostituted his life for his art and his art for his life, whether he has the right or the ability to make films.

Although $8\frac{1}{2}$ tempts critics to treat it as an abstract Pirandellian disquisition on life and art, reality and illusion, its major strength, like Fellini's, is as human drama. Fellini successfully roots the drama in Marcello's thoughts and sensations. The film begins with Marcello's nightmare: he feels trapped inside a hot, smoky automobile during a mammoth traffic jam. He longs to escape from the car, to fly high above the earth. The remainder of the film works on the man's anxiety and longing, his desire to break free of the bonds of his life, his desire to soar in life and art. He searches throughout the film for an actress to portray a pure lady in white. Is she the illusory panacea that will make sense of both his personal relationships and his artistic purpose? Is she a reference to the girl in white in *La Dolce Vita* whom Fellini now sees as a facile and naïve solution to a complex artistic and human problem? By the end of the film, Marcello seems to renounce the search. He attends a gala party for his film. The party becomes a gigantic circus composed of all the characters of his memories and of his film. Fellini's camera swirls in an excited circle as the parade of Marcello's creatures dances about a circus ring, that familiar Fellini setting. Marcello stares at the dancing creatures; he then steps into their circle and joins the dance. His life is what it is; his art is what it is. There is nothing for him to do but live it and create it. The artist's tension has been resolved; he cannot be separated from the dancing ring of his thoughts, his loves, his creations, his memories. The film that could not be made has been made because whatever Marcello's (and Fellini's) deficiencies as a human being, he is a maker of films. That is his dance.

Like Fellini, Michelangelo Antonioni's roots are in neorealism. While Rossellini and DeSica were making their documentary-style features, Antonioni was making documentary shorts about the lives of peasants and farmers. But Antonioni soon deserted the documentary for the highly polished and stylized drama of personal sensations. He quickly evolved a prin-

THE
BICYCLE
THIEF

Father and son search desperately in
a downpour for the irreplaceable bicycle.

LA STRADA

Giulietta Masina.

Gelsomina and Zampano
(Giulietta Masina and Anthony Quinn)—
human love despite the obstacles.

Fellini faces.

8½

8½

The artist (Marcello Mastroianni) among his memories.

The circle and circus of the film director's life.

ciple of art that was quite the antithesis of Zavattini's neorealism. Whereas neorealism uses the external environment to define a man, Antonioni uses the emotions of a man to define the external environment. For Antonioni, the world takes its color from the character, rather than the character taking his color from the world. In fact, when Antonioni finally adopted color photography in *The Red Desert* in 1964, the above metaphor for Antonioni's method became a cinematic reality. Whereas Fellini deserted neorealism in favor of a romantic flair that exposed the director's hand guiding every flamboyant filmic detail, Antonioni deserted neorealism by blurring objective reality and burying the action within the subjective perceptions of the central characters. After apprentice work on *I Vinti* (1952), *Le Amiche* (1955), and *Il Grido* (1957), Antonioni achieved complete mastery over his method with *L'Avventura* (1960).

Rather than using the camera merely to record dialogue, movement, and facial reaction, Antonioni's method concentrates as much on the scenic environment as on the people in the environment. The environment defines the people in it. And not just socially. The emotional resonances of the environment convey the internal states of the people within it. Among Antonioni's favorite photographic subjects are the slick, hard-surfaced materials of modern architecture: glass, aluminum, terrazzo. The cold, alien surfaces are metaphors for the hollowness a character feels at that dramatic moment. The angular furniture, the stony objects, and the glossy floor of the apartment at the beginning of *L'Eclisse* (1961) brilliantly evoke the coldness, the emptiness, the deadness in a former human relationship as Vittoria (Monica Vitti) breaks off with her lover. Significantly, Antonioni underscores the scene's shiny, hard look with silence—no music, almost no words, a few scraping sounds of hard objects on stone-like floors and furniture. *La Notte* (1960) begins with a similar feeling of hollowness and death, created by the slick, shiny glass windows and the bare white corridors of the hospital where the author and his wife (Marcello Mastroianni and Jeanne Moreau) visit a dying friend. The beginning of *Blow Up* (1966) surrounds a group of carnivalesque merrymakers with wet, shiny terrazzo courtyards and hard, cold aluminum-and-glass apartment buildings. The beginnings of Antonioni films consistently use the scenic environment to define both the film's social milieu and emotional climate.

Other Antonioni environments come to mind: the rocky, barren island where the empty, barren holidaymakers search for Anna in *L'Avventura;* the steel flagpoles with the ropes hollowly clanging against them in *L'Eclisse,* the gray-brown ugliness of the factory belching smoke in *The Red Desert,* the endless desert of *Zabriskie Point* (1970). Perhaps Antonioni's favorite object for emotional definition is the white wall: Sandro's flat in *L'Avventura,* the hospital corridors in *La Notte,* the hotel corridor in *Red Desert,* the photographer's studio in *Blow Up.* In *Red Desert,*

Giulia (Monica Vitti again) searches for some color to make the hard, white wall of her shop feel more comfortable. The Antonioni character's feeling of affinity with the hard, white wall is constantly emphasized by a piece of business that recurs through all the films—the character stands against the wall and then circles around the room, back and palms pressing against the plaster. The Antonioni characters are wall-bound.

A tendency of criticism of Antonioni is to push his films into one of two clichéd and comfortable categories. The first tendency is to turn the artistic principle of the films upside down by taking the subordinate social and material environment as the real stuff of the film. According to such critics, *L'Avventura* is about the evils of wealth, *L'Eclisse* condemns the stock exchange, *Red Desert* denounces industrialization, *Blow Up* contrasts illusion and reality. However, Antonioni accepts the fact that today's men live with the stock exchange, with factories, with ambiguities. What else can he do with a fact? What he is interested in is how do they live with them, how does it feel to do so, what are the problems in doing so. Modern life is the inescapable fact out of which all the Antonioni films grow; that fact is the foundation of his films, not the focus. Why focus on the obvious? Unfortunately, *Zabriskie Point*, lacking a subtle and complex human center, does focus on the obvious, and the result is a collection of visually stunning but intellectually predictable clichés. The great Antonioni films are not about modern society itself but about the emotional tension between the sensitive central character (Monica Vitti, Jeanne Moreau, David Hemmings) and the society surrounding him or, more often, her.

The second cliché of Antonioni criticism is that all his characters live lives that are boring and empty, meaningless and sterile, and that his subject is sterility and meaninglessness in the abstract. Ironically, all the Antonioni characters manage to survive; they do not commit suicide, which would be a logical conclusion to draw from a premise of total emptiness. Each of the central Antonioni figures finds some value that helps him live, and each of the Antonioni films ends with some cautiously positive implication. Sandro and Claudia in *L'Avventura* come together in a moment of mutual sympathy—beautifully and sensitively depicted by her placing her white hand on his black hair—without saying a word. The ending of *L'Eclisse* implies, with a long series of visual images, again without dialogue, that human relationships continue to provide temporary if not ultimate relief from loneliness. The photographer at the end of *Blow Up* realizes that his life has a meaning to him, if to no one else, that, like the carnival clowns with their invisible tennis ball, he can play his own life's game with the same energy and conviction, even if that game has no ultimate meaning or absolute meaningfulness to anyone else. The ending of *Red Desert* is so explicitly positive that it is uncomfortably inconsistent with the usual Antonioni reliance on visual image. Giulia walks by the factory exactly as she did in the film's opening sequence; the smoke stack still belches its poisonous smoke. Giulia's young son asks her if the smoke will kill the little birds that might fly through it. Giulia answers that the birds have long since learned not to fly through the smoke. The parallel of the birds to Giulia, and the smoke to the industrial world surrounding her, implies that Giulia too has learned something.

The real subject of the Antonioni films is education. So many of the films are circular; they seem to end where they began: *L'Eclisse, Red Desert, Blow Up*. Although the characters walk around in a physical circle, they do not walk around in an emotional one. In the course of their journeys, they learn the pervasiveness of emptiness and the possible if temporary ways of combating it. For such a theme, Antonioni's visual images are the only means of rendering each emotional stage of the journey clearly, convincingly, and sensitively. The images become Antonioni's "objective correlatives"; he is as dependent on visual images for these correlatives as was the director of *Broken Blossoms, The Cabinet of Caligari, The Last Laugh*, and *Greed*. No other director of sound films is as dependent on pictures and as free of words as Antonioni.

He rejects words for two reasons. First, words are not a very effective tool for communicating internal states of feeling. Vague, imprecise feelings of loneliness, uneasiness, *angst* do not lend themselves to the terse summary required of movie dialogue. The more lucidly and lengthily a man talks about his own internal feelings (either in life or in art), the more we distrust the sincerity of his feelings and the depth of his self-awareness. Second, Antonioni does not trust words as a genuine means of human communication. If his characters succeed in discovering anything meaningful at all, they inevitably do so by physical contact, by moments of laughter or calm, by a union of temporarily harmonizing vibrations rather than by discussion and conversation. Antonioni summarizes his opinion of words in *Red Desert* with the self-satisfied engineer (Richard Harris), whose commitment to his vocation and his selfish pleasures has put blinders on his ability to feel and to question. While making a play for the groping, longing Giulia, he sums up his philosophy of experience in a tidy, coherent speech of clichéd banalities. Giulia's perceptive reply deflates the man's smug complacency: "That's a fine bunch of words." Words are antipathetic to Antonioni because both his artistic premise and his philosophical vision negate their value and utility.

L'Avventura is probably Antonioni's most whole, most careful, most completely realized film. Despite the impression that the film wanders, it travels steadily toward its final moment of human reconciliation and compassion in which Claudia can feel sympathy for the weakness of Sandro and in which Sandro can feel the terrible pathos of his need to betray Claudia. The film is a series of betrayals. Anna betrays her friend, Claudia, by making her wait downstairs while she viciously devours Sandro in an afternoon of casual love-making. The middle-aged couple (Giulia and Corrado) survives daily on little betrayals—stinging, hateful words that hurt. Giulia betrays Corrado with the adolescent boy who paints nothing but nudes. Sandro has betrayed his talent as an architect by selling out to the pressures of finance. Antonioni brilliantly captures Sandro's bitterness as the former architect deliberately spills ink on a young architectural student's careful line drawing of the town's cathedral. Sandro's betrayals are also sexual. He betrays Anna by lusting after Claudia before Anna disappears. And even after the touching, fulfilling moments with Claudia, he callously flirts with the tasteless American publicity seeker in the very hotel where Claudia waits in bed for his return.

But if Sandro's education is to discover the human weakness that makes betrayal so inevitable, Claudia's education is to discover that betrayal is a fact of human life and to ignore that fact is to cut herself off completely from the human. Though Antonioni invests most of the film in exposing human weaknesses, he does so only because no genuine human relationship is possible without an understanding of the nature of the beast. The terms human and betrayal are unfortunately synonymous; any meaningful human relationship must start from that definition. *L'Avventura* is a journey and adventure that bring Sandro and Claudia to that starting point.

If *L'Avventura* is the fullest and most sensitive statement of Antonioni's vision, *The Red Desert* is the most revealing of his technique. *Red Desert,* Antonioni's first color film, is a film about colors, as its title indicates. The troubles that Giulia has with reality are mirrored by the troubles she has with colors. Color in the film is not Fellini's flamboyant visual show but Antonioni's use of the visual to mirror the character's internal states and, ultimately, to communicate the film's subject. *Red Desert* often uses a lens that blurs the background into a mass of indistinguishable colors; that effect mirrors the way Giulia herself sees color: frightening, aggressive, uncontrollable, indistinguishable. She is so uncomfortable with colors that she cannot pick one to cover the walls of her shop. Giulia's discomfort with colors is a metaphor for her discomfort with the reality that surrounds her—all of its sights, sounds, smells, uncertainties. In a later sequence in the engineer's hotel room, the walls change color from their original hard gray to warm pink. The walls are now pink because Giulia feels them pink, with her body next to a warm, strong man. He, ironically, neither cares how she feels nor how she feels the walls.

Though Antonioni's method disparages words, he does not forget sounds. Sound is a crucial element in *Red Desert* and in all Antonioni films (even his deliberate silences reveal a knowledge of the power of sound). In *The Red Desert* sound and color operate similarly. Giulia sees her everyday life as a grayish, poisonous, choking existence, punctuated by frightening, grotesque colors of the factory pipes (hence the gray-brownish-ness of the shots of the factory, the mud, the fog, and the striking blues and oranges of the pipe lines). Accompanying the shots of the oppressive factory are the incessant thumping, beating, chugging noises of the factory machines on the sound track. Later in the film, Giulia tells her child a beautiful fairy tale of an ideally serene life on a far-off paradisiacal isle. Suddenly the screen changes from its sordid browns and grays to shots of brilliant blue waters and sparkling pink sand—the same pink as in the hotel room scene, and carefully dyed pink by the director to look that way. With the appearance of beautiful, clear, inviting images, the irritating noises on the sound track melt away to be replaced by the sound of gentle waves lapping on the beach and the serene singing of an angelic soprano. By his careful control of both image and sound, Antonioni tells the story of this woman's mental journey. Despite the oppressive factory, despite her inattentive husband, despite her suicide attempt, despite her callous lover, despite her scare about her son's legs, she, like the little birds, has learned how to avoid the poisonous smoke by acknowledging its existence.

Pietro Germi is Italy's greatest film satirist. Germi made several imitative neorealist films just after the war, the most interesting being *In the Name of the Law* (1949), a contrast between social hypocrisies and the underlying moral realities in a Mafia-dominated Sicily. This contrast of the appearance and the reality, the external show and the internal emotion, later became Germi's dominant theme in his great satirical comedies, *Divorce—Italian Style* (1962), *Seduced and Abandoned* (1964), *The Birds, the Bees, and the Italians* (1966), and *Alfredo, Alfredo* (1972). In the first of these films, murder seems a practical social tool, there being no easier legal way to break a stifling marriage contract. In *Seduced and Abandoned*, a Sicilian family insists on maintaining its honor to the death. And death is precisely the result of the worship of the dead word, honor, despite the hilariously comic machinations to get the deflowered daughter engaged, disengaged, and eventually married. The concept of honor becomes an empty word that the characters frenziedly uphold with the most ludicrous, hypocritical, and silly seriousness. Reflecting the attitude of the film's director toward the archaic and artificial social code is the police inspector, a Roman, who is trying to bring civilized northern law to the chaotic southern island. The inspector, baffled by the empty words, the frenzied familial threats, the moral contradictions, the comic attempts at rape and murder, stares at the map of Italy. He puts his hand over the island of Sicily, covering it up. As he gazes at the amended Italy, he quips, "Better, much better."

Although it received less critical attention than the two earlier films, *The Birds, the Bees, and the Italians* is equal to Germi's greatest work; it is another powerful mixture of Germi's stinging, acid social commentary and his hilarious, farcical social comedy. The film leaves Sicily for a northern Italian city, Germi implying that hypocrisy and sterile social values are not indigenous to any particular region. In a town of grotesque lechers, drunkards, and gossips, a society whose every thought (if not deed) is lewd, two unmarried people openly dare to live together. Their love is the purest, tenderest human feeling in the film. The town lechers, hypocritically supporting the official moral code, refuse to let the two people live together so warmly and sincerely while their own emotional lives remain blunted and covert. Using the moral clichés, the townspeople drive the couple apart, forcing her to leave town and him to jump off a roof.

Despite the obvious seriousness of the film's stand against hypocrisy, Germi carries the story off with almost the flavor of farce. Every lecher is comically and grotesquely individuated. Richly comic are their social gatherings when they all get together, gossiping viciously out of one side of the mouth and excitedly arranging a liaison out of the other. Richly comic is the seduction scene of the young girl from the country who comes to town and succeeds in shopping at each of the stores without spending any money. Equally comic and telling is the scene in which the businessmen's wives pay a visit to the now pregnant farm girl and arrange all the details of buying her off. And richly comic is the scene in a sleazy night club, supposedly a lurid strip joint, where the tawdry, bourgeois townspeople go for a night of "fun." The night club seems a deliberate bourgeois parody of the posh night clubs of Fellini and Antonioni. Neither chic nor exotic, the tacky café wakes up and puts on its dolce vita only when the soused and senseless customers enter. The most lurid entertainment comes not from one of the hired strippers but from a nymphomaniac wife who suffers from the constant desire to take off her clothes. The Germi world in this film is the Fellini world gone bourgeois—with warts. By mixing farcical grotesques with the enormous suffering that the comic hypocrites inflict on less callous, more sincere beings, Germi achieves his particular serio-comic blend.

The descendants of neorealism took several other directions. Mario Monicelli's *The Organizer* (1964) applied neorealistic principles to a historical study, the fight for fair wages and working conditions by a group of early-twentieth-century strikers. Pier Paolo Pasolini began neorealistically with *Accattone* (1961), a study of a brash, poor young man in a Roman slum, trying to make enough money to survive and preserve enough of his identity so that survival is worth it. Pasolini later drifted from realism to *The Gospel According to St. Matthew* (1963), to moral and political allegory (*Teorema*, 1968; *Pigpen*, 1969). Vittorio de Seta, a documentary filmmaker, combined documentary and fiction for his feature, *The Bandits of Orgosolo* (1961), one of the precursors of *"cinéma vérité."* Marco Bellochio satirically examined the clumsy attempts of the bored rich to carve a meaning out of their lives by dabbling in romance and Marxian politics in *China Is Near* (1967).

Most neorealistic of the second-generation postwar directors is Ermanno Olmi. In *Il Posto* (*The Sound of Trumpets*, 1961), Olmi studies a young adolescent boy's absorption into the machinery of bureaucratic, industrialized society. The boy leaves home, takes a civil service examination, gets a job as messenger, and finally earns a clerk's desk in the bureaucratic office. The film ends with a brilliant sound effect, not the glorious sound of trumpets but the cranking of a mimeograph machine. The boy has been "duplicated," cranked through the industrial process to emerge as one more identical sheet of paper on which his future for the next fifty years has been stamped.

Although Olmi clearly condemns the dehumanizing, mechanistic pattern that turns a boy into a faceless man, he handles his subject from two perspectives: from his own view, which judges and condemns, and from the boy's, who sees the whole process as something very exciting and adult. The job frees him from his home; it gives him some sense of financial security; it brings him into contact with girls. Whereas Olmi's view condemns the prison-like, regimented process of taking a civil service examination, the boy excitedly, earnestly tries to pass it. Whereas Olmi's view exposes the hollow, tawdry sterility of the company's New Year's Eve party, a sad evening of manufactured fun that is no fun at all, the young boy fights his initial fright, drinks a bit of wine, dances, and actually enjoys himself. Perhaps Olmi's point is that "the piece of paper" is ignorant about being ground through a machine and hence can enjoy it. The two contrasting views of the same social process add both a touching humanness and artistic richness to the film.

Olmi's later film, *One Fine Day* (1969), contains the same ambivalence. An advertising executive, fiftyish, successful but not supremely successful, accidentally strikes and kills a man with his automobile on his way to the airport. The "fine" day is not fine at all. The accident shakes the man up enough so that he begins to examine his whole life: its meaning, its value, his job, his personal relationships with daughter, wife, and mistress. Although a cunning lawyer pulls legal strings to get the man acquitted, although the man returns to his wife and job (because he has nowhere else to go), he will never be quite the same again. Olmi's method views the action on two levels: his own, judging the man's unquestioning complacency and callousness; and the man's, trying to make sense of the life that he is in the process of living.

Perhaps the most interesting Italian *auteur* to emerge in the late 1960s is Bernardo Bertolucci. Bertolucci's first film, *Before the Revolution* (1964), set the pattern for his more famous films to follow—*The Conformist* (1971) and *Last Tango in Paris* (1973). Thematically, Bertolucci's primary concern is the interrelationship between political issues and sexual drives. The rich, bored dilettantes are no more committed to Marxian ideology than they are to their own lusts and seductions in *Before the Revolution*. They play around with both and succeed in fulfilling neither. In *The Conformist* the central figure's ideological emptiness is intimately connected with his lack of sexual identity, his need to assert his masculine *machismo* while covering up his inherent homosexuality. He can betray ideals, his friends, his professor, his lover, his wife, his principles because he is a zero—both ideologically and sexually. Technically, Bertolucci is a director of the sixties, much more elliptical and subjective than the neorealist masters, depending on shock- and jump-cutting, the hand-held camera for specific effects (for example, the chase and death in the forest in *The Conformist*), instantaneous switches from present to past to present, and instantaneous switches from an objective observation to a subjective experience. Bertolucci might be thought of as combining the leftist social conscience of a DeSica with the more personal, sexual, and psychological perceptions of a Visconti or Antonioni.

For twenty-five years the Italian film has started with the surface of reality as its initial premise. But the Italian filmmaker has been free to manipulate the realistic surfaces of rich or poor, of past or present, and to probe beneath those surfaces with sociological commentary, psychological insight, farce comedy, philosophical ennui, bizarre romance. Though they are both committed to realism, though they are both Italian and contemporaries, no two film directors are as dissimilar as Federico Fellini and Michelangelo Antonioni. The postwar Italian film has been so rich and diverse because the filmmakers have been encouraged to use their imaginations and because, ironically, the Italian film industry has been supported by American dollars to stimulate that encouragement.

Yet a further irony about the power of the Hollywood dollar is that it not only stimulated the Italian art films but the cheap, trash films as well. A series of quasi-Roman, quasi-Biblical "spectacle" films starring the American muscleman, Steve Reeves, could be shot for under $250,000 in Italy and then dubbed into English for mass release in American neighborhood theatres and drive-ins. A series of Italian, "Spaghetti Westerns," many of them starring Clint Eastwood and directed by Sergio Leone, not only made money but attracted a cult, a coterie of intellectual admirers: many of them French, many of them the same fans who admired the raw, garish violence of the Roger Corman horror films of the same era. Leone's success with the cheap, violent western was so great that he was given the chance to shoot a major, high-budget western, *Once Upon a Time in the West* (1969), which perhaps serves as an example of the slowest-paced, most naturalistically detailed, most ponderously heavy, and most visually dazzling collection of western clichés ever made.

In its early years the postwar Italian cinema showed the American industry how to combine ideas, social comment, realistic human observation, and poetic visual techniques with the motion picture form; in its later years it seemed to pander more and more to the very movie conventions and practices it previously tried to subvert. In the 1970s, with its best directors either working all over Europe on international co-productions or on multi-million-dollar visual extravaganzas, the question is whether any truly Italian cinema still exists at all.

The postwar Italian film sprang from the reality which the director sought to capture with camera and film; the postwar French film sprang from the director's stylistic concern with the way a camera can capture reality. Although both François Truffaut and Jean-Luc Godard attacked the formalism, the stylization, the artificiality in the films of their predecessors, their own works are as stylized, as preoccupied with cinematic form and perception as the works they sought to supplant. That the postwar French cinema should be formalistic is not surprising; the prewar French cinema was formalistic, beginning with the abstract films of the twenties through the musical romps of Clair and the literariness of Renoir and Carné. To approach reality through the manipulation of artistic form has been an aesthetic premise of the French creative mind from Racine to Proust to Ionesco. The postwar French cinema is very much in the same tradition.

The sameness is emphasized by the fact that the great prewar directors—Clair, Renoir, Carné, Cocteau—also made films after the war. René Clair returned to France to combine fantasy, song, and social satire once again in films that were frothy mixtures of physical movement, stylized decor, and music—among them, *Le Silence est d'or* (1947), a nostalgic tribute to the Zecca-Méliès years of the French film; *Beauty and the Devil* (1949), an ironic treatment of the Faust legend; and *Beauties of the Night* (1952), the romantic reveries of a daydreaming musician.

Whereas Clair returned to France to make films that were softer, sweeter, and weaker than his earlier work, Renoir returned to make at least three films that are arguably as great as or greater than his masterpieces of the 1930s. The three films—*The River* (1951), *The Golden Coach* (1953), and *French Cancan* (1954)—might be considered a kind of trilogy. All three are in color and use color not only beautifully but also as a metaphoric and thematic element in their human investigations. All three are set in periods or places far distant from postwar France: India's Bengal region (*The River*), South America of the 1800s (*The Golden Coach*), and Montmartre of the 1890s (*French Cancan*). And all three examine the conflicting human choices of contempt and consent, commitment and alienation, vocation and love. The primary duality of all three films is the usual Renoir conflict between art and nature (or life), but in these late films the conflict becomes a communion as the very artfulness of the films themselves—their visual beauty as well as their structural complexity—reveals how one can indeed make life into art and thereby synthesize the opposites of art and nature.

The River, shot in India by a French director with a Bengali crew, featuring a cast of both Indians and westerners, is about this clash of cultures and values. Using the vibrant colors of the Indian landscape, the pulsing music of the sitar, the myths of the Hindu religion, and the contemplative philosophy of the Indian people, Renoir's film shows a group of "crippled" westerners—crippled either physically or spiritually by the war, by political chaos, and by personal disappointment—healing their minds and feelings by seeking to achieve a harmony with the eternal cycles of nature: birth, life, and death. *The Golden Coach* continues the examination of clashing cultures. A group of Spanish aristocrats try to impose their decadent tastes and values on the unformed freedom of the New World. Ironically, another group of Europeans, the members of an acting troupe (led by Anna Magnani), are far more successful at communicating with their New World audience. Art is a more powerful force than politics, and the director, through his leading actress, argues for the validity of art as a human vocation. And *French Cancan* addresses the same issue. Renoir depicts a theatrical producer (played by the aging Jean Gabin who, like Renoir himself, is twenty years older than he was when he made *The Lower Depths* or *Grand Illusion*) who, also like Renoir, defines art as his life.

Marcel Carné, deprived of Jacques Prévert's scripts, never regained the power of his *Les Enfants du Paradis* though he made almost a dozen films examining human failure, lost love, and inexorable death. Jean Cocteau made several films in strikingly different, though equally formalistic film styles: the claustrophobic naturalism of *Les Parents Terribles* (1948), a complicated tangle of sexuality, incest, parental rivalry, and jealousy; the poetic symbolism of *Orphée* (1950), an expressionistic study of the artist's ambivalent relationship with love and death; and *Beauty and the Beast* (1946), which mixed Cocteau's realism and symbolism quite effectively in the story of Belle's growing love for the physically ugly yet humanly loving beast. The impression of these stylistically eclectic Cocteau films is that they are the works of a cinematic amateur (in the original sense of the word). The artist, having given birth to his personal and symbolic world on the stage, on the page, and on canvas, also decided to people the screen with his fantasies. The dominant trait of Cocteau's plays and drawings, an almost aggressive insistence on flippancy and casualness (which is a typical Dadaist trait), also asserts itself in his films. Unlike Renoir, who takes the business of art and, especially, of filmmaking very seriously, the Cocteau films reveal the director playing around with a variety of film styles and demonstrating how ably he can handle all of the possibilities of cinema, how easily he can make the immense cinema machines into his own private pens and brushes.

Of the new French directors in the fifteen years following the war, the three greatest were Max Ophuls, Robert Bresson, and Jacques Tati. All three of them made films very much in the Clair-Carné-Renoir tradition; all three of them had, in fact, made films before 1945. Whereas the end of the war signaled a shift in an entirely new direction for the Italian film, the end of the war in France extended an earlier one. The break with French tradition came in 1959, and, as we shall see, it was not a complete break.

Max Ophuls made films in Italy, Holland, and the United States after fleeing his German homeland and Hitler in 1933. Max Ophuls's reputation today rests almost entirely on three films he made in France between 1950 and his death in 1955: *La Ronde* (1950), *Madame de ...* (1953), and *Lola Montès* (1955). Ophuls is clearly an international rather than a French director. And yet he found a home in France at a particularly apt time for his particular talents—a time when French film values favored the literate, almost theatrical script and the ornate, carefully styled studio production. Ophuls's greatest artistic resemblance is to two other internationalized Germans, Ernst Lubitsch and Erich von Stroheim, whose contrasting qualities he seems to synthesize. Ophuls's films combine Lubitsch's light, mocking, sexually wise touch with von Stroheim's perception of human desire and social corruption.

The Ophuls films all revolve around sexual intrigue in conflict with the social regulations against such intrigue. The Ophuls characters continue to carry on their intrigues while either hypocritically ignoring the social tensions (as the liars do in *La Ronde* and *Madame de ...*) or openly defying social convention (as Lola does). In developing a consistent theme, Ophuls also prefers consistent stylistic conventions. The plots are not linear stories but a string of vignettes, held together either by the setting (the Vienna of *La Ronde*), an object (the earrings of *Madame de ...*), or the central character (Lola Montès). By deemphasizing the story, Ophuls illuminates key structural balances, comparisons and contrasts of similar actions in different circumstances or different actions in similar ones. Such balancing takes the viewer directly to the center of Ophuls's moral statement on love, man, and social custom, just as structural balancing fulfilled precisely the same function in *Grand Illusion* or *Rules of the Game.* Also similar to Renoir—particularly the postwar Renoir—is Ophuls's deliberate choice of an artificial, theatrical setting (the sound stage in *La Ronde,* the circus tent in *Lola Montès*), which provides not only a nonrealistically appropriate setting for Ophuls's comedies of socio-sexual manners but also raises intentional questions about the shams of real human activity and the realness of acting and impersonation.

La Ronde is one of the finest translations of a stage work into film terms. The film is completely theatrical and completely cinematic. Ophuls effected the translation in much the same way as Olivier did with his *Henry V* several years earlier—by coming to terms with the aesthetic fact that the stage is verbal and stylized and that the film is visual and intensely natural. Ophuls neither erases the stage artificiality (as so many American adaptations of stage plays try to do) nor the film's visual realism (as a few American adaptations—*Top Banana, Li'l Abner, South Pacific*—tried to do). The setting in *La Ronde* is both an undisguised sound stage and the city of Vienna around 1900. Ophuls's camera wanders about the sound stage at will between the two poles of obvious stage set and realistic bedroom, between a metaphorical carousel, symbolic of the film's ever-turning dance of sexual relationships, and a real boudoir. "To wander" is an especially appropriate verb, for Ophuls keeps his camera perpetually on the move, spinning, gliding, flowing, traveling around the sound stage. Ophuls's German heritage is especially clear in his moving camera. The gliding photography adds not only visual energy but also continuity be-tween the potentially disparate vignettes. And Ophuls's wandering camera has an ally: the director has invented a narrator, a character who does not exist in the original play, who speaks directly for the filmmaker to the audience. The urbane, perceptive, witty narrator (Anton Walbrook) wanders, as the camera wanders, as he speaks for Ophuls. Director, camera, and narrator are one.

The single view they present is of sexual desire and the lies people tell to others and to themselves to obtain the objects of their desires. Ophuls's view of human relationships is the same as Arthur Schnitzler's, author of the original play (both Lubitsch and von Stroheim also liked Schnitzler). Schnitzler's play is a series of ten wryly comic seductions, all of which, except the last, denote the sexual climax with a line of asterisks in the text. The play's unique structure gives its author several interesting perspectives, which Ophuls pointedly borrows. Because the scenes do not depict sexual activity but the events leading up to and away from the activity, the obvious focus of each scene is on the emotional reactions before (usually sexual excitement, clichéd lies, mental fencing) and after (usually disillusionment, callousness, and guilt) the asterisks. The play's aim (and Ophuls's aim, too) is decidedly psychological, not sexual—hence the ridiculousness of Roger Vadim's later, explicitly sexy version of the play (*Circle of Love,* 1964). Furthermore, Schnitzler's play uses each character in two successive seduction scenes, leading to obvious comparisons of each character's actions, words, pose, and emotions in each sexual situation. And third, the Schnitzler play is constructed with an increasing complexity; the lies that each of the characters tells gets fancier and fancier with each subsequent scene; the sexual confrontations steadily climb the social ladder beginning with whore and ending with count. All classes, all people, play the same games, each in his own way.

Ophuls preserves filmically the intentions of Schnitzler's witty play: the stylized settings, the graceful camera, the understated acting, the charming waltz that plays as the characters change beds, the elegant and careful details of each setting, the urbane and confidential patter of the narrator. Especially clever is Ophuls's discovery of cinematic equivalents for Schnitzler's asterisks, usually handled on the stage by dimming and then brightening of the lights. To denote the sexual climax, Ophuls's camera often gracefully tracks away from the lovers, riveting itself on an object, and then later (perhaps after a dissolve) tracks back to them. His cleverest device is the sequence in which the film abruptly stops and jump-cuts to the narrator holding up a strip of film and a pair of editing scissors, shaking his head in concern over the lewdness of the scene he is about to censor. The narrator snips the sensual strip from the reel and the film jumps back to the two sated lovers. Perhaps the weakest section of the film is the last few sequences; the director shies away from Schnitzler's increasing verbal complexities in the later scenes. As a result, the concluding scenes are not different enough from the early ones and the film's repetitive structure becomes a bit tedious.

The moral view of Ophuls's *La Ronde* is not simply that sex is frothy and fun. The film poses a moral tension between natural human responses and unnatural social restrictions. The result is that the only time the characters cannot lie to each other is when they are lying with each other, during the "asterisks" of each scene. There is an underlying sad antithesis of human feeling and human callousness; the human brain's subjection to social rules and theories of proper human responses devastatingly turns both men and women into masses of contradictions of which they are totally ignorant.

This same antithesis between experience and convention propels *Lola Montès,* but Lola (Martine Carol) resolves the contradiction by remaining unflinchingly true to her feelings, regardless of the risk, regardless of the consequences. The story of Lola is the story of a woman who has taken a series of brilliant lovers—a famous composer (Liszt), a Bavarian prince. But Lola falls on evil fortune; she becomes a circus performer, forced to parade her life's story in front of a crass and ogling audience, selling gossip and kisses for a quarter. Lola has, on the surface, fallen from great lover to circus freak and two-bit whore. Her new lover is the fat and slimy ring-master (Peter Ustinov) who, though he loves her, salaciously revels in Lola's past, his present mastery over her, and the money he makes from her life. Lola's conquerors are those common mortal ones, circumstance and time, as her ill and aging body requires more and more whiskey to keep it going.

Despite the change in Lola's fortunes, despite the public tawdriness of her new life and lover, Lola is still Lola. She refuses to bow to convention, to play safe. Even her deliberate public display of her past is an unconventional act of defiance. If the past is all that remains of her life, then she will live in that past, even in front of a circus audience that gets a vicarious thrill from it. Though her doctor advises her that she is too weak, too ill to make her high platform leap that climactically ends her act, she insists on making the leap. And contrary to all circus-film clichés, Lola does not leap to her death at the end of *Lola Montès* (although she will, of course, leap to it one day). Lola cannot live her life any other way than as a series of dangerous leaps. What is important is not whether the leap is successful but that she always makes the leap.

But *Lola Montès* is more than an examination of a romantic life-style. It is one of the most dazzling of visual shows—in both color and Cinema-Scope. The circus within the film is matched by Ophuls's visual circus of mammoth action, swirling colors, and brilliant decor. Each of the sequences has its own unique color and tone: the warm browns, oranges, and ambers of the rustic affair with the composer; the cold whites, silvers, and pale blues of the affair with the prince; the dazzling reds and golds of the circus, glowing in the blackness of the circus tent. The film's composition is as effective as its color. Ophuls was one of the first directors to compose not *in* the wide screen but *for* the wide screen. The big shots—in the circus tent, in the palace—truly fill the frame. Ophuls's constantly moving camera, his panoramic staging, and his careful decor decrease the impression of the screen's great width by adding fullness and balance to the frame. Ophuls constantly splits the wide screen with contrapuntal verticals, breaking the horizontal expanse with lamps, chandeliers, ropes, drapes, pillars.

For his intimate close-ups, Ophuls rejects the conventional single face in the center of the frame, a composition that clashes with the wide screen; he either frames two faces that tensely balance one another on opposite sides of the screen or frames a single face that is balanced asymmetrically by an object or rearground action on the opposite side of the frame. Ophuls's favorite camera maneuver in the film is the circular track which moves round and round the action, keeping the figures contrapuntally balanced around an invisible pole in the center of the wide frame. The circular motion is not only active and interesting pictorially; it is the perfect cinematic parallel for the film's metaphorical circus tent, which becomes a microcosm for all earthly places and all human experience. Ophuls's turning camera, his metaphorical setting, and the very structure of *Lola Montès,* turn all human experience into a vivid circus and all spectators in the film theatre into spectators in the circus tent.

Robert Bresson, though equally careful with narrative structure, details of decor and pictorial composition, is a completely different kind of filmmaker. Subdued rather than flamboyant, quiet rather than gaudy, introspective rather than extrovertedly spectacular, Bresson's and Ophuls's films are as far apart as Brittany and Vienna. Bresson has made only nine films in a career of almost thirty years, the most important of them being *The Ladies of the Bois de Boulogne* (1944–45), *Diary of a Country Priest* (1951), *A Man Escaped* (1956), and *Pickpocket* (1959). Bresson takes two, three, even five years to make a single film. His slowness and care as a craftsman seem to mirror the quietness, the slow pace, the internalized probing of his films. Whereas the Ophuls films are dizzying visual shows, the Bresson films feel more like novels. Bresson's favorite transitional device is the slow fade out and fade in, strikingly parallel to the novelistic end of one chapter and beginning of the next. Like the novelist, Bresson can either tell his story through an omniscient third person (*The Ladies of the Bois de Boulogne*) or a confessional first person (*Diary of a Country Priest*). The *Diary* even uses the narrator's voice as the priest makes entries in his journal.

Bresson's primary theme is the battle of spiritual innocence with the corruption of the world. Bresson, a devout Catholic, searches for spiritual meaning and salvation in a world that has obviously lost them. In *Diary of a Country Priest,* a young, innocent curé faces the worldly evils about him: a cynical, nihilistic doctor commits suicide; a wealthy count substitutes money and influence for morality and faith; the faith of the count's wife wavers at the loss of her son; the count's neurotic daughter viciously implicates the priest in the countess's death; the peasants of the countryside remain indifferent and hostile. As a priest, the man fails. He succeeds only in bringing a moment of faith and peace to the countess. The other members of his parish remain tied to their selfish cares and physical concerns. But as a man, the priest succeeds completely. He dies of cancer, unshaken in his faith to the end, certain that "all is grace." His spirit wins the battle with his body. The Bresson cinematic technique—unselfconscious, unspectacular, effortlessly transparent—never diverts our attention from the man's internal struggle and the thematic basis of that struggle, spiritual and physical health. The film's structure consistently contrasts the priest's spiritual stability with the weakness and fears of those around him.

Bresson's camera lingers on faces, on eyes, on the priest's hands, purposely taking the time not just to slow the pace but to allow the human details to register in our minds and feelings.

Jacques Tati is the great comic of the French film, probably the greatest film mime and visual comic since Chaplin and Keaton. Like Bresson, Tati works slowly, controlling every detail of the film himself from script to cutting; like Bresson, Tati refuses to compromise with either technicians or producers. As a result, though Tati's first film appearance was as early as 1932, he has made only five feature films: *Jour de Fête* (1949), *Mr. Hulot's Holiday* (1953), *My Uncle* (1958), *Playtime* (1968), and *Traffic* (1972). Like Chaplin and Keaton, Tati came to films from the music hall. Before taking to the stage, Tati took to sport—tennis, boxing, soccer. Tati's comedy—for example, his famous tennis pantomime—often combines the athletic field and the music hall. But Tati is sensitive not only to the comic possibilities of his body, but also to the visually comic possibilities of the film: a paint can that mysteriously floats on the water and drifts over to the painter at exactly the moment he needs it in *Mr. Hulot's Holiday;* a house that appears to roll its eyes as two people walk inside its windows in *My Uncle;* travel posters exotically beckoning the tourist with a picture of the same modern, Hiltonesque hotel in the center of every exotic locale in *Playtime.*

Like Chaplin and Keaton, Tati plays the same character in each film, and the character he plays is inevitably a loner, an outsider, a charming fool whose human incompetence is preferable to the inhuman competence of the life around him. Tati's Mr. Hulot (even the name Hulot recalls Charlot) merely goes about his business, totally unaware that the world around him has gone mad and that his naive attention to his own business turns its orderly madness into comic chaos. In *Jour de Fête,* Tati plays a clumsy rural postman who discovers the apparent efficiency and speed of the American postal system. Tati's zany attempts to convert himself into a speedy, efficient machine produce great visual gags as well as chaos in the little town. As always with Tati, that which seems efficient and modern is ultimately inefficient and wasteful.

For *Mr. Hulot's Holiday,* Tati creates Monsieur Hulot, an apparently conventional, pipe-smoking, easygoing, middle-class gentleman who comes to spend a conventional week at a completely conventional, middle-class resort. Monsieur Hulot, again like Chaplin and Keaton, unfortunately runs afoul of objects. His troubles with a canoe, with his car, with a donkey, with a warehouse full of fireworks, reduce the conventional, routinized tourist resort to unconventional hysteria.

My Uncle features Monsieur Hulot again—this time as an old-fashioned, simple, mild uncle of a family of upper-middle-class sub-urbanites. Hulot's simple, unaffected ways contrast with the complicated machinery of his suburban relatives' lives: their fancy gadgets that open the garage doors and kitchen shelves (inconsistently); their bizarrely shaped furniture that is designed for everything but comfort and functionality; their gravel-lined, flagstone-paved "garden" that is suitable for everything but growing things and enjoying the sun. In this struggle of man versus the artifact, the gadgets win the battle (they always do in physical comedy), but M. Hulot wins the satirical war.

Playtime brings a group of American tourists to Paris. Hulot, more a passive observer than the central figure of the film, accompanies a group on their tour of a modern industrial exposition and a fancy night club that has just been glued together for fashionable Parisians and American tourists. The film's joke, as well as its serious point, is that Paris—the Paris of the travel folders and romance—does not exist. The old Paris has been replaced by aluminum-and-glass skyscrapers and neon-lit, prefabricated restaurants. Paris is no different from New York—hence the irony of the American tourists. The film is a clear extension of *My Uncle*, the ultimate blow at "modernity."

But the blow wears a hilariously comic glove. Tati ridicules the slick surfaces of modern life with hysterical visual gags: the tiles of the dance floor have been pasted down so recently that they stick to the dancers' high-stepping shoes; a plate glass door is so invisible that the customers cannot tell whether the doorman actually opens the door or merely mimes it. Tati also uses sound hilariously in the film. Unlike Chaplin or Keaton, Tati is a child of the sound era; his physical comedy never ignores its possibilities. Although *Playtime* has so little dialogue that it requires no subtitles, Tati develops aural gags like a plastic-and-foam-rubber sofa that makes grotesque breathing and sucking noises when Hulot sits on it and a miraculous modern door that makes absolutely no noise even when slammed with the most violent force. The Tati blend of social satire, wry human charm, and imaginative physical gags has not been surpassed by any other postwar film comic, French or otherwise.

Two other major French directors of the years just following the war were Henri-Georges Clouzot and René Clément. Clouzot is a cinematically conventional director of suspenseful melodramas. Both *The Wages of Fear* (1953) and *Les Diaboliques* (1955) mix chills, horror, sexual intrigue, and taut suspense. *Diabolique* is the more celebrated of the two, a story of a supposedly dead man who keeps reappearing to terrify his living wife—and a shrieking audience. But *The Wages of Fear* is a purer representative of the Clouzot method: an agonizingly tense, long journey of two trucks transporting nitro-glycerin through the jungles of South America. The suspense over whether the trucks will make it or not before exploding is supplemented by the nauseatingly powerful sequence in which one of the drivers suffers a crushed leg as he founders in a pool of oil. Clouzot's visual mixture of the slimy oil with the bloodied leg, obviously dangling loose from the man's body, held only by a thread of tissue, is both a haunting and sickening image and an effective narrative device for squeezing the story's suspenseful screws still tighter. Most illustrative of Clouzot's bitter, sordid premise is the film's final sequence: One truck has finally made it; the dangerous cargo has been unloaded; the young protagonist sits at the wheel, driving the now harmless truck back home. He is on his way to see his mistress again. He turns on the radio and listens joyfully to a pleasant version of the "Blue Danube Waltz." He turns the wheel in rhythm with the music; he sways back and forth over the mountain road. He misses a curve and the truck plunges down a ravine, taking the man to his waltz-time death.

Clément's most important film is *Forbidden Games* (1952), a wartime story of two children who are both affected and infected by the murderous world of their elders. A young girl's parents and puppy are machine gunned by a strafing German airplane. The girl, too horrified by the death of her parents, fixes her fascination on the dead puppy, refusing to believe it is dead; she tries to keep it and play with it. She is adopted by a family of Pyrenees farmers who, through their young son, teach her that dead things must be buried. The girl buries the puppy. She becomes so fascinated with burying things that she and the young boy go about the countryside killing living beings—flies, spiders, toads—specifically so they can bury them.

Attached to all the burials is that symbol of the cemetery, the cross. Clément equates Christianity and the forces of death. In their quest to bury bigger and bigger things the two children attack bigger animals and steal crosses out of the town cemetery for them. Eventually their private cemetery is discovered; they are punished for their activity, which ironically merely mimics that of their elders. The little girl is sent back to Paris as an orphan, separated from the boy and the family she has come to love.

But Clément's later films fail to duplicate the thematic seriousness and artistic integrity of *Forbidden Games*. Clément has been responsible for *Gervaise* (1956), a heavy and stilted translation of Zola, with Maria Schell; for *Purple Noon* (1959), a psychological, picture-postcard mystery that uses Alain Delon's body in the same way that Roger Vadim used Brigitte Bardot's and Jane Fonda's; for *Is Paris Burning?* (1966), an epic, Franco-American coproduction shot in France but rooted in Hollywood; and for *Rider on the Rain* (1971), a horrific suspense story with sexual overtones (like *Purple Noon*) in which Clément attempted to show the New Wave directors that he too could evoke Hitchcock (the detective's name is MacGuffin) and the Monogram mysteries (he is played by Charles Bronson—the American B-picture actor catapulted to stardom in Italy and France).

In the years following the war a new generation of Frenchmen became addicted to the movies. These *cinéastes* became film critics rather than filmmakers, simply because in France, as in America, the studio establishment had solidified enough to keep new minds out. These cinephiles did not like the film establishment's ornately-staged, heavily-plotted, over-scripted, unspontaneous, leaden films. In *Cahiers du Cinéma,* the journal founded by film theorist André Bazin, the young critics François Truffaut, Jean-Luc Godard, and Claude Chabrol ripped apart the films of Clément, Clouzot, Aurenche and Bost (*Symphonie Pastorale,* 1946; *The Red and the Black,* 1948), and others of the same literary, talky, studio-crafted, theatrical type. These *Cahiers* critics retreated a generation, to the 1930s of Clair, Renoir, and Vigo, where they found the zest and spontaneity of what they considered the authentic French tradition. Just as the French directors of the 1920s leaped backward to the primitive exuberance of Cohl, Zecca, and Sennett, the French directors of the 1960s leaped backward to the films of the 1920s and 1930s. Just as the French films of the 1920s combined echoes of the past with bizarre innovations for the future, the films of Truffaut and Godard were to be full of echoes of Vigo, Bogart, Hitchcock, Howard Hawks, Renoir, combined with ingeniously elliptical, irrational techniques. The year 1959 was the year that the critics convinced adventurous financial backers to give them the opportunity to make films. It was the year of Truffaut's *The 400 Blows* (its very title an echo of Méliès's *The Four Hundred Blows of the Devil*) and Godard's *Breathless.*

For François Truffaut, as for Vigo and Renoir, the central artistic idea is freedom, both in human relationships and in film technique. Truffaut's central characters are rebels, loners, or misfits who feel stifled by the conventional social definitions. Antoine, the thirteen-year-old protagonist of *The 400 Blows,* must endure a prison-like school and a school-like prison, sentenced to both by hypocritical, unsympathetic, unperceptive adults. Charlie Kohler of Truffaut's *Shoot the Piano Player* (1960) has deliberately cut himself free of the ropes of fame and fortune as a concert pianist, preferring his job in a small, smoky bar—uncommitted, unburdened, untied. Catherine of *Jules and Jim* (1961) feels so uncomfortable with all definitions—wife, mistress, mother, friend, woman—that she commits suicide. Truffaut's cinematic style is as anxious to rip the cords as his characters are. His films are consistently elliptical, omitting huge transitional sections of time and emotional development. His construction emphasizes the key moments of interaction and conflict rather than the motivational gaps between the moments. This elliptical leaping gives the Truffaut films an intensity, a spontaneity, a lightness that a more rationally plotted film lacks.

Truffaut also delights in mixing cinematic styles. *The 400 Blows* ranges from sentimental traveling shots of Antoine's tear-stained face, underscored by Jean Constantin's lush music; to improvised, candid comic scenes in the schoolroom, echoing Vigo's candid work with school children; to a *cinéma vérité* interview between Antoine and a prying social worker; to agonizingly long, subjective traveling shots as Antoine escapes the reform school and races toward the sea. The film then ends with a deliberately startling surprise, a freeze-frame of the boy staring ahead, presumably implying the ambiguity of the future that lies ahead of him. *Shoot the Piano Player* contains one of the most audacious of irrelevant interruptions. A character swears he is telling the truth. "May my mother drop dead," he says. Truffaut then cuts to a shot of an old lady by a stove who suddenly clutches her heart and collapses on the floor. Truffaut then returns to the story without further comment. In *Jules and Jim,* Truffaut undercranks the camera for Sennettesque effects; he uses a subjective traveling shot as the three characters race across a bridge; he uses newsreel footage of World War I that is horribly distorted by his contemporary anamorphic lens; he uses a brief freeze-frame to capture a moment of Catherine's beauty; he uses slow motion as Catherine drives her car off a pier to her death, prolonging the suicide, making the moment sad and slow. The trick and the surprise are intrinsic to Truffaut's method. They perfectly accompany the stories and people he has chosen to film. They give the film's action the Truffaut spirit.

Charlie Kohler finds it impossible to divorce himself from human commitment and human emotion in *Shoot the Piano Player.* Charlie, as a flashback reveals, was once the famous concert pianist, Edouard Saroyan. Edouard's wife, the woman he loved, felt her husband's career steadily tearing him away from her. She resolves the tension by jumping out a window to her death. Saroyan resolves his guilt by becoming Charlie Kohler, honky-tonk pianist, determined to avoid any further human involvement, human conflict, love. He sits at his piano expressionless, grimly banging out his honky-tonk tunes.

But life catches up with Charlie, forcing him to make a human response—just as it catches up with Bogart in *Casablanca* and Jean Gabin in *Port of Shadows,* both of whom are specifically evoked by the film. Charlie cannot stop himself from helping Léna, from defending her against the bullying owner of the bar (whom he accidentally kills), from falling in love with her despite his decision not to love. And like his first love, Léna dies, accidentally caught in the middle of a gunfight between Charlie's brothers and two gangsters. Accidents in the film are ironic and horrifying, so senseless yet so pervasive. Truffaut captures the pathos of Léna's death in her poignant, agonizing slide down a hill of white snow; it is deliberately drawn out in slow motion, like Catherine's suicide in

Jules and Jim, to prolong its sadness. Charlie has lost his love again. In the film's final shot, he has returned to his piano once again, banging out the same haunting tune—grim, expressionless, determined. The film paradoxically maintains that it is in the nature of love to be lost but that to protect oneself from the pain of loss by not loving is not to live at all.

Jules and Jim is another study of the relationship of love and life. Catherine refuses to live any longer than she can love, feel, respond freely, act impulsively. She travels with a bottle of vitriol as a potential means of escape from a life that might one day hang too heavily about her neck. She is a creature of whim, of impulse, of change. She can dress up like a Jackie-Cooganesque kid; she can race across a bridge; she can dive into the Seine to shake up her complacent companions. The same impulsiveness later drives both her and Jim off a pier to their deaths. Truffaut establishes Catherine as a pure spirit, an incarnation of the goddess of love. Her face and smile identically match the statue of the love goddess that Jules and Jim discover on an archaeological trip. But the pure spirit of love has difficulties surviving in the real world of geographical boundaries, marriage laws, child bearing, and political wars. Though Catherine enjoys supremely sunny moments with Jim, with Jules, with the two of them together, the moments lose their sunlight when they become months and years. She cannot remain happy with anyone for very long. And so she cuts the rope that binds her to life by driving her car off a pier. Once again permanent love and human reality are mutually exclusive.

The Truffaut films get their vitality from the cinematic surprises, from the themes of love and freedom, and especially from the charm and attractiveness of the leading characters: Antoine Doinel, Charlie Kohler, Jules, Jim, Catherine. Immediately after the success of the first three films, Truffaut suffered a series of failures. *The Soft Skin* (1964), a melodramatic study of the wife-husband-mistress triangle, was so lacking in a charming central figure and so elliptically told that the film wavered between the poles of drab melodrama and unintentional parody of melodrama. *Fahrenheit 451* (1966), an adaptation of Ray Bradbury's story of a Brave-New-World-like society that bans all emotions and all books, was so overproduced, so leaden, so lacking in spontaneity that it became the kind of plodding literary film that the young critic Truffaut expressly had hated. *The Bride Wore Black* (1968), though it moved much more swiftly than *Fahrenheit 451,* was so self-consciously indebted to Hitchcock—practically a film dissertation—that Truffaut had little opportunity to flex his own creative muscles.

But *Stolen Kisses* (1969) was a return to the old Truffaut: a thoroughly charming love story between an incompetent young man who cannot keep a job and his pretty girlfriend, with whom he manages his affairs just as incompetently. The breezy Truffaut had returned with the charm of the young man, played by Jean-Pierre Léaud, who had performed so charmingly and so endearingly as Antoine in *The 400 Blows*. The breezy Truffaut returned with the man's bizarre, nonsensical jobs (night clerk in a flop house, private detective, TV repairman); with the teasing traveling shot that follows strewn clothing up the stairs, eventually (after a coy false turn) revealing the two lovers in bed; and with the delightful *non sequitur* joke with which the film ends. A man has been following the girl throughout the film. We suspect that he is a private eye, tailing her, sinisterly mixing himself up in her life as the boy tried—unsuccessfully —to mix himself up in the lives of others. But the ominous man finally walks over to the young couple, politely swears he has long loved the girl from afar, and then walks away. On that buoyant, nonsensical note the film ends.

After *Bed and Board* (1970), which closed the Doinel trilogy by marrying Antoine off and fitting him—more or less comfortably—into adult behavior and society, Truffaut embarked on a series of style pieces. One of the most interesting was *The Wild Child* (1970), on its surface an almost documentary-style study of a late eighteenth-century scientist who succeeds in taming a wild boy—a child who had spent his entire early life as a beast in the forest—and introduces him to the luxuries of civilization: speech, clothes, shelter, and—most important—love. That the film is much closer to the Doinel trilogy than it might seem from its case-history surface can be seen in the fact that Truffaut dedicated the film to Jean-Pierre Léaud (the boy who grew up in Truffaut's trilogy from childhood to manhood), that Truffaut himself played the scientist who taught the boy (just as Jean Renoir played roles in many of his own films), and that the Truffaut-Léaud relationship is unmistakably significant to *The Wild Child*. Just as both the boy and the scientist grow into fuller human beings as the result of the educational process in *The Wild Child*, both Truffaut and Léaud, who were themselves outlaws and outcasts, grew into mature and full human beings under the tutorship of the director and in the process of creating works of art, the ultimate product of civilization.

The central Truffaut theme had evolved into one that was quite close to Renoir's: the relationship of art to nature and the ability of art to contain nature and to become its own nature. *The Wild Child* looks less sympathetically at the claims of nature than *The 400 Blows* or *Jules and Jim*. In contrast to the exuberant, natural spontaneity of the earlier rebels is the savagery of the wild child who is both unfettered and inhuman. Although wild children certainly live freely, they do not live well with other human beings and they do not create works of art. The stylish artistry of the film itself is a testimony to the value of art and supports its fable. Truffaut demonstrates the powerful claims of art in his careful cinematic re-creation of the life of an earlier century (one of the cinema's unique gifts), in its sensitive human study of man and boy, and in its cinematic devices that consciously evoke the visual values of an earlier cinematic era, particularly D. W. Griffith's. Truffaut's use of irising, of scenes of silence, of black-and-white whose silvery monochrome looks more like the older orthocromatic film than the newer panchromatic stock all reveal the director retreating into the cinematic past for his study of the historical past.

Precisely the same tension between art and nature propels *Day For Night* (1973), a film that Truffaut was seemingly destined to make since its subject is the process of filmmaking itself. As with *The Wild Child*, Truffaut plays a role in his own film—a similar role—the patient, paternal teacher-master who is responsible for the success of a complex project. As with *The Wild Child*, the film develops the conflict and resultant synthesis of art and nature, for the filmmaking process is none other than that of converting the totally artificial into the seemingly natural. A film produces candle effects with electric lights, rain and fire with valves and hoses, snow with suds of foam, an artfully "artless" ironic touch (a kitten eating the remains of an amorous breakfast) with a specially selected (and unnaturally uncooperative) cat, and deadly accidents with the leaps of a nimble stuntman. The term that gives the film its title, day-for-night (in French, *La Nuit Americaine*—"American Night"), is itself a synthesis of art and nature, the term that Hollywood coined in the era when the movies inevitably produced the effect of nighttime by shooting during the day with a blue filter.

But the synthesis of art and nature in *Day For Night* goes even deeper. Those in the film business ultimately turn their lives into the service of art. Their own personal difficulties—the loss of a lover, separation from a husband, even the grief from the death of a leading player—are subservient to the end of making the picture. Whatever happens in their lives, they make the picture—for ultimately their art is their life. As in the late Renoir films, the dedication to art indeed becomes natural for people who define themselves as being artists.

That Truffaut's film is close to Fellini's *8½* is obvious not only in its subject but in the recurring dream sequence which deliberately echoes the anguished fantasies of Fellini's film as well as Bergman's ominous dream sequences in *Wild Strawberries*. But the difference between Fellini's tortured view of the tension between life and art and Truffaut's more playful view becomes clear in *Day For Night*'s turning this potential dream of *angst* into a joke, a parody. Whereas the Truffaut dream begins frighteningly, each successive repetition reveals more and more glee as Truffaut's little boy unashamedly seizes possession of his great prize—the stills for *Citizen Kane*. Whereas Fellini's director dreams of frustration and Bergman's doctor dreams of death, Truffaut's director dreams of the way the commitment to art turns the fears of death into a celebration of life.

Jean-Luc Godard took the idea for his first film, *Breathless,* from

Truffaut. Michael Poiccard, the gangster-lover-hero of the film, is very much a Truffaut figure, a synthesis of Charlie, Catherine, and Antoine Doinel. But *Breathless* and Michel Poiccard were as close as Godard's films ever came to Truffaut's. Whereas Truffaut's films are consistent in both theme and technique, the Godard films are consistent in their inconsistency, their eclecticism, their mixing of so many different kinds of ideas and cinematic principles.

Godard, paradoxically, supports several contradictory ideas and filmic methods at the same time. On the one hand, he finds human experience irrational and inexplicable: the sudden, accidental deaths at the end of *Vivre sa vie* (1962) and *Masculine/Feminine* (1966), the chance murder of the policeman in *Breathless*. On the other hand, Godard flirts with Brechtian devices and politics, and Brecht's premise was that both art and human problems must be viewed as strictly rational and hence solvable. The parable of turning a man into a soldier in *Les Carabiniers* (1963) echoes the same parable in Brecht's *A Man's a Man* (written in 1924); the explicitly numbered scenes of *Vivre sa vie* and *Masculine/Feminine* and the concrete references to B.B. in *La Chinoise* (1968) are unmistakable. On the one hand, Godard is fond of allegorical, metaphorical parables: *Les Carabiniers, Alphaville* (1965), *Weekend* (1969). On the other, he is fond of recitations of concrete facts and figures: the prostitution figures in *Vivre sa vie,* the Maoist students' speeches in *La Chinoise,* the truck drivers' debate in *Weekend.* Godard depicts both irrational moments of fleeting sensation and long-winded speeches of abstract rational argument, both moments of violent action and hours of inactive discussion, outrageous intrusions of the director's favorite film titles and sequences, and long, unedited sequences in which the director attempts to efface himself completely. The speed at which Godard makes his films—fourteen features and several shorts in ten years—also contributes to their eclecticism and unevenness. In comparison with Truffaut, although Godard's films seem the more serious, Truffaut takes making films more seriously.

Breathless is the most realistic, the strongest narrative of the Godard films. Godard examines the life of Michel Poiccard (Jean-Paul Belmondo), alias Laszlo Kovacs (the same name as the American cinematographer who began by filming B-pictures for American-International and who later shot *Easy Rider* and *Five Easy Pieces*). Poiccard is indeed a petty crook in the Monogram, B-picture tradition, a casual car thief who kills a policeman by chance, gets emotionally entangled with his girl (Jean Seberg), and is gunned down eventually by the police after the girl tips them off. The remarkable thing about the film is not its simple story, but its Bogartesque character: brazen, charming, free, refusing to warp human emotions into words or human conduct into laws. Remarkable also are the emotional moments of the film: the startlingly real interaction between

Michel and Patricia in her room and bed, Michel's buoyant good humor as he drives the car just before he sees the cop, the sentimental but touching ending (a deliberate echo of Lucy's dying gesture in *Broken Blossoms*) as the dying Michel bids a funny-sad farewell to the woman who betrayed him because she was afraid to love him.

To like Godard for *Breathless* is perhaps to like Godard for being Truffaut. But even in *Breathless* the unique Godard devices—the assault against logic, the sudden and abrupt event, the detachment of the viewer from the illusion of the film—control the work. Michel's shooting of the policeman becomes a distant puppet show as a result of Godard's nonfluid, jumbled cutting of the sequence and his games with camera speed. As Michel walks on the Champs Elysées, an automobile suddenly strikes and kills an unsuspecting pedestrian. Again Godard's jump-cutting and Raoul Coutard's hand-held camera give the accident the convincing feeling of accident, chance, the unexpected. Michel takes a casual look at the dead pedestrian, shrugs, and keeps walking. The fragments of human passion, the juggled editing and jiggled camera, are pure Godard, not Truffaut.

The primary strength of the succeeding Godard films is the director's continuing ability to catch flashing, elusive moments of passion, joy, or pain with the most surprising and unconventional narrative techniques. *Vivre sa vie,* a supposedly cold, detached, rational study of a girl who drifts into prostitution and is accidentally killed, contains perceptive and revealing moments of human interaction. In the film's first scene, the girl and her husband separate; Godard catches the emptiness, the hollowness of the relationship by shooting the film in a café, full of the sounds of tinkling cups and passing traffic, behind the two speakers' backs. The faces of the man and woman never appear in the scene, except in a brief reflection in the mirror opposite the counter at which they are sitting. Also effective in the film is the girl going about the business of being a prostitute—with the very old, the very young, the ugly and the handsome—in the most matter-of-fact way, while Godard's sound track gives us, in counterpoint, a dry recitation of facts and figures on prostitution. The girl's teasing of a young man in a pool room, her sentimental weeping at a screening of Dreyer's *Joan of Arc,* and her lengthy but touching discussion of the meaning of life with an old philosopher in a café also contribute to the roundness of her portrait.

Masculine/Feminine also succeeds because of its charming or touching moments. Godard seeks to capture the world, the feelings, the vitality of the young, the generation of "the bomb and Pepsi Cola." Godard relies on improvisational interviews with his young central figures, whose charm, spontaneity, and honesty in front of the camera are infectious. The suddenness of the boy's chance death (Jean-Pierre Léaud again) at the end of the film parallels the irrational abruptness of the deaths in *Breathless* and *Vivre sa vie*. Godard again handles death anticlimactically. We only discover that the boy has fallen off a building to his death when his girl-friends report the accident to the police. The clicking clatter of the bureaucratic typewriter recording the account in the coldest, most mechanical manner contrasts poignantly with the breathing, vital energy of the living boy. Life and death, energy and deadness are that close and that far apart in the world of Godard.

Les Carabiniers and *Weekend* get their energy from the power of Godard's fable rather than the charm of his characters. *Les Carabiniers* is a wryly comic, Brechtian parable of two country bumpkins—ironically named Michelangelo and Ulysses, a synthesis of classical, Renaissance, and modern civilization—who leave the farm to go to war. The recruiting officer promises them the world; instead, the yokels merely bring back picture postcards of the world. Except, ironically, those postcards *are* the world, just as Ulysses and Michelangelo are Western civilization. When the two clowns return to combat, whose issues, strategies, and warring sides are intentionally unclear and undeveloped, they inadvertently get tangled up in some kind of political and military intrigue. The result of this entanglement is their death—they are incomprehensibly and unexpectedly gunned down by their officer. Throughout the film the two soldiers have described their travels and exploits to their women at home on wry little postcards that make no separation between the pleasant places they visit and the numbers of people they butcher. This naively bitter, comic, Brechtian device points directly to the film's statement: those who butcher get butchered in return.

The dominant mood of *Weekend,* another film about butchery, is not wryness but animalistic brutality. The film begins realistically enough; Godard takes realistic man's animal-like possessiveness about his automobile as the film's starting point. As the central couple travel on a highway to a weekend with their in-laws, Godard transports them from the land of the living to parable land. Using an agonizingly long, stifling traffic jam on the highway—intentionally made agonizing by the director's repetitious and unending traveling shots of the jam—Godard leads us gradually from reality into metaphor: from traffic jam to a land of wrecked automobiles and mutilated crash victims, to a land of open human hostility and warfare, to a land of cannibalistic savages slaughtering pigs and people with equal appetite. Cannibalism is the ultimate metaphor for modern society.

But on his way to this ultimate reduction, Godard cannot restrain himself from adding capricious, playful touches: a journey through literature land where the characters meet figures out of books (perhaps a parody of Truffaut's *Fahrenheit 451*); a political discussion of colonialism by two truck drivers, one white, one black, as they both devour meaty sandwiches; a secret code employed by the cannibalistic bands based entirely on film titles and characters—Potemkin, Gosta Berling, Arizona Jules. The latter is one of the innest of in-group jokes, apparently a combination of Arizona Jim (the parody of Rio Jim in Renoir's *Crime of Monsieur Lange*) and *Jules and Jim*. Godard is wry when serious and serious when wry.

La Chinoise, on the other hand, is an arid film of debate and discussion, as if the truck drivers' discussion of colonialism in *Weekend* had been expanded into a whole film. The problems of the film are, first, whether two hours of static discussion make an interesting film, and, second, whether Godard is for or against his Maoist speakers. Though Godard sympathizes with the students' critique of society, he also seems to poke holes in it. As the speakers talk, Godard's camera remains riveted on their faces; the viewer's eye is free to roam, having nothing more absorbing to compel its attention. As the eye roams, the viewer discovers subtle details that reveal how dependent these rebels are on the society they want to blow up: they drink Pepsi, they listen to decadent rock music on decadent bourgeois stereo machines, they have a copy of the *Guide Michelin* on their library shelves, whose red cover is the same color as the one that encloses Chairman Mao's *Sayings*. The ending of the film also seems to deflate the political seriousness of their speeches; after the young leftists evacuate the apartment two chic lesbians move into it, obviously to use it for something other than political debate. Is the Marxist debate pure fadism? Is the leftist student dallying with revolution the way others dally with sex? The film leaves the question unanswered. But if Godard does not take their ideas seriously, why does he expose us to two hours of them? Godard's later films, *Le Gai Savoir* (1969) and *One Plus One* (1971), are further static debates on contemporary politics, sexual mores, aesthetic values, et cetera. The key questions about the Godard of the future are, will he decide whether he is a Marxist or humanist, a rationalist or irrationalist, an artist or teacher? and is the soul of his films in images or speech, action or talk? Perhaps Godard's contradictions will continue to define his films as all of these things at once.

If Godard's overall career reveals a consistent pattern it is that he began by using bizarre devices of cinematic perception as a means to tell rather conventional narratives—the means to bring his characters to life— and he became progressively more concerned with cinematic perception— irrational nonnarrative; bizarre manipulation of space and time—as an end in itself. Along with his increasing interest in the way cinema records and transforms reality came his commitment to radical political causes, heavily influenced by the Paris student riots of 1968. The late Godard is both a radical formalist and a radical ideologue, and his ultimate synthesis is probably that only by destroying the ordinary and accepted modes of cinematic perception can the filmmaker destroy the ordinary and accepted views of his conventional society.

The tension between formal experimentation and political commitment is also central to the work of Alain Resnais. Although Resnais has been consistently linked with both Truffaut and Godard, he is a completely different kind of filmmaker. Ten years older than Truffaut and Godard, Resnais's career in films began not as *cinéaste* and critic but as film editor and documentary filmmaker. His most important early films studied the works of artists (Van Gogh, Gauguin, Picasso's "Guernica") or examined the horrors of the Nazi concentration camps (*Night and Fog,* 1955), two types which set the pattern for his two interests: art (the purity of form) and ideas. But as with Truffaut and Goddard, 1959 was the year of Resnais's first feature, *Hiroshima Mon Amour,* and critics assumed his work was part of the same "wave," despite the differences in his films.

Resnais begins with a far more literary premise than Truffaut or Godard. His films are neither improvised nor spontaneous. Like Bresson and Renoir, Resnais begins with detailed, literate, highly polished scripts. Although Resnais does not adapt novels into films—he believes a work must be written specifically for the film—he asks novelists to write his original scripts: Marguerite Duras, Alain Robbe-Grillet, Jean Cayrol. Resnais respects literateness, complex construction, and poetic speech. His films are thoughtful, slow, tightly controlled, and perhaps cold and heavy in comparison with the breezy, erratic, makeshift feeling of Truffaut and Godard films. If Resnais and the younger men are constantly compared it is probably because all three share one thematic premise and one formal principle. First, Resnais films examine the possibility of love, of sincere emotional interaction, in the world as it is: with its politics, its wars, its social inequities, its "rules of the game." Second, because one of the key Resnais themes is the effect of time, the interrelation of past, present, and future, his narratives are frequently elliptical, jump-cutting in time and space even more freely than Truffaut's or Godard's.

There the similarities end. The Truffaut and Godard films are obviously works of much younger, much more optimistic, much more zestful men. There is something very sad, very cold, very dead about the life and the people in the Resnais films. In *Hiroshima Mon Amour,* a French woman and a Japanese man try to build something more between them than a single night in bed. She is an actress who has come to Hiroshima, to make a peace film; he is an architect trying to build the ruined city up from its ashes. But both of them are separated by more than cultural distance. Between them is the past. For him, there is Hiroshima, the burned-out home of his youth. For her, Nevers, the little French town where she loved a German soldier in the occupation army whom the villagers murdered when the Nazis evacuated. Both have burned-out pasts.

To show the intrusion of these pasts into the present, Resnais, the sensitive editor, continually cuts shots of Nevers and the Hiroshima carnage into the shots of the present. At the film's opening, the two embracing lovers' arms seem to be covered with radioactive dust. As they make love, Resnais's camera tracks through the Hiroshima war museum, showing the burnt buildings and mutilated bodies. When the man accuses the woman of not knowing what it was like, Resnais cuts in flashes of her experience in Nevers. The result of this assault of the past on the present is an emotional gulf between them that can never be bridged. The final sequence of the film, lasting almost an hour, is a sterile, silent walk by the couple through the city: to a restaurant, a railroad station, an empty, desolate public square. The scenes of silence, of cold stone, of harsh neon lights, of antiseptic modern buildings rising from the rubble, all underscore the emptiness and the futility of their relationship.

Last Year at Marienbad (1961) is another dazzling film of the living dead. Resnais captures the ornate details of an elegant and elaborate chateau: its mirrors and chandeliers, its carved walls and ceilings, its formal gardens. His editing adds to the visual excitement, jumping about the castle so freely that he erases time and space completely. The film's problem, however, is translating the hypnotic visual show into some kind of coherent human experience. Time and space have been so thoroughly obliterated that every character and event in the film is totally ambiguous. A man may or may not meet a woman at what may or may not be a health resort; he may or may not have met her there one year before. He may or may not ask her to leave the resort with him, to flee the man who may or may not be her husband. At the end of the film, they may or may not leave the chateau together.

In this maze of time and faces, several dominant themes are quite clear. One of them is the contrast between sincere emotional interaction and the stifling artificial conventions, as evoked by the cold, sterile ornateness of the castle itself and the woman's sinister "husband," who is both murderous (he enjoys the pistol range) and infallible (he cannot be defeated at the matchstick game). A second clear theme is time itself. The man claims to have met the woman last year, but what exactly is a year? She has photographs in her room, clear mementos of the past, but the pictures seem to be of her in the present. At one point in the film a man bumps into a woman and spills her drink. Some forty-five minutes of film time continue from this point. Then Resnais returns to the spilled-drink sequence, with the characters in exactly the same positions as when the drink was spilled. Has Resnais equated forty-five minutes of screen time with an instantaneous flash of thought and feeling in a particular character's mind? And if it is a subjective flash, whose is it? Although the film's structure strikingly resembles the stream-of-consciousness narration of modern fiction, it is difficult to determine whose consciousness is streaming in the film—the man's, the woman's, the director-*auteur's,* or some combination of all of them? Perhaps the film is not to be interpreted at all, but to be savored for its cold images and sensitive moments, much like *Chien andalou* or *Ballet Mécanique*. But these abstract-surrealist films were only two reels long.

La Guerre est finie (1966), a much less heralded Resnais film, is a much warmer, much more human film than either of his first two features. The film is also more lucid and comprehensible, reserving Resnais's jump-cutting into the past for special, isolated moments of the film which specifically evoke the past. Like the earlier films, *La Guerre est finie* asks how a man lives in the present given the fact of his past and, further, how he makes sense of his life in personal terms if it makes no absolute sense.

Thirty years after the Spanish Civil War, a man (Yves Montand) continues to work for the Spanish underground, making regular trips into Spain from France to bring the Spanish workers revolutionary literature and strategy. Though the war is indeed over, it is not over for the man who has defined his life in terms of fighting it, and whose relationships with other people—friends, lover, mistress—is defined by his vocation. The climactic moment of the film comes when his vocation is challenged by a group of young leftists who find his methods and his crusade archaic, worthless, ineffective; they advocate not intellectual conversion and organization of the workers but violent revolution and dynamiting the society. The man rejects their callous challenge and continues to make his trips to Spain, fighting the finished war in his own way. And they, so Resnais implies, will continue to fight their war in their way long after it too is over. The important thing about the war for a man is not the winning of it—for the film doubts that a just war can ever be won—but the fighting of it.

Several other French filmmakers—though not of the stature of Godard, Truffaut, and Resnais—have also contributed to the reputation of the French film in the last fifteen years. Claude Chabrol was the first of the *Cahiers* critics to make a film. In films like *Les Cousins* (1959), *Les Bonnes Femmes* (1959), *Landru* (1963), *Les Biches* (1969), and *Le Boucher* (1971), Chabrol reveals an interesting contrapuntal tension between the sexual passions of his characters and the carefully detailed social environment, which is either stiflingly bourgeois or pretentiously exotic and chic. Chabrol specializes in case studies of bizarre psychological types and personal relationships that almost inevitably culminate in a grotesque murder.

Roger Vadim's first film, *And God Created Woman* (1956), also preceded the 1959 wave. Vadim began with a rough, honest sexuality that made Brigitte Bardot a star, but his subsequent films have become ponderously ornate, tasteless style pieces that leer as coyly at sex as Cecil B. DeMille ever did: *Les Liaisons Dangereuses* (1959), *Circle of Love* (1964), *Barbarella* (1968). Compared with the honest sexuality of the opening scene of *Hiroshima Mon Amour* or the bedroom scene in *Breath-*

less, Vadim is a little boy scrawling dirty words on the restroom wall—although he uses very expensive and very colorful chalk.

If Vadim is France's DeMille, Jacques Demy is its Busby Berkeley. In *The Umbrellas of Cherbourg* (1964), Demy takes the tritest of melodramatic plots (boy loves girl; he goes into the army; she marries a rich suitor; he returns; their love can never be again) and decorates it with the richest frosting he can find. First, the film is 100% all-singing; even the most banal ideas—needing a penicillin shot, asking for a gallon of gas—get the benefit of Michel Legrand's lush score. Second, the film's art director adopted the aesthetics of the department-store window; Bernard Evein takes special care that if the wallpaper is orange with lavender flowers then the women must wear lavender dresses with orange flowers. When people match the wallpaper, more subtle principles of fictional construction get overlooked. Demy's earlier *Lola* (1960) and later *Girls of Rochefort* (1966) are also long on sentimentality, melodrama, sexual poses, stilted acting, rich decor and lush music and short on ideas, sincerity, and psychological complexity.

Demy's wife, Agnes Varda, is a totally different kind of filmmaker: probing, thoughtful, intellectually sensitive to the problems of the artist and the difficulty of making life both happy and full. In *Cleo from Five to Seven* (1962), *Le Bonheur* (1965), and *Lion's Love* (1969), her central characters are all either women or artists and their problem is to come to terms with the undeniable fact of both physical and psychic pain.

Louis Malle is one of the most eclectic French directors. In *The Lovers* (1958), he shapes a graceful, literary study of the manners and world of the very rich, culminating in the woman throwing over both industrialist husband and polo-playing lover to leave with the young student with whom she spends the night. *Zazie dans le Métro* (1960) is a delightfully breezy, illogical, spirited film that uses cinematic tricks to recreate the literary and linguistic gags of Raymond Queneau's novel. The film is one of surprise and freedom, the director's hymn to the spontaneous and unfettered. The zany illogic of the film's story, editing, and staging mirrors the illogic that little Zazie embodies by being a petite eight-year-old who knows how to talk dirty. *Murmur of the Heart* (1971) seems a synthesis of these earlier styles with its child's-eye view of the restraints of adult life and a wealthy, attractive mother's attempts to manage both her family and her love life.

The spontaneous, unconventional French film spirit of 1959 is still very much alive. The directors who first created the free spirit are still very young, very free, and very spirited. That spirit is also apparent in the works of the newer directors of the "second wave." Eric Rohmer, though older than Truffaut and Godard (and even Resnais), was a later graduate from the *Cahiers du Cinéma,* which he edited after Bazin's death, to the cinema. Rohmer's films (*La Collectioneuse,* 1967; *My Night at Maud's,* 1969; *Claire's Knee,* 1970; and *Chloe in the Afternoon,* 1971) are quiet, sensitive, experiential probings of the definitions and relationships of love, sex, life, and art. In a completely different spirit are Costa-Gavras's violent and violently political films (Z, 1968; The Confession, 1970; and State of Siege, 1973), which, like the films of Godard and Resnais, mix their political radicalism with deliberately erratic and radical film styles: mixtures of driving suspense and social comment, human spontaneity and political commitment, elliptical jumps into the past and future, freeze-frames and slow motion, satirical comedy and passionate sincerity. Costa-Gavras's ancestry is especially apparent in the refreshing camera work of Raoul Coutard—prowling over faces, running through a crowd—whose work added similar insight and energy to Breathless, Les Carabiniers, and Jules and Jim. Gillo Pontecorvo (The Battle of Algiers, 1966; Burn!, 1970) is another radical in both style and ideology, using the apparent surfaces of documentary, cinéma-vérité realism to give both life and immediacy to his studies of commitment and liberation. Of course the discovery and development of the cinéma vérité documentary style was also a French contribution (as its name implies) of the New Wave era, the most influential films in that style probably being Jean Rouch's Chronique d'un été (1961) and Chris Marker's Le Joli Mai (1962).

The French (and Italian) Revolution

Perhaps the most important contribution of the French and Italian postwar cinemas was not the addition of at least a dozen masters of the film art and several dozen masterpieces of film art to the body of world cinema. Even more significant—from the vantage point of what is now two decades of hindsight—is the fact that these two national movements (and especially the French) revolutionized the values and aesthetics of the motion picture, affecting and influencing the entire world's cinema in the sound era as much as Griffith, Murnau, or Eisenstein did in the silents. The stylistic revolution that began in Italy and culminated in France spread worldwide, eventually capturing the cinema of America and even Asia. The Italian movement was more concerned with content than style—the close, careful observation of ordinary human beings in their social contexts—but the French movement essentially created a new content through style—and hence its even greater impact. That new style came at a propitious moment to fill an aesthetic void—at a time when the American cinema had become bankrupt in both content and style. Hollywood films attempted to apply the old stylistic values to the new wide-screen, color film; the two European cinemas discovered what to do with the wide screen and, later, color.

As in the past, in both the Griffith and the Lubitsch-Clair eras, a tech-

ACCATONE

The world of neorealism.

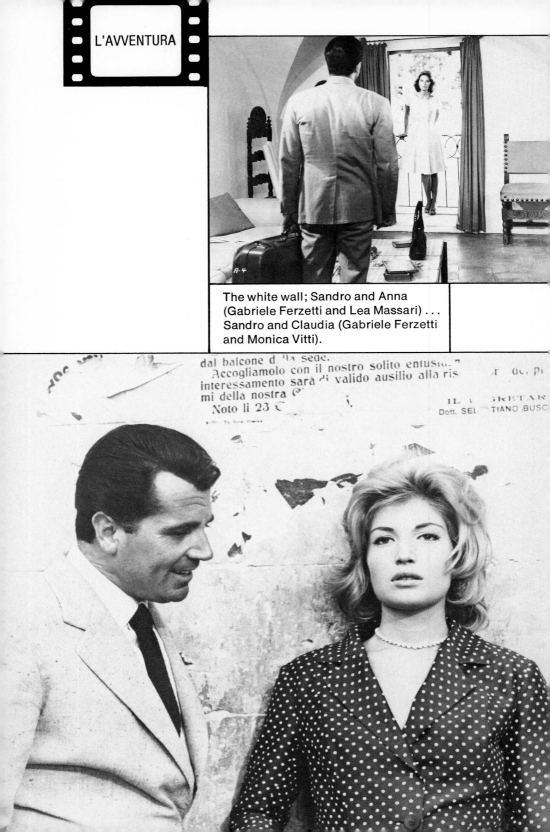

L'AVVENTURA

The white wall; Sandro and Anna
(Gabriele Ferzetti and Lea Massari) . . .
Sandro and Claudia (Gabriele Ferzetti
and Monica Vitti).

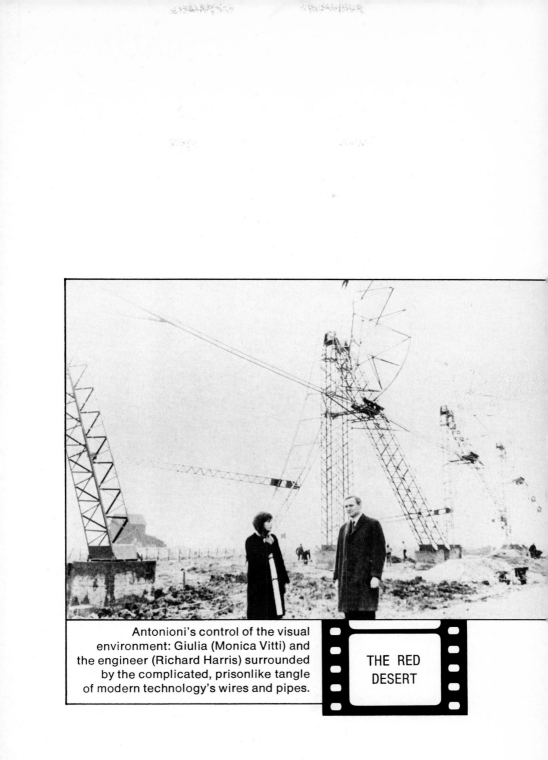

Antonioni's control of the visual environment: Giulia (Monica Vitti) and the engineer (Richard Harris) surrounded by the complicated, prisonlike tangle of modern technology's wires and pipes.

THE RED DESERT

Filling the frame.

LOLA
MONTĒS

Composition for the wide screen. Contrapuntal verticals (Martine Carol and Anton Walbrook) . . .

Balanced figures (Miss Carol and Peter Ustinov) with a central object (the cane) to link them.

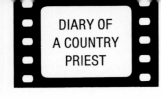

DIARY OF
A COUNTRY
PRIEST

Soft eyes and soft faces.

MY
UNCLE

The war between people and things.
M. Hulot (Jacques Tati) and
the other guests attempt to enjoy
themselves in a garden where
even the fish is an ugly
and noisy machine . . .
M. Hulot does battle
with mechanical gadgets
in a modern kitchen.

THE 400 BLOWS

Antoine Doinel (Jean-Pierre Léaud) in the classroom. Both the feeling and the candid style of Vigo's **Zéro de conduite.**

Antoine at the sea—the final freeze-frame.

Antoine caught with the typewriter—and a delicious parody of the American movie gangster.

Catherine
(Jeanne Moreau)
as a creature
of whim and
caprice.
She tightropes
along the bank
of the Seine.

Supremely
sunny moments.

JULES
AND JIM

DAY FOR NIGHT

Tragedies in life and art. The mother in the movie (Valentina Cortese) listens stoically as she hears her movie son (Jean-Pierre Léaud) inform of her husband's affair with his fiancée, but the actress breaks down when she cannot remember her blocking (with Jean-Pierre Aumont and Nike Arrighi).

BREATHLESS

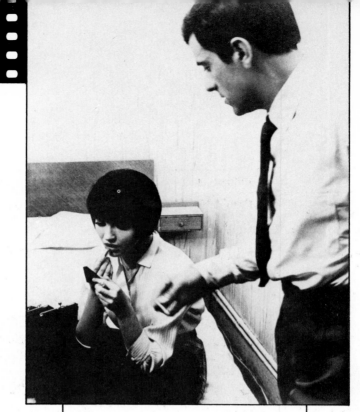

Going about the business of prostitution.

Irrational and accidental death.

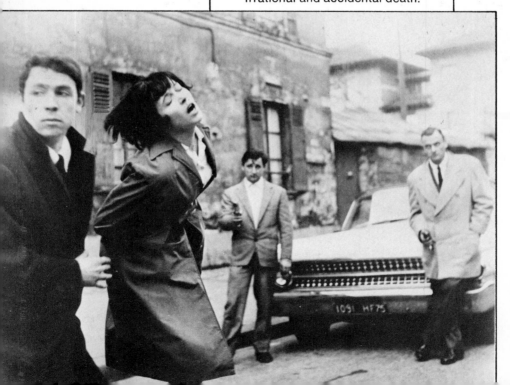

nological discovery produced a new style which determined a new content. Whereas the old narrow-screen, black-and-white film was a more distant, objective, rational experience (perfectly suited to lengthy scenes of dialogue, a rational narrative continuity, and images that essentially supported a film's story and issues), the new wide-screen, color film was a more immediate, subjective, and kinetic experience (in which the physical sensations produced by the images and sounds were often the primary basis for understanding a film's story and issues). Composition in the "Golden Frame" (as the narrow screen was called) was indeed composition *in* the frame, deriving from classical conceptions of space, balance, proportion, and perspective. Although the best Hollywood directors noted how poorly suited the stretched-out wide-screen's shape was to such compositional values, they merely tried to apply them as best they could. But effective wide-screen composition was to become composition *out of* the frame, in the sense that the screen no longer produced compositions of images to be viewed but instead used its images to strike, assault, and prod the viewer into experiencing those sensations that mirrored those of the characters. The sheer size and grandeur of the wide screen aided and necessitated its physical assault. And so all the cinematic tricks—the freeze-frames, the jiggling hand-held camera, the zoom lens, the elliptical jumps in the plot, the jump- and shock-cutting—all became ways of transferring subjective sensations to an audience.

This new stylistic assumption determined the content of the two primary kinds of films that used it. The subject of the films either became experiential itself: the feelings, sensations, and experiences of people living through an ultimate or exquisite moment of their lives, often ending with a Joycean "epiphany" of discovery (Truffaut, early Godard, Antonioni, Fellini). Or the subject of the films became political, using radical stylistic devices to produce a fuller perception of political and social realities (obviously and even admittedly influenced by Brecht), such as the later Godard, Costa-Gavras, and Pontecorvo films. Or the subject of the films became some mysterious and personal combination of politics and experiential sensations (Resnais, Bertolucci). Ultimately, the films were about perception—either of emotional or social, inner or outer, realities. And they used all the cinema's devices of perception to make the audience perceive.

It is interesting (and perhaps ironic) that these discoveries were made by the disciples of André Bazin, for Bazin's view was that cinema was the ultimate transcriber of reality, man's ultimate discovery of the means of getting nature into his power by reproducing it. For Bazin, the filmmaker's role was to efface himself completely, making the film reveal the reality in front of the lens rather than to mirror the perceptions of the filmmaker himself. Bazin's favorite filmmakers—von Stroheim, Welles, Renoir, Flaherty, Chaplin, Rossellini—were those who "put their faith in reality" rather than in the image, as Eisenstein did (who constructed his own reality by means of montage). Bazin's New Wave disciples are much more in the modernist tradition of defining reality as only that which each person can subjectively perceive. (There is no reality; there are only our own realities.) As a result, the cinematic tricks of these French directors were far more intrusive and self-conscious in their manipulations of "reality"—of spatial, temporal, and causal continuity—than Bazin's theory encouraged.

But then Bazin, who died in 1958, did not live to see the total conversion to the wide screen and color. In all fairness to Bazin, he did envision the possibility of a future period when the stylistic demands of the cinema would change. He noted that the cinema had attained a stability of style and technique that had remained constant for over two decades (which indeed they had since the introduction of synchronized sound), and he predicted that the introduction of a radically different technology might well produce a radically different cinema style and content. Then came the technological revolution, and the postwar cinemas of Italy and France (Bazin's disciples among them) brought the rest of the world into its next cinematic era.

Chapter

14

EMERGING
NATIONAL
TRADITIONS

The two decades of the 1950s and 1960s saw the emergence of other distinctive and important national movements, which were the result of many of the same causes that produced the postwar French and Italian successes. First, the postwar period encouraged personality and individuality in the cinema—new things to "say" and new ways to "say" them—because the old formulae and stylistic assumptions were breaking down. Second, and closely related, the audience, the technology, and the world were all changing. Times of instability and change tend to encourage originality rather than formula. Third—and also closely related—the American film industry was in severe trouble artistically and commercially. Prizes at international film festivals (a new sign of the times) not only brought honor to previously unknown film artists and industries but, perhaps more important, bookings. American films were no longer powerful or attractive enough to keep foreign films off the screen, either abroad or in America itself. Ironically, in the 1970s the wheel seems to have come full circle. By adopting the styles and assumptions of the foreign film movements, the American cinema has not only become strong enough to keep most foreign competition off American screens but has been winning the prizes at the international film festivals as well.

The name of Ingmar Bergman is as synonymous with the new cinematic directions of the last fifteen years as Fellini's, Antonioni's, or Godard's. Bergman, like Truffaut and Godard, is the product of a rich national film tradition. The Swedish film industry, though never producing a great number of films, enjoys a long and distinguished history. Bergman, an actor, playwright, and stage director, learned his film craft from Alf Sjöberg, Sweden's most important director in the first two decades of sound production. And Sjöberg learned his craft in the silent era of Victor Sjöström and Mauritz Stiller.

Both Stiller and Sjöström combined the visual and poetic power of the northern landscapes with stories of realistic passions and mystical influences—exactly as Bergman would do forty years later. The three consistent traits of the Swedish silents were, first: their use of natural imagery to evoke and convey human passions as in Sjöström's use of the sea in *A Man There Was* (1916), and of the mountains and fjords in *The Outlaw and His Wife* (1917), and Stiller's use of the lake of ice in *Sir Arne's Treasure* (1919), and of the snow and mountains in *The Atonement of Gosta Berling* (1923); second: their satirical and critical condemnation of social hypocrisies and injustices, as in Sjöström's *The Outlaw and His Wife,* and Stiller's *Erotikon* (1920); and third: the influence of cosmic, metaphysical forces in human affairs. The eerie, ghostly carriage that comes for the tramp who dies at precisely midnight on New Year's Eve in Sjöström's *The Phantom Carriage* (1920) is clearly the ancestor of the hearse that comes for Isak Borg in Bergman's *Wild Strawberries,* and Sjöström's figure of death with his scythe is an equally clear ancestor of Death in Bergman's *The Seventh Seal.* The films of Sjöström and Stiller were so influential that both men came to Hollywood to work for Zukor or Mayer. Even the title of Sjöström's most important American film, *The Wind* (1927), implies the story's interpenetration of nature and human response. The metaphorical unity in the Swedish film tradition is striking, for Victor Sjöström—Sweden's first film master—played the role of the old doctor in Bergman's *Wild Strawberries.*

Bergman directed his first film, *Crisis,* in 1945. For ten years Bergman and his first photographer, Gunnar Fischer, felt their way together within the film form, discovering how to synthesize the drama (Bergman's first love) with the visual image, building a stock company of actors sensitive to each other and to the director: Max von Sydow, Gunnar Björnstrand, Eva Dahlbeck, Ingrid Thulin, Harriet Andersson, Bibi Andersson. *Smiles of a Summer Night* (1955) was probably Bergman's first mature work, although critics in retrospect now point to signs of the Bergman mastery in *Thirst* (1949), *Monika* (1952), and *The Naked Night* (1953). But it was

The Seventh Seal (1956) that first conquered audiences throughout the world, and within two years Bergman had produced two more films, *Wild Strawberries* (1957) and *The Magician* (1958), to cement his reputation. These three films—*The Seventh Seal, Wild Strawberries,* and *The Magician*—make up a central unit in the Bergman canon, a complementary trilogy of films despite their differences in tone, style, and historical milieu. The films represent the best of Bergman's early period; they are also a pool of ideas and images from which all his later work seems to be drawn.

The key question about *The Seventh Seal* is whether it is a metaphysical allegory told in earthly terms, or whether it is an earthly allegory told in metaphysical terms. Its story is of a medieval knight, Antoninus Blok, who returns home from the crusades only to encounter Death waiting for him on a rocky, desolate beach. Blok challenges Death to a game of chess, knowing the inevitable result but obviously playing for time. Blok wants the time for one reason: to discover the value of living. Everywhere around him he sees death: from the crusades, from the plague, from flagellation and superstition. Is there life?

At the end of the film, Blok loses the chess game and Death inevitably overtakes him and his party. But, as Blok himself says, the delay has been most significant, for the knight has accomplished one important vital action. He has helped a young family of simple, innocent folk escape the clutches of Death. This happy family of father (significantly named Joseph), mother (named Mary), and infant becomes the film's trinity of life. At the end of the film, they stand by the sea in the sunlight, watching Death lead the knight and his party across a hilltop in shadow.

The film's central contrast is the opposition of the ways of life and the forces of death. The Church—organized, dogmatic religion—becomes emblematic of everything in the film connected with death. The Church instigated the deadly crusades. The Church decorates its walls with pictures of death. The Church inspires men to frenzies of prayer, and mourning, and mortification. The Church burns human scapegoats to keep the congregation in terror. The men of the Church wear black, the color of death. In fact, Antoninus mistakes the figure of Death for a priest when he makes confession. Bergman underscores the minions of death with darkness, shadows, and the religious smoke of the censer or the stake. This "holy" smoke dominates the religious sequences, befouling the clarity of the scene with a substance that seems like both fog and poison.

Opposed to the film's dark moments are its moment of life, clarity, and light. The scenes between Joseph and Mary—the two strolling players—are slightly overexposed, brilliantly bathed in light. The scene in which Blok partakes of their happiness, when the group sits in the sunshine to eat wild strawberries, is another scene of peace and light. Nature is not always dark and dead; it is also bright and sweet. The real religion, the real humanity in the film stems from the sincere, unselfish feelings the characters have for one another: husband for wife; parent for child; the cynical squire for his master the knight, for the tormented farm girl, and the tortured actor Joseph. In the course of the film, Antoninus Blok discovers the value of those feelings and feels them himself.

In Bergman's allegorical terms, we all play chess with Death. Life and death are inseparably close. One of the film's most haunting and, at the same time, most comic sequences is the one in which Death chops down the tree in which Skat, an actor, is hiding. Skat plummets to his death, while Bergman's camera remains riveted to the sawed-off trunk of the tree. Immediately after the sound of the crashing tree, a cute little squirrel jumps on the tree stump and twitches its nose. Life and death are that close. And so are comedy and tragedy, for Bergman uses comedy as sardonic, earthy comment on a serious film's weighty and philosophical themes. Like the gravedigger in *Hamlet,* the Squire in *The Seventh Seal* (and Granny in the later *Magician*) treats death as a bitter and hopeless joke. Since we all play chess with death, and since we all must suffer through that hopeless joke, the only question about the game is how long it will last and how well we will play it. To play it well, to live, is to love and not to hate the body and the mortal as the Church urges in Bergman's metaphor. In this sense Antoninus Blok wins the game with Death; it is the only way that game can be won.

Wild Strawberries puts the same theme in modern dress. The film begins with a vision of death, the old man's dream in which he sees a hearse roll down a desolate street, in which he sees himself inside the hearse's coffin, in which the vision of himself in the coffin grabs hold of the dreamer and tries to pull him into it, in which he sees that time has stopped, that the clocks have no hands. Bergman increases the dream's impression of whiteness, of desolation, of unreality by overexposing the whole vision, giving the dream world the pale texture of a ghostly shroud. Then the old doctor wakes up. Since he perceives the closeness of death he is haunted by questions about the value of the life he has lived. Ironically, this doctor, Isak Borg (played by Sjøstrøm), aged 78, is about to be honored by society for the value of his life's work; a university is going to award him an honorary degree. Despite the university's assessment of his life's worth, the doctor is not so certain about it. The rest of the film shows him groping for an answer. Like *The Seventh Seal,* the film is structured as a journey. As Borg travels along the road toward the university, three kinds of encounters influence his thought: encounters with his present relationships (son, housekeeper, daughter-in-law, mother), encounters with people on the road (three young, robust hikers and a bickering, middle-aged married couple), encounters with visions of his past that keep crowding into his brain.

When Borg examines his present relationships he sees nothing but emptiness and sterility. He has tyrannized his old housekeeper of some forty years, taking her completely for granted, never realizing that she has served him as faithfully and as lovingly as any wife ever could. His mother is a shell of a human being, living totally in the past, measuring her life by the little scrapbook mementos and childhood trinkets that she has dutifully preserved. But even worse is Borg's relationship with his son and daughter-in-law. He has tyrannized them, too, refusing to give his son the financial means to be independent. Borg's great legacy to his son is transferring his bitterness, his nihilism, his contempt for life. So successfully has Borg passed on this dowry that the son and daughter-in-law are in danger of separating. The son hates life so bitterly that he refuses to bring children into it.

The two groups that Borg encounters on the road are diametric opposites. The youths are shining, vital, energetic; they devour life with a callous yet honest robustness (Ibsen called it the Viking Spirit), unfettered by social convention, disillusionment, and failure. The middle-aged couple are slaves of a now empty passion, tied to one another by habit, by argument, and by the need to share futility. Both encounters trigger Borg's visions. The pair with blasted lives produces Borg's bitterest moment in which he attends a hell-like school (the scene echoes the school scene in Strindberg's *A Dream Play*) and receives pedantic, empty lectures from the husband. The doctor's life has been as empty and pedantic as that schoolroom.

But the young trio, particularly the girl, stimulates Borg to dream of his childhood, his dazzling summers at the family summer house, where he felt both bitter disappointment (in romance) and the blinding happiness of youth. Bergman shoots these summer scenes with a clarity, a brilliance, and a whiteness that echo the scenes between Mary and Joseph in *The Seventh Seal*. Summer and sunshine, in fact, are consistent Bergman metaphors for moments of human happiness in *Smiles of a Summer Night*, *Monika*, *Summer Interlude* (1950), *The Virgin Spring* (1959), and *Persona*. As in *The Seventh Seal*, there are wild strawberries, tart and sweet, alive, fresh. Borg's final vision of his summer youth is of a brilliant sunshiny day, the whole family outdoors in the clear bright air, the girls and boys in white, his mother and father, despite their emotional difficulties, alone together in a boat on the lake.

Like Antoninus Blok, Isak Borg translates his vision into human action. At the end of his journey, he realizes the irrelevancy of the university's social pageant. Instead, he shows his human responsiveness by proposing marriage to his housekeeper, by offering to ease his pressure on his son, and by, in effect, reconciling son and daughter-in-law to one another. Borg has taken a journey toward life, and the film's implication is that he has helped his son do the same, preparing him to procreate new life. Borg contentedly falls asleep, no longer haunted by clocks without hands.

In *The Magician*, Bergman turns from the relationship of death to life to examine the relationhip of art to life. *The Magician* is also a story of the road. A nineteenth-century magic lanternist and his assistants travel by coach to a town where they are stopped by the local authorities. These bureaucratic devotees of pure reason are anxious to see the lanternist display his wares, to see if his illusion is powerful enough to unsettle their rational reality. The magician's art is indeed powerful enough to drive one spectator to hang himself and another to the point of madness. And yet the bureaucrats judge the man's performance a failure. In the midst of his dejection, word comes to the lanternist that his presence is desired at court. He will be honored by both the coin and prestige of the throne. In an unexpected mood of joy and triumph and (of course) sunshine, the magician's coach sets out for the court.

The great power of *The Magician* is that the film operates on two levels simultaneously. There are, in fact, two magicians; one of them is Vogler, the lanternist; the other is Bergman, the filmmaker. Both Vogler and Bergman work on the principle that the trick, the fake, the illusion can seize the mind more powerfully than the expected reality. Vogler's life is a tissue of lies and tricks. He is not mute as he pretends to be; his hair is dyed; his assistant is not a boy but his wife. Everything about the man is false—a game of mirrors and deceptive appearances like his lantern show. But the same is true of the film director's art. Bergman plays tricks on *his* audience as ruthlessly as Vogler plays them on his. The film's opening scene is in a forest during a thunderstorm; it is a dark and ominous one: murky, shadowy, back-lit in a gothic manner that consciously evokes John Ford. In this first sequence, Bergman introduces us to a dark, shadowy figure who seems to be an apparition of death (a conscious parody of his own Death figure in *The Seventh Seal?*) and who appears to die in the coach before the magician arrives at the town. But later in the film we discover that the figure is not dead at all. The director has deliberately tricked us into believing him dead. He also tricks us with the magician's apparent muteness and his assistant's sex. But his ultimate trick on us is also the magician's ultimate trick on the bureaucrat: Vogler mysteriously lures the official to an attic, locks him in, and then reduces him to absolute terror with thumping sounds, invisible attacks, and the vision of a detached eyeball swimming in an ink well. Bergman reduces us to terror, too; the sequence is so inexplicable, so evocative of the powers of the unknown, so tensely controlled in its rhythm of sounds and cutting.

As though Bergman hasn't demonstrated the magician-director's powers convincingly enough, he ends the film with a grand artistic caprice. The film director has the instant power to change failure to victory, gloom to triumph: he can introduce a messenger with a letter from the king; he can add the music of trumpets and triumph to the sound track; he can shoot the scene in bright sunshine rather than murky shadow. The artistic principle behind all this conscious trickery is simply to show that reason, that the forces of society, have an undeniable power; society can put people in jail or decree their failure. But the irrational, the weapon of the artist, also has an undeniable power; its appearances can capture not the reason but the feelings of man. And feeling, as both *The Seventh Seal* and *Wild Strawberries* assert, is an essential human function.

The later Bergman films return again and again to the same ground as these central three. The films that Bergman himself designated as his trilogy—*Through a Glass Darkly* (1961), *Winter Light* (1962), and *The Silence* (1962)—all seek meaningful personal values—love—in a world in which human life has no absolute purpose other than to be. *The Ritual* (1969), like *The Magician*, reveals both the power of the rational bureaucrat over the artist and the power of the artist over the rational bureaucrat. *Cries and Whispers* (1973) returns to the issue of *Wild Strawberries*: the way that the awareness of an impending death defines the values of living. And *Persona* (1967) combines the self-conscious cinematic tricks of *The Magician* with a psychoanalytic study of a mind that, like Isak Borg and Antoninus Blok, views the experience of living as a bleak and lifeless lie. That *Persona* parallels *The Magician*'s concern with art and illusion is especially clear in the surname of the actress, Vogler, which is the same as the magician's.

But despite their similarities to the earlier films, the Bergman cinematic style had altered radically in these later films. Whereas the earlier films generated their philosophical meanings through lucid dialogue, supported by appropriate images and well-plotted, literary structures (revealing Bergman's origins in the theatre), the later films incorporated the elliptical and irrational cinematic devices of the French masters, their disruption of spatial, temporal, and causal continuity. Bergman's stylistic shift may be partly the result of his observation of these French manipulations of cinematic perception, partly the result of his realization that the probing of human perception and internal psychology required a more elusive technique, and partly the result of his switching to a more experimental cinematographer, Sven Nykvist, who replaced the more conventional Gunnar Fischer in the 1960s. The late Bergman films are increasingly concerned with internal psychology—the fears, anguish, and even diseases of individual human brains—as though devoting themselves entirely to the anguished dream world of Isak Borg or the irrational, illusionistic world of magician Vogler's attic. Bergman's adoption of a more elliptical technique solved the problem that seems to have defeated him in the *Glass Darkly-Winter Light-Silence* trilogy of the early 1960s, in which he rather contradictorily tried to depict human perception of the universe's irrationality by means of rational plotting and uncomfortably rational and explicit dialogue.

Persona is Bergman's late masterpiece, his most complex film, his most difficult, and his most dazzling display of technical virtuosity. On its surface, the film is a psychological case study of Elizabeth Vogler, a famous and successful actress who went blank on stage during a performance of *Electra* and has refused to speak since. Her refusal to communicate is symptomatic of her feeling that human existence is merely a collection of meaningless lies, that there is nothing to achieve, that success is an illusion and happiness the biggest lie of them all. For Elizabeth, to speak is to lie. She is treated in a mental hospital by the young, energetic, and dedicated nurse, Alma, and the cure then takes both of them out of the hospital to the seaside home of the hospital's head psychiatrist. At that seaside retreat, where the nurse does all the talking, the two women share both moments of tender intimacy and of intense hatred. The end of this process is the actress's apparent return to communication, to her life on the stage and with her family, and Nurse Alma's return to her job, somewhat shaken by the experience but continuing on her way.

What complicates the case study is Bergman's elliptical and non-linear way of telling this story, which gives rise to several motifs that extend far beyond a simple examination of an aberrant human mind. First, Bergman presents his film not as a mirror of human events but quite frankly as a film about human events. The process of making and watching the film plays a role in the film. *Persona* begins with the illumination of a projection bulb, with the spooling of a reel of film on the projector, with the familiar projection leader that counts down the numbers—11, 10, 9 . . . —on a screen before a film begins, and with several miscellaneous clips of other films interspersed (a slapstick comedy, an animated cartoon). It ends with a loop of film slipping out of the projection gate, with sprocket holes, with the white glare of a blank screen and the extinguishing of the projection bulb with which the film began. Between these two self-referential devices the film refers to itself by, at one point, showing the camera filming a scene (it is the scene of the actress onstage in *Electra* and gives rise to the question of whether she is acting on the stage or on a sound-stage), and, at another, by the film's appearing to stop, rip, and burn in the projection gate.

Bergman calls attention to the film as a film because he wants to emphasize that what follows is a fiction, an illusion—a sequence of light and shadow on a flat screen. The audience has entered the world of art and chimera, not of nature and reality. But Bergman's film then gives this clear dichotomy another twist, for is the world of nature any more solid, any more real than that of artistic illusion? That is the question that propels the rest of the film after its projectionist prologue. For example, at one point in the film Alma believes she hears Elizabeth Vogler speak to her—and we believe we hear her too. But Elizabeth denies speaking, and indeed the words were so soft and so misty that we begin to doubt what we thought we heard and wonder if she really did speak or if Alma merely imagined it. At another point in the film, Alma believes she hears a noise in the house and discovers Elizabeth's husband, who mistakes the nurse for his own wife and begins making love to Alma as Elizabeth watches. And yet he cannot possibly be there in that house; he must be the product of Alma's imagination. And yet there he stands, concretely before us and before the nurse. These are only two of the film's sequences that intentionally cast doubt on the reliability of the senses. Is the concrete world any more tangible, any more "real" than the "intangible" world of the imagination? Are the two so easily separated as the words tangible and intangible imply? And if the illusion can be as tangible as the reality, is this film (which has proclaimed itself as illusory from its start) any less real than any other phenomenon in nature?

This phenomenonological collapse of the familiar distinction between illusion and reality leads to Bergman's collapsing another familiar kind of distinction. Nothing is usually so unique and consistent, in art or in the psychoanalyst's definitions, as individual human personality. Bergman has titled his film *Persona*, a term which can refer either to a role in the drama (as in *dramatis personae*) or to a psychological type in reality (as in Jungian terminology or split persona-lity). One of the assumptions of such terminology is that individual and distinct *personae* exist. The film apparently presents us with two opposite, antithetical *personae*—nurse and patient (can an opposition be clearer?). Each has her own part to play and even her own "costume" (patient's gown, nurse's uniform).

The patient is "ill" because she has discovered the futility, the instability, the lies of all life's definitions: success, marriage, family, wealth. The head psychiatrist explains this illness as Elizabeth's escape from the lies of life by silence, as merely a role (like her roles on the stage) created out of apathy and of which she will become bored. That the psychiatrist is right is irrelevant, for the doctor fails to perceive that the very truths, terms, and definitions of her science are indeed the very lies that Elizabeth (and Bergman) has discovered and cannot accept.

Nurse Alma would appear to be Elizabeth's opposite: contented with her job, with her fiancé (whom she admittedly does not love), with her optimistic and unquestioning acceptance of reality's ambiguities as solid verities. And then Bergman collapses these two opposites—nurse and patient—into one. For the nurse does all the talking; she ironically is the one actually undergoing the psychoanalytic treatment while Elizabeth plays the psychiatrist and merely listens. (A further irony is that Alma describes herself as a good listener. And perhaps she is, for she starts listening to herself.)

The film is Alma's psychodrama, not Elizabeth's. It is Alma who confesses her doubts and insecurities; it is Alma who is driven to acts of violence, inconsistency, jealousy, frenzy, and paranoia. One suspects that Elizabeth is playing her psychiatrist's role rather deliberately, if only to prove that she is capable of reaching another human being, no matter how vicious that reaching becomes.

Bergman's film constantly emphasizes that the two women are one and the one is two. First, the two women (played by Liv Ullman and Harriet Andersson) look strikingly alike. Second, there is the magnificent, ghostly scene before the mirror (which may or may not be a dream since it looks as if it were shot through a fog or gray gauze), in which the two women embrace, their two heads seemingly emerging from a single body. Finally, there is the lengthy scene at the kitchen table which Bergman shoots in its entirety twice. First, he shoots Alma's entire story from her point of view, camera riveted on Elizabeth—wearing a black sweater and black headband—moving the camera steadily toward Elizabeth's face with a series of lap dissolves (a series of shots that overlap and seem to melt into one another). Then Bergman shoots the story over again from Elizabeth's point of view, camera riveted on Alma (a conventional film would shoot the sequence twice but cut back and forth between the two points of view in the final editing)—who is wearing an identical "costume" of black sweater and black headband—the camera again moving steadily closer to the subject's face with another series of identical lap dissolves (at exactly the same points of the speech as in Elizabeth's previous sequence). The faces begin to mirror one another. Finally, Bergman literally blends the two faces into one (thesis-antithesis-synthesis), using half of each woman's face to make the entire composite portrait (and it is impossible to tell whose face forms the left side and whose the right; it is impossible to tell at whom exactly one is looking). The two opposite *personae* are literally, tangibly one—a concrete illusion that Bergman has produced by means of the filmmaker's art.

The ultimate impression of *Persona* is of an elusive coherency, a unified but hauntingly evasive treatment of the issues of illusion and reality, art and nature, tangibility and insubstantiality, subjectivity and objectivity, definitions and definability. The result of this meeting of the two *personae* is that Elizabeth succeeds in shaking Alma, in giving her an "existential shudder" (the same shudder that produced the actress's silence initially). And Bergman's film is intended to haunt his audience with the same kind of shudder as he pulls the rug of our comfortable and functional definitions of reality and psychology out from under our feet. Bergman could only accomplish this shudder by eschewing the conventional linear narrative, by boldly proclaiming the discontinuity of time and space, by interjecting reminders that the cinema, grand illusion though it is, is no grander an illusion than the reality which we accept as tangible and real. Only Bergman's elusive, elliptical, antirational style could convey a vision of life as elusive, indefinable, and irrational without betraying it. Though the film begins by proclaiming that it is art and not life, what Bergman paradoxically means is that the film is life indeed.

Although Ingmar Bergman is the unquestioned directorial star of the postwar Swedish industry, several newer and lesser lights have appeared in the last decade: the lush, pictorial, fatalistic romanticism of Bo Widerberg's *Elvira Madigan* (1967); the close, affectionate observation of Swedish immigrants in Jan Troell's *The Emigrants* (1972); the frank sexuality and the probing of the relationship between mind and body in Vilgot Sjöman's *I Am Curious* (Yellow and Blue, 1969). This last work was very close to a Swedish "subgenre" that is familiar to many American audiences who may never have even heard of Ingmar Bergman. Using its reputation as one of the world's most sexually liberated nations, Sweden unleashed a series of sexploitation films on the world market—*Inga, Helga, 491, I a Woman* (Parts I, II, and III!)—that played extended runs on New York's 42nd Street and in the seamier neighborhoods of many other cities. Like the Italian cinema, the Swedish industry discovered it could make money from its trash as well as its art.

The English Social Realists

The British film has never quite recovered the experimental and artistic uniqueness of the era of Hepworth, Urban, Smith, Williamson, and Collings, which disappeared just before World War I. The common language made England such a Hollywood colony that the British government passed special quota laws to protect the native cinema in the era of the talkies. The quotas protected no one and produced a flood of artless, craftless cheapies that served as second features for the American films that everyone came to see. If a British film did score an international success—such as Alexander Korda's *The Private Life of Henry the Eighth* (1933) or Hitchcock's *The 39 Steps*—its director or star almost immediately departed for Hollywood. Charles Laughton and Leslie Howard were as much a part of the Hollywood of the past as Richard Burton, Julie Christie, Peter Sellers, Vanessa Redgrave, and Peter O'Toole are of the "Hollywood" of today. Alfred Hitchcock's conversion to Hollywood budgets and procedures has been duplicated by the similar conversion of David Lean— from his stylish Dickens adaptations like *Great Expectations* (1946) and *Oliver Twist* (1947), to *The Bridge on the River Kwai* (1957), *Lawrence of Arabia* (1962), *Doctor Zhivago* (1965), and *Ryan's Daughter* (1970).

Carol Reed has also gone the same route from taut, Hitchcockesque thrillers like *Odd Man Out* (1947) and *The Third Man* (1949) to *Oliver!* (1968).

For the first fifteen years following World War II, the British film seemed synonymous with four cinematically conventional genres. First, there were the highly polished, fluently acted adaptations of the literary classics: Lean's films of Dickens, Olivier's later adaptations of Shakespeare (*Hamlet*, 1948; *Richard III*, 1955), and Anthony Asquith's adaptations of Rattigan and Wilde (*The Winslow Boy*, 1949; *The Browning Version*, 1951; and *The Importance of Being Earnest*, 1952). Second, there were the suspenseful, mystery thrillers—tightly edited, subtly acted—of wartime military assignments or postwar political cabals. Third, there were the satirical, understated "little" comedies made at the Ealing Studios by Robert Hamer (*Kind Hearts and Coronets*, 1949; *Father Brown*, 1954), Alexander Mackendrick (*Tight Little Island*, 1948; *The Man in the White Suit*, 1951; *The Ladykillers*, 1955), Charles Crichton (*The Lavender Hill Mob*, 1951), and Anthony Kimmins (*The Captain's Paradise*, 1953). Most of these films starred Alec Guinness. And fourth, there were the lavish ballet spectacles of Michael Powell and Emeric Pressburger (*The Red Shoes*, 1948; *The Tales of Hoffman*, 1950). The general traits of all four of these British genres were a subtle understatement, expert acting, carefully realistic decor, and a firm control of taut narrative construction.

Perhaps the most unique and significant work in the British film between the era of Charles Urban and 1959 was the documentary film movement of the 1930s and 1940s. Sponsored by the government and directed by filmmakers like John Grierson, Paul Rotha, Basil Wright, Harry Watt, Edgar Anstey, Humphrey Jennings, and Len Lye, the British documentaries developed the craft of capturing the surfaces of reality to illuminate the essences beneath them. The realist texture that seemed to distinguish British fictional films from Hollywood's was especially obvious in the purely realist documentary films. To some extent, the new British film of 1959 began with a similar premise. This new British film was the product of several influences: of the British documentary tradition; of the new class-conscious British novels and plays by authors like John Osborne, John Braine, Arnold Wesker, Alan Sillitoe, and Alun Owen; of the Italian neorealist films; of the new spirit of free cinema that was emerging in France at the same time. The result of these many influences was a series of films that was radically different from the polished, elegant, escapist films of Lean, Asquith, and Reed.

The new British films, like the Italian neorealist ones, emphasized the poverty of the working man, the squalor of his life, the difficulty of keeping a home and keeping one's self-respect at the same time, the social assumptions that sentence a man with no education and a working-class dialect to a lifetime of bare survival. To emphasize the dreary mediocrity of the working-class life, the British directors turned their cameras on the oppressive smoke of factories, the dull and drizzly weather at their stifling seaside resorts, the dingy and smoky feel of the pubs where they try to escape, the bare and faded austerity of the rooms they can afford to rent. In the midst of this intentionally barren and gray world, the directors focus on a common man reacting to his surroundings—bitter, brutal, angry, tough. These heroes of the films, traditionally labeled "angry young men," inevitably react in one of two ways to the working-class prisons of their lives: they try to grab some of the swag of the upper-class life for themselves, or, failing that, they break things. Their tragedy is usually that their only talent is loving, and society does not reward that kind of talent.

Jack Clayton's *Room at the Top* (1959) was the first of the working-class British films to earn an international reputation and to make money. Clayton did not come to the films as a young rebel but as a tireless perfectionist-craftsman who had worked his way up in the British film industry. Clayton's care and craftsmanship was as responsible for the film's success as its sociological content. Joe Lampton (Laurence Harvey), an ambitious young man with a provincial accent and a provincial education, takes a job at Brown's factory in a northern industrial city. Joe quickly learns the economic facts of life. He becomes enamored of a posh residential area of the city known as "the top," a hill that dominates the town. Most attractive of all the houses on "the top" is Mr. Brown's, the owner of the factory and commercial lord of the town. Despite his present affluence, Brown himself worked his way out of the working class, only to don class snobbery and to join the Conservative Club once he had gotten to "the top."

Joe sets his sights on Susan, Brown's daughter, a rich, pretty but emotionally shallow girl who responds to human affection with the same intensity as to a brisk set of tennis. On his way to capturing Susan, Joe meets an older, warmer woman (Simone Signoret) who reveals to him what two people are capable of feeling for one another. She, escaping her callous, brutal husband, falls in love with Joe, and he falls in love with both the strength of her mind and the warmth of her body. But fate grabs hold of Joe. Just when Joe had decided that the relationship with Susan Brown was valueless, Susan becomes pregnant and her father compels Joe to marry her. When Joe tells his mistress that he is going to marry Susan, she becomes so upset that she kills herself in an automobile accident. And so Joe marries Susan. He gets his room at the top. Only now he does not want it. He sits in a taxi on the day of his gala, socialite wedding. It should be the great moment of his life, the realization of his driving ambition. But Susan sits next to him chattering about how "super" their life will be together. And Joe's eyes fill with tears. Their life together will be anything but super, top or no top.

Clayton's handling of the film shows his experience and craft. He gets the best English-language performance of her career from Simone Signoret, and the most virile, least mannered performance of his career from Laurence Harvey. Compositionally, Clayton has not only exerted great care in bathing the film in wet, dreary, smoky grays, but also in surrounding the characters with the importance of Brown's name and power in the industrial town. On billboards, outside railway windows, reflected in the puddles on the street, hanging on one of his smokestacks, is the name of Brown, an ever-present reminder of the temptation of money and power, the temptation to which Joe so easily yields, unwittingly damning himself.

That Clayton's commitment is more to his craft than to his class-conscious subject matter becomes clearer in his subsequent films. In *The Innocents* (1961), Clayton leaves the gray, dirty world of the present for the costumed grace of a country manor house of the nineties. Clayton adapts Henry James's *The Turn of the Screw,* a novella with one of the most debated critical questions in literary history. Has James written a story of real ghosts or a story of phantoms created by the neurotic brain of a sexually starved lady? Clayton decides, as have many literary critics, that the ambiguity in the story is intentional, that James deliberately refuses to show if the ghosts are real or imaginary. His problem is to translate this ambiguity into cinematic terms, for the camera can be quite convincing in its demonstrations that a being either is or is not there. By letting the governess's point of view control every shot of the ghosts—we never see them except from her vantage point—the director ingeniously sustains the doubt about their existence in any one else's world but her own. The result of this careful manipulation of point of view is a combination of a chilling story of terror and evil with a psychological mystery about the potential fallibility of the human brain. Does the evil in the universe torture the children to death or does the evil in the human mind kill them?

Clayton's next film, *The Pumpkin Eater* (1963), is another novelistic work (script by Harold Pinter) that depends heavily on the integration of two points of view: the world's objective view of the neurotic wife (Anne Bancroft), and the wife's subjective view of the quicksand world around her. The consistent Clayton characteristic is his subjective, psychological premise—the way the world looks and feels to the central figure. To capture these sensations, Clayton uses either the images of external reality or the tight control of the camera's point of view to mirror the workings of a character's mind. With the passing of the mid-sixties, Clayton's influence and power also passed. His direction of *The Great*

Gatsby (1974), though revealing his usual craftsmanship and stylishness, is an empty and impersonal exercise.

Tony Richardson was the first and most fortunate of the British directors to take advantage of the success of *Room at the Top.* In 1959, Richardson directed the film version of John Osborne's *Look Back in Anger,* three years after he had directed the sharp, tongue-lashing stage-play at London's Royal Court Theatre. Within three years Richardson had directed three similar films: two adaptations of realist, class-conscious plays (*The Entertainer,* 1960; *A Taste of Honey,* 1962); and an adaptation of Alan Sillitoe's antiestablishment, class-conscious novel, *The Loneliness of the Long-Distance Runner* (1962). These four early Richardson films are quite similar in their strengths and weaknesses. All of them depend heavily on the literateness of the original works. All of them are brilliantly acted, both in the major roles and in the tiny character parts. Richardson's experience as a stage director no doubt aided his actors. But actors like Richard Burton, Claire Bloom, Mary Ure, Laurence Olivier, Brenda DaBanzie, Rita Tushingham, Murray Melvin, and Tom Courtenay made his task somewhat easier. Cinematically, the Richardson films feel like stage-plays, punctuated by shots of grimy slums, run-down rooms, unamusing amusement parks, and dirty children. *Loneliness of the Long-Distance Runner* is the most adventurous of the films cinematically, allowing the freeness of the novel and the new cinematic winds blowing from across the channel to help him escape the tyrannies of stage dialogue and stage setting, of stage time and stage place.

Later Richardson films—*Tom Jones* (1963), *The Loved One* (1965), *The Charge of the Light Brigade* (1968)—leave the grime of working-class England and the bitterness of her social-outcast laborers far behind. The angry, naturalistic sincerity of the four early films is replaced by higher budgets, bigger casts, and colorful settings, thousands of miles and hundreds of years distant from industrial Britain. *Tom Jones,* a consistently delightful film, succeeds because of two Richardson strengths—its debt to the original Fielding fable and its fine performances. But there is something impersonal about the film's inconsistent weaving of cinematic styles: part romance, part Feydeau bedroom farce, part Sennett romp, part gratuitous naturalism with its shots of horsemen's spurs drawing real blood from their abused mounts.

Richardson's stylistic bankruptcy is especially clear in *The Loved One,* a desperate and outrageous attempt to copy the mixture of humor and horror of Kubrick's *Dr. Strangelove.* Even the film's opening shots, developing the comic sexuality of a jet plane's "orifices," echo the memorable sexual union of the planes at the opening of *Dr. Strangelove.* The rest of the film's satire of American burial festivities—and the culture that created such festivities—consistently falls off the tightrope that *Dr. Strange-*

love walks between farce and social polemic; it becomes heavy-handed farce and heavy-handed polemic at alternate moments. The film has its striking sequences: a cold, bitchy argument to the death between a rich husband and wife on the appropriate burial arrangements for their dog; an enormously fat lady who constantly eats and whose favorite TV programs are the food commercials. But Richardson, desperately chasing after someone else's style, splinters the film into a series of inharmonious gags and vignettes: some camp (both Liberace and Tab Hunter make cameo appearances), some grotesque (Jonathan Winters as the sex-starved king of undertakers), some symbolic (the hero's love for a girl who lives in a condemned house that teeters on the edge of a hill). From the tasteless stylistic stew of *The Loved One*, Richardson's later films have moved even further from the shrill, engaging energy of his commitment to the social rebels of his early films. For Richardson, as for his friend Osborne, success has not been altogether kind.

For five years English directors made film variations on the Clayton-Richardson themes: the young, uneducated, often unintelligent working man or woman sentenced by industrial society to an inescapable yet unendurable life of drabness and mediocrity. Quite significantly, not one of these social-realist films was shot in color. Color was as antithetical to the smoke and fog of working-class Britain as it was to the poverty of neorealist Italy. Karel Reisz's *Saturday Night and Sunday Morning* (1961) and *Morgan!* (1966) and Sidney J. Furie's *The Leather Boys* (1963) mix stories of young, rebellious have-nots with the carefully realistic depiction of the social milieu that condemns them to the prison of their economic class. Other British films of the same era, with widely different themes and characters, share the same texture and smell of cinematic naturalism—from the factory tensions of Guy Green's *The Angry Silence* (1959), to the realistically brutal world of success in Lindsay Anderson's *This Sporting Life* (1963), to the neurotic occultism of Bryan Forbes's *Seance on a Wet Afternoon* (1964), to the realism of a Midlands mining town in Jack Cardiff's *Sons and Lovers* (1960), to the fashionable social world of John Schlesinger's *Darling* (1965), to the study of pathetic senility in Forbes's *The Whisperers* (1967).

The one obvious exception to this school of social realism was the work of Richard Lester, an American expatriate who united the Beatles with the cinematic ellipticality of Truffaut and Godard. The results— *A Hard Day's Night* (1964) and *Help!* (1965)—were buoyant, seemingly effortless romps through the streets and fields of illogic. But later Lester films reveal that the quality of his pictures varies inversely with the strength of his original material. There is a tension between the realistic material in *The Knack* (1965) and *How I Won the War* (1967) and Lester's formalistic games at the editing table. This tension produces not the lightness of the Beatle films but the self-conscious heavy-handedness of a director strangling his material with his own cleverness. Tony Richardson could have made a much more sensitive film out of Ann Jellicoe's psychologically perceptive stageplay, *The Knack;* and any Hollywood director could have made a funnier film out of the farcically delightful stage musical, *A Funny Thing Happened on the Way to the Forum* (1966). Lester's ebullient success with *The Three Musketeers* (1974) is another indication that the real content of his films is his playful manipulation of lightweight material that has no intrinsic content.

Since 1963 the line dividing London and Hollywood has blurred again. Tony Richardson's desertion of native themes for Hollywood production values is a paradigm for the British industry as a whole. Karel Reisz deserted the slums for the Technicolor internationalism of *Isadora* (1968); Lindsay Anderson's surface realism continues in *If. . . .* (1968), augmented by the new Hollywood conventions of youthful romanticism, lush Technicolor pictorialism, and Pirandellian games with the inseparability of reality and illusion; Bryan Forbes directed the Technicolor all-star disaster, *The Madwoman of Chaillot* (1969); John Schlesinger was almost as comfortable with the American social fringes in *Midnight Cowboy* (1969) as he was with the British ones in *Darling.* British and American styles are so indistinguishable that there is no essential stylistic difference between two parallel film adaptations of historical stageplays, Fred Zinnemann's *A Man for All Seasons* (1966) and Anthony Harvey's *The Lion in Winter* (1968), except for Zinnemann's superior ability to translate a talky drama into a moving picture.

By the mid-1970s a new group of British directors had solidified their positions as the most interesting to watch in the future. Ken Russell is the most audacious British stylist, a director with a brilliant visual sense of decor and a strong yearning to say things of significance—the significance of which is frequently buried beneath the scenery and wallpaper. Russell, whose training came in filming biographies (mostly of composers) for television, directed his first highly acclaimed film in 1969, *Women in Love.* The solidity of the D. H. Lawrence characters and the effectiveness of the novel's symbolism helped anchor Russell's visual flights of fancy in solid fictional ground. His film of *The Boy Friend* (1972) avoids the tension between style and ideas by having none of the latter; it (like his later *Tommy,* 1975) is as pure a style piece as has ever been made, a self-contained history of the musical film. But Russell's "psychological" studies of Tchaikovsky (*The Music Lovers,* 1970) and medieval religious fanaticism (*The Devils,* 1971) seem to have more to do with stereotypic romantic and sexual poses than psychological subtlety and revelation, and both seem to lose their intended intellectual and psychological complexity beneath the striking but simple surfaces of the decor.

John Schlesinger is a completely different kind of stylist, the most literate, verbal, and psychological of the new British directors. Schlesinger's primary concern is to reveal the normal, ordinary sense behind the lives of people whom society would define as most abnormal, freaky, and bizarre. For Schlesinger, "abnormal," "aberrant" people live lives that seem completely normal and make perfect sense from their point of view, and the Schlesinger films develop precisely this subjective point of view. The young man's erratic and erotic fantasies in *Billy Liar* (1963), the bizarre sexual and career values of the world of high fashion in *Darling*, and down-and-out lives of hustlers and bums in *Midnight Cowboy*, the bisexual triangles in *Sunday, Bloody Sunday* (1971) are not examples of human freaks but examples of the way even the most bizarre-seeming human types are not so bizarre, but merely people trying to satisfy the most common human needs: security and love.

Lindsay Anderson remains the British director most devoted to rebellion against a stagnant and repressive bourgeois society and bourgeois mentality. Anderson's rebellion is embodied by his violent central characters who usually want to break (or machine gun) the elements in society that repress them: Richard Harris in *This Sporting Life* and Malcom McDowell (who is to the 1970s what James Dean was to the 1950s) in *If . . .* and *O, Lucky Man!* (1973). Anderson's rebellion also determines his cinematic style, avoiding the literate coherency of a Schlesinger or the lush pictorialness of a Russell by making violent attacks on the continuity of space, time, and action. Whereas structure, character, and dialogue are Schlesinger's strengths (the dramatic values) and spatial composition is Russell's (the pictorial values), Anderson's primary strength is his battle with continuity at the editing table. Anderson is the British director most obviously influenced by the French, particularly by Godard (and Godard's interpretation of Brechtian theory). Like the French New Wave directors, Anderson was a film critic (and editor of the film journal, *Sequence*) who turned filmmaker. The key question about his future is whether his rebellious leftist anger can remain free of cliché and his self-conscious film trickery remain fresh and functional (rather than derivative and gratuitous) in its manipulation of the cinema's devices.

As in its earlier periods, the British film is at least as notable for its actors as it is for its directors. With performers such as Tom Courtenay, Albert Finney, Rita Tushingham, Vanessa and Lynn Redgrave, Alan Bates, Richard Attenborough, Richard Harris, Julie Christie, James Fox, Dirk Bogarde, Maggie Smith, Malcolm McDowell, Michael York, Glenda Jackson, and Oliver Reed, the British industry continues to demonstrate that British actors are among the most interesting, most talented, and best trained in the world.

No cinema better demonstrates the interrelationship of film art and political freedom than the cinema of little Czechoslovakia, a country that has probably been invaded, occupied, and liberated more times in this century than any other. The Czech Golden Age of cinema (or "Czech film miracle" or "Czech New Wave" as it has also been called) was an extremely short one, a bit longer than five years (roughly, 1963 to 1969), during which time over a dozen Czech films won major awards at the important international film festivals, including two nearly successive Academy Awards for Best Foreign Language Film of 1965 (*The Shop on Main Street*) and 1967 (*Closely Watched Trains*). The years of Czechoslovakian film mastery coincided with the only years since the Munich Agreement of 1938 that the Czech people and Czech artists enjoyed a measure of intellectual and creative freedom. Before this brief eruption, the Czech cinema was one of startings and stoppings, of promising beginnings cut short by political repression and artistic censorship. Although the American filmmaker suffered the commercial repression of a Louis B. Mayer and the moral suppression of the Hays Code, the history of the Czech cinema reveals that the censorship of bureaucratic political committees can be even more devastating to the individual artist.

In the late silent and early sound periods, the Czech cinema had begun to develop an integrity and individuality (as in the films of Gustav Machatý, Otakar Vávra, and Martin Frič) that was destroyed by the Nazi occupation of 1939. After the war the Czech cinema made another new beginning. Led by a group of young filmmakers who had organized their intentions in the final year of the Nazi occupation, the cinema was the first of the industries that was nationalized after the liberation. But this promise was cut short by the Soviet occupation and Stalinization of 1948, and thereafter followed over a decade of repressive rule: the purges, the tightening of the Iron Curtain, the cultural isolation of the Cold War. The fears and repressive climate of the McCarthy years in the United States were marked and mirrored by parallel (and much more severe) activities on the other side of the Iron Curtain (as can be seen in Costa-Gavras's *The Confession,* as well as in Jaromil Jireš's Czech film, *The Joke,* 1968). Signs of a political thaw began to appear in 1961, and the Czech Golden Age of cinema sprang up through the cracks until the Soviet tanks rolled into Prague in August of 1968.

During the decades of occupation and repression two significant institutions were founded that would later contribute to the greatness of the Czech film in its years of freedom. Just as the Fascists founded a film school and built an efficient studio in Mussolini's Italy that would later be put to use by significant artists in a period of artistic freedom, the noted Czech film school, the F.A.M.U., was founded in 1947, and the Barrandov Studios were built into one of the best equipped production facilities in Europe during the Nazi occupation. The great Czech films and filmmakers would come from this film school (five intensive years of training at the State's expense) and film studio as soon as the filmmakers were free to combine their artistic imaginations with their technical capabilities.

The Czech masterpieces were of four general types, including two which had undergone a transformation in the previous years of Soviet suppression. One of these was the story of Resistance against the Nazi Occupation, a safe subject in the Stalinist era since opinion of the Nazis was quite unanimous. But under the Soviets, the Resistance film mirrored the values of socialist-realism, primarily by presenting a positive, heroic, almost super-human figure as the embodiment of political resistance—like Schors and Chapayev in those Soviet sound films. In the mature Czech films of the 1960s, however, the central figure of resistance was frequently weak, lazy, slovenly, and comic—nonheroic, all-too-human figures who eventually choose or are forced to take a political stand. This study of the comic antihero confronted by the demands of war is a long-standing Czech literary tradition, perhaps most memorable in Hašek's famous novel, *The Good Soldier Schweik*.

Such are the "heroes" of Jiří Weiss's *The Coward* (1961), the study of a cowardly rural schoolteacher who eventually decides to sacrifice himself rather than to select ten of his fellow townspeople to be slaughtered by the Nazis; of Jan Kadár's and Elmar Klos's *Death is Called Engelchen* (1963), the study of a wounded Czech partisan who wonders if his sacrifice has been worth the struggle; of Zbyněk Brynych's *The Fifth Horseman is Fear* (1964), the story of an aged and cowardly Jewish doctor who must choose between protecting himself and helping another human being who has dedicated himself to helping the doctor's people; as well as of both of the Academy-Award-winning Czech films. Significantly, the anti-Nazi genre continues in the post-1968 era of Soviet occupation since it is still not controversial to hate Nazis. Jaromil Jireš's *And My Love to the Swallows* (1971) is another story of the Resistance, but this film's protagonist—a beautiful young girl—is a saint, a perfect and perfectly contented martyr, obviously cut from the idealized cloth of socialist-realism.

A second genre, the historical, costume drama, also popular during the years of suppression, was less popular in the 1960s. As was true in Hitler's Germany and Mussolini's Italy, a film could avoid delicate political issues by avoiding contemporary life altogether. In the sixties this escapist tendency continued, but of special note are František Vláčil's *Marketa Lazarova* (1968), a mammoth and carefully detailed historical spectacle, and Jiří

Weiss's *The Golden Fern* (1963), a beautiful cinematic adaptation of a Czech fairy-tale. A shepherd discovers and steals the mystical golden fern in the forest on midsummer eve, a magical token which allows him to fulfill all his wishes so long as he keeps possession of it. Of special interest and beauty in the film are its attention to the styles of decor and costume (there are three—peasant village life, Hapsburg nobility, and High Turk) and its ability to translate such fanciful and mystical material into the concrete reality of cinema (in particular, Weiss's use of natural imagery, lighting, and camera movement to develop the conflict of man and Nature for possession of the fern). Significantly, both *Marketa Lazarova* and *The Golden Fern* were shot by the same talented cinematographer, Bedrich Batka.

The third of the Czech genres of the 1960s—the film of contemporary life, of contemporary human and social problems—had a very different analogue in the era of Soviet suppression. Under the Soviets, the Czech cinema eulogized the noble worker, limned the praises of the collective society, depicted the beauty of the factory, and dedicated itself to the idealistic proposition that with hard work and collective cooperation Life Would Be Beautiful. The mature Czech films of the 1960s doubted the values of collectivization, suggested that work did not make a man happy, and implied that the essential human problems were internal, psychological, and personal rather than external and social.

These films of contemporary life tend in two opposite directions. Many of them set their studies of human personality against a clear social and political background. Věra Chytilová, perhaps the most important and accomplished woman director of postwar Europe, makes careful studies of feminist problems (*The Ceiling*, 1962; *Daisies*, 1966; *Fruits of Paradise*, 1969). Jan Němec's *The Report on the Party and the Guests* (1966), a satire on conformity, was banned for over a year, even in the liberalized Czechoslovakia. Jaromil Jireš's *The Joke* is an explicitly anti-Stalinist and anti-Soviet film, the story of a man who seeks revenge for his earlier imprisonment and injustice in the 1950s era of the purges. Evald Schorm's *Courage for Everyday* (1964) and Jiří Weiss's *Ninety in the Shade* (1964) both use suicide as a means of exposing the potential alienation and sterility of living in such a constrained, highly regulated society. Indeed, the number of these Czech films that use the motif of suicide (either attempted or successful) is striking.

The other tendency of the contemporary films is to avoid political problems altogether and to turn themselves into pure studies of human sensations and experiences. These "experiential" films represent one of the truly unique (and most influential) accomplishments of the Czech cinema: personal, subtle, internal, touching, probing. Many have no plots; there are few incidents or events; almost nothing happens. But in the course of this nothing the audience discovers how it feels to be these people, how they feel life and how they feel about life. The purest expressions of these "experiential" films are the sympathetic satires of Miloš Forman (*Black Peter*, 1963; *Loves of a Blonde*, 1965; *The Firemen's Ball*, 1967) and the delicately sensitive film of Ivan Passer, *Intimate Lighting* (1965), who began as Forman's scenarist. But upon closer inspection, the truly unique and attractive quality of the Czech cinema—whether World War II Resistance, costume drama, or study of a contemporary social problem—is this experiential quality. Regardless of their settings, the primary focus of the great Czech films of the 1960s is the internal quality and texture of human experience.

Precisely the same is true of the fourth genre of Czech films of the period, the surreal or futuristic allegory. Jan Schmidt is the master of this genre, and his short film, *Josef Kilian* (1963), co-directed by Pavel Juráček, has been frequently compared with the work of another Czech master, Franz Kafka. Josef K's world becomes a frightening, hysterical nightmare, and the experiential quality that Schmidt and Juráček develop is that of wandering about a labyrinth of terrifying dreams. Schmidt's later science-fiction film, *The End of August at the Ozone Hotel* (1968), script by Juráček, is a brutal and frightening odyssey of survivors from atomic holocaust, all of them women, roaming about the countryside, murdering other living beings—a snake, a dog, a cow—for the sport of it. They are desperately searching for a man to renew the species, and when they find him— a gentle, civilized old man—they murder him too. Schmidt's point seems to be that such a race is better off perishing.

Perhaps the most anarchic and surreal of the directors of the era is Juraj Jakubisko, a Slovak. The Slovak and Czech production centers are separate (the Czech studio, Barrandov, is in Prague, the Slovak in Bratislava), the cultures and traditions are separate, the religions were originally separate (the Czechs Protestant, the Slovaks Catholic). Jakubisko seems to have the same relationship to the Czech cinema as Dovzhenko, a Ukrainian, had to the Moscow-based Soviet cinema. Like Dovzhenko, Jakubisko's films (*The Deserters and the Nomads*, 1968; *Birds, Orphans, and Fools*, 1969) seem anarchically poetic and erratically disconnected: a series of striking images that mix a blunt sexuality, politics, religion, audacious visual stunts, and experiential frenzy, cohering neither in plot nor in temporal continuity. As in so many of the Czechoslovakian films there is an undercurrent of fatalism and nihilism in Jakubisko. The protagonist of *Birds, Orphans, and Fools*, who has lived his life like a gleeful child (a bird, an orphan, and a fool), manages to commit one of the most super-suicides—an orgy of self-annihilation—ever seen on the screen by simultaneously hanging, drowning, and incinerating himself. It is no wonder that Juráček and Jakubisko, two of the most daring and pessimistic of the period's directors, have not been permitted to make films by the new authorities.

The Czech cinematic style reveals the pervasiveness and influence of both the French and Italian movements and might be described as a perfect synthesis of Italian neorealism—particularly the compassionate, more internal human studies of *Umberto D* or *Nights of Cabiria*—and the compositional and editing spontaneity of the French New Wave—its elliptical cutting, its jumbling of film time, its hand-held camera and *cinéma vérité* authenticity. No surer sign of French influence exists than the fact that at least a half-dozen major Czech films—Forman's *Black Peter* and Passer's *Intimate Lighting* among them—end with a Truffaut freeze-frame.

But to these foreign influences the Czechs added two uniquely Czechoslovakian traits. The first was an undiluted and unswerving commitment to illuminating internal human passions and sensations. Although the Czech films usually preferred shooting in real locations, the dominant imagery of this cinema is not natural (though nature often plays a memorable role as a film's supporting and secondary imagery). The dominant imagery of the Czech cinema is the human face, and in capturing that image the Czech directors avoid the standard "American shot" by keeping the camera much closer to the faces (many of which are those of non-professional actors). The Czech films also avoid the glossy facial lighting of the Hollywood studios, preferring much more natural and tonal lighting in much more realistic environments. These Czech devices reduce the apparent artfulness of the cinema's handling of human beings, substituting a feeling of naturalness, spontaneity, and absolute authenticity. This feeling of spontaneity is essential to the films' stories as well as their styles, for the films are frequently about the ability of people to act spontaneously.

A second Czech trait is the intermingling of comedy and seriousness, producing films that are quite remarkable in their range of emotions from hilarious laughter to touching pathos to sudden horror. And this range of effects is also one of the ideas and subjects of the films, for the Czech films imply that life is indeed a mixture of lightness and seriousness, of living through a time fraught with dangers and demanding the most difficult choices (this often subjugated people knows about difficult choices). A most difficult existence still remains rich in smiles and jokes, though death waits (and not even so unexpectedly) around the next corner. In their serio-comic blend the Czechs have distilled the tragic modern history of their little tyrannized nation into a positive vision of life that sees humor in even the darkest moments and that (with a few exceptions) refuses to surrender its faith in human exertion, commitment, and integrity.

Jiří Menzel's *Closely Watched Trains* is as good an example of this Czech spirit as any. The film's story (scripted by Bohumil Hrabak, from his short story) is of a comical young man, Miloš Hrma, who has taken a job as an apprentice at a train station during the Nazi Occupation—primarily to avoid any serious or difficult labor. Despite its wartime setting, the film seems to be a sex comedy, concentrating on the sexual inadequacies, failures, and fears of the inexperienced boy, who is a clumsy apprentice at love as well as at work. Menzel spends most of his time developing the boy's comic qualities; his ridiculously skinny and gawky body (its pathetically ostrich-like shape emphasized by his initial and repetitive appearance in only his shirt, his bird-skinny legs sticking out underneath); his naïve adoration of his train controller's uniform (symbolized by his comical worship of his cap, which he wears even in bed); his comical ancestors (the grandfather, a magician who attempted to conjure the Nazi tanks out of Czechoslovakia; the father, a former train employee who retired at the age of 48 to spend the rest of his life in bed); his naïve, bird-like, eyes-closed attempts to peck a kiss at his girlfriend, Maša, usually without success (in contrast to his coworker, Hubicka, for whom sexual intimacy is as natural as breathing). Comic sexual symbols dominate the film: the official, bureaucratic train stamps that are held up to the mouth and blown upon (in close-up); the long neck of a goose that the station master's wife rubs continually up and down, up and down, to force the food down its neck; the perpetual rip in the station master's leather sofa, a hole opened by the athletic sexual activity on the sofa.

But beneath the sexual comedy there are darker elements, even while Menzel refuses to desert his comic spirit and pratfalls at the same time. Menzel reminds us that Czechoslovakia is at war and occupied by the Nazis by depicting an air raid, yet depicting it in a strangely comic way. During the raid, the boy sleeps in a photographer's studio, where he has just failed to make love to Maša. In that same studio a giggling group of sexy girls had been photographed earlier, their bodies protruding above a cartoon drawing of an airplane. During the air raid, Menzel keeps his camera on that comic, cartoon plane while real bombs drop their potentially deadly bombs. And the air raid ends comically when the photographer awakens in his bed only to discover that he is sleeping outdoors, the walls of his studio having been blown away. His reaction is uncontrolled and exuberant laughter.

The boy's reaction to this night of lost and clumsily unfulfilled love is not comic, however. Menzel continues his subtle development of the film's serious undercurrents when the boy tries to ease his sexual failure and frustration with another act of impotency: he tries to commit suicide by slashing his wrists as he sits in a hot and steamy bathtub. But even the suicide has a comic balance, for the boy's final act of bidding the world goodbye is to remove his precious cap (he doesn't want to dishonor it), and Miloš is only saved from death when a comically clumsy workman punches a hole in the bathroom wall and sees the scrawny, limp form in the tub.

The ultimate surfacing of seriousness is the film's climax, when the boy performs the mission of blowing up a Nazi ammunition train and is suddenly and unexpectedly machine-gunned by a Nazi guard. The term climax is especially relevant to this final act, or Miloš's body lies sprawled on the top of a train car in a sexual position, and this implied coitus in which he implants his explosive charge into the passive train is as successful as his sexual intercourse of the night before with Viktoria Freie (the woman who brought him the explosive charge to blow up the train as well as provided her body for Miloš to exercise his first successful sexual charge). The result of the boy's ultimate and final "coitus" is the mammoth orgasm of the exploding train. As if the ironic juxtaposition of sex and war were not clear enough in the boy's mission and death, Menzel adds another (and comic) level by cross-cutting back and forth between the boy's mission and a ridiculous punitive inquiry taking place in the train station itself (an ironic variation on the Griffith cross-cut!), which also has a sexual basis and which serves as a diversionary tactic to allow the successful act of war. Inside the train station, the Chief Train Inspector, himself a ridiculous combination of comic and serious elements (his speeches turn Hitler's rhetoric into hilariously funny bombastic clichés), grills Hubicka about the sexual encounter with Miss Svata, in which he decorated her buttocks with the official train inspector's stamps. While the Chief Inspector is aggrieved by this "insult to the Third Reich," and the other inspectors busily study the photographs of Miss Svata's decorated *derrière,* Miloš insults the Third Reich by blowing up one of its trains.

The reaction to the train explosion and the boy's death (though Hubicka and the others do not yet know Miloš has been killed) is joy: the same exuberant laughter with which the photographer greeted the disappearance of his studio (they were, after all, American bombs—bombs of liberation). The station's clock chimes happily, just as it has chimed after each of the previous sexual encounters on the station master's sofa. Menzel's point is clearly that a clumsy boy has become a man—both sexually and politically—that his previous impotency has been succeeded by an act of fertility. But our intellectual understanding of that positive point is balanced and complicated by our emotional awareness that he will never be able to exercise his manhood again, and that in gaining his manhood he has lost his life. Maša's sad realization parallels the audience's, for she knows that Miloš is dead when the wind of the explosion blows his cap (which he would never willingly remove) to her feet. Details count for Menzel, and he transforms the comic symbol of the cap into a touching monument to the boy's memory. In this strange variation on the familiar *Buildungsroman,* the long apprenticeship produces a period of maturity that is strikingly and tragically brief.

The Shop on Main Street, produced and directed by Jan Kadár and

Elmar Klos, also mixes the comic and the serious, although not so exuberantly or contrapuntally as *Closely Watched Trains*. According to Kadár, in his collaboration with Klos he took responsibility for the shooting and the handling of the actors while Klos served as producer and supervised the cutting. If so, *The Shop on Main Street* owes its greatest debt to Kadár's work with actors while their earlier *Death is Called Engelchen*, with its brilliant leaps backward and forward in time and space, was more dependent on the cutting of Klos. The central figure of *The Shop on Main Street* is another comical figure, Tono, a lazy, poor provider who would rather spend time strolling with his dog than working at a job, and who prefers the company of the loyal and affectionate animal to that of his shrewish and grasping wife. Tono attempts to remain apolitical in a political era, in sharp contrast to his brother-in-law who has devoted himself to serving the Nazi regime so he can parade around as one of the little town's most influential (and richest) citizens. Tono is obviously a Chaplinesque figure (he even notes the resemblance to Chaplin when he wears a new derby) who wants to have as little to do with work, respectability, and the Establishment as possible. (In particular, he has nothing to do with the huge and ugly "Tower of Babel" being built by the town as a symbol of its submission and capitulation to the fascists.)

The film's central situation is that Tono's brother-in-law uses his influence to give Tono a "present," one of the spoils of Fascism. He makes Tono the "Aryan Controller" of a Jewish widow's supposedly prosperous shop. Every Jewish business must have its "Aryan Controller," who then reaps a handsome share of the profits. Several ironies proceed from this gift. First, the old widow Lautmann (played brilliantly by the Polish-Jewish actress, Ida Kaminska) is both a bit deaf and completely unaware of the new political regime in the little Slovak town. She not only cannot hear the words when Tono tells her he is her "Aryan Controller"; she cannot even comprehend what the words mean and imply. And the comic and sympathetic Tono has neither the heart nor the patience to make her understand. So he offers to work for her as her assistant (a concept she can understand), and he spends his time in assisting her in the shop and in mending her old furniture (he is a carpenter by trade) in her apartment. She believes, ironically, that he is merely helping her out of kindness and charity, while he, the "Controller," is, ironically, merely a clerk and apprentice.

Another irony is that the shop is almost bankrupt and cannot make anyone, even an "Aryan Controller," rich. The shop's only commodity is buttons. Mrs. Lautmann survives not from the shop's sales but from charity; the town's other Jewish merchants all contribute to her support. Faced with the fact that Mrs. Lautmann's shop must now support her Aryan Controller as well, the Jewish merchants agree to pay Tono handsomely to serve as her assistant. And thus history and politics create one of the strangest commercial arrangements—the Jews in effect hire Tono to serve as an Aryan Controller of a Jewish business.

The comedy, and the stability, of this commercial arrangement crumble when the fascists decide that all the town's Jews must be shipped out (obviously to concentration camps). Tono now faces a crisis of decision, one of those terrible dilemmas that so often confront the protagonists of Czech films (and must have confronted the Czechs during the years of Occupation). Does Tono protect the fragile old woman—hide her from the police to spare her the pain of leaving and of comprehension that would obviously kill her? Or does he protect himself—send the old woman packing? On the one hand, Kadár has carefully and sensitively developed Tono's affection for the pathetic, kind, and uncomprehending old lady who treats Tono as her own son. On the other, Kadár has just as clearly developed what happened to Tono's friend, Kuchar, who aided the town's Jews; he was branded a "White Jew" and brutally murdered as a result. Tono vacillates, making one decision and then the other. His crisis of indecision ultimately leads to his unintentionally murdering the old woman and then hanging himself when he feels the horror of his inhuman brutality.

Again affectionate and ironic comedy have turned to horror. The film's point perhaps is that a human being *must* choose and that apolitical stances are impossible in political times (and what times are not?). Or possibly the film's point is that in political eras of inhumanity and illegality, life presents human beings with choices that cannot be made and that cannot possibly turn out well. The film's recurring dream sequence—of Tono's waltzing with Mrs. Lautmann in slow motion, in the bright (and overexposed) sunlight—might well imply that life must make sense before human choices can make sense. On the other hand (and here is that magnificent Czech balance and complexity again), Tono's dream is a dream.

Of the pure comedies, Miloš Forman is the master. An affectionate satirist who pokes fun at human folly, he also realizes that folly is what makes people human. Forman's satire is gentle and compassionate rather than corrosive and vicious (like Kubrick's). Two of Forman's three Czech films (*Black Peter, Loves of a Blonde*) and his major American film (*Taking Off,* 1971) are youth films that examine the generation gap, while his other major film, *The Firemen's Ball,* examines the follies of bourgeois adulthood, a secondary theme of the youth films. Forman's primary satirical subjects are youthful clumsiness (in this sense Forman's work is related to Menzel's film) and adult boredom. The folly of youth for Forman is that it is so earnest and so clumsy. Sexual pursuit is the primary activity, but the pursuit is awkward, callous, and mechanical. Sexual success is the only emblem of human importance, and Forman's youths devote their lives to feeding their egos and vanities with this kind of food. Forman's adults, meanwhile, spend their lives in their apartments, conversing about nothing but the evils of their children, bored with the books they read, the television they watch, and especially bored with one another. If it were not for the follies of youth, the adults would seemingly have nothing to occupy their lives at all. In *Taking Off,* however (and here Forman senses the difference between American and Czech parents), the adults also occupy themselves by imitating the follies of youth, which is a double folly.

Forman's three favorite domains are the dance hall, the kitchen, and the bedroom—three distinct and essential social centers. Dances are society's and youth's institutionalized means of sexual pursuit, and Forman delights in examining the clumsy and self-conscious games that people play in the dance hall. Using a *cinéma vérité* method of photographing actual dance halls and mixing his players with the real "revellers" (like Mack Sennett in *Tango Tangles!*), Forman continually reveals how difficult it is for young people to act naturally and effectively in such a situation, how the major business of a dance is not dancing but finding a dance partner, and how most of the people at a dance spend most of their time defending themselves against the very thing they have come to the dance to get. The kitchen is the inevitable social center of the individual family, the place where the boring, painful, yet inevitable discussions of the worthlessness of youth take place. The clumsiness that Forman captures in this social center is that no one listens to what the others are saying (or cares), no one (father, mother, child) agrees on the issues of the discussion, and no one in the kitchen cares about the results of the discussion, since there will obviously be none, a fact which everyone in the kitchen already knows but which everyone still feels compelled to continue nonetheless because it is obligatory. The bedroom is the personal and private social center where the results of the sexual pursuit culminate. The clumsiness that Forman brilliantly captures in these scenes (in particular the seduction scenes between Mila and Andula in *Loves of a Blonde*) reveals the way that such monumentally important matters of human experience culminate in such awkward, pedestrian, and limited physical acts.

One of the most beautiful, least publicized, and most emblematic of the spirit of the Czech film is Ivan Passer's *Intimate Lighting.* The film is one of those "experiential" studies in which nothing happens; instead the film examines a collection of people—their feelings, hopes, frustrations, and contentment. The occasion for the film is the visit of a cellist from the city to play a concert at a music school in the provinces. This occasion unites a series of human oppositions: the city musician with his former chum who now runs the provincial music school; the cellist's sexy and sophisticated mistress with the wife and children of the country musician; the two musicians of a middle generation with the country musician's father (also a musician) and mother of an earlier generation; the values of city life with those of country life; the values of the educated and cultured with those of the peasant farmers; the values of the modern age with the eternal values of the countryside. The film devotes itself to the commonplace, to the banal, to the frustrations of the two musician-friends (roads not taken and successes not achieved). The best that the city musician can do is play solo performances in the provinces, and the best that the country musician can do is devote himself to a provincial music school.

But even in these modest and mediocre attainments Passer develops the satisfaction, the contentment, the comfort that life can bring. At the center of the film's style, study, and subject is music. *Intimate Lighting* may be the best film about music and with (instrumental) music ever made. Its sound track—from the opening titles in which a conductor leads the school's orchestra through a rehearsal for the concert, to its final freeze-frame—is saturated with music. There is music "to bring tears" at a funeral. There is nature's music in the waving of wheat in the fields. There is exuberant beer-barrel music and song at the wake after the funeral. The men play chamber music to relax (and bicker) after dinner. The two friends cannot talk to one another without music on the phonograph. Their friendship exists through music, in music, and with music. There is even music in the rhythmic snores of the old man at night. *Intimate Lighting* depicts the way the rhythms of music mirror the rhythms of life and the way that music can unite and synthesize all social strata and human differences. Though life has its banalities and disappointments and frustrations, it also has its music, which is beautiful and vibrant and sweet.

One further contribution of the Czech cinema that cannot be overlooked is its accomplishments in animation and in puppet cinema, most notably the work of Jiří Trnka (*The Devil on Springs*, 1946; *The Emperor's Nightingale*, 1949; *Song of the Prairie*, 1949; *The Hand*, 1964). Trnka's work is significant, not only for its new and imaginative standards in puppet films, but also for its founding an entire school and studio for animation and puppetry, of which Karel Zeman (*Baron Münchhausen*, 1962) is probably the most distinguished disciple.

The other cinemas of Eastern and Central Europe endured the same Stalinist and anti-Stalinist twists and turns as the Czech cinema, producing similar periods of fertility and barrenness. After the Czech cinema, the Polish cinema is the most interesting. The most fertile period of the Polish cinema preceded the Czech era by almost a decade (1955–1964), produced primarily by the founding of another major film school (the Lodz Film School in 1948) and the splitting of the Polish industry into individual artistic production units in 1955. These smaller production units granted the Polish directors a new freedom and allowed the exercise of more individuality; the two most talented directors, Andrej Wajda (of the KADR unit) and Roman Polanski (of the KAMERA unit), took advantage of this new opportunity.

As in Czechoslovakia, the Nazi Occupation and the Resistance against it were favored subjects of the Polish cinema, and no one made more powerful films on the Occupation era than Andrej Wajda. As opposed to the serio-comic, neorealist, intimately personal style of the Czech war films, Wajda's style is more active, more violent, more baroque, and less internalized. The Wajda films (*Kanal*, 1957; *Ashes and Diamonds*, 1958) consistently use a grotesque visual imagery (for example, the claustrophobic Warsaw sewers in *Kanal*), and the recurrent Wajda image seems to be of rubble, ashes, and garbage. His is a barren, ruined world, and the ruined landscapes are metaphoric of the ruined spirits and minds of those who must live there. *Ashes and Diamonds* is a spectacularly visual film (far more consciously spectacular than the Czech war films), with grotesque and bizarre lighting effects (its extreme back-lighting and low-angle camera work reminiscent of *Citizen Kane*), with two brilliantly climactic murder scenes that juxtapose the deaths with striking visual images (the startling eruption of fireworks at the moment of death, the dark stains of blood oozing into a white sheet drying in the sun), and with the compelling performance of one of the most interesting (and least known) stars in the history of cinema, Zbigniew Cybulski.

Roman Polanski's style is also more grotesque and externalized than the Czechs, but Polanski's primary theme is not the rubble of war but the ominousness of the universe itself. Polanski's Polish films use an extremely simple situation built around a single object and very few characters (two men carry a wardrobe out of the sea in *Two Men and a Wardrobe*, 1958; three people sail a boat out to sea in *Knife in the Water*, 1962). But Polanski endows these simple events with allegorical significance, primarily by charging the entire universe with a menacing, hostile spirit that turns the most simple and commonplace human events into terrifying combats of great magnitude. In *Knife in the Water* he endows the simple meeting of the three with menace by his use of lenses (primarily wide-angle lenses that magnify and distort distances), by his camera placement (using grotesque angles so that characters or objects dominate others or even blot them out entirely), and by the muted tension and jousting beneath the spare dialogue, props (that hypnotic knife), and movement. In *Rosemary's Baby* (1968), his first successful American film (after leaving Poland in 1964 when the nation's film policies shifted), Polanski added color as another way for the universe to manifest its terrifying presence (the comparison between the sharp, clean colors of the married couple's apartment and the baroque, warm, sickeningly rich colors of the devilish neighbors' apartment). And in *Chinatown* (1974), the evil in the universe hides beneath the most beautiful Technicolor surfaces. Polanski's weakness is for overstatement and heavy-handedness, as his more pretentious and less successful films indicate (*Cul-de-sac*, 1966; *Macbeth*, 1971).

THE
SEVENTH
SEAL

Death as confessor. The equation of black, death, darkness, and the Church.

THE
SEVENTH
SEAL

Mary (Bibi Andersson) and Joseph (Nils Poppe). Two actors in the sunlight.

The Knight (Max von Sydow) laughs with the actress in the sun.

Official societal definitions of a meaningful life—
the Doctor (Victor Sjøstrøm) honored by the University.

Summer, sunlight, whiteness, and the memories of youth.

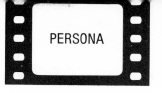

PERSONA

Two as one, one as two (Liv Ullman and Harriet Andersson).

CLOSELY
WATCHED
TRAINS

The human texture of Czech realism. Miloš (Václav Neckár)
whispers his sexual secret to the pro-Nazi train inspector (Vlastimil Brodsky).

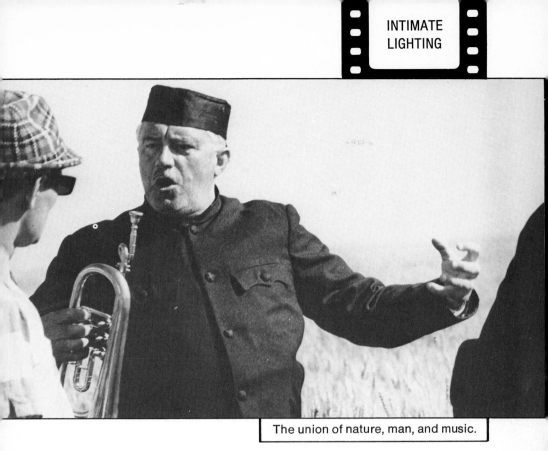

The union of nature, man, and music.

THRONE OF BLOOD

Kurosawa's use of consistent imagery—
the witch who sits blanketed by the mist of
the forest; the usurper who collapses into the
mist at the feet of the moving, human forest.

The Potter's sensual dream-life—mirrored by the sensual softness of Mizoguchi's nature (Masayuki Mori and Machiko Kyo).

UGETSU

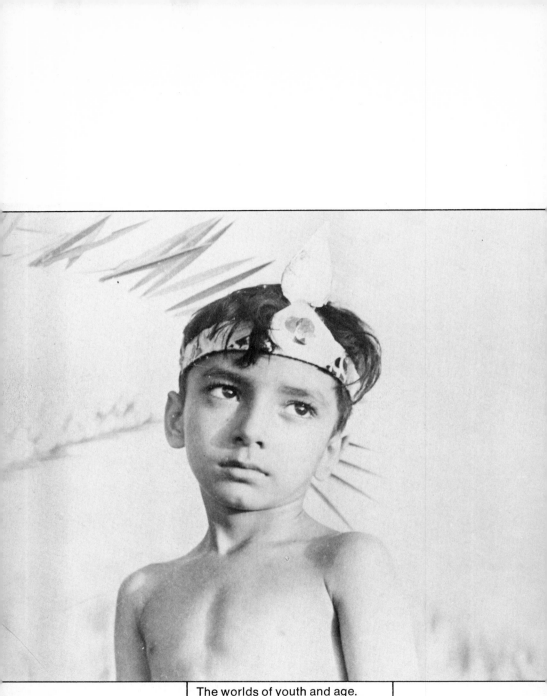

The worlds of youth and age.
The young Apu (Subir Banerji)
and the old aunt (Chunibala Devi).

VIRIDIANA

Buñuel's beggars and cripples at his parody of "The Last Supper."

There were other Polish directors who made effective films in its greatest decade: Aleksander Ford, who had been making films since 1929 (*The Young Chopin*, 1952; *Five Boys from Barska Street*, 1953), and Jerzy Skolimowski, who began as a script writer for both Wajda and Polanski (scripted *Knife in the Water*; directed *Walkover*, 1965, and *Barrier*, 1966, in Poland; directed *Le Départ*, 1967, in Belgium), were the most significant.

The early Hungarian cinema is probably most notable for the talents it exported to the rest of the world after their Hungarian apprenticeships: Béla Lugosi; Hollywood directors Michael Curtiz, Andre de Toth, and Paul Fejos; the noted British producer and director, Alexander Korda; and the international film theorists, László Moholy-Nagy and Béla Bálázs. The best known international representative of the new Hungarian cinema of the 1960s in Miklós Jancsó (*Cantata*, 1962; *The Red and the White*, 1967; *The Confrontation*, 1968). The primary contribution of the Yugoslavian cinema is its famed Zagreb animation studio, the most innovative, imaginative, and influential source of animation films in the world since 1957. In live-action films, the Yugoslavian cinema is one of the youngest in Europe, with no native production until after the Second World War. Its most influential "new wave" director is the brilliantly clever political and social satirist, Dušan Makavejev (*A Man is not a Bird*, 1965; *The Switchboard Operator*, 1967; *Innocence Unprotected*, 1968; *WR—Mysteries of the Organism*, 1971).

Cinemas East

The Japanese cinema first conquered the West when Akira Kurosawa's *Rashomon* won the Grand Prize at the Venice Film Festival of 1951. In the wake of *Rashomon* followed a series of imaginative and impressive films from Japan, directed by Kurosawa and by other masters of a cinema that had previously been unknown to Western audiences: Kenji Mizoguchi, Yasujiro Ozu, Teinosuke Kinugasa, Kon Ichikawa, Hiroshi Inagaki, and many others. The decade of the 1950s proved to be Japan's richest cinematic era—both commercially and artistically—as a result of many of the same forces that stimulated the new Western film industries in the same period: the receptivity to new forms of film expression; the new market for non-American films; and the new period of political and intellectual freedom. Like many of the European nations, the Japanese cinema emerged from over a decade of political constraints caused both by World War II and its aftermath of "normalization." What was equally surprising for both Western audiences and critics· was not simply the maturity of Japanese films in this decade but the richness and depth of the Japanese film tradition; Mizoguchi, Ozu, and Kinugasa had been directing films since the 1920s.

The Japanese cinema developed under conditions that kept it approximately ten years behind the cinemas of the West, a lag which worked in its favor in the 1950s, for the Japanese film industry felt the crippling effects of television almost a decade later than the industries of America and Europe. So too, the early period of primitivism lasted a decade longer in Japan, at least into the mid-1920s. Although there were commercial reasons for this retardation—a lag in organizing the industry, problems with machines and film—the primary reasons were aesthetic. First, women did not appear in Japanese films until the mid-1920s, women's roles being played by female impersonators, called *oyama* (Kinugasa's career began as an *oyama*). This sacrifice of naturalness and authenticity tended to keep the Japanese cinema tied to its theatrical roots (where men also played the female roles) and kept it from asserting the kind of naturalness and spontaneity that gradually evolved in the films of the West between 1905 and 1915. Second, the Japanese cinema used a narrator to explain the film to the audience. Called the *benshi,* this narrator's presence not only eliminated the need for printed titles but also for a "grammar and rhetoric" of the cinema itself. With a human being to do the speaking, the cinema itself did not need to "speak" in its own unique and powerful terms. All the early Western masters of the cinema—Griffith, Eisenstein, Murnau, et al.— were specifically those who discovered ways to make a purely visual "language" communicative.

These backward Japanese cinematic traditions died slowly and unwillingly. The *oyama* disrupted film production in 1922 by calling a strike when they saw they were to be replaced by women. The *benshi,* who had made themselves into one of the primary attractions of the Japanese cinema (often an audience attended a film merely to enjoy the commentary of a clever and popular *benshi*), fought extinction even more vigorously. In 1932 the *benshi* and the theatre musicians called a strike against the entire film industry; some *benshi* turned off the sound track of the early sound films so they could do their act; on at least one occasion the *benshi* union hired thugs to assault an official of one of the studios that was converting to sound.

When sound finally came to the Japanese cinema it too came almost a decade later than to the film industries of the West. The first successful sound film was not shot in Japan until 1931—*The Neighbor's Wife and Mine,* directed by Heinosuke Gosho. In 1932 only 45 of some 400 Japanese films used synchronized sound. Ozu did not shoot his first sound film until 1936, and silent production did not die completely until 1937.

The coming of sound to Japan was quickly followed by the coming of war, and the Japanese government demanded that the film industry support the war effort with films reflecting national militaristic policies. An equally repressive policy restricted the Japanese film industry after the war when the American Occupation Forces created SCAP, a cultural "reorientation" committee, which banned certain subjects (for example, all Japanese period dramas because they were feudalistic and militaristic) and demanded others (for example, the values of peaceful living and democratic institutions). Which brings us again to 1950 and *Rashomon*.

On the other hand, the Japanese film industry had developed a number of practices and traditions that would work for rather than against it when a period of commercial, technical, and political equality would enable it to compete on the world's screens. First, the Japanese film industry was the only other film industry in the world organized like the American one— around the studio system. Whereas studios in other countries were either buildings where individual production companies rented space (like the American studios in the 1970s) or a single, monolithic production company owned by the State, the Japanese system was composed of several competing commercial companies, with their own writers, directors, actors, and technicians working under contract, and which were in the business of conceiving, making, and selling films. The four Japanese studios that became most familiar to Western audiences were Nikkatsu (the oldest, founded in 1912—Ichikawa's studio); Shochiku (founded in 1920 and for three decades the commercial leader—Ozu's studio); Toho (founded in the 1930s by the amalgamation of several smaller companies—Kurosawa's primary studio; exploiter of Japanese monster pictures, like *Godzilla;* developer of Japan's own wide-screen, anamorphic process, Tohoscope); and Daiei (founded during the war—producer of *Rashomon, Gate of Hell,* and Mizoguchi's later films).

One of the obvious implications of such a studio system is production in quantity, and the Japanese industry regularly produced over 400 feature films each year, second only to Hollywood in its most golden Studio Era and leader in quantitative output when American production fell in the 1950s. As in the United States, this production in quantity guaranteed a very large number of very bad to passably mediocre films every year. But as in the U.S., it also guaranteed a significant number of films every year that would rank among the art's finest achievements.

The Japanese studio system avoided many of the evils of the American system, however, if only to produce others. A primary advantage was that it was a system built around the director rather than the producer or star. The Japanese "producer" is comparable to the First Assistant Director in Hollywood, a man who, despite his title, is really the assistant to the producer and who manages production details but makes no decisions. The Japanese director is a more powerful audience attraction than a film's star, and it is the director's name—not the star's—that frequently appears above the title in Japanese films. As a result, the Japanese star earns far less money than his counterparts in the West and consequently enjoys far less power. The Japanese director is the paternalistic head of his own production "family"—the Japanese film industry being modeled to some extent as a mirror of Japanese society. The disadvantages of such a comfortable and less competitive system than Hollywood's are, first, that genuinely talented directors must serve long apprenticeships in order to work themselves up the familial ladder. Japan does not import instant talents from outside its studio system—no Rouben Mamoulians or Mike Nichols who come from the theatre; no François Truffauts, Jean-Luc Godards, Lindsay Andersons, and Peter Bogdanovichs who come from film journals. A second disadvantage is that the paternalistic system tends to perpetuate mediocrity and incompetence, for no member of any family is thrown out of it for mediocrity.

In its film subjects the Japanese cinema also bears a striking resemblance to American movies; Japanese films tend to bunch themselves in clear-cut genres and cycles. In fact, Japanese genres are even more specifically defined and definable than their American counterparts. The basic division is between the *jidai-geki,* a period or costume film set in Japan's past, and *gendai-geki,* a film of modern life. But within these two basic genres there are many sub-genres. The *jidai-geki* can be further subdivided into the particular period of Japanese history it depicts—Tokugawa period, Meishi period, et cetera. The *gendai-geki* has such sub-genres as the *shomin-geki* (middle-class comedy), the "mother picture" (a mother's relationship to her children), the "wife picture" (the difficulties of marriage for women), the "nonsense picture" (farcical comedies), and the "youth picture" (the wild doings of youth, parallel to Hollywood's "Beach-blanket" genre of the fifties and sixties). As in Hollywood films, the least able directors freeze these genres into collections of their most banal and predictable conventions, whereas the most talented ones breathe life into the film either by developing those conventions with great personal intensity and sensitivity or by reversing the conventional expectations altogether.

Given the quantity and diversity of Japanese production, it is more difficult to find consistent traits of style than in the more unified movements of Italy, France, or Czechoslovakia. Again, the parallel with the American Studio Era is the illustrative one—an era in which Lubitsch, Ford, Hawks, Capra, von Sternberg, Sturges, Cukor, and W. C. Fields all made films at the same time. Two consistent structural traits seem to dominate the best Japanese films, however, and both of these traits are descendants of the Japanese theatrical traditions of the Kabuki and the Noh.

First, the best films are ruthlessly economical in their concentration on the central theme. Rather than filling up the script with flavorful and atmospheric touches that "flesh out" a film—in a sense diverting an audience from the central issue and giving the film a feeling of life's randomness—the great Japanese films seem to rivet every incident of the plot, every character, every visual image, and every line of dialogue to the film's single thematic question (and there is usually only one). A second, and related, structural trait is the Japanese concern for symmetry. Many of the best Japanese films are not close studies of individual people or pairs but of a fairly large group of people who make different choices, take different paths in life, and thereby come to different ends. This structural feeling for symmetry keeps these multi-path "journeys" moving along side by side in the audience's mind, all of the paths united, of course, by the single thematic issue that has produced the "journey" in the first place.

Unlike the French or Czech cinemas, there is no single, consistent trait of visual style that dominates the Japanese cinema. Those three directors who, at least from a Western perspective, appear to be Japan's greatest film artists—Akira Kurosawa, Kenji Mizoguchi, and Yasujiro Ozu—have three completely different visual senses and use three completely different cinematographic principles. These very visual differences are what make them such unique and individual stylists.

Akira Kurosawa is the Japanese director most popular in the West—perhaps more popular in the West than in Japan—but he also seems the Japanese director with the greatest power, the greatest range, and the greatest stylistic imagination and inventiveness. Kurosawa is the only one of the three Japanese directors with effective films in both the *jidai-* and *gendai-geki*. He is also the only one of the Japanese masters who is obviously influenced by films of the West. Kurosawa's *samurai* films are closely related to American westerns (and have been remade as westerns); his films move with the swift, violent pace of American films rather than the more leisurely pace of Japanese films; and he is clearly influenced by Western cinematic styles, especially the use of the subjective traveling camera, the use of extreme deep-focus photography, and, consequently, the use of very fast film. Kurosawa also seems to share an artistic trait with such Western directors as Hitchcock and Truffaut—the urge to tackle very difficult stylistic problems that require him to push himself beyond the artistic frontiers he has already charted and conquered.

Rashomon (1950) clearly demonstrates Kurosawa's thematic concerns and stylistic maturity (he had been directing films since 1943). The film is famous as the essential cinematic demonstration of the relativity and subjectivity of truth—and that it is. But of greater interest in the film is, first, Kurosawa's stylistic control which conveys and convinces us of that subjectivity and, second, what he says human beings should do with their lives given the fact that truth is relative and subjective.

The film uses what might be described as six different cinematic styles, six separate camera strategies, each of which corresponds to one of the levels of the film's realities. Two of the six sections are "frames," not the central incident itself but ways of telling or finding out about the incident. One of these two frames is primary: two men telling a third about the incident as they sit beneath the ruins of the Rashomon Gate during a rainstorm; the other is, in effect, a frame-within-a-frame: the testimony of the three participants in the incident to a "judge" who is attempting to discover exactly what happened and why. The remaining four sections are four different versions of what happened and why, each of them mirroring the attitudes, perceptions, and personality of the witness. The single concrete fact is that a man lies dead in the forest. But human beings need to assign a cause, to see a reason for a catastrophic fact, and the film becomes a search for this reason.

The film's primary frame introduces this search as two men, a Woodcutter and a Priest (representatives of the secular and sacred orders, respectively), feel compelled to tell their story to a stranger, perhaps to aid their search, perhaps to ease their suspicion that the search has no end. Kurosawa sets this frame during a furious and violent rainstorm, from which the only refuge is a pitiful shelter of architectural ruins. Although rainstorms are almost a cliché of the Japanese cinema, Kurosawa clearly uses this storm as a concrete, external image of both the internal, mental agony of the unfulfilled search and the chaotic social instability of the era: a period of lawlessness, bandits, plagues, famine, war, and, like the Rashomon Gate itself, ruins. Kurosawa is a master at using concrete natural imagery to evoke abstract and internal human sensations, a technique he brings to perfection in his later *Throne of Blood* (1957). What is intriguing about the Woodcutter's introduction is that he tells the Listener that this incident is especially terrible, worse even than the social chaos of the present. The Listener, whose curiosity is understandably aroused—he serves as the viewer's surrogate in this respect—agrees to listen to the tale in the course of waiting out the storm.

For these scenes at the Gate, Kurosawa uses a conventionally objective cutting and photographic method. He cuts freely—from various distances and angles—to make the viewer a privileged observer, leading him from place to place, always giving him the most interesting and revealing point of view. The dominant motif is the driving sound and image of the incessant rain. But for his frame-within-a-frame—the testimony before the "judge"—Kurosawa uses a totally different visual principle. Kurosawa keeps his camera in a single spot, at about the eye level of a seated observer, while the speakers stare directly at the camera to tell their story. The implication is obvious; the camera is the "judge" and has become the new viewer-surrogate; the camera-judge takes the evidence, attempting to provide the viewer-judge with the means to draw a conclusion. Kurosawa returns to this courtyard (it is not a court*room*, since the camera-judge, as well as the witnesses, are obviously sitting on the ground outdoors) after each of the versions of the tale, just as he returns to the Rashomon Gate after each of the testimonies in the court. So the viewer has the continual feeling of going from the version of the incident to the court, to the Gate, and returning again in the opposite direction. Kurosawa's clearly established visual perspectives and the symmetry of his structure keep the location in both space and time completely clear in the viewer's mind.

The first three versions of the incident are those of each of the three principal participants. Each is completely different in human motivation, in the sequence of events, in its emotional tone, and in its visual style. The first version is that of the bandit, Tojamaro, played as a sensual, virile, exuberant male animal by Toshiro Mifune. Tojamaro's version emphasizes the physical sensations of the confrontation—the heat of the day, the glare of the sun, the sting of the gnats which he repeatedly swats—which Kurosawa depicts subjectively, from Tojamaro's point of view. When Tojamaro first sees the woman, he describes her in sensual terms—as a cool breeze—and Kurosawa's camera watches a gust of wind ripple through the leaves and across the characters' clothes, accompanied by the rippling tinkle of a celeste. Kurosawa's primary subjective device in the sequence, however, is the violent, furious pace of his tracking and panning shots, the camera's incessant, energetic movement, translating Tojamaro's predatory stalking into visual terms. It is also Kurosawa's way of translating the way Tojamaro sees himself: aggressive, restless, dominant, assertive.

According to Tojamaro, his conquest of the woman was exactly that: an assertive masculine act in which he subdues the woman first by his strength and then by his passion. They struggle violently for a dagger—a struggle which he exuberantly enjoys—until he kisses her and she feels the earth reel. Except Kurosawa's subjective camera is quite ironic at this point, for it does not mirror the way the woman feels Tojamaro's kiss (the usual implication of "dizzy" camera movements, as in *The Last Laugh*), but the way Tojamaro feels she feels his kiss. The bandit then bests the husband in fair, violent, valiant combat ("He fought marvellously"), again the virile male displaying the theoretical characteristics of masculinity. Kurosawa's camera catches the flashy *samurai* swordsmanship and the final kill as Tojamaro perceives it: with violent movement of the participants, violent camera movement, and violent cutting. Violence, pace, and movement are the three stylistic keys of the section: in action, in emotion, in camera movement, and in editing (a perfect synthesis of form and content).

The woman (Machiko Kyo) tells a completely different version in style, tone, emphasis, and action. According to the way she sees both herself and the event, she is a "poor helpless woman" (she depicts herself as just as stereotypically "feminine" as Tojamaro's self-stereotyped "masculinity"). Although her version begins after the sexual consummation, her obvious implication is that she had no choice but to submit meekly to the rape of a strong and determined animal (as opposed to the bandit's description of her struggling like a tigercat). It serves both her self-image and her credibility for her to avoid any references to the sexual act itself. So too, the bandit plays a very small role in her version of the incident, and the few glimpses she provides are of a whooping, subrational, subhuman savage, a grotesque caricature of the bandit's masculinity in his own version. The bandit scarcely exists for her because the real object of her concern is her husband, the only one whose reactions to the rape matter. And his reaction is a cold, pitiless, piercing stare. She retrieves her dagger, still stuck in the trunk of a tree (a point of agreement with Tojamaro's version) and he continues to stare. She starts moving toward him, the dagger erect, and his hypnotic stare continues. For this sequence, Kurosawa's aim is to increase the tension and suspense, and rather than using travelling shots he uses the classic suspense device of the cinema, the cross-cut. As Kurosawa cuts back and forth between the brutally still husband and the seemingly mesmerized wife, hypnotically moving steadily toward him with the knife, the music on the sound track (which sounds unfortunately close to Ravel's "Bolero") pulses and swells, mirroring the tension of the moment for the wife who has been caught in a kind of trance. The result, however, is that she faints, and upon awaking she finds the dagger in her husband's chest (different murder weapon than in Tojamaro's story). Interestingly, Kurosawa does not depict her discovery of the knife visually but merely lets her tell that part of the story to the camera-audience-judge.

The woman's dead husband tells the third version of the story, a feat which Kurosawa accomplishes mystically by using a female medium to summon the man's spirit from the other world and to serve as the vessel of the husband's perceptions. As "he" tells "his" story, Kurosawa uses uniquely cinematic devices to convert this intangible and metaphysical presence into a concrete, tangible, and credible reality. (The Japanese were masters at turning metaphysical spirits into concrete visual realities without making them seem ludicrous, as in Kurosawa's later *Throne of Blood* and Mizoguchi's *Ugetsu*.) A man's voice issues from the woman-medium's lips, and that voice is not only foreign to the apparent sex of the speaker but also strange in its pitch, tone, and timbre—echoing, breathy, hollow, sounding like a phonograph record played at too slow a speed in an underground cavern. Kurosawa supports the bizarre sound with a striking visual image: the medium's white veils float and flap violently in the wind that has suddenly entered the courtyard, clashing with its previous stillness. The wind is a blast from the supernatural and accompanies, perhaps even carries, the voice of the spirit from that other world.

In contrast to the writhing agony of the medium is the stillness and quiet of the husband's version of the incident itself, toward which his attitude is one of sad resignation. For the husband (played with majestic silence by Masayuki Mori), the woman hardly exists. For him, the essential relationship is between himself and the bandit, two honorable men both caught in the trap of a worthless woman. Whereas the versions of both bandit and wife proceed from stereotypic sexual definitions, the husband's proceeds from the stereotype of honor. The husband sees his action as completely self-determined, completely a matter of his own conscience and his own decision. The mood of that decision is quiet stillness, and Kurosawa shoots the scene of decision from a high angle with the fixed camera and very long takes—as opposed to the predatory travelling shots and the tense cross-cutting of the earlier versions. According to the husband, he does not die by being bested in combat (Tojamaro's version), nor as a result of a hypnotic trance that impels his wife toward him with the dagger (as in hers), but as a result of his own decision—to commit *hara-kiri* according to the *samurai*'s precepts of honor.

But the Woodcutter, whom we know (from an earlier travelling shot) discovered the body and whom we now find out actually witnessed the entire incident, sees all three versions as concoctions of lies—even the dead man's: "There was no knife." One cannot even depend on supernatural beings for the truth. The Woodcutter then tells his version of the incident, an "objective account" of an outside observer. Interestingly, the Woodcutter is played by Takashi Shimura, a regular member of the Kurosawa acting family, and a figure whom Kurosawa uses consistently as the objective, rational, balanced center of an intense human action (Shimura plays the leader of the *Seven Samurai* who survives to bury his fallen comrades; he plays the equivalent of the Macduff role in *Throne of Blood*).

In the Woodcutter's "objective" account, all three characters are weaker, smaller, and sillier than in their own. The bandit sentimentally begs for forgiveness and blubberingly offers to marry the woman he defiled; the husband is a jittery coward; the wife is a selfish and cackling shrew who simply wants the two men to fight over her. Because both men are so cowardly and so comical in this version, they have a good deal of trouble working up a fight. They both shake with fright, their hands trembling so convulsively they can barely hold their swords, much less make contact with the other's. Their whoops are not masculine assertions of strength (as in the bandit's version) but nervous squeals of sheer terror. Each offers a very tentative poke of a sword-thrust only to scurry away furtively for cover.

For this sequence, Kurosawa uses the generally fixed camera, shooting at some distance from the participants, reducing their stature and the impression of violence, reducing their sloppy swordsmanship to a comic parody of their fight in the bandit's version. One of the most comic of Kurosawa's images is his shot of the tips of the two swords, each shakily and tentatively entering the frame from its opposite sides, trying (but not very hard) to cross in the middle of the frame, only to lose heart, pull back, and evacuate the frame altogether. (Kurosawa uses a similar comic image of weapons entering opposite sides of the frame in *Yojimbo*.) Accompanying these distant comic images is Kurosawa's sound track: no violent whoops (as in the bandit's version), no pulsating music (as in the wife's), no stillness (as in the husband's), but the sniveling sounds of male whimpers, sobs, and whines, punctuated by the hysterically vulgar cackles of the wife which serve as their goad to combat (and occasionally scares them apart just when they are beginning to get close enough to tangle). Eventually the fight blunders to its climax as the husband loses his weapon and backs away (a long, slow tracking shot rather than a rapid, violent one), trips, and is killed. Even as he whines for mercy, the bandit sobbingly and quiveringly pushes his sword home.

Several questions arise, however, from this "objective" report. First, can an outside observer actually feel the personal and internal resonances of such an intense event? Is his comical, low, and essentially deflating view of human passion and action accurate in terms of the participants' feelings? The Woodcutter's consistent tendency in the film has been to see all forms of human exertion as essentially low and vile. Is he any more to be trusted than the others? Second, if he is to be trusted (however warily), what does his version imply about human behavior, given the conflicting but consistent attempts of the other versions to ennoble human passions and enrich the reasons for human responses? Clearly, the participants do not see their own actions as petty and silly, or they do not say so. But there is the difficulty. Are the participants "lying"—as the Woodcutter believes—or are they telling the "truth" as they perceive it? Lying implies the intention to deceive about what they know to be true. Is that what the characters are doing? Or are they simply telling what they "know" to be true—even if each of them, including the Woodcutter, "knows" something different to be true?

This is the ambiguity that the film poses. But *Rashomon*'s final sequence, which returns us to the ruins of the Rashomon Gate, provides Kurosawa's synthesis of the conflicting versions and resolution of the ambiguity in terms of human action. As the Woodcutter's story finishes, the three men hear the cries of an infant, obviously abandoned to the storm and the ruins by its parents. The Listener's reaction is to steal the baby's clothes and blanket: "We can't live unless we act selfishly these days." The Woodcutter prevents him and protects the helpless infant by drawing a dagger—obviously the mysteriously missing knife that belonged to the wife in all versions of the story except the Woodcutter's. The sudden appearance of this concrete object serves two ironic purposes. First, it shows that the Woodcutter, too, is capable of acting selfishly, of stealing from the victims of misfortune. Second, it undermines the objectivity of his report because it proves that he is really a participant in the incident itself. He has something to hide, and so it is to his advantage to make people believe there was no dagger (as he has said all along) and that the husband died on Tojamaro's sword. The Listener backs away from the Woodcutter's stolen dagger, laughs (for he perceives these ironies that make the Woodcutter no better a man than he), and walks off into the cascades of rain.

The Woodcutter then reaches for the infant, and the Priest's assumption is that now this other thief wants to steal what little protection against life's harshness the infant still has. The Priest's faith in human beings has been so shaken that he now assumes people act from the most selfish and lowest of motives. Instead, the Woodcutter tells the Priest that he will adopt the infant, that he already has six children and a seventh will not make much difference. The two men apologize to one another—the Woodcutter for his callousness and selfishness, the Priest for his lack of faith—and the two men bow. The rain has suddenly stopped, the Woodcutter walks away from the Gate with his new child in his arms, and Kurosawa's tracking camera walks with him as he leaves the ruins of the Rashomon Gate behind him. The sun finally shines.

Kurosawa's point is that ambiguity, vanity, subjectivity, and self-interest are unavoidable facts of human existence, and that certainty, selflessness, and objectivity are unattainable. All that people can do is their best, or what they feel is their best. They must assert themselves in action as best they can, realizing that it is both impossible to know if that action is really best and to know anything about human experience except what they "know" in their own subjective perceptions.

Kurosawa might be considered the most existential of the Japanese directors: a person is what he does simply because it is impossible to discover what anything is in any other way. What a person feels, thinks, or intends is unknowable, even by that person himself. All four versions of the incident were attempts, in effect, to explain away a brutal, selfish human act that should never have occurred in the first place. Once the inhumane deed has been done, the reasons for it become irrelevant. This same view dominates the other Kurosawa masterpieces of the decade. Kurosawa's two most interesting *samurai* films—*Seven Samurai* (1954) and *Yojimbo* (1961)—work the theme into two opposite situations, both borrowed from the American western. *Seven Samurai* is a variation on the ranchers-against-the-farmers western (like *Shane*), except in Kurosawa's film they are the farmers against the bandits. *Yojimbo* is the story of the paid gun (i.e. sword) for hire who rides (i.e. stalks) into a small town, split between two warring but equally crooked rival factions, and succeeds in cleaning up both sides. *Seven Samurai* develops the theme of human assertion and action through cooperation—regardless of differences in temperament, background, social class, and personal style. *Yojimbo* develops the theme of self-assertion and individual integrity, the man who can sell his sword but not his values. Kurosawa paid his debt to the American western when both *Rashomon* and *Seven Samurai* were remade by Hollywood as westerns (*The Outrage*, 1964, and *The Magnificent Seven*, 1960, respectively). But the western's debt to Kurosawa may be even greater, for one of his startling and original stylistic devices in *Seven Samurai*—using the lyricism of slow motion to heighten the climactic moment of death in a duel—has become a cliché of the "new" western.

Kurosawa's most important *gendai-geki* is *Ikiru* (*Living*, 1952), another extension of his belief in the assertion of human dignity through action, regardless of the reasons for or the consequences of the action. Takashi Shimura plays the major role in a Kurosawa film for once (Kurosawa tends to use Shimura in a supporting role and the more active, assertive Mifune in the major role). *Ikiru* is the story of a petty bureaucrat who has wasted most of his life, and who discovers that he is dying of cancer. He decides to dedicate his final days to accomplishing one important thing before his death. The film is as sensitive, as personal, as close in its human observation as the *samurai* stories are active and violent.

But perhaps no two films reveal Kurosawa's stylistic range than his two films of 1957, both of them film adaptations of Western classics of the drama: Shakespeare's *Macbeth* (*Throne of Blood*) and Maxim Gorky's *The Lower Depths*. The two literary texts pose opposite cinematic problems: Shakespeare's magnificent language and sprawling structure; Gorky's claustrophobic, discursive, and philosophic study of a social mass rather than a single protagonist. And Kurosawa solved these opposite stylistic problems in opposite ways. He dispensed altogether with Shakespeare's text and translated the spirit of the play's theme and poetry into concrete visual symbols; he kept the text of the Gorky play almost verbatim (it is a far more literal translation of the play than Renoir's 1936 version) and shot the entire film in confined and cramped settings. The results of these opposite approaches of the same year unquestionably rank among the ten finest cinematic adaptations of dramatic works in film history.

In *Throne of Blood* Kurosawa translated Shakespeare's poetry (the references to blood, to the chaos in nature), theme (the valiant man tempted and destroyed by both the evil in himself and in the cosmos— which are identical), and characters (the strong warrior, the grasping wife) into purely visual terms. In a film that is as visually magnificent as any Kurosawa (or anyone else) ever made, it is worth noting his consistent choices: the dominant method is to depict the interrelationship and interpenetration of natural, supernatural, and psychological forces. At the beginning of the film, nature is "out of joint"—a violent wind and furious rain storm (as in *Rashomon*). Lord Washizu (the Macbeth figure, played by Mifune) and his friend, Miki (Banquo), attempt to ride through a forest, which attacks them on every side with lightning, tortuous branches, and diverting bypaths (Kurosawa's tracking shots again increase the impression of violence and fury). The tangled, "breathing" forest is both metaphoric of the internal maze in Washizu's mind as well as the ensnaring temptations of the supernatural order, which is about to angle for his soul. This imprisoning forest in the film's early sequence is mirrored by the liberating forest in the late sequence when a moving, man-made forest (the forest's new "soul" is human not superhuman) restores the balance of nature and purges the results of the initial human experience with a forest.

Another of Kurosawa's images linking man, nature, and supernature is fog: the misty white smoke of steamy clouds seemingly rising from beneath the earth. The fog is metaphoric of both the universe's poisonous temptations as well as the moral fog in Washizu's mind. When Washizu first sees the Witch, she is sitting on the earth, seemingly rising out of the fog which blankets her legs and feet. And her skin is the same chalk white as that pestilential mist. And then Kurosawa makes a dazzling leap from the metaphysical to the psychological plane, for Lady Washizu (Lady Macbeth) has the same chalk white skin, and she continually sits motionless—while she "argues" with her husband, while he performs the murder—in a position identical to that of the Witch. The Witch and Lady Washizu and the fog are white and are earthbound. While Washizu argues with his wife about their course of action, he continually stands up and paces about (the camera pacing with him) as he defends the selfless, humane position; but when he relents and accepts her arguments, he, too, sits down—earthbound, motionless. At the end of the film, when the wood comes to the castle to reclaim the initial debt of the forest, Washizu's own men shoot him full of arrows (he becomes a sort of monstrous tree himself), and he eventually collapses to the earth in a cloud of mist. He is now permanently bound to the earth and the fog.

The Lower Depths is a wide-screen film that avoids such stunning natural images and uses, instead, the imagery of the human face and the social grouping. Rather than make a dazzling, pictorial wide-screen film, which Kurosawa obviously could have done, he uses the big screen to emphasize the cramped little dwelling that serves as the physical boundary and the shelter of a social microcosm. He also uses another potential of the wide screen—its greater capability of rendering depth-of-field—to turn the film's primary visual principle into a contrasting series of planes of depth, usually by basing all his compositions on some variation of the receding triangle. (There are very few shots in which there is only a single being in the frame. Even in a character's most isolated moments there is a face or a body or two in the rearground.) *The Lower Depths* is a study of a social whole, and these triangulations in depth continually emphasize that the whole is inescapable and omnipresent.

In addition to this deliberate stylistic confinement, the film mirrors Kurosawa's vision of life as clearly as any. At its conclusion a group of characters erupt into an exuberant, rhythmic, vital dance—an absolutely compelling mixture of rhythmic sounds, physical movement, and film cutting. At the same time, another character commits suicide. That juxtaposition is the Kurosawa statement, a point he greatly emphasizes, in comparison to the Gorky play, by inventing this dance. There is life and death, dance and suicide, elation and annihilation, but life and the dance go on.

Kenji Mizoguchi was a director of an earlier generation whose career came to its artistic culmination as Kurosawa's began to expand. In comparison to Kurosawa, Mizoguchi's work reveals a more consistent and single visual style, a more consistent theme and setting, and a much narrower range of emotion and tone. Mizoguchi specializes in period dramas, and his milieu is not simply the past but the past as seen in folk legends, fairy tales, and paintings. Whereas Kurosawa saturates the past with modern realism and intellectual issues, Mizoguchi develops the distant mildness, softness, and stateliness of that past. His primary attraction to the past comes from its apparent synthesis of art and nature—the way the natural life of the past has been frozen (and enshrined) by the art of the legend and the drawing. Many of Mizoguchi's central figures are themselves artists: the actress Taki no Shiraito in the 1933 silent film of the same name; the troupe of players in *The Story of the Last Chrysanthemums* (1939); the artist Utamaro in *Utamaro and His Five Women* (1946); the potter in *Ugetsu* (1953). For Mizoguchi, the business of the artist is the conversion of life into the perfection and precision of art, and the business of the cinema is both the conversion of life into art and the reverse conversion of art (a folk tale, for example) into the "living" vitality of cinema. No clearer blending of the domains of art and nature exists than in the opening of *Ugetsu* which begins with paintings of nature (under the titles) and dissolves into shots of nature.

In his photographic style Mizoguchi mirrors this art-as-nature-as-art synthesis. As opposed to Kurosawa's traveling camera and deep focus, Mizoguchi uses a generally fixed camera (when it travels, it does so slowly and gracefully) and soft focus. Mizoguchi's shots of Japanese settings—fields, mountains, lakes—are much softer and flatter than Kurosawa's shots of nature, deliberately turning these natural settings into evocations of Japanese prints and paintings. Mizoguchi tends to use back- and side-lighting for these outdoor shots, not only softening them and reducing the depth-of-field but also giving them a hazy, limpid glow. Even in moments of human agitation (for example, the sister's suicide in *Sansho the Bailiff*, 1954), nature remains soft, still, and quiet. The girl drowns herself in a placid pool of glassy water, framed by statuesque, motionless, and gauzy trees who watch but do not react (as opposed to Kurosawa's nature whose tumult mirrors human agitation).

In his structure, Mizoguchi is also more classical and more literary than Kurosawa; Mizoguchi's major films are perfect examples of the Japanese sense of symmetry. Whereas Kurosawa's symmetry (in *Rashomon, Seven Samurai, Throne of Blood*) is often blurred by the violence and energy of his action, Mizoguchi's stately pace emphasizes his structural purity (and symmetry is another of the ways that art improves on nature). Mizoguchi's primary structural device is the separation of the leading characters, each of them traveling different paths—quite literally since the journey is essential to many Mizoguchi films. *Taki no Shiraito* traces the separate paths of the actress and the young law student, until fate draws the paths together; *Utamaro* follows the artist's "journey" as well as that of each of his women; *Sansho* is a series of separations—father from wife and children, mother from children, son from daughter—and eventual reunions with both the living and dead. The symmetry of *Sansho* is so perfect that there are two fathers in the film (Sansho and Zushio's father), two sons (Taro and Zushio), two separations (the mother from Zushio and Anju; Zushio from Anju), two children (Zushio and Anju), two reunions with the living (Zushio with Taro and Zushio with his mother), and two reunions with the dead at their shrines (Zushio at his father's tomb and at the lake where Anju drowned).

Ugetsu is a perfect Mizoguchi film in structure, theme, visual style, and tone. There are four central characters—a potter and his wife, the potter's brother and his wife—each of whom travels a separate path and comes to a different end. The men, pursuing the false goals of money, fame, and lust, both discover the worthlessness of these goals, primarily because the wives trod a road that led to their rape (one is murdered by soldiers, the other becomes a prostitute). Mizoguchi brings the film to life by the elegance of this symmetry and the magnificence of his visual technique which dissolves nature into the mystical and concretizes the mystical into nature.

As the characters travel by boat on a misty lake to bring their goods to market (the potter is driven by his desire for riches), Mizoguchi converts the lake into a misty, ethereal Acheron; the thick fog converts the natural lake into an apparently supernatural netherworld. As opposed to Kurosawa's fog, which seethes, breathes, and floats, Mizoguchi's fog seems to sit and stifle. Out of this fog, the characters see a boat floating toward them, a mystical and eerie boat, seemingly floating on the fog itself. Inside the boat lies a chalk white, corpselike figure who looks like a ghost, and is even taken for a ghost by the characters. No, he says, he is not a ghost but a man who has been beaten and robbed by pirates. He warns the characters against going further—especially because of the danger to the women. But the potter presses onward.

Not heeding this warning from a man who looks like a ghost, Mizoguchi brings the potter face-to-face with ghosts who look like people. First, the potter falls under the spell of Lady Wakasa (Machiko Kyo again, who specialized in beautiful sirens), who tempts him by flattering his artistry and gains possession of his body by satisfying his sensuality. Their moments of sensual union are echoed by the diaphanous, shiny glow of nature in Mizoguchi's typically luminous photography. But Mizoguchi keeps his comment on the action clear by continually cross-cutting between the other characters on their "paths." While the potter falls under the dreamily sensual spell of Lady Wakasa, his wife is murdered by a group of soldiers on the road, his brother cheats his way into fulfilling his dreams of becoming a *samurai,* and his brother's wife is raped on the road by bandits (a brutal sexual encounter that comments on the potter's).

The potter's diaphanous dream-world collapses when he awakes one morning to discover that Lady Wakasa has been dead for years and that her house is a mere pile of ruins (Mizoguchi shoots this "morning after" discovery in a much harsher and brighter light than is usual for him). The potter, penniless and broken, returns home to join his wife (the usual Mizoguchi reunion after separation). Although the wife who greets him appears to be a corporeal being, he discovers the next morning from his neighbors that she has been killed and that he has spent the night with yet another ghost (a second "morning after" discovery—and a sure sign of the Mizoguchi symmetry). He decides to devote his life to honoring his wife's grave (just as the son honors the graves of his sister and father in *Sansho*), and the spirit of his wife returns to him again—this time as an incorporeal voice. She tells him that her spirit will remain perpetually beside him (a beneficial supernatural presence, in contrast to the deleterious Lady Wakasa) and that he should return to his pottery. Both the potter and the brother renounce their false ambitions and return to the normal cycles of their lives.

Mizoguchi's moral system is more sentimental and more conventional than Kurosawa's. He advocates the usual humanistic virtues of love, fidelity, and selflessness as opposed to the selfish drives of lust, power, and money, but mixes these values with the traditional Japanese virtues of patience, submission, humility, and resignation. Mizoguchi, however, brings this traditional morality to life in *Ugetsu* by making his reality look so shimmeringly unreal and his unreality look so very real, by the mysticizing of nature and the naturalizing of mysticism.

Yasujiro Ozu, Mizoguchi's contemporary, is the master of the *shomin-geki*—the modern-day, middle-class comedy. Ozu's primary subjects are the surfaces, forms, rituals, and processes of middle-class (or upper-middle-class) life itself. His films are dominated by scenes of eating, both at home and in restaurants, scenes at the office, scenes of men drinking together in bars. They are films about the central social processes: work, marriage, family life, friendship. And they are films which mirror the modernization of Japanese life: television sets, neon lights, modern architecture, furniture, and offices. The women gossip, the men play golf, and the children both go to school and watch television.

As a stylist Ozu is a real oddity, in many ways challenging most of the West's cinema theory. It is probably not unfair to say that of all the world's highly respected directors in the entire history of film, there is none more visually bare (indeed barren) than Ozu. Perhaps the unkindest possible description of Ozu's style would be that he makes "women's pictures" of endless dialogue in the made-for-TV Hollywood fashion of taking pictures of faces and mouths. And all his pictures are alike, so that it is impossible to tell one from the other. In truth, the titles of many of the Ozu films are so similar that they sound like the same film (*Late Spring*, 1949; *Early Spring*, 1956; *Late Autumn*, 1960; *End of Summer*, 1961; *Autumn Afternoon*, 1962). In truth, the subjects of them are inevitably similar—parents and children; if, when, and who to marry—and the actors recur from one film to another. In truth, all of them have a similar tone—a subtly understated pathos and comedy that play against one another in delicate counterpoint.

Most striking of all, the films are consistently devoid of scenes and moments that are purely visual. There is perhaps a higher percentage of talk in an Ozu film than in anybody else's ever; the only scenes without talk tend to be either conventional "establishing shots"—the building or location where the dialogue is about to take place—or a brief (and often very effective) reaction shot after a dialogue scene. Such visual images usually last less than ten seconds. Ozu's editing is invisible (intentionally, so as not to divert attention from the talk or the people); the color is unspectacular, indeed unnoticeable or even downright ugly; the camera seems confined to eye level as if it were sitting on the floor of one of those Japanese houses (clearly to increase the sense of intimacy). And from these films it would appear that there is nothing colder, uglier, and more sterile than contemporary Japanese houses, offices, office corridors, quick-lunch restaurants, and bars, all of which have walls so hard and bare, floors so highly polished, that they appear unfit for human life. But the counterpoint of warm, vital human life in a cold, sterile environment is at the center of Ozu's vision: all of his films are indeed variations on the single theme that people *do* manage to live—and not so badly either—in the midst of spectacularly glossy ugliness simply by remaining human and trusting in the human (rather than the inanimate) institutions.

Ozu's strengths are structural and psychological rather than visual.

Like Kurosawa and Mizoguchi, Ozu inevitably uses the multiple human focus, examining parallel actions, reactions, and choices in the lives of different people. Unlike Kurosawa and Mizoguchi, Ozu's tendency is toward parallelism, the similarity of responses which play against one another contrapuntally, rather than contrast; unlike Kurosawa's multiple points of view in *Rashomon* and Mizoguchi's multiple paths in *Ugetsu,* Ozu builds his films as very subtle variations on a single issue—say, getting married—revealing the attitudes of old and young, married and single, parents and children, widowers and adolescents toward the central issue. Ozu is the master of counterpoint, in his purity, delicacy, and deceptive complexity, a kind of J. S. Bach of cinema. An inevitable Ozu effect is that just at that point when one wonders if anything is going to happen and if the film is going anywhere (some forty-five minutes into it), the film's structure, idea, warmth, subtlety, and charm grab hold of the viewer and refuse to let go until the end of the study.

Ozu's *Ohayo* (*Good Morning,* 1959), which is not one of his "seasonal" studies of marriage, is a good example of his method and concerns. The film's subject is etiquette, the formal pleasantries of life (like saying, "Good Morning") that enable human beings to live together. The film reveals the social tensions of life—women's gossip, the suspicion of a neighbor's dishonesty, the fear of being snubbed—and demonstrates that the social niceties are truly necessities for easing these tensions. At the center of the film are two children (Ozu has always liked the world of children, beginning with his first silent triumph, *I Was Born But . . .,* 1932). The two boys want their father to buy them a television set; when he refuses they get angry and he tells them that they talk too much. The oldest boy says that adults talk too much, too, that they say useless things like, "Good Morning." And so the two boys refuse to talk altogether, throwing the neighbors, their teachers, their friends, and their own family into confusion. Ozu comically and deftly shows that the "useless" amenities of life are extremely useful for keeping society at peace. Ironically, the boys have their own social ritual—a marvelous little amenity in which they have developed the ability to fart automatically as a result of being pushed on the forehead. To the boys that is a useful ritual, while to say, "Good Morning," is useless. Ozu, without any specific comment and overemphasis, reveals how necessary all our social rituals are—including a father's giving in to his kids and buying them a TV. From such a film one can see that Ozu's true subject is the extraordinary ordinary and the interesting boring.

Of the lesser Japanese directors, Kon Ichikawa is perhaps the most interesting. Ichikawa's primary distinction is for the intensity and savagery of his ideological argument, usually examining the depravity and degeneration of the human animal. Ichikawa's first noted film, *The Harp of Burma* (1956), is one of his milder studies: the examination of a soldier in Burma in the final days of World War II who first disguises himself as a priest in order to survive and who subsequently becomes a true convert to the priestly values, primarily as a result of the war horrors he has seen (and Ichikawa's camera occasionally shows us). But his *Fires on the Plain* (1959), another story of the final days of the War, concentrates on the horrors exclusively, on a man's innate determination to survive (despite the fact that he is ill with consumption), even if it means murdering and eating other human beings to keep himself alive. Ichikawa's *Odd Obsession* (1959) is set in the Ozu environment of the upper-middle-class family, but this family occupies itself with bizarre sexual games that eventually destroy all the players. Kon Ichikawa also directed the mammoth record of the *Tokyo Olympiad* (1964).

Kinugasa's *Gate of Hell* and Inagaki's *Samurai* (both 1953) were two of Japan's first color films and are visually magnificent in their application of splendid color photography to the *jidai-geki*. Hiroshi Teshigahara's *Woman in the Dunes* (1964) is remarkable for its minute, tactile examination of a bizarre human conversion. A man from a modern city on vacation in the dunes is imprisoned by the people who live there, forced to serve as the husband of a woman who lost her previous one. He begins by resisting this imprisonment, trying to escape, loathing the pervasive and omnipotent sand that seeps into his hair, clothes, food, bed, and soul. Only when he ceases to fight the sand and decides instead to study its laws and work with it (he calculates a way to distill precious, life-giving water from the sand) does his prison suddenly become a home. He discovers that sand is certainly no worse a physical environment than the sterile technological society from which he came.

The Japanese film industry, like the industries of the West, underwent severe commercial changes in the decade following 1950. The Japanese discovered that many of their cheaper and exploitative productions —monster pictures (*Godzilla, Rodan*), invasions from outer space (*The Mysterians*)—could make money abroad. And so Japan was continually invaded by prehistoric monsters or visitors from another planet who devoured or incinerated plastic models of Japan's major cities before they were repulsed by some new weapon or old bacillus. As the Japanese bought (and manufactured) more and more television sets, Japanese film attendance dropped. The Japanese film industry had learned from the West, however, that this was one monster that could not be repulsed. The Japanese studios began production for television from the start—and even began operating television stations themselves. Since the mid-1960s, however, the Japanese industry has been remarkably silent, not so much in its quantitative production, which is still high, but in the fact that Kurosawa has done little in over a decade (one magnificent color film, *Dodes' Kaden,* 1970) and there have been no new Ozus or Mizoguchis to replace those who have died.

The West discovered the Indian cinema in much the same way as it did the Japanese. Satyajit Ray's *Pather Panchali* (1955) won a special prize at the 1956 Cannes Film Festival, and his next film, *Aparajito* (1956), won the Grand Prize at Venice the following year. Unlike the Japanese cinema, however, the West discovered not a rich, unknown cache of Indian cinema artistry but instead that Satyajit Ray *was* the Indian cinema. Not that the Indian film industry was not prolific: India produced some 300 feature films in 1958, second only to Japan (but ahead of America) in the quantity of feature production. But several causes—unique both to Indian society and its film industry—kept quantity up and quality down.

First, India is a vast nation of over 500 million people, and movies remain the only form of popular entertainment accessible to the masses. There are very few television sets in India *per capita,* and the percentage of that *capita* that can afford to buy them is very small. This pressure to provide mass entertainment for a huge and highly uneducated and unsophisticated audience has led to a consistent mediocrity, a devotion to formula and convention, and a fear of experimentation.

Second, and even more difficult for the film industry, India is a nation without a common language. There are over a dozen Indian languages—all of them a mystery to every Indian except his own—the most common of which are Hindi, Bengali, Telugu, Marathi, and Tamil. This language barrier obviously caused little difficulty in the silent era. The Indian silent film industry, effectively established in 1913 by the magical, mythological films of Dadasaheb Phalke and developed by pioneers such as Dhiren Ganguly, Debaki Bose, and Chandulal Shah, may well have been more artistically advanced than the silent Japanese cinema. But the coming of sound, which liberated the Japanese cinema from the *benshi,* imprisoned the Indian cinema in the Tower of Babel. Indian film production is necessarily narrow and regional in its outlook, which reduces any attempt to appeal to an international market.

Third, the Indian cinema has been subject to ruthless government intervention and censorship. Under the British, themes of independence were forbidden; under the government of free India, "decadent" Western influences were forbidden. In addition to limiting its artistic freedom, the Indian government taxes the film industry heavily; its huge audiences provide handsome revenues, even with the extremely low ticket prices. Further, the Indian government levied severe import quotas which restricted the supply of raw film stock. Even more ironic, an Indian print that had been shown abroad was subject to duty as "imported" film upon returning home.

Fourth, the Indian Film industry itself is a victim of corrupt, profiteering practices. Independent producers who want to make a quick killing, rather than established film companies, are the rule. In the 1930s, however, India's studios were more solid organizations; the most famous of them, Bombay Talkies, was a cooperative, familial studio—modeled on Germany's UFA where Bombay Talkies' owners, Himansu Rai and Devika Rani, had worked. But the independent speculator, who usually did not have enough money to complete a film once he started it and therefore needed to beg, borrow, deal, and swindle more as the shooting went along, came to dominate the industry in the 1940s.

The speculator could only get that money because, fifth, the Indian film industry has been totally dominated by the star system since the collapse of the familial studios of the 1930s. And it has been a star system with a vengeance, making the power and salaries of the Hollywood luminaries look puny. Because only a producer with a major star could get the money to finish his film, stars became so popular and enjoyed such power that they commanded immense salaries (at least half of it paid under the table in untaxable "black money") and might work on as many as a dozen films at once, dropping in periodically on each of the production units as the star's schedule and inclinations permitted. Music was the supporting "star" of an Indian film (the music director is the second highest paid position in the Indian film industry); for decades, of the hundreds of films shot each year in India, there was *not one* without singing and dancing. The Indian film became so conventional that its foremost historians (Barnouw and Krishnaswamy) described the formula succinctly as, "A star, six songs, and three dances."

To such assumptions and conventions Satyajit Ray was, and still remains, a stranger. Ray was a student of serious Indian literature and philosophy; his father was a friend of Rabindranath Tagore, India's greatest writer of the twentieth century, and Ray was a personal student of Tagore's. But Ray was also, like many of his Western counterparts, a *cinéaste;* he was the cofounder of the first film society in India, the Calcutta Film Society, in 1947. So one might see Ray as uniting the traditions of serious Indian literature with those of Western cinema (avoiding Indian cinematic traditions altogether). The influence of Western cinema is unmistakable in Ray's films, particularly Italian neorealism and the graceful structure of the French classical cinema of the 1930s. A particular influence was Ray's observing Jean Renoir make *The River* in Calcutta in 1951, when he spoke frequently with the classical French director. Although Ray is a Bengali, his outlook is an international, humanistic one—

an attitude which perhaps makes his work more popular in the rest of the world than it is in Bengal.

In terms of Indian cinematic traditions, Ray makes "Socials"—the two opposite genres of Indian films being Mythologicals and Socials, corresponding roughly to Japan's *jidai-* and *gendai-geki*. But Indian "Socials" typically drown modern social issues (say, the caste question or the subjugation of women) in sentimental, saccharine clap-trap (there are no social solutions only tragic endings), while the Mythologicals display their fantastic hokum undiluted by reality. (Ray himself pokes gentle fun at this hokum in the film-within-a-film sequence of *The World of Apu*, 1958, which parodies one of these Mythologicals, yet, at the same time, shows the intense audience devotion to it.) Ray's *Pather Panchali* avoided all these Indian film traditions: no star (Ray, in the manner of the Soviets, Italians, and Czechs, even used some nonprofessional actors); no songs and dances (although there was a brilliant instrumental score by Ravi Shankar); a cinematographer who had never shot a motion picture before (the distinguished still photographer, Subrata Mitra); and shooting on location (Indian films were exclusively studio films, even for outdoor films, a choice that aided their flight from reality). Ray's film wanted to have as much to do with reality as possible.

Ray's Apu trilogy (*Pather Panchali, Aparajito,* and *The World of Apu*) is one film that is three and three films that are one. In adapting a mammoth novel by Bibhuti Bannerjee, Ray seems to have perceived (as did von Stroheim before him) that the best way to make a film of a novel without losing its texture and complexity was to make three films. The Ray trilogy employs a complex and carefully conceived structure that is apparent in the unity of the individual films as well as the overall conception of the trilogy as a whole. The subject of the trilogy is the growth of a young Indian boy from his peasant, rural youth to a mature and educated adulthood in the city, an Indian variation on the *Buildungsroman*. The three films devote themselves to childhood, adolescence, and adulthood respectively. In all three films deaths play a pivotal role in the boy's growth and development: the death of the old aunt and his sister in *Pather Panchali*; the death of his father and mother in *Aparajito*; the death of his wife (the hardest one for him to accept) in *The World of Apu*. In counterpoint to these deaths, all three films end identically: Apu is on the road ("Pather Panchali" means "Song of the Road"), moving from the country to the city, implying the continuity of life and growth.

At the end of *Pather Panchali*, the remains of the family battered by death leave the little peasant village to try to live better in the city. At the end of *Aparajito*, Apu pulls himself together after the death of his mother and takes the path back to the city and the university. At the end of *The World of Apu*, a film which was almost entirely Ray's own invention and which revealed his ability to graft his own material onto that of the original novel without leaving any traces of the stitching, Apu is back on the road, returning to Calcutta again, his young son on his back. For Apu, it is also his most explicit return to life, on which he had turned his back after the death of his wife. A sign of the complexity and precision of Ray's structural conception is that at the end of this final installment Apu's young son is almost exactly the same age as the child Apu in the first one, living a similar life (unfettered but fatherless), now on his way to the city with a newly returned father. The song of the road has come full circle.

Ray's themes and concerns are clear in the trilogy. First, there is his sympathetic and microscopic examination of the points of view of all the major characters. Although much of *Pather Panchali* gives the child's-eye view of life (and death), the mother's-eye view of that struggle also gets Ray's careful attention. She often acts cross and vicious, but she has the heavy responsibility of keeping the family together and alive with her husband not only penniless but absent. That responsibility proves too much for her when she fails to protect her daughter, Durga, from death. The mother is caught between her tenderness, her responsibility, and her shame—and Ray catches those conflicting pressures as well. In *Aparajito* the same (but older) mother is caught between her selfish need to keep her son with her and her selfless desire to see him do well in life, while the boy is caught between his attachment to his mother and his ambition to succeed and to study. Ray's films excel in the many-sidedness of these human portraits. Another many-sided portrait of Ray's is the wastrel husband: in *Pather Panchali* the husband is literate, sensitive, and poetic but a poor provider; in *The World of Apu* the same becomes true of Apu, his son. The wastrel husband recurs in many later Ray films—*The Music Room* (1958) and *Mahanagar* (1963) in particular.

Perhaps Ray's essential theme, however, is his ultimate commitment to life, to human exertion, and to the cycles of nature of which man is a small and uncomprehending part. Ray's films are acutely aware that life is often painful, that people can be petty, that sorrow is inescapable and death inevitable. As he shows in the Apu trilogy, life is defined by death. But despite this awareness, Ray reveals that people continue to travel the road of life, that the continuity of that road has been decreed by nature, and that the road has a clear, sweet, and compelling song.

Ray's dominant technique for rendering the human feelings that are so central to his films might be described as the prolonged reaction shot: a device which he uses constantly and which is absolutely unique to his work. Ray's concern is not human action but the essential moment of human reaction to an event of great personal significance; the prolonged moment of reaction serves as the culmination and ultimate definition of that significance. Ray leaves his camera riveted on the figure's face, a face that usually remains as motionless as his or her body, and the camera simply continues watching, watching, watching. The stillness, the silence of the facial-physical reaction, coupled with the extreme length of the take, allows that face to serve as a kind of sponge—slowly absorbing all of the events, feelings, and images that have been built around it until both the face and the audience are saturated with that feeling. These reaction shots, so still and yet so long, convert a totally external objectivity into a truly internal experience for both the character and the audience. One of the best (of many possible) examples is the painful moment of parting between mother and son in *Aparajito* as he goes off to the city, to the university, and, in effect, to his own life. Ray's camera holds on her motionless face and body; she stands still in the dusty arch of a doorway that seems to frame and to fix her forever, watching his back recede down the village path. She stands there, and stands, and stands—her feelings of loss flickering beneath the surface of her placid face, locked into the doorway of her own now empty life. It is *the* moment of separation.

Another of Ray's tools is his masterful visual imagery, often charged with symbolic connotations. In *Pather Panchali* there is the magnificent sequence of the mother's nighttime vigil beside the bed of her feverish daughter. Outside the little house a storm rages, rattling the shutters, banging at the door, sending gusts of wind through the cracks, trying to blow out the little candle of light at the bedside. The storm personifies the attack of nature and death on the little household, and the mother, in trying to save her daughter, is, in effect, trying to keep the raging natural forces outside her shaky home. Those forces win, however, as a gust slips through to extinguish the candle. Another haunting and symbolic image of the same film is the magnificent shot of a speeding train, powerfully slicing through the fields of waving grain, leaving behind its awesome trail of floating smoke. With the train, awesomely depicted as the child Apu perceives the magical monster, Ray juxtaposes the old and new worlds (one of his constant themes), the adult, modern world outside the little village and the little world of the child. (Apu's globe of the world in *Aparajito* serves a similar symbolic function, but Apu is then old enough to understand the relationship between region and world.) Significantly, trains play an increasingly important role in Apu's life, constantly carrying him from city to village and back to the city again, and so the wondrous image of his boyhood becomes a commonplace method of transportation in his adulthood.

Ray's mastery of imagery, and his awareness that pace and understatement in recording an image are essential to its effectiveness (rather than just the image itself), is especially clear in the haunting image that follows the death of Apu's father in *Aparajito*. Ray cuts to a shot of birds leaving their roost and flying off into the sky. Now this parallel of flying birds with a departing human soul is an obvious literary cliché; it is doubtful whether any verbal simile could redeem its triteness. Ray's visual simile, however, is a moment of great beauty. First, he couples the sudden collapse of the father's head on his pillow (the precise moment of death) with an unexplained crack or snap on the sound track. That snapping sound then serves as the impetus (a "gunshot") that scares the birds, for Ray cuts suddenly and sharply from the father's face to the birds making a sudden departure on precisely that sudden sound. He then follows this technique of sharp suddenness with a very brief (perhaps five seconds) shot of the birds flying, a lyrical, graceful moment of swirling shapes and floating wings, that lasts so briefly that the audience acutely feels its graceful ephemerality rather than has time to figure out the precise meaning of the symbolism. By keeping his camera riveted to the human face for long periods of time and by keeping it on his symbolic images only fleetingly and suggestively, Ray achieves his combination of maturity, subtlety, clarity, and compassion.

The Ray films that succeeded the trilogy are equally interesting in their careful views of Indian life and are often quite as effective. In *The Music Room* Ray examines the collapse of the old India—its traditions and its art—and the rise of the new bourgeoisie. *Devi* (*Goddess*, 1960) is also a clash of old and new, a study of the old religious prejudices and fanaticism that can destroy human happiness. *Mahanagar* (*The Big City*) examines family life in the new Calcutta, particularly the new status of women. And *Kanchenjungha* (1962), Ray's first color film, is a less anguished, more placid, Indian *L'Avventura*, the problems and frustrations of wealthy married couples on vacation in Darjeeling. All of these films are significant for their sensitive development of human reactions, for their social analysis (particularly the contrast of old and new), and for their resonant visual imagery. The only films shot in India other than Ray's and Renoir's *The River* that have been widely seen in the West are those of James Ivory, an American who works in India (*Shakespeare Wallah*, 1965; *Bombay Talkie*, 1970) and who has been heavily influenced by Ray.

The New Internationalism

The most striking change in film commerce since the mid-1960s has not been the introduction of individual national traditions but the leveling of national boundaries that has created a truly international market. The extent of international distribution, the extent of American investments in foreign production, the number of international coproductions, and the number of directors working outside their native industries have become more significant than any particularly national statistics. Of course, films have always received international distribution, but not until the 1970s did a major company like Columbia or Warner Brothers distribute a foreign "art film" like *The Emigrants* or *Claire's Knee*. Of course, foreign directors have always worked in America for political or financial reasons, but not since the 1920s have so many worked in the American industry—Antonioni, Forman, Polanski, Kadár, et cetera. Of course, there have always been international coproductions, but not since the earliest period of sound have so many international casts and crews worked together: Visconti shoots *The Damned* in Italy with Swedish, German, and English stars who speak English; Ingmar Bergman makes *The Touch* with Elliot Gould and, at the last minute, mercifully rejects a plan to remake *The Merry Widow* for MGM with Barbra Streisand and Max von Sydow. And through all this internationalism, flows money from American investors (how else can Fellini make a film that costs over $10,000,000?), who need pictures both for their own theatres and the world market, pictures which the American industry can no longer supply exclusively as it did before the Second World War.

Perhaps the precursor of this internationalism is the career of the vagabond director, Luis Buñuel, for forty years a man without a cinematic country, making films in France, Mexico, and only occasionally in his native Spain. Buñuel, a descendant of the surrealism of Paris in the 1920s where he learned his craft from Jean Epstein, has made films in a variety of styles: symbolic-surrealist (*Un Chien andalou*, 1929; *L'Age d'or*, 1930), documentary (*Los Hurdes*, 1932), social-realist (*Los Olvidados*, 1950), psychological case study (*El*, 1952), religious allegory (*Nazarin*, 1959; *Viridiana*, 1961), psychological-surrealist allegory (*Belle de Jour*, 1967), religious-surrealist allegory (*The Milky Way*, 1968), and social-surrealist allegorical comedy (*The Discreet Charm of the Bourgeoisie*, 1973). Through these differing styles over an amazingly long career shine the consistent Buñuel traits: the surrealist's conviction in the insubstantiality of reality coupled with the surrealist's savage humor (for to smash the solidity of reality is an act of joy as well as destruction); the psychologist's interest in the inner workings of the human brain (particularly its sexual fantasies and personal visions of experience that violate all the norms of the realists, the professional psychologists, and the Church); and, finally, his preoccupation with the Church itself (for Buñuel, its fundamentally and comically naïve and false definitions of man). Just as Ingmar Bergman, the son of a Lutheran minister, rebelled against his religious heritage in films that ironically used the images, the terms, the metaphors of that religion, Buñuel, educated by the Jesuits, broke the icons of his childhood faith and used those icons as the central artistic metaphors of his work. But whereas Bergman could supplement the northern preacher's view of life as a vale of tears with the notion that it was also a vale of sunlight, Buñuel could only supplant the Catholic cathedral of gold and silk and ruby with a pile of mortal manure.

The pre-1960 Buñuel films are strikingly lacking in most of the cinematic virtues. The stories are loose and clumsy, the acting overstated and obvious, the decor inattentive to detail and style. Nor is Buñuel's work distinguished in either its cinematography or editing; both his composition and cutting is strictly functional and quite conventional. The Buñuel films have two great strengths: the imaginativeness of the film's abstract idea and the ferocious energy of its translation into a concrete fictional metaphor.

The first event in Buñuel's first film was a close-up of a razor blade slicing the human eyeball. The brutality, the nausea, the visceral attack of this first action dominate the Buñuel canon. One of the most unflinchingly sadistic and brutal scenes ever filmed is the assault of the juvenile delinquents in *Los Olvidados* on a legless, armless beggar (cripples, dwarfs, blind men, hunchbacks, and other assorted physical freaks are as common to the Buñuel world as priests). The delinquents pull the helpless cripple out of his cart, roll the man over on the ground, kicking the stump of his body, leaving him sprawled on the street like a turtle on its back, after which they gleefully send his cart careening down the street so he can never retrieve it. The vicious hoodlums also murder the film's young, innocent boy and later dispose of his body by stuffing it in a wheelbarrow and then dumping it on the slum's garbage heap.

The equation of man and garbage is the central Buñuel theme. The teachings of the Church and the assumptions of social morality infuriate the director, who views man as not only fallen but irretrievable. Buñuel's fury becomes the starting point of a film that intentionally rubs the nose of a naive innocent in the feces of Buñuel's reality. In the process the audience gets its nose rubbed, too. In *El* a church merely serves as the means for the film's central character, a paranoid lecher, to make a sexual conquest. (The man's paranoia also climaxes in church: an insanely grotesque fantasy that everyone, including the priest, is howling at his cuckoldry.) *Belle de Jour* uses the whorehouse as the ultimate metaphor for man's genuine sexual passions, whereas marriage, the official social outlet for sexual passion, is constricting, artificial, and sterile. The result of imposing such artificial behavior on the human beast is perversion, murder, and castration. In fact, in *Belle de Jour*, as in *Los Olvidados* and *El*, such terms are synonymous.

Viridiana is one of Buñuel's most even, most whole works. The film begins in a monastery with the music of Handel's "Messiah"; it ends in the bedroom of a young lecher with rock-and-roll music. The music and the settings mirror the film's journey. The young girl, Viridiana, is a novitiate in a convent, on the threshold of taking her final vows. Before taking those vows she makes the customary trip back to the secular world to make sure she wants to leave that world. She visits her rich uncle's estate. He falls under the sexual spell of her beauty. Carried away by his passion, he drugs his niece with the intention of raping her insensate body. But instead of actually committing the rape, he merely tells her that she has been violated, daubing the sheets of her bed with blood to convince her of the physical fact of her sin. The blood of lust on her sheets convinces her she no longer carries the blood of the lamb in her soul. She decides not to return to the convent.

Rejecting the formal teachings of the Church as a means of saving man's soul, Viridiana takes the next step on the film's allegorical path. She turns to natural religion—good works, charity—as a means of helping mankind. Viridiana uses the money and the grounds of her uncle's estate to establish a utopian community for the poor. Viridiana feels her soul strengthened by this Christian-communist colony in which all work together and none go hungry. But one day when Viridiana and the other masters leave on an excursion, the peasants break into the house, set out the fancy linen and china, and begin to devour a banquet of their own. They raucously break furniture and dishes; they drunkenly bloody the white linen with wine. One of the beggars takes a picture of the loathsome group; they pose in the identical positions of the disciples in da Vinci's "Last Supper"; the beggar woman "snaps the picture" of the gathering by raising her skirt and exposing her naked groin. This lewd burlesque of the sacred scene deflates any hope of improving or helping this human scum by any means whatever. Viridiana has failed at both faith and charity. Seeing no hope at all, Viridiana wanders into the bedroom of her sensual cousin where he "plays cards," as he euphemistically puts it. As Viridiana sits down at the card table, her cousin tells her that he has always known she would one day play cards with him. Buñuel's allegory of the vile reality of the human flesh is complete.

Nazarin is also an allegory that develops the gap between the abstract, ideal teachings of Christ and Buñuel's concrete definition of the bestial human animal, while *The Discreet Charm of the Bourgeoisie* develops the gap between the simple, concrete reality that the bourgeois expectations assume (the banality of property, success, money, social intercourse, and, especially, eating dinner) and the complex levels of super-realities (wishes, dreams, imaginings, fancies) that actually exist. But one of the funniest, cleverest, and most challenging of the late Buñuel films that combines these two themes is *The Milky Way,* a film named after the route of pilgrimage from Paris to San Sebastian in Spain, where Christian pilgrims of the Middle Ages traveled to view the tomb of St. James. Buñuel's film is more a pilgrimage in time than in space, for as his two modern "pilgrims" (one old, one young; both of them "bums," reminiscent of Chaplin or Laurel and Hardy) make the same journey, their "stopping places" are a series of religious heresies that might have existed on or near that route over the past five centuries. Buñuel's film skips among the centuries, making it completely natural for the two twentieth-century pilgrims to meet two young men who continually walk back and forth between events in the seventeenth and twentieth centuries.

The heresies that the two "pilgrims" visit are magnificently bizarre, all of them based on actual historical testimony, as one would expect from Buñuel. The bizarre authenticity of these "actual" heresies is essential to Buñuel's attempt to show how bizarre are all religious beliefs and to raise the question about what makes heresy heretical. Among the bizarre heretics are a group of worshippers who combine their Latin prayers with sex orgies, continuing to speak in Latin and wear their priestly robes even as the Bacchanalia begins; a convent of nuns who literally re-enact the Crucifixion, driving nails into the palms of the chosen sister (she is so inspired that the nails do not hurt her at all); a swashbuckling duel between two devotees of different sects; a bishop's exhuming the body of one of his predecessors, presumed a saintly cleric, and excommunicating his bones for his now heretical opinions. Even in the posh restaurants and country inns of the present, the waiters and customers seem to have nothing better to discuss than matters of religious controversy, such as transsubstantiation and the credibility of miracles.

Buñuel's comic (and serious) point is that today's orthodoxy is tomorrow's heresy: heresy is simply a matter of contemporary opinion. For example, when the "pilgrims" finally arrive in San Sebastian they discover that no other pilgrims have journeyed there because the Church long ago decided that the presumed bones of St. James that lay entombed there were not the bones of St. James. (And the Church can decide whose bones are whose as it pleases. Just as it decides whose views are heretical and why.) Buñuel finds it extremely ludicrous that a body of men, calling themselves the Church, can presume to define matters of such insubstantiality with such certainty—especially when history (as Buñuel's film shows) reveals the force of that insubstantiality with great clarity.

The cinema is a useful tool for Buñuel to make such a point since it is so able to make the solid appear insubstantial and the insubstantial appear so solid. The film is capable of showing us historical phantoms in corporeal dress, of showing us supernatural figures (a clairvoyant man with a flowing black cape) in a completely natural guise; even of showing us miracles (the appearance of both the Virgin and of Christ) more concretely than any vision ever appeared to any saint. One of Buñuel's most vigorous (and amusing) demonstrations of the insubstantiality of the concrete and the concreteness of the insubstantial is a sequence in an inn where two men each go to their separate rooms alone. In one of the rooms, however, a beautiful and naked woman miraculously appears in the bed beside one of the men, despite the fact that he has not opened the door and it is impossible to enter the room in any other way. As he lies in the room next to the tempting woman who cannot possibly be there, a priest begins giving him a lecture on abstinence and chastity (what else?), sitting outside the bedroom door. Except that the priest suddenly appears inside the room, facing the man and woman (who also is not there) while he lectures, despite the fact that he too cannot possibly have entered the room. But there he is inside the room! For Buñuel the cinema has always been the realm of the impossible actual: phenomena, which in the reality of time and space cannot possibly occur, can occur before the viewer's eyes because the cinema is free of reality's time and space.

But for Buñuel this feature makes the cinema *more* like life and experience (not less), for reality is composed of thoughts, dreams, and ideas as much as by tangible objects. The heresy that transpired in a farmhouse *is there* on that Milky Way just as clearly as that farmhouse is there. In Buñuel's view, only when men realize the insubstantiality of our supposedly "objective reality," and of our opinions based on it, will we be able to avoid doing violence both to reality and to one another. Only then will Christ cease to be the messiah of war and death that He says He has been in the film's epilogue.

The pervasiveness of the new internationalism, the commercial effects of international distribution, the sudden and spectacular emergence of the Czech cinema from obscurity, the example of a Satyajit Ray who can transcend the limitations of his own film industry, and the international reputation of a radical and vitriolic director like Buñuel all seem to offer hope for the future of the "Third World" film. Perhaps films from such countries that are not only just beginning to attain an economic maturity but whose film industries are also in the process of birth and growth will eventually make an impact both on the world market and within their own boundaries. As of this writing, directorial talents have begun to emerge in Brazil (Glauber Rocha: *Antonio-das-Mortes,* 1969), Argentina (Leopoldo Torre Nilsson), Mexico (Alejandro Jodorowsky: *El Topo,* 1970, heavily influenced by Buñuel), Egypt (Shadi Abdelsalam: *The Night of Counting the Years,* 1970), Cuba, Senegal, and elsewhere. The impact of the "Third World's" films on the art and society of the future remains uncertain.

THE FOURTH AMERICAN ERA

Chapter 15

t is not entirely certain when the old American movie became the new American cinema: *Bonnie and Clyde* (1967)? *Who's Afraid of Virginia Woolf?* (1966)? *The Pawnbroker* (1965)? *Dr. Strangelove* (1963)? *Lonely Are the Brave* (1962)? *The Hustler* (1961)? *Psycho* (1960)? The exact film that triggered current American production values is not important and not definable, for America slid gradually into its latest era, just as it slid into its transitional third phase (but unlike its sudden leap into the second era with the coming of synchronized sound). All seven of the above films contain some of the seeds of the present values: the off-beat, antihero protagonist; the sterile society that surrounds him; the explicit treatment of sexual conflicts and psychological perversities; the glorification of the past and the open spaces; the slick but tawdry surfaces of contemporary reality; the mixing of the comic and the serious; the self-conscious use of special cinematic effects (slow motion, quick cutting, ironic juxtaposition of the visual and sound). All seven of the films give evidence of the two clichés that critics use to describe today's films— sex and violence. But films have always used sex: whether it was the sexiness of Griffith's Friendless Ones, the sexiness of Marlene Dietrich's veiled face in a key light, or the sexiness of bare breasts and buttocks in a Paris apartment. And films have always been violent—whether it was violent death on a Civil War battlefield in *The Birth of a Nation,* the violent death of a hoodlum on the cathedral steps in *Little Caesar,* or the violent death of the film's protagonists in a slow-motion ballet. The key question about any film style is not whether it uses sex and violence but how it uses them.

To be sure, not all new American films are examples of this new cinema. The big multi-million-dollar musicals, the family pictures that play Radio City Music Hall, the films that conscientiously seek the industry's "G" rating all prove that the old Hollywood and its former production values still survive. But each year's most discussed, most important American films do not receive the "G" rating. This new cinema in America evolved for several reasons; for one, there is a negative cause: the old, steady movie patrons stay home to watch television. The industry had to find new steady customers, not the ones who will go to a movie four times a year, but those who will go every week.

For another, the new cinema of Europe eventually converted American producers. The innovations of Godard, Truffaut, and Antonioni had already conquered the rising generation of young filmmakers and audiences at the art houses. Even more convincing, Truffaut and Antonioni could make money. The years 1959 and 1960 were as important as any to the future American film. Those were the years of *Breathless, The 400 Blows, Shoot the Piano Player, Hiroshima Mon Amour, L'Avventura,* and *La Dolce Vita.*

Third, though Hollywood repeatedly scoffed at the Underground Cinema, the underground has crawled up into Hollywood to enjoy the last laugh. Not only have underground filmmakers succeeded in Hollywood's financial terms—for example, Andy Warhol, Robert Downey, and Brian da Palma—but the underground films have conditioned a whole generation of young filmgoers (precisely those who are the steady customers at Hollywood films) to understand and accept innovations in cinematic form, visual stimulation, and illogical construction.

Fourth, the film industry has pushed its discovery of the elitism of the new film audience to its limits. Rather than attempting to make all of the films for all of the people, producers and exhibitors realize they must appeal to very special tastes. They can make a few family pictures to serve that special need. They can capitalize on the racial make-up of urban audiences by making "blaxploitation" cops-and-robbers films (*Shaft* and all his descendants). They can make "sexploitation" films for that special audience, even further catering to particular tastes by aiming the films at the specific sexual orientation of the viewers (heterosexual, homosexual, or bisexual) and at their preferred voyeuristic fantasies within those orientations (oral, anal, sado-masochistic, et cetera). *The Devil in Miss Jones* (1973), *Deep Throat* (1972), and *Boys in the Sand* (1971) are probably the three most

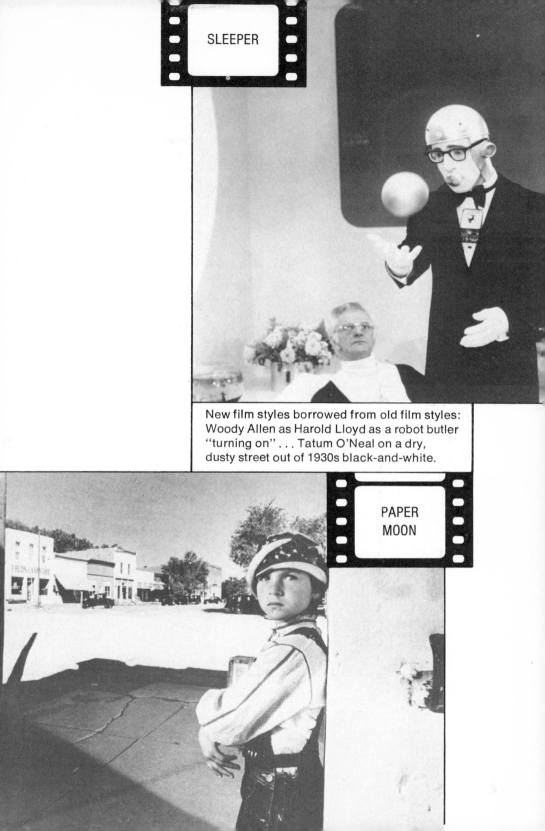

SLEEPER

New film styles borrowed from old film styles: Woody Allen as Harold Lloyd as a robot butler "turning on" ... Tatum O'Neal on a dry, dusty street out of 1930s black-and-white.

PAPER MOON

Styles of experimental cinema:
the dance of pure form in
Oskar Fischinger's **Motion Painting #1** . . .

a satirical dummy with a television head in
Stan Van Der Beek's **Breathdeath** . . .

the sexual fantasies of motorcycle fetichism in
Kenneth Anger's **Scorpio Rising ...**

and perceiving the changes in the unchanging
room of Michael Snow's **Wavelength.**

The sterility of Kubrick landscapes—the space station.

2001:
A SPACE
ODYSSEY

The milk bar.

A
CLOCKWORK
ORANGE

commercially successful films in their respective "genres." In the same way, the American industry aims its "art films" (i.e. those directed by Arthur Penn, Mike Nichols, Peter Bogdanovich, Robert Altman, and others) at the minority audience that likes those kinds of films, a group that not only represents a fraction of the American population but also of the film-going public. These films, however, are precisely those which have come to serve as America's best current examples of film art and the most important representatives of its fourth era.

And finally, the values of these new American "art films" reflect the sexual and social values of the new American film audiences. The American college student, the core of this audience, has discovered the sensual pleasures of the body and the joint as two concrete values in a world of conflicting ideals and hypocritical rhetoric. The vision of reality on the screen does not entirely shape its audience; as in the 1930s, the screen today reflects the values of those who sit in front of it. Those values have changed.

Bonnie and Clyde was perhaps the first full statement of the new cinema's values; it has been as influential on the American films that followed it as *Breathless* was in France or *Open City* in Italy. In the years since *Bonnie and Clyde,* the innovations it introduced have hardened into obligatory conventions; many of the new, "free" films are as impersonal, as subservient to convention and cliché as the Preminger films of the 1950s or the studio films of the 1930s. These conventions of the new cinema can be assembled easily into a list.

First, the protagonists of the films are social misfits, deviates, or outlaws; the villains are the legal, respectable defenders of society. The old bad guys have become the good guys; the old good guys are now the bad guys. The surprising element in *Bonnie and Clyde* (and *Easy Rider, Cool Hand Luke, Butch Cassidy and the Sundance Kid, Thieves Like Us,* et cetera.) was not simply that the protagonists were criminals, for films had had their Little Caesars, Scarfaces, and Bonnie Parkers for years. The surprise was that these new murderers were also charming, warm, loving, compassionate, good-humored. The pursuers with badges were inevitably the humorless, inhuman ones. Given the outlaw protagonists, the new obligatory ending is the unhappy rather than happy one. The protagonists die; law triumphs over lawlessness. However, good does not triumph over evil, for law and good are antithetical.

The crucial thing about the new antihero heroes is not that they die, since death is inevitable, but that they have lived as they have—free, unchained, unswervingly true to themselves. Ironically, despite this reversal of moral values, the American film is still essentially romantic and Manichean, just as it was in the 1920s and 1930s. There are still film characters who live profoundly beautiful lives and others who live profoundly vile ones—even if the definitions of beauty and vileness have changed. Even in those films that strive for the European ambivalence—*The Last Picture Show, Thieves Like Us, They Shoot Horses, Don't They?, Five Easy Pieces*—there is still an idealization of love.

Second, the new American cinema does not ask to be taken as reality but constantly announces that it is artificial. Rather than effacing the film's artfulness, as a Ford or Hawks intentionally did, the new directors throw in as many cinematic tricks as possible, which both intensify the film's moods and remind the audience that it is watching a film. Slow motion, freeze-frames, jump-cutting, mixtures of black-and-white and color are all standard, indeed obligatory tricks of the new trade. This deliberate artificiality has several consequences.

The first is that there is an emotional power in the visual assaults of the medium itself. The viewer responds not just to a story and people but to the physical stimulation of eye and ear for its own sake. One of the advantages the film enjoys over television is that its big screen is more hypnotic, its stereophonic sound more overwhelming. And it is not interrupted by commercials. In McLuhanesque terms, television is much cooler than the films, more distant from its viewers who necessarily remain more detached. The new American films take even further advantage of their "hotness" by using color and the wide screen almost exclusively. A second consequence of the film trickery is the emphasis of the films as emotional metaphors rather than as literal stories. The quick cutting, the flashes both forward and backward in time (sometimes confusingly interwoven) totally destroy the definitions of time and space, of now and then, of reality and fantasy, purposely emphasizing emotional continuity at the expense of linear continuity.

Third, the new films play as trickily with sound as they do with images. Gone is the old principle of studio scoring—to underscore a scene with music that increases the action's emotional impact without making the viewer aware of the music's existence. This early principle of film scoring was a clear extension of the piano's function in the nickelodeon. In the new films, there is little of this kind of background music. If there is to be music it must be either clearly motivated (i.e., playing on a radio or record player nearby) or deliberately artificial (a song on the sound track that exists specifically to be noticed and plays either in harmony or in counterpoint with the sequence's visuals). In *Butch Cassidy and the Sundance Kid* (1969), the story stops for an idyllic ride on a bicycle accompanied by a pleasant Burt Bacharach rock tune. In *Medium Cool* (1969), the patriotic speeches and songs inside the Democratic Convention hall accompany the riots between students and police in Grant Park. The sound track of *Thieves Like Us* (1973) is a compendium of 1930s radio broadcasts, serving to show how central the radio was to American life in that era, saturating the film with "period color," and often commenting ironically (for example, an install-ment of "Gang Busters" during a bank robbery or a radio version of *Romeo and Juliet* during a love scene) on the action.

Some sequences in the new films distort sound purposely (for exam-ple, *The Conversation*, 1974, whose subject is sound recording); others are completely silent, contrasting with the other sequences of song or noise. The new constant of film music is that no longer are scores written by Alfred Newman, Miklos Rozsa, or Max Steiner and performed by the studio's symphony orchestra. Rock and jazz composers write the new film scores and the most popular rock groups perform them. The new films use rock music heavily (the score of *Easy Rider* is a sampler of a dozen different rock hits), for rock music is the other artistic and social passion of the young audiences who now support the movies.

The danger of any set of popular conventions is that the director will substitute conventionality and surface effects for originality and get away with it because his audiences won't be able to tell the difference. A few sequences of quick cutting and rock music will add enough zip to a static, talky, pretentiously symbolic film like Frank and Eleanor Perry's *Last Summer* (1969) to hide the picture's essential dishonesty and deadness. Slick cutting, extreme deep-focus photography, and brilliant scoring will hide the fact that the cops-and-robbers story of Peter Yates's *Bullitt* (1968) is not only thin but unfathomable. A leaden film like Peter Bogdanovich's *What's Up, Doc?* (1972) believes it can get laughs by shoving a number of social stereotypes and a lot of references to other movies down an audi-ence's throat. Of course even the purely flashy, purely surface new film can generate enough excitement, vitality, and visual surprise to entertain. Rich-ard Fleischer's *The Boston Strangler* (1968), for example, flavors a rather arid journalistic study of psychopathology with split-screen effects that add genuine visual interest by showing three different points of view—the stran-gler's, the victim's, the observer's—simultaneously.

The new cinema in America has become self-consciously concerned with style—with visual texture, a careful attention to the dress, decor, and dialects of the historical era (usually from America's recent past), with a specific use of the camera and sound track to capture and mirror that au-thenticity. The days of sound-stage shooting have passed; directors prefer the naturalness and authenticity of shooting on location. Whereas the old Hollywood style was devoted to eliminating the imperfections of reality—graceless rooms, uneven lighting, uncontrollable noise—the new American films require accident and imperfection for their visual style and human credibility. This demand for authenticity is the result of the conversion of the American cinema to a uniquely European cinema value—to render the experiential texture of a human event. The new films do not depict action so much as how the action *feels*, so that character rather than plot has become the dominant interest. In the manner of Godard's *Breathless* or Truffaut's *Jules and Jim,* the American films capture and develop the feelings of people passing through an event or process. In many ways, the new American films seem as influenced by the Czechs as the French, for in their attempts to transfer the world of internal sensations to an audience, *Five Easy Pieces* (1971), *Thieves Like Us, The Conversation,* and *The Last Detail* (1974) feel like Czech films. Of course, one of the American film industry's claims is that it now makes better "European" pictures than the Europeans, so that American theatres screen fewer and fewer European films each year. On the other hand, the new American films have been losing their devoted audiences in Europe, who seem to prefer the more external, exuberant, and active old American movie.

However Europeanized the fourth American era has become, it still maintains its old inclination toward rigid genres and repetitive cycles. Producers still feel safer with a formula that has succeeded before, and so a series of films about compassionate thieves followed *Bonnie and Clyde,* a series of films about the last assertive gasp of the old frontier followed *The Wild Bunch,* a series of violent police-chase films followed *The French Connection,* a series of Mafia films followed *The Godfather,* et cetera. Despite their new experiential and stylistic commitments, the new films are descendants of the old genres: the western, the gangster, the *policier,* the screwball comedy, and so on. The basic generic division in the new films, however, is that between city films and country films. Those two metaphors for American culture—the cement canyons of New York and its other modern cities; the mountain canyons of the Great West—have become the dominant images of the American film.

The city films, which inevitably examine the harried and hurried quality of American city life, are dependent on the imagery of the city: hard, close, flat, artificial, cold. (Stone and neon.) Many of the city films develop a thematic opposition between the unnaturalness and brutality of the city compared with the freedom and openness outside the city. Such new films, however, are clearly descendants of the old *films noirs* of the transitional era (the toughness of living and growing up in "the big city"), which were themselves descendants of the reporter pictures (tough reporters were indigenous to the big city) of the Studio Era. Close cousins to the city films, thematically as well as geographically, are the suburb films—such as, *The Graduate* (1968), *Bob and Carol and Ted and Alice* (1969), and *Goodbye, Columbus* (1969). Appropriately, two of these three films use Los Angeles, that city of suburbs, as its setting and metaphor. Even those films that do not assail the inhumanity of the city or suburb have taken advantage of shooting in Manhattan, using its real settings and gifted actors for the same natural, off-beat feeling that the British realist films evoked from London, Manchester, and Birmingham: *A Thousand Clowns* (1965), *A Fine Mad-*

ness (1966), *You're a Big Boy Now* (1967), *Up the Down Staircase* (1967), *The Producers* (1968), *The Night They Raided Minsky's* (1968), *Popi* (1969), *The French Connection* (1972), to name just a few.

The new, "experiential" western—for example, Sam Peckinpah's *The Wild Bunch* (1969), George Roy Hill's *Butch Cassidy and the Sundance Kid* (1969), Robert Altman's *McCabe and Mrs. Miller* (1972)—reveals the internalization and sensualization of a previously external and active genre. For Hawks, the West was a place where a man proved his toughness in order to survive; for Ford, the West was a place where man brought civilization and order to savagery and desert. For the new films, the West, the vast plains and deserts, are the last outposts of the free spirit of man and the original pioneer spirit of America. Just as the city films need the country for contrast, the country films need the city—the place where sheriffs and policemen and businessmen reside. Both *The Wild Bunch* and *Butch Cassidy* are set in an era when the Old West was crumbling, when the city's values were swallowing the country's. The heroes of both films prefer to remain happy anachronisms rather than surrender to "decency" and the machine. The inevitable sections in slow motion in these new westerns exist to heighten, lyricize, and magnify the moment of death, in effect turning that moment into a prolonged sensual experience. If the new western differs from the old one it is not because it is more violent; plenty of men were shot dead in old westerns. But in the old western the audience merely saw a man shot dead; the emotional effect came from the suspense before the shooting (who will win the gunfight, when, and how?) and the relief after it. The new western turns the moment of death itself into the emotional experience.

The new gangster film mirrors the same basic generic division between past and present, city and country. The crime films either concern themselves with rural gangsters of the past or urban gangsters of the present or near-present. The country-crime genre is essentially a subgenre of the new western. Whereas the protagonists of the western depend on their horses, the central figures of *Bonnie and Clyde* and *Thieves Like Us* use the automobile as their means of slicing through the open prairies. Contrasted with the happy freedom of Bonnie and Clyde is a nation of economic slaves, the hungry and the poor who are victims of a political system that dwarfs people and undermines their lives with its Depressions. Contrasted with the happy freedom of Bowie, Masefield, and Chickesaw is the boring banality of middle-class drawing rooms and dinner tables, lives that are so tawdry and dull that those corny radio shows serve as their only glimpse of a more exciting existence.

A synthesis of past and present, city and country, gangster and cowboy exists in the idealization of sky, plain, and mountain in *Easy Rider*; the horse has now become the motorbike; civilization is personified by the small-town bigots, the county sheriff, institutionalized love (a New Orleans whorehouse), institutionalized fun (Mardi Gras), and institutionalized death (an immense cemetery). But even the free and romantic West is being sullied; a commune of transposed, hip city kids feels as much hostility toward the two easy riders as the "straight" bigots in the towns and city. The only freedom, the only joy is being on the road itself, and even that, as the film's ending shows, can never be enjoyed for long.

Whereas the country-crime films tend toward a softness and slowness, softening human brutality and luxuriating in the luminous beauty of nature, the city-crime films are hard, fast, and cold. If the slow-motion death sequence is obligatory in the western and country-crime film, the breathlessly rapid and assaultive chase is obligatory in the city-crime and police films. The essential technical tool of the city film is editing rather than composition as in the country films, and the basic subjective device is the violent rushing of the traveling or hand-held camera, rather than the subjective prolongation of an event in slow motion. Cops in the city-crime films (*The French Connection; The New Centurions*, 1972; *Serpico*, 1973) usually face two sources of tensions: within themselves (are they just doing their job or are they neurotically driven to violence and sadism?) and within their own departments (the pressures of politicians, bureaucrats, and incompetents). The *film noir* of the transitional era (for example, Lang's *The Big Heat*) is a truly transitional link between the detective films of the Studio Era (in which the cop fought crime) and of the new era (in which a cop fights himself and cops fight each other). The new focus of the gangster city films is less on the push to the top and the inevitable fall (*Little Caesar* or *Scarface*) and more on the mundane problems of living legitimately once having reached the top (the conflict between the old life of crime and the new respectability in *The Godfather*).

The new American cinema is not a shift in direction so much as a new use of the traditional themes and images of American literature and American film. Instead of the indoor, studio-built, glamorized, dialogue-centered films of the first thirty years of sound, the new films prefer to go outdoors, to real locations rather than staying on sets; they emphasize the kinetic effects of film as movement, picture, music, rather than as well-made, logical story. The old story of John not being able to get Jane because her parents object to him has been replaced by the complication that he cannot get her because he has had an affair with her mother and because he detests the values of Jane's world. The "swinging" married couple of Nick and Nora Charles has been replaced by the swinging Bob and Carol and Ted and Alice. But the best new American films are like those that have always been best—a unified blend of story (now pared down in the quantity of incident), human insight (now carefully textured in the quality of an experience), thematic vision (now more ambivalent in its moral positions), and cinematic style (now more intrusive and idiosyncratically stylized than ever).

Like the film industries of Europe and Japan, the American cinema has become a director's cinema, granting the proven director a higher measure of control over the scripting (he, like the European director, is often listed as one of the screenwriters), cutting, and production decisions, allowing him more freedom in selecting his projects, and essentially valuing his contribution more than Hollywood ever did in its Studio Era. The American director has become one of the film's stars, and it is significant that many directors can make films now without any major star at all (*The Last Picture Show, Thieves Like Us*), an unheard of practice for major films until 1968 (and Kubrick's *2001*). When François Truffaut in France and Andrew Sarris in America developed the *"auteur* theory" (or *auteur* policy), they did so as a means of distinguishing directorial individuality in the Studio Era, since individuality was often buried beneath the decisions of producers and the scripts of the scenario department. But the new American *auteur* is a film author in the full sense of a Truffaut, Fellini, Bergman, Forman, or Kurosawa—the man who controls the responsibility for the entire project so that his own personal vision and visual style get recorded on film.

The list of these new *auteurs* which follows is necessarily tentative. The American directors who now seem most interesting and most important are all very young; all of them are in mid-career; perhaps none of them has made the masterpiece that fulfills the general promise of his talent and craft (no *Citizen Kane, Breathless,* or *Jules and Jim* among the juvenilia). But all of them have made a cluster of films that reveal both a high level of creativity and imagination as well as a consistency of style and vision.

Peter Bogdanovich is the new American *auteur* who is most influenced by the *auteur* theory and its application to the old Hollywood movie. Like many of the New Wave French directors, Bogdanovich began as a film critic, his favorite subjects being those lesser known studio directors (Raoul Walsh, Allan Dwan) whose individuality and consistency had not been previously appreciated. Bogdanovich's first film, *Targets* (1968), in many ways his cleverest, is a film buff's film, taking its style from the Roger Corman Technicolor-terror *genre* (of which Bogdanovich is also an advocate and admirer), complete with Boris Karloff as its star. Bogdanovich also plays a role in the film: a young director who is making a horror film with Karloff as its star (Bogdanovich cast himself as a director of a film-within-a-film before Truffaut did in *Day For Night*). The point of Bogdanovich's film-within-a-film is that he can use it to examine the real horrors of American life; juxtaposed with the making of Karloff's "horrific" movie is the story of a clean-cut, good-looking, all-American boy who goes quietly berserk and turns sniper, randomly shooting strangers with his high-powered rifle. The film climaxes magnificently in a drive-in theatre (a center of middle-American values) with the premiere of the Karloff horror film (no Grauman's Chinese for this kind of film). While the Karloff film-within-a-film spins its web of "monstrous horrors," the boy sits behind the screen performing genuine horrors: picking off people one by one as they sit in their cars, totally unaware of the real horror around them because their windows are rolled up (as they inevitably are in a drive-in theatre). They sit hermetically sealed in their own little cages, totally cut off from one another, mesmerized by the fake horror on the screen. The film indicts the sterile and false values of middle-class American life as the real cause of social horrors—beings so nurtured on the puritanical pap that they "vomit" it by indulging in nihilistic orgies. But Bogdanovich, always the buff, also enjoys such caprices as evoking the memory of those two Hitchcock films with similar titles—*Sabotage* and *Saboteur*—that juxtapose movie murders with real ones.

For *The Last Picture Show* (1971) and *Paper Moon* (1973) Bogdanovich re-creates the dry, dusty aridity of America's rural past—of the 1950s and 1930s respectively. He also uses the textures of American films of those decades, in particular his radical decision to use black-and-white. Because both audiences and television packaging prefer color, Bogdanovich is one of the only American directors since 1966 (*Who's Afraid of Virginia Woolf?*) who has dared to make a major film in monochrome, a sign of his concern for absolute tonal and visual authenticity—and another parallel with Truffaut (*The Wild Child*). The danger of Bogdanovich's pure universe of art is clear in *What's Up, Doc?* (1972) and *At Long Last Love* (1975), heavy-handed and empty attempts to combine 1930s musical and screwball comedy with contemporary wide-screen, color, and star values. If there is a personal commitment in Bogdanovich other than to old movies it would be to the old American cliché of love—of warm, compassionate, sincere human interaction—as the source of redemption from life's loneliness and tawdriness.

To some extent the same is true of Robert Altman. Altman's major concern is to study very bizarre people with very bizarre lives: the military medics in *M*A*S*H* (1970), the boy who wants to become a bird and fly in *Brewster McCloud* (1971), the incompetent gunslinger and the drug-addict dance-hall girl in *McCabe and Mrs. Miller* (1971), the bizarre life-style of Philip Marlowe in *The Long Goodbye* (1973), the thieves who want to rob enough banks so they can settle down to respectable, middle-class lives in *Thieves Like Us* (1974), the clumsy gamblers in *California Split* (1974). One of the consistently attractive traits for Altman is the sheer incompetence of his less-than-heroic heroes. Altman's gift is his ability to make these bizarre folks seem completely normal, familiar, and comprehensible, primarily by capturing moments of absolutely convincing interrelationships between them. The films excel not in their stories (which tend to be somewhat wandering) but in the compelling authenticity of their individual moments—of uproarious laughter, of drunkenness, of the camaraderie of men, of the potential informality and humor in a love scene, of the starkness and loneliness of the moment of death. In his visual style, Altman has begun to cultivate a hazy, gauzy look for his period films (as opposed to Bogdanovich's dry dustiness), as if they were shot through a very soft and gentle fog. (An unfortunate experiment in this direction was the sound track of *McCabe and Mrs. Miller,* which was so intentionally fuzzy it was often unintelligible). In this respect, Altman's first film, *That Cold Day in the Park* (1969), a study of sexual repression that was remarkable only for its pervasive atmosphere of rain, mist, damp, and cold, is more typical of his later work than the more exuberant *M*A*S*H.* When one thinks of Altman landscapes, the sterility of the Astrodome (*Brewster McCloud*), the coldness of snow (*McCabe and Mrs. Miller*), and the mistiness of early morning dew (the opening scene of *Thieves Like Us*) come instantly to mind.

Francis Ford Coppola splits his time between big commercial projects (*Finian's Rainbow,* 1968; *The Godfather* I and II, 1972 and 1974) and small personal ones (*You're a Big Boy Now,* 1967; *The Conversation,* 1974). The big projects allow Coppola to exercise his craft, in particular his abilities as a script writer (he has even written scripts for films he has not directed); they also provide him with the money to make his own films as well as to run his own American Zoetrope studio in San Francisco. *The Conversation,* with its clever use of sound as both the central subject and the dominant stylistic device of the film, with its furtive and recurring *cinéma vérité* sequences shot in Union Square that are an exact visual equivalent of the sound-recording process, with its effective settings (the modern, barren, absolutely impersonal and Kafkaesque office building; the matter-of-fact detail of the commercial exposition displaying the newest products for snooping and bugging) was perhaps the first of his films to reveal Copolla's social conscience and intellectual consciousness. One might see the film's theme as the clash between a person's craft and his moral conscience, the pure devotion to artisanship as opposed to the moral responsibilities of engaging in any business that affects the lives of other human beings. One might also see the film as a mirror of Coppola's own dilemma as a film director who has perhaps been more the craftsman than the human being.

Coppola also "pays his dues" by helping younger filmmakers. George Lucas made his terrifying view of a sterile and repressive future, *THX 1138* (1971), and his affectionate view of the recent rock-and-roll past, *American Graffiti* (1973), with the aid of Coppola's advice, money, and American Zoetrope studio.

William Friedkin is the purest and most impersonal technician of the new directors, a man who sees each project as a specific tactical problem to be solved and who then proceeds to solve it in a dazzling way. Among the problems he has posed himself are the translating of talky stage plays into cinematic terms (*The Birthday Party*, 1968; *The Boys in the Band*, 1969); capturing the texture and flavor of the old burlesque houses, customers, and performers (*The Night They Raided Minsky's*, 1968); translating the violence of urban police life into visual terms (*The French Connection*, 1971); bringing the devil to the screen with convincing and terrifying effectiveness (*The Exorcist*, 1973). Friedkin's solutions are as eclectic as the problems themselves: developing the human texture of *Boys in the Band*; exercising great care with atmosphere and color textures in *Minsky's*; editing *French Connection* with overwhelming dexterity and virtuosity; employing perhaps the most disturbingly agonizing sound track ever made for *The Exorcist*. Friedkin described his own intention in all his films as that of producing powerful but crude emotional effects—terror, tension, suspense. Of all the newer directors he would have been most comfortable in the Studio Era.

There are several other directors who, just two or three years ago, seemed much more important than they do in 1975—a further warning about the ephemerality of directorial reputations and the difficulty of assessing artists in mid-career. Mike Nichols (*Who's Afraid of Virginia Woolf?*; *The Graduate*; *Catch-22*, 1971; *Carnal Knowledge*, 1972; *The Day of the Dolphin*, 1973), a very successful director of Neil Simon comedies on the stage, seems to prove with every film that he is very good at observing human beings during off-beat, comic scenes of dialogue and very weak at everything else to do with cinema. Arthur Penn is a director of the old school (*The Miracle Worker*, 1962) who came to the films from television dramas and has tried to convert to the new school. His dominant interest seems to be the creation of folk legends out of outlaws or off-beat social rebels (*The Left-Handed Gun*, 1958; *Bonnie and Clyde*; *Alice's Restaurant*, 1969; *Little Big Man*, 1971), and his dominant weakness seems to be a clumsy visual sense and intellectual equipment that is not equal to its aspirations (as in the pretentious fiasco of *Mickey One*, 1964, as well as the tendencies toward overstatement and pretentiousness in *Left-Handed Gun* and *Little Big Man*). Sam Peckinpah, who also came to the films from television, is probably the most talented of these directors (he certainly has the strongest visual sense) who have been eclipsed, if only temporarily, by a younger generation. Peckinpah's three best films study the crumbling old men (an aged Randolph Scott and Joel McCrea) who personify the crumbling free spirit of the Old West (*Ride the High Country*, 1962), the inevitability of violence in human experience and the necessity of a man's defining his relation to it (*Straw Dogs*, 1971), or both (*The Wild Bunch*). Peckinpah falls back on a series of predictable mannerisms which show through blatantly in his bad films, which are as bad as the others are good (*Major Dundee*, 1965; *The Ballad of Cable Hogue*, 1970; *Pat Garrett and Billy the Kid*, 1973): plodding, indeed incoherent (dis)continuity; gratuitous slow-motion violence; mannered treatment of existential assertion in the face of cosmic meaninglessness.

The two emerging *auteurs* of comic films, Woody Allen and Mel Brooks, have much in common with each other and with the noncomic directors. Both Allen and Brooks make style pieces that use the movies themselves as their source material, parodying the conventions, motifs, situations, and characters of movies of the past. Allen's films, however, are more scattered, more surreal, more topical, more sociological, and probably more perceptive than Brooks's. Woody Allen is like Mack Sennett in several respects: lots of jokes that come very fast; if one joke doesn't work there's another right behind it; an almost pure surrealism of pace, incoherency, and illogic. Like Mack Sennett, Allen does not make good films but good moments. In *Take the Money and Run* (1968), *Bananas* (1971), *Everything You Always Wanted to Know About Sex . . .* (1972), and *Sleeper* (1973), Allen's technique, like Sennett's, is truly flip, in two senses. First, it is casual and flippant, taking nothing as serious or sacred (racial and religious stereotypes, political philosophies, politicians, intellectuals, revolutions, conformity, cultural crazes, sexuality, psychology, et cetera), especially the making of the movie itself. He is also flip in that he leaps from gag to gag with astonishing rapidity, often wearing the audience (and his ideas) out before the end of the film and often establishing funny situations that he fails to develop (two dangers of flipping). The multilevels of the best Woody Allen sequences, however, combine film parody, psychological observation, sociological analysis, topical commentary, and an awareness of sexual fears and ploys into moments that are as funny and as perceptive as anything in American comedy since Preston Sturges. Mel Brooks (*The Producers*, 1968; *The Twelve Chairs*, 1970; *Blazing Saddles*, 1973; *Young Frankenstein*, 1975) is more coherent, more systematic in exhausting the specific conventions of a genre, and more dependent on a single kind of stereotyping and a single kind of joke. The moment when the cowboys finally ride out of the western movie and into the movie-making process itself in *Blazing Saddles* is a welcome relief, but one wonders if Brooks would have attempted the irrational without a Woody Allen as an example.

Perhaps the most important American filmmaker of the last decade is Stanley Kubrick, who is completely detached from the newest fashions of the American cinema because he has detached himself from America. (Like Henry James, Kubrick could be claimed as either an American or English artist. Also like James, but unlike his co-expatriate directors, Richard Lester and Joseph Losey, Kubrick's work remains rooted in American values and culture.) Kubrick had been making "new" movies for years before they became the fashion (which has caught up with him). Kubrick, a perfectionist who, like Welles and Bresson, controls every detail of the film himself, from scripting to cutting, works very slowly. His reputation rests on only five films: *Paths of Glory* (1957), *Lolita* (1962), *Dr. Strangelove: Or How I Learned to Stop Worrying and Love the Bomb* (1964), *2001: A Space Odyssey* (1968), and *A Clockwork Orange* (1972). Kubrick's early films, *Fear and Desire* (1953), *Killer's Kiss* (1955), and *The Killing* (1956), are melodramatic potboilers, obvious apprentice work; and on *Spartacus* (1960), Kubrick was more doctor than director, having been brought in by Kirk Douglas to help save an immobile and over-stuffed patient.

Kubrick films are unpopular with American critics. In none of the films is there a successful, fulfilling love relationship; there is something cold, sterile, and dead about the Kubrick world. Kubrick has also been attacked for being a pure craftsman and a careful imitator of other men's cinematic styles. *Paths of Glory* undeniably recalls the elegant, polite, hypocritical world of Renoir's *Grand Illusion* combined with the Germanic camera movement of Murnau and Pabst. The back-lit, shadowy, up-angle photography of *Dr. Strangelove* irresistibly recalls *Citizen Kane*. But Kubrick's work does not borrow from the work of Renoir and Welles so much as echo it, in the same way that Lester echoes Sennett or Godard echoes the Bogart films. Like Renoir and Welles, Kubrick begins with a deep thematic conviction and a refusal to compromise in developing that conviction.

The essential Kubrick theme is man's love affair with death. Kubrick seems to be a social critic in that his films consistently rip apart the hypocrisies of polite society: the military society of World War I France, the pseudo-intellectual society of suburbia, the political society of the White House and Pentagon, the scientific society that can develop rockets that fly to the moon but cannot keep nations from warring with one another, the sterilized banality of a society of the future. As with Renoir, Kubrick's social evils are human evils; men created society, not the other way around. Human society and humanness are antithetical and yet life is so constituted that human life is paradoxically impossible without human society and impossible with it. Without a society men slaughter each other individually as they do in "The Dawn of Time" sequence in *2001* after the first ape-man discovers how to use a weapon. With society men slaughter each other *en masse* under the pretext of military justice or the necessities of war and national defense.

Kubrick's great cinematic gift is not just his ability to develop this bitterly ironic theme, but his gift for finding the perfect ironic tone—part horror, part humor, a mixture of burlesque and Grand Guignol—for developing it. The historical parallel for Kubrick's tone is again Renoir and his bitterly satiric human comedy of manners, *The Rules of the Game*. No native American director except Kubrick has been able to handle social satire without turning it into a pie-throwing farce. Although several of Kubrick's characters do indeed throw pies, the cold, hard intellectual edge of Kubrick's satirical knife never lets the sad farce become silly farce. Kubrick's taste is for understatement, and it is understatement that separates satire and farce, a lesson that Kramer, Preminger, Jerry Lewis, Clive Donner, Richard Lester, and Blake Edwards have never learned. An example of the Kubrick touch is in *2001* when an American officer needs to use the toilet in a space ship. Kubrick gives us a single shot of the man studying an incredibly long list of directions for relieving himself in a nongravity toilet. Another director might have zoomed in to the instructions in close-up or somehow underlined the absurdity of a man needing instructions to perform a natural function. Instead, Kubrick merely gives us a ten-second medium-distance shot, no underlining, no emphasizing. We draw our own ironic conclusions.

Dr. Strangelove is the most perfect expression of the Kubrick theme and the Kubrick tone. The film begins with an audacious visual joke. Two jet planes, one refueling the other, look exactly like two human bodies copulating. Kubrick emphasizes the gag by photographing the coupled planes from various "loving" angles and underscoring the planes' passion with a lush, romantic version of the syrupy popular tune, "Try a Little Tenderness." The pornographic joke is more than joke. The whole film synthesizes copulation and murder. The American general, Buck Turgidson (George C. Scott), acts the same in the bedroom with his sweetie as he does in the war room discussing the bomb crisis. The crazed army commander, Jack Ripper, develops his whole theory about the Commies attacking his "precious bodily fluids" with fluoridated water because he cannot make it sexually with the ladies anymore. The American pilots in the atomic bomber work feverishly to drop their bomb on the Rooskies, despite the fact that the plane has been critically damaged. When they finally succeed in dropping it, the plane's commander (Slim Pickens) rides the bomb down to his destruction, whooping like a cowboy on a bronco, the bomb looking exactly like a surrogate phallus.

The ultimate symbol of man's romance with death is Dr. Strangelove himself, the "converted" Nazi scientist who still delights in the means of mass murder and who, despite his platitudinous respect for American democracy, cannot keep his arm from rising into an instinctive "Sieg heil." The film ends as it began, with a romantic orgy performed by death-dealing machines. The bombs explode in hypnotizingly beautiful rhythms and slow motion; as they explode, the saccharine female voice of Vera Lynn sings her optimistically romantic tune of the 1940s, "We'll Meet Again: Don't know where, don't know when." Don't know how.

Kubrick's virtuosity as a stylist tempted him into adapting two essentially unadaptable literary style pieces—Vladimir Nabokov's *Lolita* and Anthony Burgess's *A Clockwork Orange*. Both of the novels are totally dependent on a virtuoso's manipulation of language; Kubrick turned both into films with many remarkable moments and sections, but both films ultimately fail to reproduce the complexity of the original works. And for the same reason. Both novels use a first-person narrator; both narrators use language in a bizarrely abnormal and idiosyncratic way (Humbert Humbert's effusive, rhapsodic intellectualizations; Alex's private argot, Nadsat); and both novels use such unique language because this language *is* the mind of the narrator, the way he sees the world, and that narrator's mind *is* the subject of the book. That mind is not Kubrick's subject (or interest), and in losing the central intelligence of both novels Kubrick loses the essence of both original works.

But he makes some interesting substitutions. In *Lolita* there is Kubrick's deliciously vicious satire of suburban pseudo-intellectualism (Shelley Winters's terrible stabs at French, terrible pretentions to "Kulchah," and terribly clumsy and banal sexuality) and the quirkily hilarious impersonations of Peter Sellers as Claire Quilty (an almost invisible character in the novel whose best scene in the film, a bizarre ping-pong duel with Humbert Humbert, also does not exist in the novel). In *A Clockwork Orange* there is a spectacularly balletic violence in the teenage orgies of destruction, and hilarious satiric comedy in both the callous reduction of sex to a slapstick horse race (the brilliantly funny accelerated-motion seduction scene) and the tawdriness of Alex's parents' sterile bourgeois home. Kubrick's dominant concerns—social violence, social satire, and social sterility—pull the original psychological novels in interesting but more superficial directions.

To some extent, the same is true of *2001: A Space Odyssey,* which is really two films, one mystical, one cynical, which do not always harmonize with each other very well. On the one hand, Kubrick's astronauts travel toward the meaning of life itself, the life force that has specifically planted metal slabs on the earth at the "dawn of time" and on the moon to inform itself of man's progress. The traveler's discovery (and, through the subjective aid of Cinerama, our discovery) is that physical life merely is—birth, aging, death—but that the soul journeys perpetually in the void of space until the life mystery again requires its services. This metaphysical theme remains fuzzy and elusive in the film; the metal slabs never receive adequate explanation, and the force behind the slabs is not developed at all.

On the other hand, the film's social and human commentary is quite clear, a satirical study of a race that can improve its machines and weapons but not its mind and instincts. The first tool that the ape-man discovers becomes a weapon. When man travels to the moon he takes his capitalistic establishments with him—Pan Am, Howard Johnson's, Bell Telephone. He also takes his nationalistic prejudices and loyalties, not being free to discuss scientific problems with his colleagues from other countries. And when he builds super machines—the computer, Hal—he builds them with his own weaknesses. Hal is a superbrain; he also kills. Despite the tensions in the film's two quests, it remains one of the most intelligent "big" films ever made: always intriguing, often breathtaking, careful both in attention to detail and to the thematic reason for making the film in the first place. It took Kubrick five years to make it.

The Independent American Cinema

The Independent American Cinema has been called by many names: the American Underground, the American Avant-Garde, The New American Cinema, the Experimental American Cinema among them. By whatever name, another cinema tradition has existed in the United States since the 1940s with a series of assumptions that differ markedly from those of the commercial American cinema. This cinema is highly personal and individual (often one person literally makes the entire film); it has no commercial aspirations or even value (these films rarely play in theatres where one must buy a ticket to see them); and it is necessarily revolutionary in structure, or visual technique, or intellectual attitude, or all three.

There are three conflicting critical attitudes about the Independent Cinema. For many, this cinema represents the narcissistic visual scribblings of the lunatic fringe, whose work is ultimately irrelevant to the development of serious film art (i.e. commercial, feature-length "art films"). In support of this position, it is probably true that a vast majority of American filmgoers has never even heard of the most respected Independent filmmakers. A second position finds the Independent Cinema a fertile testing ground for techniques and devices that are later absorbed, refined, and extended by the mainstream (i.e. commercial, feature-length "art films") of filmmaking. In support of this position one can point to the influence of the French avant-garde on the later features of Clair, Epstein, Renoir, and Buñuel (all of whom came out of the avant-garde), as well as the fact that so many of the stylistic devices and moral attitudes of the new commercial films (their sensuality, the use of slow motion, accelerated motion, shock cutting, split screen) were first seen in Independent films. Yet a third position finds the Independent American Cinema the only significant and serious works of film art in America today. In support of this position, they cite the fact that these are the only films totally free of commercial pressures, totally dependent on the vision of a single artist, and totally aligned with the parallel modernist movements in painting, music, and literature. The business of these Independent films is perception: the way the devices of an art can aid, extend, and complicate a human being's ability to perceive his inner and outer realities. That goal might be taken as the ultimate intention of all the modernist arts.

Rather than engage in this controversy of values, it would be useful simply to trace the history of this movement, to define its principles and principal types, and to mention the accomplishments of its most distinctive filmmakers. The tendency of the earliest avant-garde American films (in the 1920s and 1930s) was to avoid the Hollywood assumptions by making films of pure visual form, films that were, in effect, moving paintings that had no content except the visual content of forms in motion. Although Robert Florey and Slavko Vorkapich's *Life and Death of 9413—A Hollywood Extra* (1928) seems to protest against the facelessness and in humanity of the modern industrial system (it uses the movie business as its industry), it is really a series of expressionist paintings made to move combining the visual settings of the German expressionists (especially *Metropolis*) with the camera trickery of the French surrealists. Ralph Steiner's *H_2O* (1929), which is nothing but a series of images of light reflecting on water, begins with beautiful and recognizable images (say, industry), it is really a series of expressionist paintings made to move abstract, so that the shots of light and shimmering water cease to look like anything except waving abstractions (a sort of moving Mondrian or Pollock painting). Among the few early exceptions to this purely formal rule were Joseph Berne's sensitive *Dawn to Dawn* (1934) and Watson and Webber's sexually symbolic *Lot in Sodom* (1933).

The best early films of pure form, movement, rhythm, and (later) music were not made in America, however (except for the early Disney films, which share many of the assumptions of these form-films), but in Europe. In the silent era, Hans Richter and Viking Eggeling excelled in rhythmically moving forms that also manipulated the restrictions of black-and-white. For example, Richter's *Rhythmus 21* (1921) features a variety of kinds of rhythmic movement: rectangular shapes move about the screen; they change their sizes and shapes (expanding and contracting into lines, squares, trapezoids, and so forth); and they change their shades (shifting from white on black to black on white to grey on black, et cetera). In the 1930s, however, Len Lye in England and Oskar Fischinger in Germany developed the film of pure form and movement to its height by using color and by accompanying the dizzily spinning and changing forms with an appropriate musical background. In effect, these films became dances—the dance of color and shape.

The first important American filmmaker who perceived that a non-commercial, personal film could do something other than make a series of shapes dance around the screen was Maya Deren, a woman who combined her interest in dance, in voodoo, and in subjective, phenomenological psychology into a series of surreal perceptual films. *Meshes of the Afternoon* (1943) and *At Land* (1944) defy the continuity of space and time, erase the line between dream and reality, turn the entire vision of the film into the streaming consciousness of the filmmaker, who is herself the central performer in the films as well. She is both the mind behind the film and the body within it. *Meshes of the Afternoon* uses a series of repeating motifs—a shadow walking dreamily down a garden path, a rose, a key, a knife, attempts to mount a flight of stairs—that echo the use of similarly repeating motifs in *Last Year at Marienbad*, almost two decades later. Deren attacks objective reality by metamorphosizing the knife into the key, the rose into the knife, by making the act of climbing a flight of stairs seem an impossibly difficult and tortuous act (simply by her use of lenses, camera angles, and slow motion), by combining suggestions of chastity, sexuality, and death without the audience's ever being able to pull the complexly woven themes apart to make solid and coherent sense out of them. The motifs weave together musically rather than rationally, tangling the viewer in a systematic labyrinth of unresolvable resonances. As such, the film serves as a clear bridge between the surrealism of *Chien andalou* and the dream-realities of *Marienbad, Persona, 8½,* and *The Milky Way.*

Greatly influenced by Maya Deren, the American avant-garde began building itself into a movement in the mid-1950s—aided by the expanding availability of 8 and 16mm. equipment—with the emergence of the work of Stan Brakhage, Robert Breer, Shirley Clarke, Bruce Conner, Kenneth Anger, Gregory Markopoulos, Jonas Mekas, and the Kuchar brothers. Since that time, the Independent Cinema has tended to gravitate toward four vague but recognizable "genres": the formal, the social-satirical, the sexual, and the perceptual-psychological. As with the avant-garde French films of the 1920s, these categories were neither rigid nor mutually exclusive. A film devoted primarily to the visual effects of imaginatively dancing forms could imply a social and perceptual dimension (most notably Robert Breer's *Jamestown Baloos,* 1957, *Horse Over Teakettle,* 1962, and *Fist Fight,* 1964). A sexual film almost inevitably satirizes the assumed social values of normalcy (say, Kenneth Anger's *Scorpio Rising,* 1964). And many of the films devoted to visual perception necessarily devote themselves to dazzling manipulations of visual forms.

The film of pure form, one of the oldest experimental styles of cinema, persisted in the American Underground, much of it influenced by the earlier work of Fischinger and Lye. The outstanding formal dances are the computer films of John Whitney, who, like Fischinger, combines his ceaselessly moving color-forms with appropriate accompanying music (*Catalog*, 1961; *Permutations*, 1968; *Matrix*, 1971). Whitney's films differ from Fischinger's in being more precise and mathematical in their symmetrical visual forms (not surprising since those forms are being spun to symmetrical perfection by a computer) yet looser and freer in their music. (Fischinger used the elegance and precision of classical music—say, a Bach Brandenburg Concerto—while Whitney uses the more improvisatory jazz or Indian raga). Other films in the formal tradition include those of Jordan Belson (heavily influenced by both Fischinger and Whitney) and some of Robert Breer: *Blazes* (1958), which assaults and smashes the viewer with 24 different images per second (more an attack than a "dance"); *69* (1968), another sequence of cleverly evolving forms and colors. Scott Bartlett's *Offon* (1967) succeeds in turning more concrete referents (the eye, eyeball, human forms, a bird, a face) into purely kaleidoscopic forms in ceaseless motion, accompanied by *musique concrète*. Indeed, this form of modernist "music"—usually a rhythmic assemblage of various abstract sounds such as buzzing, scratching, grinding, whining, et cetera—is one of the primary accompaniments of the Underground films, especially the formal and perceptual ones.

Bruce Conner is the funniest of the social satirists; he is essentially an editor, and his best films (*A Movie*, 1958; *Cosmic Ray*, 1961) simply splice together existing stock footage to make their satirical point. Conner's point is that man is murderous, violent, destructive, and, ultimately, suicidal, conducting an assault against his fellow human beings and against nature itself that will eventually kill everyone. Conner supports his view in *A Movie* with pirated film footage of violence and destruction exclusively: planes dropping bombs and then diving to earth in a retributive burst of flames; Indians and cowboys on the warpath; tanks in battle; collisions of racing automobiles; the burning of the zeppelin; the collapse of a bridge; the detonation of the atomic bomb. Conner's movie implies that the business of the movies is the chronicling of catastrophe; he splices these catastrophes together with such rhythmic, repetitive, and rapid insistence that the impression of cataclysm is complete. Man is his machines (and the movie is also the product of a machine), and his machines produce death and disaster.

Equally satirical is Stan VanDerBeek's *Breathdeath* (1964), which combines his interest in collage and cartooning with his own apocalyptic vision of a society warring, breathing, and boring itself to death. Tom deWitt's *Atmosfear* (1967) is a satirical view of "pollution": of the air, of the landscapes (with ugly factories and smokestacks and architecture), of the cities (with repressive and restrictive signs), and, ultimately, of the mind. In this same satirical tradition are the films of James Broughton (*Mother's Day*, 1948; *Loony Tom, The Happy Lover*, 1951; *The Pleasure Garden*, 1954) and, more recently, Robert Nelson (*Confessions of a Black Mother Succuba*, 1965; *Oh Dem Watermelons*, 1965). An underlying theme of many of these satirical-social films is man's war with nature, and the filmmakers are quite convinced that unfortunately man is winning.

Yet another kind of satirical Underground film burlesques the business of movie-making aboveground (also an implication of the Bruce Conner films), for society's art mirrors society's values. The comical, usually "camp" films in this tradition are those of George and Mike Kuchar (*The Naked and the Nude*, 1957; *I Was a Teenage Rumpot*, 1960; *Pussy on a Hot Tin Roof*, 1961; and their *chef d'oeuvre*, *Sins of the Fleshapoids*, 1964) and some of the early films of Andy Warhol (*Tarzan and Jane Regained . . . Sort of*, 1963; *Harlot*, 1965). Warhol's two opposite interests —the sexual-sociological and the Hollywood Camp—continue to pull his films (including those directed by Paul Morrissey) in opposite directions. His more recent parody-Camp films are *Lonesome Cowboys*, 1968 (which might be subtitled, "What Cowpokes Really Did When They Slept Together Under the Stars"), *Heat*, 1973 (a "Sunset Boulevard Revisited"), and *Frankenstein*, 1974 (or "What You Always Wanted to See in a 3-D Movie But Never Did Until Now").

As can be seen from the Warhol films, the satirical Independent films are close cousins to the sexual ones, for in his studies of bizarre, inevitably "abnormal" sexuality, the Underground filmmaker often comments satirically on society's concepts of normalcy. The master in the field is Kenneth Anger, the son of a famous Hollywood agent of its Golden Age. The young Anger translated his Hollywood experiences into an outrageously scandalous book about Hollywood sexual practices, *Hollywood Babylon*, which includes such gossipy morsels as the "real" murder weapon in the Virginia Rappe murder case, the "real" reasons for the deaths of Thomas Ince, William Desmond Taylor, and Paul Bern (Jean Harlow's husband), and the various genital sizes of the Hollywood matinee idols. Anger's outrageousness also dominates his films, beginning with his first major work, *Fireworks* (1947), which he made when he was only fifteen. The film is clearly his own adolescent and masochistic fantasy, the story of a boy (played by Anger himself) who is picked up, beaten, and raped by three sailors, climaxing (literally and figuratively) with the image of a sailor's penis metamorphosizing into a Roman candle.

Fetishism and sado-masochism dominate Anger's most important film,

Scorpio Rising (1964), an examination of the practices, perversions, and paraphernalia of the motorcycle "man," his attachment to costume and symbol (chains, boots, belts, leather, levis, jacket), his idolization of Marlon Brando (in *The Wild One*) and James Dean (another motorcycle freak), and his tendencies toward the cosmic oppositions of mildness (personified by recurring shots of a kitschy Christ in film clips from hokey Biblical movies) and cruelty (personified by film clips and stills of Hitler). The motorcycle freak's adoration of the masculine external is clearly a literal cover-up of his homosexual essence, and Anger uses the sound-track to comment contrapuntally (and comically) on this gap between self and projected self-image. Popular rock-and-roll tunes of the era (in this sense a precursor of *Easy Rider*) dominate the sound track, and at one point, as the cyclist adoringly dons his *macho* levis, the song goes, "She Wore Blue Velvet." Anger's film is also important in that it served as the basis for one of the country's crucial obscenity test cases, first seized and then judged not obscene by the State of New York in 1965.

One of the famous sexual films that has not yet been thus exonerated is Jack Smith's *Flaming Creatures* (1963), an outrageous, funny, and violent attack on sexual definitions, propriety, and normalcy. Smith's friend, Ken Jacobs (*The Death of P'town*, 1961; *Blonde Cobra*, 1962; *Tom, Tom, the Piper's Son,* 1971), is also in the sexual-social-satirical tradition, as is the later Provincetown filmmaker John Waters (*Mondo Trasho*, 1971; *Pink Flamingos*, 1972). Some of Warhol's early work—in particular, *Blow Job* (1964), a thirty-minute reaction shot of the face of a man apparently receiving one—are not only attacks on normal and accepted sexual practices but also Warhol's attack on the normal definition of a movie.

The experimental films that examine psychological and visual perception are the most varied, the most complex, the most difficult, and, perhaps, the most important contributions of the Independent Cinema. They are also probably the least fun. Whereas the purely formal films are dazzling visual shows accompanied by pleasant music (usually lasting less than ten minutes), and the social and sexual films are funny but one-dimensionally iconoclastic, the perceptual films tend to be moodier, quieter, and longer (often over thirty minutes). The films are so varied in style, tone, and emphasis because the issue of perception has so many obvious variables: the ways that human beings perceive, the ways that the cinema perceives, the different levels and kinds of perception, and the inter-relationship of all three.

Stan Brakhage is the most lyrical, poetic, and humanistic of these perceptual filmmakers; his work lacks the bitterness and agony of so many of the other experimental films. His films are highly personal renderings of his own experiences (sexual experiences in *Flesh of Morning*, 1957, and *Wedlock House: An Intercourse,* 1959; the birth of his own child in *Win-*

dow Water Baby Moving, 1959) or of his interpretation of a child's experiences (*The Wonder Ring,* 1955; *Anticipation of the Night,* 1958; *Scenes from Under Childhood,* 1968). His feeling for the beauty of nature saturates his feature-length *Dog Star Man* (1964) as well as his *The Machine of Eden* (1969), which contains some of the most spectacularly beautiful natural scenery ever photographed. The film suggests that this beauty is the product of some mystical loom that has spun it out of some miraculous cloth, but it is clear that Brakhage's real "Eden Machine" is the camera, and the miraculous cloth is made of celluloid.

The work of Bruce Baillie is very different—more violent, more nervous, more spectacularly tricky. In films like *Mass* (1964), *Quixote* (1965), and *Castro Street* (1966), Baillie uses dizzying superimpositions, complicated split screens, a personal color symbolism all, in effect, to draw his own psychological and cultural map on film and to develop his own language in the process of doing so. Ed Emshwiller's *Relativity* (1966) is one of the most intellectual and visually effective of the perceptual films. Its goal is an examination of the term in its title on two levels: first, the relativity of time and space in human experience (large, small; long, short); second, the relativity of this human experience to the absolute infinity of time and space. Using camera movement, lenses, and his selection of photographic subjects brilliantly (as well as a terse but provocative factual narration), Emshwiller's *Relativity* is as fascinating to watch as to ponder.

Perhaps the most celebrated and controversial of the perceptual films is Michael Snow's *Wavelength* (1967), a fascinating and, at the same time, excruciatingly boring film that is nothing but a forty-five minute zoom shot of a single, empty room. Snow's is a structural film (one that uses either no editing at all or in which all the editing is done in the camera) that appears to be a single zoom beginning far away from a wall of windows, moving slowly (in fact, imperceptibly slow) yet steadily closer to the windows, eventually culminating in an extreme close shot of some pictures on the wall between the windows. In its lack of editing, the film is a reminder that an experimental film can experiment by using as much editing and camera trickery as possible or as little. The point of *Wavelength,* and of many structural films, is that if one keeps looking at the same thing long enough one sees that it is not the same thing at all— that it can change both its appearance and essence in our minds while remaining apparently the same to our eyes. Snow's long film is remarkable in its lulling us into believing that nothing is changing, only for us suddenly to "'wake up" and become aware that something has indeed changed. Except we cannot say precisely what, nor can we define the exact moment when we perceived that change. *Wavelength* is also a remarkable tease. It constantly suggests that something will come along to give it meaning: two girls in the room near the beginning of the film (who are they?); a man who collapses on the floor (dead? drunk? dead drunk?); a girl who makes a furtive telephone call (who is she?); the life and traffic outside the window (is that significant?); and, ultimately, those pictures on the wall (Surely they will provide an answer. They don't.). The sound track is a similar tease—the abstraction of *musique concrète* mixed with more coherent sounds (even some synchronized dialogue) which are no more communicative than the pure noise. *Wavelength* makes something out of nothing, and yet the something it makes is simply itself, which is nothing.

And a film like *Wavelength* once again raises the issue of the value and significance of the Independent American Cinema. On the one hand, a critic can respond to *Wavelength* with a "So what." Who needs an empty, boring nothing? On the other, the critic can find it one of the most perfect examples of the way the cinema can educate the viewer to perceive the mystery, instability, and neutrality of the physical universe around him.

Postscript

To summarize eighty years of film history in a few sentences is not only an impossible task, but one that would negate the detail of the rest of the book. To summarize the attitude that this book has taken toward that eighty-year history is less difficult. This short history has been a study of the great film minds, of those men who saw something very clearly and very deeply about human experience and who possessed the art and craft to translate what they saw into something that we could see. This has not been a history of film people—stars, producers, even directors—nor a history of film events—premieres, the founding of studios, the funerals of stars—nor even a history of great individual films. There have been no apocryphal stories of what Dorothy Parker said to Irving Thalberg or what Jean Harlow drank for breakfast. The book has studied the themes, the imaginations, the techniques, the visual qualities of those artists who might have become novelists or painters or poets but became filmmakers instead.

In these eighty years, most film directors have been merely typesetters, not poets. To find the artistic individuality, the creative intelligence, the "mind" at the center of most films is an impossible and artificial exercise. For this reason, this short history has also tried to call attention to those facts of film life that turn directors into typesetters. Who is the ultimate creator of a film? the director? the producer? the writer? the photographer? the editor? How independent is the film's creator (be he director or producer) from the demands of the audience on one hand and the demands of his creditors on the other? The shooting of a film is part plan, part accident, and part chaos. Thousands of people may contribute to the final product. The relationship of a director to his film is vastly different from the relationship of a poet to his sonnet. The facts of film production would seem to nullify the possibility of any film's unique and personal spirit and vision. And yet whole canons of films (not just individual accidents) by Griffith, Chaplin, Renoir, Bergman, Antonioni, and so forth reveal that a single artist's mind can be as clear, as consistent, and as compelling in the film form as in a canon of lyric poems. If one is to discuss the film as a work of art rather than as entertainment, as business, as societal mirror, or as manufacturer of the twentieth century's new royalty, one must discuss the minds who know how to create great films and how those minds work.

This particular kind of film history is itself indicative of critical and audience opinion about the movies in the 1970s. Never before have audiences been so conscious of the film as art; never have directors been so self-conscious of their work as art. Film study is now a liberal art. The new film journals (another clear sign of current cinema intellectualism) and film magazines feature interviews with directors as well as with stars. The directors have become stars. This new cinematic self-consciousness will have an impact on the films of the future as more and more people study both the aesthetics of film art and the techniques of film production. Since this self-conscious debt to film tradition has produced exciting films in the past—Vigo's, Clair's, Truffaut's, Godard's, Bogdanovich's—it should continue to produce exciting films in the future.

The excitement, the imagination, the inventiveness, the intelligence of moving pictures have never been so obvious as they are in the 1970s. The richness of the film past of the last eighty years may well be a prelude to the greater richness of the film future. The best films of the past have consistently blended an engaging narrative, insightful human relationships, a sincere and convincing intellectual vision, and a functional cinematic style. I expect that the best films of the future will do the same.

FOR FURTHER READING AND VIEWING

The books and films below, correlated with each chapter of the text, are intended to give the reader an idea of the extent of available material for further research. Neither the bibliography nor the list of films is exhaustive. In selecting films for each director, only a representative sample of his important work has been listed. Further, only those films that circulate in 16 mm. prints have been listed. Distributors others than those listed may handle a particular film; the most reliable guide to film distribution is the current catalogue published by each distributor. A list of the major distributors in 16 mm. with their addresses and telephone numbers follows at the end of the appendix.

1. General Histories of Film and Reference Works

Bardeche, Maurice, and Brasillach, Robert. *History of Motion Pictures*. New York: Norton, 1938.
Brownlow, Kevin. *The Parade's Gone By*. New York: Alfred Knopf, 1968.
Crowther, Bosley. *The Lion's Share*. New York: Dutton, 1967.
————. *The Great Films: Fifty Golden Years of Motion Pictures*. New York: G. P. Putnam's Sons, 1967.
Everson, William K. *The American Movie*. New York: Atheneum, 1963.
Fulton, Albert R. *Motion Pictures*. Norman, Oklahoma: Oklahoma University Press, 1960.

Griffith, Richard, and Mayer, Arthur. *The Movies*. New York: Simon and Schuster, 1970.
Halliwell, Leslie. *The Filmgoer's Companion*. Fourth Edition. New York: Hill and Wang, 1974.
Jacobs, Lewis. *The Rise of the American Film*. New York: Harcourt, Brace, 1939.
Knight, Arthur. *The Liveliest Art*. New York: New American Library, 1959.
Leprohon, Pierre. *Histoire du Cinéma*. Paris: Éditions du Cerf, 1961.
Macgowan, Kenneth. *Behind the Screen*. New York: Delacorte Press, 1965.
Manvell, Roger, general ed. *The International Encyclopedia of Film*. New York: Crown, 1972.
Ramsaye, Terry. *A Million and One Nights*. New York: Simon & Schuster, 1964.
Rotha, Paul, and Griffith, Richard. *Film Till Now*. New York: Twayne, 1960.
Sadoul, Georges. *Histoire Générale du Cinéma*. 5 vols. Paris: Éditions Denoël, 1946–54.
Sarris, Andrew. *The American Cinema: Directors and Directions 1929–1968*. New York: Dutton, 1968.
Skar, Robert. *Movie-Made America*. New York: Random House, 1975.
Wagenknecht, Edward. *Movies in the Age of Innocence*. Norman, Okla.: Oklahoma University Press, 1962.

2. Birth (1825–95)

BOOKS

Dickinson, Thorold. *A History of the Kinetograph, Kinetoscope, and Kinetophonograph*. New York: Arno Press, 1970.
Marek, K. W. *Archaeology of the Cinema*. New York: Harcourt, Brace, 1965.
Ramsaye, Terry. *A Million and One Nights*. New York: Simon & Schuster, 1964, pp. xxxvii–175.

FILMS

LOUIS AND AUGUSTE LUMIÈRE

The First Programs (1895–96)—MMA
Early Lumière Films (1895–96)—EMG, MMA

THOMAS EDISON

Films of the 1890s (1894–99)—MMA
Film History #1 (1894–99)—AUD
The Edison "Black Maria" Films (1894–98)—EMG, MED

3. Film Narrative (1895–1912)

BOOKS

Arvidson, Linda. *When the Movies Were Young*. New York: Benjamin Blom, 1968.
Balshofer, Fred J., and Miller, Arthur C. *One Reel a Week*. Berkeley and Los Angeles: University of California Press, 1968.

Jacobs, Lewis. *The Rise of the American Film.* New York: Harcourt, Brace, 1939, pp. 3–67.

Low, Rachel, and Manvell, Roger. *History of the British Film.* 3 vols. (1896–1918). London: Allen & Unwin, 1948–50.

Ramsaye, Terry. *A Million and One Nights.* New York: Simon & Schuster, 1964, pp. 176–602.

Smith, Albert E., and Skoury, P. A. *Two Reels and a Crank.* New York: Doubleday, 1952.

Wagenknecht, Edward. *Movies in the Age of Innocence.* Norman, Okla.: Oklahoma University Press, 1962, pp. 30–77.

FILMS

GEORGES MÉLIÈS

Méliès Color Films (1898–1902)—AUD. Contains *An Astronomer's Dream* and *A Trip to the Moon*

Georges Méliès Program (1899–1912)—MMA. *The Conjuror, A Trip to the Moon, The Palace of the Arabian Nights, The Doctor's Secret,* and *Conquest of the Pole*

A Trip to the Moon (1902)—AUD, EMG

Magic of Méliès (1903–4)—AUD. Contains *Jupiter's Thunderbolts, The Magic Lantern, The Mermaid*

Conquest of the Pole (1912)—AUD, EMG

EDWIN S. PORTER

Edwin S. Porter: Five Films (1903–7)—MMA. *Life of an American Fireman, Uncle Tom's Cabin, The Great Train Robbery, Dream of a Rarebit Fiend, Rescued from an Eagle's Nest*

Film History #3 (1903–6)—AUD. *The Great Train Robbery, Uncle Tom's Cabin, Dream of a Rarebit Fiend*

The Great Train Robbery (1903)—AUD, EMG

A selection of Porter films (1903–7)—EMG

OTHER FILMS OF THE ERA

Ferdinand Zecca Program (1906–7)—MMA

Films of Cohl, Feuillade, and Durand (1907–12)—MMA

Three Max Linder Films (1905–12)—MMA

A selection of Linder films (1905–12)—EMG

The Beginnings of the British Film (1901–11)—MMA. *Funeral of Queen Victoria, Rescued by Rover, The Airship Destroyer,* and *Tatters: A Tale of the Slums*

Film History #5 (1907–12)—AUD. Includes Bernhardt's *Camille*

The Film d'Art (1908–12)—MMA. *The Assassination of the Duke of Guise* and *Queen Elizabeth*

Fantômas (1913)—MMA

4. Griffith (1907–31)

BOOKS

Barry, Iris, and Bowser, Eileen. *D. W. Griffith: American Film Master.* New York: Museum of Modern Art, 1965.

Gish, Lillian. *The Movies, Mr. Griffith, and Me.* Englewood Cliffs, N.J.: Prentice-Hall, 1969.

Henderson, Robert M. *D. W. Griffith: The Years at Biograph.* New York: Farrar, Straus, and Giroux, 1970.

———. *D. W. Griffith: His Life and Times.* New York and London: Oxford University Press, 1972.

Huff, Theodore. *Intolerance: Shot-by-Shot Analysis.* New York: Museum of Modern Art, 1966.

Jacobs, Lewis. *The Rise of the American Film.* New York: Harcourt, Brace, 1939, pp. 95–119, 171–201, 384–94.

Wagenknecht, Edward. *Movies in the Age of Innocence.* Norman, Okla.: Oklahoma University Press, 1962, pp. 78–137.

FILMS

ONE-REELERS

1776 or *The Hessian Renegades* (1909)—MMA

Griffith Biograph Program (1909–12)—MMA. *The Lonely Villa, A Corner in Wheat, The Lonedale Operator, The Musketeers of Pig Alley, The New York Hat*

The Lonedale Operator and *The New York Hat*—AUD. Not recommended; severely cut and clumsily titled

Excellent selection of one-reelers (1908–12)—EMG

FOUR-REELERS

The Avenging Conscience (1914)—MMA
Home Sweet Home (1914)—MMA
Judith of Bethulia (1914)—AUD, EMG, MED, MMA

FEATURES

The Birth of a Nation (1915)—AUD, EMG, MMA
Intolerance (1916)—AUD, EMG, MED, MMA
Hearts of the World (1918)—AUD
Broken Blossoms (1919)—AUD, EMG, MED, MMA
Way Down East (1920)—AUD, EMG, MED, MMA
Orphans of the Storm (1922)—AUD, MMA
America (1924)—AUD, MMA
Abraham Lincoln (1930)—EMG, FCE, MED
The Struggle (1931)—AUD
(Most of the Griffith program pictures—1916–27—can be rented from AUD or MMA, e.g., *True Heart Susie, The Idol Dancer, Dream Street, Sorrows of Satan.*)

5. Mack Sennett and Charles Chaplin (1911–18)

BOOKS

Agee, James. "Comedy's Greatest Era." In *Agee on Film: Reviews and Comments,* pp. 2–19. Boston: Beacon Press, 1964.

Chaplin, Charlie. *My Autobiography*. New York: Simon & Schuster, 1964.

Huff, Theodore. *Charlie Chaplin*. New York: Henry Schuman, 1951.

Lahue, Kalton C., and Brewer, Terry. *Kops and Custard*. Norman, Okla.: Oklahoma University Press, 1968.

Manvell, Roger. *Chaplin*. Boston: Little, Brown, 1974.

Mast, Gerald. *The Comic Mind: Comedy and the Movies*. Indianapolis and New York: Bobbs-Merrill, 1973, pp. 43-124.

Payne, Robert. *The Great God Pan*. New York: Hermitage House, 1952.

Quigley, Isabel. *Charlie Chaplin: Early Comedies*. New York and London: Dutton/Vista, 1968.

Sennett, Mack. *King of Comedy*. New York: Doubleday, 1954.

Tyler, Parker. *Chaplin: Last of the Clowns*. New York: Horizon, 1972.

FILMS

MACK SENNETT (DIRECTED OR SUPERVISED)

Mack Sennett Program (1911-20)—MMA. *Comrades, Mabel's Dramatic Career, The Surf Girl, His Bread and Butter, The Clever Dummy, Astray from the Steerage*

Barney Oldfield's Race for a Life (1913)—AUD, EMG

Teddy at the Throttle (1917)—AUD, EMG, MMA

Personalities Programs #2, 3, 5, 6, 7, and 8—AUD. Several Sennett films

His Bitter Pill (1916)—MMA

Mickey (1916-18)—MED, MMA

Excellent Sennett Selection (1912-24)—EMG

CHARLES CHAPLIN

Chaplin's Keystone Films (1914)—MMA. *Making a Living, The Knockout, The Masquerader, The Rounders, Getting Acquainted*

Complete selection of Keystone and Essanay films (1914-15)—EMG

Tillie's Punctured Romance (1914)—AUD, EMG

Chaplin's Essanay Films (1915-16)—MMA. *The Tramp, A Woman, The Bank, Police*

Carmen (1916)—AUD, EMG, MED

The Mutual Films (1916-17)—All AUD, EMG. *The Floorwalker, The Fireman, The Vagabond, One A.M., The Count, The Pawnshop, Behind the Screen, The Rink, Easy Street, The Cure, The Immigrant, The Adventurer*

The Gold Rush (1925)—AUD, EMG, JAN, MED

Most Chaplin First Nationals and all Chaplin Features—RBC. *A Dog's Life* (1918), *Shoulder Arms* (1918), *The Idle Class* (1921), *The Kid* (1921), *The Pilgrim* (1923), *The Circus* (1928), *City Lights* (1931), *Modern Times* (1936), *The Great Dictator* (1940), *Monsieur Verdoux* (1947), *Limelight* (1952), *A King in New York* (1957)

A Countess from Hong Kong (1967)—UNI

6. The American Film (1914-27)

BOOKS

Blesh, Rudi. *Keaton*. New York: Macmillan, 1966.

Curtis, Thomas Quinn. *Von Stroheim*. New York: Farrar, Straus, and Giroux, 1971.

DeMille, Cecil B. *Autobiography*. Englewood Cliffs, N.J.: Prentice-Hall, 1959.

Everson, William K. *The Films of Laurel and Hardy*. New York: Citadel, 1967.

Jacobs, Lewis. *The Rise of the American Film*. New York: Harcourt, Brace, 1939, pp. 81–395.

Keaton, Buster. With Charles Samuels. *My Wonderful World of Slapstick*. New York: Doubleday, 1960.

Lloyd, Harold. *An American Comedy*. New York: Dover, 1971.

Mast, Gerald. *The Comic Mind: Comedy and the Movies*. Indianapolis and New York: Bobbs-Merrill, 1973, pp. 125–96.

O'Leary, Liam. *The Silent Cinema*. New York and London: Dutton/Vista, 1965.

Ramsaye, Terry. *A Million and One Nights*. New York: Simon & Schuster, 1964, pp. 603–834.

Robinson, David. *Buster Keaton*. Bloomington, Ind. and London: Indiana University Press, 1969.

Rubinstein, E. *Filmguide to The General*. Bloomington, Ind. and London: Indiana University Press, 1972.

Wagenknecht, Edward. *Movies in the Age of Innocence*. Norman, Okla.: Oklahoma University Press, 1962, pp. 138–256.

Weinberg, Herman G. *The Complete "Greed" of Erich von Stroheim*. New York: Dutton, 1973.

———. *The Complete "Wedding March" of Erich von Stroheim*. Boston: Little, Brown, 1974.

FILMS

ITALIAN SPECTACLE PICTURES

Quo Vadis? (1912)—MMA
Cabiria (1913)—MMA
Anthony and Cleopatra (1914)—AUD, EMG, MED
Julius Caesar (1914)—AUD
The Last Days of Pompeii (1914)—EMG, FCE
Salammbo (1914)—AUD, EMG, MED
Spartacus (1914)—EMG, MED

CECIL B. DeMILLE

The Goose Girl (1915)—MOG
Male and Female (1919)—MMA
King of Kings (1927)—FI, TWY
Sign of the Cross (1932)—UNI
Cleopatra (1934)—UNI
Union Pacific (1939)—UNI
David and Bathsheba (1951)—FI
The Greatest Show on Earth (1952)—FI
The Ten Commandments (1956)—FI

DOUGLAS FAIRBANKS

His Picture in the Papers (1916)—EMG, MED
Two Early Films of Douglas Fairbanks (1916–17)—MMA. *The Mystery of the Leaping Fish* and *Wild and Woolly*
Flirting with Fate (1916)—EMG, MED
Reaching for the Moon (1917)—MMA

When the Clouds Roll By (1919)—EMG, MED, MMA
The Mark of Zorro (1920)—EMG, MED, MMA
The Mollycoddle (1920)—MMA
The Nut (1921)—EMG, MED
The Three Musketeers (1921)—MMA
Robin Hood (1922)—MMA
The Thief of Bagdad (1924)—AUD, MED, MMA
The Black Pirate (1926)—MED, MMA
The Gaucho (1927)—MMA
The Taming of the Shrew (1929)—MMA
Mr. Robinson Crusoe (1932)—EMG, MMA

ROBERT FLAHERTY (SILENT)

Nanook of the North (1922)—CON, MMA
Moana (1926)—MMA

THOMAS INCE (directed or supervised)

The Last of the Line (1914)—MMA
The Taking of Luke McVane (1915)—MMA. With W. S. Hart
Keno Bates, Liar (1915)—MMA. With W. S. Hart
The Coward (1915)—MMA. With Charles Ray
The Deserter (1916)—MMA. With Charles Ray
Civilization (1916)—MMA

BUSTER KEATON

Shorts (1920-23)—All AUD. *One Week, Convict 13, The Scarecrow, Neighbors, The Haunted House, The Playhouse, The Paleface, Cops, My Wife's Relations, The Blacksmith, The Frozen North, The Electric House, Daydreams, The Balloonatic*
Our Hospitality (1923)—AUD
Sherlock Jr. (1924)—AUD
The Navigator (1924)—AUD
Seven Chances (1925)—AUD
Go West (1925)—AUD
The General (1926)—AUD, EMG
College (1927)—AUD
Steambot Bill Jr. (1927)—AUD, EMG

HARRY LANGDON

Tramp, Tramp, Tramp (1926)—AUD
The Strong Man (1926)—AUD
Long Pants (1927)—AUD
A selection of Langdon shorts (1924-26)—AUD, EMG

LAUREL AND HARDY

Shorts (1927-32)—AUD. *The Finishing Touch, Two Tars, You're Darn Tootin, Leave 'Em Laughing, Bacon Grabbers, Big Business, Double Whoopee, Men O'War, Perfect Day, Below Zero, Brats, The Music Box*

Two Films of Laurel and Hardy (1928–29)—MMA. *Two Tars* and *Big Business*
Beauhunks (1932)—MED, SWA
Sons of the Desert (1934)—SWA
Blockheads (1938)—EMG, MED, SWA
Swiss Miss (1938)—EMG, SWA, WIL
A Chump at Oxford (1940)—EMG, MED, SWA
Saps at Sea (1940)—EMG, SWA

HAROLD LLOYD

High and Dizzy (1921)—MMA
Harold Lloyd's Funny Side of Life—JAN
Excellent selection of Lloyd shorts (1915–20)—EMG

ERICH VON STROHEIM

Blind Husbands (1919)—CFS, MMA, UNI
Foolish Wives (1922)—EMG, MMA, UNI
The Merry-Go-Round (1923)—CFS
Greed (1924)—FI
The Merry Widow (1925)—FI

IMPORTANT FILMS OF THE ERA

Three Vitagraph Comedies (1912–17)—MMA. *Stenographer Wanted, Goodness Gracious, The Professional Patient*
Two Broncho Billy Westerns (1913–18)—MMA
A Fool There Was (1915)—MMA. With Theda Bara (Frank Powell)
Woman (1918)—AUD (Maurice Tourneur)
Dancin' Fool (1920)—MMA (Sam Wood)
Excuse My Dust (1920)—MMA (Sam Wood)
The Last of the Mohicans (1920)—FCE, MOG (Maurice Tourneur)
The Toll Gate (1920)—MMA. With W. S. Hart (Lambert Hillyer)
Miss Lulu Bett (1921)—MMA (William C. DeMille)
Tol'able David (1921)—EMG, MMA, STA (Henry King)
Blood and Sand (1922)—AUD, MED, MMA. With Rudolf Valentino (Fred Niblo)
The Hunchback of Notre Dame (1922)—AUD, MED (Wallace Worsley)
Salome (1922)—AUD, MED (Charles Bryant)
The Covered Wagon (1923)—AUD, STA (James Cruze)
The White Sister (1923)—FI. With Lillian Gish (Henry King)
The Big Parade (1925)—FI (King Vidor)
Phantom of the Opera (1925)—AUD, MED (Rupert Julian)
Dancing Mothers (1926)—AUD, MED. With Clara Bow (Herbert Brenon)
Ben Hur (1926)—FI (Fred Niblo)
The Scarlet Letter (1926)—FI. With Lillian Gish (Victor Sjøstrøm)
Son of the Sheik (1926)—AUD, EMG, SWA. With Valentino (George Fitzmaurice)
What Price Glory? (1926)—EMG, MMA (Raoul Walsh)
Hotel Imperial (1927)—MMA (Mauritz Stiller)
The Wind (1927)—FI. With Lillian Gish (Victor Sjøstrøm)
The Crowd (1928)—FI (King Vidor)

BOOKS

Barsam, Richard Meran. *Filmguide to Triumph of the Will*. Bloomington, Ind. and London: Indiana University Press, 1975.

Eisner, Lotte. *The Haunted Screen: Expressionism in the German Cinema*. Berkeley and Los Angeles: University of California Press, 1969.

———. *F. W. Murnau*. Berkeley and Los Angeles: University of California Press, 1973.

Kracauer, Siegfried. *From Caligari to Hitler*. New York: Noonday, 1959.

Manvell, Roger. With Heinrich Fraenkel. *The German Cinema*. New York: Praeger, 1971.

Rotha, Paul, and Griffith, Richard. *Film Till Now*. New York: Twayne, 1960, pp. 252–92.

FILMS

FRITZ LANG

Destiny (Der Müde Tod, 1921)—EMG, JAN, MMA
Doktor Mabuse, Der Spieler (1922)—MMA
Die Niebelungen (1924)—JAN, MMA
Metropolis (1926)—JAN, MMA, STA
Spies (1928)—JAN, MMA
M (1931)—AUD, EMG, FCE, JAN

F. W. MURNAU

Nosferatu (1922)—MMA
The Last Laugh (1924)—EMG, MMA
Tartuffe (1927)—AUD
Sunrise (1927)—EMG, AUD, MMA

G. W. PABST

The Joyless Street (1925)—MMA
The Love of Jeanne Ney (1927)—MMA
Westfront 1918 (1930)—AUD, MMA
The Threepenny Opera (1931)—AUD
Kameradschaft (1931)—AUD

OTHER MAJOR FILMS OF THE ERA

The Cabinet of Doctor Caligari (1920)—AUD, EMG, MMA (Robert Wiene)
The Golem (1920)—EMG, MED, MMA (Paul Wegener and Henrick Galeen)
Warning Shadows (1922)—AUD, MMA (Arthur Robison)
The Street (1923)—MMA (Karl Grune)
Waxworks (1924)—AUD (Paul Leni)
Variety (1925)—AUD, EMG, MMA (E. A. Dupont)
Berlin: Symphony of a Great City (1927)—MMA (Walther Ruttmann)
Überfall (1929)—MMA (Erno Metzner)

Kuhle Wampe (1932)—AUD (Slatan Dudow and Bertolt Brecht)
Triumph of the Will (1934)—AUD, CON, MMA (Leni Riefenstahl)
Olympia (1938)—CON, MMA (Leni Riefenstahl)

8. The Soviet Film (1917–40)

BOOKS

Barna, Yon. *Eisenstein.* Bloomington, Ind. and London: Indiana University Press, 1974.
Dickinson, Thorold, and de la Roche, Catherine, eds. *Soviet Cinema.* London: Falcon Press, 1948.
Eisenstein, S. M. *Film Form* and *The Film Sense.* New York: Harcourt Brace, n.d.
———. *Notes of a Film Director.* London: Lawrence & Wisehart, 1959.
Leyda, Jay. *Kino: History of the Russian and Soviet Film.* New York: Macmillan, 1960.
Nizhny, Vladimir. *Lessons with Eisenstein.* New York: Hill & Wang, 1962.
Pudovkin, V. I. *Film Technique and Film Acting.* London: Vision Press, 1959.
Rotha, Paul, and Griffith, Richard. *Film Till Now.* New York: Twayne, 1960, pp. 217–51.
Seton, Marie. *Sergei M. Eisenstein.* New York: Grove Press, 1960.

FILMS

ALEXANDER DOVZHENKO

Zvenigora (1928)—AUD
Arsenal (1928)—AUD, MMA
Earth (1930)—AUD
Schors (1939)—AUD

S. M. EISENSTEIN

Strike (1925)—AUD, MMA
Potemkin (1925)—AUD, MMA
October or *Ten Days That Shook the World* (1928)—AUD, EMG, MMA
Old and New or *The General Line* (1929)—AUD, EMG
Thunder over Mexico (1933)—MMA
Alexander Nevsky (1938)—AUD
Ivan the Terrible, parts I and II (1944–46)—AUD
Kino-Pravda (1922)—MMA (Dziga-Vertov)
The Cloak (1926)—AUD (Kozintsev and Trauberg)
Bed and Sofa (1927)—AUD, MMA (Abram Room)
By the Law (1927)—MMA (Lev Kuleshov)
The Ghost That Never Returns (1929)—AUD (Abram Room)
The Man With the Movie Camera (1929)—AUD (Dziga-Vertov)
Turksib (1929)—AUD (Victor Turin)
The Road to Life (1931)—AUD, MMA (Nikolai Ekk)
Chapayev (1934)—AUD, MMA (the Vasiliev brothers)

OTHER FILMS OF THE ERA

The Youth of Maxim (1935)—AUD, MMA (Kozintsev and Trauberg)
We Are from Kronstadt (1936)—AUD (Yefim Dzigan)
Lenin in October (1937)—AUD (Mikhail Romm)
The Gorky Trilogy (1938-40)—AUD (Mark Donskoi)

VSEVLOD I. PUDOVKIN

Chess Fever (1925)—MMA
Mechanics of the Brain (1926)—AUD
Mother (1926)—AUD, MMA
The End of St. Petersburg (1927)—AUD, MMA, MOG
Storm over Asia (1928)—AUD, MMA
The Return of Vasili Bortnikov (1953)—AUD

9. The Transition to Sound (1927–30)

FILMS

The Coming of Sound (1927-28)—MMA. *Shaw Talks for Movietone, Steamboat Willie, Sex Life of the Polyp*, plus excerpts from *The Jazz Singer* and *The Lights of New York*

ILLUSTRATIVE TRANSITIONAL FILMS

The Jazz Singer (1927)—CON, STA (Alan Crosland)
The Singing Fool (1928)—CON (Lloyd Bacon)
Applause (1929)—UNI (Rouben Mamoulian)
The Broadway Melody (1929)—FI (Harry Beaumont)
Hallelujah (1929)—FI (King Vidor)
The Virginian (1929)—MMA, UNI (Victor Fleming)
All Quiet on the Western Front (1930)—SWA, TWY, UNI (Lewis Milestone)

ERNST LUBITSCH

Passion and *Gypsy Blood* (1919)—MMA
The Marriage Circle (1924)—MMA
Lady Windermere's Fan (1925)—AUD
So This Is Paris (1925)—CON
The Love Parade (1929)—MMA, UNI
Monte Carlo (1930)—UNI
The Man I Killed (1932)—MMA, UNI
Trouble in Paradise (1932)—MMA, UNI
Design for Living (1933)—UNI
Ninotchka (1939)—FI
The Shop Around the Corner (1940)—FI
To Be or Not To Be (1942)—AUD, MOG, UFC
Cluny Brown (1946)—FI

BOOKS

Bazin, André. *Jean Renoir*, edited by François Truffaut. New York: Simon and
    Schuster, 1973.
Braudy, Leo. *Jean Renoir*. Garden City, N.Y.: Doubleday, 1972.
Clair, René. *Reflections on the Cinema*. London: Kimber, 1953.
———. *Cinema Yesterday and Today*. New York: Dover, 1972.
Durgnat, Raymond. *Renoir*. Berkeley and Los Angeles: University of California Press,
    1973.
Gomes, P. E. Salles. *Jean Vigo*. Berkeley and Los Angeles: University of California
    Press, 1971.
Leprohon, Pierre. *Jean Renoir*. New York: Crown, 1971.
Mast, Gerald. *The Comic Mind: Comedy and the Movies*. Indianapolis and New
    York: Bobbs-Merrill, 1973, pp. 224–48, 302–11.
———. *Filmguide to Rules of the Game*. Bloomington, Ind. and London: Indiana
    University Press, 1973.
Ray, Man. *Self Portrait*. Boston: Little, Brown, 1963.
Sadoul, Georges. *French Film*. London: Falcon Press, 1953.

FILMS

MARCEL CARNÉ

Bizarre, Bizarre (1937)—AUD
Port of Shadows (1938)—AUD
Le Jour se lève (1939)—JAN
The Children of Paradise (1944–45)—CON

RENÉ CLAIR

Paris qui dort or *The Crazy Ray* (1923)—EMG, MMA
Entr'acte (1924)—MMA
The Italian Straw Hat (1927)—CON
Les Deux Timides (1928)—CON
Sous les toits de Paris (1930)—AUD
Le Million (1931)—AUD
À Nous la liberté (1931)—CON
The Last Millionaire (1934)—CON
The Ghost Goes West (1936)—AUD, MOG
I Married a Witch (1942)—MOG, TWF
It Happened Tomorrow (1944)—MOG
And Then There Were None (1945)—EMG, UFC
Le Silence est d'or (1946)—FCE
Beauty and the Devil (1949)—CON
Beauties of the Night (1952)—CON
Gates of Paris (1957)—AUD

MARCEL PAGNOL

Marius (1931)—CON
Fanny (1932)—CON

Angèle (1934)—CON
César (1936)—CON
The Baker's Wife (1938)—CON
Le Schpountz (1938)—CON
Letters from My Windmill (1955)—CON

MAN RAY

Return to Reason (1923)—AUD, MMA
Emak Bakia (1927)—AUD, MMA
Étoile de mer (1928)—AUD, MMA
Les Mystères du Chateau Dé (1929)—AUD, MMA

JEAN RENOIR

The Little Match Girl (1928)—EMG, MED, MMA
Boudu Saved from Drowning (1932)—CON
Toni (1934)—CON
The Crime of Monsieur Lange (1935)—AUD
The Lower Depths (1936)—CON
A Day in the Country (1936)—CON
Grand Illusion (1937)—JAN
La Marseillaise (1938)—CON
The Rules of the Game (1939)—JAN
The Southerner (1945)—EMG
The Golden Coach (1953)—AUD
French Cancan (1954)—AUD
Picnic on the Grass (1959)—CON
The Elusive Corporal (1961)—CON

JEAN VIGO

Zéro de conduite (1933)—AUD
L'Atalante (1934)—AUD

REPRESENTATIVE SILENT FILMS: SHORTS

Fièvre (1921)—MMA (Louis Delluc)
The Smiling Madame Beudet (1922)—MMA (Germaine Dulac)
Ballet Mécanique (1924)—MMA (Fernand Léger)
Menilmontant (1925)—AUD, MMA (Dimitri Kirsanov)
Anæmic Cinema (1926)—MMA (Marcel Duchamp)
Rien que les heures (1926)—MMA (Alberto Cavalcanti)
La Marche des machines (1928)—MMA (Eugene Deslaw)
Brumes d'automne (1928)—AUD (Dimitri Kirsanov)
The Seashell and the Clergyman (1928)—MMA (Germaine Dulac)

FEATURES

The Late Matthew Pascal (1924-26)—MMA (Marcel L'Herbier)
The Fall of the House of Usher (1928)—AUD, MMA (Jean Epstein)
The Passion of Joan of Arc (1928)—AUD (Carl-Theodore Dreyer)

IMPORTANT SOUND FILMS

La Maternelle (1934)—CON (Jean Bénoit-Levy)
Crime and Punishment (1935)—AUD (Pierre Chenal)
Carnival in Flanders (1936)—AUD (Jacques Feyder)
Razumov (1937)—FCE (Marc Allegret)
The Golem (1937)—AUD (Julien Duvivier)
They Were Five (1938)—AUD (Julien Duvivier)
Volpone (1939)—CON (Maurice Tourneur)

11. The American Studio Years (1930–45)

BOOKS

Adamson, Joe. *Groucho, Harpo, Chico, and Sometimes Zeppo.* New York: Simon and Schuster, 1973.

Agee, James. *Agee on Film: Reviews and Comments.* Boston: Beacon Press, 1964.

Bogdanovich, Peter. *John Ford.* Berkeley and Los Angeles: University of California Press, 1968.

———. *Allan Dwan: The Last Pioneer.* New York: Praeger, 1971.

Capra, Frank. *The Name Above the Title.* New York: Macmillan, 1971.

Cowie, Peter. *The Cinema of Orson Welles.* New York: Barnes, 1965.

Crowther, Bosley. *The Lion's Share.* New York: Dutton, 1967, pp. 163–283.

Eyles, Allen. *The Marx Brothers: Their World of Comedy.* New York: Barnes, 1966.

Feild, Robert. *The Art of Walt Disney.* New York: Macmillan, 1943.

Geduld, Harry. The Birth of the Talkies. Bloomington, Ind. and London: Indiana University Press, 1975.

Grierson, John. "Directors of the Thirties." In *Film: An Anthology,* edited by Daniel Talbot, pp. 110–29. Berkeley and Los Angeles: University of California Press, 1966.

Gussow, Mel. *Don't Say Yes Until I Finish Talking.* Garden City, N.Y.: Doubleday, 1971.

Higham, Charles. *The Films of Orson Welles.* Berkeley and Los Angeles: University of California Press, 1970.

Huettig, Mae D. *Economic Control of the Motion Picture Industry.* Philadelphia, Pa.: University of Pennsylvania Press, 1944.

Inglis, Ruth A. *Freedom of the Movies.* Chicago: University of Chicago Press, 1947.

Jacobs, Lewis. *The Rise of the American Film.* New York: Harcourt, Brace, 1939, pp. 419–540.

Kael, Pauline. *The Citizen Kane Book.* Boston: Little, Brown, 1971.

Lambert, Gavin. *On Cukor.* New York: Putnam, 1972.

Mast, Gerald. *The Comic Mind: Comedy and the Movies.* Indianapolis and New York: Bobbs-Merrill, 1973, pp. 249–93.

Mayer, Arthur. *Merely Colossal.* New York: Simon & Schuster, 1953.

Perry, George S. *The Films of Alfred Hitchcock.* New York: Dutton, 1965.

Rosten, Leo C. *Hollywood: The Movie Colony and the Movie Makers.* New York: Harcourt, Brace, 1941.

Sarris, Andrew. *The Films of Josef von Sternberg.* New York: Museum of Modern Art, 1966.

Schickel, Richard. *The Disney Version.* New York: Simon & Schuster, 1968.

Seldes, Gilbert. *The Movies Come from America*. New York: Scribner's, 1937.
Taylor, Robert Lewis. *W. C. Fields: His Follies and Fortunes*. Garden City, N.Y.: Doubleday, 1949.
Thomas, Bob. *King Cohn*. New York: G. P. Putnam's Sons, 1967.
———. *Thalberg: Life and Legend*. New York: Doubleday, 1969.
Thorp, Margaret. *America at the Movies*. New Haven, Conn.: Yale University Press, 1939.
Truffaut, François. *Hitchcock*. New York: Simon & Schuster, 1967.
Tyler, Parker. *Magic and Myth of the Movies*. New York: Simon and Schuster, 1970.
———. *The Hollywood Hallucination*. New York: Simon & Schuster, 1970.
Von Sternberg, Josef. *Fun in a Chinese Laundry*. New York: Macmillan, 1965.
Weinberg, Herman G. *Josef von Sternberg*. New York: Dutton, 1967.
———. *The Lubitsch Touch*. New York: Dutton, 1968.
Wood, Robin. *Hitchcock's Films*. New York: Barnes, 1965.
———. *Howard Hawks*. London: Secker and Warburg, 1967.

FILMS

FRANK CAPRA

Platinum Blonde (1931)—SWA
It Happened One Night (1934)—SWA
Mr. Deeds Goes to Town (1936)—AUD, SWA
Lost Horizon (1937)—AUD
Mr. Smith Goes to Washington (1939)—AUD, SWA
Meet John Doe (1941)—FCE, ICS
Arsenic and Old Lace (1944)—AUD, UA
State of the Union (1948)—UNI

GEORGE CUKOR

Dinner at Eight (1933)—FI
David Copperfield (1934)—FI
Camille (1936)—FI
Holiday (1938)—SWA
The Philadelphia Story (1940)—FI
Gaslight (1944)—FI
Adam's Rib (1949)—FI
Born Yesterday (1950)—AUD
Pat and Mike (1952)—FI
It Should Happen to You (1954)—AUD, ICS
A Star Is Born (1954)—TWF, TWY
My Fair Lady (1964)—SWA
Travels With My Aunt (1973)—FI

MICHAEL CURTIZ

The Charge of the Light Brigade (1936)—CWF, UA
Kid Galahad (1937)—UA, WIL
Angels With Dirty Faces (1938)—UA
Dodge City (1939)—TWY, UA, WIL
Santa Fe Trail (1940)—TWY, UA
Casablanca (1942)—AUD, CWF, UA

Yankee Doodle Dandy (1942)—AUD, CWF, UA
Mildred Pierce (1945)—UA, WIL

WILLIAM DIETERLE

A Midsummer Night's Dream (1935)—CWF, UA
The Story of Louis Pasteur (1935)—CWF, UA
The Life of Emile Zola (1937)—CWF, UA
Juarez (1939)—AUD, UA

WALT DISNEY

Steamboat Willie (1928)—MMA
The Skeleton Dance (1929)—AUD
A World Is Born (1941)—DIS. Excerpt from *Fantasia*
Dumbo (1941)—FI, SWA, TWY
The Three Caballeros (1944)—DIS
So Dear to My Heart (1948)—DIS, TWY
Ichabod and Mr. Toad (1949)—DIS
Alice in Wonderland (1951)—DIS
(None of the classic Disney cartoon features circulates in 16 mm.)

W. C. FIELDS

Shorts: *The Barber Shop* (1933), *The Fatal Glass of Beer* (1933), *The Pharmacist* (1933)—AUD, MED
Million Dollar Legs (1932)—MMA, UNI
Tillie and Gus (1933)—UNI
Six of a Kind (1934)—UNI
It's a Gift (1934)—UNI
The Old-Fashioned Way (1935)—UNI
Poppy (1936)—UNI
The Bank Dick (1940)—SWA, TWY, UNI
My Little Chickadee (1940)—SWA, TWY, UNI
Never Give a Sucker an Even Break (1941)—SWA, TWY, UNI

JOHN FORD

The Iron Horse (1924)—FI, MMA
The Lost Patrol (1934)—FI
The Informer (1935)—AUD, FI, JAN
The Prisoner of Shark Island (1936)—FI
Stagecoach (1939)—MOG, TWF, UFC
The Grapes of Wrath (1940)—FI
The Long Voyage Home (1940)—AUD, MOG WIL
How Green Was My Valley (1941)—FI
My Darling Clementine (1946)—FI
Fort Apache (1948)—AUD
She Wore a Yellow Ribbon (1949)—TWY, UFC
Wagonmaster (1950)—FI
The Quiet Man (1952)—FI, STA
The Horse Soldiers (1959)—UA
The Man Who Shot Liberty Valance (1962)—FI

HOWARD HAWKS

The Criminal Code (1930)—SWA
Viva Villa! (1934)—FI
Twentieth Century (1934)—AUD, SWA
Bringing Up Baby (1938)—FI
Only Angels Have Wings (1939)—MOD, SWA
His Girl Friday (1941)—AUD
Sergeant York (1941)—UA
To Have and Have Not (1944)—UA
The Big Sleep (1946)—AUD, CON, UA, WIL
Red River (1948)—UA
The Big Sky (1952)—FI
Rio Bravo (1959)—WAR
El Dorado (1967)—FI

ALFRED HITCHCOCK

The Pleasure Garden (1925)—AUD
The Lodger (1927)—MMA
Blackmail (1929)—MMA
The 39 Steps (1935)—FCE, MOG, UFC, WIL
Sabotage (1936)—MMA
The Lady Vanishes (1938)—CON, JAN, UFC
Rebecca (1940)—AUD
Foreign Correspondent (1940)—TWF, UFC
Suspicion (1941)—FI
Saboteur (1942)—UNI
Shadow of a Doubt (1943)—TWY, UNI
Lifeboat (1944)—FI
Spellbound (1945)—AUD, TWF
Notorious (1946)—AUD, TWF
Strangers on a Train (1951)—WAR
Dial M for Murder (1953)—SWA, TWY
The Trouble with Harry (1955)—FI
The Wrong Man (1956)—WAR
North by Northwest (1959)—FI
Psycho (1960)—SWA, TWY, UNI
The Birds (1963)—SWA, TWY, UNI
Frenzy (1972)—SWA, UNI

FRITZ LANG

Fury (1936)—FI
You Only Live Once (1937)—AUD
Rancho Notorious (1952)—SWA
The Big Heat (1953)—SWA

MERVYN LeROY

Little Caesar (1930)—AUD, CON, UA
I Am a Fugitive from a Chain Gang (1932)—UA
Waterloo Bridge (1940)—FI

Random Harvest (1942)—FI
Quo Vadis? (1951)—FI
The FBI Story (1959)—ICS, SWA, TWY, UFC
Gypsy (1962)—CWF, ICS, SWA, TWY

THE MARX BROTHERS

The Cocoanuts (1929)—TWY, UNI
Monkey Business (1931)—SWA, TWY, UNI
Horsefeathers (1932)—SWA, TWY, UNI
Duck Soup (1933)—MMA, SWA, TWY, UNI
A Night at the Opera (1935)—FI
A Day at the Races (1937)—FI
At the Circus (1939)—FI

LEO McCAREY

Ruggles of Red Gap (1935)—MMA, TWY, UNI
The Awful Truth (1937)—SWA
Make Way for Tomorrow (1937)—MMA
Going My Way (1944)—UNI

JOSEF VON STERNBERG

Underworld (1927)—MMA
The Last Command (1928)—MMA
The Blue Angel (1929)—CON, JAN
Morocco (1930)—MMA, TWY, UNI
An American Tragedy (1931)—UNI
Shanghai Express (1932)—TWY, UNI
The Blonde Venus (1932)—TWY, UNI
The Scarlet Empress (1934)—TWY, UNI
The Devil Is a Woman (1935)—MMA, TWY, UNI

PRESTON STURGES

The Great McGinty (1940)—UNI
The Lady Eve (1941)—UNI
Sullivan's Travels (1941)—UNI
The Palm Beach Story (1942)—UNI
The Miracle of Morgan's Creek (1943)—FI
Hail, the Conquering Hero! (1944)—UNI
Unfaithfully Yours (1948)—WAL

W. S. VANDYKE

Trader Horn (1931)—FI
Tarzan, the Ape Man (1932)—FI
The Thin Man (1934)—FI
San Francisco (1936)—FI
Marie Antoinette (1938)—FI

RAOUL WALSH

The Roaring Twenties (1939)—UA
High Sierra (1941)—UA
They Died With Their Boots On (1941)—UA
White Heat (1949)—UA

ORSON WELLES

Citizen Kane (1941)—AUD, FI, JAN
The Magnificent Ambersons (1942)—FI, JAN
Journey into Fear (1942)—FI
The Lady from Shanghai (1948)—AUD
Othello (1955)—JAN
Touch of Evil (1958)—TWY, UNI
Mr. Arkadin (1962)—CON, JAN
The Trial (1963)—AUD

WILLIAM WELLMAN

Wings (1929)—FI
Public Enemy (1931)—AUD, CON, UA, WIL
Wild Boys of the Road (1933)—UA
The President Vanishes (1934)—MMA
A Star Is Born (1937)—CWF, MOG
The Ox-Bow Incident (1943)—FI
The Story of G.I. Joe (1945)—MOG, WIL
Battleground (1949)—FI

MAE WEST

She Done Him Wrong (1933)—MMA, UNI
I'm No Angel (1933)—UNI
Belle of the Nineties (1934)—UNI
Goin' to Town (1935)—ICS, UNI
Klondike Annie (1936)—UNI

MUSICAL FILMS OF THE STUDIO ERA

Musicals of the Thirties (1929-35)—MMA. Excerpts from *Rio Rita, Gold Diggers of 1933* and *1935, Forty-second Street, Flying Down to Rio, Music in the Air,* and *In Caliente*
Forty-second Street (1933)—AUD, CON, UA, WIL (Lloyd Bacon/Busby Berkeley)
Gold Diggers of 1933 (1933)—AUD, CON, UA, WIL (Mervyn LeRoy/Busby Berkeley)
Dames (1934)—AUD, UA (Ray Enright/Busby Berkeley)
Footlight Parade (1934)—AUD, UA (Lloyd Bacon/Busby Berkeley)
Gold Diggers of 1935 (1935)—AUD, CON, UA, WIL (Busby Berkeley)
In Caliente (1935)—AUD, UA (Busby Berkeley)
Gold Diggers of 1937 (1936)—AUD, CON, UA, WIL (Lloyd Bacon/Busby Berkeley)

Flying Down to Rio (1933)—FI (Thornton Freeland)
The Gay Divorcee (1934)—FI (Mark Sandrich)
Top Hat (1935)—AUD (Mark Sandrich)
Swing Time (1936)—FI (George Stevens)
Shall We Dance? (1937)—FI, MMA (Mark Sandrich)

STUDIO ERA MISCELLANY

The Big House (1930)—FI (George Hill)
Dracula (1931)—MOG, UNI (Tod Browning)
Frankenstein (1931)—UNI (James Whale)
Freaks (1932)—AUD, FI (Tod Browning)
Grand Hotel (1932)—FI (Edmund Goulding)
King Kong (1933)—FI, JAN (Cooper and Schoedsack)
The Private Life of Henry VIII (1933)—AUD, MOG (Alexander Korda)
Queen Christina (1933)—FI (Rouben Mamoulian)
State Fair (1933)—FI (Henry King)
Our Daily Bread (1934)—JAN, MMA (King Vidor)
Becky Sharp (1935)—FCE, ICS, MOG (Rouben Mamoulian)
The Lives of a Bengal Lancer (1935)—MMA (Henry King)
Mutiny on the Bounty (1935)—FI (Frank Lloyd)
My Man Godfrey (1936)—UNI (Gregory LaCava)
The Petrified Forest (1936)—AUD (Archie Mayo)
Easy Living (1937)—MMA, UNI (Mitchell Leisen)
The Good Earth (1937)—FI (Sidney Franklin)
Alexander's Ragtime Band (1938)—UFC (Henry King)
Golden Boy (1938)—AUD (Rouben Mamoulian)
Jesse James (1939)—UFC (Henry King)
Dark Victory (1940)—AUD, FI, TWF, WIL (Edmund Goulding)
Since You Went Away (1944)—STA, TWY (John Cromwell)

12. Years of Transition (1945–60)

BOOKS

Alloway, Lawrence. *Violent America: The Movies 1946–64.* New York: The Museum of Modern Art, 1971.

Battcock, Gregory. *The New American Cinema.* New York: Dutton, 1967.

Conant, Michael. *Antitrust in the Motion Picture Industry.* Berkeley and Los Angeles: University of California Press, 1960.

Kael, Pauline. "Movies, the Desperate Art." In *Film: An Anthology,* edited by Daniel Talbot, pp. 51–71. Berkeley and Los Angeles: University of California Press, 1966.

———. "Zeitgeist and Poltergeist; Or, Are Movies Going to Pieces?" In *I Lost It at the Movies,* pp. 3–24. New York: Bantam, 1966.

———. "Hud, Deep in the Divided Heart of Hollywood." In *I Lost It at the Movies,* pp. 69–83.

Kitses, James. *Horizons West: Mann, Boetticher, Peckinpah.* Bloomington, Ind. and London: Indiana University Press, 1969.

MacCann, Richard Dyer. *Hollywood in Transition.* Cambridge, Mass.: Houghton Mifflin, 1962.
Manvell, Roger. *New Cinema in the USA.* New York and London: Dutton/Vista, 1968.
Ross, Lillian. *Picture.* Garden City, N.Y.: Doubleday, 1962.

FILMS

JOHN HUSTON

The Maltese Falcon (1941)—AUD
The Treasure of the Sierra Madre (1948)—AUD
Key Largo (1948)—AUD, MOD
The Asphalt Jungle (1950)—FI
The Red Badge of Courage (1951)—FI
Beat the Devil (1954)—SWA

ELIA KAZAN

A Tree Grows in Brooklyn (1945)—FI
Boomerang (1947)—FI
Gentleman's Agreement (1947)—FI
Pinky (1949)—FI
Viva Zapata! (1952)—FI
On the Waterfront (1954)—AUD, ICS, SWA
East of Eden (1955)—AUD, ICS, SWA

STANLEY KRAMER

The Defiant Ones (1958)—UA
On the Beach (1959)—UA
Inherit the Wind (1960)—UA
Judgment at Nuremberg (1961)—UA
Guess Who's Coming to Dinner (1967)—SWA, TWY

VINCENTE MINNELLI

Meet Me in St. Louis (1944)—FI
An American in Paris (1951)—FI
The Band Wagon (1953)—FI
Lust for Life (1956)—FI
Designing Woman (1957)—FI
Gigi (1958)—FI
The Reluctant Debutante (1958)—FI
Bells Are Ringing (1960)—FI

OTTO PREMINGER

Laura (1944)—FI
The River of No Return (1954)—FI
Bonjour Tristesse (1958)—CWF, TWY
Anatomy of a Murder (1959)—AUD, SWA
Advise and Consent (1962)—SWA

GEORGE STEVENS

Alice Adams (1935)—FI
Vivacious Lady (1938)—FI
Gunga Din (1939)—FI
Woman of the Year (1942)—FI
I Remember Mama (1948)—AUD
A Place in the Sun (1951)—FI
Shane (1953)—FI
Giant (1956)—ICS

BILLY WILDER

Double Indemnity (1944)—UNI
The Lost Weekend (1945)—UNI
A Foreign Affair (1948)—UNI
Sunset Boulevard (1950)—FI
Stalag 17 (1953)—FI
Sabrina (1954)—FI
Love in the Afternoon (1957)—HUR
Some Like It Hot (1959)—UA
The Apartment (1960)—UA

WILLIAM WYLER

Dead End (1937)—SAM
Wuthering Heights (1939)—SAM
The Little Foxes (1941)—SAM
The Best Years of Our Lives (1946)—SAM
Roman Holiday (1953)—FI
Friendly Persuasion (1956)—HUR
Ben Hur (1959)—FI
Funny Girl (1968)—SWA

FRED ZINNEMANN

The Men (1950)—ICS, TWY, WIL
High Noon (1952)—AUD, CON, SWA, TWY
Member of the Wedding (1952)—AUD
From Here to Eternity (1953)—AUD, CON, ICS, SWA, TWY
A Hatful of Rain (1957)—FI
The Nun's Story (1959)—AUD, TWF, TWY
A Man for All Seasons (1966)—SWA

TRANSITIONAL ERA MISCELLANY

Anchors Aweigh (1945)—FI (George Sidney)
The House on 92nd Street (1945)—FI (Henry Hathaway)
State Fair (1945)—MED (Walter Lang)
A Walk in the Sun (1946)—MED (Lewis Milestone)
Body and Soul (1947)—AUD, WIL (Robert Rossen)
Crossfire (1947)—FI (Edward Dmytryk)
The Ghost and Mrs. Muir (1947)—FI (Joseph L. Mankiewicz)

Good News (1947)—FI (Charles Walters)
The Boy with Green Hair (1948)—FI, STA (Joseph Losey)
Call Northside 777 (1948)—FI (Henry Hathaway)
Easter Parade (1948)—FI (Charles Walters)
Force of Evil (1948)—WIL (Abraham Polonsky)
The Senator Was Indiscreet (1948)—ICS, WIL (George S. Kaufman)
The Snake Pit (1948)—FI (Anatole Litvak)
All the King's Men (1949)—AUD, SWA, TWY (Robert Rossen)
I Shot Jesse James (1949)—ICS (Samuel Fuller)
A Letter to Three Wives (1949)—FI (Joseph L. Mankiewicz)
On the Town (1949)—FI (Gene Kelly and Stanley Donen)
The Set-Up (1949)—FI (Robert Wise)
All About Eve (1950)—FI (Joseph L. Mankiewicz)
Winchester '73 (1950)—UNI (Anthony Mann)
The Day the Earth Stood Still (1951)—FI (Robert Wise)
Death of a Salesman (1951)—AUD, SWA, TWY (Laslo Benedek)
The Thing (1951)—FI (Christian Nyby)
Singin' in the Rain (1952)—FI (Gene Kelly and Stanley Donen)
Lili (1953)—FI (Charles Walters)
Niagara (1953)—FI (Henry Hathaway)
The Wild One (1953)—AUD, SWA (Laslo Benedek)
The Country Girl (1954)—FI (George Seaton)
Johnny Guitar (1954)—FI (Nicholas Ray)
Seven Brides for Seven Brothers (1954)—FI (Stanley Donen)
Bad Day at Black Rock (1955)—FI (John Sturges)
The Big Knife (1955)—UA (Robert Aldrich)
The Blackboard Jungle (1955)—FI (Richard Brooks)
Marty (1955)—UA (Delbert Mann)
Night of the Hunter (1955)—UA (Charles Laughton)
Rebel Without a Cause (1955)—AUD, ICS, SWA, TWF, TWY (Nicholas Ray)
Invasion of the Body Snatchers (1956)—HUR (Don Siegel)
Picnic (1956)—AUD, ICS (Joshua Logan)
Funny Face (1957)—FI (Stanley Donen)
Twelve Angry Men (1957)—UA (Sidney Lumet)
The Goddess (1958)—AUD (John Cromwell)
I Want to Live (1958)—UA (Robert Wise)
Imitation of Life (1959)—ICS, UNI (Douglas Sirk)
The Savage Eye (1959)—AUD (Maddow, Meyers, and Strick)
Elmer Gantry (1960)—UA (Richard Brooks)
The Magnificent Seven (1960)—UA (John Sturges)

13. Postwar Cinema in Italy and France (1945–74)

BOOKS

Armes, Roy. French Cinema Since 1946. 2 volumes. New York: Barnes, 1966.
———. The Cinema of Alain Resnais. New York: Barnes, 1968.
Bazin, André. What is Cinema? Vols. I, II. Berkeley and Los Angeles: University of California Press, 1967.

Cameron, Ian, ed. *The Films of Robert Bresson.* New York: Praeger, 1970.
Cameron, Ian and Wood, Robin. *Antonioni.* New York: Praeger, 1968.
Cocteau, Jean. *Cocteau on the Film.* New York: Roy Publishers, 1954.
Cowie, Peter. *Antonioni, Bergman, Resnais.* New York: Thomas Yoseloff, 1964.
Durgnat, Raymond. *Nouvelle Vague: The First Decade.* Essex: Loughton, 1963.
Guarner, José Luis. *Roberto Rossellini.* New York: Praeger, 1970.
Houston, Penelope. *Contemporary Cinema.* Baltimore, Md.: Penguin, 1964.
Jarratt, Vernon. *The Italian Cinema.* New York: Macmillan, 1951.
Kael, Pauline. "The Come-Dressed-as-the-Sick-Soul of Europe Parties: *La Notte, Last Year at Marienbad, La Dolce Vita.*" In *I Lost It at the Movies,* pp. 162–76. New York: Bantam, 1966.
Leprohon, Pierre. *Michelangelo Antonioni.* New York: Simon & Schuster, 1963.
Manvell, Roger. *New Cinema in Europe.* New York and London: Dutton/Vista, 1966.
Mussman, Toby, ed. *Jean-Luc Godard: A Critical Anthology.* New York: Dutton, 1968.
Petrie, Graham. *The Cinema of François Truffaut.* New York: Barnes, 1970.
Rondi, Gian. *Italian Cinema Today.* New York: Hill & Wang, 1965.
Roud, Richard. *Jean-Luc Godard.* New York: Doubleday, 1968.
Siclier, Jacques. *Nouvelle Vague?* Paris: Éditions du Cerf, 1961.
Ward, John. *Alain Resnais, or The Theme of Time.* New York: Doubleday, 1968.

FILMS

ITALY

MICHELANGELO ANTONIONI

Il Grido (1957)—CON
L'Avventura (1960)—JAN
La Notte (1961)—UA
L'Eclisse (1962)—AUD
The Red Desert (1964)—AUD
Blow Up (1966)—FI
Zabriskie Point (1970)—FI

BERNARDO BERTOLUCCI

Before the Revolution (1964)—AUD, NYF
The Conformist (1971)—FI
Last Tango in Paris (1973)—UA

VITTORIO DE SICA

The Bicycle Thief (1948)—AUD
Miracle in Milan (1951)—JAN
Umberto D (1952)—JAN
Gold of Naples (1955)—AUD
Two Women (1961)—AUD
The Garden of the Finzi-Contini's (1971)—CIN

FEDERICO FELLINI

Variety Lights (1950)—AUD
The White Sheik (1952)—AUD, CON
La Strada (1954)—AUD
Il Bidone (1955)—AUD
I Vitelloni (1956)—AUD, CON
Nights of Cabiria (1957)—AUD
La Dolce Vita (1959)—AUD
8½ (1963)—AUD
Juliet of the Spirits (1965)—AUD
Fellini-Satyricon (1969)—UA

PIETRO GERMI

The Railroad Man (1956)—WAL
Divorce—Italian Style (1961)—AUD
Seduced and Abandoned (1964)—WAL
The Birds, the Bees, and the Italians (1966)—WAR

PIER PAOLO PASOLINI

Accattone! (1961)—AUD
The Gospel According to St. Matthew (1964)—AUD
The Hawks and the Sparrows (1965)—AUD
Teorema (1969)—WAL

ROBERTO ROSSELLINI

Open City (1945)—CON
Paisan (1946)—NYF
General Della Rovere (1959)—WAL
The Rise to Power of Louis XIV (1965)—AUD

LUCHINO VISCONTI

Ossessione (1942)—AUD
La Terra Trema (1948)—AUD
Senso (1954)—AUD
Rocco and His Brothers (1960)—AUD
The Leopard (1963)—FI
The Damned (1968)—WAR
Death in Venice (1971)—WAR

ITALIAN MISCELLANY

To Live in Peace (1948)—AUD (Luigi Zampa)
Without Pity (1948)—AUD (Alberto Lattuada)
Bitter Rice (1949)—AUD (Giuseppi de Santis)
Rome 11 O'clock (1952)—AUD (Giuseppi de Santis)
The Bandits of Orgosolo (1961)—CON (Vittorio deSeta)
The Sound of Trumpets (1961)—JAN (Ermanno Olmi)
The Easy Life (1963)—AUD (Dino Risi)

The Fiancés (1963)—JAN (Ermanno Olmi)
The Girl with the Suitcase (1963)—AUD (Valerio Zurlini)
The Organizer (1964)—WAL (Mario Monicelli)
The 10th Victim (1965)—AUD (Elio Petri)
China is Near (1967)—SWA (Marco Bellochio)
Once Upon a Time in the West (1969)—FI (Sergio Leone)
Investigation of a Citizen above Suspicion (1970)—SWA (Elio Petri)

FRANCE

ROBERT BRESSON

Les Dames du Bois de Boulogne (1943)—CON
Diary of a Country Priest (1951)—AUD
A Man Escaped (1956)—CON
Pickpocket (1959)—NYF
The Trial of Joan of Arc (1962)—CON

CLAUDE CHABROL

The Cousins (1959)—AUD
Les Bonnes Femmes (1959)—AUD
Les Biches (1968)—AUD
Le Boucher (1970)—SWA

RENÉ CLÉMENT

Forbidden Games (1952)—JAN
Gervaise (1956)—WAL
Purple Noon (1959)—AUD
Is Paris Burning? (1966)—FI

HENRI-GEORGES CLOUZOT

The Wages of Fear (1953)—AUD
Diabolique (1955)—WAR

JEAN COCTEAU

Blood of a Poet (1930)—AUD
Beauty and the Beast (1946)—JAN
Les Parents Terribles (1948)—JAN
Orpheus (1949)—JAN
The Testament of Orpheus (1959)—JAN

JEAN-LUC GODARD

Breathless (1959)—CON
A Woman Is a Woman (1961)—CON
Vivre sa vie (1962)—CON
Les Carabiniers (1963)—NYF
Le Petit Soldat (1963)—NYF
Band of Outsiders (1964)—SWA

A Married Woman (1964)—SWA
Contempt (1964)—AUD
Alphaville (1965)—CON
Masculine/Feminine (1966)—SWA
Weekend (1968)—GRO

LOUIS MALLE

Frantic (1958)—AUD
The Lovers (1958)—JAN
Zazie dans le Métro (1960)—AUD
Viva Maria (1965)—UA
Murmur of the Heart (1971)—WAL

MAX OPHULS

Letter from an Unknown Woman (1948)—AUD, WIL
Caught (1949)—WIL
La Ronde (1950)—JAN
The Earrings of Madame de . . . (1953)—CON
Lola Montès (1955)—AUD

ALAIN RESNAIS

Hiroshima Mon Amour (1959)—AUD
Last Year at Marienbad (1961)—AUD
Muriel (1963)—UA
La Guerre est finie (1966)—AUD

ERIC ROHMER

La Collectioneuse (1967)—CON
My Night at Maud's (1969)—CON
Claire's Knee (1970)—SWA
Chloe in the Afternoon (1971)—SWA

JACQUES TATI

Mr. Hulot's Holiday (1953)—WAL
My Uncle (1958)—CON
Playtime (1968)—WAL
Traffic (1972)—SWA

FRANÇOIS TRUFFAUT

The 400 Blows (1959)—JAN
Shoot the Piano Player (1960)—JAN
Jules and Jim (1961)—JAN
The Soft Skin (1965)—JAN
Fahrenheit 451 (1966)—SWA, TWY
The Bride Wore Black (1968)—UA
Stolen Kisses (1968)—UA
Bed and Board (1970)—SWA
The Wild Child (1970)—UA

FRENCH MISCELLANY

Symphonie Pastorale (1947)—SWA (Jean Delannoy)
Les Enfants Terribles (1950)—JAN (Jean-Pierre Melville)
Les Liaisons Dangereuses (1959)—AUD (Roger Vadim)
Lola (1960)—CON (Jacques Demy)
Cleo from Five to Seven (1961)—AUD (Agnès Varda)
Leon Morin, Priest (1961)—AUD (Jean-Pierre Melville)
Sundays and Cybèle (1962)—SWA (Serge Bourgignon)
Thérèse Desqueroux (1962)—CON (George Franju)
Judex (1963)—WAL (Georges Franju)
Le Bonheur (1965)—JAN (Agnès Varda)
Circle of Love (1965)—WAL (Roger Vadim)
The Battle of Algiers (1966)—AUD (Gillo Pontecorvo)
The Two of Us (1968)—SWA (Claude Berri)
Z (1969)—CIN (Costa-Gavras)
The Confession (1970)—FI (Costa-Gavras)
The Sorrow and the Pity (1972)—CIN (Marcel Ophuls)

14. Emerging National Traditions (1945–74)

BOOKS

Barnouw, Erik, and Krishnaswamy, Subramanyam. *The Indian Film*. New York: Columbia University Press, 1963.

Blumenthal, J. "*Macbeth* Into *Throne of Blood*." In *Film Theory and Criticism: Introductory Readings*, edited by Gerald Mast and Marshall Cohen, pp. 340–51. New York: Oxford University Press, 1974.

Cowie, Peter. *Swedish Cinema*. New York: Barnes, 1966.

Donner, Jorn. *The Personal Vision of Ingmar Bergman*. Bloomington, Ind. and London: Indiana University Press, 1964.

Durgnat, Raymond. *Luis Buñuel*. Berkeley and Los Angeles: University of California Press, 1968.

Kyrou, Ado. *Luis Buñuel: An Introduction*. New York: Simon and Schuster, 1963.

Lauritzen, Einar. *Swedish Film*. Garden City, N.Y.: Doubleday, 1962.

Richie, Donald. *The Films of Akira Kurosawa*. Berkeley and Los Angeles: University of California Press, 1965.

———. *The Japanese Cinema*. New York: Doubleday, 1971.

———. *Ozu*. Berkeley and Los Angeles: University of California Press, 1973.

——— and Anderson, Joseph. *Japanese Film: Art and Industry*. New York: Grove Press, 1960.

Seton, Marie. *Portrait of a Director: Satyajit Ray*. Bloomington, Ind. and London: Indiana University Press, 1971.

Simon, John. *Ingmar Bergman Directs*. New York: Harcourt Brace, 1927.

Young, Vernon. *Cinema Borealis: Ingmar Bergman and the Swedish Ethos*. New York: David Lewis, 1972.

FILMS

SWEDEN

INGMAR BERGMAN

Three Strange Loves (1949)—JAN
Monika (1952)—JAN
The Naked Night (1953)—JAN
Dreams (1955)—JAN
Smiles of a Summer Night (1955)—JAN
The Seventh Seal (1957)—JAN
Wild Strawberries (1958)—JAN
The Magician (1959)—JAN
The Virgin Spring (1960)—JAN
The Devil's Eye (1961)—JAN
Through a Glass Darkly (1962)—JAN
Winter Light (1963)—JAN
The Silence (1963)—JAN
Persona (1967)—UA
Hour of the Wolf (1968)—UA
Shame (1969)—UA
The Passion of Anna (1970)—UA
Cries and Whispers (1972)—FI

SWEDISH MISCELLANY

Thirst (1948)—JAN (Alf Sjøberg)
Miss Julie (1951)—JAN (Alf Sjøberg)
Dear John (1966)—AUD (Lars Magnus Lindgren)
Here's Your Life (1966)—AUD (Jan Troell)
Elvira Madigan (1967)—SWA (Bo Widerberg)
My Sister, My Love (1967)—AUD (Vilgot Sjøman)
I Am Curious (Yellow) (1968)—GRO (Vilgot Sjøman)
Adalen '31 (1969)—FI (Bo Widerberg)
The Emigrants (1972)—WAR (Jan Troell)

GREAT BRITAIN

LINDSAY ANDERSON

This Sporting Life (1963)—TWY
If . . . (1968)—FI
O Lucky Man! (1973)—WAR

JACK CLAYTON

Room at the Top (1959)—WAL
The Innocents (1961)—FI
The Pumpkin Eater (1964)—AUD, CON, ICS, SWA, TWY

DAVID LEAN

Brief Encounter (1946)—WAL
Great Expectations (1947)—AUD, TWY
Oliver Twist (1948)—JAN
Summertime (1955)—UA
The Bridge on the River Kwai (1957)—AUD, ICS, SWA, TWY
Lawrence of Arabia (1962)—SWA
Doctor Zhivago (1965)—FI
Ryan's Daughter (1970)—FI

RICHARD LESTER

A Hard Day's Night (1964)—UA
The Knack (1965)—UA
Help! (1965)—UA
Petulia (1968)—ICS, TWY

LAURENCE OLIVIER

Henry V (1944)—AUD, TWY
Hamlet (1948)—AUD, TWY
Richard III (1955)—JAN

CAROL REED

Odd Man Out (1947)—JAN, UNI
The Fallen Idol (1949)—WAL
The Third Man (1950)—TWY, WAL
Outcast of the Islands (1952)—AUD
The Man Between (1953)—AUD, WAL
The Key (1958)—AUD
Our Man in Havana (1960)—AUD, TWY
Oliver! (1968)—SWA

TONY RICHARDSON

Look Back in Anger (1959)—WAR
The Entertainer (1960)—WAL
Sanctuary (1961)—AUD, ICS
A Taste of Honey (1962)—TWY, WAL
The Loneliness of the Long-Distance Runner (1962)—AUD, TWY, WAL
Tom Jones (1963)—UA

KEN RUSSELL

Women in Love (1970)—UA
The Devils (1971)—WAR
The Boy Friend (1971)—FI

JOHN SCHLESINGER

Billy Liar (1963)—TWY, WAL
Darling (1965)—AUD

Midnight Cowboy (1969)—UA
Sunday, Bloody Sunday (1971)—UA

THE BRITISH "LITTLE COMEDIES"

Kind Hearts and Coronets (1949)—CON, TWF, TWY (Robert Hamer)
Tight Little Island (1949)—JAN (Alexander Mackendrick)
The Lavender Hill Mob (1951)—CON, TWF, TWY (Charles Crichton)
The Man in the White Suit (1952)—CON, TWF, TWY (Alexander Mackendrick)
The Captain's Paradise (1953)—AUD, WAL (Anthony Kimmins)
Father Brown or *The Detective* (1954)—AUD (Robert Hamer)
The Green Man (1957)—AUD (Robert Day)
The Horse's Mouth (1958)—UA (Ronald Neame)

BRITISH MISCELLANY

The Red Shoes (1948)—TWY, WAL (Powell and Pressburger)
The Winslow Boy (1950)—WIL (Anthony Asquith)
Tales of Hoffman (1951)—WAL (Powell and Pressburger)
The Importance of Being Earnest (1952)—JAN (Anthony Asquith)
The Doctor's Dilemma (1958)—FI (Anthony Asquith)
The Angry Silence (1959)—AUD, TWY (Guy Green)
Expresso Bongo (1960)—WAL (Val Guest)
I'm All Right, Jack (1960)—AUD (John Boulting)
Sons and Lovers (1960)—FI (Jack Cardiff)
Tunes of Glory (1960)—UA (Ronald Neame)
The Kitchen (1961)—AUD (James Hill)
The League of Gentlemen (1961)—JAN (Basil Dearden)
Saturday Night and Sunday Morning (1961)—WAL (Karel Reisz)
Whistle Down the Wind (1961)—JAN (Bryan Forbes)
Billy Budd (1962)—AUD, HUR (Peter Ustinov)
The Beggar's Opera (1963)—ICS, TWY (Peter Brook)
The Servant (1963)—AUD (Joseph Losey)
Lord of the Flies (1963)—WAL (Peter Brook)
Sparrows Can't Sing (1963)—JAN (Joan Littlewood)
The Caretaker (1964)—JAN (Clive Donner)
The Girl with Green Eyes (1964)—UA (Desmond Davies)
Nothing But the Best (1964)—AUD, CON, TWY (Clive Donner)
Seance on a Wet Afternoon (1964)—AUD (Bryan Forbes)
Morgan! (1966)—SWA (Karel Reisz)
Georgy Girl (1966)—AUD, ICS, SWA, TWY (Silvio Narizzano)
The Whisperers (1967)—UA (Bryan Forbes)
Accident (1967)—SWA (Joseph Losey)
Joanna (1968)—FI (Michael Sarne)
Isadora (1968)—TWY (Karel Reisz)
The Go-Between (1971)—SWA (Joseph Losey)

CENTRAL AND EASTERN EUROPE

MILOŠ FORMAN

Black Peter (1963)—AUD
Loves of a Blonde (1965)—AUD

The Firemen's Ball (1967)—CIN
Taking Off (1971)—SWA, TWY, UNI

JAN KADÁR AND ELMAR KLOS

Death Is Called Engelchen (1963)—AUD
The Shop on Main Street (1965)—AUD
Adrift (1971)—FI

MIKLÓS JANCSÓ

My Way Home (1964)—AUD
The Round Up (1965)—AUD
The Red and the White (1968)—AUD
Silence and Cry (1968)—AUD

DUŠAN MAKAVEJEV

Love Affair, or The Case of the Missing Switchboard Operator (1967)—AUD
WR—Mysteries of the Organism (1971)—CIN

ROMAN POLANSKI

Knife in the Water (1962)—JAN
Repulsion (1965)—SWA
Rosemary's Baby (1968)—FI
Macbeth (1971)—SWA

ANDREJ WAJDA

Kanal (1957)—JAN
Ashes and Diamonds (1958)—JAN

MISCELLANY: CZECHOSLOVAKIA, POLAND, YUGOSLAVIA

Romeo, Juliet, and Darkness (1960)—AUD (Jiří Weiss)
Baron Münchhausen (1962)—AUD (Karel Zeman)
Intimate Lighting (1965)—AUD (Ivan Passer)
Closely Watched Trains (1966)—AUD (Jiří Menzel)
Daisies (1966)—AUD (Věra Chytilová)
The Fifth Horseman is Fear (1966)—AUD (Zbyněk Brynych)
A Report on the Party and the Guests (1966)—AUD (Jan Němec)
Salto (1966)—AUD (Tadeusz Konwicki)
I Even Met Happy Gypsies (1967)—AUD (Aleksandar Petrovič)
Capricious Summer (1968)—AUD (Jiří Menzel)

JAPAN AND INDIA

KON ICHIKAWA

The Harp of Burma (1956)—JAN
Fires on the Plain (1959)—JAN

Odd Obsession (1960)—JAN
Tokyo Olympiad (1964)—AUD

AKIRA KUROSAWA

Those Who Tread on the Tiger's Tail (1945)—AUD
Drunken Angel (1948)—AUD
Stray Dog (1949)—AUD
Rashomon (1950)—JAN
Ikiru (1952)—AUD
Seven Samurai (1954)—AUD
The Lower Depths (1957)—AUD
Throne of Blood (1957)—AUD
Yojimbo (1960)—AUD
The Bad Sleep Well (1960)—AUD
Red Beard (1965)—AUD
Dodes' Kaden (1970)—JAN

KENJI MIZOGUCHI

Utamaro and his Five Women (1946)—NYF
Women of the Night (1948)—AUD
The Life of O'Haru (1952)—NYF
Ugetsu (1953)—JAN
Sansho the Bailiff (1954)—AUD
Princess Yang Kwei Fei (1955)—NYF
Street of Shame (1956)—JAN

YASUJIRO OZU

I Was Born, But . . . (1932)—NYF
Passing Fancy (1933)—AUD
There Was a Father (1942)—AUD
Late Spring (1949)—NYF
Early Summer (1951)—AUD
Tokyo Story (1953)—NYF
Early Spring (1956)—NYF
Tokyo Twilight (1957)—AUD
Ohayo (1959)—AUD
Floating Weeds (1959)—JAN
Late Autumn (1960)—NYF
End of Summer (1961)—NYF
Autumn Afternoon (1962)—NYF

SATYAJIT RAY

Pather Panchali (1955)—AUD
Aparajito (1956)—AUD
The World of Apu (1958)—AUD
The Music Room (1959)—AUD
Devi (1960)—AUD
Kanchenjungha (1962)—AUD
Mahanagar (1963)—AUD

JAPANESE MISCELLANY

Gate of Hell (1953)—JAN, SWA, TWY (Teinosuke Kinugasa)
Samurai (1953)—AUD (Hiroshi Inagaki)
The Mistress (*Gan*, 1953)—AUD (Shiro Toyoda)
Muddy Waters (*Nigorie*, 1953)—AUD (Tadashi Imai)
Ningen no joken (1959)—AUD (Masahi Kobayashi)
Bad Boys (1960)—AUD (Susumu Hani)
The Island (1961)—AUD (Kaneto Shindo)
She and He (1963)—AUD (Susumu Hani)
Kwaidan (1964)—TWY, WAL (Masahi Kobayashi)
Woman in the Dunes (1964)—CON (Hiroshi Teshigahara)
Bwana Toshi (1965)—AUD (Susumu Hani)

LUIS BUÑUEL

Un Chien andalou (1929)—MMA
Los Olvidados (1950)—AUD
El (1952)—AUD
The Adventures of Robinson Crusoe (1954)—TWY
Mexican Bus Ride (1954)—SWA
Nazarin (1958)—AUD
Viridiana (1961)—AUD
The Exterminating Angel (1962)—AUD
Belle de Jour (1966)—HUR
The Milky Way (1969)—WAR
The Discreet Charm of the Bourgeoisie (1972)—FI

15. The American Cinema (1961–74)

BOOKS

Curtis, David. *Experimental Cinema*. New York: Universe Books, 1971.
Kael, Pauline. "Commitment and Straitjacket." In *I Lost it at the Movies*, pp. 55–69. New York: Bantam, 1966.
Renan, Sheldon. *An Introduction to the American Underground Film*. New York: Dutton, 1967.
Walker, Alexander. *Stanley Kubrick Directs*. New York: Harcourt Brace, 1971.
Youngblood, Gene. *Expanded Cinema*. New York: Dutton, 1970.

FILMS

WOODY ALLEN

Take the Money and Run (1968)—FI
Bananas (1971)—UA
Everything You Always Wanted to Know About Sex . . . (1972)—UA
Sleeper (1973)—UA

ROBERT ALTMAN

M*A*S*H* (1970)—FI
Brewster McCloud (1970)—FI
McCabe and Mrs. Miller (1972)—WAR
Images (1972)—SWA

PETER BOGDANOVICH

Targets (1968)—FI
The Last Picture Show (1971)—RBC
What's Up, Doc? (1972)—WAR
Paper Moon (1973)—FI

FRANCIS FORD COPPOLA

You're a Big Boy Now (1967)—ICS, SWA, TWY
The Godfather (1972)—FI
The Conversation (1974)—FI

WILLIAM FRIEDKIN

The Night They Raided Minsky's (1968)—UA
The Boys in the Band (1970)—SWA
The French Connection (1971)—FI

STANLEY KUBRICK

Killer's Kiss (1955)—UA
The Killing (1956)—UA
Paths of Glory (1957)—UA
Lolita (1962)—FI
Dr. Strangelove (1963)—SWA
2001: A Space Odyssey (1968)—FI
A Clockwork Orange (1973)—WAR

SAM PECKINPAH

Ride the High Country (1962)—FI
Major Dundee (1965)—TWY
The Wild Bunch (1968)—WAR
The Ballad of Cable Hogue (1970)—ICS, SWA, TWY
Straw Dogs (1971)—FI
Pat Garrett and Billy the Kid (1973)—FI
The Getaway (1973)—SWA

AMERICAN MISCELLANY

Breakfast at Tiffany's (1961)—FI (Blake Edwards)
A Cold Wind in August (1961)—UA (Alexander Singer)
The Hustler (1961)—FI (Robert Rossen)
David and Lisa (1962)—AUD (Frank Perry)

Experiment in Terror (1962)—AUD, ICS, TWY (Blake Edwards)
Lonely Are the Brave (1962)—TWY, UNI (David Miller)
The Manchurian Candidate (1962)—UA (John Frankenheimer)
Whatever Happened to Baby Jane? (1962)—TWY (Robert Aldrich)
Shock Corridor (1963)—HUR (Samuel Fuller)
The Great Escape (1963)—UA (John Sturges)
Hallelujah the Hills (1963)—JAN (Adolfas Mekas)
Hud (1963)—FI (Martin Ritt)
Cat Ballou (1965)—ICS, TWY (Elliot Silverstein)
The Pawnbroker (1965)—AUD (Sidney Lumet)
The Spy Who Came in from the Cold (1965)—FI (Martin Ritt)
A Thousand Clowns (1965)—UA (Fred Coe)
Who's Afraid of Virginia Woolf? (1966)—WAR (Mike Nichols)
A Fine Madness (1966)—TWY (Irvin Kershner)
Bonnie and Clyde (1967)—ICS, SWA, TWY (Arthur Penn)
Cool Hand Luke (1967)—ICS, SWA, TWY (Stuart Rosenberg)
In Cold Blood (1967)—SWA (Richard Brooks)
Up the Down Staircase (1967)—ICS, SWA, TWF, TWY (Robert Mulligan)
In the Heat of the Night (1967)—UA (Norman Jewison)
Faces (1968)—WAL (John Cassavetes)
Bullitt (1968)—ICS, SWA, TWY (Peter Yates)
The Fixer (1968)—FI (John Frankenheimer)
Night of the Living Dead (1968)—AUD (George A. Romero)
Pretty Poison (1968)—FI (Noel Black)
Rachel, Rachel (1968)—TWY (Paul Newman)
Goodbye, Columbus (1969)—FI (Larry Pierce)
Easy Rider (1969)—RBC (Peter Fonda and Dennis Hopper)
They Shoot Horses, Don't They? (1969)—FI (Sidney Pollack)
Medium Cool (1969)—FI (Haskell Wexler)
Bob and Carol and Ted and Alice (1969)—SWA (Paul Mazursky)
Butch Cassidy and the Sundance Kid (1969)—FI (George Roy Hill)
The Great White Hope (1969)—FI (Martin Ritt)
Last Summer (1969)—HUR (Frank Perry)
Where's Poppa? (1970)—UA (Carl Reiner)
Patton (1970)—FI (Franklin J. Schaffner)
Five Easy Pieces (1970)—RBC (Bob Rafelson)
Joe (1970)—WAR (John G. Avildsen)
Klute (1971)—ICS, SWA (Alan J. Pakula)
The Reivers (1971)—SWA (Mark Rydell)
Little Big Man (1971)—SWA (Arthur Penn)
A New Leaf (1971)—FI (Elaine May)
THX 1138 (1971)—WAR (George Lucas)
Fritz the Cat (1972)—WAR (Ralph Bakshi)
Deliverance (1972)—WAR (John Boorman)
Carnal Knowledge (1972)—SWA (Mike Nichols)
Something For Everyone (1972)—SWA (Harold Prince)
Cabaret (1972)—HUR (Bob Fosse)
Bang the Drum Slowly (1973)—FI (John Hancock)
The Sting (1973)—UNI (George Roy Hill)
American Graffiti (1973)—SWA, UNI (George Lucas)

INDEPENDENT CINEMA MISCELLANY

Rhythmus 21 (1921)—MMA (Hans Richter)
Symphonie Diagonale (1921–24)—MMA (Viking Eggeling)
The Life and Death of 9413—A Hollywood Extra (1928)—MMA (Florey and Vorkapich)
H_2O (1929)—MMA (Ralph Steiner)
Lot in Sodom (1933)—AUD, CFS (Watson and Webber)
The Films of Oskar Fischinger (1933–49)—MMA
Dawn to Dawn (1934)—AUD (Joseph Berne)
Colour Box (1935)—MMA (Len Lye)
Swinging the Lambeth Walk (1940)—MMA (Len Lye)
Meshes of the Afternoon (1943)—MMA (Maya Deren)
Fireworks (1947)—CFS, FMC (Kenneth Anger)
Mother's Day (1948)—AUD (James Broughton)
Muscle Beach (1950)—AUD (Joseph Strick)
Loony Tom, the Happy Lover (1951)—AUD, MMA (James Broughton)
The Pleasure Garden (1954)—AUD (James Broughton)
Reflections on Black (1955)—AUD (Stan Brakhage)
The Wonder Ring (1955)—AUD, MMA (Stan Brakhage)
Man Is in Pain (1955)—AUD (Larry Jordan)
Star-Spangled to Death (1957)—FMC (Ken Jacobs)
Flesh of Morning (1957)—AUD, FMC (Stan Brakhage)
Blazes (1957)—MMA (Robert Breer)
Jamestown Baloos (1957)—AUD, MMA (Robert Breer)
A Movie (1958)—AUD, MMA (Bruce Conner)
Anticipation of the Night (1958)—MMA (Stan Brakhage)
Wedlock House: An Intercourse (1959)—AUD, FMC (Stan Brakhage)
Window Water Baby Moving (1959)—AUD, FMC, MMA (Stan Brakhage)
The Flower Thief (1960)—FMC (Ron Rice)
Catalog (1961)—MMA (John Whitney)
Cosmic Ray (1961)—AUD, CFS, MMA (Bruce Conner)
The Death of P'town (1961)—FMC (Ken Jacobs)
Guns of the Trees (1961)—FMC (Jonas Mekas)
Thanatopsis (1960–62)—FMC (Ed Emshwiller)
Horse Over Teakettle (1962)—FMC, MMA (Robert Breer)
Normal Love (1963)—FMC (Jack Smith)
Dog Star Man (1959–64)—FMC (Stan Brakhage)
Breathdeath (1963–64)—CFS, FMC (Stan VanDerBeek)
Blow Job (1964)—AND, FMC (Andy Warhol)
Scorpio Rising (1962–64)—FMC (Kenneth Anger)
Sins of the Fleshapoids (1964)—FMC (George and Mike Kuchar)
Mass (1963–64)—AUD, MMA (Bruce Baillie)
Fist Fight (1964)—MMA (Robert Breer)
Harlot (1965)—AND, FMC (Andy Warhol)
Confessions of a Black Mother Succuba (1964-65)—AUD, FMC (Robert Nelson)
Quixote (1964–65)—AUD, MMA (Bruce Baillie)
My Hustler (1965)—AND, FMC (Andy Warhol)
Oh Dem Watermelons (1965)—AUD, FMC, MMA (Robert Nelson)
Report (1965)—AUD (Bruce Conner)

The Chelsea Girls (1966)—AND (Andy Warhol)
Castro Street (1966)—AUD, FMC, MMA (Bruce Baillie)
Inauguration of the Pleasure Dome (1954-66)—FMC (Kenneth Anger)
Relativity (1963–66)—FMC (Ed Emshwiller)
Wavelength (1967)—MMA (Michael Snow)
Atmosfear (1967)—MMA (Tom DeWitt)
Offon (1967)—MMA (Scott Bartlett)
Chinese Firedrill (1968)—MMA (Will Hindle)
Permutations (1968)—MMA (John Whitney)
Trash (1968)—CIN (Warhol and Morrissey)
Scenes from Under Childhood (1968)—AUD, FMC (Stan Brakhage)
The Machine of Eden (1969)—MMA (Stan Brakhage)
Lemon (1969)—MMA (Hollis Frampton)
Quick Billy (1968–71)—AUD (Bruce Baillie)
Tom, Tom, the Piper's Son (1971)—MMA (Ken Jacobs)
Matrix (1971)—MMA (John Whitney)

DISTRIBUTORS

AND

Warhol Films, Inc.
33 Union Square West
New York, N.Y. 10003
(212) 924-4344

AUD

Audio-Brandon Films
34 MacQuesten Parkway South
Mount Vernon, N.Y. 10550
(914) 664-5051
        or
1619 North Cherokee
Los Angeles, California 90028
(213) 463-0357
        or
3868 Piedmont Avenue
Oakland, California 94611
(415) 658-9890
        or
8400 Brookfield Avenue
Brookfield, Illinios 60513
(312) 485-3925

CFS

Creative Film Society
8435 Geyser Avenue
Northridge, California 91324
(213) 786-8277

CIN

Cinema 5   16
595 Madison Avenue
New York, N.Y. 10022
(212) 421-5555

CON

Contemporary Films/McGraw-Hill
Princeton Road
Hightstown, New Jersey 08520
(609) 448-1700
        or
828 Custer Avenue
Evanston, Illinois 60202
(312) 869-5010
        or
1714 Stockton Street
San Francisco, California 94133
(415) 362-3115

CWF

Clem Williams Films
2240 Nobleston Road
Pittsburgh, Pennsylvania 15205
(412) 921-5810
        or
5424 West North Avenue
Chicago, Illinois 60639
(312) 637-3322

DIS

Walt Disney Productions
800 Sonora Avenue
Glendale, California 91201
(213) 845-3141

EMG

Em Gee Film Library
16024 Ventura Blvd.
Encino, California 91436
(213) 981-5506

FCE

Film Classic Exchange
1926 South Vermont Avenue
Los Angeles, California 90007
(213) 731-3854

FI

Films Incorporated
35-01 Queens Blvd.
Long Island City, N.Y. 11101
(212) 937-1110
          or
4420 Oakton Street
Skokie, Illinois 60076
(312) 676-1088
          or
offices in Atlanta, Boston, Dallas,
Hollywood, Salt Lake City, and
San Diego

FMC

Filmmakers' Cooperative
175 Lexington Avenue
New York, N.Y. 10016
(212) 889-3820

GRO

Grove Press Films
53 E. 11th Street
New York, N.Y. 10003
(212) 677-2400

HUR

Hurlock Cine World
13 Arcadia Road
Old Greenwich, Conn. 06870
(203) 637-4319

ICS

Institutional Cinema Service
915 Broadway
New York, N.Y. 10010
(212) 673-3990

JAN

Janus Films
745 Fifth Avenue
New York, N.Y. 10022
(212) 753-7100

MED

Media International
107 North Franklin Street
Madison, Wisconsin 53703
(608) 255-3184

MMA

Museum of Modern Art
Department of Film
11 West 53rd Street
New York, N.Y. 10019
(212) 956-6100

MOD

Modern Sound Pictures
1410 Howard Street
Omaha, Nebraska 68102
(402) 341-8476

MOG

Mogull's
112 West 48th Street
New York, N.Y. 10019
(212) 757-1414

NYF

New Yorker Films
43 West 61st Street
New York, N.Y. 10023
(212) 247-6110

RBC

RBC Films
933 North La Brea Avenue
Los Angeles, California 90038
(213) 874-5050

SAM

Samuel Goldwyn 16
1041 North Formosa Avenue
Los Angeles, California 90046
(213) 851-1234

STA

Standard Film Service
14710 West Warren Avenue
Dearborn, Michigan 48126
(313) 581-2250

SWA

Swank Motion Pictures
201 South Jefferson Avenue
St. Louis, Missouri 63166
(314) 534-6300

TWF

Trans-World Films
332 South Michigan Avenue
Chicago, Illinois 60604
(312) 922-1530

TWY

Twyman Films
329 Salem Avenue
Dayton, Ohio 45401
(513) 222-4014

UA

United Artists Sixteen
729 Seventh Avenue
New York, N.Y. 10019
(212) 245-6000

UFC

United Films
1425 South Main Street
Tulsa, Oklahoma 74119
(918) 583-2681

UNI

Universal Sixteen
221 Park Avenue South
New York, N.Y. 10003
(212) 777-6600
or
1025 North Highland Avenue
Los Angeles, California 90038
(213) 465-5136
or
425 North Michigan Avenue
Chicago, Illinois 60611
(312) 337-1100
or
offices in Atlanta, Dallas, and
Portland, Ore.

WAL

Walter Reade 16
241 East 34th Street
New York, N.Y. 10016
(212) 683-6800

WAR

Warner Brothers Film Gallery
4000 Warner Boulevard
Burbank, California 91522
(213) 843-7280

WIL

Willoughby-Peerless
110 West 32nd Street
New York, N.Y. 10001
(212) 564-1600

Index

Page numbers in **boldface** refer to extended discussions of particular entries; numbers in *italic* designate pages containing one or more still photographs taken from the films indexed.

À Nous la liberté, 232, 233, 245, 247–50, 252, 343
Abbott, Bud and Lou Costello, **333**
Abraham Lincoln, 89
Absalom! Absalom!, 310
Academy Award, 347, 421, 422
Accattone, 362, 389
Acres, Birt, 20
Adventurer, The, 88, 100, 101, 102, 103, 104
Adventures of Dolly, The, **54–55**
Advise and Consent, 328
African Queen, The, 330
L'Age d'or, 470
Agee, James, 144
Agfacolor monopack, 325
Aitken, Harry, 127
Alexander Nevsky, 203, **206,** 217
Alfredo, Alfredo, 361
"Alice in Cartoonland", 237

Alice Plays Cupid, 237
Alice's Restaurant, 490
Allen, Woody, 477, *491*
All Quiet on the Western Front, 175, 226, 287
Alphaville, 380
Altman, Robert, 481, 485, **488–89**
Amarcord, 352
Ameche, Don, 285
America, 85, **89**
American Film Theater, 50
American Graffiti, 490
American in Paris, An, 320, 335, **336**
American-International Pictures, 327, 380
American Mutoscope and Biograph Company ("Biograph"), 34–35, 46, 47, 48, 54, 57, 58, 59, 73, 75, 76, 91, 115, 117

"American Perforation", 16
"American shot", 56, 425
American Zoetrope studio, 489, 490
Amiche, Le, 357
Amidei, Sergio, 348
Anæmic Cinema, 241
Anamorphic lens. *See* CinemaScope.
Anatomy of a Murder, 328
And God Created Woman, 386
And My Love to the Swallows, 422
And Then There Were None, 250
Anderson, "Broncho Billy", 36, 43
Anderson, Lindsay, 418, 419, **420**, 448
Andersson, Bibi, *434*
Andersson, Harriet, 404, 412, *437*
Andy Hardy Gets Spring Fever, 287
Angel, 291
Anger, Kenneth, 479, 497, **499–500**
Angry Silence, The, 418
"Angry Young Man" films, 414– 15, 417, 418
Animation, 11, 40, **228**, **237–38**, 431, 445, 498
Anni Difficili, 346
Anticipation of the Night, 501
Antonio-das-Mortes, 474
Antonioni, Michelangelo, 343, **352**, **357–61**, 362, 364, *390, 391*, 401, 404, 470, 476, 503
Anything Goes, 287
Aparajito, 464, **466–67**, **468–69**
Apartment, The, 334
Ape Man, The, 286
Applause, 227
Apu Trilogy. *See Aparajito, Pather Panchali*, and *The World of Apu*.
Arbuckle, Roscoe C. ("Fatty"), 95, 97, 98, 118, **124**, 142, 248
Arletty, 260, *236*
Armat, Thomas, **20**, 46–47

Aronson, Max. *See* "Broncho Billy" Anderson.
Arrighi, Nike, *398*
L'Arrivé d'un train en gare, 19
L'Arroseur arrosée, 19, **30**, 91
Arsenal, 194–96, **214–15**
"Art" films, 337, **341–43**, 364, 470, 481, 495
Artaud, Antonin, *230*
Arthur, Jean, 293
Arvidson, Linda, 54
Ashes and Diamonds, 432
Asphalt Jungle, The, 330, 332
Asquith, Anthony, 414
Assassination of the Duke of Guise, The, 49–50
Astaire, Fred, 267, *269*, 285, 334, 335, 336
At Land, 497
At Long Last Love, 488
At the Circus, 294
L'Atalante, **258–59**
Atmosfear, 400
Atonement of Gosta Berling, The, 383, 404
Attenborough, Richard, 420
August, Joseph, 301
Aumont, Jean-Pierre, *398*
Aurenche, Jean and Pierre Bost, 375
Austin, Albert, *108*
"*Auteur* theory", 3, 74, 286, 287, 363, **487**, 491
L'Avventura, 357, 358, **359–60**, *390*, 469, 476

Bacall, Lauren, 304, 305
Backus, Jim, *319*
Bad Day at Black Rock, 331
Baillie, Bruce, **501**
Balazs, Bela, 445
Ballad of a Soldier, 217
Ballad of Cable Hogue, The, 491
Ballet Mécanique, 241, 386

Bananas, 491
Bancroft, Anne, 416
Bandits of Orgosolo, The, 362
Banerji, Subir, *442*
Bank, The, 102
Bank Dick, The, 296
Bannerjee, Bibhuti, 466
Bara, Theda, **117–18**
Baranovskaia, Vera, *189,* 209
Barbarella, 386
Bardot, Brigitte, 374, 386
Barney Oldfield's Race for a Life, **96**
Barrandov Studio, 422, 424
Barrault, Jean-Louis, *236,* 260
Barrie, J. M., 130, 131
Barrier, 445
Barrymore, John, 304
Barrymore, Lionel, 59, 60, 227, 285
Barthelmess, Richard, *72,* 86, 87, 118, 137
Bartlett, Scott, 498
Bates, Alan, 420
Batka, Bedrich, 423
Battle Cry of Peace, The, 159
Battle of Algiers, The, 388
Bauman, Charles, 49
Bazin, André, 39, 133, 164, 202, 348, 375, 387, **401–2**
Beach at Dover, The, 29
Beatles, The, 113, 418, 419
Beat the Devil, 330
Beaumont, Harry, 227
Beauties of the Night, 365
Beautiful Blonde from Bashful Bend, The, 334
Beauty and the Beast, 366
Beauty and the Devil, 365
Beckett, Samuel, 153, 259, 342, 343
Becky Sharp, 325
Bed and Board, 378
Bed and Sofa, 216
Beery, Wallace, 96
Before the Revolution, **363–64**

Behind the Screen, 104
Belasco, David, 37, 53, 54, 89
Belle de Jour, 470, 471
Belle of the Nineties, 295
Bellochio, Marco, 362
Belmondo, Jean-Paul, 380, *399*
Bend of the River, 331
Belson, Jordan, 498
Benedek, Laslo, 332
Bengali film production, 366, 465–66
Ben Hur (1907), 36, 327
Benshi, **446,** 464
Bergman, Ingmar, 3, 38, 166, 343, 379, **404–13,** *433–37,* 470, 471, 487, 503
Bergman, Ingrid, 306, 347
Bergson, Henri, 92, 141
Berkeley, Busby, 267, *269,* 285, 335, 387
Berlin: Symphony of a Great City, 176–77
Bern, Paul, 499
Bernhardt, Sarah, *28,* 50–51
Bertolucci, Bernardo, **363–64,** 401
Besserer, Eugenie, *229*
Best Years of Our Lives, The, 329
Bevan, Billy, 125
Biches, Les, 386
Bicycle Thief, The, 337, **345–46,** *353*
Big Heat, The, 332, 486
Big House, The, 266
Big News, 266
Big Parade, The, 138, 218
Big Sleep, The, 304, 305, 331
Big Swallow, A, 56
Billington, Francelia, *109*
Billy Liar, 420
Biograph. *See* American Mutoscope and Biograph Company.
Bioscope, 12, 20, 34
Birds, Orphans, and Fools, 424

Birds, the Bees, and the Italians, The, **361–62**
Birth of a Nation, The, 63–65, 75, **77–82,** 83, 85, 88, 116, 118, 126, 134, 314, 476
Birthday Party, The, 490
Bison Life Motion Picture Company, 49, 97
Bitter Rice, 346
Bitzer, G. W. ("Billy"), 70, 76
Bizarre, Bizarre, 259
Bjørnstrand, Gunnar, 404
Black, Alexander, 17
Black Peter, 424, 425, 429
Black Pirate, The, 324
Blackmail, 308
Blackton, J. Stuart, 36, 37, 159
Blasetti, Allessandro, 346
"Blaxploitation" films, 476
Blazes, 498
Blazing Saddles, 491
Blind Husbands, 109, 130, **132–33**
Blonde Cobra, 500
Blonde Venus, The, 272–73, **299**
Blondell, Joan, 285
Bloom, Claire, 417
Blow Job, 500
Blow Up, 357, 358, 359
Blue Angel, The, **178–79,** 267, *271,* **296–97**
Boat Leaving the Port, 24
Bob and Carol and Ted and Alice, 484, 486
Body and Soul, 382
Boetticher, Bud, 331
Bogarde, Dirk, 420
Bogart, Humphrey, 285, 304, 305, 375, 376, 380, 492
Bogdanovich, Peter, 448, *477,* 481, 483, **487–88,** 503
Bombay Talkies, **465,** 469
Bonheur, Le, 387
Bonnes Femmes, Les, 386

Bonnie and Clyde, 475, **481,** 484, 485, 490
Bose, Debaki, 464
Boston Strangler, The, 483
Boucher, Le, 386
Boudu Saved From Drowning, 252
Boy Friend, The, 419
Boys in the Band, The, 490
Boys in the Sand, 476
B-pictures, 374, 380
Brakhage, Stan, 497, **500–1**
Brando, Marlon, 290, *317,* 329, 333, 500
Brasseur, Pierre, *236,* 260
Breathdeath, 478, 498
Breathless (À Bout de souffle), 375, **379–81,** 386, 388, *399,* 476, 481, 484, 487
Brecht, Bertolt, 3, 102, 160, 172, 175–76, 177–78, 208, 216, 288, 380, 382, 401, 420
Breen Code. *See* Hollywood Code.
Breen, Joseph, **208–9,** 210
Breer, Robert, 497, 498
Bresson, Robert, 262, 367, **371–72,** 384, *394,* 492
Brewster McCloud, 488, 489
Bride Wore Black, The, 377
Bridge on the River Kwai, The, 327, 413
Bringing Up Baby, 304, 305
British film, 12, **18–19, 34, 44–46,** 140, 305, 325, **413–20,** 484
Broadway Melody, 227
Brodsky, Vlastimil, *438*
Broken Blossoms, 58, 72, 83, **85–87,** 89, 138, 342, 359, 381
Bronson, Charles, 374
Brook, Clive, 299
Brooks, Mel, **491**
Broughton, James, 499
Brown, Clarence, 287
Browning, Tod, 285, 287

Browning Version, The, 414
Brute Force, 332
Brynych, Zbyněk, 422
Buchanan, Jack, 267
Buchanan Rides Alone, 331
Buildungsroman, 427, 466
Bullitt, 218, 483
Bunny, John, 118
Buñuel, Luis, 241–42, *444*, **470–74**, 495
Burgess, Anthony, 494
Burglar on the Roof, 36, 37
Burn!, 388
Burton, Richard, 413, 417
Butch Cassidy and the Sundance Kid, 481, 482, 485
Butterfield 8, 328
By the Law, 207

Cabiria, 76, 116
Cabinet of Doctor Caligari, The, 145–46, 160, **162–64**, 168, 169, 173, 243, 343, 359
Caccia Tragica, 346
Cagney, James, 285, 332
Cahiers du Cinéma, 375, 386, 387
Caine Mutiny, The, 328
California Split, 489
"Caligarism", 164
Caligula, 342
Call Northside 777, 332
Camera obscura, 12
Campbell, Eric, 100, 102, *106*, 144
Camus, Albert, 259, 342, 343
"Canned theatre", 50, 224, 239, 256–57
Cantata, 445
Captain's Paradise, The, 414
Canudo, Ricciotto, 240
Capra, Frank, **143–44**, 292–93, 300, 301, 305, 316, 334, 448
Carabiniers, Les, 19, 380, **382**, 388
Cardiff, Jack, 418

Carmen, 95
Carnal Knowledge, 490
Carné, Marcel, *236*, **259–62**, 286, 342, 343, 365, 366, 367
Carnival in Flanders, 259
Carol, Martine, 369, *393*
Carroll, Madeleine, 306
Casablanca, 287, 376
Case, Theodore, 222
Casler, Herman, 20, 35
Castro Street, 501
Catalog, 498
Catch-22, 490
Catholic Legion of Decency, 264
Cavalcanti, Alberto, 242
Ceiling, The, 423
Celluloid film, 14, 15, 19, 217
Central Casting Corporation, 339
Chabrol, Claude, 375, **386**
Chapayev, **217**, 422
Chaplin, Charles, 41, 49, 92, 94, 95, **97–104**, *106–8*, *111*, **113–14**, 115, 117, 118, 121, 140, 141, 142, **144**, **153–55**, 156, 157–58, 171, 177, 212, 237, 248, 249, **288–90**, 309, 333, 342, 372, 373, 401, 428, 472, 503
Charge of the Light Brigade, The, 287, 417
Chess Fever, **208**
Chevalier, Maurice, 226, 228, 267
Chien andalou, Un, **241–42**, 258, 386, 470, 497
Childhood of Maxim Gorky, 217
Children of Paradise, The, *236*, **260–62**, 343, 349, 366
China is Near, 362–63
Chinatown, 432
Chinoise, La, 380, **383**
Chloe in the Afternoon, 387
Chrétien, Henri, 323
Christie, Julie, 413, 420
Chronique d'un été, 388

Chronophotograph, 14
Chukhrai, Grigori, 217
Chytilová, Věra, 423
CinemaScope, 12, **323–24,** 330, 370
Cinematographe, 12, 20, 29, 33
Cinéma vérité, 362, 376, **388,** 425, 430, 489
Cinerama, **6,** 243, **322–23,** 494
Circle of Love, 369, 386
Citizen Kane, 6–7, *280–84,* **309–13,** 314, 342, 379, 432, 487, 492
City Lights, 113, 144, **288,** 342
Civilization, 84, 126, 159
Clair, René, 96, 226, 227, *232–33,* 239, 241, **244–50,** 251, 256, 257, 286, **365,** 367, 375, 388, 495, 503
Claire's Knee, 387, 470
Clansman, The, 77–78
Clayton, Jack, *415–17,* 418
Clément, René, 373, **374,** 375
Cleo from Five to Seven, 387
Clever Dummy, The, 92
Clift, Montgomery, *277,* 304
Clockwork, Orange, A, 480, 492, **494**
Closely Watched Trains, 421, **425–27,** *428, 438*
Cluzot, Henri-Georges, **373–74,** 375
Cocoanuts, The, 293, 294
Cocteau, Jean, 240, 365, **366–67**
Cohl, Émile, *25,* **40,** 41, 237, 240, 257, 375
Colbert, Claudette, 293
Collectioneuse, La, 387
Columbia Pictures Corporation, 292, **316, 321,** 326, 470
Comden, Betty and Adolph Green, 336
Comédie Française, 50, 240
Come On Marines, 287
Computer films, 498
Comrades, 101
Confession, The, 388, 421

Confessions of a Black Mother Succuba, 499
Conformist, The, 363, 364
Conjuror, The, 38
Conklin, Chester, 97, *110*
Conner, Bruce, 497, **498,** 499
Conquest of the Pole, The, 38
Conrad, Joseph, 310–11
Constantin, Jean, 376
"Constructivism", **216**
Conversation, The, 483, 484, **489**
Cool Hand Luke, 481
Cooper, Gary, 293, 297, 333
Coppola, Francis Ford, **489–90**
Cops, 153
Corman, Roger, 364, 487
Corner in Wheat, A, 73
Cortese, Valentina, *398*
Cosmic Ray, 498
Costa-Gavras, **388,** 401, 421
Costello, Lou. See Abbott, Bud and Lou Costello.
Cotten, Joseph, *282–84,* 313, 314
Coulouris, George, *283*
Count, The, 99, 100, 101
Countess from Hong Kong, A, 290
Country Cupid, A, 73
Courage for Everyday, 423
Courtenay, Tom, 417, 420
Cousins, Les, 386
Coutard, Raoul, 381, 388
Covered Wagon, The, 96, 138
Coward, The (American), **126**
Coward, The (Czech), 422
Crabbe, Buster, 168
Cranes are Flying, The, 217
Crawford, Joan, 285
"Creative geography", 43, 45, 88, **183,** 208
Crichton, Charles, 414
Cries and Whispers, 409
Crime of Giovanni Episcopo, The, 346

Crime of Monsieur Lange, The, 251–52, 383

Criminal Code, The, 266, 304, 305

Crisis, 404

Crisp, Donald, 59, 87

Crosland, Alan, 223, 244

Cross-cut, See Editing, uses and principles of.

Crossfire, 332

Cruze, James, 124, 138

Cry of the City, 332

Cukor, George, 287, 448

Cul-de-sac, 432

Curtis, Tony, 334

Curtiz, Michael, 285, 287, 445

Cybulski, Zbigniew, 432

Czechoslovakian film, 421–31, 432, 448, 466, 474, 484

Dadaism, 241, 242, 246, 367

Dagover, Lil, 147, 161

Daguerre, Louis Jacques Mandé, 12–13

Dailey, Dan, 285

Daiei Company, 447

Daisies, 423

Dali, Salvador, 240, 241–42

Dalio, Marcel, 235, 253

Damned, The, 347, 348, 470

Darling, 418, 419, 420

Dassin, Jules, 332

Davies, Marion, 313

Davis, Bette, 285

Davis, Mildred, 111

Dawn to Dawn, 496

Day at the Races, A, 294

Daydreams, 153

Day For Night (La Nuit Americaine), 352, 379, 398, 488

Day of the Dolphin, The, 490

Dean, James, 319, 329, 333, 420, 500

Death in Venice, 347, 348

Death is Called Engelchen, 422, 428

Death of P'town, The, 500

Deception, 138

Decision at Sundown, 331

Deep Throat, 476

Defiant Ones, The, 329

de Forest, Dr. Lee, 220–21, 222, 267

Delluc, Louis, 240, 242

De Mille, Cecil B., 129–32, 139, 166, 285, 325, 386, 387

Delon, Alain, 374

Del Ruth, Roy, 287

Demy, Jacques, 387

Départ, Le, 445

Depression, 264, 265, 287, 290, 485

de Putti, Lya, 161, 173, 225

Deren, Maya, 497

de Santis, Giuseppi, 346

Deserter, 213

De Seta, Vittorio, 362

DeSica, Vittorio, 337, 343, 345–46, 347, 352, 364

Design for Living, 291

Desilu Productions, 326

Destiny (Der Müde Tod), 129, 147, 164–66, 168, 169, 171, 173

de Toth, Andre, 445

deWitt, Tom, 499

Devi, 469

Devi, Chunibala, 443

Devil in Miss Jones, The, 476

Devils, The, 419

Diaboliques, Les, 337, 373

Dial M for Murder, 322

Diamond, I. A. L., 334

Diary of a Country Priest, The, 371–72, 394

Dickens, Charles, 57, 205, 260, 413, 414

Dickson, William Kennedy Laurie, 15–16, 29, 34, 35, 219

Dieterle, William, 285, 287

Dietrich, Marlene, *271–73*, **296–300**, 475

Discreet Charm of the Bourgeoisie, The, 470, 472

Disney, Walt, **228,** *229,* **237–38,** 290–91, 325, 326, 496

Divorce—Italian Style, 361

Dixon, Thomas, 77, 78, 82

Dmytryk, Edward, 332

Docks of New York, 138

Dr. Kildare's Victory, 287

Doctor Mabuse, 165

Doctor Strangelove: or How I Learned to Stop Worrying and Love the Bomb, 157, 168, 417–18, 475, 492, **493–94**

Doctor's Secret, The, 38

Doctor Zhivago, 413

Documentary film, 139–40, 176–77, 216, 242, 316, 352, 362, 378, 384, 388, 414

Dodes' Kaden, 464

Dodge City, 287

Dog Star Man, 501

Dolce Vita, La, **350,** 351, 352, 476

Donat, Robert, 306

Donen, Stanley, 335–36

Don Juan, 221, 222, 288

Donner, Clive, 493

Donskoi, Mark, 217

Douglas, Kirk, 492

Dovzhenko, Alexander, *194–96,* 213–16, 424

Dracula, 169, 285, 287

Dream of a Rarebit Fiend, The, 40, 44

Dream Play, A, 407

Dressler, Marie, 93–94, 98

Dreyer, Carl-Theodore, *230–31,* 243–44, 381

Drunkard's Reformation, The, 58

Duchamp, Marcel, 241

Duck Soup, 287, 294

Dudow, Slatan, 177–78

Dulac, Germaine, 242

Dumbo, 238

Duping, 31, 36, 46, 48

Dupont, E. A., 138, 161, 173

Durand, Jean, 240, 245

Durbin, Deanna, 267, 285

Dunvivier, Julien, 239

Dwan, Allan, 487

Ealing comedies, 414

Earth, 215

Eastman, George, 14, 15, 34, 48, 49

Eastmancolor, 325

East of Eden, 329

Eastwood, Clint, 364

Easy Rider, 74, 380, 481, 483, **485–86,** 500

Easy Street, 100, 102, *106,* 172, 250

L'Eclisse, 357, 358, 359

Edison, Thomas (and Edison Company), **14–16,** 17, 18, 19, 20, *23,* 29, **30–31,** 33, 34, 35, 36, 37, 41, 44, 45, **46–47,** 48, 49, 53, 54, 91, 119, 121, 219, 220

Editing, uses and principles of, *26–27,* 34, **42–45, 49, 59–60,** *61,* **73,** 75, 79–80, 81, 82–83, 84, 87–88, 96, 104, 133, 138, 154, 158, 174–75, 177, 178, **182–84,** *186–87, 190–91,* **197, 200–2,** 207, 208, 209–10, 228, 268, 307–8, 310, 330, 369, 381, 384–85, 401, 412, 420, 427, 428, 450, 451, 452, 453, 460, 461, 482, 483, 486, 490, 498, 501. *See also* Creative geography; Elliptical construction.

Edwards, Blake, 493

Eggeling, Viking, 496

8½, **351–52,** *355–56,* 379, 497

Eisenstein, Sergei M., 45, 75, 84, 177, 182, 184, *185–88*, **198–207**, 210, 211, 213, 214, 215, 216, 217–18, 225, 226, 238, 243, 257, 324, 344, 388, 402, 446

Ekk, Nicolai, 216–17

El, 470, 471

El Dorado, 331

Elliptical construction, 43, 44, 45, 214, 216, 364, 375, 377, 384, 388, 401, 409, 410, 418, 425

Elvira Madigan, 413

Emak Bakia, 241

Emerson, John, 127, 128

Emigrants, The, 413, 470

Emshwiller, Ed, 501

End of August at the Ozone Hotel, The, 424

End of St. Petersburg, The, 193, **210–12,** 214

Enfants du Paradis, Les. See Children of Paradise, The.

Entertainer, The, 417

Entr'acte, 241, **245–46**

Epstein, Jean, 239, 242, 495

Erotikon, 404

Essanay (S and A) Company, 36, 41, 48, 98, 99, 114

Étoile de Mer, 241

Evein, Bernard, 387

Everything You Always Wanted to Know About Sex . . . , 491

Execution of Mary, Queen of Scots, The, **30,** 38

Exodus, **328**

Exorcist, The, 490

Experiential film, 388, 389, **423–24,** 430–31, 483–84, 485

Experimental film, 164, 218, 240, **241–43,** *478–79,* **495–502**

Expressionism, 135, *145–46, 148,* 163, 173, 176, *281,* 309, 496

Face in the Crowd, A, 329

Fairbanks, Douglas, 118, 121, 124, **127–29,** 142, 166, 324

Father Brown, 414

F.B.I. Story, The, 286

Fahrenheit 451, 377, 382

Falconetti, *230–31,* 243–44

Fall of the House of Usher, The, **242,** 343

Famous Players in Famous Plays, 51, 119

Fan magazines, 117–18

Fantasia, 238, 291

Fatima, 122–23

Faulkner, William, 310

Faye, Alice, 285

Fear and Desire, 492

Feature film, 51, 76, **77–85, 116,** 117, 119, 121–22, 222–23

Fellini, Federico, 343, **348–52,** *354–56,* 360, 362, 364, 379, 401, 404, 470, 487

Fellini—Roma, 351

Fellini Satyricon, 350, 351

Ferzetti, Gabriele, *390*

Feuillade, Louis, 240

Feyder, Jacques, 239, 259

Fields, W. C., 285, **295–96,** 448

Fièvre, 242

Fifth Horseman is Fear, The, 422

Film, 153

Film aesthetics, 113, 164, 324, 348, 388, 401–2, 461, 503

Film and

   fantasy, 39, **161–69,** 237, 245, 249, 250, 251, 365, 424, 459–60, 464, 473

   morality, 74, 77, 81–82, 100, 113, **122–25,** 128, 171–72, 264–65, 297, 312–13, 328, 369

   music, 177, 197, **203,** 206, **243,** 462, 497

Film *(Cont.)*

narrative fiction, 1, 57, **134–36,** 252, 310–11, **327–28,** 371, 374, 384, 385, 387, 414, 416, 422, 427, 466, 494

painting, 163, 164, 214–15, 243, 250, 336, 384, *478,* 496, 498

politics, **78–79,** 167–68, 179, 181–82, 208, 214, 216, 217, 383, 386, 388, 401, 421, 423, 429

psychology 42, 133, 162, 163, 170, 343, 347–48, 357, 368– 69, 409, 410–13, 416, 419–20, 470, 500–2

reality, 29, 39, 164, 335, 336, **344–45,** 346, 364, 368, 379, 410–11, 414, 418, 466, 470, 474, 482, 484, 497

society, 78–79, 82, 88–89, 100, 101–2, **122–25,** 174, 216, 252, 253, 254, 256, **287–88,** 329, 331, 332, 333, 345, 346, 369, 414–15, 448, 464, 481, 497

theatre, **2–3,** 7, 17, 29, 30, 37, 39, 44, 50–51, **56,** 120, 130–33, 136, 199, 224, 226, *236,* 256– 57, 260–62, 293, 309, 330, 335, 338, 368–69, 404, 409, 414, 417, 446, 448–49, 490

Film audience, **1–2, 5–6,** 89, 115, 123, 265, **337–40,** 341, 342, 343, 464, 476, 481, 483, 484, 503

Film critics, 6, 244, 332, 333, 338, 341, 343, 375, 420, 448, 475, 487, 492, 502

Film d'Art, **49–51,** 54, 240

Film festivals, 403, 421, 445, 464

Film genres, 128, 139, 168, 266– 67, 285, 286, 305, **331–37,** 448, 466, **484–86,** 487

Film genres *(Cont.)*

acting, 4, **50–51, 58–59,** 86–87, 170, 223, 302, 313, 314, 330, 417, 471

chases, 40, 55, 101, 240, 246, 247, 306, 486

comedy, **30, 91–104, 113–14,** 127–29, **140–44, 153–58,** 208, 245–50, **288–96, 333–34,** 361– 62, **372–73,** 414, 425, 429–30, 473, 491, 494

cycles, **266–68,** 448, 484

film noir, **332,** 484, 486

gangsters, 224, **266,** 267, 285, 305, 332, 333, *396,* 484, 485, 486

gendai-geki (Japanese film of modern life), **448,** 449, 456, 460–62, 466

horror, ghosts, and vampires, **162–69,** 285, 327, 404, 456– 57, 459–60, 487–88

jidai-geki (Japanese period or cos-tume film), **448,** 449–60, 463, 466

musicals, 227–28, 247–49, **266– 67,** *269,* 285, *320,* **334–37,** 419, 476, 488

science-fiction, 168, 327, 424, 463, 494–95

parody, 38, 41, 93, **95–96,** 127– 28, 136, 172, 220, 379, 453, 477, 491, 499

satire, 45, 101, 124, 138, 142, 199, 204–5, 209, 218, 221, 245, 246–47, 250, 334, 361– 62, 365, 373, 388, 404, 417– 18, 423, 424, 429–30, 445, *478,* 493, 494, 495, 497, 498– 99

shomin-geki (Japanese middle-class comedy), 448, 460–61

"street films", 174

Film genres *(Cont.)*
  tricks, **38–40,** 91, 129, 216
  western, 36, 43–44, 126–27, 138,
    251, *276–77,* 285, 300–1,
    302–4, 305, **331–32,** 333, 364,
    449, **455–56,** 484, 485, 491
  "White Telephone" pictures, 343–
    44, 346
Film industry, 4–5, 46–49, 113–14,
    115–25, 221–22, 223–26, **263–
    66, 315–16, 321–28, 337–40,**
    403, 445, 446, 447, 463–65,
    469–70, 474, 476, 484
  antisemitism in, 123
  anti-trust violations, 49, 116,
    315–16
  block booking, **120**
  censorship, 123, 125, 464
  distribution, 3, **47–48,** 120, 121,
    469–70, 474
  independent production, 48–49,
    116, 117, 121, 326–27
  monopolies, **48–49,** 120
  publicity, **117–18,** 124, 125
  star system, **117–18,** 124–25, 161,
    225, 447–48, 465
Film schools
  Centro Sperimentale, 344
  F.A.M.U., 422
  Lodz, 431
  Moscow, 182–83, 206
Film societies, 240, 465
Film studio, **16,** 35, 36, 53–54, 58,
    95, 121, 225, 263–64, 268,
    285–87, 339, 344, 367, 368,
    375, 422, 447–48, 483
  Black Maria, **16,** *23,* 31, 35, 36,
    44, 121, 220
  Hollywood system, 116, **119–21,**
    161, **263–64, 265–68, 285–88,**
    305, **316, 321,** 336–37, **339–
    40,** 447–48, 487, 490

Film styles, 309–10, 331, 343, 344,
    367–68, 371, 449, 458, 461,
    481–84
  accelerated motion, uses and ef-
    fects of, **92,** 95, 246, 376, 494,
    496
  color cinematography, 6, 34, 206,
    243, 250, 290, **324–26,** 330,
    331, 332, 335, 347–48, 350,
    357, **360,** 365, 370, 388–89,
    402, 418, 419, 432, 461, 463,
    469, 482, 488
  deep-focus photography, 45, 126,
    282, 310, 449, 457, 458, 483
  design and decor, 83, 131, 132–
    33, 161, 163, 165–66, 176,
    178, 248–49, 346, 348, 365,
    370, 419, 423, 471, 483
  freeze frame, *194,* 242, 376, 388,
    396, 401, 425, 431, 482
  "Golden Frame", 401
  hand-held camera, 381, 388, 401,
    425, 486
  integration of sound and picture,
    140–41, 178–79, **206,** 222,
    225, **227–28,** *229,* **237–38,**
    244, 247, *278–79,* 290, 291–
    92, 296–97, **307–8,** 310, 336,
    360–61, 373, 381, 451, 452,
    454, 458, 461, 469, 475, 482
  lighting, 4, 46, **58,** 87, 244, 251,
    268, 309–10, 405, 406, 425,
    429, 432, 458, 460
  montage, 177, 178, **182–84,** *186–
    87, 190–91,* **197,** 198–99, **200–
    2, 203,** 204–5, 206, **207,** 208,
    210, 211–12, 213, 215, 216,
    217, 218, 227, 267, 268, *277–
    78,* 289, 310, 314, 336, 402
  moving camera, **57,** 81, **170–71,**
    173, 174, 175, 201, 227, 243–
    44, 246, 298, 300, 301, 345,
    348, 368, 370–71, 376, 378,

Film styles *(Cont.)*
  moving camera *(Cont.)*
    382, 385, 449, 451, 452, 453, 454, 455, 457, 458, 486, 492, 501
  music and scoring, 226, 237, **253,** 256, 297, 307–8, 328, 348, 365, 366, 374, 376, 431, 452, 465, 466, 482, 483, 493, 494, 497, 498, 500, 502
  outdoor and indoor filming, 29, 42, 43, 44, 45, 54, 126–27, 160–61, 163, 198, 227, 254, 344, 404, 466, 483, 486
  panning (pan-shot), 43, 51, 57, 225, 345, 348, 451
  slow motion, uses of and effects of, 246, 255, 257, 376–77, 388, 456, 475, 476, 482, 485, 486, 491, 493, 496, 497
  stop-action, 30, 37, **38–40,** 41, 97, 103, 104, 166, 246
  strategy of shots, 44–45, **55–57,** 83, 97, 104, 113, 143, 158, 209, 211, 215, 223, 243–44, 268, 370–71, 372, 432, 449–54, 458, 461, 467–68, 493
  symbolism, 76–77, 86, 87, 202–3, 210, 213, 214–15, 228, 249, 254, 255–56, 298, 300, 301–2, 302–3, 330, 349, 350, 366, 368, 374, 405–6, 418, 426, 456–57, 459–60, 468–69, 483, 493, 496
  titling, 74, 77, 131, 160, 172, 244
  wide screen, 6, 250, 322, **323–24,** 331, **370–71,** 388, *392–93,* 401, 402, 447, 457, 482, 488
  zoom lens, 80, 329, 348, 401
Film technology **6–7, 9–20, 29,** 224–25, **226–27,** 310, **321–26**
  camera, invention of, 6, **9–16**

Film technology *(Cont.)*
  intermittent movement, **18,** 19, 35
  projection, invention of, 11, 15, **17–20, 29**
  stereophonic sound, 12, 220, 322, 482
  synchronized sound, 6, 15, 140, 143, 153, 175–76, 178–79, 205–7, 213, 216, 217, **219–28,** **237–38,** 247–50, 267, 288, 296, 402, 446, 452, 475, 489, 490
Film theatres, 19, 20, 29, **47–48,** 94, 119, **121–22,** 225, **321,** 323, 337, **338**
  "art" theatres, 6, 337, 476
  double features, 265, 286
  drive-in theatres, 6, 327, 488
  neighborhood movie houses, 6, 326, 327, 337, 364
Finian's Rainbow, 489
Finney, Albert, 420
Firebird, The, 287
Firemen's Ball, The, 424, 429
Fires on the Plain, **463**
Fireworks, **499**
First National Exhibitors' Circuit, 97, 114, **121,** 221
Fischer, Gunnar, 404, 409
Fischinger, Oskar, *478,* 497, **498**
Fist Fight, 497
Five Boys from Barska Street, 445
Five Easy Pieces, 380, 482, 484
Flaherty, Robert, **139–40,** 154, 401
Flaming Creatures, 500
Flash Gordon, 168
Fleischer, Richard, 483
Fleming, Victor, 127, 226, 287, 325
Flesh of Morning, 500
Floorwalker, The, 101, 103
Florey, Robert and Slavko Vorkapich, 496

Fonda, Henry, 285, 329
Fonda, Jane, 374
Fontaine, Joan, 306, 307
Fool and a Girl, A, 53
Fool There Was, A, 117
Foolish Wives, 113
Forbes, Bryan, 418, 419
Forbidden Games, 374
Force of Evil, 332
Ford, Alexsander, 445
Ford, John, 3, 126, 138, 265, *275–76,* 285, **300–3,** 304, 305, 309, 316, **331,** 408, 448, 482, 485
Foreign Affair, A, 334
Foreign Correspondent, 306
Formalism, 205–6, 213, 217, 365, 383
Forman, Miloš, 424, 425, **429–30,** 477, 487
Formula films, 31, 36, 89, 139, 181, 266, 267–68, 338, 465
Fort Apache, 331
42nd Street, 267
Four Horsemen of the Apocalypse, The, 138, 327
400 Blows, The, 375, **376,** 378, *396,* 476
491, 413
Fox, James, 420
Fox-Movietone News, 222
Fox, William, 49, 116, 221–22
Francis, Kay, 291
Frankenstein (1931), 168, 285, 287
Frankenstein (1974), 322, 499
Freaks, 287
Fred Ott's Sneeze, **15,** 16, *22,* 56
Freed, Arthur, 335
French film, 12, 14, 19–20, **29–30,** 31, 33–34, **38–41, 49–51,** 183, 219, **239–62, 365–88, 401–2,** 414, 425, 448, 465, 481, 484, 497

French Cancan, **365–66**
French Connection, The, 218, 484, 485, 486, 490
Freshman, The, 142
Fresnay, Pierre, *234,* 252
Freud, 330
Freuler, John R., 127
Freund, Karl, 161, 169, 170, 173, 176, 177
Friedkin, William, **490**
Friese-Greene, William, **18–19**
Fröhlich, Gustav, 168
From Here to Eternity, 328
Front Page, The, 266, 287
Fruits of Paradise, 423
Fuller, Samuel, 331, 332
Funny Girl, 338
Funny Thing Happened on the Way to the Forum, A, 419
Furie, Sydney J., 418

Gabin, Jean, *234,* 253, 259, 366, 376
Gable, Clark, 265, 285, 293, 313
Gai Savoir, Le, 383
Game of Cards, A, 33
Gance, Abel, 242–43, 322, 324
Garbo, Greta, 161, 174, 225, 285
Garden of the Finzi-Continis, The, 347
Garfield, John, **332**
Garland, Judy, 336
Garmes, Lee, 298
Gas Works, 199
Gate of Hell, 447, 463
Gaumont, Léon, 33, 34, 120, 219
General, The, 112, 144, 153, **155–58**
General Film Company, 48, 49, 51, 73
Gentleman's Agreement, 329
Gentlemen Prefer Blondes, 331
German film, 12, **159–79,** 219, 220

Germi, Pietro, 361–62
Gershwin, George, 267, 336
Gervaise, 374
Getting Acquainted, 95, 101
Ghost Goes West, The, 250
Giorno nella vita, Un, 346
Girls of Rochefort, The, 387
Gish, Dorothy, 59
Gish, Lillian, 35, 55, 59, 65, 71, 72,
    77, 86, 87, **88**, 118, 134
Godard, Jean-Luc, 19, 240, 365,
    375, **379–83**, 384, 386, 387,
    388, 399–400, 401, 404, 418,
    420, 448, 476, 484, 492, 503
Godfather, The—Parts I and II,
    484, 486, 489
Godzilla, 447, 468
Going My Way, 287
Goin' to Town, 295
Golddiggers of 1933, 267, 286
Golddiggers of 1935, 269
Golden Coach, The, **365–66**
Golden Fern, The, **423**
Gold Rush, The, 111, **153–55**, 156,
    157–58, 250
Goldwyn, Samuel (Goldfish), 116,
    119, 120, 326
Golem, The, 168
Gone with the Wind, 79, 287, 325,
    327
Goodbye, Columbus, 484
Goodbye, Mr. Chips, 287
Goodness Gracious, 96
Gorky, Maxim, 208, 252, 456, 457–
    58
Gosho, Heinosuke, 446
Gospel According to St. Matthew,
    The, 362
Götzke, Bernhard, 147
Gould, Elliott, 470
Go West, 294
Gowland, Gibson, 110
Grable, Betty, 285

Graduate, The, 484, 490
Grahame, Gloria, 332
Grand Illusion, 137, 234, **252–54,**
    256, 259, 343, 366, 367, 492
Grand Jeu, Le, 259
Granger, Farley, 308
Grant, Cary, 285, 304, 306, 307,
    318, 337, 346
Grapes of Wrath, The, 303, 342
Grauman, Sid, 122, 488
Great Dictator, The, 289
Great Expectations, 413
Great Gatsby, The, 416–17
Great McGinty, The, 334
Great Train Robbery, The, 42, **43–
    44,** 56, 57, 96, 126
Greatest Show on Earth, The, 327
Greed, 110, **134–36,** 154, 330, 342,
    359
Green Forest, The, 219
Green, Guy, 418
Grido, Il, 357
Grierson, John, 414
Griffith, David Wark, 3, 34, 35, 42,
    44, 46, 50, 51, **53–60, 61–72,**
    73–90, 91, 92, 93, 96, 97, 100,
    113, 115, 118, 121, 123, 125,
    126, 127, 129, 130, 133, 137,
    138, 139, 154, 156, 157, 160,
    170, 182–83, 184, 199, 207,
    209, 210, 224, 286, 288, 295,
    300, 302, 303, 304, 324, 327,
    338, 343, 379, 388, 427, 446,
    475, 503
Guerre est finie, La, **386**
Guiness, Alec, 414
Gunfight at the OK Corral, 331
Gypsy, 286
Gypsy Blood, 138

Hagen, Jean, 332
Hail the Conquering Hero, 334
Hale's Tours, 57

Hallelujah, 226
Hamer, Robert, 414
Hamlet, 406, 414
Hannibal, 327
Hard Day's Night, A, 418
Hardy, Oliver, *See* Laurel, Stan and Oliver Hardy.
Harlot, 499
Harlow, Jean, 285, 499, 502
Harp of Burma, The, 463
Harris, Richard, 359, *391,* 420
Harron, Robert, 59
Hart, William S., 118, 120, 251, 383
Harvey, Anthony, 419
Harvey, Laurence, 415, 416
Hathaway, Henry, 285, 287, 332
Hawks, Howard, 126, *277,* 285, **303–5,** 309, 375, 448, 482, 485
Hays Office. *See* Motion Picture Producers and Distributors of America.
Hays, Will H., 125, 221
Hayworth, Rita, 334
Hearst, William Randolph, 313
Heart of Darkness, 310–11
Hearts of the World, 85
Heat, 499
Hecht, Ben, 266
Helga, 413
Hello Dolly!, 336
Help!, 418
Henry V, 325, 368
Hepburn, Katharine, 285, 304
Hepworth, Cecil, 34, 44–45, 50, 51, 413
L'Herbier Marcel, 242
Hercules, 327
Herlth, Robert, 161, 165, 170
Herrand, Marcel, 261
Herschel, Sir John, 10
Hersholt, Jean, 134
High and Dizzy, 111, **142–43**

High and the Mighty, The, 287
High Noon, 331
Hill, George Roy, 485
Hiroshima Mon Amour, **384–85,** 386, 476
His Girl Friday, 305
Hitchcock, Alfred, 250, *278–79,* **305–9,** *318,* 321–22, **330–31,** 374, 375, 377, 413, 414, 449, 488
Hitler, Adolf, 160, 167–68, 176, 178, 179, 213, 216, 289, 344, 367, 422, 427, 500
Hodkinson, W. W., 121
Holden, William, 334
Hole in the Head, A, 334
Hollywood
  as metaphor, 4, 314, 316, 325, 326, 328, 337, 338, **339,** 342, 379, 413, 456, 476
  code, 264–65, 266, 267, 292, 295, 299, 325, 328, 421
  establishment as production center, **118–19**
  film versus European film, 172, 337, **341–43,** 388, 476, 481–82, 483–84
Hollywood Babylon, **499**
Holt, Tim, 314
Home Sweet Home, 76–77, 78, 81
Hopkins, Miriam, 267, *270,* 291
Horner, William George, 11
Horsefeathers, 294
Horse Over Teakettle, 497
Horton, Edward Everett, 292
House of Wax, 321, 323
Howard, Leslie, 413
How I Won the War, 418
How the West Was Won, 323
Hrabak, Bohumil, 425
H₂O, 496
Hungarian film, 445
Hunter, Tab, 418

Hurdes, Los, 470
Hustler, The, 475
Huston, John, 316, **330**, 332

I Am a Fugitive from a Chain Gang,
   286
I Am Curious (Yellow and Blue),
   413
I a Woman, 413
Ibsen, Henrik, 407
Ichikawa, Kon, 445, 447, **462–63**
I, Claudine, 300
Idol Dancer, The, 85
If . . . , 257, 339, 419, 420
Ikiru, **456**
I Married a Witch, 250
Immigrant, The, 99, 100, 101–3,
   104
Importance of Being Earnest, The,
   414
Inagaki, Hiroshi, 445, 463
Ince, Thomas, 49, 84, 119, 120,
   126–27, 129, 137, 138, 285,
   303, 499
Independent American cinema, 472,
   495–502, 478–79
Independent Motion Picture Com-
   pany (Imp), 49, 117
Indian film, **464–69**
Informer, The, 275, **301–2**
Inga, 413
Ingram, Rex, 134, 138
Inkishinov, V., 212
Innocence Unprotected, 445
Innocents, The, **416**
In the Name of the Law, 361
Intimate Lighting, 424, 425, **430–
   31,** 439
Intolerance, 66–71, 73, 75, 76, **82–
   85,** 88, 118, 132, 138, 159,
   182–83, 207, 303
Ionesco, Eugene, 241, 343, 365
Iron Horse, The, 96, 138, 302

Isadora, 419
I Shot Jesse James, 332
Is Paris Burning?, 374
Italian film, 76, **343–52, 357–65,**
   388, 401–2, 413, 414, 425,
   448, 465, 466, 481
Italian Straw Hat, The, 245, **246–47**
It Happened One Night, 293
It's a Mad, Mad, Mad, Mad World,
   323
It's a Wonderful Life, 334
Ivan the Terrible, Parts I and II,
   203, 206
I Vinti, 357
Ivory, James, 469
I Was a Teenage Frankenstein, 327
I Was a Teenage Werewolf, 327
I Was Born, But . . . , 462
Iwerks, Ub, 237

J'Accuse, 242
Jackson, Glenda, 420
Jacobs, Ken, 500
Jakubisko, Juraj, **424–25**
James, Henry, 163, 416, 492
Jamestown Baloos, 497
Jancsó, Miklós, 445
Jannings, Emil, *152,* 161, 170, 173,
   178, 225, *271,* 296, 297
Japanese film, **445–64**
Jazz Singer, The, 219, **222–23,** *229,*
   267
Jean, Gloria, 285
Jeffries-Sharkey fight, **46**
Jireš, Jaromil, 421, 422, 423
Joanna, 218
Jodorowsky, Alejandro, 474
John Rice-May Irwin Kiss, The, **30–
   31,** 122
Johnny Guitar, 331, 332
Joke, The, 421, 423
Joli Mai, Le, 388
Jolson, Al, 222–23, *229*

Josef Kilian, 424
Jour de Fête, 372
Journey Into Fear, 314
Joy Ride, 327
Joyce, James, 205, 401
Joyless Street, The, **174–75**
Joyous Microbes, The, 25, 40
Juarez, 287
Judgment at Nuremberg, 329
Judith of Bethulia, **74–75**, 80, 82, 88
Jules and Jim, 375, 376, **377**, 378, 383, 388, *397,* 484, 487
Juliet of the Spirits, 350, 351

Kadár, Jan and Elmar Klos, 422, **427–29**, 470
Kafka, Franz, 205, 343, 424, 489
Kalatozov, Mikhail, 217
Kalem (K.L.M.) Company, 36, 48, 327
Kalmus, Herbert and Natalie, 325
Kaminska, Ida, 428
Kanal, 432
Kanchenjungha, 469
Karina, Anna, *400*
Karloff, Boris, 487, 488
Karno (Fred) Pantomime Troupe, 97, 98
Kaufman, George S., 334
Kazan, Elia, **329–30**
Keaton, Buster, 41, 92, *112,* 118, 140, **144, 153, 155–58,** 283, 333, 372, 373
Keeler, Ruby, 285, 334
Kelly, Gene, 127, *320,* **335–36**
Kennedy, Jeremiah J., 49
Kessel, Adam, 49, 97, 98
Keystone Studios, 91, 97, 98
Keystone Kops, 94, 95, 96, 100–1
Kid, The, 113
Killer's Kiss, 492
Kimmins, Anthony, 414

Kind Hearts and Coronets, 414
Kinemacolor, 34, 324
Kinetograph, 15, 18, 36
Kinetophonograph, 15
Kinetoscope, 12, **15–16,** 19, 20, *23,* 29, 35, 36, 37, 119
King, Henry, 123, 137–38, 285
Kino-Eye, 182, 216
Kino-Pravda, 182
Kinugasa, Teinosuke, 445, 446, 463
Kircher, Father Athanasius, 17
Kirsanov, Dimitri, 242
Kiss Before the Mirror, The, 287
Kleine, George, 36
Klein-Rogge, Rudolf, 168
Klondike Annie, 295
K.M.C.D. Syndicate, 34–35
Knack, The, 418–19
Knife in the Water, 432, 445
Knockout, The, 98
Korda, Alexander, 413, 445
Koster and Bial's Music Hall, 20
Kovacs, Laszlo, 380
Kozintsev, Grigori and Leonid Trausberg, 217
Kracauer, Siegfried, 39, 164
Kramer, Stanley, 328, **329,** 342, 493
Krauss, Werner, *145,* 161, 162
Kubrick, Stanley, 6, 323, 417, 429, *480,* 487, **492–95**
Kuchar, George and Mike, 497, 499
Kuhle Wampe, **177–78**
Kuleshov, Lev, **182–84, 197,** 198, 207, 208, 213, 217
Kurosawa, Akira, *440,* 445, 447, **449–58,** 459, 460, 462, 464, 487
Kurz, Emilie, *151*
Kyo, Machiko, *441,* 451, 460

La Cava, Gregory, 287, 295
Ladies of the Bois de Boulogne, The, 371

Lady Eve, The, 334
Ladykillers, The, 414
Lady Windermere's Fan, 139
Laemmle, Carl, 48, 49, 116, 119, 130, 133
Land of the Pharaohs, 331
Lang, Fritz, 129, 138, *147–48,* **164–68,** 176, 179, 198, 286, 332, 486
Langdon, Harry, 41, 121, 140, **143–44,** 293
Lasky, Jesse, 116, 120, 130
Last Days of Pompeii, The, 116
Last Detail, The, 484
Last Gangster, The, 266
Last Hurrah, The, 331
Last Laugh, The, 150–52, **169–72,** 173, 174, 177, 297, 343, 359, 451
Last Picture Show, The, 74, 482, 487, 488
Last Summer, 483
Last Tango in Paris, 363
Last Year at Marienbad, 42, **385–86,** 497
Late Martha Pascal, The, 242
"Latham" Loop, 20, **46–47**
Latham, Major Woodville, Grey, and Otway, 18, 20, 34, 35, 47
Lattuada, Alberto, 346
Laughton, Charles, 300, 413
Laurel, Stan and Oliver Hardy, 92, **140–41,** 248, 333, 473
Lavender Hill Mob, The, 414
Lawrence, D. H., 419
Lawrence, Florence, 117
Lawrence of Arabia, 413
Lean, David, 413, 414
Leather, Boys, The, 418
Léaud, Jean-Pierre, **378,** 381, *396,* 398
Lee, Christopher, 169
Left-Handed Gun, The, 490
Leger, Fernand, 241

Legrand, Michel, 387
Leigh, Janet, 307
Leigh, Vivien, 329
Lemmon, Jack, 334
Leni, Paul, 168
Lenin, Nikolai, 181
Leopard, The, 347
Leone, Sergio, 364
Le Prince, Louis Augustin, **18**
LeRoy, Mervin, 285, **286**
Lester, Richard, 97, 339, **418–19,** 492, 493
Levine, Joseph E., 327
Lewis, Jerry, **333–34,** 493
Liberace, 418
Life and Death of 9413—A Hollywood Extra, The, 496
Lifeboat, 306
Life of an American Fireman, The, **42–43,** 56
Life of Emile Zola, The, 287
Lights of New York, The, **224,** 227, 267
Limelight, 153, **289**
Linder, Max, *28,* **40–41,** 98, 240
Lion in Winter, The, 419
Lion's Love, 387
Little Big Man, 490
Little Caesar, 266, 286, 476, 481, 486
Little Match Girl, The, 241, **251**
Lives of a Bengal Lancer, 287
Lloyd, Harold, 41, 92, *111,* 118, 140, **141–43,** 144, 477
Loew, Marcus, 116, 120, 221
Lola, 387
Lola Montès, 367, **369–71,** *392–93*
Lolita, 492, **494**
Lombard, Carole, 304
Lonedale Operator, The, **59–60**
Loneliness of the Long-Distance Runner, The, 417
Lonely Are the Brave, 475
Lonely Villa, The, **59,** *61,* 91

Lonesome Cowboys, 499
Long Goodbye, The, 488
Long Gray Line, The, 331
Long Pants, 144
Look Back in Anger, 417
Loos, Anita, 60, 127, 128
Loren, Sophia, 290, 347
Losey, Joseph, 492
Lost Child, The, 55
Lot in Sodom, 496
Love, Bessie, 227
Love of Jeanne Ney, The, 175
Love Parade, The, 226, 227–28
Loved One, The, 417–18
Lovers, The, 387
Loves of a Blonde, 424, 429, 430
Lower Depths, The (1936), 252, 366
Lower Depths, The (1957), 456, 457–58
Lubin, Sigmund, 36, 48
Lubitsch, Ernst, 138–39, 162, 178, 221, 225, **227–28**, 265, 267, 270, 285, **291–92**, 299, 307, 309, 328, 367, 368, 388, 448
Lucas, George, 490
Lugosi, Béla, 169, 445
Lumière, Auguste Marie Louis Nicolas and Louis Jean, **19–20**, *24*, **29–30**, 31, 33, 35, 39, 45, 46, 56, 57, 91, 181
Lupino, Ida, 285
Lye, Len, 414, 497, 498

M, 165, **179**
Mabel's Dramatic Career, **94**, 117
Macao, 300
Macbeth, 314, 432, **456–57**
MacDonald, Jeanette, 226, 227, 228, 267, 285
Machine of Eden, The, **501**
Mackendrick, Alexander, 414
Madame de . . . , 367

Mad Wednesday, 334
Madwoman of Chaillot, The, 419
Magic Lantern, 11, 13, **17**, 36, 38, 408
Magician, The, 166, 405, 406, **408–9**
Magnani, Anna, 346, 347, 348, 349, 366
Magnificent Ambersons, The, **313–14**
Magnificent Seven, The, 456
Mahanagar, 467, 469
Major Dundee, 491
Makavejov, Dušan, 445
Male and Female, **130–32**, 166
Malle, Louis, 97, 240, **387**
Maltese Falcon, The, 330
Mamoulian, Rouben, 226–27, 325, 448
Man for All Seasons, A, 419
Man in the Iron Mask, The, 287
Man in the White Suit, The, 414
Man is not a Bird, A, 445
Man of Aran, 140
Man There Was, A, 404
Man Who Knew Too Much, The, 303, 307, 330
Man Who Shot Liberty Valance, The, **302**, 331
Man With the Golden Arm, The, 328
Man with the Movie Camera, The, 216
Mankiewicz, Herman J., 310
Mann, Anthony, 331
Mann, Thomas, 342, 343, 348
Mannix, Eddie, 227
Man's Genesis, 74
"March of Time, The", 309
Marcy, Étienne-Jules, **13**
Marie Antoinette, 286
Marker, Chris, 388
Marketa Lazarova, 422, 423

Marriage Circle, The, 139
Marsh, Mae, 59, 69, 76
Marshall, Herbert, 270, 291, 299
Martin, Dean, 304, 333
Marvin, Arthur, 54
Marvin, Henry, 35, 54
Marx Brothers, The, 285, 293–94, 295, 296, 333
Marx, Karl (and Marxism), 177, 181, 198, 213, 248, 345, 362, 383
Masculine/Feminine, 380, 381–82
M*A*S*H, 488, 489
Masquerader, The, 93, 95
Masina, Giulietta, 348–49, 350, 354
Massari, Lea, 390
Mastroianni, Marcello, 350, 352, 356, 357
Matrix, 498
Max and the Quinquina, 41
Max Plays at Drama, 41
Mayer, Carl, 162, 169, 176, 343
Mayer, Louis B., 116, 119, 120, 122, 127, 134, 268, 285, 337, 404, 421
McCabe and Mrs. Miller, 485, 488, 489
McCarey, Leo, 285, 300
McCarthy era, 123, 124, 328, 329, 331, 421
McCrea, Joel, 491
McCutcheon, Wallace C. ("Old Man"), 54
McDowell, Malcolm, 420
McLaglen, Victor, 275, 302
Mechanics of the Brain, 208
Medium Cool, 218, 482
Meet Me in St. Louis, 325
Meighan, Thomas, 118, 131
Méliès, Georges, 25, 30, 33, 38–40, 41, 42, 43, 44, 46, 48, 50, 51, 57, 97, 103, 104, 166, 237, 240, 246, 324, 365, 375

Menilmontant, 242
Menjou, Adolphe, 118, 298
Menzel, Jiří, 425–27
Mercanton, Louis, 50
Merry-Go-Round, 134
Merry Widow, The, 136, 470
Meshes of the Afternoon, 497
Messter, Oscar, 219
Metro-Goldwyn-Mayer (MGM), 119, 120, 121, 127, 136, 227, 265, 267, 268, 285, 286, 287, 316, 326, 330, 335, 336, 339, 470
Metro Pictures, 120, 134
Metropolis, 148, 166–68, 176, 179, 198, 496
Metzner, Erno, 161
Meyerhold, Vsevold, 199, 216
Mickey Mouse, 229, 237–38, 290
Mickey One, 490
Midnight Cowboy, 74, 419, 420
Midsummer's Night Dream, A, 287
Mifune, Toshiro, 440, 451, 456
Mildred Pierce, 287
Milestone, Lewis, 175, 226, 287
Milky Way, The, 470, 472–74, 497
Million, Le, 247, 249
Minnelli, Vincente, 325, 335, 336
Minter, Mary Miles, 124
Miracle in Milan, 347
Miracle Worker, The, 490
Mississippi, 287
Mr. Deeds Goes to Town, 143, 293
Mr. Hulot's Holiday, 372
Mr. Smith Goes to Washington, 143, 293
Mitra, Subrata, 466
Mizoguchi, Kenji, 441, 445, 446, 447, 449, 452, 458–60, 462, 464
Moana, 140
Moby Dick, 330
Modern Times, 113, 248, 288–89

Modernism, **343,** 351, 402, 496, 498

Moholy-Nagy, László, 445

Mondo Trasho, 500

Monicelli, Mario, 362

Monika, 404, 407

Monogram Pictures, 285, 374, 380

Monroe, Marilyn, 332

Monsieur Verdoux, **289**

Montand, Yves, 386

Monte Carlo, 226, 227, **228**

Moon is Blue, The, 328

Moore, Owen, 118, 124

Moreau, Jeanne, 357, 358, *397*

Morgan!, 418

Mori, Masuyuki, *441,* 453

Morocco, 267, **297–98**

Morrissey, Paul, 499

Mother, 184, *189–92,* **208–10,** 211, 213

Mother Goose Tales, 219–20, 223

Motion Painting #1, 478

Motion Picture Patents Company (Film Trust), 48–49, 51, 55, 73, 116, 117, 118, 119, 125, 324

Motion Picture Producers and Distributors of America (M.P.P.D.A.), **125,** 264–65

Moulin Rouge, 330

Movie, A, **498**

Movietone, 222

Mozhukin, Ivan, 183, 207

Muni, Paul, 285

Murmur of the Heart, 387

Murnau, F. W., 138, 140, *149–52, 169–72,* 173, 178, 225, 342, 343, 388, 446, 492

Murray, Charlie, 95

Music Lovers, The, 419

Music Room, The, 467, 469

Musketeers of Pig Alley, The, 73

Mussolini, Benito, 343, 344, 421, 422

Mutoscope, *25,* **35,** 119

Mutual Film Corporation, 76, 99, 114, 127

Muybridge, Eadweard, **13,** 14, *21*

My Darling Clementine, 303, 331

My Fair Lady, 328

My Little Chickadee, 295

My Man Godfrey, 287

My Uncle (Mon Oncle), **372–73,** *395*

My Universities, 217

Mysteries of the Chateau Dé, The, 241

Nabokov, Vladimir, 494

Naked City, 332

Naked Night, The, 404

Nanook of the North, **139–40,** 154

Napoléon, 242, 243, 322

Narrative, development and styles of, **36–46, 55–59,** 126, 137, 184, 198

Nazarin, 470, 472

Neckár, Václav, *438*

Negri, Pola, 161, 225

Neighbor's Wife and Mine, The, 446

Nelson, Robert, 499

Němec, Jan, 423

Neo-Impressionist Painter, The, 40

Neorealism, **344–47,** 348, 352, 357, 361, 362, 363, 364, *389,* 414, 418, 425, 432, 465

New Centurions, The, 486

"New Wave" ("Nouvelle Vague"), 256, 374, **375–88,** 401–2, 414, 420, 425, 487

New York Hat, The, **60–61,** *62,* 75

Newman, Alfred, 483

Newsreels, 216, 222

Nichols, Dudley, 301, 303

Nichols, Mike, 448, 481, 482
Nickelodeon. *See* Film theatres.
Niebelungen, 168, 179
Nielsen, Asta, 161, 174
Niepce, Nicéphore, 12
Night and Day, 287
Night and Fog, 384
Night at the Opera, A, 294
Night of Counting the Years, The, 474
Night of the Iguana, 330
Night They Raided Minsky's, The, 485, 490
Nights of Cabiria, 337, 348, **349–50**, 351, 425
Nikkatsu studio, 447
Nilsson, Leopoldo Torre, 474
Ninety in the Shade, 423
Ninotchka, 291
Nordisk, 181
Normand, Mabel, 94, 96, 97, 124
Norris, Frank, 73, 134–36
North by Northwest, 306, 318, 330, 331
Nosferatu, 149, **169**
Not as a Stranger, 328
Notte, La, 357
Novarro, Ramon, 118
Nykvist, Sven, 409

O, Lucky Man!, 420
Odd Man Out, 414
October or *Ten Days that Shook the World,* 188, **203–5,** 211, 212
Odd Obsession, 463
Offon, 498
Of Mice and Men, 287
Ohayo (Good Morning), **462**
Old and New or *The General Line,* **205**
Old-Fashioned Way, The, 295
Oliver!, 338, 414

Oliver Twist, 413
Olivier, Laurence, 325, 368, 414, 417
Olmi, Ermanno, **363**
Olvidados, Los, 470, 471
Olympia, 179
On the Beach, 329
On the Waterfront, 317, 329
Once Upon a Time in the West, 364
One A.M., **103–4,** 107
One Exciting Night, 85
One Fine Day, **363**
One Million B.C., 90
One Plus One, 383
O'Neal, Tatum, 477
Onésime Horloger, 240
Only Angels Have Wings, 304
L'Onorevole Angelina, 346
Open City (Roma, Cittá Aperta), **344,** 348, 481
Ophuls, Max, 261, 262, **367–71,** *392–93*
Organizer, The, 362
Orphans of the Storm, 85
Orphée, 366
Orthochromatic film, 379
Osborne, John, 414, 417, 418
Ossessione, 347
O'Toole, Peter, 413
Out in the World, 217
Outlaw and His Wife, The, 404
Oyama, **446**
Ox-Bow Incident, The, 287
Ozu, Yasujiro, 445, 446, 447, 449, **460–62,** 463, 464

Pabst, G. W., 45, **174–76,** 179, 342, 492
Pagnol, Marcel, 257
Paisán, 346, 348
Palace of the Arabian Nights, The, 39
Pallette, Eugene, 250

Panavision, 324, 348

Panchromatic film, 7, 310, 379, 449

Panofsky Erwin, 164

Paper Moon, 477, 488

Paramount Pictures, 49, 51, 97, **119–20**, 121, 140, 205, 221, 267, **268, 285,** 339

Parents Terribles, Les, 366

Paris, Dr. John Ayrton, 10

Paris qui dort (The Crazy Ray), 245

Pasolini, Pier Paolo, 362

Passer, Ivan, 424, 425, **430–31**

Passion, 138

Passion of Joan of Arc, The, 230–31, **243–44,** 381

Patent Company. *See* Motion Picture Patents Company.

Patent war, **46–48**

Pat Garrett and Billy the Kid, 491

Pathé, Charles and brothers, **33–34,** 40, 48, 97, 120, 181

*Pather Pancali, 442–43, 464, **466–67, 468***

Paths of Glory, 492

Paul, Robert W., 18, 20, 29, 33, 34

Pawnbroker, The, 475

Pawnshop, The, **104,** *108,* 154

Peckinpah, Sam, 126–27, 485, **490–91**

Penn, Arthur, 481, 490

Pension Mimosas, 259

Perception, film's manipulation and development of, 365, 383, 401, 409, *479,* 496, 497, 498, **500–2**

Permutations, 498

Perry, Frank and Eleanor, 483

Persistence of vision, **9–12,** 35

Persona, 407, 409, **410–13,** *437,* 497

Peyton Place, 328

Phalke, Dadasaheb, 464

Phantasmagoria, 17

Phantom Carriage, The, 404

Phenakistiscope, **10–11,** 13, 16, 18

Phonofilm, 220–21, 222, 267

Phonograph, *23,* 14–15, 220

Photography, invention of, *12–14*

Pickens, Slim, 493

Pickford, Mary, 35, 59, 60, 117, 118, 120, 121, 123, 124, 129, 138

Pilgrim, The, 113

Pink Flamingos, 500

Pinky, 329

Pinter, Harold, 416

Pippa Passes, 58

Pirandello, Luigi, 160, 257, 342, 419

Piscator, Erwin, 160

Pitts, ZaSu, *110*

"Plastic material", 137, *192,* 207, 209, 212–13, 307, *318,* 331, 357

Plateau, Joseph Antoine Ferdinand, 10–11

Playtime, 372, 373

Pleasure Garden, The, 305

Poelzig, Hans, 168

Polanski, Roman, **432,** 445, 470

Police, 100, 101

Polish film, **431–32,** 445

Polonsky, Abraham, 332

Pommer, Erich, 161, 169, 178

Pontecorvo, Gillo, 388, 401

Popi, 485

Poppe, Nils, *434*

Poppy, 287, 295

Port of Shadows (Quai des brumes), **259–60,** 376

Porter, Edwin S., 36, 40, **41–44,** 49, 50, 51, 54, 56, 58, 120, 126

Postman Always Rings Twice, The, 347

Posto, Il (The Sound of Trumpets), **363**

Potemkin, 177, *185–87,* **199–203,** 204, 205, 207, 343, 383

Powell, Dick, 285, 334

Powell, Michael and Emerie Pressburger, 414

Power of the Press, The, 266

Power, Tyrone, 285

Preminger, Otto, **328,** 342, 481, 493

Prévert, Jacques, **259–62,** 343, 366

Private Life of Henry the Eighth, The, 413

Private Lives of Elizabeth and Essex, The, 287

Producers, The, 485, 491

Projecting kinetoscope, 47

Projecting phenakistiscope, 13

Prokofiev, Sergei, 203, 206

Protazanov, Yakov, 217

Proust, Marcel, 342, 365

Psycho, 307, 330, 475

Public Enemy, The, 266, 287

Public Hero Number 1, 266

Pudovkin, Vsevlod I., 137, 182, 184, *189–93,* **207–13,** 214, 215, 216, 218, 307, 344

Pullman Honeymoon, **37–38,** 39

Pumpkin Eater, The, 416

Pumpkin Race, The, 40

Purple Noon, 374

Purviance, Edna, 100, 101, 102, *106*

Que Viva Mexico!, 205

Queen Elizabeth, 28, **50–51,** 54, 81, 84, 116, 119

Queen Kelly, 136

Quiet Man, The, 331

Quinn, Anthony, 349, *354*

Quo Vadis?, (1912), 76, 116

"Quota Quickies", 413

Radio, 220, 223, 309, 310

Radio City Music Hall, 6, 122, 476

Raphaelson, Samson, 292

Rappe, Virginia, 124, 499

Rashomon, 445, 447, **449–55,** 456, 459, 462

Ray, Charles, 118

Ray, Man, **241**

Ray, Nicholas, 331, 332–33

Ray, Satyajit, *442–43,* 464, **465–69,** 474

Raye, Martha, 289

Reaching for the Moon, **128–29**

Rear Window, 330, 331

Rebel Without a Cause, 319, 333

Red and the Black, The, 375

Red Desert, The, 357, 358, 359, **360–61,** *391*

Red River, 277, 304, 305, 331

Redgrave, Lynn, 420

Redgrave, Vanessa, 413, 420

Reed, Carol, 414

Reed, Oliver, 420

Reeves, Steve, 327, 364

Reid, Wallace, 124

Reimann, Walther, 161, 163

Reisz, Karel, 418, 419

Relativity, 501

Renoir, Jean, 45, *234–35,* 239, 241, **250–56,** 257, 258, 261, 262, 286, 342, **365–66,** 367, 368, 375, 378, 379, 383, 384, 401, 456, 465, 469, 492, 493, 495, 503

Repas de bébé, Le, 19, 24, 29

Report on the Party and the Guests, The, 423

Republic Pictures Corporation, 285, 326, 332

Rescued by Rover, 26–27, **44–45,** 55

Rescued from an Eagle's Nest, **54,** 55

Resnais, Alain, 42, **384–86,** 387, 388, 401

Return to Reason, 241

Revue Productions, 326

Rex Company, 49, 120
Rhythmus 21, **496**
Richardson, Tony, **417–18,** 419
Richter, Hans, 496
Ride the High Country, 491
Rider on the Rain, 374
Riding High, 334
Riefenstahl, Leni, 179
Rien que les heures, 242
Rink, The, 100, 101
Rio Bravo, 304, 331
Rio Jim. *See* Hart, William S.
Rio Rita, 342
Riot in Juvenile Prison, 327
Rire, Le, 92, 141
Riskin, Robert, 292–93
Ritual, The, 409
River, The, **365–66,** 465, 469
R.K.O. Radio Pictures, **285,** 313, 314, 326
Roach, Hal, 90, 96, 141, 292
Road to Life, The, **216–17**
Robe, The, 323, 327
Robinson, Edward G., 285
Robison, Arthur, 169
Rocco and His Brothers, 347
Rocha, Glauber, 474
Rock music. *See* Film style, music and scoring
Rock, William ("Pop"), 36
Rodgers, Richard, 267, 335
Rogers, Ginger, 267, 285, 334
Rogers Will, 285
Rôget, Peter Mark, 10
Rohmer, Eric, **387–88**
Rohrig, Walther, 161, 163, 165, 169
Romeo and Juliet, 339
Ronde, La, 367, **368–69**
Roof, The, 347
Room, Abram, **216**
Room at the Top, **415–16,** 417
Rooney, Mickey, 265
Rope, 330

Rose Marie, 287
Rosemary's Baby, 432
Rosita, 138
Rossellini, Roberto, **344,** 346, 347, 348, 352, 401
Rossen, Robert, 332
Rota, Nino, 350
Rothafel, Samuel L. ("Roxy"), 122
Rouch, Jean, 388
Roue, La, 242
Rounders, The, 95, 98, 142
Rozsa, Miklos, 483
Ruggles, Charles, 292
Rules of the Game, The, 235, **254– 56,** 367–68, 493
Run of the Arrow, 332
Russell, Jane, 321
Russell, Ken, **419**
Russian and Soviet film, **181–84,** 197–218, 344, 345, 424, 466
Russian Revolution, 181, 183, 204, 211
Ruttmann, Walther, 176–77, 179
Ryan's Daughter, 413

Sabotage, 307, 488
Saboteur, 306, 307, 488
Safety Last, 143
Saga of Anatahan, The, 300
Salvation Hunters, 138
Samurai, 463
Sandrich, Mark, 287
San Francisco, 287
San Quentin, 266
Sansho the Bailiff, **458–59,** 460
Sarris, Andrew, 487
Saturday Night and Sunday Morn- ing, 418
S.C.A.P., 447
Scarface, 266, 305, 481, 486
Scarlet Empress, The, 274, **299–300**
Schlesinger, John, 418, 419, **420**
Schmidt, Jan and Pavel Juráček, 424

Schnitzler, Arthur, 368–69
"School of Brighton", 34, 44–46, 57
Schorm, Evald, 423
Schors, 215
Schreck, Max, *149, 169*
Schulberg, B. P., 268, 285
Scorpio Rising, 497, **500,** 479
Scott, George C., 493
Scott, Randolph, 333, 491
Screen Gems, 326
Séance on a Wet Afternoon, 418
Seberg, Jean, 380, *399*
Seduced and Abandoned, 361
Selig, "Colonel", 36, 48
Sellers, Peter, 413, 494
Selznick, David O., 326
Selznick, Lewis J., 116, 120
Senator Was Indiscreet, The, 334
Sennett, Mack, 35, 41, 49, **91–97,** 98, 99, 100, 101, 103 *105,* 114, 115, 127, 139, 140, 141, 143, 237, 245, 246, 249, 292, 293, 306, 333, 375, 376, 417, 430, 491, 492
Series pictures, 267, 287
Serpico, 486
Seven Samurai, 453, **455–56,** 459
Seven Years Bad Luck, 28, 41
1776 or *The Hessian Renegades,* 73
Seventh Seal, The, 166, 404, **405–6,** 407, 408, 409, *433–35*
"Sexploitation" films, 322, 413, 476
Shaft, 476
Shakespeare, William, 3, 73, 265, 266, 286, 342, 414, 456
Shane, 331, 332, 455
Shanghai Express, **298–99**
Shanghai Gesture, The, 300
Shankar, Ravi, 466
Shaw, George Bernard, 222, 243
Shaw Talks for Movietone, 222
She Done Him Wrong, **294–95**

She Wore a Yellow Ribbon, 331
Shearer, Norma, 285
Shimura, Takashi, 453, 456
Shochiku studio, **447**
Shoeshine, 345
Shoot the Piano Player, 375, **376–77,** 476
Shop on Main Street, The, 421, 427–29
Shostakovich, Dimitri, 203
Shub, Esther, 216
Shumyatsky, Boris, 217
Sidney, Sylvia, 307
Signoret, Simone, 415, 416
Silence, The, 409
Silence est d'or, Le, 365
Sillitoe, Alan, 414, 417
Silly Symphonies, 238, 290
Simon, Michel, 258, 260
Singin' in the Rain, 127, 220, 221, 225, *320,* **336**
Siodmak, Robert, 332
Sir Arne's Treasure, 404
Six of a Kind, 295
69, 498
Sjöberg, Alf, 404
Sjöman, Vilgot, 413
Sjöström, Victor, 138, 404, 406, *436*
Skater's Debut, A, 41
Skeleton Dance, The, **238**
Skladanowsky, Max and Emil, 20
Skolimowski, Jerzy, 445
Sleeper, 477, 491
Slippery Jim, 40
Sloane, Everett, 282, 283
Smiles of a Summer Night, 404, 407
Smiling Madame Beudet, The, 242
Smith, Albert E., 36, 46
Smith, G. A., 34, 40, 56, 413
Smith, Jack, 500
Smith, Maggie, 420
Snow, Michael, *479,* **501–2**

Snow White and the Seven Dwarfs, 290, 291
Socialist Realism, **216,** 217, 421, 422
Soft Skin, The, 377
Some Like It Hot, 334
Song of the South, 237
Sons and Lovers, 418
So This is Paris, 139
Sous les toits de Paris, 247
Spaak, Charles, 259
"Spaghetti Westerns", 364
Spartacus, 327, 492
Spellbound, 307
Spoor, George K., 36
Stagecoach, 276, **302–3**
Stalin, Joseph, 205, 217, 421, 422, 423, 431
Stanford, Leland, 13
Stanislavski, Constantin, 216
Steamboat Willie, 229, **237–38**
Steiger, Rod, *317,* 329
Steiner, Max, 302, 483
Steiner, Ralph, 496
Sterling, Ford, 94, 96, 97, 98
Stevens, George, 324, 331
Stewart, James, 302, 306
Stiller, Mauritz, 138, 225, 404
Stolen Kisses, **377–78**
Storm Over Asia, **212–23**
Story of a Simple Case, The, 213
Story of Dr. Wassel, The, 130, 325
Story of G.I. Joe, The, 287
Story of Louis Pasteur, The, 287
Story of the Last Chrysanthemums, The, 458
Strada, La, 337, 348, **349,** 351, *354*
Strand Theatre, 122
Strangers on a Train, 307, 308, 330
Straw Dogs, 491
Straw Man, The, 130
Streisand, Barbra, 470
Strike, 84, 184, **199**
Strindberg, August, 407

Stroboscope, 11
Strong Man, The, 143–44
Structural film, 501
Struggle, The, 89–90
Student of Prague, The, 168–69
Sturges, John, 331–32
Sturges, Preston, 285, 334, 448, 491
Suddenly Last Summer, 328
Suffragette in Spite of Himself, A, **45**
Sunday, Bloody Sunday, 420
Sunrise, 178
Sunset Boulevard, 137, 334, 342, 499
Surf Girl, The, 93, **95,** *105*
Surrealism, 40, 237, **241–42,** 244, 251, 350, 386, 424, 470, 491, 496, 497
Suspicion, 307
Sutherland, Edward, 287, 295
Swain, Mack, 97
Swanson, Gloria, 96, 118, 131, 137, 334
Swedish film, **404–13**
Sweet Bird of Youth, 328
Sweet, Blanche, 59
Sweethearts, 287
Swing Time, 269
Symphonie Pastorale, 375

Tagore, Rabindranath, 465
Take the Money and Run, 491
Taki no Shiraito, 458, 459
Taking Off, 429, 430
Tall T, The, 331
Tally, Thomas L., 47
Talmadge, Constance, 68
Tango Tangles, 430
Targets, **287–88**
Tarzan, 286
Tati, Jacques, 367, **372–73,** *395*
Taylor, William Desmond, 124–25, 499

Tea and Sympathy, 328
Tearing Down the Spanish Flag, 36, 159
Technicolor Corporation, 12, **324–25,** 335, 419, 487
Teddy at the Throttle, **96**
Television, 12, 218, 220, 267, **316,** 321, 324, 325, **326,** 328, 337, 338, 339, 341, 419, 446, 461, 462, 463, 464, 476, 482, 488, 490
Temple, Shirley, 267, 285
Ten Commandments, The, 132, 327
Terra Trema, La, 347, 348
Teshigahara, Hiroshi, 463
Thalberg, Irving, 120, 127, 133, 134, 136, 268, 502
That Cold Day in the Park, 489
Thaumatrope, 10, 11
Theatrograph, 33, 34
They Shoot Horses, Don't They?, 482
Thief of Bagdad, The, **129,** 166
Thieves' Highway, 382
Thieves Like Us, 481, 482–83, 484, 485, 487, 489
Thin Man, The, 286, 486
"Third World" film, 474
39 Steps, The, 278–79, **305–6, 307–9,** 413
This is Cinerama, 322, 323
This Sporting Life, 418, 420
3-D, **6,** 43, 243, **321–22,** 323, 330, 499
Three Little Pigs, The, 290
Three Musketeers, The, 339
Three Must-Get-Theres, The, 41
Three Songs of Lenin, 216
Threepenny Opera, The, 102, 172, **175–76,** 179
Throne of Blood, 440, 450, 452, 453, **456–57,** 459
Through a Glass Darkly, 409

Thulin, Ingrid, 404
THX 1138, 490
Tillie's Punctured Romance, **93–94**
Tisse, Edouard, 205
To Be or Not To Be, 291
To Catch a Thief, 330, 331
Toho Company, 447
Tol'able David, 123, **137–38**
Toland, Gregg, 301, 310, 329
Tolstoy, Leo, 216, 260
Tom Jones, 417
Tommy, 419
Toni, 252, 257
Topo, El, 474
Tosca, 53, 54
Touch, The, 470
Tourneur, Jacques, 331
Tracy, Spencer, 285, 329
Trader Horn, 286
Traffic, 372
Tramp, The, 99, 100, 102, 103
Tramp, Tramp, Tramp, 143
Treasure of the Sierra Madre, The, 330, 342
Triangle Film Corporation, **127**
Tri-Ergon Process, **220**
Trip to the Moon, A, 25, **38**
Triumph of the Will, 179
Trnka, Jiří, 431
Troell, Jan, 413
Trouble in Paradise, 228, 270, **291–92,** 328
Truffaut, François, 240, 352, 365, **375–79,** 380, 381, 382, 384, 386, 387, *396–98,* 401, 404, 418, 425, 448, 449, 476, 484, 487, 488, 503
Trucolor, 332
Trust Companies. *See* Motion Picture Patents Company.
Trust War, **48–49,** 116, 118
Turn of the Screw, The, 163, 416
Turpin, Ben, 92, 97

Tushingham, Rita, 417, 420
Twelve Chairs, The, 491
Twentieth Century, 304
Twentieth-Century Fox, 49, **285,** 323, 326, 339
Two Men and a Wardrobe, 432
2001: A Space Odyssey, 6, 323, 339, 480, 487, 492, 493, **494–95**
Two Women, 347

Ugetsu, 441, 452, 458, **459–60,** 462
Ullman, Liv, 412, *437*
Umberto D, 347, 425
Umbrellas of Cherbourg, The, **387**
Uncle Tom's Cabin, 44
Underground cinema. *See* Independent American cinema.
Underworld, 138, 224
United Artists Corporation, **121,** 326
Universal Pictures (Universal-International; Universal Studios), 49, 119, 133, 134, 285, 326, 339
Universum Film A. G. (UFA), 159–60, 161, 296, 465
Up the Down Staircase, 485
Urban, Charles, **34,** 40, 324, 413, 414
Ustinov, Peter, 370, *393*
Utamaro and His Five Women, 458, 459

Vadim, Roger, 368, 374, **386–87**
Vagabond, The, 102
Valentino, Rudolph, 118
VanDerBeek, Stan, *478, 498*
Van Dyke, W. S., 140, **286–87**
Van Fleet, Jo, 329
Varda, Agnes, 387
Variety, 161, **173,** 175, 177
Vasiliev Brothers, 217
Vaudeville, 20, 47, 122, 153, 289, 295, 372

Veidt, Conrad, *145,* 161, 162
Vernon, Bobby, 96
Vertigo, 330
Vertov, Dziga, **182,** 216
Vidor, King, 138, 218, 226
Vigo, Jean, **257–59,** 286, 375, 376, *396,* 503
Virginian, The, 226
Viridiana, 444, 470, **471–72**
Visconti, Luchino, **347–48,** 364, 470
Vitagraph Company, **35–36,** 46, 47, 48, 49, 96, 159
Vitaphone, 12, 220, **221,** 222, 223, 267, 288
Vitascope, 12, 20, 29, 36, 47
Vitti, Monica, 357, 358, *390, 391*
Vivre sa vie (My Life to Live), 380, **381,** 382, *400*
Vlatil, František, 422
von Harbou, Thea, 164, 168
von Stampfer, Simon Ritter, 11
von Sternberg, Josef, 138, 178–79, 224, 265, *271–74,* 285, **296–300,** 301, 305, 448
von Stroheim, Erich, *109–10,* 118, 129–30, **132–37,** 139, 159, 162, 170, *234,* 252, 299, 309, 330, 342, 367, 368, 401, 466
von Sydow, Max, 404, 470, *433, 435*
von Uchatius, Baron Franz, 11, 13

Wages of Fear, The, **373–74**
Wagner, Fritz Arno, 161
Wagonmaster, 331
Waiting for Godot, 153, 259
Wajda, Andrej, 431–32, 445
Walbrook, Anton, 368, *393*
Walker, Robert, 308
Walking Down Broadway, 137
Waller, Fred, 322
Walsh, Raoul, 129, 332, 487
Walters, Charles, 335

Walthall, Henry B., 59, *63, 65*
Warhol, Andy, 322, 476, 499, 500
Warm, Hermann, 161, 163, 165, 245
Warner Brothers, 221, 222, 224, 267, **285,** 286, 326, 470
Warning Shadows, 169
Warwick Trading Company, 34
Washday Troubles, 31
Waters, John, 500
Wavelength, 479, **501–2**
Waxworks, 168
Way Down East, 55, 73, 76, 85, **87–88,** 89, 137, 138, 183, 210, 301, 303, 327
Wayne, John, *276–77,* 304, 333
Wedding March, The, 136
Weekend, 380, **382–83**
Wegener, Paul and Henrik Galeen, 168
Weiss, Jiří, 422, 423
Welles, Orson, 6, *281–84,* **309–14,** 342, 401, 492
Wellman, William, 285, 287
West, Mae, 285, **294–95,** 296
Western Electric, 221, 225
Westfront 1918, **175,** 179
West Side Story, 336
Whale, James, 285, 287
What's Up, Doc?, 483, 488
Whence Does He Come?, 40
White Heat, 332
Whitney, John, **498**
Who's Afraid of Virginia Woolf?, 475, 488, 490
Widerberg, Bo, 413
Wiene, Robert, 163, 164
Wild Bunch, The, 484, 485, 490
Wild Child, The, **378–79,** 488
Wild Ones, The, 332, 500
Wild Strawberries, 379, 404, 405, **406–8,** 409, *436*
Wilder, Billy, 285, 334

Williamson, James, 34, 413
Wind, The, 404
Winter Light, 409
Winters, Jonathon, 418
Winters, Shelley, 332, 494
Wise Man, The, 199
Wizard of Oz, The, 287, 325
Woman, A, 103
Woman in the Dunes, 463
Women in Love, 419
Wood, Sam, 287
Workers Leaving the Lumière Factory, 19, 24
World of Apu, The, **466–67**
World War I, 84, **115–16,** 159, 175, 182, 211, 220, 252–54, 305, 341, 344, 376, 413, 492
World War II, 136, 217, 250, 256, 258, 262, 263, 265, 314, 316, 325, 327, 330, 332, 334, 335, 338, 341, 344, 346, 347, 374, 375, 403, 414, 421, 422, 424, 426, 428–29, 432, 445, **446– 47,** 463, 470
Wyler, William, 316, 329

Yankee Doodle Dandy, 287
Yates, Peter, 483
Yojimbo, 454, **455–56**
York, Michael, 420
You Can't Take It With You, 283
You're a Big Boy Now, 485, 489
Yugoslavian film, 445

Z, 218, 338
Zabrskie Point, 357, 358
Zagreb animation studio, 445
Zampa, Luigi, 346
Zavattini, Cesare, 344, 345, 346, 347, 357
Zazie dans le Métro, 387
Zecca, Ferdinand, 40, 41, 42, 55, 240, 245, 246, 365, 375

Zeman, Karel, 431
Zéro de conduite, **257–58,** *396*
Zinnemann, Fred, 316, 331, 419
Zoopraxiscope, 13

Zootrope (or Zoetrope), **11,** 16, *21*
Zukor, Adolph, 51, 116, 119, 120,
    121, 122, 125, 136, 221, 337,
    404